Strategies for Reading Assessment and Instruction

Helping Every Child Succeed

Second Edition

D. Ray Reutzel
Utah State University

Robert B. Cooter, Jr.
University of Texas at Arlington

Merrill
Prentice Hall

Upper Saddle River, New Jersey
Columbus, Ohio

Library of Congress Cataloging-in-Publication Data

Reutzel, D. Ray (Douglas Ray)
    Strategies for reading assessment and instruction : helping every child succeed / D. Ray
Reutzel, Robert B. Cooter, Jr.-2nd ed.
        p. cm.
    Rev. ed. of: Balanced reading strategies and practices. c1999.
    Includes bibliographical references and index.
    ISBN 0-13-098899-5 (pbk.)
    1. Reading. 2. Reading-Remedial teaching. 3. Child development. I. Title: Strategies
for reading assessment and instruction. II. Cooter, Robert B. III. Reutzel, D. Ray
(Douglas Ray) Balanced reading strategies and practices. IV. Title.

LB1050 .R477 2003
372.43-dc21

2002021941

Vice President and Publisher: Jeffery W. Johnston
Editor: Linda Ashe Montgomery
Production Editor: Mary M. Irvin
Design Coordinator: Diane C. Lorenzo
Text Design and Production Coordination: Carlisle Publishers Services
Cover Designer: Linda Sorrells-Smith
Cover Art: Eyewire
Production Manager: Pamela D. Bennett
Director of Marketing: Ann Castel Davis
Marketing Manager: Krista Groshong
Marketing Coordinator: Tyra Cooper

Photo Credits: Robert B. Cooter, Jr., p. 314; Scott Cunningham/Merrill, p. 156; Barbara Mathews/Dallas Independent School District, p. 10; D. Ray Reutzel, pp. 87, 90, 91, 92.

This book was set in Souvenir by Carlisle Communications, Ltd., and was printed and bound by Courier Kendallville, Inc. The cover was printed by Phoenix Color Corp.

Pearson Education Ltd.
Pearson Education Australia Pty. Limited
Pearson Education Singapore Pte. Ltd.
Pearson Education North Asia Ltd.
Pearson Education Canada, Ltd.
Pearson Educación de Mexico, S.A. de C.V.
Pearson Education-Japan
Pearson Education Malaysia Pte. Ltd.
Pearson Education, *Upper Saddle River, New Jersey*

10 9 8 7 6 5 4 3 2 1

For my companion and sweetheart of over 27 years, Pam; my wonderful five children and their spouses; my three grandsons; and my teacher colleagues; many thanks for making life and learning an everlasting joy!

I am also extremely grateful to the Emma Eccles Jones Foundation for its continuing support of my work in the *Emma Eccles Jones Early Childhood Education Center.*
—DRR

For Kathy
—RBC

About the Authors

D. Ray Reutzel

D. Ray Reutzel is currently the Emma Eccles Jones Endowed Chair and Distinguished Professor of Early Childhood Education and Director of the *Emma Eccles Jones Center for Early Childhood Education* at Utah State University. Ray regularly works with teachers and children in local public schools and in the Edith Bowen School on the Utah State University campus. He is a former Provost and Vice President for Academic Affairs at Southern Utah University; Associate Dean of Teacher Education in the David O. McKay School of Education; and former Chair of the Department of Elementary Education at Brigham Young University. While at BYU, he was the recipient of the 1992 Karl G. Maeser Distinguished Research Professor Award. Several years ago, he took a leave from his university faculty position to return to full-time, first-grade classroom teaching in Sage Creek Elementary School to pilot comprehensive balanced reading practices. Ray has taught in Kindergarten, 1st grade, 3rd grade, and 6th grade.

Dr. Reutzel is the author of more than 130 articles, books, book chapters, and monographs. Ray has published in *Reading Research Quarterly, Journal of Reading Behavior, Journal of Literacy Research, Journal of Educational Research, Reading Psychology, Reading and Writing Quarterly, Reading Research and Instruction, Language Arts, Journal of Reading,* and *The Reading Teacher, Instructor,* among others. He is the past Editor of *Reading Research and Instruction,* and co-author of the best selling college textbook *Teaching Children to Read: Putting the Pieces Together, 3rd Edition,* and *Balanced Reading Strategies and Practices: Assessing and Assisting Readers with Special Needs,* both published by Merrill/Prentice Hall. He is or has been a reviewer for *The Reading Teacher, Reading Research Quarterly, Reading Psychology, Reading Research and Instruction,* and a past reviewer for *The Journal of Reading Behavior, Journal of Literacy Research,* and *The Elementary School Journal.* He is also an author of Scholastic Incorporated's Literacy Place 1996 & 2000® school reading program. Dr. Reutzel received the A.B. Herr Award for Outstanding Research and Published Contributions to Reading Education from the College Reading Association in 1999. Dr. Reutzel was recently appointed with his colleague, Judith P. Mitchell, as editor of the International Reading Association's elementary section journal—*The Reading Teacher.*

Robert B. Cooter, Jr.

Dr. Robert Cooter is Professor of Reading & Urban Literacy Education and Director of the national *Center for Urban Literacy* at The University of Texas at Arlington. Dr. Cooter teaches undergraduate and graduate courses in reading, literacy, and in the assessment and correction of reading difficulties. He is particularly interested in constructing effective comprehensive literacy programs for city kids in grades K–12.

Dr. Cooter is perhaps best known for his recent service as the first "Reading Czar" (or Associate Superintendent for Reading/Language Arts) for the Dallas (Texas) Independent School District. Bob engineered the District's highly acclaimed *Dallas Reading Plan,* a collaborative project supported by Dallas area business and community enterprises, which is being accomplished through the training of approximately 5,000 teachers in "comprehensive literacy instruction."

In March of 1998, Cooter was recognized as a "Texas State Champion for Reading" by then-Governor George W. Bush and Texas First Lady Laura Bush as a result of the many successes of the Dallas Reading Plan initiative.

Cooter has worked with teachers and school district leaders around the nation. He has taught grades 1, 3, 4, 7, 11, and 12 in the public schools, and also served as a Title I reading specialist.

In addition to his best-selling text *Teaching Children to Read, 3rd Edition* (Merrill/Prentice Hall, 2000), which is currently used at over 200 universities and colleges to prepare elementary teachers, Cooter has also authored or co-authored four other professional books which include *The Flynt/Cooter Reading Inventory for the Classroom* (Merrill/Prentice Hall, 2001), *Teaching Reading in the Content Areas* (Wiley, 1996), and *The Flynt/Cooter English-Español Reading Inventory* (Merrill/Prentice Hall, 1999). Bob has just completed a new book titled *Perspectives on Rescuing Urban Literacy Education: Spies, Saboteurs & Saints* (Erlbaum, 2003), and is working on three other new books dealing with reading assessment, and the teaching of the language arts. He has had over 50 articles on reading assessment and education published in such journals as *The Reading Teacher, Journal of Reading, Language Arts,* and the *Journal of Educational Research.*

A native of Nashville, Tennessee, Bob enjoys fiction writing, houseboating, and riding his Harley-Davidson motorcycle into schools and performing Southern folktales as "Easy Reader." He lives in Arlington, Texas, with his wife, Kathy, a Special Education professor and Director of Laboratory Schools at Texas Christian University. Bob is the proud father of five children and three stepchildren, has six grandchildren, and is owned by a hound dog of unknown breed and questionable utility.

Contact Information:
Dr. Robert B. Cooter, Jr., Professor of Reading & Urban Literacy Education
School of Education, Box 19227, The University of Texas at Arlington
Arlington, TX 76019; Telephone: 817.272.5058; E-mail: cooter@uta.edu

Preface

After years of intense debate in the "reading wars," the swinging pendulum of fads and fancy in reading instruction seems to be settling into a more inclusive and complete view. *Comprehensive reading instruction* is now regarded by most classroom teachers and reading scholars as the only viable position to take in relation to philosophy and classroom practice (see, for example, Pearson, 1999; Pressley, 2002; Rayner, Foorman, Perfetti, & Seidenberg, 2002). As we have continued to work in real-world classrooms, it has become increasingly apparent that children, and the profession itself, can benefit from this settling of the pendulum on *comprehensive reading instruction.*

For the second edition of *Strategies for Reading Assessment and Instruction,* our intent was to compose a book containing the best research-proven assessment and teaching strategies from the field of comprehensive reading instruction. This is a ready reference to assist classroom teachers in identifying and solving problems encountered by students as they advance on the path of becoming fluent, strategic, and successful readers. Each chapter is self-contained and, starting with Chapter 5, includes these special segments:

- **Brief research updates** that serve as a kind of "executive summary for teachers."
- **Assessment strategies** and tools for determining each child's reading needs and abilities.
- **An Intervention Strategy Guide** for linking assessment findings for each student to the teaching strategies that can help them grow and succeed as readers.
- **Highly effective teaching strategies** from the research on comprehensive reading instruction in such areas as alphabetics (i.e., phonemic awareness, alphabetic principle, phonics), comprehension, fluency, and much more.
- **Special strategies for English Language Learners** (ELL, ESL, bilingual).
- **Accommodations for students with special needs.**

FOR THE PRACTICING EDUCATOR

Classroom reading teachers will also discover that *Strategies for Reading Assessment and Instruction* provides an extensive compendium of research-validated practices and assessment tools to (1) inform your daily instruction, (2) meet the needs of individual learners, and (3) develop an understanding of the essentials of comprehensive reading instruction. For those who teach in special education resource rooms, Title I reading programs, and university reading clinics, this volume likewise provides a wide-ranging collection of strategies to assist students with special needs.

ADVANTAGES FOR PRESERVICE TEACHERS

For preservice teachers, this second edition of *Strategies for Reading Assessment and Instruction* offers a practical resource for understanding past and present issues in reading instruction and assessment. It also provides ready-to-use assessment tools and related instructional strategies you can use in your field experiences in reading instruction, clinical experiences, and student teaching assignments.

AS A TOOL FOR PROFESSIONAL DEVELOPMENT WORKSHOPS

Strategies for Reading Assessment and Instruction is an ideal tool for ongoing professional development. This book contains the latest in research on comprehensive reading instruction, highly effective assessment, and teaching strategies, and presents this information in an easy-to-use format that makes the implementation of new methods in the classroom quick and easy. In fact, the first edition of *Strategies for Reading Assessment and Instruction* was used as the primary resource in literally hundreds of workshop sessions on comprehensive reading instruction across the United States.

ACKNOWLEDGMENTS

Our most sincere thanks go out to the reviewers of our manuscript for their insightful comments: Terry S. Atkinson, University of North Carolina, Greensboro; Diane Bottomley, Ball State University; Leonard Breen, Sam Houston State University; Judy A. Leavell, Southwest Texas State University; and Mary Sanders, Angelo State University. We also wish to thank Linda Montgomery, our taskmaster and friend; Jane Parrigin, our copy editor; Mary Irvin, our production editor; Jeff Johnston; and the entire staff assisting us at Merrill/Prentice Hall.

Thank you too for choosing this second edition of *Strategies for Reading Assessment and Instruction*. We trust that it will assist you in your efforts to develop reading instruction plans. Please send us your comments and observations about whether we have achieved our aim. Best wishes as you work to help every child become a successful reader and a personally fulfilled individual.

D. Ray Reutzel
rreutzel@coe.usu.edu

Robert B. Cooter, Jr.
cooter@uta.edu

Discover the Companion Website Accompanying This Book

THE PRENTICE HALL COMPANION WEBSITE: A VIRTUAL LEARNING ENVIRONMENT

Technology is a constantly growing and changing aspect of our field that is creating a need for content and resources. To address this emerging need, Prentice Hall has developed an online learning environment for students and professors alike—Companion Websites–to support our textbooks.

In creating a Companion Website, our goal is to build on and enhance what the textbook already offers. For this reason, the content for each user-friendly website is organized by topic and provides the professor and student with a variety of meaningful resources. Common features of a Companion Website include:

FOR THE PROFESSOR

Every Companion Website integrates **Syllabus Manager**™, an online syllabus creation and management utility.

- **Syllabus Manager**™ provides you, the instructor, with an easy, step-by-step process to create and revise syllabi, with direct links into Companion Website and other online content without having to learn HTML.
- Students may logon to your syllabus during any study session. All they need to know is the web address for the Companion Website and the password you've assigned to your syllabus.
- After you have created a syllabus using **Syllabus Manager**™, students may enter the syllabus for their course section from any point in the Companion Website.
- Clicking on a date, the student is shown the list of activities for the assignment. The activities for each assignment are linked directly to actual content, saving time for students.
- Adding assignments consists of clicking on the desired due date, then filling in the details of the assignment—name of the assignment, instructions, and whether or not it is a one-time or repeating assignment.
- In addition, links to other activities can be created easily. If the activity is online, a URL can be entered in the space provided, and it will be linked automatically in the final syllabus.
- Your completed syllabus is hosted on our servers, allowing convenient updates from any computer on the Internet. Changes you make to your syllabus are immediately available to your students at their next logon.

FOR THE STUDENT

- **Topic Overviews**—outline key concepts in literacy topic areas.
- **Strategies**—these websites provide suggestions and information on how to implement instructional strategies and activities for each topic.
- **Web Links**—a wide range of websites that allow the students to access current information on everything from rationales for specific types of instruction, to research on related topics, to compilations of useful articles and more.
- **Electronic Bluebook**—send homework or essays directly to your instructor's email with this paperless form.
- **Message Board**—serves as a virtual bulletin board to post—or to respond to—quesitons or comments to/from a national audience.
- **Chat**—real-time chat with anyone who is using the text anywhere in the country—ideal for discussion and study groups, class projects, etc.

To take advantage of these and other resources, please visit the Strategies for Reading Assessment and Instruction Companion Website at

www.prenhall.com/reutzel

Contents

Chapter 8

Chapter 9

Chapter 10

Chapter 11

Chapter 12

Chapter 13

Chapter 14

Chapter 1

No Child Left Behind:
Comprehensive Reading Instruction

Ms. George and Mr. Talango reluctantly seat themselves near the back of the school library. "So, what's on for today?" asks Mr. Talango.

"Oh, I think we're supposed to have a workshop on reading instruction again," replies Ms. George. "I wonder what we'll be told today we've been doing wrong or what we haven't done enough of. Do you know who the presenter will be?"

"I think it's Dr. Reid from the university. She is supposed to really be into this phonemic awareness stuff," responds Mr. Talango.

"I've heard her before. I wonder if she's been in a classroom since the Spanish-American War. She always makes it seem that we have the luxury of focusing on just one thing to the exclusion of everything else we have to do."

"Yeah, I know how you feel. It seems like when it comes to reading instruction, we are always caught in the middle between what parents want and what the 'experts' tell us we need to be doing."

Ruefully, Ms. George says, "Well, after years of workshops, experts, and fads, I've decided that this too will pass. So, I guess I'll just keep doing what works for me."

The scenario portrayed above is familiar for many veteran reading teachers. *Strategies for Reading Assessment and Instruction: Helping Every Child Succeed, Second Edition* has been developed as a classroom tool for teachers who are in need of practical teaching and assessment ideas to complement their existing repertoire of instructional and assessment strategies. It is also for teachers who are tired of the latest and greatest fads and want well-researched information on how to provide a *comprehensive reading program* so that *all* children can succeed.

Beginning in chapter 5, we provide a brief overview of theory and scientific research called "Background Briefing for Teachers." Next, we describe assessment tools applicable to the topic taken up in each chapter. In this latest edition of our book we have created an "Intervention Strategy Guide" showing how your assessment findings can lead to the selection of specific teaching ideas presented in each chapter. In this guide we help you use assessment data to inform the selection of intervention strategies within a comprehensive reading program to meet student needs. Next, we describe several practical teaching strategies that have been validated in research and classroom practice. Finally, we address throughout this book how the special needs of students who struggle with learning to read, and students who are learning English as a second language, can be helped to succeed.

It occurs to us that it may be useful to know what this book is *not* as much as what it is. For instance, this book is not intended to serve as a basic, survey, or introductory text on reading instruction and assessment. Rather, it is a supplemental activities book for new or experienced teachers who need an exhaustive collection of classroom-proven assessment and teaching strategies that really work! [Note: For those who are just beginning the study of reading/literacy education and require a more complete orientation to the field, we suggest our companion text *Teaching Children to Read: Putting the Pieces Together, Third Edition* (Reutzel & Cooter, 2000) as a starting point, or one of the other major textbooks used in reading methods courses.] It is also intended to serve as an activities book for use in inservice teacher training on comprehensive reading instruction.

In summary, with this book one can readily and quickly turn to a chapter that presents current information on ways to assess, teach, and organize for effective and comprehensive reading instruction. Specific chapters offer guidance on assessment and for selecting teaching strategies that relate to data drawn from the assessment tools provided. Specifics on teaching concepts about print, phonics, guided reading, word recognition, fluency, comprehension, vocabulary, and so forth are provided.

In this first chapter, we discuss recent developments in reading education and research that have influenced the direction and nature of contemporary reading instruction. We begin by describing the waning of what has been termed "Balanced Reading Instruction" and why we have chosen to take the stance of "Comprehensive Reading Instruction" based on recent research reports on reading instruction. As part of describing the waning of Balanced Reading Instruction, we briefly discuss the "reading wars" of the late 1990s and early 2000s. Finally, we describe the essential elements of a comprehensive reading program.

THE READING WARS: A TIME OF TURMOIL IN READING INSTRUCTION

In 1994, data from the National Assessment of Educational Progress (NAEP) were released showing that fourth-grade students in California and Louisiana were tied for last place among the fifty states in reading achievement. This event led to yet another round of overemphasis upon some components of reading instruction at the expense of others (e.g., phonics versus the use of literature books in instruction) (Flippo, 2001; Reutzel & Smith, in press). Battles between advocates of differing reading instruction approaches, primarily proponents of whole language and skills-based approaches, led to what became known as *The Reading Wars.* Don Holdaway (1979), a well-known New Zealand educator, summed up the reading wars in this way:

> America seems to have returned to the crudities of pendulum thinking. Despite the fact that among them are strong voices speaking from a clear vision of what might be, they are stampeded by the recurrent public outcry into a back-to-basics movement without anyone having clarified just what the basics are (p. 30).

Examples of pendulum thinking could be found almost daily in newspaper headlines, such as "Reading Wars: Endless Squabbles Keep Kids From Getting the Help They Need" (*Chicago Tribune,* Rubin, 1997) and "Lost Generation of Readers Turn to Phonics for Help" (*Atlanta Journal Constitution,* Cumming, 1998). Furthermore, some recent book titles provide cases in point of the extreme positions taken among reading educators—see for example *Misreading reading: The bad science that hurts children* (Coles, 2000); *The Case Against Standardized Testing: Raising the Scores, Ruining the Schools* (Kohn, 2000), and *The Literacy Crisis: False Claims, Real Solutions* (McQuillan, 1998). Dixie

Lee Spiegel (1999) said of the reading wars hyperbole, "Education often appears to be not just a field of dreams, but a field of extremes" (p. 8).

Recent reports (see Figure 1.1) indicate stagnating or declining scores in children's reading achievement (NAEP, 2000). Such declines or stagnation in reading achievement have raised frustration levels and concern among parents, politicians, and educators alike. Increasing numbers of children are struggling in learning to read. This is particularly so among certain ethnic groups, children of poverty, and in large urban centers. The widening achievement gap between the "rich and the poor" in reading achievement has resulted in yet another round of finger pointing and blame placing in the media, political forums, and the education establishment alike. The media has often sensationalized the extent of the reading problem (Berliner & Biddle, 1995); exaggerated the depth of the disagreement among experts (Flippo, 1999, 2001); questioned the competence of teachers, teacher educators, and school administrators; and misrepresented the research.

Two former editors of *The Reading Teacher,* a journal of the International Reading Association, have judged the "Reading Wars" as an unfruitful exercise that has diverted our collective efforts away from more weighty matters: that some children, but most especially large proportions of children living in poverty in urban centers, are failing to read on level by the end of third grade (Rasinski & Padak, 1998). Amidst the strident discourse of politicians and reading experts, teachers continue in their steady, unheralded (and we think, heroic) daily efforts to bring the gift of literacy to increasing numbers of children. But what of the children and teachers who need genuine guidance and support? Is there no basis for a common understanding of high quality reading instruction and assessment? Actually, there is.

Figure 1.1 NAEP Chart

NOTE: The average scores are based on the NAEP reading scale, which ranges from 0 to 500.
SOURCE: National Center for Educational Statistics, National Assessment of Educational Progress (NAEP), 1992–2000 Reading Assessments.

Balanced Reading Instruction: Attempted Compromise, Confused Message

The Balanced Reading movement was a much-hoped-for compromise for ending the reading wars. The quest for *balanced reading instruction* began in 1990 among a small group of educators. These educators formed an organization to support a moderate, middle ground position concerning reading instruction. They issued a manifesto entitled, *Balance: A Manifesto for Balance in the Teaching of Literacy and Language Skills* (Thompson, 1997). Early on some U.S. schools and districts caught on to the balanced reading movement. But, it was not until the results of the 1994 National Assessment of Educational Progress (NAEP) became public in California that the balanced reading movement really took on national momentum.

Bill Honig (1995), then superintendent of public instruction in California, was instrumental in focusing national attention on the deficits of whole language instruction. He contended that whole language instruction was not meeting the needs of diverse students and that what was needed was a more "balanced" reading instructional approach. Honig's (1995) call for "balanced reading" was forcefully captured in the document, *Every Child a Reader: Report of the California Reading Task Force.* Other voices of reason and moderation emerged from what became known as *the radical middle* in support of a "balanced reading approach" to reading instruction.

As the national discussion progressed, an important question came into focus—"balancing *what,* and by *whom?*" Some national voices defined balance as an approach to reading instruction that brought equilibrium to two opposing views on the teaching of reading: whole language and phonics. What emerged from trying to define balanced reading instruction was the familiar notion of the "scales of justice." The concept of "balance" was to even up the sides of the scale with equal portions of phonics and whole language on either side as shown in Figure 1.2 (Baumann, Hoffman, Moon, & Duffy-Hester, 1998; Wharton-McDonald et al., 1997).

Soon it became apparent that to define "balanced reading instruction" as an act to even up the sides of the scale invited one more round of "this versus that" thinking.

Figure 1.2   Balance as Achieving Instructional Equilibrium

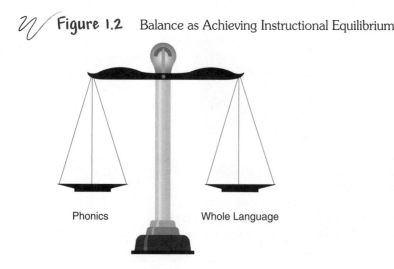

Phonics   Whole Language

Others challenged, from an historical viewpoint, the idea that balanced reading instruction was "new" and needed redefining at all (Reutzel, 1996a,b, 1999a, 1999b). This opinion held that balanced reading dated back to the popular "balanced reading" practices of the 1960s in New Zealand, also known as "READING TO, WITH, and BY" children (Mooney, 1990; Department of Education, 1985). As far as these reading educators were concerned, "balanced reading" had already been defined and proven effective for many years.

Still others felt that the concept of "balance" represented a *philosophy* rather than a defined set of practices. Balance was seen as a disciplined form of eclecticism grounded in the judgment and skill of informed teachers (Fitzgerald, 1999; Pearson, 2000; Spiegel, 1999; Strickland, 1998). In some ways this group attempted to describe balance by stating what it was and was not. Terms applied to define balanced reading instruction as a philosophy included: flexible, realistic, decision-making approach, consistency, and comprehensive (Fitzgerald, 1999; Spiegel, 1999).

THE ADVENT OF COMPREHENSIVE READING INSTRUCTION

The difficulty in defining balanced reading continued and eventually eroded much of its message and potential. David Pearson, in a presentation made for the Center for the Improvement of Early Reading Achievement (CIERA) in April 2000, stated, "I have stopped using the term 'balanced' because it seems to me that everyone has appropriated it [balance] to describe their highly particular approach. My new term is 'comprehensive'." This pronouncement was one of many signaling the waning moments of the "balanced reading" movement. Perhaps the final blow to the "balanced reading" movement was leveled by Louisa Moates (2000) in a report made to the Fordham Foundation entitled, *Whole language lives on: The illusion of "balanced" reading instruction.* Moates alleged that the term "balance" was nothing more than a cover for continuing the ineffective practices associated with whole language.

So we, like others, have abandoned the definition war associated with the term "balance" in *Strategies for Reading Assessment and Instruction: Helping Every Child Succeed, Second Edition.* We describe a **Comprehensive Reading Program** that is inclusive, research based, and one that meets the needs of all learners so that **no child is left behind!**

What is a Comprehensive Reading Program?

To develop a blueprint for a balanced reading program, we began our preparation for this new edition of *Strategies for Reading Assessment and Instruction: Helping Every Child Succeed, Second Edition* by conducting a content analysis of the findings and recommendations found in six important national reports and one international report shown in Figure 1.3.

After carefully reading each of these seven research reports, we sorted the instructional and programmatic recommendations into seven categories as found in Figure 1.4. We used these categories to help us present to you the elements of a comprehensive reading program.

Comprehensive reading programs are focused on both programs and outcomes. Comprehensive reading programs are goal driven. Many reading programs in the past have focused so heavily on measuring what goes into a reading program that measuring the results was overlooked or avoided. Reading is a complex human accomplishment and as such is not easily reduced to simplistic measurement. In fact, the extensive contents of this book

Figure 1.3   National and International Reading Reports

Flippo, R. F. (2001). *Reading Researchers in Search of Common Ground.* Newark, DE: International Reading Association.
Snow, C. E., Burns, M. S., and Griffin, P. (1998). *Preventing reading difficulties in young children.* Washington, DC: National Academy Press.
Report of the Literacy Taskforce. (1999). Wellington, New Zealand: Ministry of Education.
Teaching Reading is rocket science: What expert teachers of reading should know and be able to do. (1999). Washington, DC: American Federation of Teachers.
Report of the National Reading Panel: Teaching children to read. (2000). Washington, DC: National Institute of Child Health and Human Development.
Report of the National Education Association's Task Force on Reading 2000. (2000). Washington, DC: National Education Association.
Every Child a Reader. (1998). Ann Arbor, MI: Center for the Improvement of Early Reading Achievement.

 Figure 1.4   Seven Essential Elements of Comprehensive Reading Instruction

Points of Agreement Among National and International Reading Research Reports

Pursuit of a National Goal
School-Home-Community Partnerships
Schoolwide Reforms
Teacher Knowledge
Milestones of Reading Development
Purposeful Assessment
Student Motivation

make clear that reading assessment and instruction are complicated and multifaceted. Comprehensive reading programs:

- Embrace the national goal that 90% of third-grade or nine-year-old children will read on grade level.
- Support the effective implementation of partnerships among schools, parents, families, communities, corporations, and agencies.
- Reform the way schools organize and provide for reading instruction.
- Recognize the significant part that teachers play in helping children achieve their potential as readers.
- Identify the best practices associated with comprehensive reading instruction.
- Value the role of assessment in informing teachers' instructional choices.
- Encourage students to develop the skills to read and the love of reading.

When children receive effective, comprehensive initial reading instruction, the educational safety net is spread wide to catch them before they fail. In the pages that follow, we describe in detail each of the elements of comprehensive reading instruction to help you, the reader, thoughtfully consider how an effective, comprehensive reading program is created and implemented.

PURSUIT OF A NATIONAL GOAL

With shifts in today's employment market away from labor and manufacturing jobs toward service and information jobs, the current importance assigned to increasing children's literacy skills in the nation is amplified. Two presidents, numerous governors and legislators, parents, and educators all agree that a child who does not learn to read and use printed information has little or no chance to reach his or her potential as an individual, or to become economically mobile as a citizen in the future society and market place. In fact, it is rather depressing to note that some states plan for the number of prison beds needed for the future using the numbers of children failing to achieve basic reading proficiency by third grade. Given this grim but realistic predictor, we want all children to become fluent readers!

Our national reading goal (Fielding, Kerr, & Rosier, 1998, U.S. Department of Education—Goals 2000) is stated thus. . .

The Goal: 90% of the nation's students will read at or above grade level

by the end of third grade.

The goal, although seemingly a lofty one, is one worthy of our collective will as a nation. It will take considerable resolve among parents, teachers, administrators, and politicians to see that *no child is left behind* in learning to read competently and successfully—and that *no teacher is left behind* in providing the necessary instruction and learning conditions for achieving this important national goal.

Creating and Sustaining School-Home-Community Partnerships

The future U.S. economy and employment outlook demand greater literacy skills for all citizens to fully participate in the nation's economy and government (Fielding et al., 1998). Schools and families are finding it more difficult to work in isolation from one another and meet with much success. Families and schools, along with other agencies and businesses in the community, must partner together to support young readers so that no child is left behind.

No comprehensive reading program is complete without a school-home-community involvement program that unites our collective efforts to help children succeed in reading. Partnerships with schools, families, corporations, and government agencies that coordinate providing reading services to children and their families have increased dramatically in recent years as most notably exemplified in the *America Reads* school volunteer and tutoring programs. Research on family literacy programs has uniformly shown positive results of school-home-community partnerships on the acquisition of adult and young children's literacy skills across a variety of program types, pedagogies, and with varying populations (Au, 2000; Morrow, 1995). Requirements for receiving and retaining funds from the U.S. Government's *Reading in Excellence* grants include a strong plan for coordinating reading support services between community and government agencies and families. In the report, *Beating the Odds in Teaching All Children to Read,* issued by the Center for the Improvement of Early Reading Achievement, Taylor,

Pearson, Clark, and Walpole (1999) indicated that one of the chief characteristics associated with the most effective schools "beating the odds" in teaching all children to read was **having strong links to parents.**

We recommend broadening partnerships beyond family-school-community. Media conglomerates play an increasingly important role in providing technological support for children's development of the knowledge, concepts, skills, and dispositions toward learning to read. For example, Mates and Strommen (1996) described in an article entitled, "Why Ernie Can't Read" how the television program *Sesame Street* failed to help children grasp the "big picture" about reading and learning to read. *Ernie,* the show's main character, was typically portrayed reading words and identifying letters. He was not shown going to the library or bookstore. He did not check out or purchase a book. He did not read print in his environment, nor did he read a complete story or text. Similarly, when teachers during the early 1980s began to demand that publishing houses stop printing children's primers and basal readers using short, choppy selections (Eckhoff, 1983), corporate publishing groups began including selections of children's books, stories, and chapters in their printed materials (Reutzel & Larsen, 1995). Programs for organizing and connecting schools and families to service clubs, philanthropic foundations, government agencies, publishing houses, and media groups are no longer add-ons, extras, or optional equipment—but are rather fundamental elements of a comprehensive reading instructional program.

Cooter and his colleagues (1999) have reported dramatic results in bringing together city and community resources in the *Dallas Reading Plan.* Strategies include an annual citywide reading event known as *DEAR Dallas! (Deja todo y lee!),* an outreach videotape for parents featuring the PBS wonder dog character *Wishbone™* (ordering information follows at the end of this chapter), and *Reading Backpacks* for all K–3 classrooms so that inner city students can have books to read at home. Other outreach programs of the Dallas Reading Plan have included a summer Food and Reading program cosponsored by area churches (First Lady Laura Bush praised this program as a model for America) and a monthly newsletter for families explaining things they can do at home to support their children as developing readers (called *Refrigerator Reading* because the newsletter could be attached to the family refrigerator). These are just a few of the creative possibilities that can bring together literacy stakeholders.

In Figure 1.5, we describe several principles for connecting schools and their "communities" in the broadest sense to create collaborative partnerships that serve all children in learning to read successfully (Au, 2000; McGilp & Michael, 1994; Rasinski, 1995; Wasik, Dobbins, & Herrmann, 2001). Unfortunately, many school-home-community involvement partnerships are begun and ultimately fail because principles like those in Figure 1.5 are not followed. Observing these principles in creating and sustaining school-home-community partnerships will help to optimize chances for success in the long term as well as the short. All participants must begin with the belief that all partners want what is best for children.

In chapter 16 of this book, in a section entitled, "Family and Community Involvement Activities," we provide a greatly expanded look at school-family-community involvement programs including assessment tools, curricula for volunteer training, and effective strategies for creating and sustaining these vitally important partnerships.

Schoolwide Reading Program Reforms

Schoolwide practices are important considerations in a comprehensive reading program; they constitute the environment in which teachers teach and children learn. Most reports

ℳ **Figure 1.5**   Principles for Forging Effective School-Home-Community Partnerships
for Comprehensive Reading Instruction

Affirm the contributions of all partners to a child's success in learning to read.
Invite partners to make presentations to children on topics in which they have expertise.
Ensure that participation is open to all by providing support for their full access and participation.
Make the programs, training, and discussions enjoyable, efficient, and easy for partners.
Partner involvement needs to be consistent and require commitment.
Time, space, and resources need to be well planned so as not to waste partners' time and efforts.
Provide partners with accessible information about helping children learn to read and write suc-
cessfully such as "Raising a Reader; Raising a Writer" copublished by the International
Reading Association and the National Association for the Education of Young Children or the
publication "Starting Out Right" by the National Research Council.
Create a climate of joint ownership or shared venture. People tend to support that which they help
to create. Begin with a discussion series with partners to plan the training and program.
Provide effective communication, training, and follow-up between the school and partners.
Questions and concerns should be readily addressed and quickly resolved.
Focus on involving partners in real reading and writing with children at home, in the school,
through the media, or elsewhere in the community.
Collaborate in the development of a curriculum for training and involvement that is culturally
sensitive and respects the multiple literacies found in families of differing backgrounds.

on school reform call for increasing resources, providing consistent professional development for teachers, and having committed leadership.

Access to Print.   Access to print has been shown to be a critical element influencing children's reading development and achievement (Neuman & Celano, 2001). In the document, *Every Child a Reader: Report of the California Reading Task Force* (Honig, 1995), it was recommended that every classroom have a classroom library of at least 300 books with 1,500 books recommended as the desired collection size. A classroom library collection should contain a wide variety of reading levels and text types. The problem with this recommendation is that most school districts simply do not have the funds to create such libraries in every classroom. An alternative is to create well-stocked **literacy materials centers** in each school. These are rooms containing multiple copies of leveled books, big books, and other necessary "tools" of reading instruction set aside solely for classroom instruction (children cannot check out these books of materials, only teachers can).

For a fraction of the cost teachers can have access to all of the materials they need for instruction. Still, the cost to districts can be substantial. School district superintendents and school principals need to seek funds for and provide access to varied and sufficient quantities of reading materials if the mission of teaching every child to read is to be accomplished (Neuman & Celano, 2001; Radencich, Beers, & Schumm, 1995; Wepner, Feeley, & Strickland, 2002).

Access to Professional Development.   Teachers need continuous and coherent professional development to keep their reading instructional skills honed and to develop new understanding, insights, and skills in teaching reading. Additional resources need to be provided for schools where large proportions of children struggle learning to read—as much

A literacy materials center

as 1% of the total base district budget is recommended to be reserved for continuing professional development opportunities for teachers in reading (Snow et al., 1998), a paltry amount, really, compared to that spent by corporations (about 30%) to keep their professionals on the leading edge.

Many national policy makers are now realizing that most classroom elementary and early childhood teachers were minimally prepared in their undergraduate teacher education programs to teach reading, having had only one or two classes on the assessment and teaching of reading. Access to continuous and coherent professional development in reading instruction is essential to the success of comprehensive reading programs.

Access to Leadership.   As a group, teachers consistently remark that having strong, informed leadership supportive of quality reading instruction is an indispensable ingredient in the overall success of any reading program. The school principal, especially, must be committed to success of the program and be knowledgeable about how to support school-wide reading programs. Some states now require principals to complete a course in the supervision of school reading programs.

Access to Expertise.   The National Research Council (Snow et al., 1998) recommends that every school have a resident, certified reading specialist available to provide school-level literacy leadership, consultation, and demonstrations. Cooter (in press) describes one large urban school district that established a corps of "Lead Reading Teachers" for every elementary school to provide these and other services to classroom teachers.

The practice of giving students who struggle most in learning to read to the least trained personnel in the school (e.g., Title I aides, volunteers, or tutors) must be discontinued. The most needy must have access to the best trained reading teachers and specialists.

Access to Planning Time.   A common complaint heard among teachers is that they do not have adequate time during the school day to plan instruction, to assess individual student needs, to confer with other educational providers in the school, and/or to adapt instruction to meet the special needs of all readers. Providing teachers with adequate time to plan and coordinate services with other team members in a school stands to benefit all children, but especially those who struggle the most (Darling-Hammond, 1997, pp. 72–75).

Access to Resources for Reducing Class Size.   Reasonable restrictions on class size have been recommended in many national reports and by many national professional organizations. One encouraging sign is that some state legislatures have passed laws restricting class size in order to help our nation's teachers succeed and give our nation's students the right to learn (Darling-Hammond, 1997; Goodlad, 1994). A summary of recommendations for schoolwide reforms to support comprehensive reading programs is found in Figure 1.6.

Teacher Knowledge Is the Key

There was one clear and central theme across the seven national and international reports—*Teachers, not the method, materials, or approach, make the critical difference in the question of whether or not students will ultimately achieve and succeed in reading.* Linda Darling-Hammond, Executive Director of the National Commission on Teaching & America's Future, in a report entitled *What Matters Most: Teaching for America's Future* (1996), asserted that, "What teachers know and do is the most important influence on what students learn. Competent and caring teaching should be a student right" (p. 6).

Becoming a Nation of Readers report (1985) concluded that teacher ability was at least five times more important than the adoption of new published reading materials.

> An indisputable conclusion of research is that the quality of teaching makes a considerable difference in children's learning. Studies indicate that about 15 percent of the variation among children in reading achievement at the end of the school year is attributable to factors that relate to the skill and effectiveness of the teacher. In contrast, the largest study ever done comparing approaches to beginning reading found that about 3 percent of the variation in reading achievement at the end of first grade was attributable to the overall approach of the program. (Anderson, Hiebert, Scott, & Wilkinson, 1985, p. 85)

In the more recent report, *Preventing Reading Difficulties in Young Children,* a similar conclusion about the significant contribution of teacher competence to children's achievement in reading was asserted (Snow et al., 1998). *The National Education Association's Task Force on Reading 2000* summarized this critical point well and succinctly, *"The teacher, not the method, makes the real difference in reading success"* (p. 7).

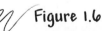 **Figure 1.6**   Schoolwide Reforms to Support Comprehensive Reading Programs

Access to Print
Access to Professional Development
Access to Leadership
Access to Expertise
Access to Planning Time
Access to Resources for Reducing Class Size

Teachers need to understand how children learn generally and how children learn to read in particular to teach them to read successfully (Smith, 1985). Studying the milestones of reading development is an important way for you, the teacher, to understand how children develop reading ability.

THE MILESTONES OF READING DEVELOPMENT: KNOWING WHICH SKILLS TO TEACH AND WHEN

In some areas of study, particularly mathematics, it is possible to say with some assurance which skills must be taught before others can be learned. For example, in order to perform division functions, one must know multiplication and subtraction skills. In reading, like mathematics, there are some skills that must be learned before others can be acquired (e.g., alphabetical order before dictionary skills, and so on). However, some reading/literacy skills may be learned within a wide span of time in the student's literacy development. Thus, knowing which reading skills are prerequisite and sequential, and which are more flexible in terms of instructional timing, can be very important indeed. In this section, we briefly summarize research pertaining to the *general* stages of reading development to assist you in accurately assessing students in the classroom. In later chapters, we describe more precisely the development of reading skills in specific areas (such as phonics, comprehension, phonemic awareness, fluency, and so on based on the National Research Council's *Starting Out Right: A Guide to Promoting Children's Reading Successes, Burns, Griffin, Snow,* 1999).

Some years ago, two teachers had a discussion about what is meant by a "beginning reader." They began to gather classroom data to create a reading development continuum (Cochrane et al., 1984). Such a continuum would, of course, be extremely helpful to them and their fellow teachers in more accurately assessing student reading development and planning future instruction. [Note: For more research on reading development that is quite compatible with Cochrane et al., see also Sulzby (1985).] Cochrane and his colleagues divided the development of reading into two overarching categories: (a) preindependent reading and (b) independent reading. Within each of these super-categories, these teachers described three more subdivisions. Within the preindependent reading category, for example, the three subordinate divisions or stages include: (a) the magical stage, (b) the self-concepting stage, and (c) the bridging stage. Within the independent reading category, the three subordinate divisions or stages are: (a) the take-off stage, (b) the independent reading stage, and (c) the skilled reading stage. Their continuum is shown in Figure 1.7 in checklist form, just as we have adapted it for our own classrooms.

THE MYSTERY OF READING: THE MAGICAL STAGE

Long before children enter school, they begin noticing print in their environment and learn that printed language stands for words they have heard others use, or that they have used themselves. Preschool children spontaneously learn to recognize billboards displaying their favorite TV channel logo. They can recognize a popular soda brand logo or pick out their favorite cereal at the local supermarket. Although they may not be able to read the print exactly on each of these objects, when asked to tell someone what the soda can says, they may respond with "soda" or "pop."

Figure 1.7   Reading Development Continuum

Observation Checklist for Reading Development

Student: _____   Year: _____
Teacher: _____   School: _____

Directions: Write in the date(s) as the child exhibits the behaviors listed below:

A. PREINDEPENDENT READING STAGES

1. *Magical Stage* [Sulzby's (1985) "Story Not Formed" level occurs about here]
   _____ Displays an interest in handling books
   _____ Sees the construction of meaning as magical or exterior to the print and imposed by others
   _____ Listens to print read to him for extended periods of time
   _____ Will play with letters or words
   _____ Begins to notice print in environmental context (signs, labels)
   _____ Letters may appear in his drawings
   _____ May mishandle books—observe them upside down; may damage them due to misunderstanding the purpose of books
   _____ Likes to "name" the pictures in a book, e.g., "lion," "rabbit"

2. *Self-Concepting Stage* [Sulzby's (1985) "Story Formed" level begins here]
   _____ Self-concepts himself as a reader, i.e., engages in readinglike activities
   _____ Tries to magically impose meaning on new print
   _____ "Reads" or reconstructs content of familiar storybooks
   _____ Recognizes his name and some other words in high environmental contexts (signs, labels)
   _____ His writing may display phonetic influence, i.e., wtbo = Wally, hr = her
   _____ Can construct story meaning from pictorial clues
   _____ Cannot pick words out of print consistently
   _____ Orally fills in many correct responses in oral cloze reading
   _____ Rhymes words
   _____ Has increasing control over nonvisual cueing systems
   _____ Gives words orally that begin similarly
   _____ Displays increasing degree of book handling knowledge
   _____ Is able to recall key words
   _____ Begins to internalize story grammar, i.e., knows how stories go together: "Once upon a time," "They lived happily ever after"

3. *Bridging Stage* [Sulzby's (1985) "Story Formed" to "Written Language-Like" level]
   _____ Can write and read back his own writing
   _____ Can pick out individual words and letters
   _____ Can read familiar books or poems that could not be totally repeated without the print
   _____ Uses picture clues to supplement the print
   _____ Words read in one context may not be read in another
   _____ Has increasing control over visual cueing system
   _____ Enjoys chants and poems chorally read
   _____ Can match or pick out words of poems or chants that have been internalized

B. INDEPENDENT READING STAGES

1. *Take-off Stage* [Sulzby's (1985) "Print Watched" to "Holistic" level]
   _____ Excited about reading
   _____ Wants to read to you often
   _____ Realizes that print is the base for constructing meaning
   _____ Can process (read) words in new (alternate) print situations
   _____ Aware of and reads aloud much environmental print (signs, labels, etc.)

continued

Figure 1.7   Continued

_____ Can conserve print from one contextual environment to another
_____ May exhibit temporary tunnel vision (concentrates on words and letters)
_____ Oral reading may be word centered rather than meaning centered
_____ Has increasing control over the Reading Process

2. *Independent Reading Stage* [Sulzby's (1985) "Holistic" level]
_____ Characterized by comprehension of the author's message by reader
_____ Reader's construction of meaning relies heavily on author's print or implied cues (schema)
_____ Desires to read books to himself for pleasure
_____ Brings his own experiences (schemata) to the print
_____ Reads orally with meaning and expression
_____ May see print as a literal truth—what the print says is right (legalized)
_____ Uses visual and nonvisual cueing systems simultaneously (cyclically)
_____ Has internalized several different print grammars, i.e., fairy tales, general problem-centered stories, simple exposition

3. *Skilled Reading Stage*
_____ Processes material further and further removed from his own experience
_____ Reading content and vocabulary become a part of his experience
_____ Can use a variety of print forms for pleasure
_____ Can discuss several aspects of a story
_____ Can read at varying and appropriate rates
_____ Can make inferences from print
_____ Challenges the validity of print content
_____ Can focus on or utilize the appropriate grammar or structuring of varying forms of print, e.g., stories, science experiments, menus, diagrams, histories

Source: Adapted from Cochrane, Cochrane, Scalena, and Buchanan. (1984), *Reading, Writing, and Caring.* Richard C. Owen Publishers, Inc., New York, New York; and E. Sulzby's (1985) "Children's emergent reading of favorite storybooks: A developmental study." *Reading Research Quarterly 20*(4), 458–481.

Children at this stage of reading development love to have books read to them. In quiet moments, these children may crawl up into a large comfortable chair to hold, look at, and tell a story from the pictures in their favorite books. When he was two years old, Jeremy enjoyed the naming of each animal in his favorite picture book. After naming each picture, he would enthusiastically make the sounds of each, such as the roaring of a lion or the crowing of a rooster. Parents and teachers of readers who find themselves journeying through the magical stage of reading development may see children who hold books upside down, turn the pages from the back to the front, and even tear out a page unintentionally. Although this may concern parents on one level, children who behave in these ways evidence a need for exposure to and understanding of the purpose of books. Withholding books from these children because they do not know how to handle them or read them at this stage would most certainly prove to be detrimental.

Children in the magical reading developmental stage develop a marked preference for a single or favorite book. Willing adults are often solicited to read this book again and again. Although parents and others may tire rapidly of this book, the affection and familiarity increases with each reading for the child. Favorite books are often repeatedly read to the point where the child memorizes them. Some parents even try to skip pages or sentences in these books, thinking their child will not notice; they soon learn, however, that their child has internalized these books, and the unsuspecting adult will be caught every time.

The reading of entire contexts such as those found on product logos and in books constitutes evidence to support the fact that young children prefer to process printed language from the whole to the parts. That is, reading the entire context of a sign or label and memorizing an entire book by young children is preferred much before they want or need to focus on the details and parts of printed language.

LOOK, MOM, I'M READING: THE SELF-CONCEPTING READING STAGE

The self-concepting reading developmental stage describes the child who has come to view himself as a reader. Although this child may not yet be able to read exactly what the print says, he is certainly aware of printed language and his own progress toward breaking the literacy barrier. Children in this stage will try to read unfamiliar books by telling the story from the pictures and from their own imaginations. Selected words are readily recognized, such as their own name, favorite food labels, and signs on bathroom doors. These readers will try to reconstruct the text of a favorite story from memory and picture clues. These children evidence an increasing awareness of words and sounds. They often ask questions about how words begin and about rhyming words. If given a chance, these children can also complete a sentence when asked to do so. For example, while reading "The Three Little Pigs," a teacher may say, "And the big bad wolf knocked at the door and said, 'Little Pig, Little Pig. . . .'" Children at this stage will immediately fill in the hanging sentence with "let me come in."

SPANNING THE GAP: THE BRIDGING STAGE

Children at the bridging stage of reading development can pick out familiar words and letters in familiar contexts and books. They often cannot, however, pick these same words out of an unfamiliar book or context when asked to do so. Children in the bridging stage can reconstruct stories from books with greater precision than can children in the previous stage. In fact, children in the bridging stage can no longer reconstruct the story completely without using the print, although they will continue to use picture clues to augment their growing control over the print system.

Children in the bridging stage can also read back what they have written. It has long been a disappointment for us when teachers and parents fail to count these early behaviors as real reading by brushing them aside as cute. Parents or teachers will often remark, "She's not reading. She's got that book memorized." Only by understanding that reading is a developmental process and that memorizing favorite print and books is universal among children will parents and teachers be able to enjoy, recognize, and support the progress their children make toward conventional reading behaviors and skills.

BLAST OFF! THE TAKE-OFF STAGE

If you are an unoccupied adult, look out for kids in the take-off stage! They are excited about reading and will perform for any reluctantly willing audience. In fact, they want to demonstrate their emerging ability as frequently as others will allow. Children at this stage of reading development have a clear understanding that print forms the basis for reading the story and constructing meaning. Words read in one book or context are now recognized in new or unfamiliar contexts. Signs and environmental print are subjects of intense interest among take-off readers. It seems as if print has a magnetic appeal for these children.

One autumn evening in a parent-teacher conference, while one of the authors was teaching first grade, a parent said that her son, Curt, had requested new breakfast cereals. When his mother asked why, Curt responded, "There's not enough to read on these boxes." His mother then bought him cereal in a box that seemed to display enough print to satisfy his appetite.

Oral reading during the take-off stage may become word or letter centered. Although oral reading before this time may have failed to perfectly represent the print on the page, it was smooth, fluent, and filled with inflection. The fact that words and letters have been discovered at this stage of development may lead to a situation in which children appear to temporarily regress in their reading development. Children in this stage need to focus on print details, which leads to less fluent and inflected oral reading for a time. With sustained opportunities to read and gain control over the reading process and print system, however, fluency and inflection will soon return.

I Can Do It by Myself! The Independent Reading Stage

The take-off reader wants an audience, but the independent reader takes great pride in reading books to himself for pleasure. The independent reader has developed control over the entire reading process and cueing systems. Reading is now carried on with simultaneous use of the author's printed clues and the reader's own store of background experiences and knowledge, called *schemata*. Fluency and inflection have returned to oral reading. In fact, chunks or phrases are now read fluently, with no laboring over single words. The independent reader is predicting ahead of the print and using context not just as an aid to decoding, but also to construct meaning (Stanovich, 1980). The ability to critically analyze print, however, has not yet been achieved. Thus, these readers may believe everything they read or may exhibit a tendency toward seeing anything in print as literal, truthful, and absolute.

Reaching the Summit: The Skilled Reading Stage

The skilled reader not only understands print, but uses print to support and extend thinking. Although this stage is the final stage of reading development, it is not a destination. The process of becoming skilled in reading is a lifelong journey. The journey to skilled reading involves processing print that is further and further removed from one's own experiences and knowledge. In other words, print is now used increasingly as a means to acquire new and unfamiliar information. The variety of printed media that skilled readers process increases from narratives and textbooks to magazines, newspapers, TV guides, tax forms, and so on. The skilled reader can talk about different types of text organizations, make inferences from print, use print to substantiate opinions, challenge the surface validity of printed materials, and vary his reading rate according to the personal purposes for reading, such as by skimming and scanning. Although more research is needed to corroborate the descriptions offered by Cochrane et al. (1984) in the reading development continuum, this model provides a useful framework for parents, teachers, and scholars through which they can view the development of a reader with increased understanding and a good deal less anxiety.

In addition to knowing the milestones of reading development, you will need to know the fundamentals of English language structure, grammar, and systems. You need to understand the reciprocal nature of oral and written language. For an in-depth study of these fundamentals, we recommend you read our other text, *Teaching Children to Read: Putting the Pieces Together, Third Edition*. In summary, we list in Figure 1.8 what competent reading teachers need to know in order to provide students with a comprehensive reading program.

Figure 1.8   What Competent Reading Teachers Need to Know

Learning theories and child development
Linguistics and language acquisition
Milestones of reading development
How to select appropriate instructional interventions based on assessment
How to address students with diverse and special needs
How to teach essential reading curriculum elements

COMPREHENSIVE READING INSTRUCTION: PURPOSEFUL ASSESSMENT

Despite persistent criticism, standardized and norm-referenced tests of reading achievement continue to dominate the educational decision-making landscape (Kohn, 2000). Policy makers in government and industry, school administrators, and the press continue to make sweeping judgments about the reading curriculum, the effectiveness of teacher's work, and the efficacy of student's learning based upon these measurement tools. As a consequence, many teachers have resigned themselves to the continued expectation that students must perform well on these types of standardized and criterion-referenced tests.

In a children's book entitled *First Grade Takes a Test,* Miriam Cohen (1980) describes the effects and shortcomings of standardized test taking on a group of first-grade children. The children are instructed that the test is timed and that they will need to hurry but that they should not worry. Next, they are told to fill in the boxes next to the "right" answers. One little boy notes that the answer options provided on the test do not adequately explain the reasons why rabbits have to eat carrots *AND* "eating carrots" was not one of the options for response. So, the little boy draws a carrot on the test response form so that the test people could know this fact!

Standardized tests do not provide adequate demonstrations of what children know or can do but rather point out only their shortcomings, deficits, and inabilities. It has been argued that the reductionistic effects of standardized, single form, high stakes testing may lead to teachers "teaching to the test" while failing to produce children who can and do read (Calkins et al., 1998; Miesels & Piker, 2001).

For you a teacher, the goals of assessment ought to be quite different from those of the public and policy makers who want to be able to determine gains and make comparisons among groups of children in schools, school districts, states, and the nation. Teachers rely on assessment leading to a "plan of action" or "next steps" in helping students develop strategic reading behaviors. They must know what children are doing *during* reading so that they can intervene where and when necessary to assist students in developing new reading skills and strategies that bring them to the next level of performance. Teachers need to *be present in the moment* with children as they read to make instructional decisions about where a student's reading processes require teaching. We offer several important principles for assessment in Figure 1.9. These principles, if followed, will help you as a teacher understand the purposes of assessment. If assessment is to be effective, teachers must use the data collected to inform their selection of appropriate teaching strategies.

Individual assessment is costly in terms of time and resources. However, if your goal in assessment is to improve instruction, and not just to make simple comparisons of group test performance, you must assess students individually. One of the goals of this book is to support you in learning alternative assessment procedures and applying the insights gained

Figure 1.9   Principles of Effective Classroom Assessment

Principle 1: Assessment should inform and improve teaching.
Principle 2: Assessment should help teachers discover what children know and can do.
Principle 3: Every assessment procedure should have a specific purpose.
Principle 4: Classroom assessment should provide teachers insights into each student's reading processes.
Principle 5: Assessment should help teachers identify each student's instructional needs.
Principle 6: Assessment should not consume so much time that it displaces instruction.
Principle 7: Individual assessment of the reading process is the only valid approach to assessment.

from assessment to your instructional planning. Continuous or ongoing assessment of instruction will help you study children's reading processes closely so that you can effectively teach those who struggle the most (Calkins et al., 1998; Kohn, 2000; Miesels & Piker, 2001). In chapter 2 of this book, we expand our discussion of general principles of effective assessment as well as how to create a successful assessment plan for your classroom and students.

ENGAGING AND MOTIVATING STUDENTS

Wigfield (1997) articulated a broad view of motivation theory related to reading as shown in the following list.

- Reading Efficacy
- Reading Challenge
- Reading Work Avoidance
- Reading Curiosity
- Involvement
- Importance of Reading
- Reading for Recognition
- Reading for Grades
- Competition in Reading
- Social Reasons for Reading
- Reading Compliance

Each of these relates to psychological constructs of engagement and motivation including beliefs, valuing, interests, rewards, goals, efficacy, ability, expectancies, attitudes, and purpose. You should understand that the selection and use of assessment tools and instructional practices could either promote or inhibit increased engagement and student effort. When you select instructional practices such as encouraging personal inquiry, social interaction, as well as providing coaching, learner-centered instruction, choice and access to a wide variety of reading materials, and coherent lesson design, students are more likely to persist in the complex task of learning to read (Wigfield & Gutherie, 1997). In chapters 10 and 15, we touch upon specific assessments and strategies/principles for increasing students' engagement and motivation as a part of a comprehensive reading instructional program.

Essential Resources, Practices, and Curricular Elements

As we planned our revision of this text to support teachers in creating and sustaining comprehensive reading programs, we carefully reviewed the recommendations of major national research reports. We knew that research had moved forward and that our new edition needed to reflect the best and most recent information about the essential curricular elements of comprehensive reading instruction. After combing through these reports for recommendations, we compiled the list shown in Figure 1.10. Elements of this list are placed in priority order based on the frequency with which they were mentioned in the research reports we reviewed.

It is important that you understand this list is neither exhaustive nor comprehensive itself. It represents the *minimal* resources, practices, and instructional content necessary to create a comprehensive reading program. These 15 individual essential curricular elements can be further reduced by placing them into three major categories: 1) *Allocated Time and Instructional Resources,* 2) *Instructional Routines,* and 3) *Essential Curricular Elements.*

Allocated Time and Instructional Resources.   Under the rubric of allocated time, it is now widely advocated that the reading/literacy instructional block should include at least 150 minutes per day of uninterrupted instructional time (Snow et al., 1998). As far as instructional resources are concerned, we have mentioned previously in this chapter the need for students and teachers to have access to a variety of reading materials at different levels of challenge to adequately support a comprehensive reading program.

Instructional Routines.   With reference to instructional routines, the work of Margaret Mooney (1990) can be used to summarize three important, even fundamental, elements of reading instruction—READING TO, READING WITH, & READING BY children. Each and every day's instructional routine ought to include reading TO children in order to model the what, why, and how of reading; reading WITH children to guide, direct, and teach the what, why, and how of reading; and reading BY children to practice, apply, and transfer knowledge of the what, why, and how of reading to novel texts and situations.

Figure 1.10   Essential Resources, Practices, and Curricular Elements of a Comprehensive Reading Program

1. Phonemic and alphabetic principle awareness instruction
2. Explicit and systematic phonics instruction
3. Oral reading fluency instruction
4. Independent reading practice
5. Access to a variety of reading and print materials
6. Comprehension strategy and text structure instruction
7. Vocabulary instruction
8. Guided reading instruction and feedback
9. Oral language development
10. Visual concepts of print instruction
11. Spelling patterns and word study skills instruction
12. Interactive read aloud
13. Technology-assisted reading instruction
14. Integrated reading, writing, and language instruction
15. Adequate daily time for reading/writing instruction and practice

Essential Curricular Elements.   These curricular elements are deemed essential because they have been shown to "cause" or are "strongly related" to increases in reading achievement among young and intermediate aged children. It is important to note also that some of these essential curricular elements need to be phased out over time as reading skill develops—such as concepts of print and phonemic awareness. To continue instruction in phonemic awareness and concepts of print past the point where they are useful would be a waste of precious instructional time and resources.

It is important for you, the teacher, to understand that these essential curriculum elements are interrelated and in some cases prerequisites for growth and development in reading. For example, oral language development is widely regarded as the foundation of learning to read and write (Hiebert, Pearson, Taylor, Richardson, & Paris, 1998). Learning about early concepts of print, letter naming, and phonemic awareness are dependent upon and build upon this critical oral language base. Likewise, phonics and word recognition instruction rely upon children acquiring an adequate grounding in the early concepts of reading such as the concepts of print, letter production and naming, and phonemic awareness. Facility in phonics and word recognition helps children to develop decoding "automaticity." Automatic decoding ability frees up limited mental capacity to allow developing readers to acquire new word meanings in print, improve comprehension, and develop fluency. Learning new word meanings and connecting these to other words and meanings stored in the oral language base is related to children's growth in comprehension performance. Learning about text structure, elaboration strategies, and self-monitoring/regulation all help to facilitate comprehension, which influences increases in children's reading fluency. Instruction in fluency and daily reading practice similarly increase students' enjoyment and comprehension. In chapters 3 and 4 of the book, we discuss in greater depth the elements, strategies, and instructional routines that support a comprehensive reading instructional program.

An Invitation . . .

In this first chapter we introduced you to the elements of comprehensive reading instruction and programs—but this is only the beginning. In the remainder of this book we offer you the most current information regarding effective classroom assessment and teaching strategies for offering comprehensive reading instruction. We urge you to read the first section of this book—*Focus on Comprehensive Reading Instruction*—to deepen your understanding of reading assessment and "Reading TO, WITH, and BY" instructional strategies.

In section two of this book—*Organizing for Instruction*—we describe in detail different ways of organizing an effective, comprehensive reading program from the primary grades through the intermediate grades. The third section of this book—*Assessment and Intervention Strategies*—once read, may be used as a handy reference tool in your professional library. For instance, if you have a group of young children who struggle with decoding, then chapters 7 and 8 on phonemic awareness and phonics will help you to assess their specific needs and select appropriate instructional interventions. However, students who want to read and comprehend nonfiction, information texts can be helped with ideas found in chapter 11—Reading Comprehension: Information Texts.

We know that your time is precious and that it is difficult to pore over all the books and journals on reading instruction to find the "just right" idea for your students. We, too, have experienced this time crunch dilemma and know how frustrating it can sometimes be when a teacher looks into the eyes of a child who is struggling with reading. With this revision, our goal was to fill the pages with current, practical, immediately useful assessment and instructional information for the experienced and the novice teacher. Along the way, we have tried out most of these ideas ourselves with children, or have asked our practicing teacher colleagues to do so. As you use this book with your students in the coming years, we trust that you will find our goal was largely met and, if time permits, you will take time to write us and suggest ways that the next edition can be even better. Best wishes for successful teaching of every child!

SELECTED REFERENCES

Anderson, R. C., Hiebert, E. F. , Scott, J. A., & Wilkinson, I. A. G. (1985). *Becoming a nation of readers: The report of the commission on reading.* Washington, D. C.: The National Institute of Education.

Au, K. H. (2000). A multicultural perspective on policies for improving literacy achievement: Equity and excellence. In M. L. Kamil, P. B. Mosenthal, P. D. Pearson, & R. Barr (Eds.), *Handbook of reading research, (vol. III.,* pp. 835–852). Mahwah, NJ: Lawrence Earlbaum Associates.

Baumann, J. F., Hoffman, J. V., Moon, J., & Duffy-Hester, A. M. (1998). Where are teachers' voices in the phonics/whole language debate? Results from a survey of U.S. elementary teachers. *The Reading Teacher, 51,* 636–50.

Berliner, D. C., & Biddle, B. J. (1995). *The manufactured crisis: Myths, fraud, and the attack on America's public schools.* Reading, MA: Addison-Wesley.

Blair-Larsen, S. M., & Williams, K. A. (1999). *The balanced reading program: Helping all students achieve success.* Newark, DE: International Reading Association.

Burns, M. S., Griffin, P., & Snow, C. E. (Eds.). (1999). *Starting out right: A guide to promoting children's reading success.* Committee on the Prevention of Reading Difficulties in Young Children, Commission on Behavioral and Social Sciences and Education, National Research Council. Washington, DC: National Academy Press.

Calkins, L. M., Montgomery, K., Santman, D., & Falk, B. (1998). *A teacher's guide to standardized reading tests: Knowledge is power.* Portsmouth, NH: Heinemann.

Cochrane, O., Cochrane, D., Scalena, D., & Buchanan, E. (1984). *Reading, writing and caring.* New York: Richard C. Owen Publishers, Inc.

Cohen, M. (1980). *First grade takes a test.* New York: Dell Publishers.

Coles, G. (2000). *Misreading reading: The bad science that hurts children.* Portsmouth, NH: Heinemann.

Cooter, R. B. (in press). *Urban literacy education.* Upper Saddle River, NJ: Merrill/Prentice Hall.

Cooter, R. B., Mills-House, E., Marrin, P., Mathews, B. A., Campbell, S., & Baker, T. (1999). Family and community involvement: The bedrock of reading success. *The Reading Teacher, 52*(8).

Darling-Hammond, L. (1997). *The right to learn: A blueprint for creating schools that work.* San Francisco: Jossey-Bass.

Department of Education. (1985). *Reading in junior classes. Wellington, New Zealand.* New York: Richard C. Owens.

Eckhoff, B. (1983). How reading affects children's writing. *Language Arts, 60*(5), 607–616.

Fielding, L., Kerr, N., & Rosier, P. (1998). *The 90% reading goal.* Kennewick, WA: New Foundation Press.

Fitzgerald, J. (1999). What is this thing called "balance?" *The Reading Teacher, 53*(2), 100–107.

Flippo, R. F. (1999). *What do the experts say? Helping children learn to read.* Portsmouth, NH: Heinemann.

Flippo, R. F. (2001). *Reading researchers in search of common ground.* Newark, DE: International Reading Association.

Goodlad, J. I. (1994). *Educational renewal: Better teachers, better schools.* San Francisco: Jossey-Bass.

Hiebert, E. H., Pearson, P. D., Taylor, B. M., Richardson, V., & Paris, S. G. (1998). *Every child a reader.* Ann Arbor, MI: Center for the Improvement of Early Reading Achievement.

Holdaway, D. (1979). *The foundations of literacy.* New York: Ashton Scholastic.

Honig, B. (1995). *Every child a reader: Report of the California reading task force.* Sacramento, CA: California Department of Education.

Kohn, A. (2000). *The case against standardized testing: Raising the scores, ruining the schools.* Portsmouth, NH: Heinemann.

Mates, B. F., & Strommen, L. (1996). Why Ernie can't read: "Sesame Street" and literacy. *The Reading Teacher, 49*(4), 300–306.

McGilp, J., & Michael, M. (1994). *The home-school connection: Guidelines for working with parents.* Portsmouth, NH: Heinemann.

McQuillan, J. (1998). *The literacy crises: False claims, real solutions.* Portsmouth, NH: Heinemann.

Miesels, S. J., & Piker, R. A. (2001). *An analysis of early literacy assessments used for instruction.* Ann Arbor, MI: Center for the Improvement of Early Reading Achievement.

Moates, L. C. (2000). *Whole language lives on: The illusion of "balanced" reading instruction.* NY: Fordham Foundation. Available online at www.edexcellence.net/library/wholelang/moats.htm

Mooney, M. E. (1990). *Reading to, with, and by children.* Katonah, NY: Richard C. Owens.

Morrow, L. M. (1995). *Family literacy: Connections in schools and communities.* Newark, DE: International Reading Association.

National Assessment of Educational Progress. (2000). Washington, D.C.: Department of Education.

National Commission on Teaching & America's Future (U.S.). (1996). *What matters most: Teaching for America's future.* New York: The Commission.

Neuman, S. B., & Celano, D. (2001). Access to print in low-income and middle-income communities: An ecological study of four neighborhoods. *Reading Research Quarterly, 36,* 8–26.

Pearson, P. D. (2000). *What sorts of programs and practices are supported by research? A reading from the radical middle.* Ann Arbor, MI: Center for the Improvement of Early Reading Instruction.

Radencich, M., Beers, P., & Schumm, J. S. (1995). *Handbook for the K–12 reading resource specialist.* New York: Allyn and Bacon.

Rasinski, T. V. (1995). *Parents and teachers: Helping children learn to read and write.* New York: Harcourt Brace.

Rasinski, T., & Padak, N. (1998). The reading wars. *The Reading Teacher, 51,* 630–31.

Reutzel, D. R. (1996a). A balanced reading approach: Spotlight on theory. In J. Baltas & S. Shafer (Eds.), *Guide to balanced reading: K–2—Making it work for you!* New York, Scholastic, Inc.

Reutzel, D. R. (1996b). A balanced reading approach: Spotlight on theory. In J. Baltas & S. Shafer (Eds.), *Guide to balanced reading: 3–6—Making it work for you!* New York, Scholastic, Inc.

Reutzel, D. R. (1999a). On balanced reading. *The Reading Teacher, 52,*(4), 2–4.

Reutzel, D. R. (1999b). On Welna's sacred cows: Where's the beef? *The Reading Teacher, 53,* 96–99.

Reutzel, D. R., & Cooter, R. B. (2000). *Teaching children to read: Putting the pieces together* (3rd ed.). Upper Saddle River, NJ: Merrill/Prentice Hall.

Reutzel, D. R., & Larsen, N. S. (1995). Look what they've done to real children's books in the new basal readers! *Language Arts, 72*(7), 495–507.

Reutzel, D. R., & Smith, J. A. (In press). Accelerating struggling readers' progress: A comparative analysis of "expert opinion" and research recommendations. *Reading and Writing Quarterly.*

Smith, F. (1985). *Reading without nonsense* (2nd ed.). New York: Teachers College Press.

Snow, C. E., Burns, M. S., & Griffin, P. (1998). *Preventing reading difficulties in young children.* Washington, D.C.: National Academy Press.

Spiegel, D. L. (1999). The perspective of the balanced approach. In S. M. Blair-Larsen & K. A. Williams (Eds.), *The balanced reading program: Helping all students achieve success* (pp. 8–23). Newark, DE: International Reading Association.

Stanovich, K. (1980). Toward an interactive-compensatory model of individual differences in the development of reading fluency. *Reading Research Quarterly, 16*(1), 37–71.

Strickland, D. S. (1996). In search of balance: Restructuring our literacy programs. *Reading Today,* Oct./Nov., 32.

Strickland, D. S. (1998). Balanced literacy: Teaching the thrills and skills of reading. *Instructor* [On line]. Available online at www.scholastic.com/instructor/curriculum/langarts/reading/balance.htm

Sulzby, E. (1985). Children's emergent reading of favorite storybooks: A developmental study. *Reading Research Quarterly, 20*(4), 458–481.

Taylor, B. M., Pearson, P. D., Clark, K. F., & Walpole, S. (1999). *Beating the odds in teaching all children to read.* Ann Arbor, MI: Center for the Improvement of Early Reading Achievement.

Thompson, R. (1997). The philosophy of balanced reading instruction. *The Journal of Balanced Reading Instruction, 4*(D1), 28–29.

Wasik, B. H., Dobbins, D. R., & Herrmann, S. (2001). Intergenerational family literacy: Concepts, research, and practice. In S. B. Neuman & D. K. Dickinson (Eds.), *Handbook of Early Literacy Research.* New York: Guilford Press.

Wepner, S. B., Feeley, J. T., & Strickland, D. S. (2002). *The administration and supervision of reading programs* (3rd ed.), New York: Teachers College Press.

Wharton-McDonald, R., Pressley, M., Rankin, J., Mistretta, J., Yokoi, L., & Ettenberger, S. (1997). Effective primary-grades literacy instruction = balanced literacy instruction. *The Reading Teacher 50*(6), 518–521.

What matters most: Teaching for America's future. (1996). New York, Teacher's College Columbia University: National Commission on Teaching & America's Future.

Wigfield, A. (1997). Children's motivations for reading and reading engagement. In J. T. Guthrie & A. Wigfield

(Eds.), *Reading engagement: Motivating readers through integrated instruction* (pp. 14–33). Newark, DE: International Reading Association.

Wigfield, A., & Guthrie, J. T. (1997). *Reading engagement: Motivating readers through integrated instruction.* Newark, DE: International Reading Association.

TO ORDER *WISHBONE*™ VIDEO AND AUDIO TAPES. . .

Products available:
DEAR Families: Paws to Read. . . with Wishbone™!—videotape/English (order # 4517)
DEAR Families: Paws to Read. . . with Wishbone™!—videotape/Spanish (order # 4518)
DEAR Schools: Paws to Read. . . with Wishbone™!—audiotape
Phone: 1-800-888-WISH
Fax: 972-390-6039
Big Feats! Entertainment
P.O. Box 9523
Allen, TX 75013-9523 (USA)
Internet: www.wwwishbone.com

Chapter 2

Classroom Reading Assessment

Jason arrived in the classroom of Ms. Catlin Spears in mid-October from a distant state. Unfortunately, his mother was not permitted to bring along his cumulative assessment files from his previous school (they must be mailed by the central office), so Ms. Spears decided she had better gather some preliminary information on his reading, writing, and mathematics abilities. But where to begin?

Catlin was a first-year teacher and felt a bit unsure of herself. And to make the situation a little more dicey, Jason's mom had informed the principal that he had attention deficit disorder (ADD) and it seemed to affect his learning, especially in reading. With that information in mind, Catlin decided to focus on reading first because it is the most fundamental.

Ms. Spears thought to herself . . . *Okay, let's stay calm. I know I can pull something together that will let me know where to begin teaching. I'll just pull out that activities book and notes from my college class on reading assessment and go from there.*

After perusing her study notes and readings, the mental haze started to lift along with Catlin's spirits. *I'll just put together a little battery of assessments that will help me find out just where Jason is in his reading. For his phonics and decoding, I'll go with a running record. For comprehension, I'll use a retelling form. Ahhh, here's a good observation checklist that'll help me gather some informal data on his reading. Maybe I should also do an interest inventory—that would help me choose some books and other texts that he would enjoy reading . . . .*

Soon Ms. Spears had enough information to begin making some judgments about where Jason was in his development, as well as discovering his "learning frontiers."

Expertise in reading assessment begins with an understanding of the learning fundamentals. The fundamentals, it seems to us anyway, can be summed up in the answers to two questions; what we refer to as the *how* and *what* questions.

How do children learn?
What should good readers be able to do?

Answer these two questions and you are ready to delve into the principles of effective classroom assessment!

LEARNING FUNDAMENTALS

How Do Children Learn?

Certainly volumes can and have been written on the subject of how children learn, so we will necessarily need to limit our conversation here to the bare essentials. For us, there are two primary beliefs as to how children learn that are indispensable in reading instruction: zone of proximal development (Vygotsky, 1986, 1990), and gradual release of responsibility (Pearson & Gallagher, 1983).

Teaching in the Zone of Proximal Development

Lev Vygotsky (1986, 1990), a Russian psychologist, teacher, and medical doctor, has had a tremendous effect on the field of education since the publication of his works in the West. According to Vygotsky, at any particular point in time a child has a range in which she can learn. Applied to reading—at one end of the range are reading skills the child can do alone, and at the other end are reading skills she could not do even with assistance. In the middle is what Vygotsky termed the **zone of proximal development.** He is well known for his statement: *What the child can do in cooperation today he can do alone tomorrow.* Vygotsky (1986) further explained:

> Therefore the only good kind of teaching is that which marches ahead of development and leads it; it must be aimed not so much at the ripe as at the ripening functions. . . . Instruction must be oriented toward the future, not the past. (pp. 188–189)

For Vygotsky, therefore, the teacher has a critical role to play in a child's learning. You might think of it this way: a child who has been riding his new bicycle using training wheels for some time asks that they be taken off so he can ride "like a big boy." The attentive parent, after removing the training wheels, runs along with the child with a hand firmly grasping the seat as he pedals his bike. Without the support of the parent, the child would not (in the beginning) have the confidence or skill to ride the bike without training wheels. This is the child's zone of proximal development for bike riding. After more practice allowing his skills to develop, he will one day ride without support. In Vygotskian terms, therefore, the effective reading teacher 1) knows *what* skills one must learn, and in what order, 2) is able to figure out *where* a student is in her reading development (i.e., *classroom assessment*), and 3) knows which skills she should learn next (her zone of proximal development). The reason classroom assessment is so important is that it should allow the teacher to know where the "frontier of learning" is for each student.

The Gradual Release of Responsibility

There is a way of operationalizing Vygotsky's notion of the zone of proximal development called the **gradual release of responsibility** (Pearson & Gallagher, 1983). When you have correctly identified the next skill for a student to learn (through classroom assessment), the process begins with your *modeling* the new skill to be learned for the student. This part of instruction and learning is *all teacher;* the student watches as you model and may ask questions to clarify his understanding of what you modeled. When you believe the student understands the new skill you have modeled, you then urge him to "try out" the skill himself with the teacher's support (like the parent firmly grasping her child's bicycle seat when he first attempts riding without training wheels). This step is known as **guided practice** and comes with massive amounts of practice (along with a gradually decreasing amount of teacher support). When we believe the student has

𝒲/ **Figure 2.1**   Gradual Release of Responsibility Model

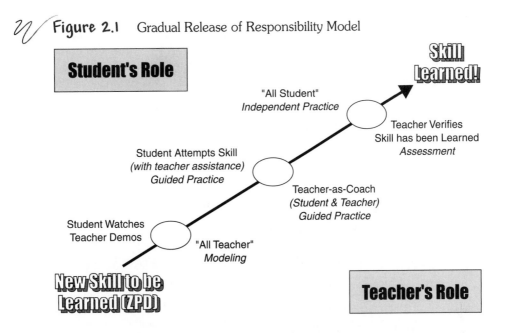

mastered the skill, we let him try it again without teacher assistance so that we can verify that permanent learning has occurred. We call this last step **independent practice.** The gradual release of responsibility concept of teaching and learning is represented in Figure 2.1. In this figure you see that teaching of a new skill moves from "all teacher" modeling for the student to observe, through guided practice and application activities involving the student with teacher support, and eventually to "all student" individual practice where the skill is finally mastered. Note the three zones of development for modeling, guided practice, and independent practice indicating that there is a gradual release of responsibility from teacher to student.

Before moving on, let's be clear about what is meant by "teacher" in the gradual release of responsibility concept. It can actually be *anyone* who is more competent in using the new skill(s) to be learned than the learner is. Thus, learners can be helped by the teacher, yes, but they can also learn from more competent classmates, family members, or a caring adult (May & Rizzardi, 2002).

WHAT SHOULD GOOD READERS BE ABLE TO DO?

Classroom assessment, more than anything else, is the ongoing process of learning just where a student is in her journey to becoming a fluent reader. Gauging where one is in any journey is done by considering the starting point and the destination. So, what is our destination for students in their reading at the end of kindergarten, first grade, second grade, and so on? What should they be able to do in reading at each level if they are progressing normally, and if they do not have significant learning problems? It stands to reason that if we understand the reading milestones students normally traverse through, then we can set out to find the best research-proven strategies for measuring each reading milestone skill.

Over the past several years, researchers have pored over the scientific literature to establish reliable and valid reading "benchmarks" for each grade level. This work has focused intently on grade K through 3 because this seems to be the place where most dysfunctional readers first have trouble. Many states (e.g., Kansas, Texas, California, Mississippi, and many more) have now established reading benchmark skills based on this type of research. One of the premier research reports that includes sections on benchmark "accomplishments" desired for normally developing children from the very young (birth to age four) through third grade is *Starting Out Right: A Guide to Promoting Children's Reading Success* (National Research Council, 1999). We have summarized their findings in Figure 2.2 to help you better understand the answer to an all-important question—*What should good readers be able to do?*

Figure 2.2   Reading Development Sequence

Kindergarten Accomplishments

- Knows the parts of a book and their functions.
- Begins to track print when listening to a familiar text being read or when rereading own writing.
- "Reads" familiar texts emergently, i.e., not necessarily verbatim from the print alone.
- Recognizes and can name all uppercase and lowercase letters.
- Understands that the sequence of letters in a written word represents the sequence of sounds (phonemes) in a spoken word (alphabetic principle).
- Learns many, though not all, one-to-one letter-sound correspondences.
- Recognizes some words by sight, including a few very common ones ("the," "I," "my," "you," "is," "are").
- Uses new vocabulary and grammatical constructions in own speech.
- Makes appropriate switches from oral to written language styles.
- Notices when simple sentences fail to make sense.
- Connects information and events in texts to life and life experiences to text.
- Retells, reenacts, or dramatizes stories or parts of stories.
- Listens attentively to books the teacher reads to class.
- Can name some book titles and authors.
- Demonstrates familiarity with a number of types or genres of text (e.g., storybooks, expository texts, poems, newspapers, and everyday print such as signs, notices, labels).
- Correctly answers questions about stories read aloud.
- Makes predictions based on illustrations or portions of stories.
- Demonstrates understanding that spoken words consist of sequences of phonemes.
- Given spoken sets like "dan, dan, den," can identify the first two as the same and the third as different.
- Given spoken sets like "dak, pat, zen," can identify the first two as sharing one same sound.
- Given spoken segments, can merge them into a meaningful target word.
- Given a spoken word, can produce another word that rhymes with it.
- Independently writes many uppercase and lowercase letters.
- Uses phonemic awareness and letter knowledge to spell independently (invented or creative spelling).
- Writes (unconventionally) to express own meaning.
- Builds a repertoire of some conventionally spelled words.
- Shows awareness of distinction between "kid writing" and conventional orthography.
- Writes own name (first and last) and the first names of some friends or classmates.
- Can write most letters and some words when they are dictated.

Figure 2.2 Continued

First Grade Accomplishments

- Makes a transition from emergent to "real" reading.
- Reads aloud with accuracy and comprehension any text that is appropriately designed for the first half of grade one.
- Accurately decodes orthographically regular, one-syllable words and nonsense words (e.g., "sit," "zot"), using print-sound mappings to sound out unknown words.
- Uses letter-sound correspondence knowledge to sound out unknown words when reading text.
- Recognizes common, irregularly spelled words by sight ("have," "said," "where," "two").
- Has a reading vocabulary of 300 to 500 sight words and easily sounded-out words.
- Monitors own reading and self-corrects when an incorrectly identified word does not fit with cues provided by the letters in the word or the context surrounding the word.
- Reads and comprehends both fiction and nonfiction that is appropriately designed for the grade level.
- Shows evidence of expanding language repertoire, including increasing appropriate use of standard, more formal language.
- Creates own written texts for others to read.
- Notices when difficulties are encountered in understanding text.
- Reads and understands simple written instructions.
- Predicts and justifies what will happen next in stories.
- Discusses prior knowledge of topics in expository texts.
- Uses how, why, and what-if questions to discuss nonfiction texts.
- Describes new information gained from texts in own words.
- Distinguishes whether simple sentences are incomplete or fail to make sense; notices when simple texts fail to make sense.
- Can answer simple written comprehension questions based on the material read.
- Can count the number of syllables in a word.
- Can blend or segment the phonemes of most one-syllable words.
- Spells correctly three- and four-letter short vowel words.
- Composes fairly readable first drafts using appropriate parts of the writing process (some attention to planning, drafting, rereading for meaning, and some self-correction).
- Uses invented spelling or phonics-based knowledge to spell independently, when necessary.
- Shows spelling consciousness or sensitivity to conventional spelling.
- Uses basic punctuation and capitalization.
- Produces a variety of types of compositions (e.g., stories, descriptions, journal entries) showing appropriate relationships between printed text, illustrations, and other graphics.
- Engages in a variety of literacy activities voluntarily (e.g., choosing books and stories to read, writing a note to a friend).

Second Grade Accomplishments

- Reads and comprehends both fiction and nonfiction that is appropriately designed for grade level.
- Accurately decodes orthographically regular, multisyllable words and nonsense words (e.g., capital, Kalamazoo).

continued

Figure 2.2 Continued

- Uses knowledge of print-sound mappings to sound out unknown words.
- Accurately reads many irregularly spelled words and such spelling patterns as diphthongs, special vowel spellings, and common word endings.
- Reads and comprehends both fiction and nonfiction that is appropriately designed for the grade.
- Shows evidence of expanding language repertory, including increasing use of more formal language registers.
- Reads voluntarily for interest and own purposes.
- Rereads sentences when meaning is not clear.
- Interprets information from diagrams, charts, and graphs.
- Recalls facts and details of texts.
- Reads nonfiction materials for answers to specific questions or for specific purposes.
- Takes part in creative responses to texts such as dramatizations, oral presentations, fantasy play, and so on.
- Discusses similarities in characters and events across stories.
- Connects and compares information across nonfiction selections.
- Poses possible answers to how, why, and what-if questions.
- Correctly spells previously studied words and spelling patterns in own writing.
- Represents the complete sound of a word when spelling independently.
- Shows sensitivity to using formal language patterns in place of oral language patterns at appropriate spots in own writing (e.g., de-contextualizing sentences, conventions for quoted speech, literary language forms, proper verb forms).
- Makes reasonable judgments about what to include in written products.
- Productively discusses ways to clarify and refine own writing and that of others.
- With assistance, adds use of conferencing, revision, and editing processes to clarify and refine own writing to the steps of the expected parts of the writing process.
- Given organizational help, writes informative, well-structured reports.
- Attends to spelling, mechanics, and presentation for final products.
- Produces a variety of types of compositions (e.g., stories, reports, correspondence).

Third Grade Accomplishments

- Reads aloud with fluency and comprehension any text that is appropriately designed for grade level.
- Uses letter-sound correspondence knowledge and structural analysis to decode words.
- Reads and comprehends both fiction and nonfiction that is appropriately designed for grade level.
- Reads longer fictional selections and chapter books independently.
- Takes part in creative responses to texts such as dramatizations, oral presentations, fantasy play, and so on.
- Can point to or clearly identify specific words or wordings that are causing comprehension difficulties.
- Summarizes major points from fiction and nonfiction texts.
- In interpreting fiction, discusses underlying theme or message.
- Asks how, why, and what-if questions in interpreting nonfiction texts.
- In interpreting nonfiction, distinguishes cause and effect, fact and opinion, main idea and supporting details.
- Uses information and reasoning to examine bases of hypotheses and opinions.
- Infers word meaning from taught roots, prefixes, and suffixes.

Figure 2.2 Continued

> - Correctly spells previously studied words and spelling patterns in own writing.
> - Begins to incorporate literacy words and language patterns in own writing (e.g., elaborates descriptions; uses figurative wording).
> - With some guidance, uses all aspects of the writing process in producing own compositions and reports.
> - Combines information from multiple sources in writing reports.
> - With assistance, suggests and implements editing and revision to clarify and refine own writing.
> - Presents and discusses own writing with other students and responds helpfully to other students' compositions.
> - Independently reviews work for spelling, mechanics, and presentation.
> - Produces a variety of written work (e.g., literature response, reports, "published" books, semantic maps) in a variety of formats including multimedia forms.

Source: From Burns, M. S.; Griffin, P., & Snow, C. E. (Eds.). (1999). *Starting out right: A Guide to promoting children's reading success.* Washington, DC: National Research Council. ISBN: 0-309-06410-4. Available online at www.nap.edu

PRINCIPLES OF CLASSROOM READING ASSESSMENT

There are several basic assumptions that govern what we do in the way of classroom reading assessment. Abiding by these principles helps us to remain focused, systematic, and purposeful in our teaching.

PRINCIPLE 1: THE TEACHER'S GOAL IS TO FIND OUT WHAT KIDS CAN DO

The development of reading follows a reasonably certain path with clear markers along the way. Your job as a teacher is to locate where each child is in her development so that you can offer appropriate instruction to continue her growth. This is done by carefully charting what a child *can* do in reading (not what she cannot do) beginning with early reading skills and moving systematically toward the more complex. This will tell you where each child is in her reading development as well as what should come next.

PRINCIPLE 2: ASSESSMENT LEADS AND INFORMS INSTRUCTION

There has been a kind of "chicken versus the egg" debate in past years about which comes first—teaching or assessment. Principle 1 resolves the debate for us; effective teaching cannot possibly begin until we first discover just where the child is in her reading development. That information helps us know the appropriate next steps for the student and, conversely, what would be a waste of her time either because the child already "owns" that reading skill, or the skill is too advanced and beyond her grasp at this time.

Reading instruction in many schools and school districts mirrors the state's mandated curriculum and reading tests—sometimes referred to as *high stakes* tests because whether or not a child is retained can be decided using these tests. In this scenario it is clear that reading tests do indeed lead instruction, and not always for the better because it is often the curriculum leading instruction instead of an assessment of the student's needs. Thus it is important that we make sure that the state tests are measuring appropriate reading skills at each grade level as determined through scientific research.

PRINCIPLE 3: BE PREPARED: GATHER YOUR ASSESSMENT "TOOLS" IN ADVANCE

The tools of assessment include such items as leveled books in the language of instruction (i.e., English and/or Spanish in many American classrooms), a cassette recorder and tapes to record student readings, student and class profiling documents (Reutzel & Cooter, 2000), carefully prepared observation checklists, a scope and sequence of reading milestone skills to be learned and charted (see previous section), perhaps an informal reading inventory for quick assessments at the beginning and mid-point of the school year (e.g., *Running Records for Classroom Teachers* [Clay, 2000]; *The Spanish & English Reading Inventory* [Flynt & Cooter, 2003]), and so forth. Chapters 5 through 15 of this book provide you with a veritable arsenal of assessment ideas, strategies, and materials.

Before conducting observations and other assessments on one or more of your students, be certain that you have gathered the necessary tools and references so that the assessments are done in a swift, efficient, and (sometimes) covert way. Being properly prepared will help you to collect valid and reliable assessments.

PRINCIPLE 4: ANALYZE ASSESSMENT FINDINGS USING IF-THEN THINKING

One of the challenges for many teachers is trying to figure out just what to do with assessment findings once they have been gathered! We sometimes get to be pretty good at *gathering* assessment evidence, but then have difficulty *analyzing* our findings and converting them into classroom action plans.

We subscribe to a method known as *If-Then Thinking* (Flynt & Cooter, 2001) for analyzing assessment data and translating it into potent lesson plans. The basic philosophy goes something like this: *If* you know that a child is able to do "X" in reading, *then* she is now ready to learn "Y." In other words, if you are able to accurately determine *where* a child is in her reading development (see Principles 1 and 2), then you will know *what* should come next instructionally. In each chapter, beginning with chapter 5, we provide you with an Intervention Strategy Guide in a section titled *Connecting Assessment Findings to Teaching Strategies* that will help you make instructional decisions based on your assessment data. For example, Figure 2.3 shows an excerpt from chapter 6 dealing with "Concepts about Print."

PRINCIPLE 5: DOCUMENT GROWTH IN READING OVER TIME

Reading assessment is not a one-shot activity done at the beginning of the year, but an ongoing and integral part of teaching and learning. Indeed assessment and good teaching are

Intervention/Strategy → Student Problem(s) ↓	Read Environmental Print	LEA	Voice Point	Frame	Masking Highlighting	Context Transfer	Error Detect	Verbal Punctuation	Shared Reading	Manipulative Letters
Book Handling	–	–	–	–	–	–	–	–	+	–
Directionality	*	*	+	–	–	*	–	–	+	*
Print Carries Message	+	+	+	+	*	+	+	–	+	*
Voice-Print Matching	*	*	+	*	+	+	*	–	+	–
Punctuation	*	+	*	*	+	*	+	+	+	–
Concept of Word/Letter	+	+	*	+	+	*	+	–	+	*
Order—Letters/Words	+	*	*	+	+	*	+	–	+	+
Pragmatic Response to Environmental Print	+	–	*	*	*	+	*	–	–	*
Reader relies on a single strategy to unlock unknown words.	*	*	–	*	*	*	*	–	+	*

Key: + excellent strategy
  * adaptable strategy
  – unsuitable strategy

virtually seamless. It is critical that we carry a veritable arsenal of assessment ideas in our teaching battery to aid us in our daily reading assessments. It is equally critical that we devise ways to document what we learn about each student's reading development to aid us in instructional decision making.

Finding Out What Kids Can Do: Basic Assessment Strategies

Decoding Assessment: The Running Record

In the early development of readers, teachers often focus on two very basic areas in their assessments: decoding, or the translation of letters and words into language, and comprehension of what has been read. An assessment procedure frequently used to measure decoding skill is the running record (Clay, 1997; Wiener & Cohen, 1997). To assess comprehension of story elements, such as setting, characters, problem, and solution, many teachers now prefer to use retellings (Tompkins, 2001). In this section we present the most current methods and ideas regarding the use of running records and retellings as important components in a teacher's reading assessment arsenal.

What Are Running Records?

From the earliest days of formal reading instruction and research, the ability to decode words in print has been viewed as essential. In 1915, for example, William S. Gray published the Standardized Oral Reading Paragraphs for grades 1 through 8, which focused on oral reading errors and reading speed exclusively. In the 1930s and 1940s, Durrell (1940) and Betts (1946) discussed at length the value of studying oral reading errors as a way to inform reading instruction. These and other writings began the development of what we now refer to as informal reading inventories (IRI), in which oral reading errors are analyzed.

Half a century after Gray's test was published, Marie Clay (1966) began publishing landmark research detailing a systematic analysis of oral reading errors of emergent readers. The examination and interpretation of the relative "value" of oral reading errors (i.e., semantic and syntactic "acceptability") by Clay helped usher in a new age of understanding of the decoding processes. A year later, it appears that Y. Goodman (1967) and other researchers mirrored Clay's thinking by employing careful studies of oral reading errors, or "miscue analysis," to better understand decoding patterns of emergent readers.

In the 1970s, Y. Goodman and Burke (1972), in an assessment manual called the *Reading Miscue Inventory* (RMI), and Clay (1972), in her manual called *The Early Detection of Reading Difficulties,* sought to formalize methodology for teachers who wish to focus on decoding assessment. Because of its complexity and impractical nature for classroom use, the RMI never really gained much acceptance beyond university research settings, although its theoretical base was widely heralded among reading education scholars. Of the two methodologies, Clay's "running records" for analyzing oral reading errors proved to be the more functional for most classroom teachers because of time and other real-world constraints. In the next section we describe in detail how running records are constructed and used to inform classroom teaching.

Conducting Running Records

Marie Clay (1972, 1985, 1997), a New Zealand educator and a former president of the International Reading Association, described the running record as an informal assessment procedure with high reliability (.90 on error reliabilities) that can inform teachers regarding a student's decoding development. The procedure is not difficult, but does require practice. Clay estimates that it takes about two hours of practice for teachers to become relatively proficient at running records. In essence, the teacher notes everything the student says or does while reading including all the correct words read orally and all miscues (Wiener & Cohen, 1997). Clay recommends that three running records be obtained for each child on various levels of difficulty for initial reading assessment. Her criteria for oral reading evaluation are based on words correctly read aloud:

Independent Level (easy to read)   95–100% correct
Instructional Level (ideal for teaching) 90–94% correct
Frustration Level (too difficult)   80–89% correct

Running records, with Clay's method, are taken without having to mark a prepared script and may be recorded on a sheet of paper; requiring about 10 minutes to transcribe. Guidelines for administration follow:

1. A sample from the book(s) to be used is needed that is 100–200 words in length. For early readers, the text may fall below 100 words. Allow the student to read the passage one or two times before you take the running record.

2. Sit alongside the student while she reads so that you can both see the page. It is not really necessary to have your own photocopy of the text; a blank sheet of paper will do. Record all accurate reading by making a check mark on a sheet of blank paper for each word said correctly. Errors or "miscues" should be noted using the notations indicated in Figure 2.4. Figure 2.5 shows an example of a running record taken using the book *Martha Speaks* (Meddaugh, 1992, pp. 1–4) using the marking system. The box on the left is a copy of the text the student is reading. The box on the right is the running record taken by the teacher with each of the miscue types noted. Next, we will take a look at how you go about analyzing miscues so that you will know what the reader *can* do.

UNDERSTANDING MISCUES: M-S-V ANALYSIS

Marie Clay (1985) developed a way of interpreting miscues for use in her widely acclaimed Reading Recovery program. This way of thinking enables you to determine the extent to which the student uses three primary **cueing strategies** when she encounters a new word and a miscue occurs: Meaning Cues (M), Syntax Cues (S), and Visual Cues (V). Here is a summary based on the work of Flynt and Cooter (1999):

- *M = Semantic (Meaning—Does it make sense?)* In reviewing each miscue, consider whether the student is using meaning cues in her attempt to identify the word. Context clues, picture cues, and information from the passage are examples of meaning cues used by the reader.

- *S = Structure (or Syntax—Does it sound right?)* A rule system or *grammar,* as with all languages, governs the English language. For example, English is essentially based on a "subject-verb" grammar system. *Syntax* is the application of this subject-verb grammar system in creating sentences. The goal in studying *syntax cues* as part of your miscue analysis is to try and determine the extent to which the student unconsciously uses rules of grammar in attempting to identify unknown words in print. For example, if a word in a passage causing a miscue for the reader

Figure 2.4   Notations for a Running Record

Reading Behavior	Notation	Explanation
Accurate Reading	√ √ √ √ √ √	*Notation:* A check is noted for each word pronounced correctly.
Self-Correction	√ √ √ √ attempt SC word from text	The child corrects an error himself. This is not counted as a miscue. *Notation:* "SC" is the notation used for self-corrections.
Omission	———— Word from text	A word or words are left out during the reading. *Notation:* A dash mark is written over a line above the word(s) from the text that has been omitted.
Insertion	Word inserted ————	The child adds a word that is not in the text. *Notation:* The word inserted by the reader is placed above a line and a dash placed below it.
Student Appeal and Assistance	———— A Word from text	The child is "stuck" on a word he cannot call and asks (verbal or nonverbal) the teacher for help. *Notation:* "A" is written above a line for "assisted" and the problem word from the text is written below the line.
Repetition	√ √ √ **R** √ √ √	Sometimes children will repeat words or phrases. These repetitions are not scored as an error, but *are* recorded. *Notation:* Write an "R" after the word repeated and draw a line back to the point where the reader returned.
Substitution	Substituted word Word from text	The child says a word that is different from the word in the text. *Notation:* The student's substitution word is written above a line under which the correct word from text is written.
Teacher Assistance	———— T Word from text	The student pauses on a word for five seconds or more, so the teacher tells him/her the word. *Notation:* The letter "T" is written to the right of a line that follows the word from text. A blank is placed above a cross-line to indicate that the student did not know the word.

2/ **Figure 2.5** Running Record Example

Student _____ Paco (Grade 2) _____	

Title: **The Pig and the Snake**

One day Mr. Pig was walking to	✓ ✓ ✓ ✓ ✓ ✓ ✓
town. He saw a big hole in the	✓ ✓ $\frac{sam|sc}{saw}$ ✓ ✓ ✓ ✓ ✓
road. A big snake was in the	✓ ✓ $\frac{-}{big}$ ✓ ✓ ✓ ✓
hole. "Help me," said the snake,	✓ ✓ ✓ $\frac{ouT}{-}$ ✓ ✓ ✓
"and I will be your friend." "No, no,"	✓ ✓ ✓✓ $\frac{-}{friend}$ | A ✓ ✓
said Mr. Pig. "If I help you get	✓ ✓ ✓ ✓ ✓ ✓ ✓ ✓
out you will bite me. You're	✓ ✓ ✓ R ✓ ✓
a snake!" The snake cried and	✓ ✓ ✓ ✓ ✓ ✓
cried. So Mr. Pig pulled the	✓ ✓ ✓ ✓ $\frac{popped}{pulled}$
snake out of the hole.	✓ ✓ ✓ ✓ ✓
Then the snake said, "Now I am	✓ ✓ ✓ ✓ ✓ ✓ ✓
going to bite you, Mr. Pig."	✓ ✓ ✓ ✓ ✓ ✓
"How can you bite me after	✓ ✓ ✓ ✓ ✓ $\frac{-}{after}$ | T
I helped you out of the hole?"	✓ ✓ ✓ ✓ ✓ ✓ ✓
said Mr. Pig. The snake said,//	✓ ✓ ✓ ✓ ✓ ✓
"You knew I was a snake	✓ ✓ ✓ ✓ ✓ ✓
when you pulled me out!"	✓ ✓ ✓ ✓ ✓

Source: Flynt, E. S., & Cooter, R. B. (2001). *The Flynt/Cooter Reading Inventory for the Classroom, 4/e.* Upper Saddle River, NJ: Merrill/Prentice Hall. Used with permission of the authors.

is a verb, ask yourself whether the student's miscue was also a verb. Consistent use of the appropriate part of speech in miscues (i.e., a noun for a noun, a verb for a verb, articles for articles, etc.) is an indication that the student has internalized the rule system of English grammar and is applying that knowledge in attacking unknown words.

- *V = Visual (Graphophonic—Does it look right?)* Sometimes a miscue looks a good bit like the correct word appearing in the text. The miscue may begin with the same letter or letters, for example saying the *top* for *toy*, or *sit* for *seat*. Another possibility is the letters of the miscue may look very similar to the word appearing in text (e.g., *introduction* for *introspection*). Use of visual cues is essentially the student's ability (or inability) to apply phonics skills. The extent to which readers use visual cues is an important factor to consider when trying to better understand the skills employed by developing readers when attacking unknown words in print.

Applying MSV thinking is fairly simple once you get the hang of it. In Figure 2.6 we return to the miscues previously noted in Figure 2.5 and conduct an MSV analysis on each. Do you see why each interpretation was made?

The Miscue Grid: An Alternative Running Records Scheme

As useful as the running record can be for teachers in planning instruction, many feel that the time required for administering and analyzing running records can be prohibitive in public school classes of 25 or more students. To make the process go more quickly and reliably, Flynt and Cooter (1999, 2001) developed a simplified process for completing running records that makes them more practical for classroom use. In their assessment instrument, *The Flynt/Cooter Reading Inventory for the Classroom*, teachers learn how to follow along during oral reading, noting miscues on a specially prepared protocol form called the Miscue Grid. They then complete the process by noting in a type of table or grid the kind of miscues that were made. By totaling the number of oral reading errors in each miscue category (i.e., word call errors, attempted decoding, and so on.), the teacher is able to quickly determine "miscue patterns" and to plan instruction accordingly. Field-tested with hundreds of Title I reading teachers, the Miscue Grid has proven to be an extremely effective classroom tool. Figure 2.7 shows an example of a completed Flynt/Cooter (1999) Miscue Grid for a student named Grace, again using *Martha Speaks* (Meddaugh, 1992) as the text.

TRANSLATING RUNNING RECORD FINDINGS INTO CLASSROOM INTERVENTIONS

In the example shown in Figure 2.7 we note that Grace had some difficulty with the text sample from *Martha Speaks*. Note that for each miscue, a mark " | " was recorded under the appropriate column heading, classifying each miscue as a word call error, repetition, or other mistake. After all miscues have been studied and their category identified, the tick marks in each column are totaled. This process reveals that with this passage, most of Grace's miscues are word call errors (3), insertions (2), and repetitions (2). With a total of 10 miscues of 100 words read (note that we do not count any miscues after the 100th word), simple subtraction tells us that Grace read with 90% accuracy, placing her within the "instructional" reading level according to Clay's system mentioned earlier. However, conclusions should not be drawn from only one running

Figure 2.6 Running Record with MSV Analysis

Student _____ Paco _____ (Grade 2) _____

Title: **The Pig and the Snake**		E MSV	SC MSV
One day Mr. Pig was walking to	✓ ✓ ✓ ✓ ✓ ✓ ✓		
town. He saw a big hole in the	✓ ✓ sam|sc / saw ✓ ✓ ✓ ✓ ✓		Ⓜ Ⓢ Ⓥ
road. A big snake was in the	✓ ✓ — / big ✓ ✓ ✓ ✓	M S V	
hole. "Help me," said the snake,	✓ ✓ ✓ ouT / — ✓ ✓ ✓	Ⓜ Ⓢ V	
"and I will be your friend." "No, no,"	✓ ✓ ✓ ✓ — | A / friend| ✓ ✓	M S V	
said Mr. Pig. "If I help you get	✓ ✓ ✓ ✓ ✓ ✓ ✓ ✓		
out you will bite me. You're	✓ ✓ ✓ R ✓ ✓		Ⓜ Ⓢ Ⓥ
a snake!" The snake cried and	✓ ✓ ✓ ✓ ✓ ✓		
cried. So Mr. Pig pulled the	✓ ✓ ✓ ✓ popped / pulled	Ⓜ Ⓢ Ⓥ	
snake out of the hole.	✓ ✓ ✓ ✓ ✓		
Then the snake said, "Now I am	✓ ✓ ✓ ✓ ✓ ✓ ✓		
going to bite you, Mr. Pig."	✓ ✓ ✓ ✓ ✓ ✓		
"How can you bite me after	✓ ✓ ✓ ✓ ✓ — / after | T	M S V	
I helped you out of the hole?"	✓ ✓ ✓ ✓ ✓ ✓ ✓		
said Mr. Pig. The snake said,//	✓ ✓ ✓ ✓ ✓ ✓		
"You knew I was a snake	✓ ✓ ✓ ✓ ✓ ✓		
when you pulled me out!"	✓ ✓ ✓ ✓ ✓		

Source: Flynt, E. S., & Cooter, R. B. (2001). *The Flynt/Cooter Reading Inventory for the Classroom, 4/e.* Upper Saddle River, NJ: Merrill/Prentice Hall. Used with permission of the authors.

Figure 2.7   Grace's Running Record Miscue Grid Using *Martha Speaks* (Meddaugh, 1992)

	Word call error	Attempt decode	Self-correct	Insertions	No word given	Teacher assist	Repeti-tion
The day Helen gave Martha dog her							
understood alphabet soup something ~~unusual~~	I						
I . . . let . . . letters happened. The ~~letters~~ in the soup went		I					
brin . . . brain sc *in* up to Martha's ~~brain~~ instead of down ^			I	I			
to her stomach. That evening, Martha							
spoke. "<u>Isn't it</u> time for my dinner?"							I
TA Martha's family had many questions to						I	
ask her. Of course, she had a lot to							
tell them. "<u>Have you always</u> understood							I
are what we were saying?" "You bet! Do	I						
Betty you want to know what Benjie is really	I						
saying?" "Why don't you come when we							
always call?" "You people are ^ so bossy. Come!				I			
Sit! Stay! You never say please."							
"Do dogs dream?" "Day and night. (100 wrds)							
This morning I dreamed I was chasing							
a giant meatloaf!"							
TOTALS	3	1	1	2	0	1	2

Source: Based on Flynt, E. S., & Cooter, R. B. (1999). *The English-Español reading inventory for the classroom.* Upper Saddle River, NJ: Merrill/Prentice Hall.

record. As already noted, a minimum of three running records should be taken and comparisons made across all three to determine whether a pattern of reading behavior exists.

If, in Grace's case, there seem to be consistent patterns of miscues as seen in the *Martha Speaks* selection, then the teacher may reasonably conclude that some sort of classroom intervention may be needed (usually in the form of minilessons). For the sake of efficiency, most teachers form short-term groups for children having the same needs (to help with insertion miscues, for example). Running records, when applied using the Flynt/Cooter (1999) grid system, can be a most informative addition to one's reading assessment program.

COMPREHENSION ASSESSMENT BASICS: USING RETELLINGS

Retellings are one of the best and most efficient strategies for finding out whether a child understands what he has read (Gambrell, Pfeiffer, & Wilson, 1985; Hoyt, 1998; Morrow, 1985), especially when compared to the seemingly endless and tedious question/answer sessions that so often characterize basal readers and their workbook pages (what we like to call the "Reading Inquisition"). Teachers who routinely use retellings for comprehension assessment find that they can monitor student progress effectively and thoroughly, and can do so in a fraction of the time required by traditional methods.

There are usually two phases in conducting a retelling with elementary students: unaided recall and aided recall. In the first phase, unaided recall, students simply retell the story they have just completed without being questioned by the teacher concerning specific details. (Note: This is a story that the students have already self-selected and read independently. It is also a different selection than the one[s] chosen for the running record[s].) While each student retells the story, the teacher notes important information that has been retold, such as characters, setting, central problem or challenge, conclusion, and theme/moral. It is critical that the teacher keep careful notes in student retellings. Thus, a story grammar retelling record like the one shown in Figure 2.8 can be most helpful to teachers. Of course, a teacher is not limited to using a specific format for making notes, but it is essential that careful and thorough notes be made for each retelling.

We have found that after students conclude the unaided recall portion of the retelling, it is often helpful to ask, "What else can you remember about the story?" Students will often eagerly offer more information. You can usually use this "What else. . ." strategy each time the student seems to be finished for as many as three times before exhausting the student's ability to recall information in the unaided recall segment.

Once the student has seemingly recalled all the information he can without assistance, the assessment progresses to the second phase, aided recall. This is the act of questioning students about story grammar elements that were not recounted during the unaided recall portion of retellings. When using the story grammar retelling record sheet, it is relatively simple for the teacher to quickly survey the sheet for missing information, then use the generic questions provided to evoke further story memories by the student. For example, if a student retold most of the story during unaided recall, but neglected to describe the setting, the teacher might use the first question under SETTING (see Figure 2.8) on the Story Grammar Retelling Record, asking, "Where did this story take place?" As in the first phase with unaided recall, the teacher records all memories the student has of the story and notes any story elements the student is unable to recall. If it appears that the student is consistently unable to remember certain story elements, then a minilesson should be offered to help him learn appropriate comprehension strategies.

Figure 2.8   Story Grammar Retelling Record Sheet

Student's Name: _____   Date: _____
Story: _____
Source/Book: _____

Category	Prompt Questions (after retelling)	Student's Retelling
SETTING	Where did this story take place? When did this story happen?	
CHARACTERS	Who were the characters in this story? Who was the main character(s) in the story? Describe _____ in the story	
CHALLENGE	What is the main challenge or problem in the story? What were the characters trying to do?	
EVENTS	What were the most important things that happened in the story? What did _____ do in the story?	
SOLUTION	How was the challenge/problem solved? What did _____ do to solve the problem? How did the other characters solve their problems?	
THEME	What was this author trying to tell us? What did _____ learn at the end of the story?	

ANALYZING ASSESSMENT INFORMATION: IF-THEN THINKING

One of the more difficult tasks for many teachers is to *analyze* the assessment data they have gathered on each child and come up with appropriate next steps in instruction. **Analysis** involves what has been termed IF-THEN thinking (Flynt & Cooter, 2001); "IF" your assessment leads you to conclude that a student has developed up to a specific point in reading, "THEN" you should know what should come next in his learning. Put another way, "IF" you know what a student can do alone in reading (his *independent* reading level), "THEN" you can accurately predict which reading skill(s) he should learn next with your assistance (his *zone of proximal development*).

Observation and *collection* are your primary assessment tools for gathering information that helps you understand where the student is in his reading development. **Observation** is the part of assessment where you document students' reading behaviors using indirect methods. Teachers commonly focus on just two or three students daily (without their knowledge, if possible) for observation and activities. Here are a few examples of observation tools and processes commonly used by teachers (many more are provided throughout this book beginning in chapter 5):

- **Anecdotal Notes**—Notes are taken while observing a student reading. They are very structured and focus on major milestones in the student's reading development and/or reading skills the teacher may be emphasizing or about to emphasize in class. Many teachers like to make their notes on self-adhesive labels such as those used on a computer printer to print addresses. These notes can then be dated and easily attached to the inside of a student's reading folder at the end of the day.

- **Reading Logs**—Daily records of student reading habits and interests are usually kept during independent reading periods, or DEAR time (Cambourne & Turbill, 1990). Students keep these records by completing simple forms held in a reading log folder at students' desks or in other appropriate locations.

- **Observation Checklist**—Teachers often find it helpful to use checklists as a quick reference classroom tool that incorporates what we know about reading development. Some teachers find that checklists that include a kind of Likert scale can be useful in student portfolios, because many reading behaviors become more fluent over time. Diffily (1994), while teaching kindergarten and first grade, developed the checklist shown in Figure 2.9 for use with her students. Although the reading behaviors listed in any scale or checklist naturally vary according to the grade level, these formats have proven to be quite helpful.

- **Literature Response Projects**—There are many ways students can demonstrate their reading comprehension. In the past and in many classrooms today, workbook pages and skill sheets have been used in great numbers as a postreading assessment activity. Unfortunately, these kinds of activities are a poor substitute for actual demonstrations of competence (Sizer, 1994). As an alternative, a growing number of classroom teachers are having students complete literature response projects to demonstrate their understanding of what they have read.

  Literature response projects can take many forms and may be completed by individual students or in literature response groups. The idea is for the student(s) to choose a creative way to demonstrate their competence. As we explore many aspects of reading comprehension, you will find numerous literature response ideas described in this book. For example, one group of sixth graders (Cooter & Griffith, 1989) decided to develop a board game in the form of Trivial Pursuit based on their reading of *The Lion, The Witch, and the Wardrobe* (Lewis, 1961). In an Ohio classroom, a student working independently decided to create a kind of comic strip that retold the book he had just completed. And a second-grade teacher in south Texas had her class make a "character report card" in which students graded a villain in a book on such character traits as honesty, trustworthiness, and so forth using inference skills and examples from the story to justify their opinions.

- **Writing Samples**—Reading and writing are reciprocal processes (Reutzel & Cooter, 2000), that is, as one skill is developed, it tends to help the student to develop the other. Writing is often a marvelous window for viewing students' understanding of phonics elements, use of context clues, and story elements, for example. Later in this book we directly address reading and writing connections and ways that writing samples can be used to assess reading development.

Collection is much more overt than observation strategies and involves direct assessment of student reading abilities, often in small groups or one-on-one situations. Throughout this book we provide you with both observation and collection tools that will assist you in gathering myriad data for charting students' reading development.

Figure 2.9   Diffily's Literacy Development Checklist

Literacy Development Checklist					
Student's Name: _____ Date: _____					
	Seldom				Often
Chooses books for personal enjoyment	1	2	3	4	5
Knows print/picture difference	1	2	3	4	5
Knows print is read from left to right	1	2	3	4	5
Asks to be read to	1	2	3	4	5
Asks that story be read again	1	2	3	4	5
Listens attentively during story time	1	2	3	4	5
Knows what a title is	1	2	3	4	5
Knows what an author is	1	2	3	4	5
Knows what an illustrator is	1	2	3	4	5
In retellings, repeats 2+ details	1	2	3	4	5
Tells beginning, middle, end	1	2	3	4	5
Can read logos	1	2	3	4	5
Uses text in functional ways	1	2	3	4	5
"Reads" familiar books to self/others	1	2	3	4	5
Can read personal words	1	2	3	4	5
Can read sight words from books	1	2	3	4	5
Willing to "write"	1	2	3	4	5
Willing to "read" personal story	1	2	3	4	5
Willing to dictate story to adult	1	2	3	4	5

Source: Gratefully used by the authors with the permission of Deborah Diffily, Ph.D., Southern Methodist University.

- **Interest Inventories**—One of the most important and elusive aspects of reading assessment is affect, which deals with a student's feelings about the reading act (Mathewson, 1994). Attitude, motivation, interest, beliefs, and values are all aspects of affect that have profound effects on reading development. Teachers building balanced literacy programs require information in student portfolios that not only provides insights into reading materials and teaching strategies that may be employed, but also into positive affective aspects that drive the reading process. Ultimately, selection of materials and strategies should be based at least in part on affective considerations. A starting point for many teachers is the interest inventory. Students are asked to complete or verbally respond to items on a questionnaire such as that shown in Figure 2.10. Responses give teachers a starting point for choosing reading materials that may interest the student and elicit the best reading possible, according to her abilities.

- **Retellings**—An ideal way to find out if a child understands a story she has read is through retellings (Hoyt, 1998). This is accomplished not by simply asking, "Do you understand the story?", but by asking her to retell the story in her own words.

∅∕ **Figure 2.10**   Interest Inventory

Interest Inventory

Student's Name: _____

Date: _____

Instructions: Please answer the following questions on a separate sheet of paper.

1. If you could have three wishes, what would they be?
2. What would you do with $50,000?
3. What things in life bother you most?
4. What kind of person would you like to be when you are older?
5. What are your favorite classes at school, and why?
6. Who do you think is the greatest person? Why do you think so?
7. Who is your favorite person? Why?
8. What do you like to do in your free time?
9. Do you read any parts of the newspaper? Which parts?
10. How much TV do you watch each day? What are your favorite shows, and why?
11. What magazines do you like to read?
12. Name three of your favorite movies.
13. What do you like best about your home?
14. What books have you enjoyed reading?
15. What kind of books would you like to read in the future?

- **Teacher-Made Tests**—Though often overused in many classrooms, paper-and-pencil tests do sometimes serve a purpose. However, we favor teacher-made tests that are taken from the books, songs, poetry, and other text forms used in the classroom. Note that the tests should always follow the same format as any teacher modeling examples presented to the student(s) to ensure transfer of learning. For instance, suppose that a teacher has chosen to use a cloze passage drawn from an old favorite classroom book such as *The Napping House* (Wood, 1984) to teach how context clues may be used to choose appropriate rhyming words. The teacher-made test developed to assess an individual student's understanding of this skill should then be in the form of a cloze passage (as opposed to a multiple-choice test).

- **Family Surveys**—When one is attempting to develop a clear understanding of a student's reading development, her reading behavior at home is obviously of great importance. Family surveys are brief questionnaires (too long, and they will never be answered!) sent to the student's parents or primary caregivers periodically to provide the teacher with insights into her home reading behaviors. Teachers can then combine the family survey response with other assessment evidence from the classroom to develop a reliable profile of the student's reading ability. An example of a family survey is provided in Figure 2.11.

- **Story Maps**—Story maps (Beck, Omanson, & McKeown, 1982; Routman, 1988) may be used to determine whether a student understands the basic elements of a narrative text or passage: setting, characters, challenge, events, solution, and theme. After reading the story, a student completes a story map. A generic format for the story map, such as the one shown in Figure 2.12, may be applied to almost any narrative text. Reading comprehension assessment and teaching procedures are discussed in detail in chapters 8 and 9 of this book.

Figure 2.11 Family Survey

September 6, 200_

Dear Adult Family Member:

As we begin the new school year, I would like to know a little more about your child's reading habits at home. This information will help me provide the best possible learning plan for your child this year. Please take a few minutes to answer the questions below and return this survey in the self-addressed stamped envelope provided. Should you have any questions, feel free to phone me at the school between 3:00 and 5:00 P.M. at 648-7696.

Cordially,

Mrs. Spencer

---

1. **My child likes to read the following at least once a week (check all that apply):**

   comic books _____   sports page _____

   magazines (example: *Highlights*) _____   library books _____

   cereal boxes _____   cooking recipes _____

   TV Guide _____   comics page _____

   others (please name): _____

2. **Have you noticed your child having any reading problems? If so, please explain briefly.**

3. **What are some of your child's favorite books?**

4. **If you would like a conference to discuss your child's reading ability, please indicate which days and times (after school) would be most convenient.**

Figure 2.12   Story Map

Story Map

Name: _____   Date: _____
Title: _____   Author: _____
 	
SETTING (Where and when did this story take place?)
 	
CHARACTERS (Who were the main characters in this story?)
 	
CHALLENGE (What is the main challenge or problem in the story?)
 	
EVENTS (What were the events that happened in the story to solve the problem/challenge?)
    Event 1:
    Event 2:
    Event 3:
(List all the important events that happened.)
 	
SOLUTION (How was the challenge/problem solved or not solved?)
 	
THEME (What was this author trying to tell the reader?)

Source: Adapted from Routman, 1988.

- **Audio-Videotapes**—Using audiotapes to record oral reading and retelling and videotapes to record students performing a variety of reading activities is a great way to periodically map reading growth. Recordings made at regular intervals, such as monthly, can be played back for careful analysis by the teacher and during parent–teacher conferences to demonstrate growth over time.

- **Self-Rating Scales**—It is often true that no one knows better how she is doing at reading than the reader herself. In the process of assessment, a teacher should never fail to ask the student how she feels about her reading ability. Although this may be best achieved in a one-on-one reading conference, large public school class sizes frequently make this impractical. A good alternative to one-on-one interviews for older elementary children, however, is a student self-rating scale. Students complete a questionnaire that is tailored to obtain specific information about the reader—from the reader's point of view.

- **Rubrics** (teacher- or school district-made)—As scoring guides or rating systems used in performance-based assessment (Farr & Tone, 1997; Reutzel & Cooter,

2000; Webb & Willoughby, 1993), rubrics assist teachers in two ways. First, rubrics make the analysis of student exhibits in the portfolio simpler. Second, rubrics make the rating process more consistent and objective. Whereas any assessment process is rarely objective, value-free, or theoretically neutral (Bintz, 1991), rubrics clearly have an important role. Webb and Willoughby (1993, p. 14) explained that "the same rubric may be used for many tasks [once established] as long as the tasks require the same skills."

Although there may be any number of ways to establish a rubric, Farr and Tone (1997) suggested a seven-step process of developing rubrics that may be adapted to reading assessment. Reutzel and Cooter (2000) modified the method slightly to conform to reading assessment needs and shortened the process to five relatively easy steps:

Step 1: Identify "anchor papers." Begin by collecting and sorting into several stacks reading exhibits from the portfolio (e.g., reading response activities, student self-analysis papers, content reading responses, and so on) according to quality. These are known as anchor papers. Try to analyze objectively why you feel that certain exhibits represent more advanced development in reading than others, and also why some exhibits cannot be characterized as belonging in the more "advanced" categories.

Step 2: Choose a scoring scale for the rubric. Usually a three-, four-, or five-point scoring system is used. A three-point scale may be more reliable, meaning that if other teachers were to examine the same reading exhibits, they would be likely to arrive at the same rubric score (1, 2, or 3). However, when multiple criteria are being considered, a five-point scale or greater may be easier to apply. Yet a major problem with reading rubrics is that they imply a hierarchy of skills that does not really seem to exist in many cases. For example, in the upper grades, is the ability to skim text for information a higher or lower level skill than scanning text for information? Probably neither label applies in this instance. This brings us to Farr and Tone's (1997) third step.

Step 3: Choose scoring criteria that reflect what you believe about reading development. Two points relative to reading rubrics need to be considered in Step 3: scoring and learning milestones. A rubric is usually scored in a hierarchical fashion. That is, using a five-point scale, if a student fulfills requirements for a 1, 2, and 3 score, but not the criteria for a 4, even if she may fulfill the criteria for a 5, she would be ranked as a 3. In disciplines such as mathematics, certain skills can be ranked hierarchically in a developmental sense. However, many reading skills cannot be ranked so clearly, and thus we recommend a procedure slightly different from that typically used to rank reading skills: If a five-point rubric is being used, survey all five reading skills or strategies identified in the rubric when reviewing exhibits found in the portfolio. If the student has the ability to do four of them, for example, then rank the student as a 4 regardless of where those skills are situated in the rubric. We hasten to add that this modification may not always be appropriate, however, especially with emergent readers for whom clearer developmental milestones are evident.

Step 4: Select sample reading development exhibits for each level of the rubric as exemplars and write descriptive annotations. It is important for teachers to have samples of each performance criterion in mind when attempting to use a rubric. From the Step 1 process in which anchor papers or other kinds of exhibits (e.g., running records, literature response activities, story grammar maps, and so on.) were identified, the teacher will have in her possession good examples or *exemplars* of each reading skill or strategy being surveyed. After a careful review of these anchor papers it will be possible to write short descriptive statements, or annotations, that summarize what the teacher is searching for in the assessment for each level of the rubric.

Figure 2.13 shows a sample rubric developed for a fifth-grade class wherein students were to describe (orally and through written response) cause-effect relationships based on in-class readings about water pollution.

Step 5: Modify the rubric criteria as necessary. In any assessment, the teacher should feel free to modify the rubric's criteria as new information emerges.

Standardized test data are usually included in teacher portfolios and are sometimes discussed in parent-teacher conferences. These data do not really inform instruction—a prime motive for classroom assessment—but they do present a limited view of how the student compares to other students nationally who have also taken that particular test. Many times parents or guardians want to know how their child compares to others. Standardized tests are somewhat useful for that purpose. They may also help teachers who work mainly with students with learning problems to maintain perspective. It is sometimes easy to lose sight of what "normal reading development" is when you work only with students having learning problems. Although we feel that standardized tests are not useful for making instructional decisions, they may be helpful in the situations previously mentioned.

Figure 2.13   Sample Rubric for a Fifth-Grade Reading Class

Cause-Effect Relationships: Scale for Oral and Written Response

Level 4: **Student clearly describes a cause and effect of water pollution and provides concrete examples of each.**
Student can provide an example not found in the readings.
"We read about how sometimes toxic wastes are dumped into rivers by factories and most of the fish die. I remember hearing about how there was an oil spill in Alaska that did the same thing to fish and birds living in the area."

Level 3: **Student describes a cause and effect of water pollution found in the readings.**
Student can define *pollution*.
"I remember reading about how factories sometimes dump poisonous chemicals into rivers and all the fish die. *Pollution* means that someone makes a place so dirty that animals can't live there anymore."

Level 2: **Student can provide examples found in the readings of water pollution or effects that pollution had on the environment.**
"I remember reading that having enough clean water to drink is a problem in some places because of garbage being dumped into the rivers."

Level 1: **Student is not able to voluntarily offer information found in the readings about the cause and effects of pollution.**

ONLY THE BEGINNING . . .

The purpose of this book is to provide you with myriad classroom assessment strategies to help you with your daily planning and teaching. This chapter, while proving some of the mainstays of classroom assessment, only scratches the surface. Chapters 5 and beyond each contain a section on assessment strategies that can help you determine each student's zone of proximal development. Each has been carefully researched, and we have used most in our classrooms. So we invite you to keep reading along with us about classroom assessment. . . this is only the beginning!

SELECTED REFERENCES

Beck, I. L., Omanson, R. C., & McKeown, M. G. (1982). An instructional redesign of reading lessons: Effects on comprehension. *Reading Research Quarterly, 17,* 462–481.

Betts, E. (1946). *Foundations of reading instruction.* New York: American Book.

Bintz, N. P. (1991). Staying connected—Exploring new functions for assessment. *Contemporary Education, 62*(4), 307–312.

Cambourne, B., & Turbill, J. (1990). Assessment in whole language classrooms: Theory into practice. *Elementary School Journal, 90,* 337–349.

Clay, M. (1966). *Emergent reading behaviour.* Unpublished doctoral dissertation, University of Auckland, New Zealand.

Clay, M. (1972). *The early detection of reading difficulties.* Portsmouth, NH: Heinemann.

Clay, M. (1985). *The early detection of reading difficulties* (3rd ed.). Portsmouth, NH: Heinemann.

Clay, M. (1997). *An observation survey of early literacy achievement.* Portsmouth, NH: Heinemann.

Clay, M. (2000). *Running records for classroom teachers.* Portsmouth, NH: Heinemann.

Cooter, R. B., Jr., & Griffith, R. (1989). Thematic units for middle school: An honorable seduction. *Journal of Reading, 32*(8), 676–681.

Diffily, D. (1994, April). Portfolio assessment in early literacy settings. Paper presented in a Professional Development Schools workshop at Texas Christian University, Fort Worth, TX.

Durrell, D. D. (1940). *Improvement of basic reading abilities.* New York: World Book.

Farr, R., & Tone, B. (1997). *Portfolio and performance assessments.* Fort Worth, TX: Harcourt Brace College Publishers.

Flynt, E. S., & Cooter, R. B. (1999). *The English-Español reading inventory for the classroom.* Upper Saddle River, NJ: Merrill/Prentice Hall.

Flynt, E. S., & Cooter, R. B. (2001). *The Flynt/Cooter reading inventory for the classroom* (4th ed.). Upper Saddle River, NJ: Merrill/Prentice Hall.

Gambrell, L. B., Pfeiffer, W., & Wilson, R. (1985). The effects of retelling upon reading comprehension and recall of text information. *Journal of Educational Research, 78,* 216–220.

Goodman, Y. M. (1967). *A psycholinguistic description of observed oral reading phenomena in selected young beginning readers.* Unpublished doctoral dissertation, Wayne State University.

Goodman, Y. M., & Burke, C. L. (1972). *Reading miscue inventory manual: Procedures for diagnosis and evaluation.* New York: Macmillan.

Hoyt, L. (1998). *Revisit, reflect, retell.* Portsmouth, NH: Heinemann.

Lewis, C. S. (1961). *The lion, the witch, and the wardrobe.* New York: Macmillan.

Mathewson, G. (1994). Toward a comprehensive model of affect in the reading process. In H. Singer & R. B. Ruddell (Eds.), *Theoretical models and processes of reading* (4th ed.). Newark, DE: International Reading Association.

May, F. B., & Rizzardi, L. (2002). *Reading as communication* (6th ed.). Upper Saddle River, NJ: Merrill/Prentice Hall.

Meddaugh, S. (1992). *Martha speaks.* New York: Houghton Mifflin.

Morrow, L. M. (1985). Retelling stories: A strategy for improving children's comprehension, concept of story structure and oral language complexity. *Elementary School Journal, 85,* 647–661.

National Research Council. (1999). *Starting out right: A guide to promoting children's reading success.* Washington, D.C.: National Academy Press.

Pearson, P. D., & Gallagher, M. C. (1983). The instruction of reading comprehension. *Contemporary Educational Psychology, 8*(3), 317–344.

Reutzel, D. R., & Cooter, R. B., Jr., (2000). *Teaching children to read: Putting the pieces together.* Upper Saddle River, NJ: Merrill/Prentice Hall.

Routman, R. (1988). *Transitions: From literature to literacy.* Portsmouth, NH: Heinemann.

Sizer, T. (1994). *Reinventing our schools.* Bloomington, IN: Phi Delta Kappa.

Tompkins, G. E. (2001). *Literacy for the 21st century.* Columbus, OH: Merrill/Prentice Hall.

Vygotsky, L. S. (1986). *Thought and language.* Cambridge, MA: MIT Press.

Vygotsky, L. S. (1990). *Mind in society.* Boston: Harvard University Press.

Webb, K., & Willoughby, N. (1993). An analytic rubric for scoring graphs. *The Texas School Teacher, 22*(3), 14–15.

Wiener, R. B., & Cohen, J. H. (1997). *Literacy portfolios: Using assessment to guide instruction.* Columbus, OH: Merrill/Prentice Hall.

Wood, A. (1984). *The napping house.* New York: Harcourt.

Chapter 3

Understanding Reading Instruction

"You are teaching my child phonics, aren't you?" questions Mrs. Jenkins, the local PTA President. "I've been hearing that your teachers aren't teaching children to read with phonics."

"Of course we are teaching your child and all children phonics as a tool for learning to read," replies Mr. Salinger, the school principal. "But, as I am sure you know, there is more to teaching a child to read than phonics instruction alone. Children need to be read to from good books regularly. They need to talk about those books with others. Children need to see and hear good readers reading. Our teachers are concerned that every child be read to daily at school and at home. They make sure that they teach children phonics, vocabulary, comprehension, and fluency strategies as well. They guide the children very carefully in learning to read. They also make sure they get guided and independent reading practice daily. Our teachers not only teach children how to read; they go one step beyond and show them what to do in different reading situations, when and how to apply specific strategies, and make sure they understand why they do it."

"I guess that sounds pretty good, but I just wanted to make sure my child gets phonics instruction as well as books."

"I understand," answers Mr. Salinger soothingly. "We want your child and all children to be successful. That is why our teachers have chosen to use the best, research-validated practices known today. You can have complete confidence that your child will receive a comprehensive reading instructional program in phonics and other critical skills at Dapper Hill Elementary."

READING TO, WITH, AND BY CHILDREN

A teacher's first order of business is to understand best practices for effective reading instruction. Literacy scholars and practitioners working in New Zealand and Australia have developed and demonstrated "best practices" in reading instruction compatible with comprehensive reading instruction for over three decades (Anderson et al., 1985; Holdaway, 1979; Mooney, 1990; Reutzel, 1996a, 1996b; Weaver, 1998; Department of Eduction, Wellington, NZ, 1985). In this chapter, we share the "best practices" of reading instruction associated with the Reading TO, WITH, and BY Children instructional framework as found in Figure 3.1.

W/ **Figure 3.1**   Reading TO, WITH, and BY Children Instructional Framework

READING TO

- Interactive Read Aloud
- Echoic Choral Reading
- Technology Assists

READING WITH

- Learning About Language Lessons
- Language Experience
- Shared Reading
- Guided Reading

READING BY

- Popcorn Reading
- Read Around the Room
- SSR

For reading instruction to be effective, teachers need to teach; and children need to learn. Optimal reading instructional conditions actively involve teachers and students in reading. In the beginning, teachers may take the major responsibility for reading while students actively listen to and interact with the teacher as he reads aloud. As time goes along, teachers release to students the responsibility for the reading until such a time comes when they can read independently. The "best practices" found in the Reading TO, WITH, and BY Children instructional framework balance the active involvement of children and teachers in reading instruction as well as gradually releasing from the teacher to children the responsibility for reading the text. In Figure 3.2, we show how each practice within the Reading TO, WITH, and BY Children instructional framework gradually releases responsibility for reading the text or print from the teacher to the children.

READING TO CHILDREN

Some school administrators and parents truly wonder why a teacher would spend limited instructional time each day reading aloud to children. Although reading aloud to children can be taken to extremes, robbing children of the opportunity to read and teachers of the time to teach, there are nevertheless many good reasons why teachers should read aloud to children for ten to fifteen minutes daily. Jim Trelease offered this insight about the value of reading aloud to children as an important part of high-quality, comprehensive reading instruction:

> [The] reasons are the same reasons you talk to a child: to reassure, to entertain, to inform or explain, to arouse curiosity, and to inspire—and to do it all personally, not impersonally with a machine. All those experiences create or strengthen a positive attitude about reading. (1995, p. 2)

Figure 3.2   Gradual Release of Responsibility for Reading

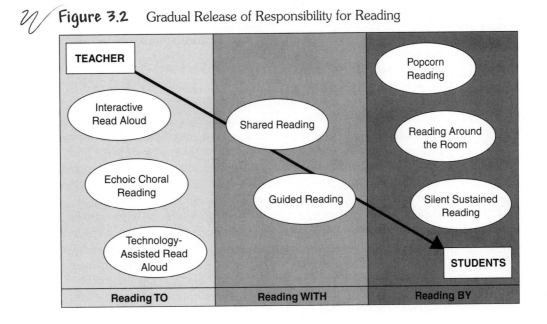

Research by Dolores Durkin (1966) revealed that children who learned to read early without formal instruction often came from homes where parents had read aloud to them regularly. Other researchers have asserted that read-aloud activities help young children develop a sense of how stories and other texts are constructed (Barrentine, 1996; Beck & McKeown, 2001; Campbell, 2001; Hoffman, Roser, & Battle, 1983; Morrow, 2001; Neuman & Roskos, 1993; Opitz & Rasinski, 1998; Reutzel, 2001; Reutzel & Fawson, 2002; Teale & Martinez, 1986). During read alouds, teachers model the reading process (Reutzel, 2001). Children witness firsthand the enjoyment of reading and are exposed to many genre and reading materials (Mooney, 1990; Reutzel, 1996a, 1996b; Reutzel & Cooter, 2000).

So, as a teacher, you can readily see that reading aloud to children offers them an important exposure to the world of oral and printed language. In addition, read alouds expand children's understanding of the world around them. By listening to stories, books, and texts read aloud, children learn new ideas, concepts, and vicariously experience events that are within their ability to understand but are well beyond the boundaries of their immediate location. The major purpose for reading aloud TO children is to model how to read for them, what to read, and why reading is important and enjoyable.

READING TRADE BOOKS ALOUD

Interactive reading of trade books with younger children helps them become successful readers as they progress in school (Bennett, 2001; Campbell, 1992; Labbo, 2001; Neuman, 1999; Rosenhouse, Feitelson, & Kita 1997). Preschool children who are read to at home, and who have access to books prior to the time they enter school, become better readers. Wells (1986) found that listening to stories read aloud and taking part in the discussion of stories was strongly related to children's later reading achievement and literacy development. Children learn about books and how they work from being read to by parents, siblings, peers, and teachers (Meek, 1984; Strickland & Morrow, 1989).

Heath (1982, 1983) found that not all reading aloud is created equal. To make reading aloud effective, parents and teachers must read aloud *interactively;* this means that when children or the parents feel a need, they stop and talk about the text and the pictures. It is important for children to be actively involved during read-aloud experiences to make sure they understand what is being read!

Morrow (1988) demonstrated that reading aloud to an entire classroom might not be sufficient to stimulate reading growth for all students. In this study, children were read to in small groups and in one-to-one settings. At the conclusion of the study, children read to in small groups or in one-to-one settings made significant progress over those students who were read to in a whole class setting.

Meyer, Stahl, and Wardrop (1994) conducted a study of reading aloud to children. The study showed that time spent reading traditional-sized books aloud to children resulted in lower achievement test scores. For many students, reading achievement is only influenced when they actually engage with the print. These researchers did find, however, that students who experienced read alouds developed new oral language concepts.

Rosenhouse, Feitelson, and Kita (1997) investigated how reading aloud stories written by the same author compared with reading stories written by different authors on children's reading achievement. It was found that reading stories aloud from the same author in a classroom of children led them to greater increases in decoding, comprehension, and picture storytelling. A "books aloud" project in inner city Philadelphia was designed to flood child-care centers with books and to train the staff in these centers on effective read-aloud techniques. This project showed that when adults were trained to read aloud effectively and often to very young children (in addition to having access to books), children's early literacy growth was positively and significantly affected (Neuman, 1999).

The effectiveness of reading books aloud to children is conditioned by a variety of factors and expectations. Reading aloud has an impact on children's reading achievement. However, simply reading books aloud is insufficient to produce such effects. Teachers and parents must consider the nature of the read-aloud experience. They need to actively involve the child in the reading aloud experience. They need to talk about the text together (Beck & McKeown, 2001). They need to consider whether or not it is best to read aloud in whole class, small group, or one-to-one settings to engage children in the print and the conversation about books. They need to realize that reading aloud to children is not a reading achievement panacea. It is only a part, albeit an important part, of an effective reading instruction (Campbell, 2001; Edwards, 1999; Reutzel, 2001). Reading aloud needs to be augmented by efforts to develop oral language facility, decoding, comprehension, and fluency. Involving children in print rich, print engaging activities with books read aloud coupled with literacy-related play, guidance, and conversation in a variety of social settings will likely produce the optimal outcomes producing later reading achievement.

SELECTING READ-ALOUD BOOKS

When selecting books to be read aloud to children, you should look for books and stories that will challenge children's intellectual development but not exceed their emotional maturity. When the concepts and experiences in books exceed a young child's emotional maturity levels, she will not enjoy the experience. For example, children who are read poetry about romance or the symbolic beauties of nature at young ages typically do not enjoy poetry, or even worse, develop contempt for poetry. Instead wise teachers and parents recognize that five- and six-year-olds are not yet emotionally ready for romantic relationships in poetry, so they read children humorous poetry by Silverstein or Prelutsky instead. When teachers observe this simple suggestion, the read-aloud experience becomes a far more enjoyable and comprehensible experience for young children.

Books selected for read alouds should challenge children's intellectual levels, offering to them new concepts, ideas, and experiences. However, books selected for read aloud should not be books children could read independently, rather select books that exceed students' current independent reading abilities. We have created, based on Trelease's (1995) *The New Read Aloud Handbook,* a listing of the "do's" and "don'ts" of read aloud (Figure 3.3).

INTERACTIVE READING ALOUDS

When teachers read aloud to children, they very often begin with a brief introduction and discussion of the book or text to be read aloud. In 1986, Teale and Martinez summarized research in which they sampled journal articles, books, and textbooks on guidelines for reading aloud to children. This study of guidelines revealed that there is no one best way to read aloud to children. But, the general findings of this research did lead to the guidelines summarized in Figure 3.4.

 Figure 3.3   The Do's and Don'ts of Reading Aloud

Do's

- Do begin reading to children as early in their lives as they can be supported to sit and listen.
- Do use rhymes, raps, songs, chants, poetry, and pictures to stimulate their oral language development, listening, and interaction with others.
- Do read aloud to children at least 10–15 minutes daily, more often if possible.
- Do set aside a time for daily reading aloud in your curriculum schedule.
- Do read picture books to all ages, but also gradually move to reading longer books without pictures as well.
- Do vary the topics and genre of your read-aloud selections.
- Do read aloud books to children that stretch their intellectual and oral language development.
- Do allow plenty of time for interaction before, during, and after the reading.
- Do read aloud with expression and enthusiasm.
- Do add another dimension to your reading sometimes, such as using hand movements, puppets, or dressing up in costume.
- Do carry a book with you at all times to model your love of books and reading.

Don'ts

- Don't read aloud too fast.
- Don't read aloud books children can read independently—give a "book talk" instead!
- Don't read aloud books and stories you don't enjoy yourself.
- Don't read aloud books and stories that exceed the children's emotional development.
- Don't continue reading a book you don't like. Admit it, and choose another.
- Don't impose your interpretations and preferences on children.
- Don't confuse quantity with quality.
- Don't use reading aloud as a reward or punishment.

Source: Based on *The New Read-Aloud Handbook* (pp. 79–85), by J. Trelease, 1995, NY: Penguin.

Figure 3.4 Suggested Reading Aloud Strategies

- Designate a legitimate time and place in the daily curriculum for reading aloud.
- Select high-quality books.
- Select literature that relates to other literature.
- Prepare by previewing the book.
- Provide the appropriate physical setting.
- Group children to maximize opportunities to respond.
- Provide a brief introduction.
- Read with expression.
- Discuss literature in lively, invitational, thought-provoking ways.
- Encourage children's responses to the book.
- Allow time for discussion and interaction about the book.
- Offer a variety of response and extension opportunities.
- Reread selected stories or books when students indicate a desire.

Source: Based on "Getting on the Right Road to Reading: Bringing Books and Young Children Together in the Classroom" by W. H. Teale and M. G. Martinez, 1988, *Young Children, 44*(1), pp. 10–15; and "Reading Aloud in Classrooms: From the Modal to a 'Model' " by J. V. Hoffman, N. Roser, and J. Battle, 1993, *The Reading Teacher, 46*(6), pp. 496–503.

As you can see from this list of guidelines for successful teacher read alouds, emphasis was placed on an introduction to the text *prior to* reading and interacting with students.

In another study of read-aloud practices in classrooms, preservice teachers were surveyed about the teacher read-aloud practices they were observing in classrooms (Hoffman et al., 1993). Preservice teachers were asked to identify the amount of time teachers were spending on reading aloud. Results indicated that teachers spend between 10 and 20 minutes per day in read aloud in elementary schools. Of the total time spent on read alouds, only 5 minutes was devoted to interaction of teachers and children around the book. Typically these discussions occurred either before or after reading the book. *Interactions between teachers and students about text as it is read aloud is of critical importance in developing children's emerging comprehension abilities* (Beck & McKeown, 2001; Campbell, 2001).

Because reading aloud to children is recognized as a critical aspect of any successful literacy program, it is only natural that over time this practice has been strengthened in its ability to support the development of reading for enjoyment and knowledge acquisition. Current read-aloud practices make use of new knowledge of the reading process. Although there is no single right way to read aloud to children, as a profession we have recognized the important influence that talking about text and interaction play in children's understanding. Barrentine (1996) reported that some teachers are beginning to encourage more student interaction with the teacher, peers, and the text during read-aloud sessions. One potential criticism of interactive read alouds might be that encouraging too much discussion of a book during reading may undermine the aesthetic characteristics of the literature and the experience for students. Although we certainly agree too much analysis and interaction during read aloud can disrupt the flow of the book and the pleasure of listening to the story, we also believe that interaction during read aloud draws on student experiences, heightening the relevance of the read-aloud experience. The goal during read alouds is to create a balance between student reactions to the text and ensuring a minimum of distractions and interruptions.

Although most reading aloud to children in school takes place with the entire class, Morrow (1988) reminded teachers to take advantage of the benefits associated with reading aloud to smaller groups of young children and individuals. Children whose reading development lags behind that of their peers can be helped a great deal by teachers, volunteers, or older peers who take time to read to them in small-group or one-to-one settings. Reading aloud to children who are lagging behind their peers can have added benefits from read-aloud sessions when these are offered in smaller groups and individually. Here are our suggestions for conducting interactive read alouds in your classroom (see Figure 3.5) based on Barrentine (1996).

Figure 3.5   Using Interactive Read Alouds in Classrooms

Carefully select books.

- Books with high quality illustrations, lively characters, rich plots, creative language, predictable patterns, and repeated rhythm encourage student attention to the text. Whereas multiple readings of a text are appropriate for read alouds, introducing new text helps to maintain student interest in this part of the routine. A good place to start is with your favorite books that are also suitable for your students.

Prepare for a successful interactive read aloud.

- Be thoroughly familiar with the book before the read aloud. With picture books this might mean making several readings of the text before the read aloud. With chapter books, it might be necessary to skim the selection you intend to read and familiarize yourself with the structure, plot, problem/resolution, setting, or characters. Be aware of areas of the book that require clarification or enrichment.
- Think about the goals for reading that you have identified for your students and identify what process and strategy are at work in your story. Keep your students in mind as you review the text. What elements in the text need to be expanded on to aid your students in their development as readers? When you think about your students' needs as readers, the read aloud becomes much more relevant in helping each student benefit from the reading.
- Identify where you will encourage students to share predictions about the developing story. Inviting students to make predictions about the story at strategic points in the reading will assist them as they develop an understanding of the text. Allowing class predictions of the story will support the less-able reader in clarifying key information in the story.
- Identify where students' background knowledge may be lacking and needing support. It is important to remember that students' listening comprehension will generally be ahead of their reading comprehension. Some concept or vocabulary development may help students to interact with stories that they otherwise would not be willing or able to handle.
- Give some thought to how you will phrase questions and anticipate student responses. Although it is possible to organize questions you would like to ask before, during, and after the reading, it is not always possible to anticipate student responses to those questions. Remember that your students will probably not grasp elements of the book at the same level that an adult will. Use this as an opportunity to gain a glimpse of their development in understanding the story and use this information to inform your future questioning.
- Be flexible and willing to relinquish your plans. Interactive read alouds are not unidirectional conversations. They are very dynamic and require a great deal of flexibility on the part of the teacher. Student interactions may add insights that you had not considered previously. Be willing to accept these slight detours as rich additions to the conversation.

continued

Figure 3.5 Continued

- Create opportunities for students to explore and extend the book in meaningful ways. It is often appropriate to explore the book in greater detail following the readings. This allows children to achieve greater personalization of the story in their own minds.

Consider the literacy environment.

- It is very important to have a general idea about how you will access books for interactive read alouds and what you will do with the book when you have completed the reading. Will you put all of your books in the classroom library at the beginning of the year or will you hold selected titles back that you will use for interactive read alouds? Will you select books that support an instructional theme that is being presented during the same time frame? How will you arrange the children so that they will all be able to see or hear the text being read?

Where will my read aloud fit into the instructional routine?

- Teachers should negotiate time in their daily literacy routine for reading aloud to students. If it is not integrated into the schedule where it becomes a part of the plan, then the chances are good that it will not occur. Twenty minutes per day is a general figure for read aloud. Understand, however, that interactive read alouds may take longer depending on the experience of the students.

Source: Based on "Engaging with Reading through Interactive Read-Alouds" by S. B. Barrentine, 1996, *The Reading Teacher, 50*(1), pp. 36–43.

ECHOIC CHORAL READINGS

Echoic choral readings involve teachers and students together in orally reading a story, poem, or text; just as one hears her own voice *echo* in a deserted canyon. The teacher reads or sings aloud a line of text from a poem, book, or song and students repeat it back just like an echo. Because the text is first read aloud by the teacher, students experience how fluent reading aloud sounds and feels. And because students and teachers are involved in echoic choral readings together, an active, lively, and participatory experience is had by all. What's more, the support offered to shy or reticent students in a group echoic reading shields them from potential embarrassment and from being singled out for attention while learning to read. The echoic experience has intrigued many people throughout time. And echoic readings are a way for teachers to begin sharing the read-aloud responsibility for a text or story with children.

To engage children in an echoic choral reading, begin by selecting a book, poem, or song that can be read a line at a time. To get your feet wet with this activity you might try Paul Fleishman's *A Joyful Noise: Poems for Two Voices,* Maurice Sendak's *Chicken Soup with Rice,* or favorite song lyrics from *Oh My Aunt Came Back.* Tell children that you are going to read them a line from a text, poem, or story and they are to copy you. You should model this with them as you get started. At this point, an example may be helpful. Let's say we selected the song lyrics from *Oh My Aunt Came Back* to use as our choral echoic reading. We would begin by singing the first line—"Oh my aunt came back from Timbucktwo" and have them sing it back as an echo. Then continue, "And she brought with her a wooden shoe." You may want to add some body movements to make it more interesting at this point by continuous tapping the toe of your right foot. This process continues line by line until you finish the song. We provide our version of the words and actions to this song in Figure 3.6 to get you started.

Echoic choral read alouds are fun and they gradually move the responsibility for reading aloud a text to the children for their full participation. Reading aloud poems and sto-

Figure 3.6   Oh My Aunt Came Back

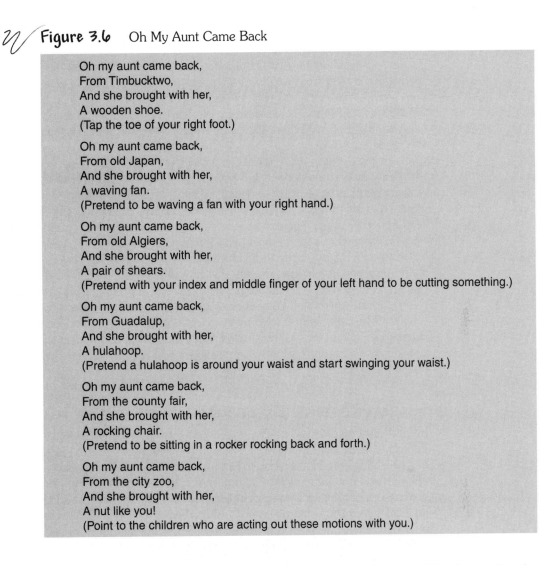

Oh my aunt came back,
From Timbucktwo,
And she brought with her,
A wooden shoe.
(Tap the toe of your right foot.)

Oh my aunt came back,
From old Japan,
And she brought with her,
A waving fan.
(Pretend to be waving a fan with your right hand.)

Oh my aunt came back,
From old Algiers,
And she brought with her,
A pair of shears.
(Pretend with your index and middle finger of your left hand to be cutting something.)

Oh my aunt came back,
From Guadalup,
And she brought with her,
A hulahoop.
(Pretend a hulahoop is around your waist and start swinging your waist.)

Oh my aunt came back,
From the county fair,
And she brought with her,
A rocking chair.
(Pretend to be sitting in a rocker rocking back and forth.)

Oh my aunt came back,
From the city zoo,
And she brought with her,
A nut like you!
(Point to the children who are acting out these motions with you.)

ries in an echoic choral reading help children accept limited responsibility for reading the text aloud as well as learning about fluent and expressive reading.

TECHNOLOGY-ASSISTED READING

Technology-assisted read alouds make use of computers and audiocassette tapes. Audiocassettes effectively support readers as they look at the print in a new or relatively unfamiliar book and try to read along with the tape. CD-ROM programs are commercially available for a wide variety of predictable books. When commercially produced tapes are not available or resources do not allow the purchase of commercially produced audiocassette tapes, teachers may record their own or involve parent volunteers. These carefully paced, prerecorded read alouds support children through the reading of a book they cannot yet read on their own. Tapes or CD-ROM programs can, for example, be color coded for representing varying levels of text difficulty (e.g., green for emergent, yellow for easy reading, and blue for independent reading) and stored in specially designed storage cases for easy retrieval by the teacher and children.

READING WITH CHILDREN

The purposes of reading WITH children are explicitly instructional. Although some children learn to read from exposure to models of fluent and expressive reading, many children require more explicit guidance and teaching to be successful in learning to read. The practices of shared and guided reading provide opportunities for teachers to teach children using a variety of text types, sizes, and levels to become independent, fluent, and expressive readers.

In *shared reading experiences,* the teacher controls the reading of an enlarged text. She explicitly teaches students how to operate on the print in the text and encourages students to participate in group repeated readings of the text. In *guided reading,* students begin to take responsibility for controlling the reading of leveled text. Through the *guided reading experience,* students accelerate their development of reading strategies and fluency. With teacher support, instruction, and guidance, students read "just right" texts selected to match their ability to handle stories and books at that level.

In the pages that follow, we describe how shared and guided reading practices can be used in reading WITH children to gradually release more and more of the responsibility for reading to the children. The goal of reading WITH children is to help them develop what Clay (1993b) called *self-extending systems* leading toward independence in reading. Developing self-extending systems helps children select appropriately and apply successfully an extensive repertoire of reading strategies to become self-directed, critical, and independent readers.

SHARED READING EXPERIENCE

In 1979, Don Holdaway described bedtime story reading as one of the earliest and most significant elements supporting the reading development of young children. *Shared reading,* or what is sometimes called the *shared book experience,* is used with very young readers to model how readers look at, figure out, and operate on the print using an enlarged text in front of an entire group of children rather than reading a traditional-sized book with an individual child. To participate in a shared book experience, children and teachers must be able to share the print simultaneously. This requires that the print be enlarged so that every child can see it and process it together under teacher guidance (Barrett, 1982).

When selecting books or stories for shared reading experiences, try to find those most loved by children that are available in a "big book" or enlarged print format that the entire group of children can see as easily as if they were sitting on your knee. Shared reading books should have literary merit, engaging content, and high interest. Illustrations in shared reading books and stories must augment and expand upon the text. Pictures should tell or support the reading of the story in proper sequence. Shared reading books are best if they contain repetition, cumulative sequence, rhyme, and rhythm to entice children into the melody and cadence of language. The proper selection of big books for shared reading experiences "hook" children on the sounds and patterns of language and the multiple purposes of reading.

Also, books chosen for shared reading ought to put reasonable demands on younger readers' capabilities. The number of unknown words in relation to known words in a new book selected for shared reading should not overwhelm them. Big books selected for initial shared reading experiences should largely carry the storyline. Print in these initial shared reading big books may amount to little more than a caption underneath the pictures such as is found in the books *Brown Bear, Brown Bear* or *Polar Bear, Polar Bear* by Martin (1990, 1991).

Conducting a Shared Book Experience

You begin a shared book experience by introducing the book. An introduction is intended to heighten children's desire to read the story, and to help them draw on their own experiences and prior knowledge so that they can more fully enjoy and interpret the story. Once a book is selected for shared reading, begin by inviting children to look at the book cover while reading the title aloud. Talk about the front and back of the book and point out certain features of the cover and title page, such as the author and illustrator names, publisher, and copyright date. Next, say to the students, *"Look at the pictures. What do you think the words will tell you?"* This typically begins a dialogue and discussion leading to children sharing personal connections and making predictions. Next, read the book with "full dramatic punch, perhaps overdoing a little some of the best parts" (Barrett, 1982, p. 16). While reading the story, invite children to join in reading any repeated or predictable phrases or words. At key points during the shared reading you should pause to encourage children to predict what is coming next in the story.

After reading, invite children to share their responses to the story. Ask them to talk about their favorite parts, connect the story to their experiences, as well as discuss how well they were able to predict and participate. The shared reading book is reread on subsequent days and will eventually become a part of a selection of "old favorite" stories to be reread. Using hand and body movements, simple props related to the story, or rhythm instruments are excellent ways we have used to increase student involvement and activity in any rereading of a shared reading book. A sample shared reading lesson is shown in Figure 3.7.

Figure 3.7   Teaching a Shared Reading Lesson

Ms. Harris selects the big book, *Each Peach Pear Plum* (Alhberg, 1978), for shared reading in her first-grade class. She invites her children to come up to the front of the room to be seated on a large carpeted area. As the children quietly but excitedly move to their places, Ms. Harris places the big book on an easel for all to see. "Boys and girls, what do you see here?" she asks. Several children immediately blurt out—A CAT, A COW, FRUIT! "That's right," she affirms. "What do you think the print in the title is telling us?" "It's going to tell us the title of the story," says Megen. "It's going to tell us about the things in the picture," offers Jona. "Well, you've all made some very good predictions. I'll read the title and you watch where I am pointing," instructs Ms. Harris. "EACH PEACH PEAR PLUM," reads Ms. Harris as she points to the words in the title. "Let's turn to the first page. What do you see here?" "A PIE WITH A MOUSE SNIFFING IT," several children respond. "Let's read together what the print tells us about this picture." Ms. Harris reads with a mysterious intonation while pointing to the print, "EACH PEACH PEAR PLUM. In this book, with your little eye, take a look, and play 'I spy.'"

The first reading continues as the children and the teacher read this book together. They interact about the pictures and print until the story is completed. After the reading, the children and teacher discuss other books that are like this, such as "Where is Waldo?" Ms. Harris shows the children several different types of "I Spy" books.

"Shall we read it again?" "YES," the children reply. "O.K. let's think about some hand actions and sounds we can put with our second reading." After a brief discussion it is decided to use their hands shaped like binoculars to look carefully at the pictures as they play "I spy." At the end of the story, they will open their arms to signal "everyone." "Remember boys and girls, you can join in with me any time as we read this book again." The second reading goes smoothly with the students all participating in the hand actions, the sounds, and in the reading.

Once a shared reading book has been reread twice, select something from the print in the book to examine in a "close reading." For example in the big book, *The Carrot Seed* (Krauss, 1945), the teacher may decide that students should begin to notice the sight word "the" in the text. To direct students' eyes to the word "the" in the text, the teacher takes stick 'em notes from a pad and cuts several to the size necessary to cover or mask the word "the" in the text. As children and teacher engage in a "close reading," they note the masked words. The teacher unmasks the first "the" and asks students to look carefully at this word. What are the letters in the word? Invite a student to come up and copy the word from the book onto a large card. Each time the word "the" is encountered in the close read, it is unmasked and stressed aloud in the reading. After the close reading for "the," the teacher gives each child a "the" word card. The children are instructed to pick up a pair of scissors from the basket and return to their seats. While at their seats, they cut the card into its three letters and scramble the letters. Each child unscrambles the letters to form the word "the" on his desktop. Each child is given a new index card to write the word "the" to keep in his own word collection.

Research by Ribowsky (1985) compared the shared book experience approach to a phonics-emphasis approach, the J. B. Lippincott basal reading series, and found that the shared book experience resulted in higher end-of-year achievement scores and phonic analysis subtest scores than did the direct-instruction phonics approach used in the Lippincott basal. Reutzel, Hollingsworth, and Eldredge (1994) and Eldredge, Reutzel, and Hollingsworth (1996) showed that the shared book experience resulted in substantial reading progress for second-grade children across measures of word recognition, vocabulary, comprehension, and fluency when compared to other forms of oral reading practice.

GUIDED READING

Guided reading is an essential part of reading WITH children (Fountas & Pinnell, 1996, 2001). Unlike basal readers that often claim to engage children and teachers in "guided reading" activities through questioning, purpose setting, and silent reading, guided reading, as we describe it here, is a teaching approach that focuses on teachers reading leveled books WITH children that would often present too many challenges for them if they were to take full responsibility for the first reading.

One of the first tasks in guided reading is to assess children's individual reading performance using "benchmark" leveled books. "Benchmark" leveled books are reserved for assessment purposes only and are *not* used for instruction or for independent reading in the classroom. Books at different levels can be selected as "benchmark" books. During assessment, children are asked to read from different levels of "benchmark" books until they read a book with 90% accuracy.

Before students can be assessed, teachers must understand how to level books or find leveling information about the books they want to use. Based on Fountas and Pinnell (1996, 1999), we have described a text gradient summary by grade level for selecting guided reading books to provide the "just right" match for children in each guided reading group as well as approximate grade level equivalents for guided reading levels A–Z (see Figures 3.8 and 3.9). Criteria for guided reading levels Q–Z are found in chapter 4.

Placing Children in Guided Reading Groups

Students are placed into guided reading groups based upon the level of the benchmark book they can read with 90% accuracy in word recognition, or "just right" books. "Just right" books present children with a reasonable challenge but also with a high potential

Figure 3.8   Leveling Criteria for Books, Levels A–P

Levels A & B
- Single idea or story line
- Pictures and text are interdependent to carry the story
- Topics are familiar to children's experiences
- Uses natural oral language structures
- Print and layout are consistent and easy to follow
- Print is separate from pictures
- Full range of punctuation use
- Spacing is sufficient to easily determine word boundaries
- Words are repeated throughout the story
- Pages contain 1–4 lines of print, with Level A less and Level B more

Level C
Level C books are similar to Level A & B books with the following changes:
- Pages contain 2–5 lines each
- Story is carried more by the print than the pictures but pictures remain important
- Print may carry across a two-page layout in columns
- Sentences are longer
- More words

Level D
Level D books are similar to Level C books with the following changes:
- Stories still simple but more complex story line
- Pictures still important but story is increasingly based on the print
- Pages contain up to 6 lines of print per page
- Sentences are longer
- More words—including those with inflected endings

Level E
Level E books are similar to Level D books with the following changes:
- Pages contain up to 8 lines of print per page
- Placement of the text may begin to vary locations on the page within the book
- Pictures contain several ideas and the text carries the story
- Problem solving is needed to connect text and pictures
- Words require word analysis skills to a greater degree
- Concepts in the story may be less familiar to children
- Long stories and more words

Level F
Level F books are similar to Level E books with the following changes:
- Print is smaller
- Literary language is mixed with oral language patterns
- Frequently used words are expanded in the stories
- Stories have a distinct beginning, middle, and end
- Increased use of dialogue
- Word analysis skills are increasingly needed at this level

Levels G & H
Level G & H books are similar to Level F books with the following changes:
- More challenging ideas and vocabulary
- Content is increasingly distant from children's experiences

continued

Figure 3.8   Continued

- Stories contain repeated language patterns in multiple episodes
- Stories are longer with more pages per book than in previous levels
- Repetition within episodes becomes less in level H books

Level I
Level I books are similar to Level G & H books with the following changes:
- Greater variety of texts—including information texts
- Story structure is more complex, more episodes, and themes less related to experiences of children
- Point of view is introduced
- Texts increase in length and there are more than 8 sentences per page
- Texts include large numbers of unfamiliar words requiring word analysis skills

Level J
Level J books are similar to Level I books with the following changes:
- Variety of genre of texts increases
- Books are 30–60 pages in length
- Chapter books start at this level
- Longer books have easier text to sustain interest
- Shorter books have more difficult text requiring greater word analysis and interpretive abilities
- Character development is enhanced in these texts

Level K
Level K books are similar to Level J books with the following changes:
- Easy chapter books that have a picture on each or every other page
- Print is relatively easy in these books, helping children sustain the reading of longer books
- Literary picture books with about 15 lines per page are about this level
- Oral reading is now moving toward more silent reading

Level L
Level L books are similar to Level K books with the following changes:
- Includes some longer, more complex picture books that guided reading groups can use for discussion
- Chapter books have more complex plots over longer periods of time and represent a full range of genre
- Most chapter books are 70–80 pages long
- Print size is varied and often smaller

Level M
Level M books are similar to Level K books with the following changes:
- Chapter books are longer with fewer pictures
- Themes and topics vary widely and are more complex
- Print size is smaller with more lines and words per page
- Ancillary information materials may be included, such as maps, glossaries, vignettes, biographies, time lines, and so on.

Level N
Level N books are similar to Level M books with the following changes:
- Books are now 100 pages or more

W/ **Figure 3.8**   Continued

- Chapters are about 15–20 pages in length
- More emphasis on reading informational texts
- Still have one plot and episodic structures in stories
- Books require a cultural or historical context for interpretation

Level O
Level O books are similar to Level N books with the following changes:
- Multiple characters with interwoven plots, flashbacks, and other complex writing styles
- Longer books of up to 200 pages including realistic fiction, biographies, science fiction, folk and fairy tales, and so on.
- Black and white illustrations are used primarily and are quite infrequent
- Many new multisyllable words are used in these texts

Level P
Level P books are similar to Level O books with the following changes:
- Figurative language is used but explained by the writer
- Longer, more complex texts with greater variety of types and genre
- Texts are largely distanced from the children's personal experiences, requiring greater ability to understand historical contexts and interpret new meanings from the text

Source: Taken from *Matching Books to Readers: Using Leveled Books in Guided Reading, K-3* (pp. 83–91), by I. C. Fountas and G. S. Pinnell, 1999, Portsmouth, NH: Heinemann Educational Books.

for success. Books used for initial guided reading experiences should demonstrate a close match of text and pictures, gradual introduction of unfamiliar concepts and words, as well as sufficient repetition of predictable elements to provide support. In most schools where guided reading is practiced in the primary grades, there is a large, centralized collection of leveled reading books, or *literacy materials center.* Teachers check out leveled materials from the school's literacy materials center to support guided reading in the classroom, a very cost-effective way of providing teachers with a kind of communal classroom library.

Guided reading is done in small, homogeneous groups of children who reflect a similar range of competencies, experiences, and interests (Fountas & Pinnell, 1996, 2001). Guided reading instruction is intended to focus on teaching children in the "zone of their proximal development" (Vygotsky, 1978) or at that point in their development where they can succeed at a task with some expert help but cannot yet succeed on their own. Therefore, an important consideration in forming guided reading groups is matching children in the group with "just right" books. Guided reading groups change as children progress through the year. This is a crucial point because failure to modify group composition can result in static ability groups like the "Eagles, Bluebirds, and Buzzards" as practiced in previous decades. The static nature of these ability groups, particularly for those children in the "lower" developmental groups, caused children to suffer documented self-esteem damage and lowered academic expectations.

In guided reading lessons, teachers lead children to understand that there are three important cueing systems good readers use to unlock unfamiliar text: 1) meaning, 2) structure-sentence organization or syntax, and 3) the visual-sound system (Fountas & Pinnell, 1996; Mooney, 1990). As shown in Figure 3.10, these three cueing systems are interlinked and interdependent.

Figure 3.9   An Approximate Grade Level Correspondence
of Leveled Books for Guided Reading

Grade Levels	A B C D E F G H I J K L M N O P
	(Guided Reading Book Levels)
Kindergarten	
First Grade	
Second Grade	
Third Grade	
May need extra support to sustain reading efforts	
Grade Levels	**K L M N O P Q R S T U V W X Y Z**
	(Guided Reading Book Levels)
Fourth Grade	
Fifth Grade	
Sixth Grade	
Approximate level expectations by grade	

Source: Taken from *Guided Reading: Good First Teaching for All Children* (p. 192), by
I. C. Fountas and G. S. Pinnell, 1996, Portsmouth, NH: Heinemann Educational Books;
and Leveled Books for Readers, Grades 3–6 (p.13), by G. S. Pinnell and I. C. Fountas,
2002, Portsmouth, NH: Heinemann.

Figure 3.10   Interlinked Cueing Systems

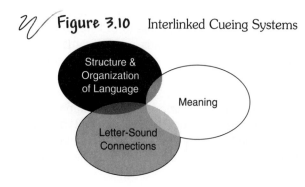

Figure 3.11   Guided Reading Teacher Prompts

Sampling Prompts:
- Read this with your finger.
- Do the words you say match with words on the page?
- Try this word. Would that make sense?
- Try this sound. Does that sound right?
- Can you find the word (or) letter?
- Does that make sense?
- Does this sound right to you? (Repeat what the child said.)
- Do you know a word like that?
- What can you do if you do not know a word?

Confirming Prompts:
- Were there enough words?
- Read that again.
- Try starting the word at the beginning with the first letter and sound.
- What did you notice?
- Does it start that way?
- Does it end with those letters or sounds?
- You almost got it. Can you find what was wrong?

Self-Correction Prompts:
- Why did you stop?
- Check that word again. Does it look right? Sound right?
- Something was not quite right. Try it again.

To help children use these three cueing systems for fluent reading, you should model their application. This is accomplished by showing children how to select and apply one or more reading strategies: 1) predicting, 2) sampling, 3) confirming, and 4) cross-checking to self-correct. Fountas and Pinnell (1999) give several examples of prompts teachers may use to direct or guide children to select and apply these reading strategies as shown in Figure 3.11.

In the earliest stages of guided reading, teachers begin by leading the first reading of the text with students. Thus, early guided reading looks in practice much like a shared reading experience; the main differences are the size of the group, the close reading of the text with individual guidance, and the use of multiple copies of the same title at the "just right" level of challenge.

Children are encouraged to use their fingers to finger-point read in the earliest stages of guided reading instruction (Ehri & Sweet, 1991). Finger-point reading involves pointing to the words as they are spoken (Reutzel, 1995). During guided reading lessons, teachers focus children's attention on print concepts such as directionality (i.e., left to right, top to bottom) and on processing text using multiple reading strategies such as predicting, sampling, confirming, cross-checking, and self-correcting. Following the guided reading of a text, children are asked to summarize or retell the text. With time and development, children assume more responsibility for the first reading of the text with the teacher taking a supporting role through echoing, coaching, and helping where needed. This gradual release of responsibility generally occurs as children understand basic print concepts, acquire a basic sight word vocabulary, and select and apply appropriate reading strategies.

Figure 3.12   Seven-Part Guided Reading Lesson

Picture Walk-Talk: Guide children through the pictures of a new book. Ask them, "What do you see here?"

First Reading: Depending on children's experiences with text, the first reading may be done by the teacher, who will gradually release responsibility for the first reading to the children as they develop greater capacity.

Language Play: After carefully analyzing the text for challenges children may encounter with the layout, print placement, words, sentence structure, picture-text match, and so on, the teacher develops a lesson around a "close reading" of the text to talk about and teach students about these challenges and how to overcome them as independent readers.

Rereading: Children reread the text aloud again (or silently as they develop oral fluency) while the teacher listens in on each child's quiet oral rereading.

Retelling: Children take turns retelling each other and/or the teacher what they have read. During this time, children are helped by the teacher to understand that stories have a beginning, middle, and end.

Sharing Competence: Children take the guided reading books home to read and share with their parents, caregivers, or siblings. Sharing emerging competence with guided reading texts increases children's self-confidence and motivation.

Extending Meaning: Children engage in projects that extend their understanding of the texts through storytelling, puppetry, plays, murals, hand actions, and so on.

As fluency is demonstrated in oral reading situations, teachers gradually help children convert their oral reading to silent reading. As children increase their fluency and comprehension, teachers broaden guidance to include an understanding of story structure, characterization, and the use of literary devices.

The stages of independent and critical reading are typically achieved in the intermediate, upper elementary, and middle school years. Once children reach these stages of reading development, teachers expand children's strategies and understandings of text to include studies of genre, reading like a writer (stylistic examinations), text structure, and study/reference skills. A basic lesson pattern employed in guided reading lessons consists of seven phases. These phases are shown in Figure 3.12 and a sample guided reading lesson is shown in Figure 3.13.

As children develop increasing fluency and expanding interests in the intermediate years, guided reading experiences change with them. At this level, guided reading can include:

- reading workshop
- writing workshop
- working with language

All of the activities associated with guided reading in the intermediate years are intended to sharpen, refine, and hone children's reading fluency and critical thinking with text (Fountas & Pinnell, 2001; Reutzel & Cooter, 1991, 2000). Whether these students are reading the novel, *The Hatchet,* or reading information text like *The Titanic,* the goal is to read orally with appropriate rate, phrasing, and intonation as well as with the purpose of understanding the text. The purpose of guided reading with children of this age group is to help them not only understand the text but also develop a deeper understanding of, and appreciation for, language. Guided reading instruction is aimed at help-

Figure 3.13   Teaching a Guided Reading Lesson

Ms. Silva gathers her seven children around her U-shaped table where she has laid out the guided reading books, one for each child, on the table. The book for today is *My Little Sister Ate One Hare* by Bill Grossman (1996). The teacher asks the children, "What do you see on the cover of this book?" Bonny replies, "I see a little girl with her mouth open like she is going to swallow a rabbit!" "That's right," Ms. Silva responds approvingly. "Now let's open the book to the first page. What do you see here?" "I see the same little girl about to swallow a rabbit," responds Maggie. "What do you think the print is telling us about this picture?" asks Ms. Silva. "It probably says she ate a rabbit," Danny intones with pleasure. "Now let's turn to the next page," Mrs. Silva says. "What do you see here?"

"The girl is eating snakes," is the reply. Ms. Silva continues the picture walk through the rest of the book and says, "Now that we have looked at the pictures in the book, let's start with the cover and read what it says. Put your finger on the cover where we should begin reading." The group reads together with the teacher. "MY LITTLE SISTER ATE ONE HARE." The children and Ms. Silva turn to the second page and read, "MY LITTLE SISTER ATE TWO SNAKES." Ms. Silva stops, "Do you boys and girls see a pattern here? What is it?" They respond, "MY LITTLE SISTER ATE_____." "That's right," and they continue reading to the end.

"Now, let's look at the cover again. Can someone point to the word, 'ATE'? Children all point. "Well done," Ms. Silva observes. "How do we write, 'ATE'?" What letters do we see here?" The children respond with "a", "t", and "e." "Now let's make the sounds of the letters together, 'AAAA TTTT'—'ATE.' What would happen if I put a 'DDDD' sound before 'ATE', what would I get? Let's try it, 'DDDD AAA TTTT—DATE.' What would it be if I put an 'RRRR' sound?" Josey blurts out, "rate!" "Let's make a list of words we could make with 'ATE.' " Ms. Silva engages children in discussion about the phonogram or rime, "ATE," and making words.

"Now let's reread the story again. Each of you read it aloud in a quiet mumble voice. I will listen in as you reread." The children reread the story again in a quiet mumble reading so the teacher can eavesdrop on each student's reading. "After reading, I want you to tell the person next to you what you read by taking turns. Because there are seven, Josey, you will tell me the story and I will tell you."

After retellings, Ms. Silva tells the children that they may take their copies of the book *My Little Sister Ate One Hare* home to read with their parents. She encourages them to read it aloud and then retell the story to their parents as well. "Now tomorrow," Ms. Silva continues, "We will make a list of all the things that 'We could eat' and make another book like this one to read together."

ing intermediate-aged students gain insights into how texts are created from a writer's point of view. They are introduced to strategies and tools to increase their general enjoyment and satisfaction from reading. We will discuss the routines and organizing for guided reading instruction including the **Reading and Writing Workshops** in chapter 4, Organizing for Effective Reading Instruction.

TEACHING SKILLS AND STRATEGIES: MINILESSONS

Teaching skills and strategies are well taught via *minilessons* (5–10 minutes per session), rather than lengthy lessons of 30–45 minutes. Minilessons are typically whole-class or small-group lessons used to: 1) teach reading strategies and skills, 2) promote student responses to what they have read, or 3) teach a necessary procedure (Hagerty, 1992). Because minilessons are brief, it usually takes several repetitions of these 5 to 10 minute minilessons for most skills or strategies to be fully taught and learned. Minilessons allow teachers to quickly get to the application of a skill or strategy and end a lesson before student attention fades.

They are not, by the way, always meant to be lessons in which "outcomes" are required. Sometimes minilessons are simply opportunities for students to take part in a literate behavior (i.e., enjoy reading a book, poem, or song, or participate in writing).

Hagerty (1992) described three types of minilessons: 1) procedural, 2) literary, and 3) strategy/skill. A listing of possible minilesson topics is found in Figure 3.14.

A *procedural reading minilesson,* for example, might involve the teacher and students in learning how to handle new books received for the classroom library corner, as well as how to repair worn books. The teacher may demonstrate how to break in a new book's binding by standing the book on its spine and opening a few pages on either side of the center of the book and carefully pressing them down. Cellophane tape and staplers may be used to demonstrate how to repair tears in a book's pages or cover.

Figure 3.14   Possible Minilesson Topics

Procedural Minilessons	Literary Minilessons	Strategy/Skill Minilessons
Where to sit during reading time	Differences between fiction and nonfiction books	How to choose a book
Giving a book talk		Selecting literature log topics
How to be a good listener in a share session	Learning from dedications	Connecting reading material to your own life
	Books that show emotion	
What is an appropriate noise level during reading time	Books written in the first, second, or third person	Tips for reading aloud
		Figuring out unknown words
What to do when you finish a book	Author studies	Using context
What kinds of questions to ask during a share session	How authors use quotations	Substituting
	How the story setting fits the story	Using picture clues
Running a small group discussion	Characteristics of different genres	Using the sounds of blends, vowels, contractions, and so on.
Self-evaluation	Development of characters, plot, theme, mood	Using Post-its to mark interesting parts
Getting ready for a conference		
How to have a peer conference	How leads hook us	Monitoring comprehension (Does this make sense and sound right?)
Where to sit during minilessons	How authors use the problem/event/solution pattern	Asking questions while reading
Taking care of books	Differences between a picture book and a novel	Making predictions
Keeping track of books to read		Emergent strategies
Rules of the workshop	Titles and their meanings	Concept of story
	Characters' points of view	Concept that print carries meaning
	Examples of similes and metaphors	Making sense
	Examples of foreshadowing	Mapping a story
	How authors use dialogue	How to retell a story orally
	Predictable and surprise endings	Looking for relationships
	Use of descriptive words and phrases	Looking for important ideas
	How illustrations enhance the story	Making inferences
	Secrets in books	Drawing conclusions
		Summarizing a story
		Distinguishing fact from opinion
		Emergent reader skills: directionality, concept of "word," sound/symbol relationships

Note: From *Readers workshop: Real reading* (pp. 113–115), by P. Hagerty, 1992, Ontario, Canada: Scholastic Canada. Copyright 1992 by Scholastic Canada. Reprinted by permission.

A *literary reading minilesson* for early readers might involve a child presenting the teacher with a small booklet written at home in the shape of a puppy that retells favorite parts from the book *Taxi Dog* (Barracca & Barracca, 1990). An upper elementary level student may be shown how to assemble a poster resembling the front page of a newspaper in order to depict major events from a novel just read, such as Betsy Byars' *The Summer of the Swans* (1970).

An example of a *strategy/skill reading minilesson* for early readers might occur during the reading of a big book entitled *Cats and Mice* (Gelman, 1985), in which the teacher makes note of the fact that many of the words in the book end with the participle form of *-ing*. Noticing this regularity in the text, the teacher draws children's attention to the function of *-ing*. For example, while rereading *Cats and Mice* the next day, the teacher may cover each *-ing* ending with a small self-adhesive note, then peel it away while reading to emphasize the word ending. A minilesson for more advanced readers might pertain to patterns used by nonfiction writers to make information books easier to understand (i.e., cause-effect, description, problem-solution, comparisons, and so on). This could involve 1) describing the patterns used, 2) searching for examples in science, mathematics, and social studies materials, then 3) writing/creating examples of these patterns pertaining to a topic of the student's choice.

READING BY CHILDREN

Recent research confirms what many educators have known for years; the more children read books at appropriate levels of challenge, the better readers they become! The axiom that "practice makes perfect" seems to be at least partially true with respect to the effect of reading books on children's reading progress. Many years ago a very good question was asked in one of the nation's leading reading journals (Allington, 1977, 2001)—"If they don't read much, how they ever gonna get good?" Teachers at all levels can promote better reading achievement by providing children with adequate time to read daily from good books appropriately chosen for interest and for levels of reading challenge. Reading books during independent reading time positively affects ALL students' reading growth, motivation, and achievement.

ACCESS TO PRINT MAKES INDEPENDENT READING POSSIBLE

Studies over the past two decades demonstrate convincingly the impact of access to print and books on reading growth and achievement (Allington, 1983; Anderson et al., 1985; Anderson, Wilson & Fielding, 1988; Duke, 2000a, 2000b; Elley & Mangubhai, 1983; Neuman, 1999; Taylor, Frye, & Maruyama, 1990).

Once again, access to books has taken center stage among researchers. Neuman (1999) conducted a study examining the effects of "flooding" local child-care centers in inner city Philadelphia with books. Access to books significantly improved young children's learning of many early print and reading concepts. Nell Duke (2000b) studied differences in the print environment, access to books, magazines, and displayed language in the rooms provided to children in 20 first-grade classrooms of very low or very high socioeconomic status. Site visits showed substantial differences between socioeconomic levels. Children in lower socioeconomic classrooms were exposed to lower amounts, types, and uses of print. In another study investigating access to information texts in first grades, Duke (2000a) found a scarcity of informational texts and information books in classrooms (particularly the low socioeconomic status schools). The most startling finding was that children in low socioeconomic classrooms had access to, and read information in, trade books about 3.6 minutes per day on average.

Beck and McKeown (2001) supported having a wide variety of trade books to read aloud to young children because, "Vivid, delightful pictures are a hallmark of children's trade books, and children are naturally drawn to them" (p. 11).

Fader (1976) wrote about the value of reading books independently, "If teachers would see themselves first as purveyors of pleasure rather than instructors in skill, they may find that skill will flourish where pleasure has been cultivated" (p. 4). Jim Trelease (2001) summed up well the value of reading books independently when he wrote, "Expecting children living in a 'print desert' to become competent readers by simply drill and skill, repeatedly teaching the sounds and letters, is the equivalent of expecting children in Israel to become competent skiers with only instruction booklets but no *snow*" (p. 4).

INDEPENDENT READING IMPROVES READING ACHIEVEMENT

Research shows independent reading produces reading achievement across a wide spectrum of measurements: knowledge base, language development, comprehension skills, story sequencing, vocabulary, reading fluency, linguistic competence, confidence to move on to more sophisticated and difficult reading, improved spelling and writing quality, and improved use of language mechanics (Caldwell & Gaine, 2000; Cantrell, 1999; Farris & Hancock, 1991; Fredericks, 1992; Krashen, 1989; Taylor et al., 1990). Anderson et al. (1988) showed that time spent reading books and other print materials resulted in consistent reading achievement gains. The highest achievers in fifth grade read up to 200 times as many minutes per day than did the lowest achievers.

The Report of the National Reading Panel (2000) reviewed a large body of research indicating a clear association or relationship of reading time to reading achievement. Although this same panel was unable to demonstrate a "causal" effect of reading on reading achievement, the preponderance of correlation data indicate a consistent positive relationship of reading books and other printed materials on gains in reading achievement. The most recent report of the National Assessment of Education Progress (2000), *The Nation's Report Card—Fourth-Grade Reading Highlights,* showed an interesting summary finding for the nation (see Figure 3.15).

Results from the 2000 National Assessment of Educational Progress (NAEP) reading assessment show a consistent, positive relationship between the number of pages read daily in school and for homework and reading performance. Students who reported reading 11 or more pages per day scored higher than students who reported reading fewer pages daily. These recent research reviews and findings consistently point out the value and importance of independently reading books and other printed materials on children's later reading achievement.

READING INDEPENDENTLY MOTIVATES STUDENTS TO READ

For 40 years, studies have also shown students are more motivated to read trade books than basal readers or content textbooks (Asher, 1980; Csikszentmihalyi & Csikszentmihalyi, 1988; McQuillan & Conde, 1996; VanSledright, 1995; Wigfield, 1996, 1997; Worthy, Moorman, & Turner, 1999). Asher found that high interest in reading materials resulted in greater desires to read and increased reading comprehension in the early 1980s. Worthy et al. (1999) reported a study entitled, "What Johnny likes to read is hard to find in school."

Figure 3.15 Higher Reading Scores for Those Who Read 11 or More Pages Daily—Grade 4

Percentage of students reporting on the number of pages read daily, 1992–2000				
	'92	'94	'98	'00
11 or more pages	56*	54*	57	60
6 to 10 pages	23*	23*	22	20
5 or fewer pages	21	23*	21	19

Average scores by number of pages read daily

5 or fewer	6 to 10	11 or more
202	215	222

* Significantly different from 2000.
NOTE: Percentages may not add to 100 due to rounding.
SOURCE: National Center for Education Statistics, National Assessment for Educational Progress (NAEP), 1992–2000 Reading Assessments.

This study examined the reading preferences and access to a variety of reading materials of sixth-grade students in three large middle schools in the southwestern United States. Results indicated that sixth-grade students enjoyed reading scary books and stories, comics and cartoons, magazines about popular culture, and books and magazines about sports. Comparisons of student preferences for reading were examined by gender, income, reading attitude, and achievement and found more similarities than differences. Surveying students and interviewing teachers and librarians determined access to the most preferred reading materials. Results showed that the majority of students obtained preferred reading materials from home and stores rather than from schools and libraries. Classrooms ranked a distant last for accessing interesting books or magazines even among low-income students! Interviews with teachers and librarians showed limited availability of the most popular reading books and magazines in school classrooms and libraries.

INDEPENDENT READING HELPS STRUGGLING AND SECOND-LANGUAGE LEARNERS

Students learn at different rates, using many learning styles, and with varying degrees of ability, confidence, and self-efficacy. Trade books offer one of the most powerful tools for meeting the needs of a variety of students with special learning needs in schools. Mangubhai and Elley (1982) asserted, "The provision of a rich supply of high-interest storybooks is a much more feasible policy for improving English learning than any pious pronouncements about the urgent need to raise teacher quality" (p. 159). Because trade books offer a wide variety of reading levels, interest, content areas, and cultures, they can be used to meet the needs of a variety of special-needs learners with some amazing results (Flippo, 1999; Hart-Hewins, 1999; Vandergrift, 2001).

Trade books play a major role in helping second-language learners become skilled and fluent readers and speakers of English (Elley, 1991; Laumbach, 1995). Elley (1991) stated, "Those children who are exposed to an extensive range of high-interest illustrated story books and encouraged to read and share them, are consistently found to learn the target language more quickly" (p. 375). Krashen (1997/1998) declared that, "We must build critically needed reading environments for all our learners—book by book" (p. 21).

Morrow (1992) found in a study of using trade books in a literature-based reading program that minority children from a variety of backgrounds experienced increases in achievement, voluntary reading, and attitudes. Routman (1991) related:

> I started combing local bookstores and buying multiple copies of appealing children's books. These books I used to teach reading. The results with low-ability first graders were impressive. Four three years in a row, typically, two of the five children would test out in June [on a Standardized test] as high-ability readers, two would be at the average level, and one would remain as a low-ability reader. The results also included students filled with high self-esteem, pride in their accomplishments, and the joy of being competent readers. (p. 10)

It is clear from this brief review of research that reading by students is a powerful ingredient in a comprehensive reading program.

We have found several excellent practices for involving students in independent reading: 1) Reading Around the Room, 2) Popcorn Reading, and 3) Sustained Silent Reading (SSR). In *Reading Around the Room,* the teacher controls the process and students participate. In *Popcorn Reading,* the responsibility for reading independently is subtly shifted to the students with the teacher exerting less control. In *SSR,* the children assume the full responsibility for reading independently.

- **Reading Around the Room.** In *reading around the room,* the teacher or a student uses a pointer to read words, charts, big books, signs, displays, or other classroom printed materials as a group in unison. Some teachers close the blinds, turn out the lights, and use a flashlight for a pointer to direct students' attention to print in the classroom environment for reading around the room. Tompkins (1998) described another approach, called *Reading Around,* where students read aloud their favorite sentences or paragraphs one at a time to others. The key to this approach is to allow children time for rehearsal of the text prior to reading aloud. If there is more than one child wanting to read the same passage or text, invite these children to rehearse together a longer piece of text than a sentence or paragraph so that each student gets to read aloud.

- **Popcorn Reading.** *Popcorn reading* (McCool, 1982) is a very common practice in many elementary classrooms. Children in the whole class or in a small group all have the same book to read. Someone, either the teacher or a child, begins reading aloud. At some point, that person calls out "popcorn," and calls on another person to continue reading. Although this process seems very simple, it does motivate students to pay careful attention and to follow along. A variation on "popcorn reading" is to stop, say "popcorn," and anyone who wants to start reading jumps in and continues the reading. Many teachers, especially those in the intermediate grades, have found that "popcorn" reading is a highly motivating form of reading practice.

- **Sustained Silent Reading (SSR).** An important part of reading by children is the opportunity to enjoy reading self-selected materials of appropriate challenge on a regular basis (Pilgreen, 2000). *Sustained silent reading* (SSR) is a structured approach that provides needed reading opportunities for students. Hunt (1970) explained that SSR is a structured activity in which children are given regular, fixed time periods for silently reading self-selected materials. Put differently, SSR is an activity where everyone in the classroom—students, teachers, parents, volunteers—reads silently something they have personally selected for a designated period of time.

The purposes of SSR are grounded in the belief that anyone—children or adults—gets better at anything they practice regularly: the time-on-task principle. We know that the more children read, the more they will learn about the process of becoming a successful reader. To help children derive greater purpose and understanding from SSR, we offer the following eight factors for SSR success based on Pilgreen's *The SSR Handbook* (2000).

- Access to Books
- Appeal of Books
- Conducive Environment for Reading
- Encouragement and Motivation
- Staff Training to Involve the School
- Nonaccountability
- Follow-Up Activities
- Regular Time to Read

McCracken and McCracken (1978) described several reasons for implementing an SSR program:

1. Reading books is important. Children come to understand what teachers value by taking note of what they are asked to do.
2. Anyone can read a book. Readers with special needs do not feel singled out for attention when they engage in reading or looking at a book during SSR.
3. Children learn that reading is interacting with an author through sustained engagement with a self-selected text.
4. Children develop the ability to remain on task for an extended period of time during SSR.
5. Books were meant to be read in large chunks for extended periods of time. Children may get the wrong idea that reading is done during small segments of time and focus on short texts such as those often found in basal readers.
6. Comprehension is improved through SSR activities (see also Reutzel & Hollingsworth, 1991).
7. Finally, children learn to judge the appropriateness of the materials they select for reading during SSR. (Note: Reutzel and Gali [1998] found that for most children the hardest part of learning to read was choosing the right book.)

Implementing an SSR program is a relatively straightforward process. Here is what you do:

- **Designate a specific daily time for reading.** Teachers have found that three time slots work well for SSR. The first is as children enter the classroom first thing in the morning. The second is following lunch or recess, and the third is right before children go home for the day. Typically, teachers allocate about 15 to 20 minutes per day for SSR. For younger children, teachers might begin with a 10-minute SSR time and lengthen this time throughout the year as children indicate a desire for more time. We have found that a cooking timer with a bell is a welcome addition for younger children so they do not become worried about watching the clock.

Figure 3.16   The Rules for SSR

Children must select their own books or reading materials.

1. Changing books during the SSR period is discouraged to avoid interruptions.
2. Each individual in the classroom is expected to read silently without interruptions during the fixed period of time for SSR.
3. The teacher and other visitors in the classroom are expected to read silently materials of their own choosing as well.
4. Children are not expected to make reports or answer teacher questions about the books they have been reading during SSR.

- **Hold a procedural minilesson to describe the rules of SSR.** To set the stage for successful experiences with SSR, we suggest that teachers conduct a brief lesson on the rules and expectations associated with SSR time. Begin by stating the purposes of SSR shown previously. Second, review with children the rules for participation in SSR. We have found that enlarging these rules and placing them on a chart for the class helps students take responsibility for their own behavior. Finally, explain how students can ready themselves for this time each day. The rules for SSR are shown in Figure 3.16 in chart form.

- **Extend the experience through sharing.** Children can be asked to share their books with other students at the conclusion of SSR through a "say something" or "turn to your neighbor" activity. In addition to these informal share sessions, groups of children may organize a response to a book through art, drama, writing, or musical performances to be shared with others. In any case, beginning an SSR program with young children, even in kindergarten, convinces children of the value of reading and gives them important practice time. Clearly, SSR has the potential to help children develop life-long reading enjoyment and habits.

As adults, many of the books we choose to read for pleasure are texts that were introduced to us through interactions with others. We have acquired knowledge of various sources we can turn to for suggestions about what we might read such as the "Best Seller" lists that are available. Perhaps we are having an informal conversation with a friend or associate and find ourselves discussing a new or favorite book. Chances are very good that through this recommendation we will seek out the text to read for ourselves. This interaction provides a driving force for us to want to share the text with others and perhaps even seek out additional books to read.

An opportunity for independent reading in most classrooms, which generally allows for student choice and interest, occurs far too infrequently. Many teachers only allow independent reading when students have completed other instructional tasks such as worksheet or workbook activities. Not all teachers make regularly scheduled independent reading time available to students. However, it is an activity that can bring great gains in student reading achievement and interest. We offer one last observation about SSR to increase its success in promoting reading growth and performance. Students experience greater satisfaction from independent reading when they select reading materials of interest from books on their independent reading level. Many teachers provide children "browsing boxes" in which a variety of interesting books are placed at the child's reading level for selection. Children choose from their browsing box or from the classroom library materials to be read during independent reading time.

LIBRARY CORNER

Books should be displayed in a well-lit and accessible area. The library corner should, where possible, be located out of the traffic flow in the classroom. It is important that this area is relatively quiet so that children are not distracted or disturbed. Bookshelves should be the appropriate size and height so that children can reach the books without standing on a chair or step stool. There should be room enough for children to sit comfortably to read alone or together with another reader. Children should be taught how to care for the books in the library corner, how to keep it clean and well organized, and how to manage a check-out system. If children are to value the time and resources of a classroom library, they must take responsibility for the care of the books and the classroom library space. For additional information on how to create and sustain an effective classroom library, consult a recently published book by Reutzel and Fawson (2002).

Reading TO, WITH, and BY children provides an instructional framework that helps teachers use best practices of interactive read aloud, choral reading, technology, shared reading, guided reading, skill and strategy instruction, read around the room, popcorn reading, and sustained silent reading (SSR) to model good reading behaviors, teach specific reading skills and strategies, and provide time, resources, and conditions for students to apply their knowledge and skills to reading each and every day. Teachers who have used these practices have consistently provided excellent instruction with equally stellar results (Morrow, Tracey, Woo, & Pressley, 1999; Wharton-McDonald, Pressley, & Rankin, 1997).

SELECTED REFERENCES

Ahlberg, J. (1978). *Each peach pear plum: An "I spy" story.* New York: Viking Press.

Allington, R. L. (1977). If they don't read much, how they ever gonna get good? *Journal of Reading, 21,* 57–61.

Allington, R. L. (1983). The reading instruction provided readers of differing reading abilities. *The Elementary School Journal, 83,* 548–559.

Allington, R. L. (2001). *What really matters for struggling readers: Designing research-based programs.* New York: Addison-Wesley/Longman.

Anderson, R. C., Hiebert, E. F., Scott, J. A., & Wilkinson, I. A. G. (1985). *Becoming a nation of readers: The report of the Commission on Reading.* Washington, D.C.: The National Institute of Education.

Anderson, R. C., Wilson, P. T., & Fielding, L. G. (1988, Summer). Growth in reading and how children spend their time outside of school. *Reading Research Quarterly, 23,* 285–303.

Asher, S. R. (1980). Topic interest and children's reading comprehension. In R. J. Spiro, B. C. Bruce, & W. F. Brewer (Eds.), *Theoretical issues of reading comprehension* (pp. 525–534). Hillsdale, NJ: Lawrence Erlbaum.

Barracca, D., & Barracca, S. (1990). *Taxi dog.* New York: Dial Books.

Barrentine, S. B. (1996). Engaging with reading through interactive read-alouds. *The Reading Teacher, 50*(1), 36–43.

Barrett, F. L. (1982). *A teacher's guide to shared reading.* Richmond Hill, Ontario, Canada: Scholastic-TAB Publications.

Beck, I. L., & McKeown, M. G. (2001). Text talk: Capturing the benefits of read aloud experiences for young children. *The Reading Teacher, 55*(1), 10–20.

Bennett, W. J. (2001, April 24). A cure for the illiteracy epidemic. *Wall Street Journal,* p. A24.

Byars, B. (1970). *The summer of the swans.* New York: Viking.

Caldwell, K., & Gaine, T. (2000). *"The Phantom Tollbooth" and how the independent reading of good books improves student's reading performance.* CA: Reading and Communication Skills Clearinghouse. (ERIC Document Reproduction Service No. ED449462).

Campbell, R. (1992). *Reading real books.* Philadelphia: Open University Press.

Campbell, R. (2001). *Read-alouds with young children.* Newark, DE: International Reading Association.

Cantrell, S. C. (1999, Fall). The effects of literacy instruction on primary students' reading and writing achievement. *Reading Research Quarterly, 39*(1), 3–26.

Clay, M. M. (1993a). *An observation survey for early literacy achievement.* Portsmouth, NH: Heinemann.

Clay, M. M. (1993b). *Reading recovery: A guidebook for teachers in training.* Portsmouth, NH: Heinemann.

Csikszentmihalyi, M., & Csikszentmihalyi, I. S. (Eds.). (1988). *Optimal experience: Studies of flow in consciousness.* New York: Cambridge University Press.

Department of Education. (1985). *Reading in junior classes. Wellington, New Zealand.* New York: Richard C. Owens.

Duke, N. K. (2000a). 3.6 minutes per day: The scarcity of informational texts in first grade. *Reading Research Quarterly, 35*(2), 202–224.

Duke, N. K. (2000b). For the rich it's richer: print experiences and environments offered to children in very low- and very high-socioeconomic status first-grade classrooms. *American Educational Research Journal, 37,* 441–478.

Durkin, D. (1966). *Children who read early: Two longitudinal studies.* New York: Teachers College Press.

Edwards, P. (1999). *A path to follow: Learning to listen to parents.* Portsmouth, NH: Heinemann.

Ehri, L. C., & Sweet, J. (1991). Fingerpoint-reading of memorized text: What enables beginners to process the print? *Reading Research Quarterly, 26,* 442–462.

Eldredge, J. L., Reutzel, D. R., & Hollingsworth, P. M. (1996, Summer).Comparing the effectiveness of two oral reading practices: Round-robin reading and the shared book experience. *Journal of Literacy Research, 28*(2), 201–225.

Elley, W. B. (1991, September). Acquiring literacy in a second language: The effect of book-based programs. *Language Learning, 41,* 375–411.

Elley, W. B., & Mangubhai, F. (1983, Fall). The impact of reading on second language learning. *Reading Research Quarterly, 19,* 53–67.

Fader, D. N. (1976). *The new hooked on books.* New York: Berkley Pub. Corp.

Farris, P. J., & Hancock, M. R. (1991, November/December). The role of literature in reading achievement. *The Clearing House, 65,* 114–117.

Flippo, R. F. (1999). *What do the experts say?: Helping children learn to read.* Portsmouth, NH: Heinemann.

Fountas, I. C., & Pinnell, G. S. (1996). *Guided reading: Good first teaching for all children.* Portsmouth, NH: Heinemann Educational Books.

Fountas, I. C., & Pinnell, G. S. (1999). *Matching books to readers: Using leveled books in guided reading, K–3.* Portsmouth, NH: Heinemann Educational Books.

Fountas, I. C., & Pinnell, G. S. (2001). *Guiding readers and writers (grades 3–6): Teaching comprehension, genre, and content literacy.* Portsmouth, NH: Heinemann Educational Books.

Fredericks, A. D. (1992). *The integrated curriculum: Book for reluctant readers, grades 2–5.* Englewood, CO: Teacher Ideas Press.

Gelman, R. G. (1985). *Cats and mice.* New York: Scholastic.

Grossman, B. (1996). *My little sister ate one hare.* New York: Crown Publishers.

Hagerty, P. (1992). *Reader's workshop: Real reading.* Ontario, Canada: Scholastic Canada.

Hart-Hewins, L. (1999). *Better books! Better readers!: How to choose, use, and level books for children in the primary grades.* York, ME: Stenhouse Publishers.

Heath, S. B. (1982). What no bedtime stories means: Narrative skills at home and school. *Language and Society, 11,* 49–76.

Heath, S. B. (1983). *Ways with words: Language, life and work in communities and classrooms.* Cambridge, UK: Cambridge University Press.

Hoffman, J. V., Roser, N., & Battle, J. (1993). Reading aloud in classrooms: From the modal to a "model." *The Reading Teacher, 46*(6), 496–503.

Holdaway, D. (1979). *The foundations of literacy.* New York: Ashton Scholastic.

Hunt, L. C. (1970). Effect of self-selection, interest, and motivation upon independent, instructional, and frustrational levels. *Reading Teacher, 24,* 146–151.

Krashen, S. D. (1989, Winter). We acquire vocabulary and spelling by reading: Additional evidence for the input hypothesis. *The Modern Language Journal, 73,* 440–464.

Krashen, S. (1997, December/1998, January). Bridging inequity with books. *Educational Leadership,* 18–22.

Krauss, R. (1945). *The carrot seed.* New York: Scholastic, Inc.

Labbo, L. D. (2001). Supporting children's comprehension of informational text through interactive read alouds. *Literacy and Nonfiction Series, 1*(2), 1–4.

Laumbach, B. (1995, Spring). Reading interests of rural bilingual children. *Rural Educator, 16,* 12–14.

Mangubhai, F., & Elley, W. (1982). The role of reading in promoting ESL. *Language Learning and Communication, 1,* 151–160.

Martin, B. (1990). *Brown bear, brown bear, what do you see?* New York: Henry Holt.

Martin, B. (1991). *Polar bear, polar bear, what do you hear?* New York: Henry Holt.

McCool, M. (1982). *Reading with a special touch.* Urbana, IL: ERIC Language Arts Center. (Government Documents No. ED220798).

McCracken, R. A., & McCracken, M. J. (1978). Modeling is the key to sustained reading. *Reading Teacher, 31,* 406–408.

McQuillan, J., & Conde, G. (1996). The conditions of flow in reading: Two studies of optimal experience. *Reading Psychology, 17,* 109–135.

Meek, M. (1984). Forward in J. Trelease (Ed.), *The read aloud handbook*. Harmondsworth, UK: Penguin.

Meyer, L. A., Stahl, S. A., & Wardrop, J. L. (1994 Nov/Dec). Effects of reading storybooks aloud to children. *The Journal of Educational Research. 88,* 69–85.

Mooney, M. E. (1990). *Reading to, with, and by children.* Katonah, NY: Richard C. Owens.

Morrow, L. M. (1988). Young children's responses to one-to-one story reading in school settings. *Reading Research Quarterly, 23,* 89–107.

Morrow, L. M. (1992). The impact of a literature-based program on literacy achievement, use of literature, and attitudes of children from minority backgrounds. *Reading Research Quarterly, 27*(3), 251–275.

Morrow, L. M. (2001). *Literacy development in the early years: Helping children read and write* (4th ed.). Boston, MA: Allyn and Bacon.

Morrow, L. M., Tracey, D. H., Woo, D. G., & Pressley, M. (1999). Characteristics of exemplary first-grade literacy instruction. *The Reading Teacher, 52*(5), 462–76.

National Institute of Child Health and Human Development. (2000). *Report of the National Reading Panel: Teaching children to read, an evidence-based assessment of the scientific research literature on reading and its implications for reading instruction* (NIH pub. NO. 00-4769). Washington, D.C.: U.S. Government Printing Office.

Neuman, S. B. (1999). Books make a difference: A study of access to literacy. *Reading Research Quarterly, 34*(3), 2–31.

Neuman, S. B., & Roskos, K. A. (1993). *Language and literacy learning in the early years: An integrated approach.* Fort Worth, TX: Harcourt Brace Jovonvich College Publishers.

Optiz, M. F., & Rasinski, T. V. (1998). *Good-bye round robin: 25 effective oral reading strategies.* Portsmouth, NH: Heinemann.

Pilgreen, J. L. (2000). *The SSR handbook: How to organize and manage a silent sustained reading program.* Portsmouth, NH: Heinemann.

Pinnell, G. S., & Fountas, I. C. (2002). *Leveled books for readers, grades 3–6: A companion volume to Guiding readers and writers.* Portsmouth, NH: Heinemann.

Reutzel, D. R. (1995). Fingerpoint-reading and beyond: Learning about print strategies (LAPS). *Reading Horizons, 35(4),* 310–328.

Reutzel, D. R. (1996a). A balanced reading approach. In J. Baltas & S. Shafer (Eds.), *Scholastic guide to balanced reading: K–2.* New York: Scholastic, 6–12.

Reutzel, D. R. (1996b). A balanced reading approach. In J. Baltas & S. Shafer (Eds.), *Scholastic guide to balanced reading: Grade 3–6,* 7–11. New York: Scholastic.

Reutzel, D. R. (2001 May/June). New research helps you reap the biggest benefits from read aloud. *Scholastic Instructor,* pp. 23–24.

Reutzel, D. R., & Cooter, R. B., Jr. (1991). Organizing for effective instruction: The reading workshop. *The Reading Teacher, 44*(8), 548–555.

Reutzel, D. R., & Cooter, R. B. (2000). *Teaching children to read: Putting the pieces together* (3rd ed.). Upper Saddle River, NJ: Merrill/Prentice Hall.

Reutzel, D. R., & Fawson, P. C. (2002). *Your classroom library: New ways to give it more teaching power.* New York: Scholastic Professional Books.

Reutzel, D. R., & Hollingsworth, P. (1991). Reading time in school: Effect on fourth graders' performance on a criterion-referenced comprehension test. *Journal of Educational Research, 84*(3), 170–176.

Reutzel, D. R., & Gali, K. (1998). The art of children's book selection: A labyrinth unexplored. *Reading Psychology, 19*(3), 3–50.

Reutzel, D. R., Hollingsworth, P. M., & Eldredge, J. L. (1994). Oral reading instruction: The impact on student reading development. *Reading Research Quarterly, 23*(1), 40–62.

Ribowsky, H. (1985). *The effects of a code emphasis approach and a whole language approach upon emergent literacy of kindergarten children* (Report No. CS-008-397). (ERIC Document Reproduction Service No. ED 269 720).

Rosenhouse, J., Feitelson, D., & Kita, B. (1997). Interactive reading aloud to Israeli first graders: Its contribution to literacy development. *Reading Research Quarterly, 32,* 168–183.

Routman, R. (1991). *Invitations: Changing as teachers and learners, K–12.* Portsmouth, NH: Heinemann.

Strickland, D. S., & Morrow, L. M. (1989). Interactive experiences with storybook reading. *The Reading Teacher, 42*(4), 322–323.

Taylor, B. M., Frye, B. J., & Maruyama, G. (1990, Summer). Time spent reading and reading growth. *American Educational Research Journal, 27,* 351–362.

Teale, W. H., & Martinez, M. (1986). Reading in a kindergarten classroom library. *The Reading Teacher, 41*(6), 568–73.

Teale, W. H., & Martinez, M. G. (1988). Getting on the right road to reading: Bringing books and young children together in the classroom. *Young Children, 44*(1), p. 10–15.

Tompkins, G. (1998). *Fifty literacy strategies step by step.* Upper Saddle River: Merrill/Prentice Hall.

Trelease, J. (1995). *The new read-aloud handbook* (4th ed.). New York: Penguin.

Trelease, J. (2001). Research, trends, essays: 'It's the climate, stupid!'. *What's New* pp. 1–6. Retrieved May 9,

2001 from http://www.trelease-on-reading.com/whatsnu_2.html

U.S. Department of Education: Office of Educational Research and Improvement. (2001). *The nation's report card: Fourth-grade reading 2000.* Jessup, MD: National Center for Educational Statistics 2001–513.

Vandergrift, K. E. (2001). *Linking literature with learning.* Retrieved May 25, 2001, from http://www.scils.rutgers.edu/special/day/linkages.html

VanSledright, B. A. (1995). *How do multiple text resources influence learning to read American history in fifth grade?: NRRC ongoing research.* Athens, GA: NRRC News: A Newsletter of the National Reading Research Center p. 4–5. (ERIC Document Reproduction Service No. ED385832).

Vygotsky, L. S. (1978). *Mind in society.* Cambridge, MA: Harvard University Press.

Weaver, C. (1998). *Reconsidering a balanced approach to reading.* Urbana, IL: National Council of Teachers of English.

Wells, C. G. (1986). *The meaning makers: Children learning language and using language to learn.* Portsmouth, NH: Heinemann.

Wharton-McDonald, R., Pressley, M., & Rankin, K. (1997). Effective primary-grades literacy instruction = Balanced literacy instruction. *The Reading Teacher, 50*(6), 518–21.

Wigfield, A. (1996). *The nature of children's motivations for reading and their relations to frequency and reading performance* [microform]. Athens, GA: National Reading Research Center. (Government Documents No. ED1.310/2:398550).

Wigfield, A. (1997). Children's motivations for reading and reading engagement. In J. T. Guthrie & A. Wigfield (Eds.), *Reading engagement: Motivating readers through integrated instruction* (pp. 14–33). Newark, DE: International Reading Association, Inc.

Worthy, M. J., Moorman, M., & Turner, M. (1999, January, February, March). What Johnny likes to read is hard to find in school. *Reading Research Quarterly, 34*(1), 12–27.

Chapter 4

Organizing for Effective Reading Instruction

Several teachers are talking in the teachers' lounge about the start of school in a few days. Ms. Cella makes a somewhat sarcastic remark about the so-called "super teachers" about whom she is always hearing. "Yeah, I hear Mrs. Luna over in Washington Elementary has five learning centers in her classroom, does guided reading groups, conducts individual assessment of each of her students every two-three weeks, and walks on water too! I've tried for years to organize my instruction to make use of small groups, centers, and individual assessment, but it's just too complex for me. It seems like one big mass of confusion for me and for the students. Every time I've tried to do it, I gave up because I can't manage the students, the materials, the centers, the assessment, the classroom setup, and on and on it goes!"

Several other teachers nod their heads in agreement.

Mrs. Johnson states conclusively, "We just don't have the time, the resources, and the support to teach like that. And even if we did, I'm just not sure how I would even begin to create and manage the 'wonder' classrooms we hear about."

CREATING EFFECTIVE CLASSROOMS

An inviting, print-rich classroom environment is essential for creating and maintaining a classroom context that supports successful readers. How the classroom is arranged and managed and how the time is allocated each day all affect the general impact of reading instruction. Past research has demonstrated a clear relationship among the arrangement, management, and variety of books and printed materials found in classroom environments and how well young children eventually develop reading ability (Morrow, 2001; Neuman & Roskos, 1990, 1992; Roskos & Neuman, 2001). Teacher decisions about creating and sustaining effective classroom literacy environments typically focus on at least three separate considerations: (1) preparing and organizing the classroom environment, (2) "scaffolding" classroom reading instruction, and (3) scheduling and managing time and resources. We discuss each as a way of guiding teachers through the process of organizing for effective reading instruction.

ORGANIZING AN EFFECTIVE LITERACY ENVIRONMENT

Preparing an effective literacy learning environment in the classroom *begins* with "provisioning" or supplying the classroom with a variety of printed materials. Spivak (1973) referred to children who are taught in print-impoverished classrooms as "setting deprived." Access to a wide variety and large quantities of printed materials has been shown to significantly affect children's literacy development and achievement (Allington, 2001; Neuman & Celano, 2001a, 2001b). Once a list of print-related and literacy-related materials has been developed and acquired, the task of organizing, arranging, and storing these materials for optimal use comes next. Finally, in this section on classroom environments we discuss how to plan, prepare, and organize classroom space for a variety of instructional and learning activities to engage children with printed materials and literacy tools.

Access to a Variety of Literacy Tools and Print Materials

Access to a rich variety of literacy tools and printed materials is fundamental in preparing a classroom environment to support literacy learning (Allington, 2001; Heald-Taylor, 2001). In Figure 4.1, we provide a list of literacy tools teachers may consider for inclusion in their classroom literacy environments.

The number of books necessary for creating a print-rich literacy classroom environment varies with the functions to be served in and out of the classroom such as read aloud, shared reading, guided reading, and independent reading. If access to books is needed

Figure 4.1   Literacy Tools for "Provisioning" a Print-Rich Classroom Environment With Reading Materials

Reading Materials

Books	Manipulative letters
Textbooks	Business cards
Pamphlets/Brochures	Computer programs
Bumper stickers	Internet access
Magazines	Instructions and directions
Cookbooks	Maps
Newspapers	Calendars
Greeting cards	Schedules
Letters	Application forms
Notes	Reference books
Journals	Comics and cartoons
Message boards	Word puzzles
Pocket charts	Books on tape
Sentence and word strips	Songs on tape
Word cards	Flashlights and pointers
Poetry, rap, and chants	Highlighting tape
Play scripts	Stick 'em notes
Nursery rhymes	Word frames
Telephone books	Easels
Product labels	Costumes and props for drama
Signs	Take-home book bags or backpacks
Posters	Pictures
Charts	Felt story board
Big books	Felt story characters and pictures
Displays	

continued

Figure 4.1   Continued

Writing Materials	Blank sentence strips
Blank books	Blank word cards
Blank comics	Elkonin boxes
Pattern books	Chart paper
Word books—no illustrations	Blank calendars, charts, and maps
Illustrated books—no words	Assorted paper sizes, types, and colors
Application forms	Scissors
Recipe cards	Product labels
Handwriting models	Stapler
Manipulative letters	Hole punch
Stencils	Binding supplies
Stationary	Markers
Envelopes	Crayons
Message boards	Pens
White lap boards	Pencils
Rubber stamps	Erasers
Ink pads	Glue
Blank greeting card stock	Blank business cards
Blank big books	Poetry pattern guides
Index cards	Editing tape
Clipboards	Old magazines for pictures
Writing folders	Ledger paper
Poster paper	Daily planner sheets
Mural paper	Diary or journals
Writing paper	Blank checks (facsimile)
Construction paper	Computer programs
Wallpaper	Word processing
Library pockets and cards	Illustrations
Blank address books	Clip art
Notepads	Digital camera
Typewriter	Desktop publishing
Computer and printer	E-mail
Telephone	Internet access
Magnetic letters	

only to support students' independent reading choices, then about 10–12 titles per student in the class is needed as a minimum (Neuman, 2000; Veatch, 1968). This means if a teacher has 30 children in her classroom, then an adequate book collection for independent reading would be between 300–350 book titles. However, if you intend to support cross-curricular studies, take-home reading, guided reading, shared reading, reading aloud, and professional development for the teacher, then the size of the classroom library collection may range from 1,500–2,000 titles, including many titles with multiple copies. Figure 4.2 lists recommended size ranges and book types for a minimum classroom library collection of 300–350 titles.

Classroom book collections should support and invite students to engage in reading a variety of texts—both narrative and expository (Allington, 2001; Burke, 2000; National Institute of Child Health and Human Development, 2000). As expository texts require that students study, gather, think about, and organize information, so too narrative texts invite students to connect with personal experiences and empathize with the characters in a book.

𝒲 **Figure 4.2**   Recommended Minimum Classroom Book Collection

Poetry collection books: 3–5 titles
Pattern/Predictable books: 50–60 titles
Leveled books: 120–140 titles
Decodable books: 40–50 titles
Information books: 40–50 titles
Award-winning books: 30–40 titles
Reference books such as dictionaries (5–10), thesaurus (1–2), CD-ROM encyclopedia
   (1–2 disks), atlases (1–2)
Newspapers (1–2), magazines (1–3 subscriptions), recipe books (1–3), catalogs (3–4)
Series books such as *Dear America, Goosebumps, Harry Potter,* etc.: 3–4 series
Play scripts, reader's theater scripts, skits, etc.: 1–3 titles

Supporting developing readers requires that every teacher have access to a collection of leveled text materials, both narrative and expository. As noted in chapter 2, many schools are establishing what we term "literacy materials centers," central collections of leveled books (multiple copies) in English and Spanish available for teachers to check out for their instruction. Sufficient quantities of leveled books need to be available to comply with the "Goldilocks principle" of achieving a "just right" match between the challenges within the text and each student's interests and needs (Ohlhausen & Jepsen, 1992). In Figure 4.3, we suggest several examples of the types and varieties of printed materials that might be included in print-rich literacy classroom environments.

Teachers need to thoughtfully consider whether or not the literacy tools and printed materials selected for inclusion in their classrooms are *developmentally appropriate.* To determine *appropriateness,* teachers might ask themselves, "Can children read these print materials successfully and purposefully? Can children use these print materials in age-appropriate ways to communicate and interact?" Next, teachers might determine if reading and print materials selected for inclusion in the classroom are *authentic.* To decide if reading and other print materials fit this criterion, teachers might ask, "Are these literacy tools and reading materials typically used by people outside the school classroom environment?" *We agree with research findings, by the way, indicating that teachers should teach children to read using far greater numbers of information texts and nonfiction materials than has been typical in the past* (Duke, 2000a, 2000b). We say this because the typical adult uses reading to learn and gather information roughly 80% of the time. However, adults read for entertainment only about 20% of the time (Ogle, 2001). Finally, teachers might ask if reading and print

𝒲 **Figure 4.3**   Suggested Text Types for Print-Rich Classroom Environment

Textbooks including the classroom reading basal
Computers with bookmarked web pages, National Archives, Library of Congress, etc.
Stories and narrative accounts, i.e., fairy tales, folk tales, biographies, etc.
Picture books that provoke images and display unique uses of artistic talent
Tests, quizzes, and worksheets for "test prep"
Drivers license manuals, auto mechanic guides, maps, telephone books, reports,
   photographs, posters, diaries, letters, etc.
Joke books, comic books, word puzzle books, etc.
Essays, editorials, critiques, etc.

materials are *functional.* That is, "Do these print materials serve a relevant literacy function valued in society at large?"

In the next section, we discuss how teachers can store, arrange, and display this rich collection of print materials to maximize their utility and impact on the reading development of children.

Storing, Arranging, and Displaying Literacy Tools and Print Materials

Morrow and her colleagues (Morrow, 2001, Morrow & Tracey, 1996; Morrow & Weinstein, 1986) have determined that the arrangement of literacy materials in a classroom can significantly affect children's literacy-related play, talk, and development. The classroom environment needs to nurture and support the teaching and learning that occur in the classroom. How teachers store, arrange, and display literacy tools and reading materials affects children's access, understanding, and use of those materials.

Literacy materials are best accessed, used, and understood when they are stored and displayed in well-organized, clearly marked containers or shelves where they are easily accessed and put away by children without teacher or adult assistance. Children will not use materials as readily if they have to ask teachers to get them. Likewise, teachers will not want to allow children access to literacy tools materials if they must clean up, reorganize, and store them after children use them. Rules and uses of literacy materials should be clearly understood and posted in independent learning centers. With the growing availability of digital photography, some teachers have found that creating a photo poster display of children appropriately using literacy tools and reading materials helps students to understand how to use literacy materials appropriately in learning centers and elsewhere in the classroom (Dragan, 2001). Just as their adult models do, children grow weary of the same old things. They need variety, too! Consequently, literacy tools and print materials should be added, deleted, and rotated on a regular basis—at least monthly if not more often.

A comfortable and functional classroom library

Storage areas in the classroom provide much needed organization for classroom literacy learning activities. For example, in a *writing storage area,* author's folders, response logs, and learning logs may be neatly filed in corrugated cardboard file boxes inside personal file folders. Children's written drafts can be stored in three-ring binders with the child's name clearly displayed on the spine of the binder for easy retrieval from a bookshelf location. A small tablet for recording spelling words can be inserted into the pocket of the writing draft three-ring binder. Rubber tubs can be used to store children's personal writing materials, pencil boxes, and belongings and can double as an individual post office box. Each tub should have the child's name and a P.O. box number written on the front.

Rubber tubs may be stored in specially constructed shelves or along coat racks and windowsills. Properly cleaned and covered with contact paper, 2- to 5-gallon ice cream buckets can be stacked along coat racks, cupboards, and windowsills for the same purposes without the expense of purchasing rubber tubs. Supplies and materials typically found in a publishing area such as staplers, paper punches, construction paper, and unlined paper need to be arranged for easy accessibility and clean up. The location of each item in the publishing area needs to be labeled. For younger children, it works well if the teacher traces around the shape of each item in the publishing center and labels the item with the word underneath the object outline. These labeled object outlines can be laminated and taped to the countertop or on the inside of cupboards or bookshelves. Children can easily recognize the object and return it to its place without adult involvement.

It is best if books stored in the *reading nook,* loft, or classroom library are organized to reflect the functions and activities of the classroom reading program. For example, guided, shared, and independent reading books should be shelved on separate bookshelves and clearly marked. Browsing boxes, multiple copies of single titles, and theme or topic book collections could be stored in separate containers on the bookshelves or clearly labeled plastic tubs. Plastic pants hangers with clothespins may be used to store or display big books and chart tablets. Bookshelves and countertops can be lined with vinyl rain gutters to display books, covers out.

Reference materials such as dictionaries, atlases, *The Guinness Book of World Records,* encyclopedias, almanacs, and spellers are best placed near an editing area in the classroom. Writing materials are best stored so that they can be easily transported throughout the classroom to where they are needed. Small plastic tubs or baskets, boxes, cut-down milk containers, and the like can be used for both storage and transporting of crayons, markers, pencils, pens, erasers, and chalk. Organizing and arranging materials in the ways suggested allow children to easily sort and clean up following busy writing output times. In some cases, it works well if small containers are emptied into large-capacity storage bins for storage after transporting to other classroom areas. In so doing, small transport containers can be used for a variety of literacy materials throughout the classroom and then returned, emptied, and used again for other classroom storage and transport needs.

ARRANGING CLASSROOM SPACE FOR INSTRUCTION

Classroom space is more effectively used when broken up into specific learning areas. Just like homes and offices, the space is less useful and functional if built without smaller, purposeful spaces. The work of a kitchen belongs in a space designed expressly for that purpose. Likewise, the work of a *publishing center* belongs in a space designed expressly for that purpose. Dividing classrooms into functional spaces encourages children to be more cooperative and engaged in literacy learning tasks (Roskos & Neuman, 2001).

One effective and often attractive way of cordoning off specific activity areas in the classroom is to use furnishings (i.e., sofas, chairs, bookcases, and so on). Another way of specifically designating activity areas is through the use of displays, labels, and signs. Although classroom space cannot be specifically designated for every content activity, space can be allocated for specific types of activities across content areas. Such spaces may include large gathering areas for the whole class, small learning centers, small group instruction areas, and so on. In any case, with respect to literacy learning, space planning in the classroom is best organized around the elements of a TO, WITH, and BY comprehensive reading program as previously described in chapter 3. Space designed to support a TO, WITH, and BY comprehensive reading program would include at a minimum the following areas:

- Environmental print and word study displays
- Shared reading
- Guided reading
- Literacy learning centers
- Content learning centers
- Independent reading
- Individual conferencing and assessment

We describe how to organize each of these classroom spaces to support the functions and elements of an effective comprehensive reading program.

Environmental Print and Word Study Displays

Classroom displays are intended to immerse students, or as master teacher Adaliese Harris (May & Rizzardi, 2002) puts it—"marinate children" in an environment of interesting and functional print. Displays may be located almost anywhere in the classroom from the ceiling to the walls, from the floor to the windows. Displays are most valued by children when they are student generated rather than teacher produced. In our experiences, a *message board* for leaving notes is a wonderful method of communication between teachers and students. A sign-in *attendance board* encourages even the very youngest children to write their names to begin the school day. *Window writing* using water-soluble ink pens allows students to transcribe their stories, poems, jokes, riddles, and messages onto the window glass. Children find window writing a fun and novel way to display words, stories, and messages largely because it seems like a "taboo" activity. *Sidewalk chalk* is another fun and engaging medium for making displays for outside games, playground science field trips, art, and mapmaking for social studies.

Creating a display of *logo language* or an *environmental print wall* can be used to show product labels and print that children bring from home. Using product labels and other environmental print items to teach reading and writing is both fun and instructionally sound. Environmental print has been shown to help even the youngest child to know she can already read and to provide a familiar bridge to the unfamiliar world of decontextualized print (Kuby & Aldridge, 1994). To create a logo language or environmental print wall display, children bring labels from cans, cereal boxes, old packages, bumper stickers, newspaper ads, and so on into the classroom. Children are asked to read these print items to the class before they are placed onto the logo language wall. Environmental print items on display are often used by children as writing or reading resources for word study lessons throughout the year. (Be sure to remind children that they must ask if they may remove the label on a can before it is used!)

Another effective classroom display often seen in today's classrooms is the *word wall*. In this display, high-frequency words or collections of word families (e.g., "-ake" words such as *take, make, bake, shake,* and so on), help students learn word patterns and remember sight words for reading and writing (Cunningham, 2000). Word wall displays

A collection of logo print displayed for children to read

A classroom word wall is a ready reference for young writers and readers

become environmental reference points for children when they are reading and come to a word they do not know or need to spell a word they do not know yet how to spell conventionally. We will talk more about word walls in chapter 9.

Prominent locations throughout the classroom can be used for posting rules, calendars, lunch menus, TV guides, and charts. *Informational displays* can be used also to exhibit such things as classroom schedules, hints on successful reading and comprehension monitoring, stages of the writing process, steps and media for publishing writing projects, lists of words the class knows, songs the class likes, favorite books, and so on. Other information displays in the classroom can be used to provide children helpful reference information such as numbers, colors, alphabet letters, lunchtime, and classroom helpers.

Scheduling displays may be used for showing the daily flow of classroom events as well as managing appointments with peers and teachers for reading and writing conferences and other individual classroom activities. Labeling objects in the classroom is useful for younger children and for those children learning English as a second language.

Setting Up a Shared Reading Area

A *shared reading area* is best located near chalkboards and well away from designated quiet areas in the classroom. We suggest using a large piece of well-padded carpet to comfortably seat the entire class or a smaller group of the children in this area. To help with classroom management of student behavior while seated on the carpet together, many teachers divide the carpet into smaller squares for each child to have individual space. Children are reminded that they are not to encroach upon another child's space and to keep their hands, arms, and feet within their own space.

Audiovisual equipment should be easily accessible. Such equipment might include a wall-mounted television; video player; overhead projector; tape/CD player; easels for displaying enlarged print of books, poems, riddles, songs, and group experience charts; and electronic keyboards for music accompaniment. A shared reading area should be clear of obstructions and may occupy up to 20% of the total space in the classroom.

Big books and pocket charts are essentials for a shared reading area

A teacher takes a running record while other children re-read a familiar book in the Guided Reading Area

Guided Reading Area

A *guided reading area* is ideally located in or near the center of the classroom at a kidney- or U-shaped table large enough to seat five to eight students comfortably and within an arm's length of the teacher. Leveled books used for guided reading should be located near the guided reading area and easily accessible. A *pocket chart display;* sentence, word, and letter strips, frames, highlight tape, stick 'em notes, markers, and a pointer are also found in this area of the classroom. Small, dry erasable lapboards, erasers, and markers for writing letters, words, and making words may also be stored in or near this area of the classroom. Plastic bins with leveled guided reading books should be placed here for each group's scheduled use of the guided reading area. We have found it helpful to have a small file cabinet adjacent to the guided reading area to store our student assessment portfolios including such things as the observation survey materials, running records, and literacy checklists.

Literacy Learning Centers

Literacy learning centers can include a number of stations or locations designed to engage children in a wide variety of independent and guided literacy learning activities. We suggest several examples of literacy learning centers:

- Listening Center—audiocassettes/CD player, books, and headphones
- Drama Center—costumes, props, play scripts, reader's theater, puppets, etc.
- Reading Around the Room Center—flashlights, laser pointers, wooden pointers, etc.
- Writing Center—writing supplies, writing ideas, editing services, peer conferencing

- Publishing Center—bookmaking supplies, publishing materials
- Paired Shared Literacy Activity Center—big books, word cards, pocket charts, poetry and song charts, etc.
- Reading Response Center—art, music, writing, and drama
- Working With Letters and Words—manipulative letters, stencils, sight word cards, word family creating and sorting activities, environmental print, etc.
- Reading Nook—comfortable, quiet area with classroom library
- Content Area Learning Centers—focused on themes or topics in science, math, social studies, art, music, etc.
- Play Centers—blocks, kitchen, newspaper office, Store, etc.
- Computer Center—Internet, e-mail, and CD ROM-based literacy activities

Literacy learning centers may be designed to reinforce word study, fluency lessons, strategy selection and application, and writing. Other stations may be designed to elaborate literacy learning through responses in art, music, and drama. Literacy learning centers are usually located at a small table or pair of desks just right for a pair of students or a small group. Supplies and materials appropriate to the focus of the center are provided at the center location. If, for example, a center is designed to focus on letter and word study, it would be stocked with plastic letters, word family tiles or cards, and word cards. Children in literacy learning centers are given specific activities or tasks to complete. For example, in our *word study center,* children might be asked to make words (Cunningham, 2000). They are given several word family cards such as "-ate, -ick, -in, and -ink" along with a tray of manipulative letters. Children are instructed to make as many words using the letters as they can for each word family and write these words down on a "Word Making" record sheet. Directions for completing the activity are clearly displayed and reviewed prior to the literacy center time period. Displays in the center include a posted list or photo display of appropriate behaviors and uses for the materials provided in the center. In the beginning, it is best if learning centers are treated as stations with a time limit and rotation schedule. As children become accustomed to the classroom routine and center expectations, children are no longer expected to rotate from center to center on a time schedule. Rather, they are given a large block of time and a series of activities and tasks they are expected to complete within that time frame. This can occur successfully only when children have learned minimal time and behavior management strategies.

Content Learning Centers

Content learning centers are designated for in-depth study of information, topics, research projects, themes, and so on, related to science, social studies, health, mathematics, art, music, and drama. Each subject-specific center includes reading and print materials as well as related activity supplies. Content learning centers create opportunities for students to expand their vocabularies and learn concepts related to the topic of study. The use of nonfiction materials is demanded in content learning centers, giving primary purpose to using these materials for reading to learn. It is also helpful if the teacher designs a means for recording student work and progress in content learning centers. A content learning center activity log can be found in Figure 4.4. Children record in this log the activities they complete in the center.

Figure 4.4   Content Area Learning Center Activity Log

Name of Student_____   Date_____

Monday
Name of Activity Completed_____
Print Materials or Books Read_____

Tuesday
Name of Activity Completed_____
Print Materials or Books Read_____

Wednesday
Name of Activity Completed_____
Print Materials or Books Read_____

Thursday
Name of Activity Completed_____
Print Materials or Books Read_____

Friday
Name of Activity Completed_____
Print Materials or Books Read_____

Independent Reading Area

An *independent reading area* is ideally located well away from the mainstream, often noisy activity of the classroom. Books and other printed materials stored in this area are organized into shelves and sections for supporting the reading program (e.g., shared, guided, and independent). Independent reading books can be divided into general levels of reading challenge such as easy reading, early reading, and fluency reading materials in a classroom library. Within each of these general categories of reading difficulty, books may be organized in alphabetical order by titles. When multiple copies of a single title are available, old cereal boxes cut in half, covered in contact paper, and displaying the title of the books on the side can be used to store these books as a group.

To match children with the "just right" book, individual *browsing boxes* can be shelved in this center as well. Children pick up their browsing box and select a book within their browsing box for independent reading. Each browsing box has between 8 and 12 titles at the child's independent reading level and on topics of expressed interest. Parent volunteers regularly rotate the contents of students' browsing boxes.

Big books can be stored on shelves, hooks, pant hangers, or easels near this area. This location can also be used to store the adopted basal readers. Whether basal stories or multiple copies of trade books are used, this area is ideal for small-group or one-to-one story reading. It should be comfortable and well lit. Carpeting, beanbag chairs, a bathtub filled with pillows, pillow chairs, and the like can be used as a comfortable place for children to curl up with a favorite book. A large rocking chair can be located here for lap reading with younger children. Plants, aquariums, and so on can do much to create a peaceful atmosphere for this part of the classroom. Record keeping for silent reading can be easily managed by using a book title and time log for each child, as shown in Figure 4.5. Children record the amount of time in minutes spent reading silently and the titles they had sampled or finished that day.

Figure 4.5   Book Time and Title Log

Name of Student_____ Week of_____

Monday
Names of Book(s) Read_____
Time Spent Reading_____ One Word Response_____

Tuesday
Names of Book(s) Read_____
Time Spent Reading_____ One Word Response_____

Wednesday
Names of Book(s) Read_____
Time Spent Reading_____ One Word Response_____

Thursday
Names of Book(s) Read_____
Time Spent Reading_____ One Word Response_____

Friday
Names of Book(s) Read_____
Time Spent Reading_____ One Word Response_____

If books or basal texts are to be checked out from the independent reading center for out-of-school reading, a librarian's center can be located near the silent reading area for check outs. A storage container can be kept here for take-home reading back-packs (Richgels & Wold, 1998) so that take-home books can be protected. Children who serve as librarians keep records on books checked out and those overdue from the class library. All children are asked to be responsible for keeping the classroom library orderly.

Based on the book *Alexander and the Terrible Horrible No Good Very Bad Day* by Judith Viorst (1972), teachers might establish an *Australia Escape Corner*. When things in the classroom or a student's personal life are just too much to handle at the moment, they may retreat to Australia, just like Alexander, for 10 minutes, no questions asked, once a day. If they need to remain longer than 10 minutes, they should explain their reasons to the teacher privately. Teachers may also retreat on occasion to Australia. This action alone was found to be one of our best classroom discipline techniques!

Individual Reading Conference and Assessment Area

The individual reading conference and assessment area is usually small and quiet. It is typically located near the teacher's desk where student records may be stored and easily accessed. This area is used for conducting reading conferences and assessing each individual student's reading performance. Students are asked to make an appointment to meet with the teacher for an individual reading conference. This is accomplished by signing up at the individual reading conference sign-up board, which is shown in Figure 4.6.

The teacher and an individual student meet together briefly, about five minutes, to read and discuss a selected or assigned trade book or basal reader story passage. As the student reads, the teacher listens, encourages, and assesses performance.

Figure 4.6   Reading Conference Sign-Up Board

(This board works best if produced on a poster board and laminated. Use an overhead water-ink marker for signing up that can be easily erased.)

Monday
Student Name _____
Name of Book or Story _____
Page Number(s) _____
Student Name _____
Name of Book or Story _____
Page Number(s) _____

Tuesday
Student Name _____
Name of Book or Story _____
Page Number(s) _____
Student Name _____
Name of Book or Story _____
Page Number(s) _____

Wednesday
Student Name _____
Name of Book or Story _____
Page Number(s) _____
Student Name _____
Name of Book or Story _____
Page Number(s) _____
ETC.

Making a Classroom Floor Plan

Having described various functional spaces for an effective literacy learning classroom environment, we know that teachers will find it helpful if we provide a few examples of how to design a total classroom space floor plan. Entering a new classroom can be a daunting task of determining how to design the use of the total space so that it integrates the essential functions of a comprehensive reading program. We have developed two examples of classroom floor plans—one for the primary grades and one for the intermediate grades. These are found in Figures 4.7 and 4.8.

Assessing the Classroom Literacy Environment

Roskos and Neuman (2001) recently reviewed the research on classroom environmental influences on children's literacy learning. They found that space allocation and arrangement, complexity and accessibility of materials, and variation and ownership of literacy learning tools influenced children's literacy learning in a variety of ways. Intervention studies (Morrow, 1990; Neuman & Roskos, 1992; Reutzel & Wolfersberger, 1996; Vukelich, 1991, 1994) have shown that creating authentic play settings, such as offices, libraries, veterinary center, flower shops, and so on, positively influenced children's literacy play, talk, and acts. From these studies, it is clear that having a classroom environment rich in literacy tools and reading materials is a key feature of supportive classroom environments. In Figure 4.9, we provide a simplified instrument for examining the "print richness" of classrooms.

Figure 4.7   Fifth-Grade Classroom Arrangement

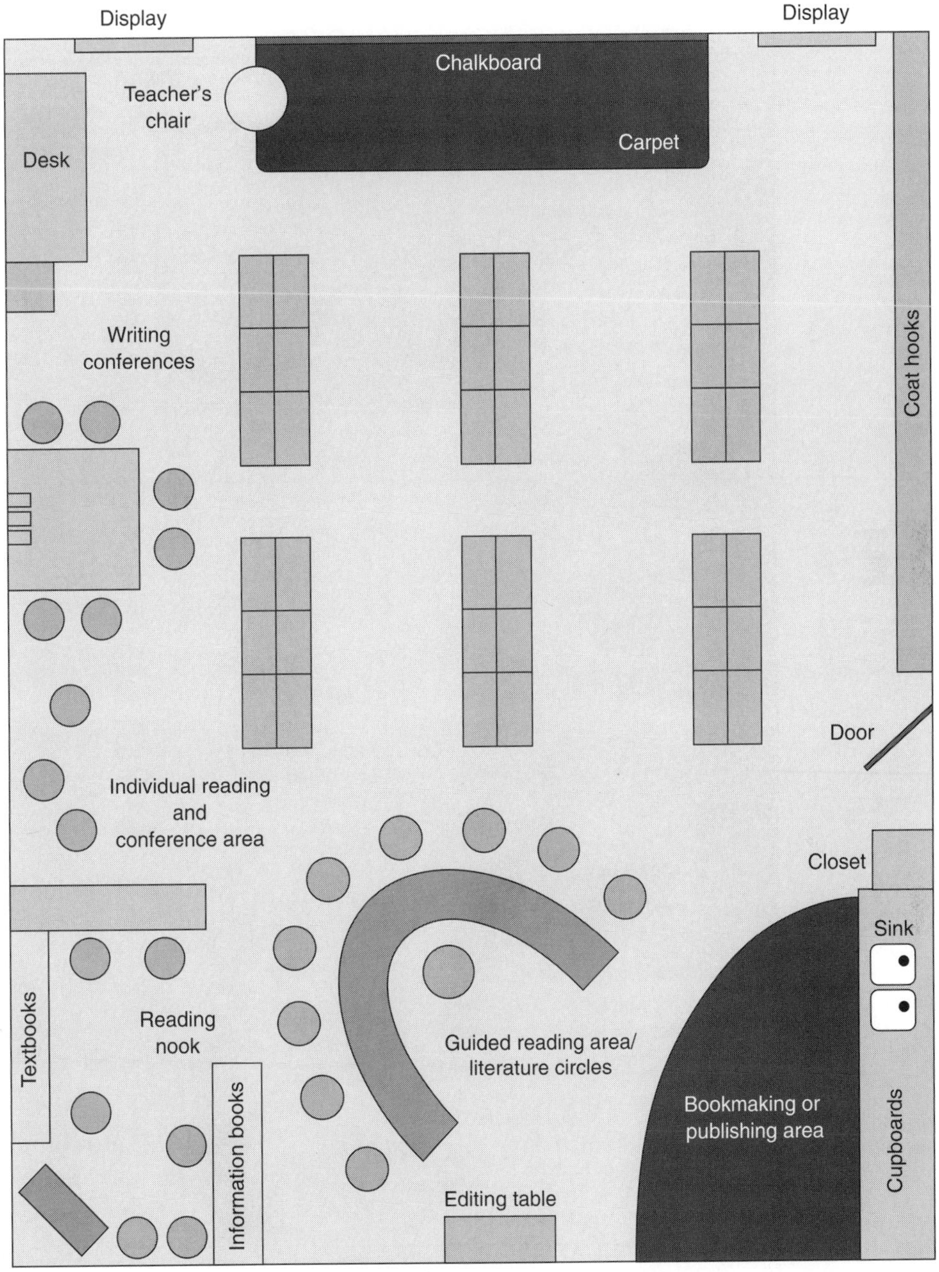

Display

Display

Chalkboard

Teacher's chair

Carpet

Desk

Coat hooks

Writing conferences

Door

Individual reading and conference area

Closet

Sink

Textbooks

Reading nook

Guided reading area/ literature circles

Bookmaking or publishing area

Cupboards

Information books

Editing table

Figure 4.8 First-Grade Classroom Arrangement

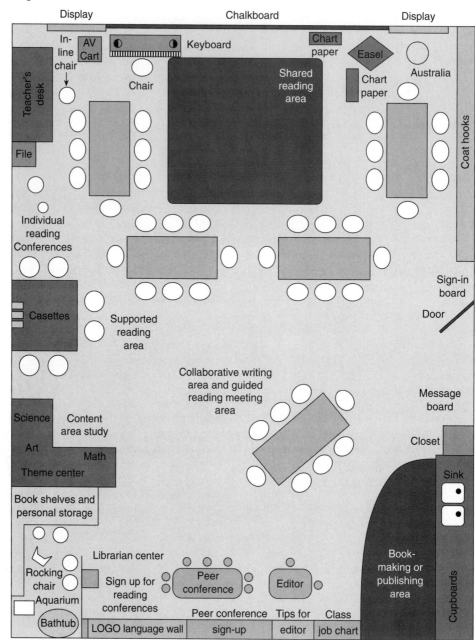

Figure 4.9 Print-Rich Classroom Environmental Survey

Teacher's Name_____ Grade Level of Classroom_____

Directions: *Read each item carefully. Scan the classroom quickly to estimate the level of compliance with each item's description. Score each item as follows: 1 = fails to meet the description, 3 = meets the description, and 5 = exceeds the description.*

1. Literacy tools provided in the classroom contain print (charts, books, displays); are used to produce print (markers, crayons, pencils, paper); and support literacy learning (computers, tape recorders, pointers, pocket charts).
       1   3   5

2. Books and print materials are adequate in number ranging between 300 and 500 individual titles or volumes (Count multiple copies of a single title as one title).
       1   3   5

3. Print materials available in the classroom represent at least five separate genres (fiction, nonfiction, poetry, magazines, newspapers, reference volumes).
       1   3   5

4. Levels of print materials in the classroom span at least three grade levels.
       1   3   5

5. Displays in the classroom represent at least three different purposes and invite student involvement such as information, schedules, sign-in boards, message boards, and labels/directions, etc.
       1   3   5

6. Student and class literacy product displays are mostly student-produced print and prominently displayed in the classroom.
       1   3   5

7. Reference materials are abundant in the classrooms with at least 15 different displays or books.
       1   3   5

8. Writing tools are abundant and represent a wide variety such as pens, pencils, markers, computer processing, sidewalk chalk, overhead markers, stamps, and stencils.
       1   3   5

9. Writing surfaces represent a wide variety of places to write including wall-mounted chalk or marker boards, paper types, stationery, sentence strips, word cards, magnetic letter boards, etc.
       1   3   5

10. Publishing materials include a variety of tools to edit, assemble, and decorate written products.
        1   3   5

11. Furnishings represent a variety of items to divide and make the room comfortable and functional such as tables, chairs, carpets, rocking chairs, beanbag chairs, play centers, author's chair, etc.
        1   3   5

12. Displaying and storing literacy tools is accomplished in a variety of ways including rain gutters, pocket charts, easels, boxes, tubs, shelves, counter tops, etc.
        1   3   5

13. Classroom library has adequate floor space, shelving, and displays to entice students into sustained reading.
        1   3   5

14. Classroom floor space is divided into areas supporting best practices such as read alouds, shared reading, guided reading, independent reading, and learning centers.
        1   3   5

continued

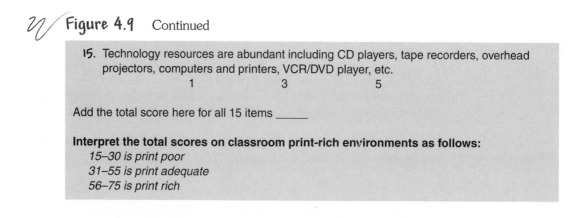

Figure 4.9   Continued

> 15. Technology resources are abundant including CD players, tape recorders, overhead projectors, computers and printers, VCR/DVD player, etc.
>
>   1   3   5
>
> Add the total score here for all 15 items _____
>
> **Interpret the total scores on classroom print-rich environments as follows:**
>   *15–30 is print poor*
>   *31–55 is print adequate*
>   *56–75 is print rich*

SCAFFOLDING CLASSROOM READING INSTRUCTION (K–2): THE PRIMARY GRADES LITERACY WORKSHOP

Children develop a sense of security when the events of the school day revolve around a sequence of anticipated activities. Although variety is the spice of life for children too, they find comfort in familiar instructional routines in a well-organized classroom (Holdaway, 1984). (*A tip for beginning teachers or veterans who may experience problems with behavior management:* We *highly* recommend *The First Days of School* [Wong & Wong, 1998] as a resource book. It's great for helping teachers get the school year off to a good start with very basic routines and expectations. See references at the end of this chapter for ordering information.)

There are any number of ways to organize the activities and instruction of the school day. However, it is important that children experience a variety of interactive settings in which to learn each day; they should be taught as a whole class, in small groups, and individually. Groupings should be flexible and meet the needs of the students and involve the "best practices" of literacy instruction.

One such approach that has been widely used to organize the school day is the "reading workshop." Although this organizational framework was originally proposed for intermediate and adolescent-aged students, we have adapted it successfully for use in the primary grades in a framework known as **The Primary Grades Literacy Workshop.** We have found this instructional framework to be both effective and manageable for many classroom teachers of young children.

The Primary Grades Literacy Workshop is an organizational framework for organizing and planning daily reading and writing instruction in the primary grades. It is a variation on the "Reading and Writing Workshops" as described for the intermediate and middle school grades (Atwell, 1987; Calkins, 1994, 2001; Fountas & Pinnell, 2001; Reutzel & Cooter, 1991). The organizational framework of the Primary Grades Literacy Workshop is a functional and flexible instructional scaffolding for providing primary grades interactive, shared, guided, and independent reading and writing experiences.

The Primary Grade Literacy Workshop consists of five parts: 1) Reading and Writing Together, 2) Word and Strategy Study, 3) Guided Reading, 4) Fluency Development, and 5) Learning Center Study and Individual Assessment. The five components of the Primary Grade Literacy Workshop incorporate elements of reading instruction recommended in several recent national reading research reports including decoding instruction, fluency development, vocabulary and comprehension strategy instruction, and guided oral reading (Snow, Burns, & Griffin, 1998; National Institute of Child Health and Human Development, 2000). The Primary Grades Literacy Workshop is designed to run for 150–180 minutes daily during an uninterrupted instructional time block. The structure of the Primary Grades Literacy Workshop is outlined in Figure 4.10.

READING AND WRITING TOGETHER (35–40 MINUTES)

During this group instructional time, teachers engage young readers in three sequenced reading and writing experiences: 1) Interactive Read Aloud, 2) Shared Reading, and 3) Interactive and/or Shared Writing. Interactive and shared readings were discussed in depth in chapter 3. Interactive writing and shared writing offer teachers and students a way to respond to interactive and shared reading through writing. Interactive writing is an important part of a comprehensive literacy program (McCarrier, Pinnell, & Fountas, 1999). An *interactive writing session* focuses on the teacher writing WITH children or

Figure 4.10   The Primary Grades Literacy Workshop (150–180 Minutes)

Reading and Writing Together [T & S]			
(35–40 Minutes Per Day)			
1. Interactive Read Aloud	2. Shared Reading		3. Interactive or Shared Writing
Working With Strategies [T & S]			
(30 Minutes Per Day)			
1. Decoding and Spelling Instruction		2. Vocabulary and Comprehension Strategy Instruction	
Workshop Time–*(60 Minutes Per Day)*			
Block 1–15 Minutes	Block 2–15 Minutes	Block 3–15 Minutes	Block 4–15 Minutes
A. Centers [S]	**A. Centers [S]**	**A. Centers [S]**	**A. Centers [S]**
Working With Strategies Writing/Handwriting Reading Response Content Study Independent Reading	Working With Strategies Writing/Handwriting Reading Response Content Study Independent Reading	Working With Strategies Writing/Handwriting Reading Response Content Study Independent Reading	Working With Strategies Writing/Handwriting Reading Response Content Study Independent Reading
B. Guided Reading I [T & S^1]	**B. Guided Reading II [T & S^2]**	**B. Guided Reading III [T & S^3]**	**B. Guided Reading IV [T & S^4]**
Fluency Workshop [S]	**Fluency Workshop & Assessment** *(30 Minutes Per Day)*		**Assessment [T & S_1]**
1. Repeated Reading Practice 2. Paired or Buddy Reading Practice 3. Performance/Recorded Reading	1. Reading Accuracy, Fluency & Comprehension Assessment 2. Spelling, Writing & Handwriting Assessment		
Closing Sharing Time: 10–15 Minutes			

Note: [T & S] means Teacher and Students. Superscript represents a hypothetical group number. Subscript represents a student number.

what is sometimes called "sharing the pen." Teachers focus an interactive writing lesson on:

- Connecting reading and writing by using literature as a take-off point for writing reproductions, innovations, and new texts *(reproducing the text in a new format such as a big book; making innovations on the language in the texts such as "The Three Quarter Horses" for "The Three Billy Goats"; and changing a story to an information book, map, mural, etc.)*
- Developing increasingly sophisticated writing strategies
- Demonstrating saying words slowly and connecting sounds in words to letters and letter combinations
- Expanding children's repertoire of writing genre and forms
- Helping children learn how the spelling process works

The subject and form of interactive writing may vary greatly depending upon the developmental levels of the children and the context of experiences in the classroom. Typically in the early years, the teacher helps children write a sentence or what some call a "story." As children learn more about the writing process and different types of writing forms and genre, the teacher makes different decisions about how to *share the pen* during interactive writing. There is no one correct way to teach an interactive writing lesson, but based upon the writings of McCarrier, Pinnell, and Fountas (1999), we recommend the following:

1. ***In the early stages of writing, the teacher helps children compose a simple message drawn from literature or from the group's experiences that is repeated several times.*** For example, consider this line from *The Very Hungry Caterpillar* (Carle, 1981), "On Monday he ate through one apple." If the teacher asked children to innovate on what the caterpillar ate on Monday, a child could offer the following: "On Monday he ate through one *tomato.*" When the teacher asks children to add new words to a line, the entire message is re-read from the beginning to help children remember how composing proceeds.

2. ***The teacher and children "share the pen" as a message is written word by word.*** When new words are added to a line of text, the children re-read the line up to the new or added word. In the earliest stages of writing development, the teacher may write the word for children. With time and development, the teacher shares the pen, inviting children to contribute a letter, several letters, or an entire word.

3. ***Where appropriate, the teacher encourages the child to stretch the word and say it slowly to predict the letters by analyzing the sounds*** (see word rubber banding in chapter 8). Children may attempt any letter in the word in any order. Working within the child's zone of proximal development *a la* Vygotsky (1986), the teacher fills in those letters that the child is unable to analyze on her own.

4. ***A word wall, like those recommended by Cunningham (2000), can be used as a writing resource for children in the classroom.*** Words can be listed on the wall as *words we know and can write, words we almost know,* and *words we need to analyze and write with help.*

5. ***As teachers and children write interactively, the teacher helps children learn directionality, punctuation, spaces, features of print, and capitalization.*** In this fashion, children learn the mechanics and the authoring processes necessary to eventually produce high-quality writing products.

Interactive writing sessions typically last from 5 to 15 minutes depending upon the nature of the text to be produced. The goal of interactive writing is a neat, legible, and sensible text.

WORKING WITH STRATEGIES (30 MINUTES)

The purpose of the *working with strategies* instructional block is to develop children's emerging decoding, spelling, vocabulary, and comprehension strategy awareness. During this time we also teach children how to select the appropriate application and apply it in a variety of reading situations and contexts. Chapters 6,7, 8, 9, 10, and 11 contain a rich array of strategies for teaching these essential aspects of the reading process. We cannot emphasize enough the importance of providing students with direct, explicit instruction. This means that teachers do not rely on discovery approaches; rather, teachers should model, explain, demonstrate, guide, and engage students in directly applying the strategies taught. We also strongly recommend that daily lessons focus on both decoding/spelling instruction and vocabulary/comprehension instruction. This provides children a comprehensive collection of strategies to enable successful reading performance and growth throughout their elementary school years and beyond.

WORKSHOP TIME (60 MINUTES)

Workshop time is divided into four blocks of 15 minutes each. The structure of workshop time is fairly rigid in the beginning as students learn to rotate from center to center, use their time wisely in completing center tasks, and manage themselves so as to minimize off-task behaviors. Within each 15-minute block of time two major types of activities dominate: *guided reading* and *centers*. The teacher is stationed in the guided reading area of the classroom prepared to offer guided reading instruction as explained in chapter 3. The children, however, may be called to their guided reading group or assigned to a "center rotation" group. *Centers* (i.e., learning centers) are teacher selected, designed, and provisioned. We strongly recommend centers that focus on decoding, spelling, handwriting, the writing process, content area studies, reader response, and independent reading. Management of centers is a primary concern for teachers; they must be designed so that the activities and tasks are clearly understood, independent of teacher supervision, and able to be completed within the time allowed. It is also important that tasks completed in learning centers have a component of accountability and performance. We show in Figure 4.11 two possible approaches for managing learning center group rotations.

Managing the workshop is a complex effort for most teachers. We caution teachers against the creation of too many learning centers. At the early part of the year, fewer centers are easier for both teachers and students to handle. As the year progresses, adding a few new centers, especially optional centers, can add variety to the workshop. We have also found that very little flexibility is needed in the group rotation schedule early in the year. As time progresses and children acquire more experience with the rotation between learning centers, we have found it better to assign children specific tasks to be completed during this time period rather than a time-controlled rotation through various learning centers.

Figure 4.11a   Center Group Rotation Wheel

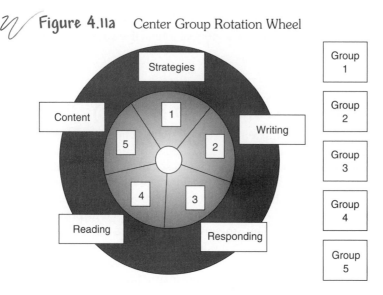

Figure 4.11b   Center Group Rotation Chart

Working with Strategies	Writing	Reader Response	Content Study	Independent Reading
1	2	3	4	5
5	1	2	3	4
4	5	1	2	3
3	4	5	1	2
2	3	4	5	1

FLUENCY WORKSHOP AND ASSESSMENT (30 MINUTES)

This 30-minute period of the Primary Grades Literacy Workshop is divided into two separate sets of activities for teacher and students, fluency development learning centers and individual reading and fluency assessment. For the teacher, the bulk of this time is devoted to meeting individually with five students, five minutes each, to hold an individual reading/writing assessment conference. Five students per day sign up for a reading/writing assessment conference on their own or at the urging of the teacher. Children who are scheduled for a reading/writing assessment conference are instructed to bring 1) an assigned "benchmark" book or text to read aloud for assessment purposes, or 2) a completed writing project to be assessed for style, structure, coherence, handwriting, form, spelling, punctuation, and so on, depending on what is being emphasized in current or past instruction.

Benchmark books are used to assess all students' reading decoding accuracy, comprehension through an oral retelling, and fluency in terms of words-correct-per-minute rates, phrasing and intonation. A benchmark book is a teacher-selected, leveled text that represents the "average" level of text difficulty expected that a child should read at that point in the year. Assessment tools to measure decoding accuracy, oral retellings, and fluency assessment are discussed in chapters 8, 10, and 13 of this book. Information garnered in these assessment conferences is used to shape later *working with strategies* instruction. If a piece of writing is brought to the assessment conference, it is evaluated for handwriting legibility, conventional spelling, appropriate presentation, and general readability.

For students, this period of time is devoted to a variety of center-based activities designed to increase reading fluency. Children engage in repeated readings by going to a listening center where books on audiocassette tapes are available along with multiples copies of a single title. Or, children can go to the computer center to read a book presented on a CD-ROM. Children may read with a partner by reading around the room, re-reading big books together, practicing sight words on word cards in pairs, re-reading charts of poems and songs, or re-reading sentence strips or interactive writing strips in pocket charts. And still other children will be in a drama center practicing the reading of a play or reader's theater script for performance. Another area of the classroom is stocked with individual audiocassette tapes for children to place into a cassette recorder and record their own reading. After reading into the tape recorder, children rate their own fluency using an adapted student version of the *Multidimensional Fluency Scale* found in chapter 13. They may erase the audiocassette recording of their first reading. The repeated reading recording should be rated again noting any improvements in their oral fluency. Each student must come to the final class sharing session from the fluency development period prepared to perform a reading selection for the whole class, a small group, or a peer. Periodically, if the teacher has assessed all of his/her students as planned, the teacher may offer a whole-class or small-group fluency lesson using strategies such as the *Fluency Development Lesson* described in chapter 13.

Student Sharing Time (10–15 Minutes)

As a daily closing activity for the Primary Grades Literacy Workshop, the teacher calls the class together to share a reading selection each child has prepared previously. The idea here is to bring closure to the day's work and give children a chance to share their reading with the group or a friend. Children can perform reader's theater productions, their own writing products, puppet shows, individual reading recitations, reader's/author's chair read alouds, and plays. We have found that there is only one problem with sharing time: keeping it to the time frame of 10–15 minutes. Once students get used to this idea, they plan for reading books, scripts, jokes, poems, and even their own writing to share with their classroom friends. As a wrap-up to this discussion, we use a *teacher's planning book* in Figure 4.12 to show how one teacher scheduled a week of activities in the Primary Grades Literacy Workshop.

𝒲 **Figure 4.12**   Primary-Grades Literacy Workshop Week Planner

Monday	Tuesday	Wednesday	Thursday	Friday
Reading and Writing Together 8:30–9:10 A.M.				
Read Aloud—Very Hungry Caterpillar *Shared Reading*—On Market Street *Interactive Writing*—"And I bought . . . ."	*Read Aloud*—Very Quiet Cricket *Shared Reading*—Re-read book masking sight word "the." *Interactive Writing*—Cricket Talk	*Read Aloud*—Grouchy Ladybug *Shared Reading*—If you Give a Mouse a *Interactive Writing*—"If you give a mouse a cookie, he will. . . ."	*Read Aloud*—Very Lonely Firefly *Shared Reading*—Re-read for "en & ill" words *Interactive Writing*—Word building	*Read Aloud*—Very Busy Spider *Shared Reading*—How Spiders Live *Interactive Writing*—"Spiders live. . ."
Working With Strategies 9:10–9:40 A.M.				
Decoding & Spelling: Phoneme Counting & Spelling—Elkonin Boxes Vocabulary & Comprehension: Listening for directions	Decoding & Spelling: Building words—"-ake, -ick" rimes Vocabulary & Comprehension: Taking a picture walk for predicting	Decoding & Spelling: Pocket chart Sponnerisms—Initial consonant substitution Vocabulary & Comprehension: Insect semantic web	Decoding & Spelling: Consonant riddles Vocabulary & Comprehension: Picture story map prediction of Three Billy Goats Gruff	Decoding & Spelling: Sound search—What's in the middle, beginning, end? Vocabulary & Comprehension: Author study—Eric Carle
Workshop Time 9:40–10:40 A.M.				
Learning Centers: Paired Language Listening Center Insect Center Word Center Environmental Print Guided Reading Groups: Intro books—Levels C-E, *Chicken Pox:* F-G, *My Computer:* H-I. *Tents*	Learning Centers: Paired Language Listening Center Insect Center Word Center Environmental Print Guided Reading Groups: Re-read for strategies & retell	Learning Centers: Paired Language Listening Center Insect Center Word Center Environmental Print Guided Reading Groups: Re-read for language features & extensions	Learning Centers: Paired Language Listening Center Insect Center Word Center Environmental Print Guided Reading Groups: Intro books	Learning Centers: Paired Language Listening Center Insect Center Word Center Environmental Print Guided Reading Groups: Re-read for strategies & retell
Fluency Workshop and Assessment 10:40–11:10 A.M.				
Fluency Centers: Read Around Room Computer Center CD/Tape Reading Record Your Reading Reader's Theater Assessment: Mica & Heather	Fluency Centers: Read Around Room Computer Center CD/Tape Reading Record Your Reading Reader's Theater Assessment: Montage & Mitchell	Fluency Centers: Read Around Room Computer Center CD/Tape Reading Record Your Reading Reader's Theater Assessment: Ginger & Jessica	Fluency Centers: Read Around Room Computer Center CD/Tape Reading Record Your Reading Reader's Theater Assessment: Austin & Sabrina	*Class Fluency Development Lesson* *Three Billy Goats Gruff* Assessment:
Closing Sharing Time 11:10–11:25 A.M.				
Turn to Your Neighbor	Reader's Theater Performance	"Today I read. . . ." *Interactive Writing*	Think, Pair, Shair	Fact Web on Spiders

SCAFFOLDING CLASSROOM READING INSTRUCTION (3-6): THE READING WORKSHOP

As children develop increasing fluency and expanding interests in the intermediate years, organizing for classroom reading instruction changes with them. **The Reading Workshop** (Atwell, 1987; Fountas & Pinnell, 2001; Reutzel & Cooter, 1991) is an organizational framework intended for intermediate and adolescent-aged learners. There are a number of different formats possible for the Reading Workshop; the one we discuss has five parts based on the work of Reutzel and Cooter (1991): 1) Teacher sharing time, 2) Minilesson, 3) State of the class, 4) Workshop, and 5) Student sharing time. A visual organizer representing these five components is shown in Figure 4.13.

TEACHER SHARING TIME (5-10 MINUTES)

During this time teachers share a variety of reading materials with students to broaden and deepen their understandings of language and literature. Myriad reading and writing examples are shared during this period of time. For example, a teacher might bring in a collection of greeting cards and share several special occasion cards, such as Halloween, Valentine's Day, birthday, anniversary, holiday, and thank you cards as examples. Or, the teacher might read aloud a magazine article or newspaper editorial from a recent magazine or newspaper.

The purpose of this part of the Reading Workshop is to introduce students to varied genres of reading materials such as folktales, tall tales, fables, handbooks, newspapers, cards, forms, and the like. This time is also to make sure students receive a balanced exposure to

Figure 4.13   The Reading Workshop

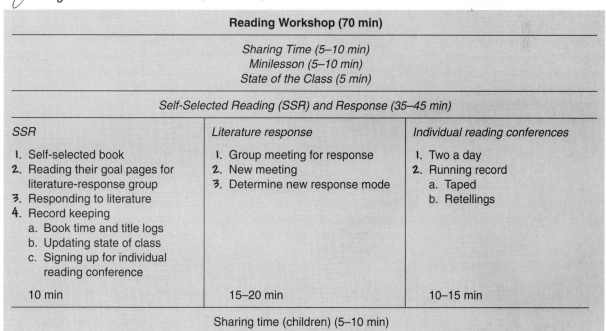

Reading Workshop (70 min)		
Sharing Time (5–10 min) Minilesson (5–10 min) State of the Class (5 min)		
Self-Selected Reading (SSR) and Response (35–45 min)		
SSR	**Literature response**	**Individual reading conferences**
1. Self-selected book 2. Reading their goal pages for literature-response group 3. Responding to literature 4. Record keeping a. Book time and title logs b. Updating state of class c. Signing up for individual reading conference	1. Group meeting for response 2. New meeting 3. Determine new response mode	1. Two a day 2. Running record a. Taped b. Retellings
10 min	15–20 min	10–15 min
Sharing time (children) (5–10 min)		

Source: "Organizing for Effective Instruction: The Reading Workshop" by D. R. Reutzel and R. B. Cooter, Jr., 1991, *The Reading Teacher, 44*(8), pp. 548–555. Copyright 1991 by International Reading Association. Reprinted by permission.

the major types of reading materials, both fiction and nonfiction. The reading sharing time block is intended to help students to "tune in" to printed materials and the formal register of printed language in order to instill in them a desire to read as well as the knowledge of how to read successfully. Sometimes, Teacher Sharing Time can also serve as a catalyst for launching various writing projects in the classroom or as the introduction for a mini-lesson to be taught the same day.

WORKING WITH LANGUAGE MINILESSONS (5–10 MINUTES)

The purpose of teaching and working with language minilessons is to meet the needs of intermediate-grade readers in becoming independent and critical readers of text. There are typically three types of minilessons: 1) Procedural, 2) Skills and Strategies, and 3) Literary Devices, (see Figure 4.14).

Figure 4.14   Possible Minilesson Topics

Procedural Minilessons	Literary Minilessons	Strategy/Skill Minilessons
Where to sit during reading time	Differences between fiction and nonfiction books	How to choose a book
Giving a book talk		Selecting literature log topics
How to be a good listener in a share session	Learning from dedications	Connecting reading material to your own life
What is an appropriate noise level during reading time	Books that show emotion	Tips for reading aloud
	Books written in the first, second, or third person	Figuring out unknown words
What to do when you finish a book	Author studies	Using context
What kinds of questions to ask during a share session	How authors use quotations	Substituting
	How the story setting fits the story	Using picture clues
Running a small-group discussion	Characteristics of different genres	Using the sounds of blends, vowels, contractions, etc.
Self-evaluation	Development of characters, plot, theme, mood	Using Post-its to mark interesting parts
Getting ready for a conference		
How to have a peer conference	How leads hook us	Monitoring comprehension (Does this make sense and sound right?)
Where to sit during minilessons	How authors use the problem/event/solution pattern	
Taking care of books	Differences between a picture book and a novel	Asking questions while reading
Keeping track of books to read		Making predictions
Rules of the workshop	Titles and their meanings	Emergent strategies
	Characters' points of view	Concept of story
	Examples of similes and metaphors	Concept that print carries meaning
	Examples of foreshadowing	Making sense
	How authors use dialogue	Mapping a story
	Predictable and surprise endings	How to retell a story orally
	Use of descriptive words and phrases	Looking for relationships
	How illustrations enhance the story	Looking for important ideas
	Secrets in books	Making inferences
		Drawing conclusions
		Summarizing a story
		Distinguishing fact from opinion
		Emergent reader skills: directionality, concept of "word," sound/symbol relationships

Source: From *Readers workshop: Real reading* (pp. 113–115), by P. Hagerty, 1992, Ontario, Canada: Scholastic Canada. Copyright 1992 by Scholastic Canada. Reprinted by permission.

The *Working With Language Minilessons* daily time block is intended to provide an intensive instructional experience to help students develop: 1) overall reading strategies and 2) strategies for meaning construction (Fountas & Pinnell, 2001). Readers have available to them two major sources of information for constructing meaning and keep reading moving forward—the text and their own background knowledge and experiences. During the "Working With Language Minilesson" period, teachers select and teach a variety of minilessons to the whole class, in needs groups, and with individual students where necessary to help them sustain forward reading progress and expand upon their strategies for constructing meaning.

Fountas and Pinnell (2001) indicated that strategies for sustaining student's forward progress in reading include: 1) solving words, 2) finding important information, 3) predicting, 4) maintaining fluency, 5) monitoring and correcting, and 6) adjusting. Intensive, focused minilessons help refine and develop students' use of these "reading sustaining" strategies in order to meet the challenges of more difficult words, books, and texts and understand authors' uses of more interesting and sophisticated literary elements.

Word Solving

Word-solving minilessons provide students with an assortment of word-solving strategies (recognize, decode, and word analysis) to unlock and learn word meanings. Suggested topics for word-solving minilessons are found in Figure 4.15.

Finding the Important Information

Effective reading involves separating the important information from the less important details. Students can be asked to read a text with you and make a list of the important information. For example, using the book, *The Trojan Horse: How the Greeks Won the War* (Little, 1988), students, with the assistance of the teacher, can sort out of this book the important aspects of winning a war from details that detract from this understanding.

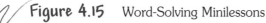

Figure 4.15   Word-Solving Minilessons

Making words:

- That start or end with the same letters
- That contain silent letters
- Into contractions
- Into compound words
- That use prefixes and suffixes
- That sound the same, but are spelled differently
- Using Latin or Greek roots
- Using a common rime or word family part such as -ick, -an, -un, or -ast
- That have the same number of syllables

Counting sounds to make simple one-syllable words

Sorting words into categories children discover (open sorts) or into teacher-directed/predetermined categories (closed sorts) using sounds, spelling, or meaning as the basis for sorting. Making word-meaning webs or semantic maps to organize words around meaning categories such as tools, colors, actions, etc.

Making Predictions

Making predictions helps students not only construct meaning from text but also helps them solve new words. Sharing books with children that not only invite predictions but also require the application of such strategies is an effective way to engage them in making predictions. A favorite book for this purpose is entitled *Bunnicula* (Howe, 1979). The teacher asks children what they know about vampires. Do they know what a vampire looks like? Do they know what a vampire is afraid of? Or, do they know what a vampire needs to drink to live? As they read the text, ask them to watch for any clues that may suggest what Chester believes about the pet in the house—a bunny who is no regular bunny.

Maintaining Fluency

Fluency involves reading at an appropriate rate with a high degree of accuracy, phrasing, and expression. Choral readings of texts in unison or in echo voices helps students get a sense of how to read with fluency. Encouraging students to re-read a passage helps them read more fluently, thus enabling greater comprehension. One very effective strategy is to engage students in the performance of reader's theater productions. A range of reader's theater scripts can be obtained on the Internet at: http://www.aaronshep.com/rt/RTE.html, http://scriptsforschools.com/, and http://www.geocities.com/Athens/Thebes/9893/readerstheater.htm.

Monitoring and Correcting

Developing the ability to notice errors and correct them is critical to successful and fulfilling reading. Prompts or cue charts are best displayed in a prominent and unobstructed area of the classroom. Such prompts or cue charts might invite students to ask themselves the following questions:

- What makes sense here?
- Does that sound right?
- Does what I said and what is on the page match?
- That sounds right but does it look right?
- That makes sense but does it look right?
- That looks right but does it make sense?

When students notice that their reading is not making sense, they then need to take action to "fix" their broken comprehension. A cue chart displaying actions to "fix" their broken comprehension could include the following prompts:

- Keep on reading to see if something will come up in the next pages to help
- Re-read the previous sentence or paragraph
- Stop and think about what you have read and re-read if necessary
- Ask someone for help
- Look at any pictures, maps, tables, or other reference material provided in the text

Adjusting Reading

Students need to learn how to adjust their reading rate to match the type of text or reading task to be accomplished. Skimming or scanning may be used to locate information in a telephone book, on a list, or in a bus schedule. Looking through a book at the chapter titles, headings, and subheadings may help students get a sense of the layout and structure of the book. Teachers need to model for students how to pick the right reading strategies adjusted to the book, the text, or the task.

Strategies for Constructing Meaning

Strategies for expanding students' understanding and comprehension in reading include 1) connecting, 2) inferring, 3) summarizing, 4) synthesizing, 5) analyzing, and 6) evaluating. These strategies help students organize information, determine the importance of information, and move between their experiences with other books and texts they read. During the intermediate years, students profit from considerable instructional attention given to this interrelated set of expanding strategies. By using "think-alouds" and demonstrating how, when, and why these expanding meaning strategies should be selected and applied, the teacher models correct practice and application for students. Minilessons help refine and develop student's use of these expanding strategies to meet the challenges of organizing information, reducing information, and connecting information to previous experience and to other knowledge. Information on these elements of instruction is found in chapters 10 and 11.

STATE OF THE CLASS (5 MINUTES)

A major concern for teachers who use the Reading Workshop organization is monitoring student activity and assessing student growth during the workshop period. *State of the Class* is a time when students are asked to report to the teacher how they plan to spend their workshop time that day. As a roll is called, the teacher writes from each student's verbal response on a chart like the one shown in Figure 4.16.

The students briefly explain their planned activities for the workshop period for that day. Atwell (1987) describes this time as a 3–5 minute time where the teacher can "eavesdrop" on each student's plan for the activity of the day. When the teacher observes a problem either in a repeated pattern of the same activity day after day or no progress, then a "house call" or student-teacher conference is scheduled. This simple monitoring process keeps students from "falling through the cracks" and ensures that those experiencing difficulties will get much needed attention. In addition, *state of the class* provides for teachers an accountability record of student's activity and work that can be referred to when making future instructional plans and when talking with parents.

THE WORKSHOP PERIOD (40 MINUTES)

The heart of the Reading Workshop period involves three interrelated daily activities: 1) Sustained Silent Reading or *SSR* (10 minutes), 2) Literature Response Group Meetings (or) Literature Circles (20 minutes), and 3) Individual Reading Conferences (10 minutes).

SSR (10 Minutes)

During the 10 minutes of **SSR,** the teacher and students silently read a book of their own choosing. It is critical that books selected for reading during this period be of interest to students and at a level of challenge that is appropriate. Otherwise, the time students spend reading will not yield the benefits anticipated. Fountas and Pinnell (2001) and Pinnell and Fountas (2002) extended their text gradient, a method of "leveling" books according to difficulty and complexity, from levels A–R to A–Z to give teachers in the intermediate grades even more levels of graded texts from which to choose for guiding reading (Daniels, 2002). Selected criteria for leveling books Q–Z is shown in Figure 4.17.

Figure 4.16   State of the Class Chart

State of the Class Chart					
Student Name	M	T	W	TH	F
John	LR-GM	LR-GM			
Maria	LR-NM	IRC			
Jalissa	LR-NM	LR-GM			
Sue	IRC	LR-NM			
Miguel	SSR-LRG	SSR-LRG			
Yumiko	IRC	SSR-LRG			
Jamie Lee	LR-NM	LR-GM			
Seth	SSR-SSB	SSR-SSB			
Andrea	SSR-SSB	SSR-RL			
Martin	IRC	SSR-SSB			
Heather	SSR-SSB	SSR-SSB			
April	LR-NM	LR-GM			
Jason	ABSENT	SSR-SSB			
Malik	LR-GM	IRC			
Juanita	SSR-LRG	SSR-LRG			
J.T.	SSR-LRG	SSR-LRG			
Francesca	ABSENT	IRC			
Shelley	LR-NM	LR-GP			
Melanie	SSR-SSB	SSR-LRG			

Key
SSR: Self-selected reading
SSB: Self-selected book
LRG: Literature-response group goal
         pages
RL: Responding to literature

RK: Record keeping
LR: Literature-response group
GM: Group meeting for response
NM: New meeting
RM: Determining new response
IRC: Individual reading conference

Source: "Organizing for Effective Instruction: The Reading Workshop" by D. R. Reutzel and R. B. Cooter, Jr., 1991. *The Reading Teacher, 44*(8), pp. 548–555. Copyright 1991 by the International Reading Association. Reprinted by permission.

Figure 4.17   Selected Criteria for Leveling Intermediate-Grade Guided Reading Books by Level

Level Q
Very few illustrations in narrative
Detailed and important illustrations in information texts
Complex sentences and more difficult vocabulary
Complex plots, themes, and ideas
Various perspectives and points of view

Level R
Represent a range of time in history, books are longer
Vocabulary is sophisticated, simile and metaphor are used
Topics deal with events and places distant from the students' time and space contexts, and require connecting concepts from history to current times and conditions

Level S
Many works of historical fiction are included in this level
Complex ideas, text structures, and sophisticated vocabulary make for good group discussions

Level T
Variety of genres using symbolism such as fantasy, historical fiction, biographies, and realistic fiction
Themes include growing up, demonstrating courage, experiencing hardship, persecution, and prejudice

Level U
Contain technical information such as tables, graphs, charts, etc.
Narratives contain plots and subplots
Writers use more technical, symbolic, and abstract constructions

Level V
Biographies at this level provide a significant amount of history beyond the stories
Fiction books focus on science fiction including complex concepts and ideas
Print is smaller with 200–300 words per page

Level W
Very similar to level V but with increasing length of books and complexity of content
Students will need to have high interest to sustain reading over a relatively long period of time

Level X
Science fiction books incorporate more technical knowledge along with high fantasy showing the struggle between good and evil
More complexity, length, and sophistication are a part of this level of books

Level Y
Complex and subtle themes and plots including social issues
Includes the use of satire, irony, and other literary devices that go beyond the literal meaning of text
Heroic journeys and sagas are a part of this level

Level Z
Information books deal with controversial social topics and political issues
These books provide a great deal of technical information

Source: Taken from *Leveled Books for Readers: Grades 3–6,* by G. S. Pinnell and I. C. Fountas, 2002, Portsmouth, NH: Heinemann.

During the SSR time, some students may read "goal" pages from a literature book chosen for participation in a Literature Response Group **(LRG)** or Literature Circle—a small group of students who have all chosen to read the same book together. "Goal" pages are a predetermined number of pages to be read by members of the LRG before they get together again to discuss or respond to a literature book.

Literature Response Group (20 Minutes)

To form the Literature Response Groups initially, the teacher presents, using "book talks," a menu of three to four books to the class for a vote. Students vote for their favorite title of the three to four books presented by the teacher. The teacher then places students into three LRGs based on their votes for a favorite book. This is typically done as a part of the "Teacher Sharing" time block.

Once the initial 10-minute SSR period is concluded in the Reading Workshop period, the class divides into two different activities. For a majority of the students in the classroom, the SSR period will continue for the remainder of the workshop time (30 minutes). These students will read books of their own choosing, complete a literature response activity, or read LRG "goal" pages.

For a small group of students each day, the teacher calls an LRG group together for a meeting to discuss the "goal" pages completed. At the LRG meeting, a literature response activity is used to guide and shape the discussion. For example, a literature response activity called *Character Report Card* might be selected to talk about the goal pages already read by the LRG members. Using a *Character Report Card* offers a wonderful opportunity for students to grade the behavior of characters in a story. The steps for completing a *Character Report Card* response activity for the book *The Best Christmas Pageant Ever* (Robinson, 1988) are shown in Figure 4.18.

The *Character Report Card* for responding to literature books helps encourage a spirit of risk taking among students as they realize that there is no single "correct" response and that interpretations depend on a reader's background knowledge and interests. After responding to goal pages using the response activity, a new set of "goal" pages is determined in anticipation of the next group meeting. Also, a new literature response activity for responding to the goal pages is selected by the group or assigned by the teacher. For example, during the next meeting students asked to make a "wanted poster" of their favorite character and describe what the character did in this part of the book to be "wanted." Finally, the next meeting date and time is scheduled, and the LRG members are dismissed to their seats to read and respond to the next set of goal pages. LRG meetings are rotated, one each day, until all three LRGs have met to discuss their goal pages and set new goal and literature response activities.

Individual Reading Conferences (10 Minutes)

During the final 10 minutes of the Reading Workshop period, the teacher meets individually with two students, 5 minutes each, to hold an individual reading conference. The teacher schedules two students daily to read aloud either a book of their own choosing or an assigned "benchmark" book or text for assessment purposes. A "benchmark" book is a teacher-selected, leveled text that represents the "average" level of text difficulty for that point in the year. "Benchmark" books are used to assess all students' reading performance against this standard.

The teacher makes notes about each student's reading processes and errors as well as asks them to retell what they have read aloud and/or answer questions. Information gar-

Figure 4.18   Character Report Card

Place children in groups of about five to eight with multiple copies of the same story chosen for the right level of reading challenge and for their interests as a group (either basal story or trade book).

After reading the story; each child independently selects a character from the story. Then the student completes the report card shown below:

Character Report Card

Character's Name_____ *Imogene* _____ Grade Level of Character _____2_____
Teacher's Name (student filling out the report) _____

Subject	Grade	Comments
Kindness	F	*She was mean and nasty!*
Cooperative	C	*She wasn't at first but improved.*
Brave	A	*She was willing to try new things.*
Learn	A+	*She was very different at the end.*

Teacher Signature _____

Next, each student shares his/her *Character Report Card* and allows the other group members to offer comments on the grades, the characters, or the reasons for the grades.

After each child in the group has shared his/her *Character Report Card,* the group may wish to pick one to share with the whole class later on during Closing Sharing Time.

nered in these conferences is used to shape "needs group" skill or strategy instruction. A "needs group" is a small, temporary group of children who evidence similar needs for a skills or strategy lesson to help them progress and extend their reading processes. Individual reading conference information is also used by the teacher to plan the next few whole-class minilessons as many or most children may be evidencing a need for the teacher to share a particular strategy, skill, or reading insight.

STUDENT SHARING TIME (5 MINUTES)

As a daily closing activity for the Reading Workshop, the teacher calls the class together to share with each other the reading activities in which children have engaged that day. Sharing time can be a time for "turn taking" in which children share their reading response activities or talk about a book they are reading. The idea here is to bring closure to the day's work and give children a chance to talk about their reading with their peers and the teacher. A very effective approach is the technique called "turn to your neighbor" in which children share in pairs with each other. The only problem with student sharing time is keeping it to a 5-minute time frame. Once students get used to this idea, they plan for ideas and projects to share with their friends. As a wrap-up to this discussion, we use a teacher's planning book in Figure 4.19 to show how one teacher scheduled a week of activities in the Reading Workshop.

Figure 4.19   Intermediate-Grades Reading Workshop Week Planner

Monday	Tuesday	Wednesday	Thursday	Friday
Teacher Sharing Time 8:30–8:40 A.M.				
Share: Bumper stickers	Share: Reading a bus and airplane schedule	Share: Thesaurus	Share: Finding books at Amazon.com	Share: Book talk on The Titanic
Working With Language Minilessons 8:40–8:55 A.M.				
Minilesson: Figurative Language—A Sixteen Hand Horse	Minilesson: Summarizing	Minilesson: Synonyms & Antonyms	Minilesson: Locating relevant information	Minilesson: K-W-L strategy
State of the Class Time 8:55–9:00 A.M.				
Workshop Period 9:00–9:40 A.M.				
SSR: 10 Min. All Literature Response Groups: 1. Set goal pages 2. Determine response activity 3. Next meeting date Individual Reading Conference: Jeff & Candice	SSR: 10 Min. Literature Response Group: *Superfudge* Group Response, new goals, new response—wanted poster, next meeting on Friday. Individual Reading Conference: Maggie & Marilyn	SSR: 10 Min. Literature Response Group: *Maniac Magee* Group Response, new goals, new response—wanted poster, next meeting on Monday. Individual Reading Conference: Su Lan & Matt	SSR: 10 Min. Literature Response Group: *Maniac Magee* Group Response, new goals, new response—wanted poster, next meeting on Tuesday. Individual Reading Conference: Juan & Will	SSR: 10 Min. Literature Response Group: *Superfudge* Group Response, new goals, new response—character report card, next meeting on Wednesday. Individual Reading Conference: Misha & Danny
Closing Sharing Time 9:40–9:45 A.M.				
Book Talk Corners	Book Advertisement	Radio Reading	Turn to Your Neighbor	Book Password

SELECTED REFERENCES

Allington, R. L. (2001). *What really matters for struggling readers: Designing research-based programs.* New York: Addison-Wesley/Longman.

Atwell, N. (1987). *In the middle: Writing, reading, and learning with adolescents.* Portsmouth, NH: Heinemann.

Burke, J. (2000). *Reading reminders: Tools, tips, and techniques.* Portsmouth, NH: Heinemann.

Calkins, L. (1994). *The art of teaching writing* (new ed.). Portsmouth, NH: Heinemann Educational Books.

Calkins, L. (2001). *The art of teaching reading.* New York: Addison-Wesley.

Cunningham, P. M. (2000). *Phonics they use: Words for reading and writing* (3rd ed.). New York: HarperCollins.

Daniels, H. (2002). *Literature circles: Voice and choice in book clubs and reading groups* (2nd ed.). York, Maine: Stenhouse Publishers.

Dragan, P. B. (2001). *Literacy from day one.* Portsmouth, NH: Heinemann.

Duke, N. K. (2000a). For the rich it's richer: Print experiences and environments offered to children in very low- and very high-socioeconomic status first-grade classrooms. *American Educational Research Journal, 37,* 441–478.

Duke, N. K. (2000b). 3.6 minutes per day: The scarcity of informational texts in first grade. *Reading Research Quarterly, 35*(2), 202–224.

Fountas, I. C., & Pinnell, G. S. (2001). *Guiding readers and writers (grades 3–6): Teaching comprehension, genre, and content literacy.* Portsmouth, NH: Heinemann Educational Books.

Heald-Taylor, G. (2001). *The beginning reading handbook: Strategies for success.* Portsmouth, NH: Heinemann.

Holdaway, D. (1984). *Stability and change in literacy learning.* Portsmouth, NH: Heinemann.

Howe, D. (1979). *Bunnicula: A rabbit tale of mystery.* New York: Atheneum.

Kuby, P., & Aldridge, J. (1994). Direct versus indirect environmental print instruction and early reading ability in kindergarten children. *Reading Psychology, 18*(2), 91–104.

Little, E. (1988). *The Trojan horse: How the Greeks won the war.* New York: Random House.

May, F. B., & Rizzardi, L. (2002). *Reading as communication* (6th ed.). Upper Saddle River, NJ: Merrill/Prentice Hall.

McCarrier, A., Pinnell, G. S., & Fountas, I. C. (1999). *Interactive writing: How language & literacy come together, K–2.* Portsmouth, NH: Heinemann.

Morrow, L. M. (1990). Preparing the classroom environment to promote literacy during play. *Early Childhood Research Quarterly, 5,* 537–54.

Morrow, L. M. (2001). *Literacy development in the early years: Helping children read and write,* (4th ed.). Boston, MA: Allyn and Bacon.

Morrow, L. M., & Tracey, D. H. (1996). Instructional environments for language and learning: Considerations for young children. In J. Flood, S. B. Heath, & D. Lapp (Eds.), *Handbook for literacy educators: Research on teaching the communicative and visual arts.* New York: Macmillan.

Morrow, L. M., & Weinstein, C. S. (1986). Encouraging voluntary reading: The impact of a literature program on children's use of library centers. *Reading Research Quarterly, 21,* 330–46.

National Institute of Child Health and Human Development. (2000). *Report of the National Reading Panel: Teaching children to read, an evidence-based assessment of the scientific research literature on reading and its implications for reading instruction* (NIH pub. NO. 00–4769). Washington, D.C.: U.S. Government Printing Office.

Neuman, S. B. (2000). *The importance of classroom libraries.* New York: Scholastic.

Neuman, S. B., & Celano, D. (2001a). Books aloud: A campaign to put books in children's hands. *The Reading Teacher, 54*(6), 550–57.

Neuman, S. B., & Celano, D. (2001b). Access to print in low-income and middle-income communities: An ecological study of four neighborhoods. *Reading Research Quarterly, 36*(1), 8–26.

Neuman, S. B., & Roskos, K. (1990). The influence of literacy-enriched play settings on preschooler's engagement with written language. In J. Zutell & S. McCormick (Eds.), *Literacy theory and research: Analysis from multiple paradigms* (pp. 179–187). *39th yearbook of the National Reading Conference.* Chicago, IL: National Reading Conference.

Neuman, S. B., & Roskos, K. (1992). Literacy objects as cultural tools: Effects on children's literacy behaviors in play. *Reading Research Quarterly, 27*(3), 203–225.

Ogle, D. (2001). *Literacy around the world.* Presidential address given at the annual meeting of the Utah Council of the International Reading Association, Salt Lake City, UT.

Ohlhausen, M. M., & Jepsen, M. (1992). Lessons from Goldilocks: "Somebody's been choosing my books but I can make my own choices now!" *New Advocate, 5*(1), 31–46.

Pinnell, G. S., & Fountas, I. C. (2002). *Leveled books for readers, grades 3–6: A companion volume to guiding readers and writers.* Portsmouth, NH: Heinemann.

Reutzel, D. R., & Cooter, R. B., Jr. (1991). Organizing for effective instruction: The reading workshop. *The Reading Teacher, 44*(8), 548–555.

Reutzel, D. R., & Wolfersberger, M. (1996). An environmental impact statement: Designing supportive literacy classrooms for young children. *Reading Horizons, 36*(3), 266–282.

Richgels, D. J., & Wold, L. S. (1998). Literacy on the road: Backpacking partnerships between school and home. *The Reading Teacher, 52*(1), 18–29.

Robinson, B. (1988). *The best Christmas pageant ever.* New York: Harper-Collins.

Roskos, K., & Neuman, S. B. (2001). Environment and its influences for early literacy teaching and learning. In S. B. Neuman & D. K. Dickinson (Eds.), *Handbook of early literacy research* (pp. 281–294). New York: Guilford Press.

Snow, C. E., Burns, M. S., & Griffin, P. (1998). *Preventing reading failure in young children.* Washington, D.C.: National Academy Press.

Spivak, M. (1973). Archetypal place. *Architectural Forum, 140,* 44–49.

Veatch, J. (1968). *How to teach reading with children's books.* New York: Richard C. Owens.

Viorst, J. (1972). *Alexander and the terrible horrible no good very bad day* (Ray Cruz, Illustrator). New York: Atheneum.

Vukelich, C. (1991). Materials and modeling: Promoting literacy during play. In J. F. Christie (Ed.), *Play and early literacy development* (pp. 215–231). Albany, NY: SUNY Press.

Vukelich, C. (1994). Effect of play intervention on children's reading of environmental print. *Early Childhood Research Quarterly, 9,* 153–170.

Vygotsky, L. S. (1986). *Thought and language.* Cambridge, MA: MIT Press.

Wong, H. K., & Wong, R. T. (1998). *The first days of school: How to be an effective teacher* (2nd ed.). Mountain View, CA: Harry K. Wong Publications. ISBN: 0–9629360–2–2. Online ordering at www.effectiveteaching.com.

Chapter 5

Oral Language Assessment and Development

Life is good this year in fifth grade. Janet was able to move into that vacant classroom on the corner with lots of windows, and the students seemed eager to learn. So far, so good. The first challenges on Janet's horizon are Molly and Roberto. They both seem to have limited abilities in speaking English, and for very different reasons.

Molly is one of four children born to a single mother. Molly's mom, Teresa, works hard as a waitress, but simply doesn't earn enough to make ends meet. Molly's family moves around a lot, which has taken its toll on her language learning. When Janet asked Teresa about how things were going, her eyes welled up as she explained their situation. Here's the pattern: the rent comes due and Teresa rarely has sufficient resources to pay the bill. After two or three months of nonpayment eviction is threatened, so she gathers up her children and moves to another apartment complex running a $99 move-in special. This state of affairs is repeated time and again because Teresa's income remains in the poverty range. In the end, she has very little time to work with Molly, who stays at home alone with her younger siblings while mom works.

Roberto's situation is quite different. His family recently immigrated to the United States from Chile when his father, a civil engineer, was transferred with his company. Roberto studied some English at his private Catholic school in Chile, and can read and understand English fairly well. His main problem seems to be oral communication.

It seems obvious that both Molly and Roberto need to build their English vocabulary and develop oral speaking fluency. The questions in Janet's mind are: 1) How can I find out what they already know?, and then 2) Where should I begin oral language instruction for each of these students?

BACKGROUND BRIEFING FOR TEACHERS

Oral language is critical to the development of reading and writing. Children must be relatively fluent in oral language in order to communicate effectively with the teacher while learning takes place, and to use it as a tool for communicating with other students in "learning networks" (Pinnell, 1998). Above all, oral language precedes the successful learning of such reading skills as phonemic awareness, alphabetic principle, phonics and decoding abilities, and comprehension.

THE CONSTRUCTIVIST VIEW OF ORAL LANGUAGE DEVELOPMENT

There are essentially two predominant theories about how children acquire oral language skills: *constructivist theory,* and *social interactionist theory.* We tend to fall somewhere in the radical middle on this and subscribe to parts of both theories. **Constructivist theory** springs from the work of Jean Piaget (1959) who believed that language development is a feature of cognitive development. Even though he believed that cognition and language were independent of each other, Piaget contended that language development was deeply rooted in the development of cognition; that concept development preceded language (Cox, 2002).

Noam Chomsky (1957,1965,1997), a leading constructivist scholar, explained that children are constantly forming and testing hypotheses about the way oral language works. Chomsky's *generative theory of language* contends that each of us has what he termed a *language acquisition device* that helps us interpret and create sentences we have never heard before. Thus, it is possible for children to understand and/or create an almost infinite number of sentences using a finite number of known words.

Carole Cox (2002) offered a summary of the stages of language development using her own children as examples. The stages are as follows:

- **Preverbal: Sensorimotor Stage (0–2 years).** Preverbal language, from birth to 6 months, is characterized by crying and babbling. Imitation of others' speech also occurs sometimes. From 12 to 18 months, you will see repetition of one-syllable sounds typically beginning with consonant phonemes, such as "nananana." First "words" also begin to appear such as Da-Da, Ma-Ma, and bye-bye.

- **Vocabulary and True Language: Preoperational Stage (2–7 years).** *From 18 months to 2 years of age,* students become skillful at naming things in their environment, using two-word sentences, called *telegraphic speech,* and grow in their ability to use simple sentences. *Children 3 to 4 years of age* begin using simple and compound sentences, understand present and past tenses, but overgeneralize sometimes (*goed* for *went*); understand numerical concepts like few and many, first and second; and may have a speaking vocabulary of up to 1,500 words. Children at this stage are still quite egocentric and do not always use words correctly—like Rob, who after fake-coughing a few moments said, "I have a *carburetor* stuck in my throat!" *From ages 4 to 7 years,* sentence length continues to grow both in terms of complexity and number of words. Children commonly use grammatically correct sentences, learn the rudiments of reading and writing, and expand their speaking vocabularies to between 3,000–8,000 words.

- **Logical and Socialized Speech: Concrete Operational Stage (7–11 years).** Speech becomes more adult-like and English is essentially mastered, though language skills will continue to grow in complexity. *At ages 7 and 8,* children use more symbolic language such as concepts (e.g., courage, freedom, time, seasons). *From 8 to 10 years,* their language becomes more flexible and students are able to engage in abstract discussions, facilitate and nurture less developed language users, and expand ideas into lengthy discourse. Responses to questions become more logically developed, and children often use language to establish and cement relationships.

- **Abstract Reasoning and Symbolism: Formal Operations Stage (11–15 years—and beyond).** At this stage, children's speech becomes, at least in function and form, indistinguishable from adult speech. As with abstract thought, some learners seem to never quite reach this level of sophistication, which is why we have inserted the phrase "and beyond" as a caveat.

One of the key points about Piaget's constructivist notions was that children move through the previous stages at fairly predictable times, and that external influences, such as schooling, can only minimally affect their evolution. In other words, we progress through these stages according to a biologically linked timetable, and external influences (i.e., environment) have very little effect on the pace of growth. This notion is very much at odds with the social interactionist perspective.

Social Interactionist View of Oral Language Development

Environment plays a leading role in the development of language according to social interactionist thinking. **Social interactionist theory** assumes that language development is greatly influenced by physical, social, and, of course, linguistic factors (Cox, 2002).

Lev Vygotsky (1986, 1990) demonstrated that adult interactions with children could not only assist in language development, but could also affect the pace of language learning (a point Piaget eventually embraced in his later years). In chapter 2 we discussed Vygotsky's *zone of proximal development,* which explains how teachers can help students move from where they are developmentally into new frontiers of learning. This concept is at the heart of the social interactionist view and is the means by which teachers are able to create a kind of *scaffolding* (Bruner, 1978) or temporary structure that helps students construct new language from what they have previously learned.

In summary, we agree with the constructivists that oral language follows cognitive learning. We also agree that children move through very predictable stages of language learning with observable traits. However, we agree with Vygotskian social interactionists that oral language learning can be positively affected and accelerated by a skillful teacher who scaffolds instruction in the student's zone of proximal development.

Uses of Language

Oral language is an amazingly potent communication tool. Language can be used as an instrument to get things done or to regulate the behavior of others. It can serve as a creative tool at the disposal of a writer, or to express our individuality. Children learn to use language quickly when they are able to use it for real purposes, rather than as a rote exercise (Pappas, Kiefer, & Levstik, 1999).

M. A. K. Halliday (1975) wrote about these functions of language and more, which are summarized in Figure 5.1. As teachers, it is important for us to understand these functions and to weave them into the fabric of our curriculum so that children will become truly fluent users of oral language. In Figure 5.1, each language function is listed along with a verbal example and possible classroom activities.

Factors That Negatively Affect Oral Language Development

It is all well and good to talk about how oral language develops for most children in "normal" situations. This is important information because the majority of your students will usually fall within normal ranges of development if you teach in a suburban or private school. However, our primary goal as teachers is to do our best to make sure *all* students succeed, not just those who fall into the normal range. In that spirit, let's take a look at students who may have less developed oral language and begin to unravel any mysteries about their ability to learn and better understand how we can help *all children succeed.*

Figure 5.1   The Functions of Language

Language Function	Example	Classroom Activities
Instrumental Language to accomplish a task	"May I have a banana?"	Problem solving Describing sequence of activities
Regulatory Language to control persons or circumstances	"I think it's time for us to all sit down."	Following directions Establishing procedures and rules
Interactional Social relationship language	"*We* don't like horror movies."	Group etiquette Discussion (guided)
Personal Language to express one's individuality or personality	"Merry Christmas . . . y'all!"	Sharing feelings Interactive discussion
Heuristic Using language to learn	"What got Benjamin Franklin interested in electricity?"	Questioning strategies Graphic organizers
Imaginative Creative language; exploratory	"Here's what I think it would be like to be the president . . ."	Storytelling Dramatic presentations Raps, rhymes, riddles
Representational Language that explains	"This is a finite amount of fuel for gas-powered engines."	Expounding about a known topic Time sequence (retelling) Explaining cause/effect relationships

Source: Based on *Learning How to Mean: Explorations in the Development of Language,* by M. A. K. Halliday, 1975, London: Edward Arnold.

Language Deficits and Reading

Language deficits can limit a child's ability to make himself understood and retard his literacy learning in reading and writing (Lyon, 1999; Snow, Scarborough, & Burns, 1999). Research shows that children with weak oral language abilities, sometimes called *language impairments* (LI), tend to have 1) small vocabularies that are characterized by lots of short words that are used frequently, 2) high usage of nonspecific words, and 3) fewer complex sentences and less elaboration (Greenhalgh & Strong, 2001; Paul, 2001; Wiig, Becker-Redding, & Semel, 1983). Simply put, research confirms that good readers "bring strong vocabularies and good syntactic and grammatical skills to the reading comprehension process" (Lyon, 1999, p. 10).

Language-related disorders affect several million children in U.S. schools each year and are the single most common reason for referrals to special education (Warren, 2001). However bleak that may sound, we do know that early intervention with children having language problems can enhance literacy learning (Warren & Yoder, 1997). So let's take a closer look at specific groups of children who sometimes struggle in their oral language development.

Student Groups Who Commonly Experience Oral Language Deficits

Though we certainly want to avoid stereotyping of any sort, there are some groups of students who have a higher incidence of oral language deficits. Here is a short list.

- **Culturally Different Students and Second Language Learners.** It seems almost absurd to speak of some children as being "culturally different," because all inhabitants of our country (except perhaps American Indians) at some point or another came here as foreigners! Language differences seem to be most obvious with individuals who enter the American mainstream as immigrants (Wiig, 2000). Many southwestern states, for example, including California and Texas, have seen a rapid increase in recent years of new citizens whose native language is Spanish. When immigrants begin to learn English as a second language (ESL), many experience some of the same problems with language deficits as students who are native English speakers. Similarly, many students whose families have been in the United States for multiple generations may have significant cultural differences at home that can have an effect on oral language learning, either due to a different language being spoken in the home, or differing levels of language stimulation available to young children. Two books that can help you gain deeper knowledge into the needs of diverse student populations, and for the selection of appropriate literature for read-alouds, are as follows:

  Delpit, L. *(1996)*. Others people's children. *New York: The New Press.*

  Harris, V. J. *(Ed.). (1997)*. Using multiethnic literature in the K–8 classroom. *Norwood, MA: Christopher-Gordon.*

  One final point related to English Language Learners (ELL): Do not be fooled into thinking all students whose conversational English is good are fully competent. The language of teaching and learning is an almost entirely different knowledge set and some ELL students may appear to be competent when in fact they are deficient in the kind of oral language knowledge needed for academic success.

- **Effects of Poverty.** Poverty is a vicious entity that commonly squelches oral language development. Regardless of race or culture, children of poverty are denied access to experiences that are common to most children in our society, from a trip to Taco Bell, to youth clubs, to summer vacations. Because the working poor often have to work several jobs just to make ends meet, parents frequently have little or no time to verbally interact with their children. The net effect of poverty is children with capable minds but poorly developed language. According to the latest report of the National Assessment of Educational Progress (2000) for reading, children from poverty score significantly lower in reading proficiency than their more affluent counterparts. These are the children at greatest risk of failing in school and eventually dropping out.

- **Learning Disabilities.** Certainly there are myriad learning disabilities that can negatively affect oral language development. Hearing and visual impairments, attention deficit disorder (ADD), problems with hyperactivity, and behavioral disorders are a few of the most common issues that can impact language development. Federal law mandates that these and other students who qualify for special education services have their needs met in the least restrictive environment, which may include specific interventions in oral language development.

- **Slow Learners.** These are students whose measured intelligence quotient (IQ) falls between 70 and 85. Slow learner adults, by the way, make up the vast majority of those who are incarcerated (about 80% in Texas, for example). Though they were once considered "educable mentally retarded" students, special education laws created in the early 1970s left slow learners without any guaranteed services. Slow learners make up about one in six in the general population and commonly have much poorer oral language vocabularies than their peers, and develop in literacy at a much slower pace. For instance, a fourth-grade student (nine-year-old) who is a slow learner can be expected to read on a first-grade level if he is developing normally. You may have three to four slow learners in your classroom each year that will need extra assistance in their learning.
- **Highly Mobile Students.** We all live in a highly mobile society, thus students often move around, particularly in large urban centers. These drop-in/drop-out children, even with good teaching, miss consistent planned instruction and their oral language development can suffer. They have an almost serendipitous education and the results are devastating (Cooter & Cooter, 2002).

ASSESSING ORAL LANGUAGE DEVELOPMENT

In this section we examine some of the ways oral language can be assessed. We begin with a description of the phases of oral language development so that you will have a way to "benchmark" students and determine whether special interventions may be needed.

WHAT ARE THE PHASES OF ORAL LANGUAGE DEVELOPMENT?

Whether you are working with slow learners, gifted students who are English Language Learners, or rather typical children in the suburbs, the development of oral language proceeds along a predictable continuum. These **phases of oral language development** are observable and can be used to help you decide just where a student is in his development and what he is ready for next (i.e., his *zone of proximal development*). The *phases of oral language development* are shown in Figure 5.2, which is based on the work of Cox (2002). Use it as an ongoing assessment tool with students who need language development.

We now turn our attention to strategies that may be used to assess oral language development.

INFORMAL LANGUAGE INVENTORY (ILI)

Purpose

This is a simple and quick way to measure students' growth in everyday oral speech. This is a very traditional approach first described by Melear (1974) and Burns (1980). As an *informal* inventory (i.e., not norm referenced), it is up to the teacher to look for patterns and compare these results with classroom observation before coming to conclusions about student needs. Refer to Figure 5.2 to help judge progress and needs.

Materials

You will need to have one or two pictures that have been drawn by the student. He may either draw one just before you conduct the interview, or have him preselect drawings from past school assignments. For older learners, you may want the student to bring in a photograph of a favorite friend or experience. A tape recorder is also recommended.

Figure 5.2   Phases of Oral Language Development

Phase	Description
Preproduction	This is a short period in which the learner is silent but is actively listening to the more capable language users in his environment.
Early Production	This phase can last up to a year or more. The learner begins using single words and short phrases.
Emergent Speech	Learner is capable of sentences and short narratives.
Developing Fluency	Learner becomes capable of longer narratives/conversations, begins reading and writing, and uses invented spellings in his writing.
Advanced Fluency	Learner uses conventions of speaking, reading, and writing.

Procedure

Begin by turning on the tape recorder and asking the student to tell you about the picture(s). Transcribe the recording, then analyze the student's language as follows:

1. Number of sentences
2. Number of grammatically correct sentences
3. Number of descriptive terms
4. Number of modifying phrases
5. Number of morphemes (these are "meaning-bearing language units" such as prefixes, suffixes, and root words)
6. Number of "mazes" in the student's language (maze, in this context, means confused or tangled groups of words such as uh . . . uh . . . mmm . . . you know . . . like . . .)

We have constructed a worksheet for conducting an ILI that you may enlarge on a copy machine and use in your assessments (see Figure 5.3).

THE STUDENT ORAL LANGUAGE OBSERVATION MATRIX (SOLOM): A TOOL FOR USE IN ESL CLASSROOMS AND OTHER LIMITED ENGLISH POPULATIONS

Purpose

Teacher judgment is one of the most important and accurate measures of English learners' oral language development (Peregoy & Boyle, 2001, p. 131). One observational tool created by the California State Department of Education is the *Student Oral Language Observation Matrix (SOLOM),* which is found in Figure 5.4. It is designed to be used in everyday classroom activities and is organized as a rubric to focus your attention on general oral language traits. The SOLOM was developed for use in ESL classrooms (English

Figure 5.3   Information Language Inventory Worksheet

Transcription of Oral Discussion	# of sentences	# of correct sentences	# of descript. terms	# of mod. phrases	# of morphemes	# of mazes

Figure 5.4 SOLOM: Student Oral Language Observation Matrix

	1	2	3	4	5
COMPREHENSION	Cannot understand simple conversation	Only understands conversational language spoken slowly	Can understand most conversations if the speech is slow and includes repetitions	Understands almost everything at normal speed, but may require some repetitions	Understands class conversations and discussions without difficulty
FLUENCY	Speech is halting and fragmentary; makes it extremely difficult to initiate a conversation	Usually silent or hesitant due to language limitations	Often speech is interrupted while the student searches for the right word or expression	Generally fluent in class discussions, but may lapse sometimes into word searches	Fluent and effortless conversation
VOCABULARY	Very little vocabulary makes conversation nearly impossible	Limited vocabulary and often misuses words	Frequently uses incorrect words, and speech is limited by insufficient vocabulary	Sometimes uses inappropriate terms or must rephrase due to limited vocabulary	Fully capable in using vocabulary and idioms
PRONUNCIATION	Difficult to understand due to severe pronunciation problems	Pronunciation problems make it necessary to repeat himself a great deal	Pronunciation problems cause listeners to have to listen closely; some misunderstandings	Always intelligible, but may have heavy accent or inappropriate intonation patterns	Normal pronunciation and intonation
GRAMMAR	Acute problems with grammar and syntax making speech nearly unintelligible	Grammar and syntax problems often force him to repeat himself and stick to simple/familiar patterns	Frequent errors with grammar and syntax that sometimes alters meanings	Sometimes makes grammar or syntax errors	Appropriate grammar and syntax usage

Stages of Development
Stage I: Score of 5–11 = Not Proficient in English
Stage II: Score of 12–18 = Limited English Proficiency (Emergent)
Stage III: Score of 19–24 = Limited English Proficient (Developing)
Stage IV: Score of 25 = Fully English Proficient

Source: Adapted from an instrument developed by the California State Department of Education.

as a Second Language), but has also been found to be useful with native English speakers having limited vocabularies.

Materials

You will need a copy of the SOLOM for each student in a file folder.

Procedure

Observe students during normal classroom activities where a good bit of language is going on, such as small-group work. Try to make sure that each time you make an observation, the situational context is similar. Limit your observations for each student to about 5 minutes each time, but make multiple observations to ensure greater reliability and generalizabilty of your conclusions.

For each trait, place an "X" in the box that best describes what the student is able to do and note the point value (1–5). For example, a student who, in the "Comprehension" category, understands nearly everything spoken at normal speed would receive a score of 4 for Comprehension. After you have placed an "X" in a box best describing the student in each trait category, add up the point values to determine his stage of development in English proficiency.

A key for scoring your observations is found at the bottom of the SOLOM. As an example, let's say that you have rated Jaime's oral language performance using the SOLOM traits and come up with the following rating:

Comprehension	4
Fluency	4
Vocabulary	4
Pronunciation	3
Grammar	4
Total	**19**

A score of 19 would be Stage III or "Limited English Proficient" on the SOLOM.

ORAL LANGUAGE CHECKLIST

Purpose

Many times, teachers are able to learn a great deal by simply making anecdotal records of students they wish to observe, then transferring that information to a checklist. Johnson (1993) developed an oral language checklist based on the research, which is well suited to this type of assessment.

Materials

Duplicate the oral language checklist found in Figure 5.5 for each student whose oral language development you wish to study. A clipboard with a legal pad or peel-off sticky computer labels is also needed for making anecdotal notes during observations.

Procedure

First, carefully review the oral language checklist found in Figure 5.5 for key points to observe. Then, identify one or two children per day whose language development you wish to study. During the school day, keep your clipboard handy and make anecdotal notes on each child according to the criteria represented in the questions on the oral language

Figure 5.5   Oral Language Checklist

While interacting with the child your wish to study in your classroom, note any of the following:

1. Was there any indication that the child misperceived words?   Yes   No
   List examples:

2. Did the child have difficulty understanding directions for various tasks?   Yes   No
   Examples:

3. Did the child have difficulty understanding any specific vocabulary?   Yes   No
   Examples:

4. Did the child have difficulty comprehending complex/lengthy sentences?   Yes   No
   Examples:

5. Did the child have difficulty listening to and comprehending extended
   discourse? (e.g., stories)   Yes   No
   Examples:

6. Did the child have difficulty remembering series of instructions?
   How many?   Yes   No
   Give examples:

7. Did the child have difficulty retrieving (recalling) words?
   Under what conditions? Picture naming, spontaneous
   conversation?   Yes   No
   Other:

8. Did the child have difficulty pronouncing multisyllabic words?
   Give examples: Yes   No

9. Did the child make grammatical mistakes when speaking?   Yes   No
   List examples:

10. Could the child convey thoughts clearly when relating an event
    or telling a story?   Yes   No
    Give examples of problems such as sequencing of events, lack
    of transition words, failure to include relevant information.

11. Did the child have good nonverbal communication?   Yes   No
    Give examples: (eye contact, gesture)

12. Did the child have any specific articulation problems?   Yes   No
    Give examples:

13. Were any of the above problems reflected in the child's
    oral reading or reading comprehension?   Yes   No
    Give examples:

14. Were any of the above *oral language* problems reflected
    in the child's written *language?*   Yes   No
    Give examples:

Source: From "Relationships between oral and written language" by D. J. Johnson, 1993, *School Psychology Review, 22*(4), 595–610. Used with permission.

checklist. At the end of each observation day, transfer your notes to a folder for each child and answer all questions that apply. Observations should be repeated about once every six weeks in order to identify growth trends and determine educational (i.e., language development) needs.

Connecting Assessment Findings to Teaching Strategies

Once you have determined who in your class may need further language development as well as the areas to be developed, then you should begin selecting appropriate learning activities. Most structured oral language development activities tend to fall into certain types: conversations, discussions, description/comparison/evaluation, reporting, storytelling, and creative drama or choral reading. In the Intervention Strategy Guide for Oral Reading we have listed the teaching strategies that appear in the next section and linked them to key need areas your assessments are likely to encounter.

Teaching Strategies for Developing Oral Language

Children's oral language is improved when teachers and family members provide good language models and opportunities to practice oral language in authentic situations, and when students receive supportive feedback for their attempts at approximating proficient English usage (Morrow, 1999). Whether teaching English as a second language or working to shore up the language abilities of native speakers, learning activities selected by teachers should help children improve their receptive (listening/reading) and expressive (speaking/writing) language skills. In this section we provide a menu of teaching strategies that have served many teachers well in the classroom.

Poetry Potpourri

Purpose

Nancy Hadaway and her colleagues (Hadaway, Vardell, & Young, 2001) assembled a wonderful collection of classroom activities that use poetry to stimulate oral language development, particularly for students learning English as a second language. They point out that reading and re-reading poetry through read-aloud and choral reading activities promote fluency, develop concept knowledge and vocabulary, and serve as splendid springboards into writing. In this section we highlight several of the poetry activities Hadaway and her colleagues recommended.

Materials

You will need a variety of poetry for language development activities. Here is a listing of the selections cited, many of which are found in school libraries:

Children's poetry books cited by Hadaway and others (2001) . . .

Ada, Alma Flor, Harris, Violet, & Hopkins, Lee Bennett. (1993). *A chorus of cultures anthology.* Carmel, CA: Hampton Brown.

Fleischman, Paul. (1985). *I am phoenix.* New York: Harper-Collins.

Fleischman, Paul. (1988). *Joyful noise.* New York: Harper-Collins.

Intervention Strategy Guide for Oral Reading

Student Problem(s) ↓ / Intervention/Strategy →	Teacher Modeling	Unison Reading	Repeated Lines/Refrain	Antiphonal Call & Response	Singing Poems	Poetry Response	Storytelling	One Looks/One Doesn't	KWHLS	Animal Crackers
Comprehension: Can be Understood	+	*	*	-	*	+	+	+	+	+
Fluency	-	+	+	+	+	+	+	-	-	-
Vocabulary	+	+	+	+	+	+		+	+	+
Pronunciation	+	+	+	+	+	+	+	+	+	-
Grammar	+	+	+	+	+	+	*	+	-	-
Understand Others	*	-	-	-	*	+	*	+	+	+
Organization of Ideas	+	-	-	-	-	+	+	+	+	*
Includes Supporting Ideas	+	-	-	-	-	+	+	-	*	-

Key: + excellent strategy
     * adaptable strategy
     – unsuitable strategy

Fleischman, Paul. (2000). *Big talk: Poems for four voices.* Cambridge, MA: Candlewick Press.

Florian, Douglas. (1994). *Bing bang boing.* San Diego, CA: Harcourt Brace.

Greenfield, Eloise. (1978). *Honey, I love.* New York: Harper & Row.

Herrera, Juan F. (1998). *Laughing out loud, I fly: Poems in English and Spanish.* New York: Harper-Collins.

Holbrook, Sara. (1996). *The dog ate my homework.* Honesdale, PA: Boyds Mills Press.

Holbrook, Sara. (1997). *Which way to the dragon!: Poems for the coming-on-strong.* Honesdale, PA: Boyds Mills Press.

Hughes, Langston. (1932/1994). *The dreamkeeper and other poems.* New York: Knopf.

Johnston, Tony. (1996). *My Mexico-Mexico mio.* New York: Penguin Putnam.

Kuskin, Karla. (1975). *Near the window tree.* New York: Harper & Row.

Kuskin, Karla. (1980). *Dogs and dragons, trees and dreams.* New York: Harper-Collins.

Mora, Pat. (1999). *Confetti: Poems for children.* New York: Lee & Low.

Nye, Naomi Shihab. (1995). *The tree is older than you are.* New York: Simon & Schuster.

Pappas, Theoni. (1991). *Math talk: Mathematical ideas in poems for two voices.* San Carlos, CA: Wide World/Tetra.

Prelutsky, Jack. (1984). *The new kid on the block.* New York: Greenwillow.

Shields, Carol Diggory. (1995). *Lunch money.* New York: Dutton.

Silverstein, Shel. (1974). *Where the sidewalk ends.* New York: Harper-Collins.

Silverstein, Shel. (1981). *A light in the attic.* New York: Harper-Collins.

Soto, Gary. (1992). *Neighborhood odes.* San Diego, CA: Harcourt.

Soto, Gary. (1995). *Canto familiar.* San Diego, CA: Harcourt Brace.

Wong, Janet. (1996). *A suitcase of seaweed.* New York: Simon & Schuster.

Procedure

Following are brief descriptions of oral language development activities that have been recommended using poetry as the primary catalyst.

- *Teacher Modeling.* It is hard to sell something you do not love yourself, so begin with poems that you particularly like. Introduce key words and phrases at the chalkboard so that students can see as well as hear new vocabulary and concepts. If you need help with this, try "Three Wishes" by Karla Kushin (1975). All of us "kids" have made wishes and can relate to this poem. For those of us with, shall we say, *wacky* relatives, Gary Soto's (1992) "Ode to Family Photographs" can be great fun with older students.

- *Unison Reading.* After the previous activity, students will usually be loosened up a bit and ready to take on more of the performance role. Choose shorter poems with repeating lines, and read the poem aloud first yourself to help students get the feel. When we each taught first grade, we found that children could hardly be *stopped* from joining in on the second reading of a fun poem! "My Monster" (Florian, 1994) is very popular from grades 1–4 for example.

- *Repeated Lines and Refrains.* Another great choral activity has students learn about timing and come in just when their assigned line comes up, or as a group when a refrain appears. Sometimes a key word is said extra loud for emphasis, such as with the poem "Louder" by Jack Prelutsky (1984).

- *Antiphonal: Call and Response.* Teachers divide the class into two groups and one side repeats the lines first spoken by the other. This is a form of antiphonal reading, an ancient tradition begun by monks in monasteries during medieval times. Try out the "call and response" method using "Copycat" by Sara Holbrook (1997).

- *Singing Poems.* Children love to put poetry to song; matching poems and songs having the same meter. It works best when using tunes that are familiar to all such as "Row, Row, Row Your Boat" or "Mary Had a Little Lamb." If you give students a copy of the poem, they will end up reading and singing the poem over and over, providing them with needed repetition of high-frequency words and a chance to develop language fluency. Try "The Dog Ate My Homework" by Sara Holbrook (1996) sung to "On Top of Old Smokey," or the poem "School Cafeteria" (Florian, 1994) sung to the tune of "Ninety-nine Bottles of 'Pop'."

- *Poetry Response.* A good language development exercise should elicit a great deal of oral language in an authentic discussion situation for student practice and teacher coaching. Draw students into discussions about interesting poems using such questions as:

> *What did this poem make you think?*
>
> *What did you like about this poem?*
>
> *What do you think the poet was trying to say?*
>
> *Does this remind you of anything you know about?*
>
> *Let's talk about what is going on here . . .*
>
> *What is this poem about?*

STORYTELLING

Purpose

Many cultures have strong oral traditions to describe their religious beliefs, politics, triumphs, and family stories (McHenry & Heath, 1994). As a tool for language development, storytelling can be powerful. As an art form, storytelling has certain aspects that should be respected for the storyteller to be effective in her communications. Here we discuss a teacher-directed method for bringing storytelling to the table as a valuable tool in your teaching arsenal.

Materials

It is best, if at all possible, to provide students with what we term "limited choice;" several stories that would be appropriate for retelling from which they can choose one. The story should be easy to read and be in concert with the student's interests and background. You will also need copies of Figure 5.6, *The Storyteller's Planning Guide.*

Procedure

Begin with a storytelling experience for the students where you model telling one of your favorite stories from memory. Next, introduce *The Storyteller's Planning Guide* (Figure 5.6)

Figure 5.6   The Storyteller's Planning Guide

Storyteller _____

Story _____

Source _____

Motivation- *I want to tell this story because . . .*

Props- *What kinds of props ("properties"), if any, would I need to tell this story? (Clothing, sound-making devices, other?)*

Introduction- *How will I begin the story? What are the exact words I should use?*

Setting- *How do I describe the setting? How can I make the listener feel like she is there? Is time and place important to the story?*

Characters- *How can I best describe each character? What makes the main character "tick"? How should I present each character to the audience? Should I use different voices for the different characters? If not, how can I make the audience understand who is talking?*

Sequence of Events- *What are the key events I will describe in my story? What is the correct order for each "scene"?*

Conclusion- *How will I bring my story to a successful end? What are my final words? (Exact words, please) How do I want my audience to feel at the conclusion?*

Rehearsal- *Have I practiced telling my story alone at least three times, and before a friend at least once?*

and explain each of its key points. Walk through a planning session where you model how you went about planning to share the story they witnessed you sharing earlier. Be sure to include discussion about any props, voices, and other points that add drama to the telling. Place students into groups of two and have them select one of the stories you have available for them to use in storytelling. Have them account for each step in the planning process using the storyteller's planning guide. When each group of two feels they are ready, have them take turns practicing the storytelling to each other. The final "act" will be for each student to perform his or her favorite part of the story to you (or the entire group, if they are not too nervous). Follow up the performance with questioning, such as, "Why did you choose that part of the story to tell?" or "Why was that your favorite part of the story?" This draws students into even more dialogue.

ONE LOOKS, ONE DOESN'T

Purpose

It is important for us to help students expand their oral communications abilities because, as "producers" (speaking) of language, they will also become better *"receivers" (reading) of language; these are reciprocal processes.* In *One Looks, One Doesn't* (Peregoy & Boyle, 2001), students are able to take turns practicing their oral communications with a peer as they describe a picture or object selected by the teacher.

Materials

You will need stimulus objects for students to describe. These can include interesting pictures from magazines or books, pictures on transparencies shown at the overhead projector for all groups to see and describe, objects that can be held, and so forth. A blindfold for each group (one only for each group) can add a little spice to this activity, too!

Procedure

First, place students in groups of two for this activity (also called *dyads*). If possible, arrange it so that in each twosome you have a more capable speaker of English, such as pairing a native English speaker with an English Language Learner (ELL), or perhaps a sixth-grade student paired with a third grader.

If using a transparency of a picture, place the transparency on the overhead projector after explaining that one student will look at the transparency while the other turns away (or wears a blindfold). The student who looks at the picture describes it to his partner and the listener attempts to guess what the partner is describing.

A variation is for the listener to try to draw what his partner is describing. After about five minutes (use an egg timer to keep it fair for all), the one drawing the picture can turn around and compare his drawing with what his partner was describing.

Areas that could be stressed in teacher-led minilessons for this activity include:

- Expressing ideas clearly and with variety
- Organizing ideas effectively before speaking
- Word usage is appropriate for the situation
- Appropriate articulation
- Listening to questions carefully from your partner, and asking for clarification as necessary
- Politely asking the speaker to repeat or explain

K-W-H-L-S Chart

Purpose

This is a teacher-directed activity in which we lead students into discussions about science, mathematics, social studies, and other real-world subjects. The *K-W-H-L-S Chart* (Baloche, 1998; Cox, 2002) helps students structure new knowledge, build concept knowledge, develop questioning skills, and strengthen vocabulary.

Materials

Multiple copies of the *K-W-H-L-S Chart* (Figure 5.7) will be needed for this activity.

Procedure

The K-W-H-L-S Chart is a super tool for leading a class discussion about a topic of study. The idea is to name a topic from your curriculum that you wish to introduce to the class. Perhaps you will be studying with older students events of the September 11, 2001 terrorist attack on New York City and Washington D.C. Discussion that resulted with one group of sixth-grade students a few months after the event occurred are shown in Figure 5.8. Note that this was the first discussion and only the first three columns of the K-W-H-L-S Chart have been completed. Remember, in our use of this procedure the teacher transcribes the discussion offerings onto the chart. This enables her to question, clarify, and modify offerings in a "teachable moment" kind of method.

Animal Crackers

Purpose

As teachers of language, we must always have a wide range of exercises of varying complexity, interest level, and difficulty available to reach children where they are in their oral language development (Avery & Bryan, 2001). For young learners this can be as simple and basic as describing familiar things in their environment, such as animal crackers!

Materials

You guessed it . . . you will need a box of animal crackers from your neighborhood grocery for each group of two or four students (whatever you decide).

Procedure

The idea is to have groups of students (groups of either two or four) sit together and generate words that describe the arrangements of animal crackers. Their descriptions can either be tape recorded or written by a recorder in the group (invented spellings are acceptable for this activity).

Here are some animal cracker themes that can be used for this activity (Brovero, 1996):

- Classify the animals by habitat/environment (graphing could be used here as well).
- Draw each animal and add speech in a cartoon-like bubble.
- Classify animals by their eating habits.
- Have small groups of students invent mathematics word problems involving a variety of animals found in their box.
- Match animals to the printed word from your word wall (see chapter 9 for a discussion of word walls).

At the end of your activities students get to eat the animals, of course!

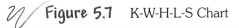 **Figure 5.7**   K-W-H-L-S Chart

Topic:

K What I *know*	W What I *want* to learn	H *How* I can learn more about this topic	L What I *learned*	S How I can *share* this new knowledge

Figure 5.8   K-W-H-L-S Chart (partially completed on the 9–11 Attack)

Topic:	September 11			
K What I *know*	**W** What I *want* to learn	**H** *How* I can learn more about this topic	**L** What I *learned*	**S** How I can *share* this new knowledge
Many innocent people were killed that day. Planes were used as flying bombs. Bin Laden was the person behind the attacks. Many of us think he is a coward. President Bush said that this is an act of war. Mayor Giuliani has been called the "Mayor of All America." We all felt afraid when this horrible thing happened. We feel so sad for the families who lost a loved one. Most Islamic people are good and are worried that some Americans will blame them for this horrible event because of bin Laden.	Where is Afghanistan? What are the countries that are on its borders? How far is it from the United States? How are the children in Afghanistan doing? Do they have enough food? What does the religion of Islam teach? What is happening now in the war on terrorism? Did the families of those killed receive help? What is an "act of war" according to the Constitution? Are we safe?	Get a map from the library to locate Afghanistan. Ask an expert about the distances from here to Afghanistan. Look on the Internet for the latest news on Afghan children and the war on terrorism. Go to the American Red Cross web site to find out about aid to surviving families. Interview a law professor from an area university about acts of war as described in the U.S. Constitution. Invite a police officer to speak to the class about our safety and things we can do.		

SELECTED REFERENCES

Avery, S., & Bryan, C. (2001). Improving spoken and written English: From research to practice. *Teaching in Higher Education, 6*(2), 169–183.

Baloche, L. A. (1998). *The cooperative learning classroom: Empowering learning.* Upper Saddle River, NJ: Prentice Hall.

Brovero, M. (1996). Class menagerie. *Teaching PreK–8, 27*(2), 64.

Bruner, J. (1978). The role of dialog in language acquisition. In A. Sinclair, R. J. Jarvella, & W. M. Levelt (Eds.), *The child's conception of language* (pp. 241–256). New York: Springer-Verlag.

Burns, P. C. (1980). *Assessment and correction of language arts difficulties.* Columbus, OH: Merrill.

Chomsky, N. (1965). *Aspects of the theory of syntax.* Cambridge, MA: MIT Press.

Chomsky, N. (1997). *Perspectives on power.* Montreal, Canada: Black Rose Books.

Chomsky, N. A. (1957). *Syntactic structures.* The Hague, The Netherlands: Mouton.

Cooter, R. B., & Cooter, K. S. (2002). Challenges challenges to change: Implementing balanced reading instruction in an urban school district. *The Journal of Balanced Reading Instruction,* 8–26.

Cox, C. (2002). *Teaching language arts* (4th ed.). Boston: Allyn & Bacon.

Greenhalgh, K. S., & Strong, C. J. (2001). Literate language features in spoken narratives of children with typical language and children with language impairments. *Language, Speech, & Hearing Services in Schools, 32*(2), 114–126.

Hadaway, N. L., Vardell, S. M., & Young, T. A. (2001). Scaffolding oral language development through poetry for students learning English. *The Reading Teacher, 54*(8), 796–807.

Halliday, M. A. K. (1975). *Learning how to mean: Explorations in the development of language.* London: Edward Arnold.

Johnson, D. J. (1993). Relationships between oral and written language. *School Psychology Review, 22*(4), 595–610.

Lyon, G. R. (1999). Reading development, reading disorders, and reading instruction: Research-based findings. *ASHA Special Interest Division I Newsletter. Language Learning and Education, 6*(1), 8–16.

McHenry, E., & Heath, S. B. (1994). The literate and the literary. *Written Communication, 11*(4), 419–445.

Melear, J. D. (1974). An informal language inventory. *Elementary English, 41,* 508–511.

Morrow, L. M. (1999). Where do we go from here in early literacy research and practice. *Issues in Education, 5*(1), 117–125.

National Assessment of Educational Progress. (2000). *The nation's report card: Reading.* Jessup, MD: Education Publications Center (ED Pubs).

Pappas, C. C., Kiefer, B. Z., & Levstik, L. S. (1999). *An integrated language perspective in the elementary school* (3rd ed.). New York: Longman.

Paul, R. (2001). *Language disorders from infancy through adolescence* (2nd ed.). St. Louis, MO: Mosby.

Peregoy, S. F., & Boyle, O. F. (2001). *Reading, writing, & learning in ESL* (3rd ed.). New York: Longman.

Piaget, J. (1959). *The language and thought of the child* (3rd ed.). London: Routledge & Kegan Paul.

Pinnell, G. S. (1998). The language foundation of reading recovery. Keynote address to the Third International Reading Recovery Institute (Third, Cairns, Australia).

Snow, C. E., Scarborough, H. S., & Burns, M. S. (1999). What speech-language pathologists need to know about early reading. *Topics in Language Disorders, 20*(1), 48–58.

Vygotsky, L. S. (1986). *Thought and language.* Boston: MIT Press.

Vygotsky, L. S. (1990). *Mind in society.* Boston: Harvard University Press.

Warren, S. F. (2001). The future of early communication and language intervention. *Topics in Early Childhood Special Education, 20*(1), 33–38.

Warren, S. F., & Yoder, P. J. (1997). Emerging model of communication and language intervention. *Mental Retardation and Development Disabilities Research Reviews, 3,* 358–362.

Wiig, E. H. (2000). Authentic and other assessments of language disabilities: When is fair fair? *Reading & Writing Quarterly, 16*(3), 179–211.

Wiig, E. H., Becker-Redding, U., & Semel, E. M. (1983). A cross-cultural, cross-linguistic comparison of language abilities of 7- to 8- and 12- to 13-year-old children with learning disabilities. *Journal of Learning Disabilities, 16*(10), 576–585.

Chapter 6

Children's Concepts About Print

Ms. Solomon's kindergarten class excitedly gathered around her on the carpet. She had a big book displayed on the easel entitled *On Market Street* (Lobel & Lobel, 1981), and was ready to start reading. As the children settled in, Ms. Solomon pointed to the cover of the book and asked, "What do you see here?"

"A girl carrying a bunch of stuff!"

"Yes, she is. It's quite a stack of things. Where do you suppose she has been to get all that stuff?"

Bobby responded somewhat quizzically, "I guess she's been to a junkyard."

"No, No, she's been shopping!" interrupted Brit.

"Why do you say that, Brit?"

"Because in the picture she is walking away from a town and some buildings."

"Good observation! What do you think the words will tell us about the picture on the cover of this book?"

"It's the title," Jana blurts out confidently.

"Thank you, Jana. That is what the writing on the cover is called. So, let me ask my question another way. What do you think the writing in the title will tell us about the picture on the cover?"

"Oh, I think it will say something about going shopping," answers Brit.

"OK, shall we see? Listen to me read the title and watch as I point to the words with my pointer." Ms. Solomon points to the words one at a time while reading, "ON—MARKET—STREET." Ms. Solomon continues into the book and comes to a picture of a girl covered with clocks.

"What is the letter at the top of this page?"

"C" says Mica.

"Good, what do you think the girl is going to buy on Market Street by looking at the picture on this page?"

The children cry out as a group, "Clocks."

"Good thinking. Let's look at this word, 'clocks.' Does the word clocks start with the letter 'c'? Look carefully and compare the first letter in 'clocks' with the letter 'c' at the top of the page." The teacher and children interactively share this book noting the pattern in the book—letter at the top of the page, a picture, the letters, and a word on each page that begins with the letter at the top of the page.

After the first reading of the big book, *On Market Street*, Ms. Solomon talks with the children about making their own *On Market Street* big book. "Now, let's see if we can make our own big book of what we would buy on Market Street," she says. Ms. Solomon lays out a big pile of labels and print taken from the children's everyday environment. There are soda drink, candy, cereal box, and canned good labels all over the floor. "So, we are going to Market Street and we are going to buy something that begins with a 'B'. What will we buy?"

One little boy, Jackson, pulls up a candy bar wrapper and says, "Let's buy a *Butterfinger* or *Baby Ruth* candy bar." They all agree and Ms. Solomon pastes the two candy bar wrappers on the page of the class's innovation on the big book *On Market Street.*

BACKGROUND BRIEFING FOR TEACHERS

Many children enter school already knowing a great deal about how books work and how to carefully look at printed language, while others do not (Yaden & Templeton, 1986). Some children know the difference between a word and a letter; others know where a story begins in a book; and others have had little access to books and guided experiences with print (Neuman, 1999; Neuman & Celano, 2001). Concepts associated with printed text, known as **print concepts** (also concepts about print), are a critical part of early literacy development and understanding among beginning readers (Clay, 2000b; Hiebert, Pearson, Taylor, Richardson, & Paris, 1998). Assessing print concepts in the early years is important so that children who come to school without prior learning opportunities, access to books and print, or guided experiences with printed language can be helped to develop these necessary concepts to prevent possible reading problems later on (Clay, 2000b; Durkin, 1989; Snow et al., 1998).

Research studies have shown that some children require direct instruction in learning print concepts (Hiebert et al., 1998). For example, Yaden (1982) found that even after a year of reading instruction, some readers' concepts of letters, words, and punctuation marks had not yet developed to a level that was functionally useful. Johns (1980) also learned that first-grade students' end-of-first-grade reading achievement could be reliably predicted using students' entering-kindergarten knowledge of print concepts. Further, Morrow (1993) found that mastery of certain characteristics, conventions, and details associated with printed language is necessary for successful literacy development. Several other researchers have shown that children's early learning of concepts about print influence language development, initial writing development, phonemic awareness, phonics learning, word reading, and reading development (Lomax & McGee, 1987; Morris, 1993; Roberts, 1992). As a result of these and other findings, Hiebert et al. (1998), in a document disseminated through the Center for the Improvement of Early Reading Achievement (CIERA) called *Every Child a Reader,* have called for teachers, administrators, curriculum developers, and publishers to focus on assessing and developing print concepts among all young learners. You can access this document, *Every Child a Reader,* by going to www.ciera.org on the Internet. We focus in the next section on defining and explaining print concepts to children.

WHAT ARE THE CONCEPTS ABOUT PRINT?

Concepts about print can be divided into three distinct and different print aspects (Clay, 2000b; Taylor, 1986): 1) the functional aspects of print, 2) the mapping aspects of print, and 3) the technical aspects of print. We will discuss each one separately.

Functions of Print

Children learn early that written language is useful for a variety of purposes. Halliday's (1975) landmark research described how oral and written language functions in our daily lives. The purposes children and adults have for using language can be divided into three parts: 1) *Ideational,* or expressing one's thoughts, 2) *Interpersonal,* or intimate social language, and 3) *Textual,* or informational language. Smith (1977) expanded Halliday's teachings to purposes for which language can be used. Each of the ten purposes or *functions of language* (Smith, 1977, p. 640) is detailed below with related examples:

Instrumental: "I want." (Language is used as a means of getting things and satisfying material needs.)

Examples in Written Language: Classified ads, notes, sign-up sheets, applications, bills, invoices, etc.

Regulatory: "Do as I tell you." (Language is used to control the attitudes, behaviors, and feelings of others.)

Examples in Written Language: traffic signs, procedures, policies, traffic tickets, prompts, etc.

Interactional: "Me and you." (Getting along with others, establishing relative status) Also, "Me against you." (establishing separateness)

Examples in Written Language: love notes, invitations, dialogue journals, friendly letters, etc.

Personal: "Here I come." (Expressing individuality, awareness of self, pride)

Examples in Written Language: opinion papers, letters to the editor, etc.

Heuristic: "Tell me why." (Seeking and testing world knowledge)

Examples in Written Language: letters of inquiry, requests, and registration forms, etc.

Imaginative: "Let's pretend." (Creating new worlds, making up stories, poems)

Examples in Written Language: stories, tall tales and yarns, etc.

Representational: "I've got something to tell you." (Communicating information, descriptions, expressing propositions)

Examples in Written Language: arguments, lists, problem solving, etc.

Divertive: "Enjoy this." (Language for humor and fun)

Examples in Written Language: Puns, jokes, riddles, etc.

Authoritative/contractual: "How it must be." (Rules)

Examples in Written Language: Statutes, laws and regulations, etc.

Perpetuating: "How it was." (Records)

Examples in Written Language: personal histories, diaries, journals, scrapbooks, etc.

Children make varied use of oral language in their own lives, at least in a subconscious way. As you help students become aware of these oral language functions, they will readily apply this knowledge in their written language use as well.

Mapping Speech Onto Print

The ability to match or *map* speech sounds onto the printed symbols (letters) develops rather slowly. Some researchers believe that the ability to map speech sounds onto printed language and knowledge of the sound-symbol code, or phonics knowledge, may develop simultaneously (Lomax & McGee, 1987). Several important concepts for students to learn are listed below:

The student . . .

- Understands that speech can be written down and read, and what is written down can be spoken
- Is aware of print in the environment and can read at least some signs and logos
- Understands that the message of the text is constructed from the print more than the pictures
- Knows written language uses different structures (see Halliday, 1975, and Smith, 1977, mentioned earlier) from spoken language
- Comprehends that the length of a spoken word is usually related to the length of the written word
- Demonstrates that one written word equals one spoken word
- Identifies some correspondences between spoken sounds and written symbols
- Uses context and other language-related clues to construct meaning and identify words

Mapping speech onto print helps students become successful readers and benefit from further experiences with written language (Johnston, 1992; Reutzel, Oda, & Moore, 1989). For some readers, failing to acquire an understanding of mapping principles can slow their progress in reading and writing development (Clay, 1993; Ehri & Sweet, 1991; Johns, 1980).

Technical Aspects of Print

Knowing technical aspects of print refers to the rules or *conventions* that govern written language. Examples include directionality (left-to-right/top-to-bottom progression across the page in reading), spatial orientation, and instructional terms used in classrooms to refer to written language elements. Because many of these technical concepts are commonsense matters for adults, it is little wonder that sometimes teachers and parents mistakenly assume that children already understand them. There is, however, ample evidence that this knowledge of the technical aspects of written language develops slowly for many learners (Clay, 1979; Day & Day, 1979; Downing & Oliver, 1973; Johns, 1980; Meltzer & Himse, 1969). A listing of the technical aspects of print follows:

Levels of Language Concepts

Ordinal

- First, second, third, etc.
- Beginning
- Last
- Book
- Paragraph
- Sentence
- Word
- Letter

Visual Clues Embedded in Books and Print

- Cover, spine, pages
- Margins, indentations
- Spacing
- Print size
- Punctuation

Location Concepts

- Top
- Bottom
- Left
- Right
- Beginning (front, start, initial)
- Middle (center, medial, in-between)
- End (back, final)

It is very important that teachers assess what young children know about the technical aspects of printed language. In the next section of this chapter, we describe five useful assessment tools for teachers to gain insights into children's understanding of the concepts about print.

ASSESSING CHILDREN'S CONCEPTS ABOUT PRINT

The assessment strategies offered in this section provide you with a comprehensive approach for assessing all three aspects of the concepts about print: 1) the functional aspects of print, 2) the mapping aspects of print, and 3) the technical aspects of print.

CONCEPTS ABOUT PRINT (CAP) TEST

Purpose

The Concepts About Print Test (CAP) was designed by Marie Clay (1972, 2000b) to assess children's mapping and technical aspects of print knowledge such as letter, word, sentence, story, directionality, *text versus picture,* and *punctuation.* The CAP test is based upon four small booklets, two published in 1972 and two published in 2000. The two booklets published in 1972 are entitled *Sand* and *Stones.* The two booklets published in 2000 are entitled *New Shoes* and *Follow Me, Moon.* All four of these text booklets are viewed and read by a teacher and an individual student together. One set of booklets may be used as a pretest and a posttest in the kindergarten year and the other two may be used as a pretest and a posttest during the first-grade year to measure concepts about print growth.

Instructions for administering the *Concepts About Print Test* are in Clay's (2000b) book, entitled *Concepts About Print: What Have Children Learned About the Way We Print Language.* More information about the *Concepts About Print* test booklets and the manual for administration, scoring, and interpretation can be found on the Internet by going to www.heinemann.com.

Materials

You will need the following items, authored by Marie M. Clay (2000b) and published by Heinemann: The *Concepts About Print: What Have Children Learned About the Way We Print Language;* and the four forms of the actual test booklets: *Sand, Stones, New Shoes* and *Follow Me, Moon.*

Procedure

Procedures for administering, scoring, and interpreting these tests are found in *Concepts About Print: What Have Children Learned About the Way We Print Language* pages 8–15. Print concepts tested include: front of book; proper book orientation to begin reading; beginning of book; print rather than pictures carry the message; directional rules of left to right; top to bottom on a page; return sweep to the beginning of a line of print; matching spoken words with written words; concepts of first and last letters in a word; mapping spoken word and letter order onto the print, beginning and ending of a story; punctuation marks; sight words; identifying printed letters, words, and upper- versus lowercase letters.

In order to adequately test children's print concepts, the *Sand, Stones, New Shoes,* and *Follow Me, Moon* booklets include some rather unusual features. At certain points the print or pictures are upside down, letter and word order are changed or reversed (*saw* for *was*), and line order is reversed as well as paragraph indentions removed or inverted.

The CAP test has established a long and excellent record as a valid and reliable screening test to be used as part of a battery of screening tasks for young, inexperienced, or at-risk readers. A major limitation of this test, however, is that it is based on error-detection tasks that require the child to find problems and explain them. Because of the somewhat tedious nature of this test and its tasks, children need to be tested in a calm environment and to have a trusting relationship with the examiner in order to obtain reliable results.

READING ENVIRONMENTAL PRINT

Purpose

This task is designed to assess students' ability to read commonplace or "highly frequent" print accessible in their local and daily environment, such as signs in the school like STOP, EXIT, or NO SMOKING. Other examples of environmental print include signs on the outside of businesses and stores, and on products commonly available across the nation such as McDonalds, Cheerios, Diet Coke, and so forth. Environmental print information can be used to assess the access a child has had or the attention given to printed language in the environment. Further, teachers can discover ways that environmental print may be used to help each child develop successful reading and writing behaviors. An added advantage of environmental print is that it encourages beginning readers to develop an "I can read!" attitude. Researchers who have examined the value of teaching children using environmental print have consistently shown it useful (Kuby & Aldridge, 1997; Neuman & Roskos, 1993; Orellana & Hernandez, 1999; Proudfoot, 1992; Vukelich, 1994; West & Egley, 1998).

Materials

Materials selected for this task are based upon a survey of children's recognition and access to environmental print completed by Briggs & Richardson (1994). To begin, three sets of ten plain index cards (30 cards total) are needed to construct this task. The first set of ten cards is used to display traffic signs or informational logos found on roads and in public buildings. The second set of ten cards is used to display logos of restaurant chains, television shows, gasoline stations, and national chain stores such as K-Mart. The third set of ten cards is used to display food product logos such as Pepsi, Alphabits, and Butterfinger.

Procedure

Classification procedures, shown in Figure 6.1: *Written Language Knowledge Taxonomy,* are used to sort student responses to the set of 30 cards into pragmatic response,

Figure 6.1   Written Language Knowledge Taxonomy

Response Category	Level	Examples
Pragmatic perspective	Attempts to read	
	Maintains communication contract	
	single word or name (with no article),	"potato chips," "bread"
	phrases (not beginning with article "a"),	"trouble with the football team"
	letters, numbers	"A" to telephone (index letter)
	Renegotiates communication contract	"7:30" to TV Guide
	names print object (usually with article)	"a newspaper"
	describes something in picture of print item	"a man"
	describes what can be found on the print item	"words," "telephone numbers,"
	describes what can be done with the print item	"pictures," "take it to the store"
	Refuses to respond	no response or "I don't know"
Inclusion of text from print item	Attempt to read includes text of print item	"State Times" to paper
	Attempt partially includes text of print item (at least one word of response is included in text of print)	"Gulf State" for "State Times" in text
	Attempt does not include text of print item	"gum, candy" not in text of grocery list
Meaning	*Meaningful*	
	Attempt includes print text central in meaning	"eggs" to grocery
	Attempt does not include text but makes sense	"tomato" to grocery list (not in text)
	Nonmeaningful	
	Attempt includes print text not central in meaning	"by," "is" to newspaper
	Attempt does not include text and does not make sense	"redfish" to book (not in text)
	Naming letters embedded in words	"S" "T" to "State" text
Attention to graphic detail	*Evidence of attention to graphic detail*	
	Attempt includes print text for item with no picture	"dog food" to grocery list
	Attempt includes print text when child points to correct text	"potato chips" and points to text "potato chips"
	Attempt practically includes print text (one word plus one letter same)	"Sunday Times" for text "State Times"
	Attempt does not include text, but it's obvious child referred to text	"the" and child points to "to"
	Attempt includes identification of letters in text	"S" "T" to newspaper

Source: Reprinted with permission from the National Reading Conference and Lea McGee, from, "Young Children's Written Language Knowledge: What Environmental and Functional Print Reading Reveals" by L. McGee, R. Lomax, and M. Head, 1988, *Journal of Reading Behavior, 20*(2), pg. 105. Copyright 1988 by the National Reading Conference.

inclusion of part of the print response, meaning conversion response, and attention to graphic detail response (Harste, Burke, & Woodward, 1981; McGee, Lomax, & Head, 1988). This taxonomy has been used to help reading researchers determine how well children process print in their environment. The environmental print task helps teachers gain insights into students' growing understanding of print concepts using environmental language. Children who show little awareness of print in the environment are also likely to have had few experiences with printed text in other contexts, such as books and writing.

MOW MOTORCYCLE TASK

Purpose

As children begin to learn to read and write, some discover how spoken words/sounds are mapped onto letters and printed words in books and other written language sources. One concept students need to discover is that the length of the *printed* word is related to the length of the same *spoken* word. The Mow Motorcycle Task (Rozin, Bressman, & Taft, 1974) taps students' awareness of this basic mapping relationship between speech and print.

Materials

Prepare ten *pairs* of word cards (20 cards total) to be used for this task. Each *pair* of word cards should contain two words beginning with the same letter and differing in written and spoken length as shown in Figure 6.2. Print each word card neatly with all uppercase manuscript or printed letters using a computer printer. Use a plain, block, or print style font rather than calligraphic or stylized fonts.

Procedure

Seat the child comfortably next to you at an appropriately sized table or desk. Displaying only one pair of cards at a time, show the child ten pairs of cards bearing printed words beginning with the same letter. For example, tell the student, "One of these words is *mow* and the other is *motorcycle*. Which one is *mow*?" The child responds by pointing. The total score is the number of correct responses, with 0 to 10 points possible. Items should be varied so that the "target" word (the one you name) and the foil (the incorrect choice) are not always in the same position. This helps prevent the possibility that mere guessing on the student's part—always choosing the left-hand word, for example—will result in a high number of false correct responses.

Figure 6.2   Mow Motorcycle Task

One of these words is *mow* and the other is *motorcycle.* Which one is *mow*?	
MOTORCYCLE	MOW

METALINGUISTIC INTERVIEW (MI)

Purpose

The Metalinguistic Interview is a set of questions designed to assess children's understanding of academic/instructional language—language teachers use in instruction as they talk about printed language in books and displayed elsewhere. For example, researchers (Clay, 1966; Denny & Weintraub, 1966; Downing, 1970, 1971–72; Reid, 1966) interviewed young children and found that they often do not have a clear understanding about many of the common academic/instructional terms used in beginning reading instruction, such as alphabet, letter, word, and sentence. Obviously, knowledge of these terms is most likely linked to how well children understand and respond to early reading and writing instruction.

Academic or instructional language terms/concepts assessed in the Metalinguistic Interview include:

- That the term *alphabet* and/or *ABCs* refers to letters
- That the actual location on a page of a single letter, word, or sentence is an indication of directionality L–R (left to right), T–D (top/down), and so on
- Punctuation
- How to differentiate upper- and lowercase letters
- Terms such as the *front* and *back* of a book, and an understanding of *page(s)*

Materials

Any children's trade book or literature book containing both pictures and print may be used. For the best early assessment, locate a book that has print on one page and a full-page picture on the adjoining page. A scoring sheet can be easily constructed by duplicating Figure 6.3. For scoring, write a 0 or 1 following each of the 20 questions. Scores on the interview range from a low of 0 to a high of 20. Carefully examine which items were missed to determine areas of future instructional focus.

Procedure

Make a copy of the 20 tasks or questions in Figure 6.3. Seat the child comfortably next to you. Hand the student a picture book such as *The Gingerbread Man* (Schmidt, 1985) or *The Little Red Hen* (McQueen, 1985) upside down, with the spine of the book facing the child. Once the child takes the book, tell him that the two of you are going to read the book together. Then ask him to respond to the 20 tasks listed in Figure 6.3 and mark the responses on the question sheet.

THE BURKE READING INTERVIEW

Purpose

The purpose of the *Burke Reading Interview* (Burke, 1980) is to help you discover what students understand about the reading process and the strategies students use to unlock unknown words and construct meaning. Children are asked to describe how they learned to read, as well as what they can do to become better readers (Burke, 1980; Harste & De-Ford, 1982). You can determine whether students recognize that the goal of reading is to understand the author's message, or if they mistakenly think that the only goal of reading is to recode letters into sounds.

Figure 6.3   The Metalinguistic Interview

1. "What are books for? What do books have in them?"
2. "Show me the front cover. Show me the back cover."
3. "Show me the title of the story."
4. "Show me the author's name."
5. "Open the book to where I should begin reading."
6. "Show me which way my eyes should go when I begin reading."
7. "Show me the last line on the page."
8. Begin reading. At the end of the page ask, "Now where do I go next?"
9. "Show me where to begin reading on this page. Will you point to the words with your finger as I say them?"
10. "Show me a sentence on this page."
11. "Show me the second word in a sentence."
12. "Show me a word."
13. "Show me the first letter in that word."
14. "Show me the last letter in that word."
15. "Show me a period on this page."
16. "Show me a question mark on this page."
17. Show the child a quotation mark and ask, "What is this?"
18. Ask the child to put his fingers around a word.
19. Ask the child to put his fingers around a letter.
20. Ask the child to show you an upper- and lowercase letter.

Correct responses are given a 1 and incorrect responses are scored 0.

Materials

Use the Burke Reading Interview (Burke, 1980) and a cassette tape recorder to record the child's responses to the interview questions. Interpretation of this instrument is based on the response to each question. A total score is not useful to guide instructional decision making. Each response must be examined to reveal to the teacher the next steps necessary for this child to progress in her reading and writing development.

Procedure

Seat the child comfortably near you and the cassette recorder's microphone for effective recording purposes. Visit with the student for a moment to establish rapport. Tell the student that you will be asking her a few questions and that you will be recording her answers. Then, turn the recorder on and begin by asking the child her name. Next ask the questions found in the Burke Reading Interview in Figure 6.4. The tape recording can be used later to analyze student responses.

CONNECTING ASSESSMENT FINDINGS TO TEACHING STRATEGIES

Before discussing intervention strategies, we have constructed a matrix connecting assessment to intervention and/or strategy choices. It is our intention to help you, the teacher, select the most appropriate instructional inventions and strategies to meet students' needs based on assessment data.

In the next part of this chapter, we offer strategies for intervention based on the foregoing assessments.

Figure 6.4 The Burke Reading Interview

Name: _____ Age: _____ Date: _____
Occupation: _____ Educational level: _____
Sex: _____ Interview setting: _____

1. When you are reading and come to something you don't know, what do you do? Do you ever do anything else?
2. Who is a good reader you know?
3. What makes _____ a good reader?
4. Do you think _____ ever comes to something he/she doesn't know?
5. "Yes" When _____ does come to something he/she doesn't know, what do you think he/she does?
   "No" Suppose _____ comes to something he/she doesn't know.
   What do you think he/she would do?
6. If you knew someone was having trouble reading, how would you help that person?
7. What would your teacher do to help that person?
8. How did you learn to read?
9. What would you like to do better as a reader?
10. Do you think you are a good reader? Why?

Source: From *Reading Miscue Inventory: Alternative Procedures* by Y. Goodman, D. Watson, C. Burke, 1987; New York: Richard C. Owen, Publisher, Inc.

INSTRUCTIONAL INTERVENTIONS AND STRATEGIES: HELPING EVERY STUDENT LEARN THE CONCEPTS ABOUT PRINT

After a careful assessment of a student's reading progress, one or more of the following strategies may be appropriately applied. Perhaps the most important thing to remember is that children with poorly developed print concepts must be immersed in a multitude of print-related activities in a "print-rich" classroom environment. Authentic reading and writing experiences coupled with the informed guidance of a caring teacher or other literate individuals (e.g., parents, peers, and volunteers) can do much to help students learn necessary print concepts.

ENVIRONMENTAL PRINT READING

Purpose

The purpose of reading environmental print is to give children an experience that allows them to read familiar print drawn from the world around them they are likely to have seen. Such experiences not only bring the outside world of print closer to the classroom but these experiences also build children's confidence in their ultimate ability to learn to read (Orellana & Hernandez, 1999; West & Egley, 1998).

Materials

Use product labels and logos from a variety of items including cans, cups, wrappers, packaging, and so on. Blank books or template books modeled after other children's books can be prepared for children to use in creating their own "I Can Read" environmental print books.

Intervention Strategy Guide for Concepts About Print

Student Problem(s) ↓ / Intervention Strategy →	Read Environmental Print	LEA	Voice Point	Frame	Masking Highlighting	Context Transfer	Error Detect	Verbal Punctuation	Shared Reading	Manipulative Letters
Book Handling	−	−	−	−	−	−	−	−	+	−
Directionality	*	*	+	−	−	*	−	−	+	*
Print Carries Message	+	+	+	+	*	+	+	−	+	*
Voice-Print Matching	*	*	+	*	+	+	*	−	+	−
Punctuation	*	+	*	*	+	*	+	+	+	−
Concept of Word/Letter	+	+	*	+	+	*	+	−	+	*
Order—Letters/Words	+	*	*	+	+	*	+	−	+	+
Pragmatic Reponse to Environmental Print	+	−	*	*	*	+	*	−	−	*
Reader relies on a single strategy to unlock unknown words	*	*	−	*	*	*	*	−	+	*
Reader doesn't understand academic or instructional language.	−	*	*	*	+	*	*	−	+	*

Key: + excellent strategy
     * adaptable strategy
     − unsuitable strategy

Procedure

Teachers and children can use environmental print commonly found in student's daily lives to learn about important print concepts. One application of using environmental print involves creating "I Can Read" books. Topics for environmental print "I Can Read" books may include: *My Favorite Foods, Signs I See, A Trip to the Supermarket, My Favorite Things, My Favorite Toys,* and so on. Children begin by choosing a topic. Next, they can select to use blank books or a template book. Following their choice of a blank or template book, they select from the environmental print collection product labels to construct their own "I Can Read" books. Using a template book, based on the well-known children's book, *On Market Street* (Lobel & Lobel, 1981), students innovate on the contents of the original book by selecting what they would have purchased "on market street" using the product labels to create their own "I Can Read" book. Because students select logos they can already read, they can easily read environmental books while acquiring print concepts. Further, these books become a source of confidence building and enjoyment.

Teachers can create logo language displays in the classroom as well as placing labels on furniture and fixtures in the classroom. Using a pointer or flashlights, teachers and children can "Read the Room" together by reading the labels in the classroom environment or the logos on the logo language display. By using print familiar to children from their homes and out-of-school world experiences, they very quickly develop an "I can do this . . . I can read!" attitude.

LANGUAGE EXPERIENCE APPROACH (LEA): CREATING GROUP EXPERIENCE CHARTS

Purpose

The **Language Experience Approach** (LEA) uses children's firsthand and/or vicarious experiences to create personalized reading materials. Children learn print conventions and concepts by seeing how their speech looks in printed form. They learn mapping of speech onto print and the technical aspects of print (i.e., directionality, punctuation marks, and so on) from LEA reading materials. Teachers have found that children's dictated LEA stories can be recorded in at least two different ways: *The Group Experience Chart,* and *The Individual Language Experience Story.*

Materials

- Large chart paper displayed on an easel. The upper half of each page should be blank for a picture and the lower half of each page should be one-inch lines for printing the students' dictated story.
- Illustration/drawing supplies for illustrating the stories.
- Cut-out pictures/magazines for cutting out pictures to illustrate the stories.

Procedure

The *Group Experience Chart* is a means of recording the experiences of a group of children. In all group LEA activities it is essential that students have a shared experience about which they can talk and dictate lines, sentences, and stories. The typical steps associated with the creation of a Group Experience Chart are:

- The children participate in a shared experience such as a field trip, an experiment, or a guest speaker.
- Teachers and children discuss the shared experience.
- Children dictate the story while the teacher transcribes the dictation onto chart paper.
- Teachers and children share in reading the chart story.
- The chart is used to teach about print concepts, words, and other important language concepts.

The selection of an interesting and stimulating experience or topic for children can spell the success or failure of an LEA group activity. Topics and experiences must capture the interest of children in order to provide the motivation necessary for learning. Some examples of previously successful topics and themes are:

- Our classroom pet had babies last night.
- Let's describe our field trip.
- Writing a new version of a favorite book.
- What we want for Christmas.
- Planning our Valentine's Day party.
- What did Martin Luther King do?
- Scary dreams we've had . . ..
- Once I got into trouble for. . . ..
- A classmate is ill. Let's make a get well card from the class.

Be sure to discuss the experience or topic carefully. This helps children to self-assess what they know about the topic and to make personal connections. Also, it motivates them to share their knowledge, experiences, and personal connections with others. Be careful not to dominate the discussion, however. Asking too many focused questions can turn what would otherwise be an open and exciting discussion into an interrogation. Questions should invite discussion, instead of encouraging short and unelaborated responses. Be careful not to make the mistake of beginning dictation too early in the discussion, as this may lead to a dull, even robotic, recounting of the experience or topic.

After plenty of discussion, ask children to dictate the ideas they wish to contribute to the chart. With special-needs learners in the early grades, you may want to record each child's dictation in different colored markers to help him identify his contribution to the chart.

Later in the year, write the child's name by his dictation rather than using different marker colors. When the chart is complete, read the children's composition aloud in a natural rhythm, pointing to each word as you read. After the first reading, invite students to read along on the second reading. Next, ask volunteers to read aloud portions of the story. Other strategies for reading the composition include:

- Read aloud a selected dictation line from the chart and ask a child to come up to the chart and point to the line you just read aloud.
- Copy several lines of the chart onto sentence strips and have children pick a sentence strip and match it to the line in the chart.
- Copy the LEA story onto a duplicating master and make copies to go home with students for individual practice.
- Put copies of favorite words in the chart story onto word cards for word banks and matching activities.

LANGUAGE EXPERIENCE APPROACH (LEA): CREATING INDIVIDUAL LANGUAGE EXPERIENCE STORIES

Purpose

The **Language Experience Approach** (LEA) as explained in the previous section uses children's firsthand and/or vicarious experiences to create personalized reading materials. Children learn print conventions and concepts by seeing how their speech looks in printed form. They learn mapping of speech onto print and the technical aspects of print (i.e., directionality, punctuation marks, and so on) from LEA reading materials. *The Individual Language Experience Story* is not only useful for teaching children concepts about print but this LEA variation is tremendously motivating because children have their own story produced in book format.

Materials

- Small booklets containing between eight and ten 8 1/2″ × 11″ pages. The upper half of each page should be blank for a picture and the lower half of each page should have 1/2-inch lines for printing the students' dictated story.
- Illustration/drawing supplies for illustrating the stories.
- Cut-out pictures/magazines for cutting out pictures to illustrate the stories.

Procedure

For most young students who are typically in an egocentric stage, no one is more important and exciting to talk or read about than themselves. *Individual Language Experience Stories* provide an excellent opportunity for learners to talk about their own experiences and to have these events recorded in print to learn about the concepts of print.

Ask the children to tell their stories into a tape recorder and listen to them. Listening and editing on tape can have a very positive transfer value for the writing process. This oral editing encourages children to retell or revise their stories until they are satisfied with the final product. We also suggest, where circumstances permit, that parent volunteers be invited to transcribe students' Individual Language Experience Stories from audiotapes to paper copy.

Next, turn these Individual Language Experience Stories into books. Recognize the value of students' Individual Language Experience Stories by placing a card pocket and library card in each child's book. These books are added to the classroom library for other children to read. A story reader's chair can be established to encourage children to read their Individual Language Experience Stories aloud to peers in their own classroom and other classrooms in the school.

One variation of Individual Language Experience Stories that children particularly like is shape books. As shown in the illustration, the cover and pages of the dictated Individual Language Experience Story are drawn and cut into the shape of the book topic. For example, if a child has created a story about a recent family trip to Disneyland, the book could be cut into the shape of Mickey Mouse's head; a trip to Texas may be recorded in a book cut into the shape of the state of Texas.

VOICE POINTING

Purpose

Pointing to the print in an enlarged book, on a chart, or on a white board while reading aloud interactively with a group of children draws the eyes of the readers into contact with the print (Clay, 1993). Otherwise, children in the earliest stages of reading acquisition will have a tendency to study the illustrations and listen to the story language without paying a great deal of attention to the print. Voice pointing shows children that: 1) the print rather than the picture carries the message of reading, 2) the beginning, ending, and directionality of the print, 3) how the spoken language of the reader is represented or mapped onto print on the page or display, and 4) the technical concepts of print such as word, letter, or punctuation.

Materials

- A pointer ranging from something as simple as an unsharpened pencil to a ruler, from a telescoping pen pointer to a laser pointer
- An enlarged copy of a story, poem, song lyrics, or book

Procedure

Clay (1979) indicated that pointing to the print while reading, or *voice pointing,* is a critical strategy to develop during the early stages of learning to read. To help beginning readers make the connection that the print is guiding the speech of the reader, teachers point to the print as they interactively read aloud.

If the teacher wants to demonstrate the beginning point of print, the flow and directionality of print from top to bottom, left to right, and so on, and where the print ends on the page, then run the pointer smoothly under the print as he reads aloud. However, if the teacher wants to demonstrate how each word read aloud is represented by its corresponding "word" in print, move the pointer in a broken, word-by-word method. To draw attention to letters, single words, or punctuation, the teacher should point using a circular motion around the print element to be given attention by the readers.

FRAMING PRINT

Purpose

Some young readers have not yet grasped the idea that a given word is the same every time it appears in print. For instance, the word *football* is always *football* whenever and wherever it appears in print, whether it is handwritten text or text appearing in a book. Understanding this basic concept is a major milestone in reading development. *Framing* is one strategy that can help students grasp this important print concept (Holdaway, 1979).

Materials

Several types of framing tools can be constructed using oak tag or poster board materials. A razor knife and stapler are also needed. A simple frame constructed of white poster board is illustrated.

A more complicated shutter frame allows teachers to not only frame words on the page, but also to expose words to students one letter at a time from left to right to encourage the use of verbal blending of letter sounds in temporal sequence. A shutter frame constructed of white poster board with a white poster board shutter is illustrated on page 158.

Procedure

Begin by reading aloud an enlarged text several times without interruption or discussion about print features. This can be text from an LEA Group Chart or a big book such as *Brown Bear, Brown Bear* (Martin, 1983). Remember to voice point to the text as you read. Highlight aspects of written language by pointing and framing a word or words using the simple frame. For example, frame the text which asks, "Brown Bear, Brown Bear, what do you see?" one word at a time. Frame each highlighted word (e.g., *brown, bear, what, do, you, see*) using the simple frame. After framing several words,

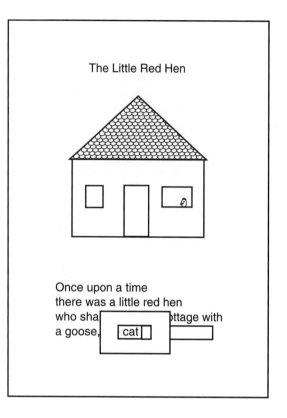

ask children to look carefully at a word with only one letter exposed using the shutter frame. Ask children to notice the letters as you expose them. Once all letters are exposed, ask children to look carefully at the word. Talk with them about how words are made up of letters demonstrating to them the difference between letters and words. Using the shutter frame, teachers can also frame punctuation marks for attention and discussion.

MASKING—HIGHLIGHTING PRINT

Purpose

Some young readers do not yet know how to look at print or what to look for on the printed page. Helping young children know where to look and what to look for on the printed page is the major purpose for using masking and highlighting techniques. Understanding the basics of how to look at print and knowing what to look at is a critical milestone in the development of young readers before they can profit from instruction about letters, words, and punctuation.

Materials

Use highlight tapes of differing colors *to highlight* selected print concepts in big books or enlarged print on chart paper. Use stick-on notes of differing sizes *to mask* selected print concepts in big books or enlarged print on chart paper.

Procedure

Select the print concept to be taught such as attention to the concept of word, concept of letters, punctuation, or figuring out an unknown word. To direct students' visual attention to spaces between words, to letters within words, to specific words, or to punctuation marks, use semitransparent highlighting tape. For example, use light blue highlighting tape to direct students' visual attention to the use of periods in text. Or, use light pink highlighting tape to direct students' attention to the letter "w" in the big book, *Mrs. Wishy-Washy.*

Use stick-on notes to mask from students' view selected concepts about print such as words, letters, and punctuation. Once masked from view, point to the masked print feature and discuss with students what they think would be behind the stick-on note. Once discussion has led to a reasonable prediction, unmask the print feature by removing the stick-on note. Using stick-on notes in this manner to mask print features directs students' attention very specifically to the covered print feature.

Use stick-on notes and enlarged text or big books to also create cloze passages. Masking specific words or masking every fifth word in a pattern creates a cloze passage. Students use the surrounding text and pictures to decide which word(s) would make sense in the place of the masked word. When students determine the masked word and the stick-on notes are removed, this focus of attention to the masked words brings "closure" to the cloze passage. Masking emphasizes the differences between words and sentences as well as basic concepts about print, while also demonstrating the importance of context clues in understanding the author's message.

Two variations of cloze that can be used to focus young readers' attention on either content or structure words in predictable books are progressive and regressive cloze. In *progressive cloze,* the text is read aloud. Next, several words are masked using stick-on notes, as shown in Figure 6.5, then the text is read aloud again. Each time a deleted word is encountered, children are asked to identify the missing word. When the deleted word is correctly identified, it is uncovered. For example, in the story *The Gingerbread Man,* the entire text of the book may be read and then several pages used for a progressive cloze procedure.

In *regressive cloze,* the process is also begun by reading the entire text aloud. Next, the text is reduced to only its structure words by covering all content words with stick-on notes. Children are then asked to identify the missing words. As each content word is identified, it is uncovered. By using these cloze variations, children begin to focus on identifying individual words within the context of familiar stories. Teachers can repeat these cloze variations in another context such as on charts, sentence strips, or a chalkboard, as shown in Figure 6.6.

PRINT CONTEXT TRANSFER

Purpose

In the earliest stages of reading acquisition, students' recognition of print concepts, words, or letters are "context bound." This means that print concepts, words, or letters encountered and recognized in one print setting are not necessarily transferred from one print setting to another. For children to pay close attention to features of print and transfer, their recognition of print elements, from one context to another, text must be removed from the original context to a new context. The purpose of the print context transfer strategy is to help students come to recognize various print concepts, words, and letters in other print settings outside the big book or chart text where they were originally encountered.

 **Figure 6.5** Progressive Cloze Covering the Content, Action, or Descriptive Words

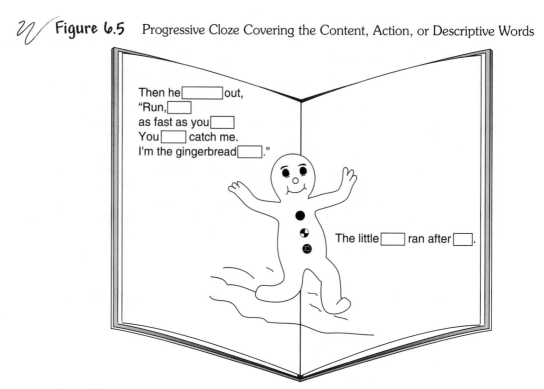

Then he ☐ out,
"Run, ☐
as fast as you ☐
You ☐ catch me.
I'm the gingerbread ☐."

The little ☐ ran after ☐.

Source: From "Fingerpoint Reading and Beyond: Learning About Point Strategies (LAPS)" by D. Ray Reutzel, 1995, *Reading Horizons, 35*(4), pp. 310–328. Copyright 1995 by Western Michigan University.

Figure 6.6 Moving the Text to Sentence Strips for Progressive or Regressive Cloze Activities

Then he ☐ out,

"Run, ☐

as ☐ as you can.

☐ can't ☐ me.

I'm the gingerbread ☐."

The little ☐ ran after him.

Source: From "Fingerpoint Reading and Beyond: Learning About Point Strategies (LAPS)" by D. Ray Reutzel, 1995, *Reading Horizons, 35*(4), pp. 310–328. Copyright 1995 by Western Michigan University.

Materials

Materials necessary to teach the print context transfer strategy include a pocket chart, sentence strips, and word cards to display sentences or words taken from an original chart text or a big book.

Procedure

Read an enlarged text selection projected onto a screen, in a big book, or on chart paper with the children. For example, sentences can be copied from the big book, *The Napping House* (Wood & Wood, 1984) onto sentence strips and displayed in a wall pocket chart, as shown in Figure 6.7.

Demonstrate for students the exact match between the print in the big book or chart text and the print copied onto the sentence strips in the pocket chart. Next, ask children to match the text framed in the original book or chart text with sentence strips or word strips displayed in the wall pocket chart. By observing and participating in this process, young or struggling readers make visual connections between the print in the book and the same print displayed on sentence strips, word card, or other print displays.

Variations on this print context transfer strategy involve children in selecting a sentence strip and placing it directly beneath the matching print in the big book or chart text. After making the direct match, students explain to a peer or classmates how the two sets of print are the same. If children are invited to match words in charts or big books to word cards, it is best if structure or function words, such as *the, and, a,* and *there,* are not used. Only concrete nouns, action words, and descriptive words that are easy to see in the mind's eye should be highlighted for this type of exercise.

Figure 6.7   Substituting Words to Draw Attention to Print Detail

Original Text	Substitution Text
And on that cat	And on that chicken
there is a mouse,	there is a worm,
a slumbering mouse	a slimy worm,
on a snoozing cat	on a snoozing chicken
on a dozing dog	on a lazy lamb
on a dreaming child	on a dreaming child
on a snoring granny	on a snoring granny
on a cozy bed	on a cozy bed
in a napping house,	in a napping house,
where everyone is sleeping.	where everyone is sleeping.

Source: From "Fingerpoint Reading and Beyond: Learning About Point Strategies (LAPS)" by D. Ray Reutzel, 1995, *Reading Horizons, 35*(4), pp. 310–328. Copyright 1995 by Western Michigan University.

ERROR DETECTION

Purpose

The purpose of the error detection strategy is to cause children to look closely at text to match what is on the page with what is said. Children need to learn to inspect words visually to determine if they "look right" in relation to what is said when the text is read aloud. This type of close reading of the text helps students develop self-correction strategies because they develop the habit of looking carefully at what they said during reading to make sure it "looks right" and matches the print.

Materials

Materials necessary to teach the print context transfer strategy include a pocket chart, sentence strips, and word cards to display sentences or words taken from an original chart text or a big book.

Procedure

In the error detection strategy, teachers substitute other words for the words in the original text. These word substitutions, along with the words found in the original text, can be interchanged in a pocket chart display during subsequent re-readings. Exchanging the substitution words with the words found in the original text helps children carefully focus on print details to determine which words have been switched in the text and how such word play can change the author's message.

For example, in the text of the book entitled *Mrs. Wishy-Washy* (Cowley, 1990), the word *mud* can be substituted with the word *dud* on a sentence strip using a white sticky note or a word card if the words on the sentence strip are cut into individual words in the pocket chart.

> "Oh, lovely dud," said the pig, and he rolled in it.

The teacher reminds the children that this text should say, " 'Oh, lovely *mud,*' said the pig, and he rolled in it," but something is wrong here. The teacher then asks, "Can you find what has been changed?" Students are invited to explain what is wrong, how the error was detected, and how the error can be corrected. Once the concept is grasped from this example, other familiar text can be copied to sentence strips. Words on these sentence strips can be substituted using word cards or stick-on notes and presented for students to analyze.

VERBAL PUNCTUATION

Purpose

Drawing students' attention to punctuation is often difficult for both students and teachers. Nonetheless, taking note of punctuation is important for students to achieve reading fluency and comprehension. Students who ignore punctuation often read without proper phrasing, rate, or intonation, which in turn interrupts comprehension. Students who skip or miss punctuation marks often run sentences together, resulting in confused or broken comprehension. The purpose of the verbal punctuation strategy is to help students notice punctuation in a playful and engaging fashion. This strategy was first made famous by the talented comedian, Mr. Victor Borge, in a nationally acclaimed comedy routine.

Materials

To use verbal punctuation, the students and the teacher must share a common text for reading aloud. This common text can be a big book, chart text, projected overhead transparency, computer-projected text, enlarged text on the classroom "black or white" board, or multiple copies of the same text for students at their seats.

Procedure

The Verbal Punctuation strategy is a process where each punctuation mark in a piece of text is given a sound. For example, a period may be represented by making the &$*@#) raspberry sound. When a question mark comes up, a rising "uh" sound can be made. This process continues, giving a sound to each punctuation mark found in a text. Once all punctuation marks have been assigned a sound, the teacher may read aloud the first few sentences, modeling for students how to make the sounds for each punctuation mark as a part of the re-reading. After the teacher has modeled the process, students join in the re-reading of the text, making the sounds of each punctuation mark in the text. Children find this strategy highly engaging and will continue its use spontaneously on later occasions.

SHARED READING

Purpose

It has been known for many years that children can learn to read by having books read with them at bedtime or on a loved one's lap (Durkin, 1966; Holdaway, 1979; Taylor, 1983). The practice of *shared reading* in the classroom is intended to help teachers replicate all of the important characteristics of bedtime or lap reading (Holdaway, 1979, 1981) with an entire classroom of children. For teachers and children to share a book together, the print needs to be enlarged so that every child can see it and process it together under the guidance of the teacher (Barrett, 1982). Shared reading, or what is sometimes called the *shared book experience,* is used by teachers with very young readers to model aspects of the reading process for an entire group of children rather than an individual child. In the case of print concepts, the Shared Reading Experience is the perfect instructional context for teachers to guide children's eyes toward significant parts of print to clarify for them print-related concepts and academic metalanguage or language used to talk about language.

Materials

To use the shared book or shared reading experience, teachers must enlarge the text so that a text can be seen by an entire group of children in a classroom. As children advance in their reading acquisition, multiple copies of the same text can be used for shared reading as well.

Procedure

Begin a shared book experience by introducing the book. The book introduction is intended to heighten children's desire to read the story, and to help them draw on their own experiences and prior knowledge so to more fully enjoy and interpret the story. Once a book is selected for shared reading, begin by asking children to look at the book cover while you, the teacher, read the title aloud. Talk about the front and back of the book and point out certain features of the book, such as author and illustrator names, publisher, copyright date, and title page. Next, instruct the students to *"Look at the pictures."* Then ask the children, *"What do you think the words will tell you?"* This request typically opens up a discussion leading to students making personal connections and predictions. Next, read the book with "full dramatic punch, perhaps overdoing a little some of the best parts" (Barrett, 1982, p. 16).

During the first reading of the story, invite children to join in on any repeated or predictable phrases or words. At key points during the shared reading, you should pause to encourage children to predict what is coming next in the story.

After the first reading, invite children to share their responses to the story. Ask them to talk about their favorite parts, connect the story to their experiences, as well as discuss how well they were able to predict and participate. The shared reading book is re-read on subsequent days to study the language and print concepts contained in the book as a part of reading instruction.

LETTER MANIPULATIVES

Purpose

One purpose for using letter manipulatives is to help students grasp the concept of letter versus the concept of word or the concept that print rather than pictures carry the author's message. By using manipulative letters, students can discover not only that words are made up of smaller discrete elements called letters but they also learn about the L–R directionality of letters within words (Fountas & Pinnell, 1998). Of course, such letter manipulatives can also be used to learn letter names and letter sounds, and to learn to build and blend words later on. But for the purposes inherent in this chapter, using manipulative letters to match or copy words in a text allows students to discover the concept of letter as compared with the concept of word or the concept that print carries the message in a text.

Materials

To use this strategy, magnetic plastic letters are best for a variety of reasons. These letters are easy to pick up, move, and trace for even the youngest of children. To keep these letters together, many teachers have found that a metal cookie sheet is excellent for storage of magnetic letters. Words in pocket charts can also be cut into individual letters for manipulation as well and stored in small, personal letter-sized envelopes.

Procedure

Two activities useful for helping students grasp the concept of letters include matching letters to other letters in text or on word cards and sorting multiple sets of manipulative letters into alphabet letter categories. In the first activity, students are given a stack of word cards drawn from the shared reading texts of the class. They are to take a word card and place it in front of them. Next, they match the letters on the word card with plastic magnetic letters from the cookie sheet collection of letters by placing these letters on top of the letters on the word card. In the second activity, students are given a mixed collection of upper- and lowercase letters to sort into single letter categories underneath the alphabet letters displayed on an oak tag laminated alphabet on a table top. Students sort small "a" and capital "A" underneath the alphabet letters until all letters are sorted underneath their alphabet letter category.

ADDITIONAL STRATEGIES FOR ENGLISH LANGUAGE LEARNERS

CONTEXTUAL DIAGRAMS

Purpose

Pictures and diagrams, in which objects in the scene are labeled, are of great help to students learning a second or new language. The purpose of labeled pictures and diagrams is to allow students to experience the new language usage in settings other than the school classroom. Associating words and pictures together not only adds to ESL or LEP students' oral language, but also serves to help them learn new English words and concepts while learning about words, letters, and print concepts in the new language. Diagrams of the kitchen, bedroom, or bathroom at home can help students begin to learn and associate second-language terms with familiar or even somewhat unfamiliar objects in another setting. Other labeled pictures and diagrams of stores, libraries, mechanic shops, or hospitals can move students' potential for language learning well beyond the physical and social confines of the classroom.

Materials

Enlarged diagrams or photographs of culturally or socially accepted settings such as restaurants, hospitals, stores, homes, or churches are needed to create labeled pictures and diagrams. Objects and actions in each of these may need to be labeled in both the first and second languages. In Figure 6.8, a labeled diagram of a house is shown.

Procedure

Typically, a large piece of butcher paper or poster board can be used to make labeled pictures or diagrams. Teachers with some artistic talent can freehand draw these, although many teachers simply choose to use an enlarged photocopy of a picture or diagram. Label the objects portrayed as shown in Figure 6.8. Enlarged labeled pictures and diagrams can be displayed in the classroom on the walls. Labeled pictures and diagrams that are not poster sized can be stored in folders or binders as references for ESL and LEP students.

Figure 6.8   Labeled Picture for Language Learning

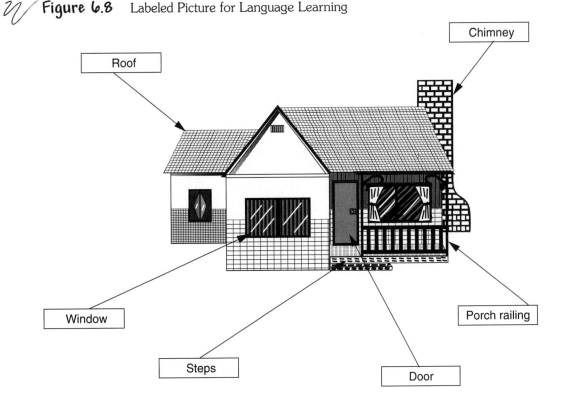

INCLUDING ALL STUDENTS

DRASTIC STRATEGY

Purpose

In 1980, Patricia Cunningham developed the "drastic strategy" to help students learn to focus carefully on printed words and letters. Although this strategy was intended to be used for teaching and learning function, glue words, or structure words, the strategy can be adapted for a close reading of print to develop struggling readers' attention to the print on the page.

Materials

Word cards, envelopes, markers, scissors, and classroom chalk or a dry erase board are needed to use the "drastic strategy" with struggling readers to develop awareness of the concepts of print.

Procedure

The "drastic strategy" uses a six-step process in which not all steps are necessary. There-fore, teachers should carefully observe the progress of children to determine at which step the strategy has produced the desired behaviors and understandings in the children. The six steps follow:

Step 1: Teacher Storytelling

Select a word, letter, or punctuation mark and enlarge it on a card for each child in the class or group. ⌐the⌐ Tell a story in which the displayed word, let-ter, or punctuation mark is used. Before you begin your story, tell the children that you and they are to hold up their cards each time they hear where the word, letter, or punctuation mark is used in your story. As you tell the story, be sure to pause briefly at the points where the word, letter, or punctuation mark is used to "emphasize" the concept of print element to which children should attend.

Step 2: Child Storytelling

Invite children to volunteer to tell a story in which the element displayed on the card is used. Again, use the same instructions for you and the other chil-dren relative to holding up the card each time the print element is used in the child's story. The teacher will need to be an active listener and model for the children during this step.

Step 3: Scramble, Sort, and Find

If the card contains a word, the teacher cuts the word into letters and scram-bles these letters on the students' table or desktop. The student's task is to un-scramble the letters to create the word three times. If the card contains a let-ter, the teacher passes out to the children an alphabet display of random letters, both uppercase and lowercase. The task for the children is to circle with a pencil each occurrence of the letter on the card in the random alpha-bet letter display. If the card contains a punctuation mark, the teacher hands out a piece of running text from a big book or chart text the children have been reading in shared reading. Students are instructed to find and circle all the instances of the punctuation mark on their card in the text distributed.

Step 4:   Take a Picture and Write It

Write the word, letter, or punctuation mark on the board. Ask children to pretend their eyes are the lens and shutter of a camera. They are to carefully look at the word, letter, or punctuation mark on the board and close their eyes to take a picture of it in their minds. After this, they should open their eyes to see if they had correctly imaged the item in their minds. This can be repeated three times if necessary. Then, the word, letter, or punctuation mark is erased and the children are to write the word, letter, or punctuation mark on a card at their seats. After all children have written on their cards, the teacher puts the word, letter, or punctuation mark back on the board for checking.

Step 5:   Fill in the Blank

Using a pocket chart, place several sentence strips on display containing a blank in the place of the word, letter, or punctuation mark under study. Select sentences from previously read text in a big book or other enlarged text from shared reading. As you read the sentence strips and come to the missing element, be it a word, letter, or punctuation mark, invite a child to come forward and write the missing element on a card or strip and place it in the sentence strip at the correct location.

Step 6:   New Text Close Reading

Using a new piece of enlarged text during shared reading, tell children to be on the lookout for the word, letter, or punctuation mark under study. When they detect the print element they have studied in the new text, they are to make a signal or sound that the group predetermines before engaging in the shared reading.

SELECTED REFERENCES

Barrett, F. L. (1982). *A teacher's guide to shared reading.* Richmond Hill, Ontario, Canada: Scholastic-TAB Publications.

Briggs, L. D., & Richardson, W. D. (1994). Children's knowledge of environmental print. *Reading Horizons, 33*(3), 225–235.

Burke, C. (1980). The reading interview: 1977. In B. P. Farr & D. J. Strickler (Eds.), *Reading comprehension: Resource guide.* Bloomington, IN: School of Education, Indiana University.

Clay, M. (1966). *Emergent reading behavior.* Unpublished doctoral dissertation, University of Auckland.

Clay, M. (1972). *Sand and Stones.* Exeter, NH: Heinemann Educational Books, Inc.

Clay, M. (1979). *Reading: The patterning of complex behaviour.* Exeter, NH: Heinemann Educational Books, Inc.

Clay, M. (1993). *An observation survey of early literacy achievement.* Portsmouth, NH: Heinemann.

Clay, M. (2000a). *New Shoes and Follow Me, Moon.* Portsmouth, NH: Heinemann.

Clay, M. (2000b). *Concepts about print: What have children learned about the way we print language.* Portsmouth, NH: Heinemann.

Cowley, J. (1990). *Mrs. Wishy-washy.* San Diego, CA: The Wright Group.

Cunningham, P. (1980). Teaching were, with, what, and other "four-letter" words. *The Reading Teaching, 34,* 160–163.

Day, K. C., & Day, H. D. (1979). Development of kindergarten children's understanding of concepts about print and oral language. In M. L. Damil & Moe, A. H. (Eds.), *Twenty-eighth yearbook of the National Reading Conference* (pp. 19–22). Clemson, SC: National Reading Conference.

Denny, T. P., & Weintraub, S. (1966). First graders' responses to three questions about reading. *Elementary School Journal, 66,* 441–448.

Downing, J. (1970). The development of linguistic concepts in children's thinking. *Research in the Teaching of English, 4,* 5–19.

Downing, J. (1971–72). Children developing concepts of spoken and written language. *Journal of Reading Behavior, 4,* 1–19.

Downing, J., & Oliver, P. (1973). The child's concept of a word. *Reading Research Quarterly, 9,* 568–582.

Durkin, D. (1966). *Children who read early: Two longitudinal studies.* New York: Teachers College Press.

Durkin, D. (1989). *Teaching them to read* (5th ed.). New York: Allyn & Bacon.

Ehri, L. C., & Sweet, J. (1991). Fingerpoint-reading of memorized text: What enables beginners to process the print? *Reading Research Quarterly, 26*(4), 442–462.

Fountas, I. C., & Pinnell, G. S. (1998). *Word matters: Teaching phonics and spelling in the reading/writing classroom.* Portsmouth, NH: Heinemann Educational Books.

Halliday, M. A. K. (1975). *Learning how to mean: Explorations in the development of language.* London: Edward Arnold.

Harste, J. C., Burke, C., & Woodward, V. A. (1981). *Children, their language and world: The pragmatics of written language use and learning.* NIE Final Report #NIE-G-80-0121. Bloomington, IN: Indiana University, Language Education Department.

Harste, J. C., & DeFord, D. (1982). Child language research and curriculum. *Language Arts, 59*(6), 590–600.

Hiebert, E. H., Pearson, P. D., Taylor, B., Richardson, V., & Paris, S. G. (1998). *Every child a reader.* Ann Arbor, MI: Center for the Improvement of Early Reading Achievement.

Holdaway, D. (1979). *The foundations of literacy.* New York: Ashton Scholastic.

Holdaway, D. (1981). Shared book experience: Teaching reading using favorite books. *Theory Into Practice, 21,* 293–300.

Johns, J. L. (1980). First graders' concepts about print. *Reading Research Quarterly, 15,* 529–549.

Johnston, P. H. (1992). *Constructive evaluation of literate activity.* New York: Longman Publishers.

Kuby, P., & Aldridge, J. (1997). Direct vs. indirect environmental print instruction and early reading ability in kindergarten children. *Reading Psychology, 18*(2), 91–104.

Lobel, A., & Lobel, A. (1981). *On Market Street.* New York: Scholastic, Inc.

Lomax, R. G., & McGee, L. M. (1987). Young children's concepts about print and reading: Toward a model of word reading acquisition. *Reading Research Quarterly, 22*(2), 237–256.

Martin, B. (1983). *Brown Bear, Brown Bear, what do you see?* Pictures by Eric Carle. New York: Henry Holt.

McGee, L. M., Lomax, R. G., & Head, M. H. (1988). Young children's written language knowledge: What environmental and functional print reading reveals. *Journal of Reading Behavior, 20*(2), 99–118.

McQueen, L. (1985). *The little red hen.* New York: Scholastic Books Inc.

Meltzer, N. S., & Himse, R. (1969). The boundaries of written words as seen by first graders. *Journal of Reading Behavior, 1,* 3–13.

Morris, D. (1993). The relationship between children's concept of word in text and phoneme awareness in learning to read: A longitudinal study. *Research in the Teaching of English, 27*(2), 133–154.

Morrow, L. M. (1993). *Literacy development in the early years: Helping children read and write,* (2nd ed.). Englewood Cliffs, NJ: Prentice Hall.

Neuman, S. B. (1999). *The importance of classroom libraries: Research monograph.* New York: Scholastic Inc.

Neuman, S. B., & Celano, D. (2001). Access to print in low-income and middle-income communities: An ecological study of four neighborhoods. *Reading Research Quarterly, 36*(1), 8–26.

Neuman, S. B., & Roskos, K. (1993). Access to print for children of poverty: Differential effects of adult mediation and literacy-enriched play settings on environmental and functional print tasks. *American Educational Research Journal, 30*(1), 95–122.

Orellana, M. F., & Hernandez, A. (1999). Talking the walk: Children reading urban environmental print. *Reading Teacher, 52*(6), 612–619.

Proudfoot, G. (1992). Pssst! There is literacy at the laundromat. *English Quarterly, 24*(1), 10–11.

Reid, J. (1966). Learning to think about reading. *Educational Research, 9,* 56–62.

Reutzel, D. R., Oda, L. K., & Moore, B. H. (1989). Developing print awareness: The effect of three instructional approaches on kindergartners; print awareness, reading readiness, and word reading. *Journal of Reading Behavior, 21*(3), 197–217.

Roberts, B. (1992). The evolution of the young child's concept of "word" as a unit of spoken and written language. *Reading Research Quarterly, 27*(2), 124–138.

Rozin, P., Bressman, B., & Taft, M. (1974). Do children understand the basic relationship between speech and writing? The mow-motorcycle test? *Journal of Reading Behavior, 6,* 327–334.

Schmidt, K. (1985). *The gingerbread man.* New York: Scholastic Books.

Smith, F. (1977). The uses of language. *Language Arts, 54*(6), 638–644.

Snow, C. E., Burns, M. S., & Griffin, P. (1998). *Preventing reading failure in young children.* Washington, D.C.: National Academy Press.

Taylor, D. (1983). *Family literacy: Young children learning to read and write.* Portsmouth, NH: Heinemann.

Taylor, N. E. (1986). Developing beginning literacy concepts: Content and context. In D. B. Yaden, Jr., & S. Templeton (Eds.), *Metalinguistic awareness and beginning literacy* (pp. 173–184). Portsmouth, NH: Heinemann Educational Books.

Vukelich, C. (1994). Effects of play interventions on young children's reading of environmental print. *Early Childhood Research Quarterly, 9*(2), 153–170.

West, L. S., & Egley, E. H. (1998). Children get more than a hamburger: Using labels and logos to enhance literacy. *Dimensions of Early Childhood, 26*(3–4), 43–46.

Wood, A., & Wood, D. (1984). *The napping house.* Illustrated by Don Wood. San Diego: Harcourt Brace Jovanovich.

Yaden, D. B., Jr. (1982). *A multivariate analysis of first graders' print awareness as related to reading achievement, intelligence, and gender.* Dissertation Abstracts International, 43, 1912A (University Microfilms No. 8225520).

Yaden, D. B., Jr., & Templeton S. (Eds.). (1986). *Reading Research in metalinguistic awareness: A classification of finding according to focus and methodology* (pp. 41–62). Portsmouth, NH: Heinemann Educational Books.

Chapter 7

Phonemic Awareness and Alphabetic Principle

Mr. Sinclair began his kindergarten class every day with a game. Today's game was a version of the game *Concentration*. There was a large poster sign on the board at the front of the room that read *Start It!* Two dozen picture cards were placed facing away from the children in a pocket chart hung beneath the sign. Excitedly the children gathered on the carpeted square at the front of the room to start the day. Mr. Sinclair explained that today's game was called *Start It* as he pointed to the sign above the pocket chart. He told the children that he would choose someone to start the game and each one would have a turn until all the cards were picked. Joshua was picked first. He was told that he could take two picture cards from the pocket chart. If the pictures on the cards began with the same sound, then he could keep the picture cards until the end of the game. Everyone was told to watch carefully and remember where each card was located. The game progressed until all 24 picture cards had been picked and matched by beginning sounds.

After the game, the children who had picture card pairs placed these on the wall underneath the alphabet letter representing the letter that started the words for their picture pair. Following this activity, Mr. Sinclair read the children a new book about the alphabet. Today he read the book *Animalia*. Following read-aloud time, the children sang different alphabet songs together with Mr. Sinclair. Today was a special day for Nigel. Why? Because Nigel had made an important discovery. At the end of the period, he raised his hand and anxiously waited to be called upon. In front of all the other children Nigel shared his new insight. "Mr. Sinclair," he blurted out, "I get it, I get it! The *albaphet* is just like the *ABCs!*"

BACKGROUND BRIEFING FOR TEACHERS

As young children learn to talk, they develop the ability to string basic speech sounds together into words. When they speak words, their goal is, of course, to make themselves understood to others. For students to use reading and writing skills, they must first develop phonological awareness (Adams, 2001; Goswami, 2000, 2001), the understanding that spoken language is composed of smaller units such as *phrases, words, syllables, onsets, rimes,* and *phonemes* (sounds). We know that children first become aware of individual words in spoken language. Following word awareness, children develop an awareness of the syllables within words. Next they become aware that syllables are made up of onsets (all the sounds in the syllable *before* the vowel) and rimes (the vowel and everything following it). Then children become aware of individual sounds, or *phonemes,* in spoken language. Finally, children develop the ability to manipulate individual sounds in language. From these findings, the teacher of reading realizes that children's awareness of spoken language progresses from the whole (ideas shared through speech) to the part (individual words, syllables, onsets and rimes, and then phonemes).

In recent years, a number of researchers and research reports have emphasized the importance of developing phonemic awareness among beginning readers (Adams, 1990, 2001; Adams, Foorman, Lundberg, & Beeler, 1998; Bear, Invernizzi, Templeton, & Johnston, 2000; Blevins, 1997; Byrne & Fielding-Barnsley, 1989, 1993; Castle, Riach, & Nicholson, 1994; Chall, 1996; Cunningham, 1990, 2000; Ericson & Juliebo, 1998; Fox, 2000; Goswami, 2000, 2001; Goswami & Bryant, 1990; Mason, 1980; Moustafa, 1997; National Reading Panel, 2000; Richgels, Poremba, & McGee, 1996; Snow et al., 1998; Stahl & Murray, 1994; Strickland, 1998; Wilde, 1997). It is estimated that roughly 20% of young children lack phonemic awareness (Blevins, 1997). Phonemic awareness is defined both *conceptually* and in terms of *performance.* Phonemic awareness, *conceptually,* is defined as an understanding that spoken language and words are made up of individual sounds. In terms of *performance,* phonemic awareness is defined as the ability to pick out and manipulate sounds in spoken words and language. So, when speaking of phonemic awareness, simple *awareness* is not enough! Children also must be able to perform specified tasks—they must be able to *manipulate* spoken sounds.

Learning that sounds in language and words are represented by symbols or letters **(graphemes)** is another milestone achievement among beginning readers (Adams, 2001). Once children are aware of sounds in language and the symbols used to represent spoken language, they become aware that there are systematic relationships between speech sounds and words in print known as the **alphabetic principle** (Adams, 1990; Anderson et al., 1985; Harris & Hodges, 1995). As children learn the logic of the alphabetic system, they are ready to receive and benefit from phonics instruction (Adams, 2001; Juel, 1991). The ability to perform phonemic awareness tasks develops from least difficult to more difficult tasks as listed below:

1. Rhyming
2. Hearing sounds in words (oddity and same-different judgment tasks)
3. Counting syllables and sounds
4. Isolating beginning, ending, and middle sounds in words
5. Substituting and deleting sounds in words and syllables
6. Blending syllables, onset and rimes, and sounds into words
7. Segmenting words into syllables, onset and rimes, and sounds
8. Representing sounds in language and words with symbols in spelling and writing

In this chapter, we first suggest ideas for teachers to use in assessing young children's phonemic awareness and the alphabetic principle. Next, we help you to connect your assessment findings (student needs) to appropriate teaching strategies. Finally, we provide you with details of a number of classroom-proven teaching strategies that assist beginning readers in acquiring phonemic awareness and an understanding of the alphabetic system.

ASSESSING STUDENTS' UNDERSTANDING OF PHONEMIC AWARENESS AND THE ALPHABETIC PRINCIPLE

Developing phonemic awareness is very often accompanied by learning the *concepts about print* covered in detail in chapter 6. Because of the way in which phonological and phonemic awareness develop, we present assessment tools in three categories in this chapter: 1) *Assessing Phonemic Awareness,* 2) *Assessing Letter Knowledge,* and 3) *Assessing Knowledge of the Alphabetic System.* In terms of the phonemic awareness assessment category, we begin by presenting assessment tools that follow the levels and types of assessments previously described: rhyming, "oddity tasks," same-different, counting, blending, and segmenting tasks. In the second category of assessment, letter knowledge, we present two assessment tools, letter recognition and a letter production task. In the final category, understanding the alphabetic principle, we present the alphabet awareness task and a dictation task.

ASSESSMENT CATEGORY 1: ASSESSING PHONEMIC AWARENESS

RECOGNIZING RHYMING WORDS: DO THESE RHYME?

Purpose

Students are asked to recognize whether or not pairs of words rhyme to assess levels of basic phonemic awareness. According to Adams (1990, 2001) and Adams, Foorman, Lundberg, and Beeler (1998), the ability to determine rhyme is the easiest of all phonemic awareness tasks.

Materials

Use a list of 20 word pairs. At least 50% of the word pairs should rhyme.

Procedure

Model the concept of rhyming by giving several examples and nonexamples. Explain that rhyming words end with the same sound(s). Then, using the word pairs shown in Figure 7.1, read aloud each pair of words asking the child if they rhyme. Note his response to each pair. According to Yopp (1988), kindergarten children usually achieve a mean score of 75% correct, or 15 out of the 20 target word pairs identified correctly. If students score poorly on this task, teachers should provide contextual reading and writing experiences to hear sounds in words with a particular emphasis upon rhyming texts.

ODDITY TASK: WHICH ONE DOESN'T BELONG?

Purpose

Bradley and Bryant (1983) designed the oddity task to measure children's development of onset and rime awareness versus phoneme awareness. Oddity tasks require that students spot the "odd word out" of a list of spoken words. Typically, children listen to (or say from pictures) a group of spoken words and then select the word that has a different sound from the others. Oddity tasks can focus on rhyming words, beginning, ending, and middle sounds in words.

Figure 7.1   Rhyming Word Pair Task List

plate	dog
fat	cat
book	hook
desk	shelf
fish	swish
shoe	ball
tree	grass
flower	power
key	lock
pen	tape
swing	thing
sat	rat
box	clock
bark	smart
berry	hairy
cow	milk
brick	thick
malt	halt
wall	call
toy	love

Materials

Use a list of 10 word sets of three words each or a collection of 10 picture sets of three pictures each. The word set in Figure 7.2 demonstrates a beginning consonant oddity task. Children pick the "odd word out" from the list or picture collections with at least 70% accuracy.

Procedure

Seat the child across from you at a table. Place the list in your lap so that you can see the words. Using a puppet, demonstrate how the puppet listens and picks out the odd word. For example say, "Kermit the Frog is going to listen to three words I will say or will look at three pictures I put on the table." Next, say the three words—pan, pig, and kite. Then let the puppet figure, in this case Kermit the Frog, select which of the three words is the odd word out. Demonstrate this again with the words coat, bus, and ball, if necessary.

Have a puppet figure pronounce the words in Figure 7.2 very slowly and clearly. Ask the child to tell the puppet which word is the odd word out. Make a record of how well the child does directly on a copy of the word list. This word list task can be modified to include oddity tasks related to rhyming words, ending, and middle sounds as well.

SAME-DIFFERENT WORD PAIR TASK

Purpose

Treiman and Zukowski (1991) designed the same-different task to measure children's development of syllable, onset and rime, and phoneme awareness. Same-different tasks require that students say whether a pair of words or a pair of pictures share the same beginning, ending, or middle syllable or sounds. Typically, children listen to (or say from pictures) a pair of spoken words and then say if the word pair is the same or different.

Figure 7.2   Beginning Consonant Oddity Task List

Soap	Six	Dog
Car	Man	Mop
Duck	Dog	Five
Pig	Pack	Fan
Fish	Fan	Leaf
Nest	Nut	Wheel
Cat	Cake	Nine
Sun	Tree	Tie
Clock	Bee	Bat
Sock	Feet	Fish

Same-different tasks can focus on rhyming words, beginning, ending, and middle syllables, and sounds in words.

Materials

A list of 10 word pairs or a collection of 10 picture pairs is needed for the same-different task. The word set found in Figure 7.3 demonstrates a beginning syllable same-different task. Children should be able to respond if the word or picture pairs have the same syllable or sound with at least 50% accuracy.

Procedure

Seat the child across from you at a table. Place the list in your lap so that you can see the words. Using a puppet, demonstrate how the puppet listens and says whether the word pair is the same or different. For example say, "Peter the Bunny is going to listen to two words I will say or will look at two pictures I put on the table." Next, say the word pair—partly and partition. Then let the puppet figure, in this case Peter the Bunny, say whether the two words are the same or different. Demonstrate this again with the words, dandy and dislike, if necessary.

Have a puppet figure pronounce the words in Figure 7.3 very slowly and clearly. Ask the child to tell the puppet if the word pairs are the same or different. Make a record of how well the child does directly on a copy of the word list. This word list task can be modified to include same-different tasks related to ending and middle syllables and sounds as well.

Figure 7.3   Beginning Syllable Same-Different Task List

Hammer	Hammock
Little	Local
Window	Winner
Single	Sickle
Maple	Motor
Donkey	Dinky
Camera	Camshaft
Twinkle	Twinkie
Belly	Balloon
Fabric	Furnish

Figure 7.4   Picture Sound Counting Task

Syllable and Sound Counting Task

Purpose

The counting task is a variation of the tapping task developed by Liberman, Shankweiler, Fischer, and Carter (1974). The counting task is designed to measure children's development of syllable and phoneme awareness. Counting tasks require that students count the number of syllables or sounds in a word or shown in a picture. Typically, children listen to (or say from a picture) a word and then they count the number of syllables or sounds. Counting tasks can focus on beginning, ending, and middle syllables and sounds of words.

Materials

A list of 10 word pairs or a collection of 10 picture pairs is needed for the counting task. The picture set found in Figure 7.4 demonstrates a sound counting task. Children should be able to accurately count the number of sounds or syllables within the words or pictures with at least 50% accuracy.

Procedure

Seat the child next to you at a table. Place the pictures in Figure 7.4 on the tabletop so that you and the child can see the words. Demonstrate how to count the sounds in samples A and B. For example say, "I am looking at this picture (point)." Next, say the word aloud and count the sounds you hear with your fingers. Tell the child the number of sounds in sample A is four—f-r-o-g. Demonstrate this again with the picture in sample B if necessary.

Have the child look at picture number one in Figure 7.4 very carefully. Ask the child to say what the picture is and count the sounds with her fingers. Then ask her to tell you the number of sounds in the word. Make a record of how well the child does on a word list.

Figure 7.5   Word Lists for Blending

at	l-ap	l-o-ck
two	t-ip	s-t-e-m
in	m-an	b-ea-k
if	st-ate	h-i-de
be	b-ox	c-a-sh
as	sc-ab	m-i-c-e
sea	r-ug	sh-ee-t
now	m-ind	f-r-o-g
go	th-ink	j-u-m-p
sew	p-ig	t-ur-key

This counting can be modified to include pictures related to ending and middle syllables and sounds as well.

Auditory Sound Blending Task

Purpose

Students are asked to recognize words by blending the sounds in words that teachers stretch out into segmented units, i.e., m-an or sh-i-p (we call this "word rubber banding"). According to Griffith and Olson (1992), the ability to guess what the word is from its blended form demonstrates a slightly higher level of phonemic awareness than recognizing rhyming sounds.

Materials

Prepare a list of 30 words divided into three sets of 10 each (See example in Figure 7.5).

- The first 10 words should be two-phoneme words.
- The second set of 10 words should be three- to four-phoneme words that are divided before the vowel demonstrating the onset and rime, e.g., c (onset)-ap (rime).
- The third set of 10 words should be three- to four-phoneme words that are segmented completely, e.g., ch-i-p.

Procedure

Tell the child that you will be stretching words out like a rubber band, saying each sound. Model several of these stretched words for the child as well as telling him the word you have stretched. For example, stretch the word s-i-t. Then say the word—sit. Do this several times. Next, stretch a word and ask the child to tell you the word. Once this has been accomplished, tell the child you are going to play a game where you say a word stretched out and he or she is to answer the question—What am I saying? According to Yopp's (1988) research, kindergarten children achieve a mean score of 66% correct, or 20 out of the 30 target words identified correctly. If students score poorly on this task, teachers should provide reading and writing experiences that help children hear sounds in words. Creating invented spellings for writing new words and using word rubber banding to sound out new words found in trade books are just two examples.

Figure 7.6   Word List for Segmenting Sounds

d ime	*h* ome
hu*sh*	yar*d*
fi *v* e	k *i* ss
clo*ck*	g e t
cu *t*	raf*t*
f ool	*b* ike
l *oo* p	mu *g*
r ode	

Segmenting Sounds

Purpose

Students are asked to listen to and isolate sounds in the initial, medial, and final positions in a word. A child's ability to isolate sounds in words is an excellent indication of whether she can profit from decoding instruction.

Materials

Construct a list of 15 words consisting of three phonemes each. Target sounds in the beginning, middle, and end of the words such as those shown in Figure 7.6.

Procedure

Model how phonemes can be pronounced by showing how *sit* starts with /s/, *hike* has the /i/ sound in the middle, and *look* ends with the /k/ sound. Next, tell the child you are going to play a quick game together. You will say a word, then you will ask him to tell you the sound he hears in a specific place in the word, such as beginning, middle, or end. For example, you may say: "*Slam.* Say the sound at the end of the word *slam.*" The child responds correctly by articulating the sound /m/. Now, begin the list of words shown in Figure 7.6. Record each response.

   According to Yopp's (1988) research study, kindergarten children achieve a mean score of 9% correct, or one to two correct responses out of 15 target words. If students score poorly on this task, teachers should provide reading and writing experiences focusing on hearing sounds in specific locations within words.

Assessment Category II: Assessing Letter Knowledge

Letter Identification

Purpose

Similar to the activity described previously, this task, based on the work of Marie Clay (1993), determines whether readers with special learning needs can identify letters of the alphabet.

Materials

Reproduce the randomized alphabet letter display (shown in Figure 7.7) on a sheet of paper or chart paper for use in this exercise.

Figure 7.7 Alphabet Letter Display

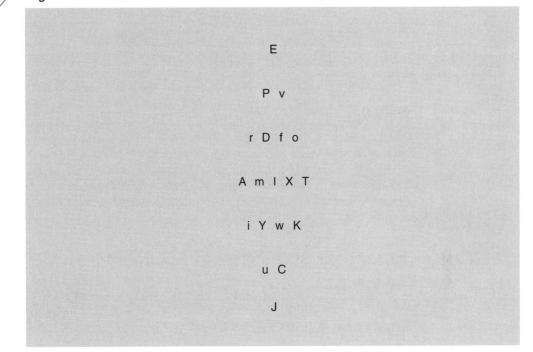

Procedure

Invite the student to be seated next to you and explain that you would like to find out which letters of the alphabet she can name as you point to them on a chart. Begin pointing at the top of the alphabet letter display, working line by line and left to right to the bottom of the display, keeping letters below your line of focus covered. Using a photocopy of the display, mark which of the letters were correctly named. Next, ask the child to point to the letter you named in the display. Record this information. Most children, even readers with special learning needs, will be able to identify at least 50% of the letters requested. However, students who have little familiarity with letters may perform poorly.

LETTER PRODUCTION TASK

Purpose

This task is designed to determine whether or not students know and can write letters of the alphabet. Unlike simple letter identification, this task requires that students be able to produce letters from memory. Letter knowledge is an indication of how well students have sorted out sound/symbol processes, but is not logically necessary for successful reading. It does, however, make learning to read easier (Venezky, 1975). Letter naming/production can be likened to a bridge that helps children cross the river of early reading and writing.

Materials

Create a list of 10 letters drawn randomly from the alphabet. Be sure to include at least three vowel letters in the selection, as shown in Figure 7.8.

Figure 7.8   Random Letter Production Task

1. b	2. m	3. e	4. f	5. t
6. i	7. p	8. o	9. s	10. h

Provide the child with a pencil and a blank piece of paper.

Procedure

Ask the student if she knows any letters. Next, ask her to write down any letters she may know and name them. Following this exercise, invite her to write the letters you name from the random letter list you created. Most students in grade 1 will score at least 70% on this task. However, students who have little familiarity with letters may perform poorly. This should be interpreted as a need to engage in strategies and activities outlined later in this chapter.

ASSESSMENT CATEGORY III: ASSESSING ALPHABETIC PRINCIPLE KNOWLEDGE

ALPHABET AWARENESS TASK

Purpose

The purpose of this task is to determine whether or not children can in some way identify the concept of an alphabet in written and spoken language. Walsh, Price, and Gillingham (1988) found that letter naming was strongly related to early reading achievement for kindergarten children. Simple awareness that an alphabet exists is necessary for understanding any alphabetic language system.

Materials

One copy of the alphabet awareness task form shown in Figure 7.9.

Procedure

Begin this task by seating the child next to you. Ask each question on the Alphabetic Awareness Task form. On question 3, if another alphabet display is available in the immediate area (such as those typically displayed over chalkboards), point to this display and ask the same question. Results of this task should give teachers a sense of alphabetic awareness. Teachers should view these results as a means to inform and direct their selection of alphabetic and phonemic awareness activities discussed later in this chapter.

DICTATION

Purpose

Students are asked to listen to several words stretched out or "rubber banded." Next, students are asked to rubber band the word(s) as the teacher dictates them and write the sounds heard in each word. Calkins (1986) related how word rubber banding was used in her Teacher's College Writing Project to help children learn how to listen for sounds.

Figure 7.9   Alphabet Awareness Task

1. Have you ever heard of the alphabet or abc's? Yes _____   No _____

2. Can you tell me what this is? Answer _____
   A B C D E F G H I J K L M N O P Q R S T U V W X Y Z

3. Can you tell me any alphabet letters you know?

4. Do you know any songs, poems, books, or rhymes about the alphabet?
   Yes _____   No _____
   Give me an example:

5. Can you tell me the order of the alphabet letters beginning with the letter A?
   Yes _____   No _____

   Answer _____

Carnine, Silbert, and Kameenui (1990) referred to a similar approach for stretching words called *auditory telescoping*. Yopp (1992) indicated that the ability to speak the phonemes within a word is a very difficult level of phonemic awareness to achieve. The ability to both speak and write phonemes in words indicates an advanced level of phonemic awareness that can be used effectively in reading and writing instruction.

Materials

Compile a list of 22 words of two or three phonemes each in length. Be sure to include a variety of words with varying consonant and vowel patterns (i.e., some that begin with consonants, others that begin with vowel sounds).

An example list is shown below in Figure 7.10.

Procedure

Demonstrate how several words can be stretched or rubber banded into sounds—both orally and in writing. Invite the child to rubber band and write the words in your list as you did. This task assesses whether or not children have developed an ability to hear and "map" sounds through writing using invented spellings. Yopp (1988) found the response rate for kindergartners to this task was 12 out of 22 or about 55% correct. Griffith and Olson (1992) indicated that the word rubber-banding task has been shown to be a highly reliable, authentic measure of phonemic awareness and a good indication as to whether a child is ready for decoding instruction.

Figure 7.10   Dictation Word List

page	me	my	now
live	can	this	but
big	get	have	come
sat	on	some	tile
men	at	back	
no	did	say	

Intervention Strategy Guide for Phonemic Awareness and Alphabetic Principle

Intervention Strategy → / Student Problem(s) ↓	Playing with Rhymes and Alliteration	Grab the Odd One Out	Picture Box Counting	Add/Take a Sound	Sing It Out	Word Rubber Banding	Environmental Print	Playing With the Alphabet/Books	Song Chant, and Poetry	The Sounds Rhythm Band
Rhyming	+	*	–	–	*	–	*	*	+	–
Oddity/Same-Different	*	+	–	*	*	–	*	–	*	*
Counting or Tapping	–	–	+	–	–	*	–	*	*	+
Blending	–	–	–	*	+	*	*	–	*	*
Segmenting	–	–	–	*	–	+	*	–	*	*
Letter Knowledge or Production	–	–	–	–	–	–	+	+	–	–
Awareness of Alphabet	*	*	–	*	–	*	*	+	*	–
Dictation	*	*	–	*	–	*	*	–	–	*

Key: + excellent strategy
* adaptable strategy
– unsuitable strategy

CONNECTING ASSESSMENT FINDINGS TO TEACHING STRATEGIES

Before discussing phonemic awareness/alphabetic principle intervention strategies, we have constructed a guide connecting assessment to intervention and/or strategy choices. It is our intention to help you, the teacher, select the most appropriate instructional interventions and strategies to meet your students' needs based on assessment data.

In the next part of this chapter, we offer phonemic awareness/alphabetic principle strategies for intervention based on the foregoing assessments.

DEVELOPING PHONEMIC AWARENESS AND THE ALPHABETIC PRINCIPLE

Several effective strategies for helping readers with special learning needs in the areas of simple alphabet knowledge, the alphabetic principle, and phonemic awareness are described in the following sections.

INTERVENTION CATEGORY I: STRATEGIES FOR TEACHING PHONEMIC AWARENESS

PLAYING WITH RHYMES AND ALLITERATION

Purpose

As teachers get to know their students' phonemic and alphabet needs, they often search for opportunities to teach these concepts in books, songs, or poems. When the teacher consciously searches for and locates books, songs, poems, or other print opportunities to teach language concepts like rhyming and alliteration, this act is called *language watching* (Reutzel, 1992). Books, songs, and poems typically contain many examples of rhyming and alliterative words that may be used to teach the concepts of rhyming and alliteration.

Materials

Texts, stories, or poems may be used to highlight rhyming and alliterative sounds in words.

Procedure

Option 1. Select a poem, for instance *Sister for Sale* (Silverstein, 1976), for a shared reading experience. After reading, analyze this poem—**S**ister for **S**ale. It provides an excellent opportunity to demonstrate the alliterative beginning sound associated with the letter /s/.

Option 2. Select a poem or song. For example, the song *Do Your Ears Hang Low*. After singing, analyze this song for pairs of rhyming words. Then, invite the children to think of other words that rhyme with pairs of rhyming words found in the song. Make a "Rhyming Word Wall" from the songs, poems, and stories read in the classroom during shared reading or singing experiences.

GRAB THE ODD ONE OUT

Purpose

The purpose of the *Grab the Odd One Out* game is to help children develop phonemic awareness through a playful "oddity task" activity. The ability to discriminate which spoken word does not fit among three choices relates to the oddity task described in the assessment section of this chapter. This game may focus children's attention on beginning, ending, or middle sounds in words. Once a list of beginning syllable words is created, then a list of ending sounds and medial sound should be created for this game as well.

Materials

- One paper sack
- A list of 10 sets of three words (hen, hammer, and pencil)
- Objects for the "odd word out"

Procedure

This game is played by seating a group of children on the floor or table comfortably. Begin by saying that you have a "Grab Bag" filled with objects while showing children the bag. Next, tell the children you will be saying three words and that they are to listen carefully for the word that does not fit. If they know the word, they are to raise their hand but not to call it out. A child is selected to reach into the "Grab Bag" without looking and feel around to find the object. When he finds it, he can say the word and show the object to the group. This process continues until all the objects in the "Grab Bag" have been used. When an object has been used, it is to be returned to the "Grab Bag" for use with the next set of words.

PICTURE BOX SOUND COUNTING

Purpose

Learning to hear sounds in words requires that students hear syllables and sounds (phonemes). Students need to develop the ability to hear syllables and sounds in words in proper sequence. Counting the number of syllables and sounds in words helps children attend more carefully to the sounds and syllables in words (Yopp & Troyer, 1992). A version of this activity (Elkonin, 1963) has been used successfully for a number of years in intervention programs such as Reading Recovery.

Materials

Prepare 5–10 cards with pictures as shown in Figure 7.11 using words already familiar to the student.

Procedure

This activity uses a word card with a picture, such as the one shown in Figure 7.11 for the word CAT. The teacher begins by pronouncing the word very slowly while placing a chip into a box below for each letter/sound heard—progressing sound by sound (CCCCC—AAAAAAA—TTTTT). After an initial demonstration, the child is encouraged to join in the activity by saying the next word for the picture on the card while the teacher places a chip into a box below each letter/sound.

Figure 7.11   Elkonin Box for Sound Counting in Words

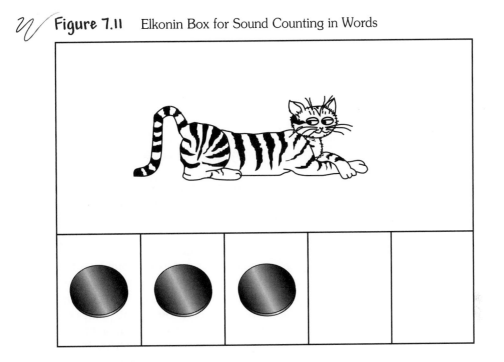

The teacher gradually releases responsibility to the child by exchanging roles. For example, the teacher can pronounce the word and the child can place chips into the boxes below each letter/sound. Finally, the child both says the word and places a chip into a box below each letter/sound entirely on his own. Eventually, children should be able to count the number of sounds in a word and be able to answer questions about the order of sounds in words (Griffith & Olson, 1992).

ADD A SOUND/TAKE A SOUND

Purpose

Adding or substituting sounds in words in familiar songs, stories, or rhymes may help special-needs and younger readers attend to the sounds in their speech. The ability to add or substitute sounds in words in familiar language is easier than segmenting sounds and benefits students in many of the same ways.

Materials

Any song, rhyme, chant, or song will be useful.

Procedure

Two strategies add enjoyment to developing awareness of phonemes and the alphabetic principle. The first of these is *consonant substitution*. When using this strategy, initial, final, or medial consonants in words found in a phrase or sentence can be exchanged. For example in the Shel Silverstein poem *Jimmie Jet and His TV Set,* change the consonants from /j/ to /n/ or /b/ to produce:

> *Nimmie Net and His TV Set*
> *Bimmie Bet and His TV Set*

Another approach is to delete the sound /j/ as follows:

> *Jimmie Jet and His TV Set*
> *immie et and His TV Set*

Young children find the nonsensical result to be both humorous and helpful in understanding how consonants work in connected text. Other consonants may be exchanged in the future to vary the number of consonants exchanged and the position of the consonants in the words.

A second strategy is *vowel substitution.* When using a vowel substitution strategy, a single vowel (and sound) is selected and substituted in key words in the text. For example, in the poem *Mary Had a Little Lamb,* the vowel sounds can be changed to produce a completely nonsensical version with *Miry hid a little limb* by substituting the /i/ short vowel sound in place of the vowels in the original poem.

Children find that adding, changing, or substituting sounds in this way turns learning about letters and sounds into a game. One first-grade, chapter 1 student who had been working with his teacher late one afternoon using these strategies remarked on his way out the door to catch his bus, "Teacher, can we play some more games tomorrow?" This statement sums up the enthusiasm these two strategies generate among young children as they learn to focus their attention on phonemic awareness.

SING IT OUT

Purpose

The purpose of *sounding it out* when one reads is to blend spoken sounds together to form words. Blending is a critical skill for learning to read successfully. Hearing individual sounds and then putting these together quickly to hear a word that is already known orally is an instructional command often used by teachers when they say, "Sound it out!" Listening to spoken sounds and saying these sounds quickly to blend them together into words is what most teachers mean when they say to sound it out.

Materials

Use one copy of the song *When You're Happy and You Know It.*

Procedure

Teacher modeling is needed in the beginning to help children understand the process. Sing the song *When You're Happy and You Know It* several times so that children learn the song and the words. Change the words at the end of the song from "clap your hands" to "say this word." Then give letters of a word in your mind you want the children to blend together. For example, the sounds b/rrr/d are spoken slowly for the children. When you clap, they are to say the word—bird! The song can go on for as long as you wish, engaging children in auditory blending of the spoken sounds you offer to make words. By singing and saying words phoneme by phoneme, students blend these sounds together to discover words.

WORD RUBBER BANDING

Purpose

Segmenting refers to isolating individual sounds in a spoken word. Segmenting can be one of the more difficult phonemic awareness tasks for students. It is, however, an important skill for children to develop if they are to profit from implicit or indirect instruction related to letter names, sounds, and the connections between the two. Segmenting sounds in words can be done by rubber banding or stretching a word into its sounds like a rubber band as described below.

Materials

Any song, poem, rhyme, chant, or story may be used.

Procedure

Begin by singing a favorite song such as *Old MacDonald Had a Farm*. Next, ask the children to repeat the first sounds of selected words as follows: "Old m-m-m-MacDonald had a f-f-f-farm, e i e i o, and on this f-f-f-farm he had a c-c-c-cow, e i e i o. With a m-m-m-moo here and a m-m-m-moo there, here a moo there a moo everywhere a moo moo. . . ." Children's names can be used in this fashion, such as J-J-J-JASON, or K-K-K-KATE. Still another variation involves drawing a sound out or exaggerating the sound, for example, MMMMMaaaaarrrrryyyy had a little llllllllaaaaammmmm. Beyond this iterative technique, children can be asked to segment entire words. Yopp (1992) recommended a song set to the tune of *Twinkle, Twinkle Little Star* for this purpose.

> Listen, listen
> To my word
> Tell me all the sounds you heard: *race (pronounce this word slowly)*
> /r/ is one sound
> /a/ is two
> /s/ is last in race
> It's true.

When working with the segmentation of entire words, it is best to use words of no more than three to four sounds because of the difficulty of these tasks for younger or special-needs learners. Children seem to enjoy these tasks and with careful guidance can enjoy high levels of success as they develop phonemic awareness through segmentation tasks.

INTERVENTION CATEGORY II: STRATEGY FOR LEARNING ABOUT LETTERS

USING ENVIRONMENTAL PRINT

Purpose

The purpose of this strategy is to use familiar examples of writing from the students' environment (such as cereal boxes, signs, bumper stickers, and candy wrappers) to help them begin to understand how sounds and letters go together (the alphabetic principle). Hiebert and Ham (1981) found in their research that children who were taught using environmental print learned significantly more letter names and sounds than did children who learned alphabet letters without using environmental print. Familiar print in the environment can be used in interesting ways to give children confidence in reading and writing and to help them understand how print works.

Figure 7.12   Environmental Print Chart

Alphabet Wall		Aa	Bb Butterfinger	Cc Coca-Cola	Dd	Ee
Ff	Gg	Hh	Ii	Jj	Kk	Ll
Mm	Nn	Oo	Pp	Qq	Rr	Ss
Tt	Uu	Vv	Ww	Xx	Yy	Zz

Materials

The only materials needed for this strategy are collectibles from home and school. Can labels, empty cereal boxes, bumper stickers, advertisements from the local papers, and other old boxes or containers are usually available in large quantities.

Procedure

Begin by setting aside a classroom display area, bulletin board, or wall that is designated as an *Environmental Print* wall. Children may be asked to bring environmental print or product logos from home to put on this display wall in random order. Next, environmental print can be taken down and rearranged in an alphabet display with 26 blocks or areas reserved for each alphabet letter as shown in Figure 7.12. For example, specific print items such as *Butterfinger, Baby Ruth,* and *Batman* can be placed in a block for the letter "B".

In some cases, children can be asked to bring environmental print to school for a specific letter name or sound. After discussing and displaying letter-specific environmental print, teachers and children can cut and paste environmental print items onto 5″ × 7″ plain index cards. These letter environmental print collections are often bound together to be read in small groups or by individuals in an alphabet and letter play center.

Selected letters can be taught from known environmental print items such as "C" in Figure 7.13. Environmental print logos can be collected and bound together to represent the selected letter, such as *S*nicker, *S*prite, *S*ugar, and so on. Other possibilities for using environmental print to produce letter knowledge include cutting up environmental print to make new words, or making letter collages for an art activity.

Figure 7.13   Environmental Print Ring

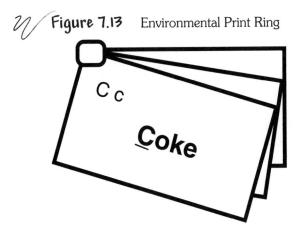

INTERVENTION CATEGORY III: TEACHING THE ALPHABETIC SYSTEM

PLAYING WITH THE ALPHABET

Purpose

Morrow (2001) suggested that children can learn the alphabetic principle by enjoying playful activities centering on letter naming, letter sounds, and the connection between letter names and sounds. Providing relaxed and game-like learning opportunities can often spark the desire to learn the letters and sounds.

Materials

Alphabet puzzles, magnetic letters, sand paper letters, alphabet games, letter stencils, letter flashcards, alphabet charts, dry-erase boards, clay trays, paper, pencils, markers, painting easels, alphabet logos, cereals and foods, and commercially published alphabet books all may be used in constructing alphabet play games.

Procedure

An alphabet station or center stocked with alphabet puzzles, magnetic letters, sand paper letters, alphabet games, stencils, flashcards, and alphabet charts can be a part of every kindergarten or first-grade classroom station or learning center. Children are invited to write, trace, or copy alphabet letters. Individual-sized chalkboards, dry-erase boards, clay trays, tracing paper, and painting easels naturally draw children into copying, tracing, and experimenting with letters.

Delicious possibilities can be periodically added to this rich alphabet activity menu. Samples of alphabet soup, animal crackers, and *Alphabits* cereal may be provided. Children may be encouraged to sort the letters or animals into alphabet letter categories prior to eating. Children can be encouraged to eat in pairs or small groups and talk about which letter they are eating. This playful interaction increases children's awareness of letters, sounds, and alphabetical order. Other playful experiences may be used as well. To emphasize specific letter sounds found in the course of language watching, activities involving a sip of *Sprite,* a bite of a *Snickers* candy bar, a long spaghetti noodle to munch on, and a handful of *Skittles* to taste may be used successfully to emphasize /s/. Art experiences can be designed where children create pictures using an *S* as the beginning point. Collages of things that begin with /s/, such as a sack, screw, safety pin, salt, silver, or sand can be created and displayed.

Environmental print logos can be used to make *I Can Read Alphabet* pattern books. These books are often patterned after well-known alphabet books such as *The Z Was Zapped* (Van Allsburg, 1987) and *On Market Street* (Lobel, 1981). Children select a product label to represent the /c/ sound from a group of alphabetized logos such as Coca Cola®, Cocoa Puffs®, Captain Crunch®, and so on. Other alphabetized product labels are selected to represent the remaining letters of the alphabet in child-produced *I Can Read Alphabet* pattern books. Because children select product logos they can already read, every child easily reads these pattern books. They become a source of confidence building and enjoyment.

READING PUBLISHED ALPHABET BOOKS

Purpose

The purpose of using alphabet books is to assist young and special-needs readers to discover the order and elements of the alphabet, both names and sounds. To do this, teachers may wish to acquire collections of quality alphabet trade books. *On Market Street* (Lobel, 1981), *Animalia* (Base, 1986), and *The Z Was Zapped* (Van Allsburg, 1987) are just a few of the many delightful books that can be used to teach children the alphabet.

Materials

Use commercially published alphabet books.

Procedure

After multiple readings of commercially produced alphabet books, teachers and children can construct their own highly predictable *alphabet books* using the commercial books as patterns. In an established writing center, young students can create both *reproductions* and *innovations* of commercial alphabet books shared in class. A *reproduction* is a student-made copy of an original commercially produced alphabet book. Children copy the text of each page exactly and draw their own illustrations for a reproduction. *Innovations* borrow the basic pattern of commercially produced alphabet books, but change the selected words. For instance, one group of first-grade students made innovations on the book *The Z Was Zapped* (Van Allsburg, 1987). Each child chose a letter and made a new illustration as an innovation. One child, Kevin, picked the letter *D* and drew a picture of the letter *D* in the shape of a doughnut being dunked into a cup of hot chocolate. The caption underneath the picture read—THE "D" WAS DUNKED. Reproductions and innovations of alphabet books help students take ownership of familiar text and encourage them to learn about the alphabetic principle through experimentation. Reproductions and innovations of alphabet books also help children sense that they can learn to read successfully.

ADDITIONAL STRATEGIES FOR ENGLISH LANGUAGE LEARNERS

SONG, CHANT, AND POETRY

Purpose

The purpose of using songs, chants, and poetry is to explore and discover how letter sounds combine to create words, word parts, and, when combined, written and oral language. Weaver (1988, 1990) suggested that many teachers use songs, poetry, raps, and chants to convey the alphabetic principle as an alternative to the more tedious direct teaching and drill of phonic generalizations and letter sounds.

Materials

Use suggested songs, chants, and poems organized by alphabet letter themes.

Procedure

When using poetry, songs, and chants, teachers can watch for specific letters that are repeated in texts to be used as examples for learning the alphabetic principle and developing phonemic awareness. For example, to emphasize the letter /s/ for a day or so, teachers might select and enlarge onto chart paper the text of the chants *Sally Go Round the Sun* or *Squid Sauce* to be read aloud by the group. Songs such as *See Saw, Margery Draw* or *Sandy Land* may be selected and the lyrics enlarged onto charts for practice and group singing. Shel Silverstein's (1976) *Sister for Sale* or Jack Prelutsky's (1984) *Sneaky Sue* poems could be likewise enlarged and used to emphasize the name and sound of the letter "S" through repeated group readings.

THE SOUNDS RHYTHM BAND

Purpose

The tapping task developed by Liberman, Shankweiler, Fischer, and Carter (1974) is the basis for the *Sounds Rhythm Band* activity. Using this activity, children learn to hear sounds in words in sequence. This is a critical prerequisite for blending sounds together to make words in reading and for segmenting words into sounds for writing and spelling.

Materials

Prepare a list of 5–10 words containing two, three, and four sounds.

Procedure

This activity uses different rhythm band instruments to "tap out" the number of sounds in spoken words. Rhythm band instruments include sticks, bells, tambourines, metal triangles, and so on, that can be used to make a noise for each sound heard in a word. Begin by modeling a word very slowly while striking the rhythm band instrument for each letter/sound, progressing sound by sound (C—AAAAAAA—T). After an initial demonstration, the children are encouraged to join in the activity by saying the next word with the teacher while striking their instruments for each sound they hear.

The teacher gradually releases responsibility to the children by exchanging roles. For example, the teacher can pronounce the word and the children strike the number of sounds they hear on their instruments. Or conversely, the children say the word slowly and the teacher strikes the number of sounds she hears on her instrument. Finally, the children both say the word slowly and strike their instruments for each sound they hear in the word. We suggest this activity begin as a choral activity with all the children participating together and progress to a point where individual children are asked to "solo" the saying of a word and striking the sounds they hear in a word. Eventually, children should be able to count the number of sounds in a word and be able to answer questions about the order of sounds in words (Griffith & Olson, 1992).

SELECTED REFERENCES

Adams, M. J. (1990). *Beginning to read: Thinking and learning about print.* Cambridge, MA: MIT Press.

Adams, M. J. (2001). Alphabetic anxiety and explicit, systematic phonics instruction: A cognitive science perspective. In S. B. Neuman & D. K. Dickinson (Eds.), *Handbook of early literacy research.* New York: Guilford Press.

Adams, M. J., Foorman, B. R., Lundberg, I., & Beeler, T. (1998). *Phonemic awareness in young children: A classroom curriculum.* Baltimore, MD: Paul H. Brookes Publishing Co.

Anderson, R. C., Hiebert, E. F., Scott, J. A., & Wilkinson, I. A. G. (1985). *Becoming a nation of readers: The report of the commission on reading.* Washington, D. C.: The National Institute of Education.

Base, G. (1986). *Animalia.* New York: Harry N. Abrams.

Bear, D. R., Invernizzi, M., Templeton, S., & Johnston, F. (2000). *Words their way: Word study for phonics, vocabulary, and spelling instruction.* Upper Saddle River, NJ: Merrill/Prentice Hall.

Blevins, W. (1997). *Phonemic awareness activities for early reading success: Easy, playful activities that prepare children for phonics instruction.* New York: Scholastic Inc.

Bradley, L., & Bryant, P. E. (1983). Categorising sounds and learning to read: A causal connection. *Nature, 310,* 419–421.

Byrne, B., & Fielding-Barnsley, R. (1989). Phonemic awareness and letter knowledge in the child's acquisition of the alphabetic principle. *Journal of Educational Psychology, 81,* 313–321.

Byrne, B., & Fielding-Barnsley, R. (1993). Evaluation of a program to teach phonemic awareness to young children: A 1-year follow-up. *Journal of Educational Psychology, 85*(1), 104–111.

Calkins, L. (1986). *The art of teaching writing.* Portsmouth, NH: Heinemann Educational Books.

Carnine, D., Silbert, J., & Kameenui, E. (1990). *Direct instruction reading* (2nd ed.). Columbus, OH: Merrill.

Castle, J. M., Riach, J., & Nicholson, T. (1994). Getting off to a better start in reading and spelling: The effects of phonemic awareness instruction within a whole language program. *Journal of Educational Psychology, 86*(3), 350–359.

Chall, J. S. (1996). *Stages of reading development.* Fort Worth, TX: Harcourt Brace.

Clay, M. M. (1993). *An observation survey of early literacy acheivement.* Portsmouth, NH: Heinemann.

Cunningham, A. E. (1990). Explicit versus implicit instruction in phonemic awareness. *Journal of Experimental Child Psychology, 50,* 429–444.

Cunningham, P. M (2000). *Phonics they use: Words for reading and writing.* New York: Longman.

Elkonin, D. B. (1963). The psychology of mastering the elements of reading. In B. Simon & J. Simon (Eds.), *Educational psychology in the U.S.S.R* (pp. 165–179). London: Routledge & Kegan Paul.

Ericson, L., & Juliebo, M. F. (1998). *The phonological awareness handbook for kindergarten and primary teachers.* Newark, DE: International Reading Association.

Fox, B. J. (2000). *Word identification strategies: Phonics from a new perspective* (2nd ed.). Upper Saddle River, NJ: Merrill/Prentice Hall.

Goswami, U. (2000). Phonological and lexical processes. In M. L. Kamil, P. B. Mosenthal, P. D. Pearson, & R. Barr (Eds.), *Handbook of reading research,* vol. 3, Mahwah, NJ: Lawrence Erlbaum Associates.

Goswami, U. (2001). Early phonological development and the acquisition of literacy. In S. B. Neuman & D. K. Dickinson (Eds.), *Handbook of early literacy research.* New York: Guilford Press.

Goswami, U., & Bryant, P. (1990). *Phonological skills and learning to read.* East Sussex, UK: Lawrence Earlbaum Associates.

Griffith, P. L., & Olson, M. W. (1992). Phonemic awareness helps beginning readers break the code. *The Reading Teacher, 45,* 516–523.

Harris, T. L., & Hodges, R. E. (1995). *The literacy dictionary: The vocabulary of reading and writing.* Newark, DE: International Reading Association.

Hiebert, E., & Ham, D. (1981). *Young children and environmental print.* Paper presented at the annual meeting of the National Reading Conference, Dallas, TX.

Juel, C. (1991). Beginning reading. In R. Barr, M. Kamil, P. Mosenthal, & P. D. Pearson (Eds.), *Handbook of reading research,* vol. 2. New York: Longman.

Liberman, I. Y., Shankweiler, D., Fischer, F. W., & Carter, B. (1974). Explicit syllable and phoneme segmentation in the young child. *Journal of Experimental Child Psychology, 18,* 201–212.

Lobel, A. (1981). *On market street.* Pictures by Anita Lobel; Words by Arnold Lobel. New York: Scholastic.

Mason, J. M. (1980). When do children begin to read: An exploration of four-year-old children's letter and word reading competencies. *Reading Research Quarterly, 15,* 203–227.

Morrow, L. M. (2001). *Literacy development in the early years: Helping children read and write.* Needham Heights, MA: Allyn & Bacon.

Moustafa, M. (1997). *Beyond traditional phonics: Research discoveries and reading instruction.* Portsmouth, NH: Heinemann Educational Books.

National Reading Panel (NRP). (2000). *Report of the National Reading Panel: Teaching children to read.* Washington, D.C.: National Institute of Child Health and Human development.

Prelutsky, J. (1984). *The new kid on the block.* New York: Greenwillow Books.

Reutzel, D. R. (1992). Breaking the letter a week tradition: Conveying the alphabetic principle to young children. *Childhood Education, 69*(1), 20–24.

Richgels, D. J., Poremba, K. J., & McGee, L. M. (1996). Kindergarteners talk about print: Phonemic awareness in meaningful contexts. *The Reading Teacher, 49*(8), 632–642.

Silverstein, S. (1976). *A light in the attic.* New York: Harper & Row.

Snow, C. E., Burns, M. N., & Griffin, P. (1998). *Preventing reading difficulties in young children.* National Academy Press.

Stahl, S. A., & Murray, B. A. (1994). Defining phonological awareness and its relationship to early reading. *Journal of Educational Psychology, 86*(2), 221–234.

Strickland, D. S. (1998). *Teaching Phonics today: A primer for educators.* Newark, DE: International Reading Association.

Treiman, R, & Zukowski, A. (1991). Levels of phonological awareness. In S. Brady & D. Shankweiler (Eds.), *Phonological processes in literacy* (pp. 67–83). Hillsdale, NH: Lawrence Erlbaum Associates.

Van Allsburg, C. (1987). *The z was zapped.* Boston: Houghton Mifflin.

Venezky, R. L. (1975). The curious role of letter names in reading instruction. *Visible Language, 9,* 7–23.

Walsh, D. J., Price, G. G., & Gillingham, M. G. (1988). The critical but transitory importance of letter naming. *Reading Research Quarterly, 23,* 108–122.

Weaver, C. (1988). *Reading process and practice: From socio-psycholinguistics to whole language.* Portsmouth, NH: Heinemann Educational Books.

Weaver, C. (1990). *Understanding whole language: From principles to practices.* Portsmouth, NH: Heinemann Educational Books.

Wilde, S. (1997). *What's a schwa sound anyway? A holistic guide to phonetics, phonics, and spelling.* Portsmouth, NH: Heinemann Educational Books.

Yopp, H. K. (1988). The validity and reliability of phonemic awareness tests. *Reading Research Quarterly, 23,* 159–177.

Yopp, H. K. (1992). Developing phonemic awareness in young children. *The Reading Teacher, 45,* 696–703.

Yopp, H. K., & Troyer, S. (1992). *Training phonemic awareness in young children.* Unpublished manuscript.

Chapter 8

Phonics and Word Attack Skills

George is seated next to his teacher, Ms. Abrams, reading from that wonderful classic, *Elmer* by David McKee (1968). The first sentence in the book reads— *There was once a herd of elephants.*

Ms. Abrams says, "George, I'm so happy you've chosen one of my favorite read-aloud books to read for *me* today. Let's start at the very beginning."

Excited and pleased, George begins: "Th-th-there w-was o-o-only . . . ."

Wanting to help, Ms. Abrams offers: "That word is 'once,' George."

George repeats, "There was once a h-h-hard . . . ."

Ms. Abrams: "HERD"

George, with beads of perspiration now forming on his brow, reads, "Herd! There was once a *herd* of elephants."

Ms. Abrams responds, "GREAT, George! Let's continue," all the while thinking to herself—*Hmmmm. Not so great. I need to take a closer look at George's phonics knowledge. He's really struggling with what I thought would surely be an independent reading book for him . . .*

Phonics refers to teaching practices that emphasize how spellings are related to speech sounds in systematic ways (letter-sound relationships) and to the reader's use of this knowledge to decode unknown words (National Research Council, 1999; Rasinski & Padak, 1996). Phonics is an extremely important element of reading instruction. In the context of great literature and varied language experiences, children can learn to read with the aid of a strong phonics program and a caring and skillful teacher (Blevins, 1996).

Phonics instruction is an essential part of comprehensive reading programs in the early grades and is one component of a larger constellation of word analysis students learn, known as **word attack.** Other word attack skills (besides phonics) include structural analysis, onset and rime, and use of sight words. Each are discussed in this chapter. A comprehensive approach to reading instruction emphasizes both meaning and word attack cues and provides numerous opportunities to practice these cueing systems.

In this chapter we summarize some of the more recent research on word attack skills, particularly phonics, and suggest activities we have found useful in assessing and developing this important area.

BACKGROUND BRIEFING FOR TEACHERS

RESEARCH ON PHONICS

Recent surveys conducted by the International Reading Association (IRA) indicated that phonics is one of the most talked-about subjects in the field of reading education (second only to the topic of balanced reading). In reviewing the literature, we have concluded that there are two essential areas for you to know about: *which* phonics skills and generalizations are important for student to learn, and *how* you might teach these skills in your classroom.

Because teachers should be THE phonics expert in the classroom, we thought you might want to begin with a little self-assessment. We have included a *Phonics Quick Test* in Figure 8.1 so that you can determine just how much you already know. (The results may surprise you.) Please complete the exercise in Figure 8.1 before reading on.

PHONICS THEY WILL USE

We have compiled a little phonics *primer* for you, summarizing the main content of instruction, beginning with the most simple, individual sound-symbol relationships, and proceeding to the more complex.

Letter Sounds

Though the English alphabet has only 26 letters, there are actually some 44 speech sounds. These 44 sounds can be represented in about 350 different ways; hence, English can become a formidable challenge for children when they try to "crack the code." Fortunately, there is a high degree or regularity in English upon which teachers can focus to introduce phonics rules and relationships.

The place to begin is at the beginning: individual letter sounds. In Figure 8.2, we have compiled a list of the 44 speech sounds and the most common way they are represented by various alphabet letters. Note that in many cases we have listed the percentage of the time each sound is represented by a specific letter. For instance, speech sound /b/ (pronounced "buh" as in the beginning sound heard in *basket* and *bunk*) is represented by the letter *b* 97% of the time in written English.

Common Rules Governing Letter Sounds

There are several rules governing letter sounds that have a high degree of reliability and are certainly worth teaching. Here they are.

The C Rule. The letter c is an irregular consonant letter that has no phoneme of its own. Instead, it assumes two other phonemes found in different words: /k/ and /s/. In general, when the letter c is followed by a, o, or u, it will represent the sound /k/ we usually associate with the letter k, also known as the hard c sound. Some examples are the words *cake, cosmic,* and *cute.* However, the letter c can sometimes represent the sound /s/ commonly associated with the letter s. This is referred to as the soft c sound. The soft c sound is usually produced when c is followed by e, i, or y. Examples of the soft c sound are in the words *celebrate, circus,* and *cycle.*

The G Rule. G is the key symbol for the phoneme /g/ we hear in the word *get*. It is also irregular, having a soft g and a hard g sound. The rules remain the same as they are for the letter c. When g is followed by the letters e, i, or y, it represents a soft g or /j/ sound,

W **Figure 8.1**   Checking Phonics Knowledge

A Phonics Quick Test*

1. The word *charkle* is divided between _____ and _____ . The *a* has an _____ - controlled sound, and the *e* is _____ .

2. In the word *small, sm-* is known as the *onset* and *-all* is known as the _____ .

3. *Ch* in the word *chair* is known as a _____ .

4. The letter *c* in the word *city* is a _____ sound; in the word *cow*, the letter *c* is a _____ sound.

5. The letters *bl* in the word *blue* are referred to as a consonant _____ .

6. The underlined vowels in the words *author*, *spread*, and *blue* are known as vowel _____ .

7. The words *tag, run, cot,* and *get* have which vowel pattern? _____

8. The words *glide, take,* and *use* have the _____ vowel pattern.

9. The single most powerful phonics skill we can teach to emergent readers for decoding unfamiliar words in print is _____ sounds in words. We introduce this skill using _____ sounds first because they are the most _____ .

10. The word part *work* in the word *working* is known as a _____ .

11. The word part *-ing* in the word *working* is known as a _____ .

12. Cues to the meaning and pronunciation of unfamiliar words in print are often found in the print surrounding the unfamiliar, also known as the _____ .

*Answers to the *Phonics Quick Test* are found at the end of this chapter.

as in the words *gently, giraffe,* and *gym.* If g is followed by the letters a, o, or u, then it usually represents the hard (or regular) sound, as in the words *garden, go,* and *sugar.*

The CVC Generalization.   When a vowel comes between two consonants, it usually has a short vowel sound. Examples of words following the CVC pattern include *sat, ran, let, pen, win, fit, hot, mop, sun,* and *cut.*

Vowel Digraphs.   When two vowels come together in a word, usually the first vowel is long and the second vowel is silent. This occurs especially often with the oa, ee, and ay combinations. Some examples are *toad, fleet,* and *day.* A common slogan used by teachers,

Figure 8.2   The 44 Sounds of English and Their Most Common Spellings

Sound	Spellings	Examples
1. /b/	b (97%), bb	ball
2. /d/	d (98%), dd, ed	dot
3. /f/	f (78%), ff, ph, lf	fun
4. /g/	g (88%), gg, gh	goat
5. /h/	h (98%), wh	hall
6. /j/	g (66%), j (22%), dg	jug
7. /k/	c (73%), cc, k (13%), ck, lk, q	kite
8. /l/	l (91%), ll	leap
9. /m/	m (94%), mm	moat
10. /n/	n (97%), nn, kn, gn	no
11. /p/	p (96%), pp	pit
12. /r/	r (97%), rr, wr	rubber
13. /s/	s (73%), c (17%), ss	sat
14. /t/	t (97%), tt, ed	tap
15. /v/	v (99.5%), f	vast; of
16. /w/	w (92%)	wood
17. /y/	i (55%), y (44%)	onion; yell
18. /z/	z (23%), zz, s (64%)	zip
19. /ch/	ch (55%), t (31%)	chair
20. /sh/	ti (53%), sh (26%), ssi, si, sci	shorts
21. /zh/	si (49%), s, ss, z	Asia; azure
22. /th/	th (100%)	(voiceless sound) bath
23. /th/	th (100%)	(voiced) than, together
24. /hw/	wh (100%)	what, wheat
25. /ng/	ng (59%), n (41%)	rung, sing
26. /ā/	ā (45%), ā_e (35%), āi, āy, eā	A; bāke
27. /ē/	ē (70%), y, ēā (10%), ēē (10%), iē	frēē
28. /ī/	ī_ē (37%), ī (37%), y (14%)	fīvē
29. /ō/	ō (73%), ō_ē (14%), ōw, ōā, ōē	gō
30. /yōō/	u (69%), u_ē (22%), ēw, uē	cubē

continued

Figure 8.2 Continued

Sound	Spellings	Examples
31. /ā/	ā (96%)	cāb
32. /ē/	ē (91%), ē_ē (15%)	bēst
33. /ī/	ī (66%), y (23%)	brīck
34. /ō/	ō (79%)	hōt
35. /u/	u (86%), ō, ōu	bug
36. /ə/ (schwā)	ā (24%), ē (13%), ī (22%), ō (27%), u	Amērīcā
37. /â/	ā (29%), -ā rē (23%), -ā īr (21%)	dā rē
38. /û/	-ēr (40%), -īr (13%), -ur (26%)	bīrd
39. /ä/	ā (89%)	bā r
40. /ô/	ō, ā, ā u, ā w, ōugh, ā ugh	fōr
41. /ōī/	ōī (62%), ōy (32%)	bōīl, bōy
42. /ōu/	ōu (56%), ōw (29%)	trōut
43. /ōō/	ōō (38%), u (21%), ō, ōu, u_ē	bōōm
44. /oo/	oo (31%), u (54%), o (8%), ould, ou, o	cook

Source: Adapted from Phonics from *A to Z: A Practical Guide,* by W. Blevins, 1998, New York: Scholastic Professional Books.

which helps children remember this generalization, is "when two vowels go walking, the first one does the talking."

The VCE (Final E) Generalization.   When two vowels appear in a word separated by a consonant *and* the final one is an *e* at the end of the word, the first vowel is generally long and the final *e* is silent. Examples include *cape, rope,* and *kite.*

The CV Generalization.   When a consonant is followed by a vowel, the vowel usually produces a long sound. This is especially easy to see in two-letter words such as *be, go,* and *so.*

R-Controlled Vowels.   Vowels that appear before the letter r are usually neither long nor short, but tend to be overpowered or "swallowed up" by the /r/ sound. Examples include *person, player, neighborhood,* and *herself.*

Special Consonant Rules

Single Consonants.   Single consonants nearly always make the same sound. We recommend that they be taught in the following order due to their frequency in our language: T, N, R, M, D, S (sat), L, C (cat), P, F, V, G (got), H, W, K, J, Z, Y.

Consonant.   This is defined as two consonants together in a word that produce only one speech sound (*th, sh, ng*).

Initial Consonant Blends or "Clusters".   Two or more consonants coming together in which the speech sounds of all the consonants may be heard are called consonant blends *(bl, fr, sk, spl)*. Consonant blends that come at the beginning of words are the most consistent in the sounds they make. It is recommended that they be taught in the following order due to their frequency in English:

Group 1	Group 2	Group 3	Group 4
st	pl	sc	sm
pr	sp	bl	gl
tr	cr	fl	sn
gr	cl	sk	tw
br	dr	sl	
	fr	sw	

Double Consonants.   When two consonants come together in a word, they typically make the sound of a single consonant (e.g., *all, apple, arrow, attic,* and so on).

PH and the /f/ Sound.   Ph is always pronounced as /f/ (e.g., *phone, phoneme, philosophy, phobia, phenomenon,* and so on).

Special Vowel Rules

Schwa /ə/.   Vowel letters that produce the "uh" sound (*A* in *America*). The schwa is represented by the upside-down *e* symbol (/ə/).

Diphthongs.   Two vowels together in a word that produce a single, glided sound (*oi* in *oil, oy* in *boy*).

Y Rules.   When the letter *y* comes at the end of a long word (or a word having at least one other vowel), it will have the sound of long *e* (/ē/) as in *baby.* When *y* comes at the end of a short word or in the middle of a word, it will make the sound of long *i* (/ī/) as in *cry* and *cycle.*

RESEARCH ON OTHER WORD ATTACK SKILLS

Onset and Rime ("Word Families")

We need to keep in mind that knowing letter names is not all there is in learning to decode. Learning to analyze a printed word into component sounds followed by blending of those sounds requires knowledge of other reliable letter-sounds associations (Pressley, 1998). There has been significant research in recent years confirming that certain word elements known as *onset* and *rime* are extremely reliable sound-symbol patterns and can be very helpful to new decoders. Simply put, **rimes** are the vowel at the beginning of a syllable and the **onset** is the consonant or consonants that come just before the vowel. For example, in the word *tack, t* is the onset and *-ack* is the rime; in the word *snow, sn* is the onset and *-ow* is the rime. In Figure 8.3, we have provided a comprehensive list of rimes for your use. The rimes in bold should be taught first, and when combined with various onsets (i.e., beginning consonants, consonant blends, or consonant digraphs) produce some 500 primary-level words (Adams, 1990).

Syllabication

The ability to segment words into syllables is yet another form of "phonic awareness" that can be useful when encountering unknown words. The research has been very inconclusive indeed as to whether teaching syllabication actually helps students with identifying un-

Figure 8.3   Rimes (Word Families)

Note: Rimes in bold type have some of the most reliable sounds and, when adding an onset (consonant, consonant blends, or digraphs) create some 500 primary-level words.

-ab	-ang	-ear (short e)	**-ice**	**-ir**	-out
-ace	**-ank**	**-eat**	**-ick**	-it	-ow (snow)
-ack	**-ap**	-ed	-id	-ob	-ow (sow)
-ad	-ar	-ee	**-ide**	**-ock**	-ub
-ade	-are	-eed	-ies	-od	**-uck**
-ag	-ark	-eek	-ig	-og	-uff
-ail	**-ash**	-eep	**-ight**	**-oke**	**-ug**
-ain	**-at**	-eet	-ile	-old	-um
-ake	**-ate**	**-ell**	**-ill**	-one	**-ump**
-ale	-ave	-ell	-im	-ong	-ung
-all	**-aw**	-end	-ime	-oop	**-unk**
-am	**-ay**	-ent	**-in**	**-op**	-ush
-ame	-aze	-ess	**-ine**	-ope	-ust
-amp	-eak	**-est**	**-ing**	**-or**	-ut
-an	-eal	-et	**-ink**	**-ore**	-y
-ane	-eam	-ew	**-ip**	-ot	

Source: Adapted from *Beginning to Read: Thinking and Learning about Print,* by M. J. Adams, 1990, Cambridge, MA: MIT Press; *The Reading Teacher's Book of Lists,* by E. B. Fry, J. E. Kress, and D. L. Fountoukidis, 1993, Paramis, NJ: Prentice Hall; and *Reading Instruction that Works: The Case for Balanced Teaching,* by M. Pressley, 1998, New York: Guilford Press.

known words in print. Nevertheless, we include in Figures 8.4 and 8.5 the syllabication rules that seem to be the most reliable for 1) dividing words and 2) pronouncing words (Manzo & Manzo, 1993). (Note: We tend to favor teaching students to use common onset and rime knowledge whenever possible to segment words in print.)

Structural Analysis

Structural analysis refers to the study of words to identify their individual meaning elements (called *morphemes*). Words are made up of two classes or morphemes: free and bound. *Free morphemes* are word parts (words, really) that sometimes stand alone. They are also known as "root words." For example, in the word *working, work* is the root word (free morpheme). In contrast, *bound morphemes* must be attached to a root word to carry meaning. Prefixes and suffixes (together referred to as *affixes*) are bound morphemes. Common prefixes, which come *before* a root word, include: *intro-, pro-, post-, sub-,* and *dis-*. Some of the more common suffixes, which come *after* a root word, include: *-ant, -ist, -ence, -ism, -s,* and *-ed.*

Figure 8.4   Syllabication Rules for Dividing Words

1. When two identical consonants come together, they are divided to form two syllables. Examples: *ap / ple, but / ter, lit / tle.*
2. The number of vowel sounds that occur in a word usually indicate how many syllables there will be in the word. Examples: *slave* (one vowel sound/one syllable); *caboose* (four vowels, but only two vowel sounds, hence, two syllables—*ca / boose*).
3. Two unlike consonants are also usually divided to form syllables, unless they form a consonant digraph. Example: *car / pet.*
4. Small words within a compound word are syllables (as with onset/rimes). Examples: *book / store, fire / fly.*

Source: From *Literacy Disorders: Holistic Diagnosis and Remediation,* by A. V. Manzo and U. C. Manzo, 1993, Fort Worth, TX: Harcourt Brace Jovanovich College Publishers.

Figure 8.5   Syllabication Rules for Pronouncing Words

1. *le* is pronounced as *ul* when it appears at the end of a word. Examples: *shuttle, little, remarkable.*
2. Syllables that end with a vowel usually have a long vowel sound. Examples: *bi / lingual, re / read.*
3. When a vowel does not come at the end of a syllable, and it is followed by two consonants, it will usually have a short sound. Examples: *let / ter, all, attic.*

Source: From *Literacy Disorders: Holistic Diagnosis and Remediation,* by A. V. Manzo and U. C. Manzo, 1993, Fort Worth, TX: Harcourt Brace Jovanovich College Publishers.

Sight Words

Many reading experts and researchers feel that the learning of high-frequency vocabulary or **sight words** is an important component of word attack for beginning readers. These are words that occur frequently in print and are usually best learned through memorization; words such as *is, are, the, was, this,* and so on. We agree that sight words are an element of word attack, but because sight words are also "vocabulary," we have chosen to include this information in chapter 9, *Teaching and Assessing Vocabulary Development.* So stay tuned for that information in the next chapter.

WHEN TO TEACH SPECIFIC PHONICS AND OTHER WORD ATTACK SKILLS: THE SCOPE OF INSTRUCTION

When should word attack skills be taught? Does research suggest a specific order? As with so many things in life, the answer is not entirely clear. For instance, there is no set rule about how quickly or how slowly to introduce sound-letter relations (Chard & Osborn,

Figure 8.6   Recommended Scope and Sequence of Instruction

Kindergarten
- Sound structure of spoken words
- Recognition and production of letters
- Basic print concepts
- Familiarity with the basic purposes and mechanisms of reading and writing
- Phonemic awareness
- Alphabet recognition
- Sense of story
- Vocabulary development (oral, some high-frequency words)

First Grade
Explicit instruction on phonemic awareness (if not previously developed in kindergarten)
Letter-sound correspondences and common spelling conventions and uses in identifying printed words

1. Consonants in beginning, ending, and medial positions as part of a decoding strategy. Letters pronounced the same regardless of context: d, f, l, n, r, v, z
2. Short vowels: a, e, i, o, and u
3. Consonant-vowel-consonant (cvc) pattern. Use simple words that begin with consistent sounds to introduce simple blending such as *fan, lad, ran.*
4. Vowel-consonant-e (vce) pattern
5. Long vowel digraphs (ai, ay, ea, ee, oa, ow)
6. Consonant blends (tr, br, bl, cl, st, etc.)
7. Early structural analysis such as suffixes

   Sight recognition of frequent words
   Use of context clues
   Independent reading including reading aloud (A wide variety of well-written and engaging texts that are below the children's frustration level should be provided)

Second Grade and Above
- Sound out and identify visually unfamiliar words.
- Recognize words primarily through attention to letter-sound relationships.
- Context and pictures should be used only to monitor word recognition.
- Accuracy in word recognition and fluency should be assessed regularly.

1999), but there is adequate scientific research data for us to set down a comprehensive listing of important skills.

In Figure 8.6, we suggest a scope and sequence of word attack instruction based on some of the most credible research (e.g., Bear et al., 1996; Blevins, 1997; Eldredge, 1995; Moustafa, 1997; National Research Council, 1999; Pressley, 1998). Instead of trying to enumerate each minute skill, in most cases we simply recommend major categories in sequence and leave decisions about the fine points to you. This knowledge of *what* and *when* to teach can be extremely helpful in 1) assessing phonics knowledge in students and 2) planning instruction and grouping effectively to meet their needs.

WHAT DOES A GOOD PHONICS AND WORD ATTACK PROGRAM LOOK LIKE?

Three main accomplishments characterize good readers: 1) They understand the alphabetic system of English to identify printed words. 2) They have and use background knowledge and strategies to obtain meaning from print. 3) They read fluently (National Research Council, 1999, p. 6). Similarly, successful phonics instruction has a number of common qualities (Stahl, 1992). First of all, it builds on children's knowledge about how print functions. In the early stages, phonics and word attack instruction also builds on students' phonological awareness when the alphabet is introduced.

We also know that exemplary instruction is clear and direct (explicit). Phonics is integrated into a comprehensive reading program and focuses, ultimately, on reading words, not memorizing rules. Research confirms that effective programs include onset and rime instruction. It is also woven into writing instruction (for instance, using "temporary" or *phonemic* spellings). A prime objective of exemplary phonics instruction is to develop independent word recognition strategies, focusing attention on the internal structure of words (structural analysis).

All effective instruction is preceded by an assessment of student knowledge, our next topic.

ASSESSING PHONICS AND WORD ATTACK KNOWLEDGE

The goal of phonics and word attack assessment is to discover what students understand about sound-symbol relationships. Knowing what a student can and cannot do makes it clear what your course of action should be in the classroom. There are a number of basic strategies that one can use to discover which skills have been learned and which need attention. In general, assessment should proceed developmentally according to the sequence in which skills are learned: phonemic awareness to alphabetic principle knowledge to phonics and other word attack skills.

Assessment of phonics and word attack knowledge often begins with a running record. Using words in context, running records permit teachers to observe how well a student's phonics skills are developing while reading real text. In chapter 2, we discussed how to conduct running records, so we will not bother to duplicate that information in this chapter; just know that we see running records as THE way to assess phonics and decoding in context.

Another assessment procedure we recommend is the *Starpoint Phonics Assessment* (Williams, Cooter, & Cooter, 2003). It uses nonsense words read in a list (without context). A similar test of phonics knowledge included in this section is the *Reutzel/Cooter Word Attack Survey,* which focuses on common vowel and consonant generalizations discussed earlier. Together with running records, you will learn a great deal about students' phonics and word attack knowledge using these two assessment tools. (Note: We have included a Student Phonics Knowledge Checklist [Figure 8.10] to help you tally up areas of strength and need based on your assessments and observations.)

THE STARPOINT PHONICS ASSESSMENT (SPA)

Purpose

For many years, nonsense words ("made-up words" having common phonics patterns) have been used in reading assessment to determine students' knowledge of English spelling pat-

Figure 8.7   SPA Nonsense Words

1. runk	mip	bor
2. pight	caw	jor
3. wunk	lemmock	zatting
4. nash	soug	zad
5. battump	dapping	yod
6. mur	hote	seg
7. lattum	yinter	poat
8. telbin	vike	leat
9. dar	mur	foat
10. pice	gar	whesp
11. dop	femmit	yadder
12. gapple	sheal	telbis
13. lome	ridnip	hade
14. tade	chogging	vappel
15. minzif	kosh	waig
16. tain	demsug	nater
17. festrip	bowunk	thiping
18. wapir	polide	wabor
19. polide	siler	jiper
20. atur	niping	quen

terns. These nonsense words are usually read in a list and the teacher records any miscues. Critics say that nonsense words, because they are not real words, do not permit students to use their prior knowledge—a primary reading tool used in decoding unfamiliar words in print. Advocates counter that nonsense words, because they deny the student the ability to use background knowledge, force the student to use only those phonics skills that he has internalized. We support the limited use of nonsense words as simply one tool in a teacher's toolbox of assessment ideas that may shed some light on a student's phonics skills development.

The *Starpoint Phonics Assessment (SPA)** (Williams et al., 2003) was designed to provide a beginning-of-the-year phonics assessment for children attending the Starpoint Laboratory School at Texas Christian University. Areas of special focus include initial consonant sounds (onsets), correct pronunciation of common rimes, syllabication, affixes (prefixes/suffixes), and r-controlled vowels. These phonics areas are embedded within nonsense words that students are asked to read (see Figure 8.7). Analysis of children's' phonics abilities focus on these five areas.

Materials

Reproduce each row of nonsense words from Figure 8.7 on cardstock as flashcards (example: Row 1 words on one card—*runk, mip, bor*). You will also need a copy of the *SPA Analysis Grid Form* (Figure 8.8) for each student to be assessed. Finally, it is important to record students as they read each group of words so that you can check your analysis, so appropriate equipment will be needed.

Procedure

Seat the student at a table directly across from where you are sitting. Turn on your cassette tape player and say the student's name aloud and the date to mark the record, then continue. Beginning with the first flashcard you have prepared from Figure 8.7, say to the student, "Please read the words on each card as I hold them up. The words are all *nonsense* words. That means they are not real words. Just pronounce them the way you think they would sound. For instance, this first word is *runk*. Go ahead and try to say the other words for me as I hold them up."

As the student reads each word, make a notation to the right of each grouping of words on the *SPA Analysis Grid Form* (Figure 8.8) indicating whether the child said the word correctly. Words pronounced correctly should be noted with a check (√) mark. Incorrect pronunciations should be written phonetically. For example, if a student mispronounced the nonsense word *wabor* (line 18), it might be written as "way-bee" to the right of the word cluster on line 18, reflecting the way the student said it. Continue having the student read each cluster of words, marking any "miscues" (a mispronounced word) in the blank area to the right of each word cluster on the *SPA Analysis Grid Form*.

Analyzing the Miscues. The *Starpoint Phonics Assessment (SPA)* is quick and easy to analyze. Analysis begins after the student has read all of the words from Figure 8.7 and has returned to his normal school activities.

First, replay the cassette recording to be sure that any miscues have been correctly recorded. Next, for each miscue noted, simply place a hash mark " | " in the box to the right, indicating which phonics skill(s) the student seems to be lacking when trying to decode that particular nonsense word: beginning sounds (onset), rimes, syllabication, affixes (common prefixes and suffixes), and/or r-controlled vowels. You should have at least one box marked for each miscue. If none of the phonics categories seems to be appropriate, which is possible, then make a note of the miscue at the bottom of the sheet in the area marked "Examiner's Notes" along with your interpretation of what the student may need to learn (e.g., cvc rule, hard g sound, vowel digraphs, and so on). If this happens, be sure to administer the *Reutzel/Cooter Word Attack Survey* discussed in the very next section.

Finally, add up the number of miscues in each column and record that number in the appropriate "Totals" box. In instances where the student has had two or more miscues in that category (i.e., beginning sounds/onset, rimes, syllabication, affixes, or r-controlled vowels) you should consider developing explicit instruction plans to teach that skill.

THE REUTZEL/COOTER WORD ATTACK SURVEY

Purpose

The *Reutzel/Cooter Word Attack Survey (WAS)*, like the *Starpoint Phonics Assessment (SPA)*, uses nonsense words to help you diagnose students' needs and abilities in phonics. The primary focus in the *WAS* is on vowel and consonant generalizations.

Figure 8.8   SPA Analysis Grid Form

			Initial Sound	Rimes	Syllab.	Affixes	R-contr.
1. runk	mip	bor					
2. pight	caw	jor					
3. wunk	lemmock	zatting					
4. nash	soug	zad					
5. battump	dapping	yod					
6. mur	hote	seg					
7. lattum	yinter	poat					
8. telbin	vike	leat					
9. dar	mur	foat					
10. pice	gar	whesp					
11. dop	femmit	yadder					
12. gapple	sheal	telbis					
13. lome	ridnip	hade					
14. tade	chogging	vappel					
15. minzif	kosh	waig					
16. tain	demsug	nater					
17. festrip	bowunk	thiping					
18. wapir	polide	wabor					
19. polide	siler	jiper					
20. atur	niping	quen					
Totals							

Examiner's Notes:

Materials

You will need to reproduce the word cards provided at the end of this chapter for the students to read. Also, make copies of the Word Attack Survey Form (see Figure 8.9) for use in noting student responses.

Procedure

Directions for administering the Reutzel/Cooter Word Attack Survey:

1. Seat the student across from you at a small table.
2. Begin by showing him the examples provided using the premade flash cards (see word cards at the end of the chapter). Say, "I would like for you to read aloud some words on these flash cards. These are not real words, but are make-believe words, so they may sound kind of funny to you. Just try to say them the way you think they should be pronounced. For example, this first word (sim) is pronounced 'SIM.'" (Note: The teacher pronounces the word for the student). "Now I'd like for you to pronounce the next word for me." (Show the word *cip*.) Praise the child for saying the word correctly (or explain again the instructions, if necessary). After asking the student to do the third example word *(sar),* go ahead to the next step.
3. Say, "Now I would like for you to say each word as I show it to you. These are also make-believe words, so they will not sound much like any word you know. Just say them the way you think they should be pronounced." Then, work your way through the words and note any mispronunciations on the Word Attack Survey Form (Figure 8.9).
4. Once the student has completed reading through the word cards, praise him for his hard work and allow him to go on to other activities. Tally up any miscues using the Word Attack Survey Form (Figure 8.9).
5. Determine areas of phonic knowledge the student may be having difficulty with based on repeated miscues. We recommend that your instructional decisions be based on a pattern of errors repeated over time. Thus, you will need to hear the child read more than once before deciding which areas must be addressed in phonics minilessons.

Figure 8.9   The Reutzel/Cooter Word Attack Survey Form

Student name: _____	Date: _____

Part 1: Vowel Generalizations

Sample Item:	sim	cip	sar

A. CVC/Beginning Consonant Sounds

1. tat	_____		6. sim	_____
2. nan	_____		7. loj	_____
3. rin	_____		8. cal	_____
4. mup	_____		9. pif	_____
5. det	_____		10. fek	_____

continued

Figure 8.9 Continued

B. Vowel Digraphs
11. geem _____
12. hoad _____
13. kait _____
14. weam _____

C. VCE Pattern
15. jape _____
16. zote _____
17. gipe _____
18. tope _____

D. CV Pattern
19. bo _____
20. ka _____
21. fi _____
22. tu _____

E. R-Controlled Vowels
23. sar _____
24. wir _____
25. der _____
26. nur _____

F. Schwa Sound
27. ahurla _____
28. thup _____
29. cremon _____
30. laken _____

Part 2: Consonant Generalizations

G. Hard and Soft *C*
31. cale _____
32. cose _____
33. cimmy _____
34. cyler _____

H. Hard and Soft *G*
35. gare _____
36. gob _____
37. gime _____
38. genry _____

I. Consonant Digraphs
39. chur _____
40. thim _____
41. shar _____
42. whilly _____
43. thar _____

J. Double Consonants
44. nally _____
45. ipple _____
46. attawap _____
47. urrit _____

K. Ph (f sound)
48. phur _____
49. phattle _____
50. phenoblab _____

L. Single Consonants*

M. Syllabication Rule**
51. lappo _____
52. pabute _____
53. larpin _____
54. witnit _____

*See section A
**Besides Items 51–54, there are many other syllabication examples throughout the *R/CWAS*.

Comments:

Figure 8.10   Student Phonics Knowledge Checklist

Student Phonics Knowledge Checklist	
Student's name: _____	
Skill(s)	**Date Observed**
Level 1: Phonemic Awareness	
1. Rhyming	_____
2. Alliteration	_____
3. Oddity tasks	_____
4. Oral blending: syllables, onset/rime, phoneme by phoneme	_____
5. Oral segmentation: syllables, onset/rime, phoneme by phoneme	_____
6. Phonemic manipulation: substitution *(i, f, v)*; deletion *(s, i, f)*	_____
Level 2: Alphabetic Principle	
7. Making the connection between sounds and symbols	_____
Level 3: Explicit Phonics Instruction	
8. Specific letter sounds/Specific letter names	
a. Onset/consonants and rimes	_____
b. Continuous consonants	_____
c. Short vowel sounds	_____
d. Continue teaching both vowels and consonants	_____
e. Consonant digraphs: *wh, ch, th, sh,* etc.	_____
f. Vowel dipthongs: *oi, oy, ou*	_____
g. Vowel digraphs: *ee, ea, ai, ay,* etc.	_____
9. Word play with onset and rime blending	_____
10. L → R blending of letter-sounds in words	_____
11. Segmentation of sounds in words, and writing segmented sounds	_____

Source: Sequence based on *Phonemic Awareness Activities for Early Reading Success,* by W. Blevins, 1997, New York: Scholastic.

One of the challenges for busy classroom teachers is organizing assessment information so that you can make enlightened teaching decisions and group effectively for instruction. To help you in this process, we offer a Student Phonics Knowledge Checklist, shown in Figure 8.10.

ASSESSING VIA RUNNING RECORDS

Okay, we just couldn't resist putting in one last reminder that you should use running records as your primary assessment for analyzing student decoding ability. Chapter 2 gives you the full picture on using this valuable diagnostic procedure.

CONNECTING ASSESSMENT FINDINGS TO TEACHING STRATEGIES

Before discussing phonics and word attack teaching strategies, we have constructed a guide connecting assessment findings to intervention and/or strategy choices. It is our intention to help you select the most appropriate instructional interventions and strategies to meet your students' needs based on assessment data. This is in keeping with the "If-Then" mode

Intervention Strategy Guide for Phonics and Word Attack Skills

Intervention Strategy → / Student Problem(s) ↓	Explicit Instruction (Glazer, 1998)	Letter-Sound Cards	Phonics Fish	Sound Swirl	Button Sounds	Stomping, Clapping...	Tongue Twisters	Nonsense Words	Making Words	Wide Reading
Letter Sound(s)	+	+	*	+	+	–	+	+	+	+
C Rule	+	*	*	*	–	–	–	+	+	+
G Rule	+	*	*	*	–	–	–	+	+	+
CVC Pattern	+	+	+	–	–	–	–	+	+	+
Vowel Digraphs	+	+	+	–	–	–	–	+	+	+
VCE Pattern	+	+	+	–	–	–	–	+	+	+
CV Pattern	+	+	+	–	–	–	–	+	+	+
R-control Vowels	+	+	+	–	–	–	–	+	+	+
Consonant Digraph	+	+	*							
Consonant Blends	+	+	*		+	–	–	+	+	+
Onset	+	+	*	+	+	+	+	+	+	+
Rime	+	+	+	+	*	+	+	+	+	+
Syllabication	+	–	–	–	–	+	*	+	+	+
Morphemic (Structural) Analysis	+	*	*	*	–	–	–	+	+	+

Key: + excellent strategy
* adaptable strategy
– unsuitable strategy

of thinking we discussed in chapter 2. Teaching strategies described in the next section are listed across the top of the Intervention Strategy Guide. Potential problems are listed vertically in the left-hand column.

In the next part of this chapter, we offer instruction strategies for interventions based on the foregoing assessments.

TEACHING STRATEGIES: HELPING STUDENTS INCREASE PHONICS AND WORD ATTACK KNOWLEDGE

APPROACHES TO TEACHING PHONICS

Phonics instruction is often categorized as *explicit* or *implicit* (Chard & Osborn, 1999). Beginning reading instruction that depends on the teaching of isolated letters, letter sounds, and phonics generalizations is known as explicit phonics instruction (Reutzel & Cooter, 2000). **Explicit phonics** methods are based on "bottom-up" theories of learning, indicating that readers mentally process information letter by letter, word by word, and sentence by sentence until comprehension occurs. With explicit phonics methods, children are first taught regular sounds and sound patterns in words. Then, examples of words having those patterns are shown, followed by reading texts that include words having those patterns. Sometimes explicit phonics teachers have students practice new skills by having them read from books containing what is known as "decodable text." These are books with language contrived to prominently display a given phonics pattern. For example, for the short a sound in CVC patterns (i.e., consonant-vowel-consonant), a sentence might read, "The fat cat sat on the mat." *Synthetic phonics instruction* is another common term for explicit phonics.

Implicit phonics instruction teaches students to decode unfamiliar words using their knowledge of sound-symbol clues from known words. For example, you might draw students' attention to the rime *-all* in words you have already taught them, such as *ball, call, fall,* and *wall;* then show them how to use this knowledge as a tool for decoding unknown words in print containing that same pattern (e.g., to decode *stall, mall, hall,* and *tall*). This could also be done with individual letter-sound relations, such as noticing the consistent sound that the letter "v" makes (the sound is written as /v/: *van, vase, Volkswagon*) to help students recognize the /v/ sound in words like *volcano, visitor,* and *villain.* This kind of teaching is also known as *analytic phonics instruction.*

TIPS ON TEACHING PHONICS

Research over the past decade or so has taught us much about the best ways to teach phonics (Stahl, 1992; Blevins, 1998; National Research Council, 1999; Cooter, 2001). Here is our advice about what you should (and should not) do to establish solid phonics instruction.

Ten things to do . . .

1. **Sequence your instruction**—Earlier in the book we provided you with a scope and sequence of instruction (see Figure 8.6).

2. **Be very direct (explicit and implicit) in your teaching**—Model each new skill thoroughly, offer students a good bit of practice under your guidance, then assess to make sure they have it.

3. **Have daily lessons and review sessions**—Phonics instruction should be an everyday occurrence in the early grades (K–2) and include a great deal of repetition. Teachers sometimes forget that even our best students need as much as 30 days of repetition for a new phonics skill to become their own (Cooter, 2001). According to the National Research Council (1999)

> . . . [Children] need sufficient practice with a variety of texts to achieve fluency, so that both word recognition and reading comprehension become increasingly fast, accurate, and well-coordinated. (p. 6)

4. **Focus on one skill at a time**—All too often we try to do too much in introducing new skills and, consequently, teach few skills well. Phonics lessons should keep a tight focus and work on the target skill until the student becomes proficient.

5. **Keep lessons brief**—If, in fact, you are teaching within the student's "frontier of learning," then you must limit instruction sessions to 10–15 minutes. Otherwise, the student's attention wanders and your teaching will be ineffective.

6. **When practicing a new phonics skill, use easy reading materials**—Many times the very best way to introduce new phonics skills is through the use of great books, poems, songs, chants, or raps. Be sure that reading materials are predominantly at the students' independent reading level with the "target" words (i.e., words unknown to the student in print that you will use to introduce a new phonics skill) woven into the text. That way, students can use what they already know, as well as some context information, to aid them in practicing the new skill.

7. **Help kids become "wordsmiths"**—We have noticed that great readers and writers are also word watchers; they seem to always notice new and interesting words in their text encounters. We must do whatever we can each day to model the attitude of fascination with words and how they are put together. This makes word study far more interesting to students—"a spoonful of sugar helps the medicine go down."

8. **Adjust the pace of instruction to meet the individual needs of students**—This can only be done consistently in small-group instruction where students come together based on a common need to know.

9. **Link phonics instruction to spelling**—Enough said on this one?!

10. **Make it clear what you want kids to do**—Be sure to say in clear terms (i.e, the words of a seven-year-old instead of college-level jargon) what the skill is, why it is worth knowing, and what you will expect them to do as a result of this lesson.

What NOT to do . . .

1. **Avoid round-robin teaching**—Do not have kids waiting continually for their turn. Small-group instruction usually makes this problem go away.

2. **Try not to correct students too quickly**—Let kids have an opportunity to self-correct before intervening.

3. **Avoid drill-and-kill teaching**—There is no question that phonics knowledge is important. However, we need to avoid militaristic teaching that drums information into young readers' heads at the cost of killing their interest in reading. Some things must be learned by rote, but be sure to include ample practice in rich and interesting texts.

In this section we recommend several activities that may be used with many of the phonics skills enumerated earlier. Therefore, please note that if we recommend an activity that is useful in teaching, say, consonant sounds, it may be just as useful in teaching consonant digraphs, rimes, or vowel generalizations.

A FORMAT FOR EXPLICIT PHONICS INSTRUCTION

Purpose

Glazer (1998) developed a step-by-step procedure for teaching phonics skills. Try it as one way to provide explicit instruction for your students.

Materials

Tongue twisters, riddles, jokes, songs, poems, or stories specially selected for the phonics pattern you wish to teach are needed for this procedure.

Procedure

Step 1: Bombard students with correct models.

New phonics knowledge is heavily dependent on students having already internalized in their listening and speaking vocabularies correct pronunciations and usages of thousands of words.

After deciding which phonics element you wish to teach, select reading materials that use the element. Read, retell, organize simple plays or raps involving students, or other means to build in many encounters with the words you want to emphasize.

As you use the target words in your readings or retellings, write the word on your easel chart paper or highlight it when using a big book. Say, "Read these words with me as I say them." Then say, "What is the same about these words we just read?" to guide them to the phonic element you want to emphasize. Always provide the correct answer if the students are in doubt.

Step 2: Provide structured practice.

With students gathered in a small group, write the letter(s) being emphasized at the top of your easel chart. If, for instance, we were emphasizing the consonant digraph "ch," then the following words could be written and said aloud slowly by the teacher: *cheese, church, cherry.* Then, students would be encouraged to contribute others having that same beginning sound (perhaps *chain, change, charm, child*).

Step 3: Assess learning using this phonics game.

The object of this game is to assess student learning by matching the letter or letter combination being emphasized with pictures beginning with that sound(s). Here's how to do it:

- Create cards for each student having the letter(s) being studied.
- Collect several pictures of objects or creatures from magazines whose names begin with that letter(s).
- Cut a sheet of tag board into several pieces about flashcard size.
- Place students into pairs. Then, demonstrate to students how to cut and paste pictures from magazines onto tag board that have the beginning sound you are emphasizing. Repeat the exercise, only this time, students are doing the task with you in their groups of two (i.e., finding pictures of objects or creatures that begin with that sound).
- Check the products from each group with the students. Ask them to name the picture that begins with that sound.

Step 4: Share what they have learned.

Children love to share (and brag) about their accomplishments. Help them create word banks, pocket dictionaries, or word charts showing off how many words they could find containing the phonics element you have been studying together. These may include the names of animals, food, toys, friends, family members, and objects from their environment having the target letter-sound combination. Have students share their accomplishments in small groups or with the whole class in a kind of author's-chair format. They will love showing off their new knowledge!

LETTER SOUND CARDS

Purpose

Letter sound cards are intended as prompts to help students remember individual and combination (i.e., digraphs and blends) letter sounds that have been introduced during mini-lessons or other teachable moments.

Materials

You will need to have a word bank for each child (children's shoe boxes, recipe boxes, or other small containers in which index cards can be filed), alphabetic divider cards to separate words in the word bank, index cards, and colored markers.

Procedure

This is essentially the same idea as the word bank activity shown in chapter 9 on vocabulary instruction. The idea is to provide students with their own word cards on which you (or they) have written a key letter sound or sounds on one side and a word that uses that sound on the other. Whenever possible, it is best to use nouns or other words that can be depicted with a picture, so that, for emergent readers, a drawing can be added to the side having the word (as needed). Two examples are shown in Figure 8.11.

PHONICS FISH (OR FONIKS PHISH?) CARD GAME

Purpose

Remember the age-old children's card game *Fish* (sometimes called *Go Fish*)? This review activity helps students use their growing visual awareness of phonics sounds and patterns to construct word families (i.e., groups of words having the same phonetic pattern). It can be played in small groups, at a learning center with two to four children, or during reading groups with the teacher.

Materials

You will need a deck of word cards. The words can be selected from the students' word banks or chosen by the teacher or parent/teaching assistant from among those familiar to all students. The word cards should contain ample examples of at least three or four phonetic patterns that you wish to review (e.g., beginning consonant sounds, r-controlled vowels, clusters, digraphs, rime families, and so on).

Procedure

Before beginning the game, explain which word families or sound patterns are to be used in this game of Phonics Fish. Next, explain the rules of the game:

1. Each child will be dealt five cards.
2. The remaining cards (deck of about fifty) are placed facedown in the middle of the group.

Figure 8.11   Letter Sound Card Examples

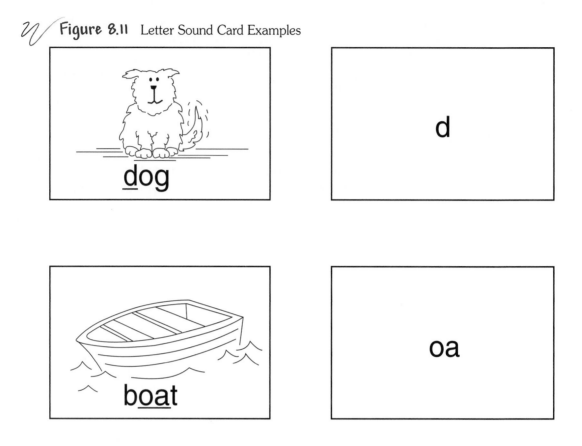

3. Taking turns in a round-robin fashion, each child can ask any other if he is holding a word having a particular sound or pattern. For example, if one of the patterns included is the /sh/ sound, then the first student may say something like, "Juanita, do you have any words with the /sh/ sound?" If the student being asked does not have any word cards with that pattern, he can say "Go Fish!" The student asking the question then draws a card from the deck.

4. Cards having matching patterns (two or more) are placed faceup in front of the student asking the question.

5. The first student to get rid of all his cards wins the game.

SOUND SWIRL

Purpose

Sound Swirl is a simple activity that is used to 1) help students think of "words in their head" that have a certain sound element and 2) to then use invented or "temporary" spellings to construct the words they have recalled. This helps students learn to sound out words and to notice particular word sounds as their phonics awareness grows. This activity is usually best applied as a guided practice or for review.

Materials

You will need some chart paper and markers in different colors.

Procedure

Gather a group of children around you with whom you wish to review a phonics sound pattern (for our example here, we will use the beginning sound represented by the letters /ch/ as in *church*). Write the letters representing the sound you wish to emphasize (/ch/ in our example) on the chart paper using a colorful marker. Say, "Boys and girls, I want us to see just how many words we can think of that begin with the sound made by the letters ch, which make the /ch/ sound. So, get your mouth ready to make the /ch/ sound, swirl around all the letters in your head (Note: Here, the teacher makes a grand gesture of a swirling motion above her head), and say the first words that come to your mind, right now!!!" At this point, the students will call out such words as *church, chump, change, child, chirp,* and so on. Select a few of the words they called out and, in whole-group fashion (using volunteers), have them sound out the written words (beginning each time with /ch/ in a different color from the rest of the word) so they can recognize visually how words can be sounded out and written.

"Button" Sounds

Purpose

Children often enjoy wearing buttons that are unique. Similarly, many schools have button-making machines that can inexpensively produce buttons for special projects. "Button sounds," as we call them, take advantage of children's attraction to buttons to help cement their understanding of introductory sounds in words. (Note: This is recommended only as an adjunct to other more comprehensive minilessons.)

Materials

You will need access to a button-making machine and materials, or a local vendor who can make the buttons for you inexpensively.

Procedure

Identify the phonics sounds/symbols you wish to emphasize. For example, we first used this activity with first-grade students to help them learn alphabet letters as initial sounds in words (e.g., Bb together with a picture of a butterfly, Cc with a picture of a cat, Gg with a picture of a goat, and so on). However, any sound/symbol relationship can be used that can be illustrated with a picture. Once you have introduced the "sound for the day" and linked it to a key illustration (e.g., a witch for the letters Ww, or a ship for the digraph sh), distribute the buttons to all students in the group or class. You should instruct the children that whenever they are asked by anyone about their button, they should respond with a statement such as, "This is my sh and ship button." An example of a button is shown in Figure 8.12.

Stomping, Clapping, Tapping, and Snapping Sounds

Purpose

Helping children hear syllables in words enables them to segment sounds. This knowledge can be used in myriad ways to improve writing/spelling, increase awareness of letter combinations used to produce speech sounds, and apply knowledge of onsets and rimes. All these skills and more enable students to sound out words in print more effectively. For ages, teachers have found success in helping children hear syllables by clapping them out when reading nursery rhymes, such as "Mar-y had a lit-tle lamb, lit-tle lamb, lit-tle lamb. . . ."

Figure 8.12   Button from "Button Sounds" Activity

wh

wheelchair

Materials

We prefer to use rhyming poetry, songs, chants, or raps for these syllabication activities. Use an enlarged version produced for an overhead projector, a big book version, or simply rewrite the text on large chart paper using a colored ink marker.

Procedure

First, model read the enlarged text aloud in a normal cadence for your students. Reread the selection at a normal cadence, inviting students to join in as they wish. Next, explain that you will reread the selection, but this time you will clap (or snap, or stomp, and so on) the syllables in the words. (Note: If you have not already explained the concept of syllables, you will need to do so at this point.) Finally, invite students to clap (or make whatever gesture or sound that you have chosen) as you reread the passage.

TONGUE TWISTERS

Purpose

Many students enjoy word play. Tongue twisters can be a wonderful way of reviewing consonants (Cunningham, 1995) in a way that is fun for students. We have found that Tongue Twister activities can combine reading and creative writing processes to help children deepen their understanding of phonic elements.

Materials

There are many traditional tongue twisters in published children's literature that may be used. However, we find that children enjoy creating their own tongue twisters perhaps even more. All you need to do is decide which sounds/letter pattern families are to be used.

Procedure

Cunningham (1995) suggested that you begin by simply reciting some tongue twisters aloud and inviting students to join in. We recommend that you produce two or three examples on chart paper and post them on the wall as you introduce the concept of tongue twisters. For example, you might use the following:

Silly Sally sat in strawberries.

Peter Piper picked a peck of pickled peppers.
If Peter Piper picked a peck of pickled peppers,
Then how many peppers did Peter Piper pick?
Peter Piper panhandles pepperoni pizza,
With his pint-sized pick-up he packs a peck of pepperoni pizzas,
For Patti his portly patron.

Simple Simon met a pieman going to the fair,
Said Simple Simon to the pieman,
"Let me taste your wares!"
Said the pieman to Simple Simon,
"Show me first your penny!"
Said Simple Simon to the pieman,
"I'm afraid I haven't any."

Children especially love it when teachers create tongue twisters using names of children in the class, such as the following example:

Pretty Pam picked pink peonies for Patty's party.

Lastly, challenge students to create their own tongue twisters to "stump the class." It may be fun to award students coupons that can be used to purchase take-home books for coming up with clever tongue twisters.

CREATING NONSENSE WORDS

Purpose

Many of the most popular poets, such as Shel Silverstein and Jack Prelutsky, have tapped into children's fascination with word play in their very creative poetry. For instance, when Silverstein speaks of "gloppy glumps of cold oatmeal," we all understand what he means, even though gloppy and glumps are really nonsense words. Getting students to create nonsense words and apply them to popular poetry is a motivating way to help students practice phonic patterns.

Materials

First decide which phonic sound/letter pattern families you wish to emphasize. For instance, it may be appropriate to review the letter/sound families represented by -ack, -ide, -ing, and -ore. Also needed are books of poetry or songs with rhyming phrases, chart paper or overhead transparencies, and markers.

Procedure

As with all activities, begin by modeling what you expect students to do. On a large sheet of chart paper or at the overhead projector, write the word family parts that you wish to emphasize (for this example, we used -ack, -ide, -ing, and -ore). Illustrate how you can convert the word parts into nonsense words by adding a consonant, consonant blend, or consonant digraph before each one, such as shown by the following:

-ack	-ide	-ing	-ore
gack	spide	gacking	zore
kack	mide	zwing	glore
chack	plide	kaching	jore

In the next phase of the demonstration, select a poem or song that rhymes and review it with students first (use enlarged text for all of your modeling). Next, show students a revised copy of the song or poem in which you have substituted nonsense words. Here is one example we have used with the song "I Know an Old Lady Who Swallowed a Fly." We show only the first verse here, but you could use the entire song, substituting a nonsense word in each stanza.

Original version:

I know an old lady who swallowed a fly,
I don't know why,
she swallowed the fly,
I guess she'll die.

Nonsense word version:

*I know an old lady who swallowed a **zwing**,*
I don't know why,
*she swallowed the **zwing**,*
I guess she'll die.

MAKING WORDS

Cunningham and Cunningham (1992) described making words as a hands-on manipulative activity in which students look for patterns in words. Students also learn how new words can be created by simply changing one letter or letter combination. Making words can be useful for either vocabulary building or for developing phonetic understanding. For a complete explanation of making words, please see the discussion of this activity in chapter 9.

WIDE READING

John J. Pikulski (1998), a recent president of the International Reading Association, noted the importance of massive amounts of reading in high-quality texts as a tool for developing decoding fluency. Specifically, he pointed out that children can benefit from three main types of practice: wide reading, independent-level reading, and multiple rereadings of texts.

Wide reading simply refers to the notion of encouraging children to read in a variety of topics and genre. Teachers can encourage wide reading by regularly conducting "book talks." With book talks, the teacher reads aloud a particularly interesting portion of a great book or other text form, but leaves the students "hanging" at a particularly suspenseful point in the narrative. This often makes students mad with desire to finish reading the selection!

Independent-level reading refers to helping children find many and varied books of interest that are easy for them to read. In this case, "easy" reading refers to books in which students will be able to read about 98% or more of the words without difficulty. In addition to improving phonics fluency, research shows that independent-level reading for at least 20 minutes each day will also greatly improve reading rate.

Multiple rereadings of texts means just what the words imply—rereading favorite books, poems, or other text forms. Multiple rereadings will essentially provide the same benefits as independent-level reading.

To make wide reading, independent-level reading, and multiple rereadings happen every day, we recommend that you institute *DEAR* time (*Drop Everything And Read*) in your classroom. For about 20 to 30 minutes each day, have students stop at a designated time and read a book of their choosing. DEAR can be broken into two shorter time segments just as effectively, if you wish. The teacher may participate and read a book for fun, or work with a small group of struggling readers rereading familiar texts in choral fashion. You will love the results.

A Phonics Quick Test (Answer Key)

1. The word *charkle* is divided between r and k. The *a* has an r- controlled sound, and the *e* is _silent_.
2. In the word *small, sm-* is known as the *onset* and *-all* is known as the *rime*. (See chapter 8 for a full explanation.)
3. *Ch* in the word *chair* is known as a _consonant digraph_.
4. The letter *c* in the word *city* is a _soft_ sound; in the word *cow*, the letter *c* is a _hard_ sound.
5. The letters *bl* in the word *blue* are referred to as a consonant _blend_.
6. The underlined vowels in the words _author_, _spread_, and _blue_ are known as vowel _digraphs_.
7. The words *tag, run, cot,* and *get* have which vowel pattern? <u>consonant - vowel - consonant (CVC)</u>
8. The words *glide, take,* and *use* have the <u>vowel - consonant - "e"</u> vowel pattern.
9. The single most powerful phonics skill we can teach to emergent readers for decoding unfamiliar words in print is <u>beginning</u> sounds in words. We introduce this skill using <u>consonant</u> sounds first because they are the most <u>constant (or "dependable" or "reliable")</u>.
10. The word part *work* in the word *working* is known as a <u>root (or "base" or "unbound morpheme")</u> word.
11. The word part *-ing* in the word *working* is known as a <u>suffix (or "bound morpheme")</u>.
12. Cues to the meaning and pronunciation of unfamiliar words in print are often found in the print surrounding the unfamiliar, also known as the <u>context</u>.

Grading Key for Teachers

Number Correct	Evaluation
12	Wow, you're good! (You must have had no social life in college.)
10–11	Not too bad, but you may need a brushup. (Read this chapter.)
7–9	Emergency! Take a refresher course, quick! (Read this chapter.)
0–6	Have you ever considered a career in telemarketing?! (Just kidding, but read this chapter . . . right away!)

SELECTED REFERENCES

Adams, M. J. (1990). *Beginning to read: Thinking and learning about print.* Cambridge, MA: MIT Press.

Bear, D. R., Templeton, S., Invernizzi, M., & Johnston, F. (1996). *Words their way: Word study for phonics, vocabulary, and spelling instruction.* Columbus, OH: Merrill/Prentice Hall.

Blevins, W. (1996). *Phonics: Quick-and-easy learning games.* New York: Scholastic Professional Books.

Blevins, W. (1997). *Phonemic awareness activities for early reading success.* New York: Scholastic.

Blevins, W. (1998). *Phonics from A to Z: A practical guide.* New York: Scholastic Professional Books.

Chard, D. J., & Osborn, J. (1999). Phonics and word recognition instruction in early reading programs: Guidelines for accessibility. *Learning Disabilities Research & Practice, 14*(2), 107–125.

Cooter, K. S. (2001). *Teaching phonics skills to urban student populations.* Unpublished manuscript, Texas Christian University, Fort Worth, Texas, November, 2001.

Cunningham, P. M. (1995). *Phonics they use* (2nd ed.). New York: Harper-Collins.

Cunningham, P. M., & Cunningham, J. W. (1992). Making words: Enhancing the invented spelling-decoding connection. *The Reading Teacher, 46,* 106–107.

Eldredge, J. L. (1995). *Teaching decoding in holistic classrooms.* Columbus, OH: Merrill/Prentice Hall.

Glazer, S. M. (1998). A format for explicit phonics instruction. *Teaching PreK–8, 28*(4), 102–105.

Manzo, A. V., & Manzo, U. C. (1993). *Literacy disorders: Holistic diagnosis and remediation.* Fort Worth, TX: Harcourt Brace Jovanovich College Publishers.

McKee, D. (1968). *Elmer.* New York: McGraw-Hill.

Moustafa, M. (1997). *Beyond traditional phonics: Research discoveries and reading instruction.* Portsmouth, NH: Heinemann.

National Research Council. (1999). *Starting out right: A guide for promoting children's reading success.* Washington, D.C.: National Academy Press.

Pikulski, J. J. (1998). *Improving reading achievement: Major instructional considerations for the primary grades.* Commissioner's Reading Day Statewide Conference, Austin, Texas, February 25, 1998.

Pressley, M. (1998). *Reading instruction that works: The case for balanced teaching.* New York: Guilford Press.

Rasinski, T., & Padak, N. (1996). *Holistic reading strategies: Teaching children who find reading difficult.* Columbus, OH: Merrill/Prentice Hall.

Reutzel, D. R., & Cooter, R. B. (2000). *Teaching children to read: Putting the pieces together.* Upper Saddle River, NJ: Merrill/Prentice Hall.

Stahl, S. (1992). Saying the "p" word: Nine guidelines for exemplary phonics instruction. *The Reading Teacher, 45*(8).

Williams, S. G., Cooter, K. S., & Cooter, R. B. (2003). *The starpoint phonics quick test.* Unpublished manuscript.

Word Cards for The Reutzel/Cooter Word Attack Survey

tat
nan
rin
mup

det
sim
loj
cal
pif

fek
geem
hoad
kait

weam
jape
zote
gipe
tope

bo
ka
fi
tu

sar
wir
der
nur
ahurla

continued

Continued

mup
cremon
laken
cale

cose
cimmy
cyler
gare
gob

gime
genry
chur
thim

shar
whilly
thar
nally
ipple

attawap
urrit
phur
phattle

phenoblab
lappo
pabute
larpin
witnit

Chapter 9

Teaching and Assessing Vocabulary Development

The sun was streaming into the classroom on a crisp October morning as Mr. Roberts sat with a group of fifth-grade students. They were about to begin learning about the rainforests of the Amazon. Tomorrow they would begin an interactive exploration via the Internet on a site called passporttoknowledge.com, so Mr. Roberts thought a little vocabulary lesson would help the kiddos get the most out of the experience. Because they lived in an urban setting in a desert region of the West, he knew there would be some fairly alien notions for his students.

Mr. Roberts wrote the following words on the easel chart: *Amazon River, South America, biodiversity, canopy, Brazil, photosynthesis, species,* and then said, "As I mentioned this morning, we're going to begin an exciting unit of study on the rainforests of the Amazon. These are a few of the words from the lesson guide that will be coming up in our Internet experiences, so I thought we should talk about them a little. Let's begin with the basics—who can tell me where South America is?"

James eagerly responded, "I think it's near Orlando."

LaJean retorts, "I don't think so. It's where Chile is, isn't it."

Mr. Roberts says, "Very good, LaJean. Let's all take a look at the map and see exactly where South America is." He then proceeded with a short geography lesson using the global map. Roberts then returned to the vocabulary words he had written on the easel chart.

"Okay, then, can anyone tell me something about the word *biodiversity*? I'll give you a hint: if you break away the first part of the word, '*bio,*' which means 'life,' that leaves you with a pretty familiar word—'*diversity.*' What does diversity mean?"

After a long silence and blank stares, Mr. Roberts tried another tack.

"Okay, forget that one for now. What about the word 'canopy'?"

Again, no takers.

Finally, Julio took a chance, "Isn't *canopy* the stuff they make tents out of?"

Clearly, these students didn't have the slightest notion what these words meant, so some serious vocabulary development was in order. Fortunately, Mr. Roberts had prepared for this possibility.

"Good try, Julio! I think you're referring to *canvas*, which looks a lot like *canopy*, but its meaning is very different. Well, not to worry—I have a few games we can play [teacher-talk for "learning activities"] that will get us ready to explore the rainforests. So let's go."

Words are the symbols we use to express ideas; *captions,* you might say, that describe our life experiences. Vocabulary development is a process that goes on throughout life and can be enhanced in the classroom through enticing learning experiences. Except for economically deprived or handicapped children, most acquire a vocabulary of over 10,000 words during the first five years of their lives (Smith, 1987). Most school children will learn between 2,000 and 3,600 words per year, though estimates vary from 1,500 to more than 8,000 (Clark, 1993; Johnson, 2001; Nagy, Herman, & Anderson, 1985).

Clearly, vocabulary development is a critical aspect of successful reading (Rupley, Logan, & Nichols, 1999). There seems to be a cyclical effect between vocabulary knowledge and reading. As Johnson and Rasmussen (1998) stated: Word knowledge affects reading comprehension, which in turn helps students expand their knowledge bases, which in turn facilitates vocabulary growth and reading comprehension (p. 204). As students progress in their schooling, vocabulary becomes even more important in content-area instruction because it constitutes both information students must learn and concepts they need to understand to function within the subject (Rekrut, 1996).

Since the latter part of the nineteenth century in America, there has been a great deal of research and debate about the role of vocabulary knowledge in learning to read. James M. Cattell in 1885 argued that children should learn entire words as a method of beginning reading. Though learning "sight words" alone is no longer recommended as an effective beginning reading approach, most teachers and researchers still believe that the acquisition of a large number of sight words should be part of every child's beginning reading program.

BACKGROUND BRIEFING FOR TEACHERS

There are actually several different "vocabularies" housed in one's mind and usable for language transactions. The largest of these is known as the **listening vocabulary.** These are words you are able to hear and understand, but not necessarily use in your own speech. For example, when the famous Hale-Bopp comet visited our solar system in 1997, most children in the middle and upper elementary grades were quite capable of watching news telecasts about the comet and understanding most of what was reported. However, if you were to ask many of these same children to explain what they had just learned, many of the technical words and factual bits of information would not be included in their description. It is not that the children somehow forgot everything they had just learned; rather, they did not "own" the words for speech purposes quite yet—they were able only to hear and understand the technical words.

Words that a student can hear, understand, *and* use in her speech are known as her **speaking vocabulary.** It is a subset of the listening vocabulary and, thus, is smaller. The gap between peoples' listening and speaking vocabularies is greatest in youth. The gap tends to narrow as adulthood approaches, though the two vocabularies are never equal. The next largest vocabulary is the **reading vocabulary.** As you might guess, it is a subset of one's listening and speaking vocabularies and consists of words one can read and understand. The smallest vocabulary that one acquires is the **writing vocabulary**—words that one can understand when listening, speaking, and reading, *and* can reproduce when writing.

Cooter and Flynt (1996) grouped listening and reading vocabularies into a collective category known as the *receptive vocabulary* and writing and speaking vocabularies into a category known as the *expressive vocabulary.* These descriptors reflect the broader language functions of these vocabularies for the student as either information receiver or spoken or written language producer.

For a student to be able to read and understand a word, she must have first acquired it at the listening and speaking levels. Teachers, then, must somehow find out which words are already "owned" by their students as listening and speaking vocabulary and teach the unknown words that may be critical in their assigned reading. Without this kind of knowledge, adequate context for word identification will be missing and can threaten further reading development and, of course, damage comprehension.

A primary way of increasing vocabulary is through wide reading on a daily basis (Irwin, 1990, Johnson, 2001). This helps readers gain greater fluency and improves their ability to use context from the passage to interpret word meanings. Effective readers can maintain satisfactory comprehension when up to 15% of the words in a passage are unknown or new. However, research shows that students who are learning English as a second language (Johnson & Steele, 1996) and, we believe, others having weak vocabularies tend to be word-by-word readers and are much less able to tolerate unknown vocabulary. The teacher's role is to help these learners with special needs, as well as normally developing readers, to learn the largest possible vocabularies.

DIRECT INSTRUCTION AND VOCABULARY LEARNING

Even though many new words are added to our vocabulary through indirect means (e.g., conversations with family members and peers, television, environmental print such as signs, and so on), some must be learned through direct instruction (Rekrut, 1996). It is estimated that many words require between five and twenty-six minutes to be learned (Jenkins, Matlock, & Slocum, 1989), depending on such factors as context, number of encounters with the new word, and, of course, prior knowledge. Studies have shown that direct instruction can be especially powerful in such content areas as science and mathematics (Bradley, 1988; Monroe, 1998).

Students learn words at one of three levels (Beck, McCaslin, & McKeown, 1980; Ryder & Graves, 1994): words whose meanings are already known concretely, words that are familiar, and unknown words. All vocabulary words must become known in such depth that they can be recognized and used in a variety of contexts and related to a range of experiences (Rekrut, 1996). Direct instruction methods, such as those presented in this chapter, can be most effective in helping students learn unknown or barely familiar vocabulary effectively. One group of students who especially benefit from direct instruction are English Language Learners, the subject of the next section.

MEETING THE NEEDS OF ENGLISH LANGUAGE LEARNERS: ESL CONNECTIONS

A growing percentage of students in our schools are learning to read in a second language—English. According to the National Center for Educational Statistics (1999), about 17% of all students are classified as Hispanic (14%) or Asian/Pacific Islander (3%). Many of these students speak a language other than English as their native tongue. As it was in the earliest days of our country for most newcomers, learning to read and write in English can be a formidable challenge, but one that must be successfully addressed if these students are to reach their potential in our society. *Literacy is in so many ways the gateway to social equity.*

One of the common needs of English Language Learners (ELLs) is assistance with unfamiliar vocabulary they encounter while reading. Peregoy and Boyle (2001), in their book *Reading, Writing, & Learning in ESL,* recommended some guidelines for vocabulary development. First, select words to emphasize that you consider important to comprehending the assigned passage. Next, create several sentences loaded with context using these target words. This will give them an opportunity to use context to predict the meaning of the target words. Teacher modeling of prediction strategies using context is a must for students to grasp this strategy. Follow these modeling and guided practice sessions with discussion using excerpts from the text they will be assigned in which the target words appear.

Two vocabulary development activities that appear later in this chapter are highly recommended for ELL students (May & Rizzardi, 2002; Peregoy & Boyle, 2001): the Vocabulary Cluster, and Semantic Map. Certainly, any of the strategies found in this chapter are appropriate for ELL students so long as you are direct and explicit in your teaching. Direct instruction helps ELL students create mental scaffolding for support of new vocabulary and concepts.

Johnson's Vocabulary Instruction Guidelines

Dale Johnson, a well-known reading researcher having a particular interest in vocabulary instruction, suggested guidelines for instruction in his book entitled *Vocabulary in the Elementary and Middle School* (2001, pp. 41–48). They are based on his extensive review of the research and are very congruent indeed with the philosophy of comprehensive instruction. Following is a summary of Johnson's vocabulary instruction guidelines:

- *Word knowledge is essential for reading comprehension.* Vocabulary instruction should utilize activities like the ones found in this chapter that link word learning to concept and schema development.

- *Wide reading should be encouraged and made possible in the classroom.* Literally thousands of words are learned through regular and sustained reading. Time should be set aside each day for this crucial learning activity. As an example, Johnson advocates the use of a program called "Read-a-Million-Minutes," which was designed to foster wide reading throughout Iowa. All students set their own in-school and out-of-school reading goal, which contributes to the school's goal.

- *Use direct instruction to teach words that are necessary for passage comprehension.* Considering how critical some words are for comprehending a new passage, teachers should not leave vocabulary learning to incidental encounters, but rather plan regular direct instruction lessons to make sure that essential words are learned.

- *Active learning activities yield the best results.* According to research conducted by Stahl (1986), vocabulary instruction that provided only definitional information (i.e., dictionary activities) failed to significantly improve comprehension. Active learning opportunities; such as creation of word webs, playing word games, and discussing new words in reading groups or literature circles, are far more effective in cementing new knowledge and improving comprehension.

- *Students require a good bit of repetition to learn new words and integrate them into existing knowledge (schemas).* In some cases, student may require as many as 40 encounters to fully learn new vocabulary. To know a word well means knowing what it means, how to pronounce it, and how its meaning changes in different contexts. Repeated exposures to the word in different contexts is the key to successful learning.

- *Students should be helped to develop their own strategies for word learning from written and oral contexts.* This includes the use of context clues, structural analysis (root words, prefixes, suffixes), and research skills (use of the dictionary, thesaurus, and so on).

ASSESSING VOCABULARY KNOWLEDGE

In truth, most vocabulary assessment done by master teachers is through careful classroom observations of student reading behaviors. As teachers work with their pupils each day in needs-based group instruction, they discover high-utility words that seem to cause trouble for one or more students. Teachers can work these words into vocabulary instruction activities like those featured later in this chapter. But this is not to suggest that more cannot be done early in the school year to discover which words most of your students need to learn. Following are a few classroom-proven ideas to help with that process.

ORAL READING ASSESSMENT

Purpose

Oral reading assessment is a method by which problem vocabulary words in print can be distinguished by the teacher in a quick and efficient manner. It is drawn from the running record style of assessment frequently used to note reading miscues.

Materials

You will need photocopies (two copies each) of three or four passages for the student to read that you believe to be at the *instructional* or *frustration* reading level. The passages should be drawn from reading materials commonly used in your classroom curriculum. Ideally, the passages are sufficiently challenging so that students will have trouble with about 5 to 10% of the words. It will be necessary for you to do a quick word count to determine if the passages are appropriate once the student has read them. It is also essential that you have a range of passages, in terms of difficulty, to account for the vast differences between students' reading ability. (Note: If the student calls less than 10% of the words correctly, she may not be getting enough context from the passages for adequate comprehension.)

Procedure

Give the student a copy of the first passage you want him to read and keep one for yourself. Ask the student to read the passage aloud. While he does, note any words that he either does not know or mispronounces. Repeat the procedure until the student has read all of the passages. We recommend that you discontinue a passage if the student consistently has trouble with more than one or two words in any one sentence. After the student has finished, tally the number of miscalled words and determine if the passage is acceptable for analysis (no more than about 10% miscalled or unknown words). List any words that seem to be problematic for the student.

Repeat this procedure with all of your students during the first week or so of the new school year and 1) create a master list of words that seem to be problematic and 2) determine the number or percentage of the class who seem to find each word difficult or unknown. Use the more frequent problem words as part of your vocabulary instruction program.

CLOZE PASSAGES

Cloze passages are short (250 words) passages drawn from typical reading materials found in your instructional program. These passages have key words deleted and replaced with a blank line (Johnson, 2001). Students are asked to read the cloze passage(s) and see if they can fill in the missing words based on what they believe makes sense using context clues. Cloze tests cause students to use their "schema knowledge" of a subject, understanding of basic syntax (word order relationships), and/or word and sentence meaning (semantics) knowledge to guess what a missing or familiar word in print might be. We encourage teachers to administer cloze passages to the whole class at once as a starting point to determine vocabulary needs.

Vocabulary Flash Cards

Purpose

One of the most traditional ways to do a quick assessment of a student's vocabulary knowledge is the flash card technique. High-frequency words, those appearing most in print, as well as other high-utility words for specific grade levels, are printed individually on flash cards and shown to students for them to identify. Though some reading researchers argue that flash cards are not a valid assessment tool—because the words are presented in isolation instead of in complete sentences and paragraphs—flash cards continue to be used by many master teachers as one way to determine the direction of classroom instruction.

Materials

Obtain a list of high-frequency sight words (Note: We provide a copy of the Fry [1980] word list in Figure 9.12). Copy each word, one word each, onto index cards using a bold marker. An alternative is to type the words into a classroom computer and print them in a large font size onto heavy paper stock. Then, cut the words into a uniform flash card size. For recording purposes, you will also need a photocopy/master list of the words for each student in your class.

Procedure

"Flash" each card to the student one at a time and ask him to name the word. Allow about five seconds for the student to identify each word. Circle any unknown or mispronounced words on a copy of the master sheet you are using for that student (simply note the student's name at the top of the photocopy along with the date of testing). After you have shown the flash cards to all students, compile a master list of troublesome words for whole-class or small-group instruction. The word banks activity found later in this chapter is one way to use this information that we highly recommend. The flash cards can be reused periodically to determine if students have learned the words being taught.

Connecting Assessment Findings to Teaching Strategies

Before discussing vocabulary instruction strategies, we have constructed a guide connecting assessment findings to intervention and/or strategy choices. It is our intention to help you select the most appropriate instructional interventions and strategies to meet your students' needs based on assessment data. This is in keeping with the "If-Then" mode of thinking we discussed in chapter 2. Teaching strategies described in the next section are listed across the top of the Intervention Strategy Guide for Vocabulary Development. Potential problems are listed vertically in the left-hand column. Here is a brief description of each problem area named in the guide.

Intervention Strategy Guide for Vocabulary Development

Student Problem(s) ↓ / Intervention Strategy →	Word Walls	Morph Analy.	Five-Step	Frayer	Cubing	Bingo!	Vocab SAVOR	Peer Teach	Pers. Word List	Semantic Maps	Making Words	Word Banks	Comp. Grid	Vocab. Cluster	Content Redef.
Reading	+	+	+	−	+	+	*	*	+	+	+	+	−	+	+
Writing	+	+	+	*	−	+	*	+	+	+	+	+	*	+	+
Concept/Schema	−	−	−	+	*	*	+	+	−	+	*	−	+	+	+
Technical	*	+	*	+	*	*	+	+	+	+	−	+	+	+	+
Context	−	*	−	*	−	*	+	*	−	−	−	−	−	−	+
Morphemic	+	+	−	*	*	−	−	+	*	−	*	*	−	−	−
Sight Words	+	−	+	−	−	+	−	*	+	−	*	+	−	−	−

Key: + excellent strategy
      * adaptable strategy
      − unsuitable strategy

231

- *Reading*—Word is in the student's listening and speaking vocabularies, but is not yet recognized in print.
- *Writing*—Word is in the student's listening, speaking, and reading vocabularies, but is not yet known well enough to be used when writing compositions.
- *Concept/schema*—The student does not comprehend the new word due to a lack of conceptual knowledge related to the word.
- *Technical*—The new word is unknown to the student and is directly related to a content area (i.e., science, social studies, mathematics, and so on).
- *Context*—Student has trouble using context clues to figure out the meaning of an unknown word.
- *Morphemic*—Student lacks sufficient knowledge about word parts such as prefixes, suffixes, and root words. This is also known as structural analysis.
- *Sight words*—Some common words in print are unknown.

In the next part of this chapter, we offer vocabulary instruction strategies for intervention based on the foregoing assessments.

TEACHING STRATEGIES: HELPING STUDENTS INCREASE THEIR READING VOCABULARIES

Susan Watts (1995) described five attributes of effective vocabulary instruction. You will discover that we have selected teaching activities that fulfill these criteria in this chapter.

- Students should be provided with 1) multiple exposures to new words, 2) in a variety of contexts, 3) over time. This will help you move new vocabulary from short-term to long-term (permanent) memory.
- Words should be taught within the context of a content-area unit/topic, theme, or story. This helps the new vocabulary to find the right "schema home."
- Teachers should help students activate prior knowledge when learning new words.
- Relationships should be emphasized in your lesson between *known* words and the *new* vocabulary you are introducing. This provides the all-important *scaffolding* for learning.
- Students should be taught to use context clues and reference tools in their reading and writing (i.e., dictionary, thesaurus) for building word knowledge.

WORD WALLS

Purpose

Pat Cunningham (2000) provided us with a wonderful description of *Word Walls:* a place where teachers can direct students' attention to high-frequency words, important words in a content unit of study, or useful words for books they are reading. There are many possible types of word walls. In essence, you simply post important words on a section of wall, usually on butcher paper or a pocket chart, and categorize them according to your purpose.

Materials

Most word walls are made from large sheets of butcher paper, on pocket charts, or bulletin boards. They need not be fancy.

Figure 9.1 Word Wall (A portion of high-frequency and other common words)

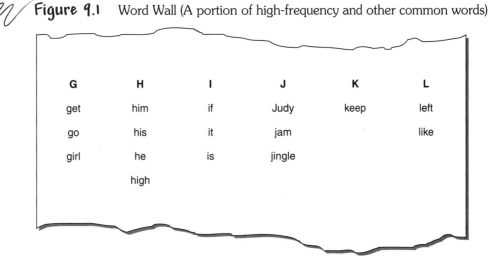

G	H	I	J	K	L
get	him	if	Judy	keep	left
go	his	it	jam		like
girl	he	is	jingle		
	high				

Procedure

Begin by making a blank word wall with a section for each letter of the alphabet. Then, introduce two or three words every few days or each week. As you introduce them, draw students' attention to common word parts, inflectional endings, meanings, and so forth. Be sure to write the words clearly using a dark marker and make letters large enough for everyone to see. An example is shown in Figure 9.1.

MORPHEMIC ANALYSIS (STRUCTURAL ANALYSIS)

Purpose

Morphemic analysis, also referred to as *structural analysis,* is the process of using one's knowledge of word parts to deduce meanings of unknown words. A *morpheme* is the smallest unit of meaning in a word. There are two types of morphemes: free and bound. A *free morpheme* is a freestanding root or base of any word that cannot be further divided and still have meaning. In the word *farmer, farm* is the root word or free morpheme. The *-er* portion of the word *farmer* is considered to be a bound morpheme. *Bound morphemes* carry meaning, but only when attached to a free morpheme. The most common bound morphemes are *prefixes (in-, pre-, mono-), suffixes (-er, -ous, -ology),* and *inflectional endings (-s, -es, -ing, -ed, -est).*

There are several ways that teachers commonly introduce morphemic analysis to students as a way of learning the meaning of new words. Sometimes we use students' knowledge of morphemes to analyze the meaning of a new word by showing a list of similar words having the same morpheme. Other times teachers simply tell students the meanings of new morphemes and let them figure out the meanings of new words containing the morpheme on their own or in small groups.

Materials

The essential activity for teachers is to research the meanings of morphemes and, in the case of activities involving word family lists, examples of other words having the morphemes to be used. A resource we have found helpful in planning many vocabulary activities is *The Reading Teacher's Book of Lists* (Fry, Kress, & Fountoukidis, 1993).

Procedure

Preselect words to be learned from the reading selection, then do the necessary background research and planning about the morphemes found in the new words. One activity is to construct *word family lists* that help students determine morpheme meanings. For example, a middle school teacher might decide to focus on the word *claustrophobia.* Her research into the morpheme *-phobia* might lead to the construction of the following list:

claustrophobia
cardiophobia
olfactophobia
telephonophobia
verbaphobia

This activity causes students to use *compare-and-contrast methods* of morphemic analysis. That is, they must look at the unfamiliar word and use their prior knowledge of other words that look like parts of the unfamiliar word to figure out what each word probably means. For example, *cardio-* probably reminds you of *cardiac,* which deals with the heart, and *-phobia* means "fear of." Therefore, *cardiophobia* must mean a fear of heart disease. To use this compare-and-contrast technique with students, first select words that have morphemes that can be compared to other words students are likely to know, then present both the new word and other words that begin or end like the unfamiliar word. Look at the following example from Cooter and Flynt (1996):

Because of my expansive vocabulary, my teacher called me a verbivore.

verbi-	vore
verbal	carnivore
verbose	herbivore
verbalize	omnivore

The teacher would write the sentence on the chalkboard and list below it examples of words that begin and end like the unfamiliar word. Then, through questioning, the teacher would lead students to specify the word's meaning by comparing and contrasting the known words to the unfamiliar one, thus concluding: A *verbivore* is a person who loves (eats) words.

Another way of using morphemic analysis to help students deduce meaning is to present unfamiliar terms along with explanations of the morphemes that make up the unfamiliar terms. The following procedure might be used as part of an introduction to a new text containing the words listed.

Step 1: Identify the terms that need preteaching.
pro-life
illegal
pro-choice
rearrest
unable
forewarn

Step 2: Along with these terms, write on the board a list of appropriate morphemes and their meanings.

pro = in favor of

il = not

fore = earlier

re = to do again

un = not

Step 3: Engage students in a discussion of what each term means and how the terms are interrelated. When there is confusion or disagreement, direct students to the terms in the text and/or the glossary for verification.

As useful as morphemic analysis can be, Cooter and Flynt (1996) offered a word of caution concerning morphemic analysis:

> Although we encourage the teaching of how to use context and morphemic analysis, we in no way advocate the overuse of these two techniques nor the memorization of lists of morphemes or types of context clues. Teachers who make students memorize common prefixes and suffixes run the risk of having students view the task as an end and not a means to help them become better readers. The story is told of a student who memorized the prefix "trans-" as meaning "across." Later the same week, the student was reading a science text and was asked what the word "transparent" meant. He replied confidently "a cross mother or father." The point being that all vocabulary instruction in the upper grades should be meaning-oriented, connected to text, functional, and capable of being used in the future. (p. 154)

FIVE-STEP METHOD

Purpose

Smith and Johnson (1980) suggested a five-step direct method of teaching new vocabulary for instant recognition. It uses multiple modalities to help students bring new words into the four vocabularies: listening, speaking, reading, and writing.

Materials

A variety of materials may be used in the five-step method, including a dry-erase board or chalkboard, an overhead projector, flash cards, and different color markers.

Procedure

1. Seeing   The new vocabulary word is shown on the overhead projector, chalkboard, or dry-erase board in the context of a sentence or (better) a short paragraph.

2. Listening   The teacher next discusses the word with students and verifies that they understand its meaning.

3. Discussing   Students are asked to create their own sentences using the new word, or, perhaps, to think of a synonym or antonym for the word. This is done orally.

4. Defining   Students try to create their own definitions for the new word. This is often much more difficult than using it in a sentence, and may not even be

possible for some words (i.e., is, the, if, and so on). Sometimes it is help-ful to ask students questions such as, "What does this word mean?" or "What does this word do in the sentence?"

5. Writing   We advocate using word banks or similar strategies in grades K–3. Stu-dents, sometimes requiring help, add each new word to their word bank and file it in alphabetical order. List the word in isolation on one side of an index card and in the context of a sentence on the reverse side. Emer-gent readers may want to draw a picture clue on the word bank card to remind them of the word's meaning.

FRAYER MODEL

Purpose

The Frayer Model (Frayer, Frederick, & Klausmeir, 1969) is a classic strategy that helps students understand new vocabulary and concepts in relation to what is already known. Frayer is especially useful for nonfiction terms—especially in the sciences—because it pre-sents essential and nonessential information related to the term, as well as examples and nonexamples.

Materials

Use a blank Frayer Model form on a transparency and an overhead projector for demon-stration purposes. Students will need paper and pencils for notetaking.

Procedure

The teacher presents or helps students determine essential and nonessential information about a concept, find examples and nonexamples of the concept, and recognize coordi-nate and subordinate relationships of the concept. This classification procedure can be done as a group, in dyads, or individually. Figure 9.2 shows an example for the concept of mammals.

Figure 9.2   Frayer Model: Mammals

Concept: MAMMALS

Essential Information or Attributes:
1. higher-order vertebrates
2. nourish young with milk from mammary glands
3. warm blooded
4. have skin covered with hair

Examples:
1. dogs
2. humans
3. monkeys
4. whales

Nonessential Information or Attributes:
1. size of the mammal
2. number of young born
3. where the mammal lives (i.e., water, land, etc.)

Nonexamples:
1. spiders
2. fish
3. reptiles

CUBING: THE DIE IS CAST!

Purpose

Cubing (Cowan & Cowan, 1980) is a postreading activity requiring students to analyze, discuss, and write about important new terms. By so doing, they activate prior knowledge or schemata that relate to the new term, which in turn helps the new information to become part of their long-term memory.

Materials

You will need a large foam or wooden cube covered with contact paper. On each side of the cube is written a different direction or question. Here are some examples that might be used for the term wheelchair:

1. Describe what it looks like.
2. What is it similar to or different from?
3. What else does it make you think of?
4. What is it made of?
5. How can it be used?
6. Where are you likely to find one?

Procedure

Once the cube is rolled and the direction facing the class or group is seen, each student is given a set number of minutes to record her answer. All six sides of the cube can be used in the activity, or, if you prefer, only a few. Once the cubing has ended, students can share their responses with the class or in small groups.

VOCABULARY BINGO!

Purpose

Vocabulary Bingo! (Spencer, 1997) is a whole-group word review activity in the format of the popular game bingo. This activity is an especially useful review for students learning English as a second language (ESL) and students in language enrichment programs, as well as for students whose first language is English.

Materials

For all students, make *Vocabulary Bingo!* boards on which you have printed new words learned in reading and writing activities during the year. The *Vocabulary Bingo!* cards can all be the same or can differ from one another, depending on the size of the group and the abilities of the learners. These words can be chosen from a classroom word bank, if one is being kept. For each word found on the cards, you will also need definitions written on slips of paper for the "caller" to read aloud during the game.

Procedure

Unlike traditional bingo games in which participants cover spaces on their boards when a number such as "B23" is called, students playing *Vocabulary Bingo!* cover board spaces upon which are printed review vocabulary words matching the definition that is read aloud by a caller. When all spaces in a row are covered, they call out bingo! An example of a *Vocabulary Bingo!* card is shown in Figure 9.3.

Figure 9.3   Vocabulary Bingo Card

VOCABULARY BINGO!				
silo	desert	umpire	dromedary	elevator
aviatrix	conifer	photography	precious	caravan
financier	meteoric	flank	declaration	cleats
maladjusted	payee	odoriferous	seizure	oasis
biannual	proceed	semicircle	humorous	proverb

SUBJECT AREA VOCABULARY REINFORCEMENT ACTIVITY (SAVOR)

Purpose

The Subject Area Vocabulary Reinforcement activity (SAVOR) (Stieglitz & Stieglitz, 1981) is an excellent postreading vocabulary learning procedure. As its name implies, SAVOR is intended for use with factual readings. Students combine research and rereading skills to identify similarities and differences between new terms.

Materials

Construct a SAVOR grid on a bulletin board or worksheet to be photocopied. Base it on a topic being studied in science, social studies, mathematics, health, history, or another content area. Make a content analysis of the unit of study and select new terms, to be listed in the left-hand column of the SAVOR grid, and characteristics related to the terms, to be listed across the top row. An example is shown in Figure 9.4.

Figure 9.4   SAVOR Grid: Solar System

Planets	Inner planet	Outer planet	Made up of gas	Has more than one moon	Longer revolution than Earth's 365 days	Has rings	Has been visited by a space probe	Stronger gravity than Earth's
Venus	+	−	−	−	−	−	+	−
Neptune	−	+	+	+	+	?	+	+
Saturn	−	+	+	+	+	+	+	+
Mercury	+	−	−	−	−	−	+	−

Procedure

SAVOR is intended to be used as a postreading activity to reinforce learning of new vocabulary. After students have completed their initial reading of the subject matter text, introduce the SAVOR grid bulletin board or photocopied worksheet. Discuss how to complete each grid space with either a plus (plus sign) or minus (minus sign), based on whether the term has the trait listed across the top of the grid. As with all minilessons, the teacher should first model the thinking process she is using to determine whether to put a plus or minus in the space provided. In Figure 9.4, we show an example of a SAVOR grid that was completed by children in a school in southern Texas as they studied the solar system.

PEER TEACHING

Purpose

An activity that has been proven to be effective with ESL students is called peer teaching (Johnson & Steele, 1996). It is considered to be a generative strategy, or one that is student initiated and monitored and can be used in different situations. Peer teaching first has individual students choosing from the reading selection a word that they feel is new and important. Next, one child teaches her term to another student, then vice versa.

Materials

Materials needed include only a reading selection to be shared with the whole group and the kind of supplies usually found in a writing center for students to use as they wish. It is also helpful to list several ways of teaching new vocabulary words to others, like those techniques found in this chapter that you commonly use with the students in your class.

Procedure

First, conduct a one- or two-session minilesson in which you model how you might choose a word from the reading selection that seems to be important to understanding what the author is saying. As an example, in Betsy Byars' Newbery Award-winning book *The Summer of the Swans* (1970), the main character, Sara, has a "grudging tolerance" of her Aunt Willie. Because this is important to understanding Sara and her feelings, you might select "grudging tolerance" as a term to teach someone reading the book. Next, model how you would choose one of the common strategies you use in class (on a list you post for all to see) and demonstrate how you would plan to teach your term to another. Finally, ask someone to role-play with you as you teach grudging tolerance.

PERSONAL WORD LISTS

Purpose

Most words are learned through repeated encounters in a meaningful context in spoken and written forms. All too often, however, when students come to a word they do not know, they simply run to the dictionary or to someone else for a quick definition, instead of using sentence or passage context to figure out for themselves the word's meaning. Although, certainly, we want students to develop dictionary skills, the first line of attack for gaining word meaning should be sentence or passage context. Personal word lists, as described in this section, have been around elementary and secondary classrooms for a very long time and have recently found success with ESL learners (Johnson & Steele, 1996). A personal

Figure 9.5   Personal Word List: *Lincoln* (Donald, 1995)

New Word	What I think it means . . .	Clues from the book or passage . . .	Dictionary definition (only when I needed to look)
1. abolitionists	people against slavery	John Brown was called one and was the leader of the Harper's Ferry raid.	
2. Republican	the party that Lincoln joined and ran for President	Lincoln went to the first meeting in 1855 (page 187) and later became its candidate in 1860.	
3. dispatches	a telegraph	Lincoln and Lee sent dispatches to people during the Civil War.	a message sent with speed

word list is a structured way of helping students develop the habit of using context to determine vocabulary meaning and to permanently fix the vocabulary in long-term memory.

Materials

Multiple blank copies of the personal word list, as shown in Figure 9.5, and a transparency version for demonstrations on the classroom overhead projector are required.

Procedure

Distribute blank copies of the personal word list sheet for students to review as you explain its function. Using a passage read recently by the class, model two or three examples of how you would complete the form for words you found in the passage that seemed important. Next, do a guided practice exercise with the whole group in which you provide several more words from the passage. Ask them to complete the form for each word and have volunteers share what they found with the class. Once students seem secure with the personal word list form, ask them to make several new entries with words of their own choosing in the next reading assignment. This will serve as a kind of individual practice exercise. Further use of the personal word list will depend on your class needs and how well you feel it works with your students. An example of a personal word list for the book *Lincoln* (Donald, 1995) is shown in Figure 9.5.

SEMANTIC MAPS

Purpose

Semantic maps are useful in tying together new vocabulary with prior knowledge and related terms (Johnson & Pearson, 1984; Monroe, 1998). Semantic maps are essentially a kind of "schema blueprint" in which students map what is stored in their brain about a topic and related concepts. Semantic maps help students relate new information to schemata already in the brain, integrate new information, and restructure existing information for greater clarity (Yopp & Yopp, 1996). Further, for students having learning problems,

Figure 9.6   Tennessee Semantic Web

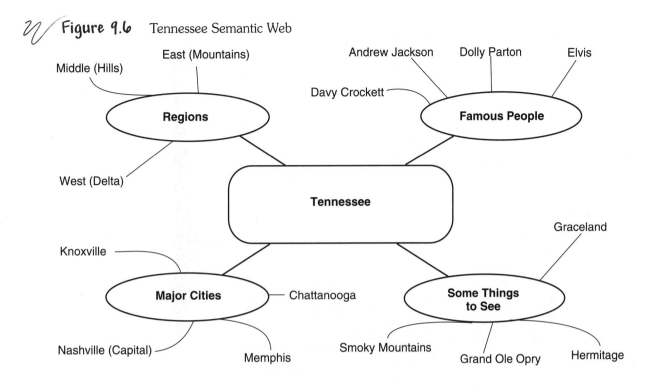

using semantic maps prior to reading a selection has also proven to promote better story recall than traditional methods (Sinatra, Stahl-Gemake, & Berg, 1984).

Materials

Writing materials are the only supplies needed.

Procedure

There are many ways to introduce semantic mapping to students, but the first time around you will likely want to use a structured approach. One way is to introduce semantic maps through something we call "wacky webbing." The idea is to take a topic familiar to all, such as the name of one's home state, and portray it in the center of the web, inside an oval. Major categories related to the theme are connected to the central concept using either bold lines or double lines. Details that relate to the major categories are connected using single lines. Figure 9.6 shows a semantic web for the topic "Tennessee."

Semantic webs can also be constructed that relate to a story or chapter book the students are reading. In Figure 9.7, we share one example of a semantic web from a story in the book *Golden Tales: Myths, Legends, and Folktales from Latin America* (Delacre, 1996).

MAKING WORDS

Purpose

Making Words (Cunningham & Cunningham, 1992) is a word learning strategy that might fit just as well in our chapter on phonics. It is a strategy that helps children improve their phonetic understanding of words through invented or "temporary spellings" (Reutzel &

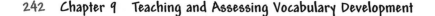

Figure 9.7   Semantic Web: "Guanina"

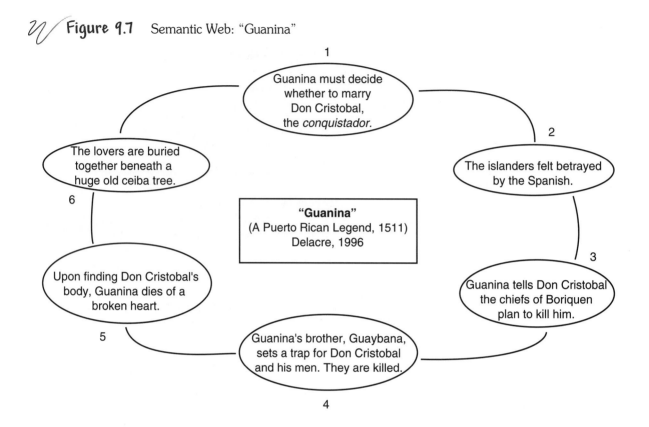

Cooter, 2000) while also increasing their repertoire of vocabulary words they can recognize in print. Making Words will be a familiar strategy for anyone who has ever played the cross-word board game Scrabble.

Materials

You will need a pocket chart, large index cards, and markers.

Procedure

In the Making Words activity, students are given a number of letters with which to make words. They begin by making two- or three-letter words using the letters during a set amount of time, then progress to making words having more letters until they finally arrive at the teacher's target word that uses all of the letters. This final word can be the main word to be taught for the day, but the other words discovered during the activity may also be new for some students. By manipulating the letters to make words of two, three, four, and more letters using temporary spellings, students have an opportunity to practice their phonemic awareness skills. Making words is recommended as a 15-minute activity when used with first and second graders. In Figures 9.8 and 9.9, we summarize and adapt the steps in planning and teaching a Making Words lesson as suggested by Cunningham and Cunningham (1992). Figure 9.10 provides details necessary for making two more Making Words lessons suggested by Cunningham and Cunningham (1992) that may be useful for helping students learn the procedure.

Figure 9.8   Planning a "Making Words" Lesson

1. Choose the final word to be emphasized in the lesson. It should be a key word from a reading selection, fiction or nonfiction, to be read by the class, or it may be of particular interest to the group. Be sure to select a word that has enough vowels and/or one that fits letter-sound patterns useful for most children at their developmental stage in reading and writing. For illustrative purposes, in these instructions we will use the word *thunder* that was suggested by Cunningham and Cunningham (1992).

2. Make a list of shorter words that can be spelled using the main word to be learned. For the word *thunder,* one could derive the following words: *red, Ted, Ned/den/end* (Note: these all use the same letters), *her, hut, herd, turn, hunt, hurt, under, hunted, turned, thunder.*

    From the You Were Able To list, select 12–15 words that include such aspects of written language as a) words that can be used to emphasize a certain kind of pattern, b) big and little words, c) words that can be made with the same letters in different positions (as with *Ned, end, den*), d) a proper noun, if possible, to remind students about using capital letters, and especially e) words that students already have in their listening vocabularies.

3. Write all of these words on large index cards and order them from the smallest to the largest words. Also, write each of the individual letters found in the key word for the day on large index cards (make two sets of these).

4. Reorder the words one more time to group them according to letter patterns and/or to demonstrate how shifting around letters can form new words. Store the two sets of large single-letter cards in two envelopes—one for the teacher, and one for children participating during the modeling activity.

5. Store the word stacks in envelopes and note on the outside of each the words/patterns to be emphasized during the lesson. Also, note clues you can use with the children to help them discover the words you desire. For example, "See if you can make a three-letter word that is the name of the room in some people's homes where they like to watch television." *(den)*

 Figure 9.9   Teaching a "Making Words" Lesson

1. Place the large single letters from the key word in the pocket chart or along the chalkboard ledge.

2. For modeling purposes, the first time you use Making Words, select one of the students to be the "passer" and ask that child to pass the large single letters to other designated children.

3. Hold up and name each of the letter cards and have students selected to participate in the modeling exercise respond by holding up their matching card.

4. Write the numeral 2 (or 3, if there are no two-letter words in this lesson) on the board. Next, tell the student "volunteers" the clue you developed for the desired word. Then, tell the student volunteers to put together two (or three) of their letters to form the desired word.

5. Continue directing the students to make more words using the clues provided and the letter cards until you have helped them discover all but the final key word (the one that uses all the letters). Ask the student volunteers if they can guess the key word. If not, ask the remainder of the class if anyone can guess it. If no one is able to do so, offer students a meaning clue (e.g., "I am thinking of a word with _____ letters that means . . .").

6. As a guided practice activity, repeat these steps the next day with the whole group using a new word.

$\mathcal{U}$ **Figure 9.10**   Making Words: Additional Examples

Lesson Using One Vowel:

Letter cards: u k n r s t

Words to make: us, nut, rut, sun, sunk, runs, ruts/rust, tusk, stun, stunk, trunk, *trunks* (the key word)

You can sort for . . . rhymes, "s" pairs (run, runs; rut, ruts; trunk, trunks)

Lesson Using Big Words:

Letter cards: a a a e i b c h l l p t

Words to make: itch, able, cable, table, batch, patch, pitch, petal, label, chapel, capital, capable, alphabet, *alphabetical* (the key word)

You can sort for . . . el, le, al, -itch, -atch

Source: Based on "Making Words: Enhancing the Invented Spelling-Decoding Connection" by P. M. Cunningham and J. Cunningham, 1992, *The Reading Teacher, 46*(2), 106–115.

WORD BANKS

Purpose

It is important for students to learn to recognize a number of words on sight to facilitate the decoding process. Many words carry little meaning (the, of, and, a), but provide the "glue" of language that helps us represent thoughts. One question for teachers is how to go about helping students increase the numbers of words they can recognize immediately on sight. *Word banks* are used to help students collect and review these "sight words." Word banks also can be used as personal dictionaries. A word bank is simply a student-constructed box, file, or notebook in which newly discovered words are stored and reviewed.

Materials

In the early grades, teachers often collect small shoe boxes from local stores to serve as word banks. The children are asked at the beginning of the year to decorate the boxes in order to make them their own. In the upper grades, more formal-looking word banks are used. Notebooks or recipe boxes are generally selected. Alphabetic dividers can also be used at all levels to facilitate the quick location of word bank words. In addition, use of alphabetic dividers in the early grades helps students rehearse and reinforce knowledge of alphabetical order. Figure 9.11 shows an example of a word bank.

Procedure

Once students have constructed word banks, the next issue for the teacher is helping students decide which words should be included and from what sources. At least four sources can be considered for sight word selection and inclusion in word banks (Reutzel & Cooter, 2000): basal reader sight word lists; "key vocabulary" words that students have self-selected for learning (Ashton-Warner, 1963); "discovery" words (i.e., words that are discovered during class discussions); and "function words" (words that supply structure to sentences, but carry little or no meaning, such as with, were, what, is, of). A more complete list of high-frequency sight words is supplied in Figure 9.12.

Figure 9.11   A Word Bank

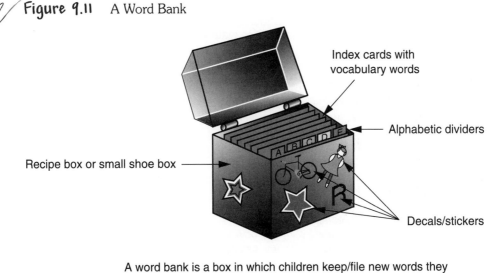

Index cards with vocabulary words

Alphabetic dividers

Recipe box or small shoe box

Decals/stickers

A word bank is a box in which children keep/file new words they are learning. The words are usually written in isolation on one side of the card, and in a sentence on the back of the card (usually with a picture clue).

Example:

Front

Back

bicycle

Jason rode his bicycle to school.

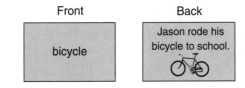

Source: From *Teaching Children to Read: Putting the Pieces Together,* by D. Ray Reutzel, and Robert B. Cooter, Jr., 2000, Upper Saddle River, NJ: Merrill/Prentice Hall.

COMPARISON GRIDS (FOR CONTENT-AREA VOCABULARY)

Purpose

In content-area instruction, it is important to try to create conceptual bridges between new vocabulary and their meanings, and their relationships to other concepts (Harmon, Hedrick, & Fox, 2000). Comparison grids can create a kind of two-dimensional framework for students that greatly simplifies abstract thinking.

Materials

All you will need is a simple grid that has one set of terms along the left-hand column and the vocabulary you want students to compare and contrast along the top row. See Figure 9.13 for an example adapted from Harmon, Hedrick, and Fox (2000) for the new vocabulary terms *executive, legislative,* and *judicial.*

Figure 9.12   High-Frequency Sight Words

The first 10 words make up about 24% of all written material, the first 100 words about 50% of all written material, and the first 300 about 65%.

1. the	44. each	87. who	130. through	173. home	216. never	259. walked
2. of	45. which	88. oil	131. much	174. us	217. started	260. white
3. and	46. she	89. its	132. before	175. move	218. city	261. sea
4. a	47. do	90. now	133. line	176. try	219. earth	262. began
5. to	48. how	91. find	134. right	177. kind	220. eyes	263. grow
6. in	49. their	92. long	135. too	178. hand	221. light	264. took
7. is	50. if	93. down	136. means	179. picture	222. thought	265. river
8. you	51. will	94. day	137. old	180. again	223. head	266. four
9. that	52. up	95. did	138. any	181. change	224. under	267. carry
10. it	53. other	96. get	139. same	182. off	225. story	268. state
11. he	54. about	97. come	140. tell	183. play	226. saw	269. once
12. was	55. out	98. made	141. boy	184. spell	227. left	270. book
13. for	56. many	99. may	142. following	185. air	228. don't	271. hear
14. on	57. then	100. part	143. came	186. away	229. few	272. stop
15. are	58. them	101. over	144. want	187. animals	230. while	273. without
16. as	59. these	102. new	145. show	188. house	231. along	274. second
17. with	60. so	103. sound	146. also	189. point	232. might	275. later
18. his	61. some	104. take	147. around	190. page	233. close	276. miss
19. they	62. her	105. only	148. form	191. letters	234. something	277. idea
20. I	63. would	106. little	149. three	192. mother	235. seemed	278. enough
21. at	64. make	107. work	150. small	193. answer	236. next	279. eat
22. be	65. like	108. know	151. set	194. found	237. hard	280. face
23. this	66. him	109. place	152. put	195. study	238. open	281. watch
24. have	67. into	110. years	153. end	196. still	239. example	282. far
25. from	68. time	111. live	154. does	197. learn	240. beginning	283. Indians
26. or	69. has	112. me	155. another	198. should	241. life	284. really
27. one	70. look	113. back	156. well	199. American	242. always	285. almost
28. had	71. two	114. give	157. large	200. world	243. those	286. let
29. by	72. more	115. most	158. must	201. high	244. both	287. above
30. words	73. write	116. very	159. big	202. every	245. paper	288. girl
31. but	74. go	117. after	160. even	203. near	246. together	289. sometimes
32. not	75. see	118. things	161. such	204. add	247. got	290. mountains
33. what	76. number	119. our	162. because	205. food	248. group	291. cut
34. all	77. no	120. just	163. turned	206. between	249. often	292. young
35. were	78. way	121. name	164. here	207. own	250. run	293. talk
36. we	79. could	122. good	165. why	208. below	251. important	294. soon
37. when	80. people	123. sentence	166. asked	209. country	252. until	295. list
38. your	81. my	124. man	167. went	210. plants	253. children	296. song
39. can	82. than	125. think	168. men	211. last	254. side	297. being
40. said	83. first	126. say	169. read	212. school	255. feet	298. leave
41. there	84. water	127. great	170. need	213. father	256. car	299. family
42. use	85. been	128. where	171. land	214. keep	257. miles	300. it's
43. an	86. called	129. help	172. different	215. trees	258. night	

Source: From "The New Instant Word List," by Edward Fry, *The Reading Teacher*, December 1980, pp. 284–289. Reprinted with permission of Edward Fry and the International Reading Association.

_W_ **Figure 9.13**   Comparison Grid: Branches of Government

Directions: Decide which of the words or phrases in the left-hand column can be used to describe each of the three branches of government. Write "yes" or "no" in each block, and be prepared to share your ideas with a partner.

	Executive	Legislative	Judicial
Elected			
Veto power			
President			
Judges			
Representatives			
Senators			
Commander-in-chief			
Constitutional authority			
Checks and balances			
Amendment			
Declares war			
Protects and defends the Constitution			

Procedure

This activity is usually best done after students have read and learned a significant amount about the topic and concepts at hand; in other words, this is a good review activity. First, have a brief discussion with students wherein they have an opportunity to refresh their memories about the new vocabulary (represented in the row across the top of the comparison grid). Then, ask them to decide which terms or phrases in the left-hand column apply to each of the new vocabulary terms. They should write "yes" or "no" in each box to indicate their judgment. After everyone has done this task independently, allow students to compare their responses in small groups before having a class discussion to confirm responses.

VOCABULARY CLUSTER

Purpose

It is especially important that students who struggle with reading use the context of a passage, the vocabulary they know, to understand new words in print. English Language Learners (ELLs) and students who have language deficiencies due to poverty are two large groups of students who benefit from direct instruction of this kind (Peregoy & Boyle, 2001). With the Vocabulary Cluster strategy, students are helped to read a passage, gather context clues, and then predict the meaning of a new word targeted for learning by you, the teacher.

Materials

Multiple copies of a text students are to read, an overhead transparency and projector, and erasable marking pens for transparencies are needed.

Procedure

First, select vocabulary you want to teach from a text the students will be reading. This could be a poem, song, novel, nonfiction textbook, or other appropriate reading. Next, gather the students around the overhead projector and draw their attention to the transparency you have prepared. The transparency should contain an excerpt from the text with sufficient context to help students predict what the unknown word might be. The target word should have been deleted and replaced with a blank line, much the same as with a cloze passage (discussed earlier in this chapter). In Figure 9.14, you will see a passage prepared in this way along with a Vocabulary Cluster supporting the new word to be learned. This example is based on the book *Harry Potter and the Prisoner of Azkaban* (Rowling, 1999). Through discussion you will lead students into predicting what the unknown word

Figure 9.14   Vocabulary Cluster Based on *Harry Potter and the Prisoner of Azkaban*: Target Word "Irritable"

> Tom woke Harry the next morning with his usual toothless grin and a cup of tea. Harry got dressed and was just persuading a disgruntled Hedwig to get back into her cage when Ron banged his way into the room, pulling a sweatshirt over his head and looking _____ . (Rowling, 1999, p. 69)

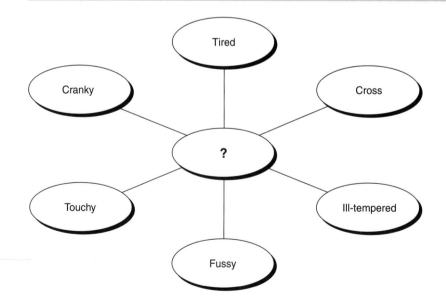

might be. If the word is not already in students' listening vocabulary, as with ELL students or those with otherwise limited vocabularies, then you will be able to introduce the new word quite well using the context and synonyms provided in the Vocabulary Cluster.

CONTEXTUAL REDEFINITION (FOR TECHNICAL VOCABULARY)

Purpose

Although there has been some debate over the years about the extent to which context should be emphasized, it is clear that learning from context is a very important component of vocabulary acquisition (Adams, 1990, p. 150). An excellent method of introducing terminology in context, such as that found in informational readings, as well as demonstrating to students why they should use context whenever possible to figure out unfamiliar words, is a strategy called contextual redefinition (Cunningham, Cunningham, & Arthur, 1981).

Materials

This is an activity that can be conducted mainly at the chalkboard, overhead projector, and/or by using teacher-constructed activity sheets.

Procedure

The steps in this procedure, as adapted by Cooter and Flynt (1996), follow:

Step 1: Select five or six terms that are unfamiliar or probably known by only a few students in the class. Introduce the topic and display the new terms on the chalkboard or overhead. Ask each student or pair of students to predict a brief definition for each term. Encourage students to guess at word meanings, reminding them that the goal is to try to come up with logical ideas and not to worry about being "right." After the students have had an opportunity to discuss probable definitions, call for individuals to share their ideas and write them on the chalkboard or overhead projector transparency. Briefly discuss why the students were unable to do much more than guess at the word's meanings.

Step 2: Next, tell the students that you have these same words written in sentences or short paragraphs and that you want them to read each passage to see if they want to revise their original guesses. Be sure to present each word in a contextually rich sentence. During the ensuing discussion, encourage students to explain why they think the word means what they now think it means. Record varying responses next to each term as they occur.

Step 3: Finally, if there are differences, have students find the word in either the text or the glossary and read its definition. Then have students copy the finalized sentences in their notebooks/journals.

Contextual redefinition provides students with opportunities to share their skills in using context and can be helpful in promoting independent use of context clues. Teachers find it an invigorating means for preteaching terms and showing that the glossary is not the first tool readers can use in figuring out the meaning of new words; context usually is.

SELECTED REFERENCES

Adams, M. J. (1990). *Beginning to read: Thinking and learning about print.* Cambridge, MA: MIT Press.

Ashton-Warner, S. (1963). *Teacher.* New York: Simon & Schuster.

Beck, I. L., McCaslin, E. S., & McKeown, M. G. (1980). *The rationale and design of a program to teach vocabulary to fourth grade students.* (LRDC No. 1980–25). Pittsburgh: University of Pittsburgh, Learning Research and Development Center.

Bradley, C. A. (1988, April). *The relationship between mathematics language facility and mathematics achievement among junior high school students.* Paper presented at the Annual Meeting of the American Educational Research Association, New Orleans, LA. (Educational Resources Information Center No. ED 293 727).

Byars, B. (1970). *The summer of the swans.* New York: Puffin Books.

Cattell, J. M. (1885). Veber die zeit der erkennung und bennenung von schriftzeichen, bildem und farben. *Philosophische Studien, 2,* 635–650.

Clark, E. (1993). *The lexicon in acquisition.* Cambridge, UK: Cambridge University Press.

Cooter, K. S. (2001). *Vocabulary instruction in the elementary grades.* Unpublished manuscript, Texas Christian University, Fort Worth, TX.

Cooter, R. B., & Flynt, E. S. (1996). *Teaching reading in the content areas: Developing content literacy for all students.* Columbus, OH: Merrill/Prentice Hall.

Cowan, E., & Cowan, G. (1980). *Writing.* New York: John Wiley & Sons.

Cunningham, J., Cunningham, P., & Arthur, S. V. (1981). *Middle and secondary school reading.* New York: Longman.

Cunningham, P. M. (2000). *Phonics they use* (3rd ed.). New York: Addison-Wesley.

Cunningham, P. M., & Cunningham, J. (1992). Making words: Enhancing the invented spelling-decoding connection. *The Reading Teacher, 46*(2), 106–115.

Delacre, L. (1996). *Golden tales: Myths, legends, and folktales from Latin America.* New York: Scholastic.

Donald, D. H. (1995). *Lincoln.* New York: Simon & Schuster.

Frayer, D., Frederick, W. C., & Klausmeir, H. J. (1969). *A schema for testing the level of concept mastery* (Working paper No. 16). Madison: University of Wisconsin, Wisconsin Research and Development Center for Cognitive Learning.

Fry, E. (1980). The new instant word list. *The Reading Teacher,* December, 284–289.

Fry, E. B., Kress, J. E., & Fountoukidis, D. L. (1993). *The reading teacher's book of lists* (3rd ed.). Paramis, NJ: Prentice Hall.

Harmon, J. M., Hedrick, W. B., & Fox, E. A. (2000). A content analysis of vocabulary instruction in social studies textbooks for grades K–8. *The Elementary School Journal, 100*(3), 253–271.

Irwin, J. L. (1990). *Vocabulary knowledge: Guidelines for instruction. What research says to the teacher.* Washington, D.C.: National Education Association (ERIC Document Reproduction Service No. ED 319 001).

Jenkins, J. R., Matlock, B., & Slocum, T. A. (1989). Two approaches to vocabulary instruction: The teaching of individual word meanings and practice in deriving word meaning from context. *Reading Research Quarterly, 24*(2), 215–235.

Johnson, A. P., & Rasmussen, J. B. (1998). Classifying and super word web: Two strategies to improve productive vocabulary. *Journal of Adolescent & Adult Literacy, 42*(3), 204–209.

Johnson, D. D. (2001). *Vocabulary in the elementary and middle school.* Boston: Allyn & Bacon.

Johnson, D. D., & Pearson, P. D. (1984). *Teaching reading vocabulary.* New York: Holt, Rinehart and Winston.

Johnson, D., & Steele, V. (1996). So many words, so little time: Helping college ESL learners acquire vocabulary strategies. *Journal of Adolescent & Adult Literacy, 39*(5), 348–357.

May, F. B., & Rizzardi, L. (2002). *Reading as communication* (6th ed.). Upper Saddle River, NJ: Merrill/Prentice Hall.

Meddaugh, S. (1992). *Martha speaks.* Boston: Houghton Mifflin.

Monroe, E. E. (1998). Using graphic organizers to teach vocabulary: Does available research inform mathematics instruction? *Education, 118*(4), 538–542.

Nagy, W. E., & Herman, P. A. (1984). *Limitations of vocabulary instruction.* (Technical Report No. 326). Champaign, IL: University of Illinois Center for the Study of Reading.

Nagy, W. E., Herman, P. A., & Anderson, R. C. (1985). Learning words from context. *Reading Research Quarterly, 20*(2), 233–253.

National Center for Educational Statistics. (1999, September). *NAEP 1998: Writing report card for the nation and the states.* Washington, D.C.: U.S. Department of Education.

Peregoy, S. F., & Boyle, O. F. (2001). *Reading, writing, & learning in ESL.* New York: Longman.

Rekrut, M. D. (1996). Effective vocabulary instruction. *High School Journal, 80*(1), 66–78.

Reutzel, D. R., & Cooter, R. B., Jr. (2000). *Teaching children to read: Putting the pieces together* (3rd ed.) Upper Saddle River, NJ: Merrill/Prentice Hall.

Rowling, J. K. (1999). *Harry Potter and the prisoner of Azkaban.* New York: Scholastic.

Rupley, W. H., Logan, J. W., & Nichols, W. D. (1999). Vocabulary instruction in a balanced reading program. *The Reading Teacher, 52*(4), 336–347.

Ryder, R. J., & Graves, M. F. (1994). *Reading and learning in content areas.* Columbus, OH: Merrill.

Sinatra, R., Stahl-Gemake, J., & Berg, D. (1984). Improving reading comprehension of disabled readers through semantic mapping. *The Reading Teacher, 38,* 22–29.

Smith, F. (1987). *Insult to intelligence.* Portsmouth, NH: Heinemann.

Smith, R. J., & Johnson, D. D. (1980). *Teaching children to read.* Reading, MA: Addison-Wesley.

Spencer, K. M. (1997). *Vocabulary bingo!: A language review activity.* Unpublished manuscript, Texas Christian University.

Stahl, S. (1986). Three principles of effective vocabulary instruction. *Journal of Reading, 29*(7), 662–668.

Stieglitz, E. L., & Stieglitz, V. S. (1981). SAVOR the word to reinforce vocabulary in the content areas. *Journal of Reading, 25,* 46–51.

Watts, S. (1995). Vocabulary instruction during reading lessons in six classrooms. *Journal of Reading Behavior, 27,* 399–424.

Yopp, H. K., & Yopp, R. H. (1996). *Literature-based reading activities.* Boston: Allyn & Bacon.

Chapter 10

Story Comprehension

"Gather around, boys and girls." Mrs. Jensen spoke gently, "I have a new story to read to you today. How many of you know the story of *Peter Cottontail?*"

"Teacher, I know what a cottontail is, it's a tiny bunny with a tail that looks like a cotton ball," exclaims Julianna.

"Very good, Julianna. But this story isn't really about a bunny. It is a story about something that all little boys and girls need to learn. Have any of you ever been disobedient to your parents? Can you share with us what it was you did and what happened when you disobeyed?"

"Oh, once my Mom told me not to ride my scooter off jumps or I would wreck and hurt myself. I didn't listen and did it anyway. One day I made a big jump off a wooden ramp at Georgio's house and landed sideways and fell over. I put my hand out to stop from falling and broke my wrist real bad. It had to be in a cast for six weeks," explained José.

"Well that is a very good example, José. Our story today tells us about a little rabbit named Peter, who always liked to stop in the best garden in the country for a snack on the way home from school; Mr. McGregor's garden. And Mr. McGregor didn't like having bunnies in his garden patch eating his prize vegetables. Peter's mom bought him some nice new clothes and reminded him NOT to go into Mr. McGregor's garden. What do you think might have happened?"

BACKGROUND BRIEFING FOR TEACHERS

Mrs. Jensen skillfully introduced this age-old tale, helping children connect with experiences they or others may have had with disobedience to parents' instructions. But more importantly, Mrs. Jensen's focus was on helping students remember relevant information that relates to the message of the story to help guide their comprehension. According to Keene and Zimmerman (1997), the central purpose of reading is to comprehend! Comprehension is developed through several lower order or word-level processes including decoding and vocabulary development (Pressley, 2000). Words and letter sounds exist largely to help readers construct meaning. We must never lose sight of the purpose for reading—to comprehend the author's message.

As teachers, we must help students understand from the outset of reading instruction that comprehension is the goal. Reading and listening to stories are key developmental experiences for children (Campbell, 2001; Neuman, 2000). From the time children first experience *Peter Cottontail* in kindergarten to the time they experience *Romeo and*

Juliet in high school, students are learning about life, human dilemmas, and the triumph of the human spirit.

Stories capture moral principles, provide escape from the problems of the moment, and allow imagination to soar beyond the bounds of the here and now. Children begin to internalize how stories are written by hearing books read aloud and by hearing stories told to them in their earliest years. They learn, for example, that stories begin with vivid descriptions of when and where a story takes place, called *setting.* An understanding of problems, goals, and attempts to solve problems often follows children's development of knowledge about the setting in stories. And finally, children learn how the major characters resolve the problems in the story. Internalization of story language, such as *Once upon a time . . .* and *. . . they lived happily ever after,* is often our first clue that children are attending carefully to story parts and structure.

WHAT DOES IT MEAN TO COMPREHEND A STORY?

Reading comprehension instruction has been profoundly influenced by **schema theory,** a theory that explains how we store information in our minds and how what we already know helps us gain new knowledge. A **schema** (plural is *schemata* or *schemas*) can be thought of as a kind of file cabinet of information in our brains containing related: 1) concepts (chairs, birds, ships), 2) events (weddings, birthdays, school experiences), 3) emotions (anger, frustration, joy, pleasure), and 4) roles (parent, judge, teacher) drawn from our life experiences (Rumelhart, 1981).

Researchers have described schemas as neural or brain networks connecting related meanings (Collins & Quillian, 1969; Lindsay & Norman, 1977). Each schema is connected to other related schemas, forming our own unique and interconnected network of knowledge and experiences. The size and content of each schema is influenced by past opportunities to learn or *prior experience.* Thus, younger children typically possess fewer, less developed schemas than mature adults.

During the 1970s and 1980s, cognitive psychologists began to study how authors constructed stories or narratives. Next, they examined how or if children developed an understanding of how the events of stories were structured or networked (Applebee, 1979). It became clear that authors, usually subconsciously, craft stories by following a set of patterns or schemas for how stories should be constructed. Researchers also found that children who were exposed to stories read aloud and discussed with others developed a sense of story structure and how to use this knowledge to comprehend and create text (Santa & Hayes, 1981). Researchers then developed a generalized set of rules to describe how stories are composed. These rules became known as story grammars (Mandler & Johnson, 1977; Stein & Glenn, 1979; Thorndyke, 1977).

Typical elements found in story grammars include:

- Setting
- Problem
- Events
- Resolution
- Moral or theme

Usually, a story or *narrative text* begins with a description of the setting. A *setting* includes information about the story location and the introduction of the main character(s). Setting also establishes the general time frame of the events in the story. Watson (1991) explained that setting involves more than just describing *when* and *where* a story takes place. Setting usually begins by introducing characters, who in turn reveal the time and place of the story, which drives the plot into action and sets the mood or tone of the story, and which finally leads to disclosing the main theme of the story. Discussions of setting should probe this chain of events carefully.

The *problem* propels the story characters into action. This is often followed by the main character devising some sort of plan to solve the problem set up in the early part of the story. Attempts to solve the problem or achieve some goal, as outlined, are called *events*. Stories may be composed of a single event, but more complex stories may contain several events that may use such stylistic devices as flashbacks, dream states, and so on. Results of the character's attempts are revealed as the story progresses. Finally, the story reaches a point of *resolution,* with some hint of the character(s) current and future state. A moral or theme of the story is sometimes also evident, such as in the classic tales "The Boy Who Cried Wolf" and "The Little Red Hen." Although labels used to describe these story grammar elements may vary slightly, all stories contain these essential parts. This chapter deals with helping readers attend to, learn about, and use their knowledge of story structure to increase reading comprehension and fluency.

Assessing Children's Story Comprehension

How can students' understanding of story structure be assessed? How can students be helped to use the structure of stories to increase their reading enjoyment and comprehension? Teachers need to have a repertoire of successful and proven assessment and instructional alternatives available to assist children in developing a sense of story structure. The assessment strategies outlined in this section provide you with the means to assess a variety of factors that influence children's comprehension of stories.

Oral Story Retellings

Purpose

One of the most effective ways to find out if a child understands story structure is to use oral story retellings (Brown & Cambourne, 1987; Gambrell, Pfeiffer, & Wilson, 1985; Morrow, 1985). Asking children to retell a story involves reconstructing the entire story including the story sequence, recalling important elements of the plot, making inferences, and noticing relevant details. Thus, oral story retellings assess story comprehension and story structure knowledge in holistic, sequenced, and organized ways.

Materials

For an oral retelling, you will need the following materials:

- blank audiotape
- portable audiocassette recorder with internal microphone
- brief story

- "parsing" of the story (see below)
- scoring sheet

Procedure

Select a brief story for students to listen to or read. For example, *The Carrot Seed* by Ruth Krauss (1945) could be selected. Next, type the text of the story onto a separate piece of paper for parsing. *Parsing,* in this instance, refers to dividing a story into four major and somewhat simplified story grammar categories: setting, problem, events, and resolution, as shown.

Story Grammar Parsing of "The Carrot Seed"

Setting

A little boy planted a carrot seed.

Problem (Getting the seed to grow)

His mother said, "I'm afraid it won't come up."
His father said, "I'm afraid it won't come up."
And his big brother said, "It won't come up."

Events

Every day the little boy pulled up the weeds around the seed and sprinkled the ground with water.
But nothing came up.
And nothing came up.
Everyone kept saying it wouldn't come up.
But he still pulled up the weeds around it every day and sprinkled the ground with water.

Resolution

And then, one day, a carrot came up just as the little boy had known it would.

Oral retellings may be elicited from children in a number of ways. One way involves the use of pictures or verbal prompts from the story. As pictures in the story are flashed sequentially, the child is asked to retell the story as remembered from listening or reading. Morrow (1985; 2001) suggested that teachers prompt children to begin story retellings with a statement such as: "A little while ago, we read a story called [Name the story]. Retell the story as if you were telling it to a friend who has never heard it before." Other prompts during the recall may be framed as questions:

- "How does the story begin?" Or, "Once upon a time. . . ."
- "What happens next?"
- "What happened to [the main character] when . . . ?"
- "Where did the story take place?"
- "When did the story take place?"
- "How did the main character solve the problem in the story?"
- "How did the story end?"

Morrow (2001) said that teachers should offer only general prompts such as those listed rather than asking about specific details, ideas, or a sequence of events in the story. Asking questions such as those listed is a form of *assisted recall* and may be especially useful with struggling readers.

A second way to elicit oral story retellings from students is to use *unaided recall,* in which students retell the story without picture or verbal prompts. Asking the child to tell the story "as if she were telling it to someone who had never heard or read the story be-

Figure 10.1   Oral Story Retelling Summary Coding Form

Student's name: _____   Grade: _____
Title of story: _____   Date: _____

General directions: Give 1 point for each element included, as well as for "gist." Give 1 point for each character named, as well as for such words as *boy, girl,* or *dog.* Credit plurals (*friends,* for instance) with 2 points under characters.

Setting
    a. Begins with an introduction   _____
    b. Indicates main character _____
    c. Other characters named _____
    d. Includes statement about time or place _____

Objective
    a. Refers to main character's goal or problem to be solved _____

Events
    a. Number of events recalled _____
    b. Number of events in story _____
    c. Score for "events" (a/b) _____

Resolution
    a. Tells how main character resolves the story problem _____

Sequence
Summarizes story in order: setting, objective, episodes, and resolution. (Score 2 for correct order, 1 for partial order, 0 for no sequence.) _____

Possible score: _____   **Student's score:** _____

fore" begins an unaided oral story retelling. To record critical elements of the story structure included in the child's oral retelling, use an audiotape recording and coding sheet like the one shown in Figure 10.1. The information gleaned from an oral retelling may be used to help teachers focus their future instruction on enhancing students' understanding of story structure.

SCRAMBLED SCHEMA STORY TASK

Purpose

A scrambled schema story task assesses how well readers can reconstruct the order of a story based on their innate understanding of story structure. In this task, a story or major portions of a story are divided into its components, such as setting, problem, events, and resolution, and then scrambled. Students are asked to read each element of the story and then organize the story elements in order on a storyboard. Results from this analysis can be used to help teachers know whether to increase interactions about story parts during read alouds and/or provide explicit instruction in story parts to help readers build a better internal sense of story structure.

Story Board		Story Board
Beginning	**OR**	**Setting**
		Problem
Middle		**Attempts**
End		**Resolution**

Materials

You will need to select a short story or storybook.

- A simple storyboard like that shown above made of laminated poster board
- Parts of the story typed onto regular 8 1/2″ × 11″ write paper and cut into story part strips
- One white legal-sized envelope for storing the typed story part strips
- A oral retelling story scoring sheet based on the design of the storyboard to score each student's response

Procedure

Choose a simple story for this activity. Parse or divide the story selected into story grammar elements, as shown for the story of *The Carrot Seed* in the "Oral Story Retellings" assessment activity. After parsing the story, transcribe the entire story text if it is a simple story—a story with no more than two lines of text per page. If not, transcribe only a few sentences from the story that provide the reader sufficient clues about where the story parts were in the sequence and structure of the story. Type the transcribed text onto plain white paper and, with scissors, cut the text into the parts of the story. Scramble the pieces and place them into a plain white legal-sized envelope. Hand the child the envelope and ask her to read each part of the story. You may want to assist her with any decoding problems. Next, ask her to put the pieces of the scrambled story in order on the storyboard. Ask her to reread the story strips on the storyboard to check that her ordering of the story makes sense. Record the child's responses to this task on the form shown in Figure 10.1. Poor performance on this task is typically due to limited exposure hearing stories read aloud and discussing these with others. As a consequence, daily interactive read alouds along with explicit story structure instruction are logical means for helping children who perform poorly on this task to develop an improved sense of story.

STORY GRAMMAR QUESTIONING

Purpose

Questions are an integral part of life in and out of school. From birth, we learn about our world by asking questions and questioning our answers against the confines of reality. Beck and McKeown (1981) and Sadow (1982) suggested that teachers follow a logical model of questioning. Research (Mandler & Johnson, 1977) indicates that story grammars provide such a model for asking questions about stories. And these same researchers have found that developing questions for stories using a story grammar framework or structure produced improved reading comprehension among children as measured by the ability to correctly and completely answer comprehension questions (Beck, Omanson, & McKeown, 1982). Other evidence from research on story grammars suggests that good readers have well-developed understanding of story structure, whereas poor readers do not (Whaley, 1981). Therefore, using a story grammar to guide self-questioning can help teachers and students to assess understanding of story structure.

Materials

You will need:

- One simple story to be read aloud or individually and silently
- One copy of an empty or blank story grammar map (see Figure 10.2)
- One set of questions dealing with each element shown in blank or empty on the story map (Hint: It is best if questions are sequenced in the order of the story map.)
- One story grammar questioning summary scoring sheet

Procedure

Select a simple story like *Jack and the Beanstalk.* Construct a story grammar map for the story as shown in Figure 10.2 for the story of *Jack and the Beanstalk.* Next, write one question for selected major elements in the story grammar map, as shown in the example questions in Figure 10.3. Students can be asked, depending on their level of writing development, to answer the questions orally or in written form. Answers to each question are evaluated for accuracy and completeness. Story elements missed in the story grammar questioning should be stressed in future story discussions and/or in future explicit story structure instruction.

SUMMARY WRITING

Purpose

Writing a summary for assessment purposes can provide teachers with insights into a student's memory of important (and unimportant) information for retelling a story. When writing summaries, students organize text information in a manner that is meaningful for them; therefore, they also reveal how they select information and how they represent that information to construct their comprehension of a text (Bromley, 1985). By examining the elements of the story and the sequencing of those elements students include or exclude in their summary writing, teachers can adjust their instruction to highlight specific story elements or the sequencing of story elements accordingly. Much like oral retellings, teachers can examine written summaries for both inclusion of major story grammar elements and the sequence in which these elements were presented to inform their interactions with children and their instruction with stories.

Materials

You will need:

- One brief story
- One "parsing of that story" (see Figure 10.4)
- One written summary scoring sheet

Figure 10.2   Story Grammar Map of "Jack and the Beanstalk"

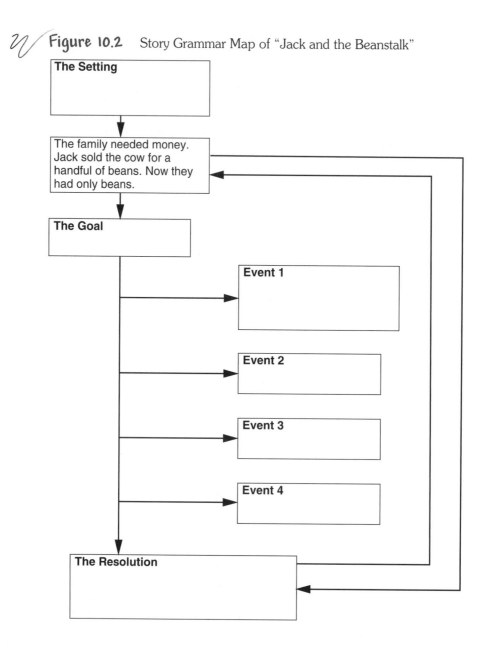

Figure 10.3   Story Grammar Questioning for "Jack and the Beanstalk"

Setting:	In the beginning of the story, why did Jack's mother want him to sell the cow?
Problem:	When Jack traded the cow for a handful of beans, what kind of a problem did this decision create for Jack and his mother?
Events:	When Jack climbed the beanstalk the first time, relate what happened to him. Why did Jack climb the beanstalk a second time?
Resolution:	At the end of the story, what had happened to Jack and his mother to solve the problem of trading the cow for a handful of beans?

Figure 10.4 Story Grammar Parsing of *The Day Jimmy's Boa Ate the Wash*

The Setting
"How was your class trip to the farm?"

The Problem
"Oh . . . boring . . . kind of dull . . . until the cow started crying."

The Events
"A cow . . . crying?"
"Yeah, you see, a haystack fell on her."
"But a haystack doesn't just fall over."
"It does if a farmer crashes into it with his tractor."
"Oh, come on, a farmer wouldn't do that."
"He would if he were too busy yelling at the pigs to get off our school bus."
"What were the pigs doing on the bus?"
"Eating our lunches."
"Why were they eating your lunches?"
"Because we threw their corn at each other, and they didn't have anything else to eat."
"Well, that makes sense, but why were you throwing corn?"
"Because we ran out of eggs."
"Out of eggs? Why were you throwing eggs?"
"Because of the boa constrictor."
"THE BOA CONSTRICTOR!"
"Yeah, Jimmy's pet boa constrictor."
"What was Jimmy's pet boa constrictor doing on the farm?"
"Oh, he brought it to meet all the farm animals, but the chickens didn't like it."
"You mean he took it into the hen house?"
"Yeah, and the chickens started squawking and flying around."
"Go on, go on. What happened?"
"Well, one hen got excited and laid an egg, and it landed on Jenny's head."
"The hen?"
"No, the egg. And it broke—yucky—all over her hair."
"What did she do?"
"She got mad because she thought Tommy threw it, so she threw one at him."
"What did Tommy do?"
"Oh, he ducked and the egg hit Marianne in the face."
"So she threw one at Jenny but she missed and hit Jimmy, who dropped his boa constrictor."
"Oh, I know, the next thing you knew, everyone was throwing eggs, right?"
"Right."
"And when you ran out of eggs, you threw the pigs' corn, right?"
"Right again."

Resolution
"Well, what finally stopped it?"
"Well, we heard the farmer's wife screaming."
"Why was she screaming?"
"We never found out, because Mrs. Stanley made us get on the bus, and we sort of left in a hurry without the boa constrictor."
"I bet Jimmy was sad because he left his pet boa constrictor."
"Oh, not really. We left in such a hurry that one of the pigs didn't get off the bus, so now he's got a pet pig."
"Boy, that sure sounds like an exciting trip."
"Yeah, I suppose, if you're the kind of kid who likes class trips to the farm."

Based on *The Day Jimmy's Boa Ate the Wash,* by T. H. Noble, 1980, New York: Scholastic.

- One to two lined sheets of paper for the written summary
- Two pencils or pens for writing the summary

Procedure

Select a brief story for students to listen to or read. For example, *The Day Jimmy's Boa Ate the Wash* by Trinka Hakes Noble (1980) might be selected. Type the text of the story onto a separate piece of paper for parsing. Divide the story into the four major story grammar categories mentioned earlier: setting, problem, events, and resolution (see Figure 10.4). Ask the child to prepare a written summary of the story after they complete reading this book silently. Written summaries may be elicited from children in a number of ways. One way involves the use of pictures or verbal prompts from the story. As pictures in the story are flashed sequentially, students write a summary of the story as remembered from listening or reading. Morrow (1985) suggested that teachers prompt children to begin writing story summaries with a statement such as: "A little while ago, we [or you] read a story called [name the story] . . . Write a story summary as if you were telling it to a friend who has never heard it before" (p. 659). Other prompts during summary writing may be framed as questions:

- "How does the story begin?" Or, "Once upon a time. . . ."
- "What happens next?"
- "What happened to [the main character] when . . . ?"
- "Where did the story take place?"
- "When did the story take place?"
- "How did the main character solve the problem in the story?"
- "How did the story end?"

As noted earlier with oral retellings, teachers may use both aided and unaided recall prompts to help students produce written story summaries. To record and examine critical elements of the child's story summary, use a coding sheet (see Figure 10.1.).

The information gleaned from a written story summary may be used to help teachers focus their instruction on enhancing students' understanding of story structure, the sequence of events in a story, or important story information. Story summary analyses may also indicate the nature of information to be focused upon in future story summary writing instructional sessions or the nature of the prompts to be given during summary writing. Assessment of children's written story summaries can reveal much about their understanding of story structure, story sequence, and the major elements of the story plot from a reading and writing perspective.

THE READER SELF-PERCEPTION SCALE

Purpose

A sense of personal or self-efficacy in learning and using comprehension strategies plays a key role in every reader's development of competence and confidence. *Self-efficacy* denotes one's beliefs about her own capabilities to learn or to perform a given task at specified or designated levels of proficiency (Bandura, 1986; Paris & Winograd, 2001; Schunk & Zimmerman, 1997). Previous research has clearly demonstrated a strong link between learners' sense of self-efficacy, motivation, and self-regulatory processes (Schunk, 1996).

Self-efficacy has been shown to influence task choice, effort, persistence, and ultimate achievement. Effective comprehension strategy instruction requires that students develop a sense of self-efficacy as well as self-regulating behaviors and dispositions. Henk and Melnick (1995) developed an instrument for measuring how children feel about themselves as readers, an indicator of self-efficacy, called the *Reader Self-Perception Scale (RSPS)* (see Figure 10.5.).

Figure 10.5   The Reader Self-Perception: Scale Directions for Administration, Scoring, and Interpretation

The reader Self-Perception Scale (RSPS) is intended to provide an assessment of how children feel about themselves as readers. The scale consists of 33 items that assess self-perceptions along four dimensions of self-efficacy (Progress, Observational Comparison, Social Feedback, and Physiological States). Children are asked to indicate how strongly they agree or disagree with each statement on a 5-point scale (5 = Strongly Agree, 1 = Strongly Disagree). The information gained from this scale can be used to devise ways to enhance children's self-esteem in reading and, ideally, to increase their motivation to read. The following directions explain specifically what you are to do.

Administration
For the results to be of any use, the children must: (a) understand exactly what they are to do, (b) have sufficient time to complete all items, and (c) respond honestly and thoughtfully. Briefly explain to the children that they are being asked to complete a questionnaire about reading. Emphasize that this is not a *test* and that there are no *right* answers. Tell them that they should be as honest as possible because their responses will be confidential. Ask the children to fill in their names, grade levels, and classrooms as appropriate. Read the directions aloud and work through the example with the students as a group. Discuss the response options and make sure that all children understand the rating scale before moving on. It is important that children know that they may raise their hands to ask questions about any words or ideas they do not understand.

The children should then read each item and circle their response for the item. They should work at their own pace. Remind the children that they should be sure to respond to all items. When all items are completed, the children should stop, put their pencils down, and wait for further instructions. Care should be taken that children who work more slowly are not disturbed by children who have already finished.

Scoring
To score the RSPS, enter the following point values for each response on the RSPS scoring sheet (Strongly Agree = 5, Agree = 4, Undecided = 3, Disagree = 2, Strongly Disagree = 1) for each item number under the appropriate scale. Sum each column to obtain a raw score for each of the four specific scales.

Interpretation
Each scale is interpreted in relation to its total possible score. For example, because the RSPS uses a 5-point scale and the Progress scale consists of 9 items, the highest total score for Progress is 45 (9 × 5 = 45). Therefore, a score that would fall approximately in the middle of the range (22–23) would indicate a child's somewhat indifferent perception of herself or himself as a reader with respect to Progress. Note that each scale has a different possible total raw score (Progress = 45, Observational Comparison = 30, Social Feedback = 45, and Physiological States = 40) and should be interpreted accordingly.

Materials

You will need:

- One copy for each student of the RSPS shown in Figure 10.6
- One copy for each student of the RSPS scoring sheet shown in Figure 10.7

Procedure

The RSPS assessment tool is group rather than individually administered. In order to obtain valid results, it is imperative that students clearly understand the nature of the task and be given sufficient time to thoughtfully and honestly respond to each item. Children are to be told that this is not a *test* and that there are no right or wrong answers. Responses will be kept strictly confidential. Ask children to fill in the personal information at the top of the RSPS. Read the directions aloud to the group and guide them through the completion of the example item. Make sure children understand the response categories and understand the task. Then have them complete their response for each item of the RSPS. When children finish the RSPS, ask them to quietly take out a book, write, or draw at their seats so as not to disturb others who are still completing the scale.

Scoring is accomplished by using the RSPS scoring sheet. Sum the numerical rating for each RSPS item within the categories listed on the RSPS scoring sheet. Interpretation of the scores obtained for the RSPS are found at the bottom of the scoring sheet.

THE CLASSROOM MODIFIED READING STRATEGY USE SCALE (CMRSUS)

Purpose

Metacognition refers to two important concepts related to reading comprehension: 1) a reader's knowledge of the status of his own thinking and the appropriate strategies to facilitate ongoing comprehension; and 2) the executive control one has over one's own thinking and the use of comprehension strategies to facilitate or repair comprehension as he reads (Paris, Wasik, & Turner, 1991). For many readers, problems in comprehension result from failures related to one or both of these two important concepts. The purpose of metacognitive assessment is to gain insight into how students select strategies to use in comprehending text and how well they regulate the status of their own comprehension as they read. We have modified the *Reading Strategy Use (RSU)* scale developed by Pereira-Laird and Deane (1997) for classroom application. Scores obtained from administering the CMRSUS provide insights into how well students select, apply, and regulate their use of comprehension strategies.

Materials

The classroom modified *Reading Strategy Use* scale shown in Figure 10.8 can be used with most story selections.

Procedure

The CMRSU scale is group administered. Tell students that the CMRSUS is not a *test* and that there are no right or wrong answers. Ask students to fill in the personal information

Figure 10.6   The Reader Self-Perception Scale

Listed below are statements about reading. Please read each statement carefully. Then circle the letters that show how much you agree or disagree with the statement. Use the following:

SA = Strongly Agree
A = Agree
U = Undecided
D = Disagree
SD = Strongly Disagree

Example: **I think pizza with pepperoni is the best.**   SA   A   U   D   SD

If you are *really positive* that pepperoni pizza is best, circle SA (Strongly Agree).
If you *think* that it is good but maybe not great, circle A (Agree).
If you *can't decide* whether or not it is best, circle U (undecided).
If you *think* that pepperoni pizza is not all that good, circle D (Disagree).
If you are *really positive* that pepperoni pizza is not very good, circle SD (Strongly Disagree).

	1. I think I am a good reader.	SA	A	U	D	SD
[SF]	2. I can tell that my teacher likes to listen to me read.	SA	A	U	D	SD
[SF]	3. My teacher thinks that my reading is fine.	SA	A	U	D	SD
[OC]	4. I read faster than other kids.	SA	A	U	D	SD
[PS]	5. I like to read aloud.	SA	A	U	D	SD
[OC]	6. When I read, I can figure out words better than other kids.	SA	A	U	D	SD
[SF]	7. My classmates like to listen to me read.	SA	A	U	D	SD
[PS]	8. I feel good inside when I read.	SA	A	U	D	SD
[SF]	9. My classmates think that I read pretty well.	SA	A	U	D	SD
[PR]	10. When I read, I don't have to try as hard as I used to.	SA	A	U	D	SD
[OC]	11. I seem to know more words than other kids when I read.	SA	A	U	D	SD
[SF]	12. People in my family think I am a good reader.	SA	A	U	D	SD
[PR]	13. I am getting better at reading.	SA	A	U	D	SD
[OC]	14. I understand what I read as well as other kids do.	SA	A	U	D	SD
[PR]	15. When I read, I need less help than I used to.	SA	A	U	D	SD
[PS]	16. Reading makes me feel happy inside.	SA	A	U	D	SD
[SF]	17. My teacher thinks I am a good reader.	SA	A	U	D	SD
[PR]	18. Reading is easier for me than it used to be.	SA	A	U	D	SD
[PR]	19. I read faster than I could before.	SA	A	U	D	SD
[OC]	20. I read better than other kids in my class.	SA	A	U	D	SD
[PS]	21. I feel calm when I read.	SA	A	U	D	SD
[OC]	22. I read more than other kids.	SA	A	U	D	SD
[PR]	23. I understand what I read better than I could before.	SA	A	U	D	SD
[PR]	24. I can figure out words better than I could before.	SA	A	U	D	SD
[PS]	25. I feel comfortable when I read.	SA	A	U	D	SD
[PS]	26. I think reading is relaxing.	SA	A	U	D	SD
[PR]	27. I read better now than I could before.	SA	A	U	D	SD
[PR]	28. When I read, I recognize more words than I used to.	SA	A	U	D	SD
[PS]	29. Reading makes me feel good.	SA	A	U	D	SD
[SF]	30. Other kids think I'm a good reader.	SA	A	U	D	SD
[SF]	31. People in my family think I read pretty well.	SA	A	U	D	SD
[PS]	32. I enjoy reading.	SA	A	U	D	SD
[SF]	33. People in my family like to listen to me read.	SA	A	U	D	SD

Figure 10.7   The Reader Self-Perception Scale Scoring Sheet

Student name _____

Teacher _____

Grade _____   Date _____

Scoring key: 5 = Strongly Agree (SA)
4 = Agree (A)
3 = Undecided (U)
2 = Disagree (D)
1 = Strongly Disagree (SD)

Scales

General Perception	Progress	Observational Comparison	Social Feedback	Physiological States
1. _____	10. _____	4. _____	2. _____	5. _____
	13. _____	6. _____	3. _____	8. _____
	15. _____	11. _____	7. _____	16. _____
	18. _____	14. _____	9. _____	21. _____
	19. _____	20. _____	12. _____	25. _____
	23. _____	22. _____	17. _____	26. _____
	24. _____		30. _____	29. _____
	27. _____		31. _____	32. _____
	28. _____		33. _____	
Raw score	_____ of 45	_____ of 30	_____ of 45	_____ of 40

Score interpretation				
High	44+	26+	38+	37+
Average	39	21	33	31
Low	34	16	27	25

at the top of the CMRSUS. Read the directions aloud and ask children if they have any questions about the nature of the responses to be given to each statement. Once you, the teacher, are sure that the students understand, instruct them to read each item and circle the number under the response that best represents their behavior in relation to each statement. When children finish the CMRSUS, ask them to remain in their seats. They should quietly take out a book, write, or draw so as not to disturb others who are still completing the scale.

Scoring is accomplished by summing the response numbers circled and dividing by the total of the 15 items in the CMRSUS—Sum of individual responses/15 items = the

Figure 10.8 A Classroom Modified Version of the Reading Strategy Use Scale

Name _____ Grade _____

Teacher_____ School _____

Directions: Read each item and the number of the word that best describes how often you do what is stated. Let's do number 1 together to make sure you understand how you are to respond to each item.

1. I read quickly through the story to get the general idea before I read the story closely.
   Always   Sometimes   Never
   3   2   1

2. When I come to a part of the story that is hard to read, I slow my reading down.
   Always   Sometimes   Never
   3   2   1

3. I am able to tell the difference between important story parts and less important details.
   Always   Sometimes   Never
   3   2   1

4. When I read, I stop once in a while to go over in my head what I have been reading to see if it is making sense.
   Always   Sometimes   Never
   3   2   1

5. I adjust the speed of my reading by deciding how difficult the story is to read.
   Always   Sometimes   Never
   3   2   1

6. I stop once in a while and ask myself questions about the story to see how well I understand what I am reading.
   Always   Sometimes   Never
   3   2   1

7. After reading a story, I sit and think about it for a while to check my memory of the story parts and the order of the story parts.
   Always   Sometimes   Never
   3   2   1

8. When I get lost while reading, I go back to the place in the story where I first had trouble and reread.
   Always   Sometimes   Never
   3   2   1

9. When I find I do not understand something when reading, I read it again and try to figure it out.
   Always   Sometimes   Never
   3   2   1

10. When reading, I check how well I understand the meaning of the story by asking myself whether the ideas fit with the other information in the story.
    Always   Sometimes   Never
    3   2   1

11. I find it hard to pay attention when I read.
    Always   Sometimes   Never
    3   2   1

12. To help me remember what I read, I sometimes draw a map or outline the story.
    Always   Sometimes   Never
    3   2   1

13. To help me understand what I have read in a story, I try to retell it in my own words.
    Always   Sometimes   Never
    3   2   1

14. I learn new words by trying to make a picture of the words in my mind.
    Always   Sometimes   Never
    3   2   1

15. When reading about something, I try to relate it to my own experiences.
    Always   Sometimes   Never
    3   2   1

mean score. A mean score near 3 indicates strong selection, use, and self-regulation of comprehension monitoring strategies. A mean score near 2 indicates occasional selection and use of comprehension monitoring strategies. The pattern of responses should be carefully studied to see which of the comprehension monitoring strategies are in use and which are not to inform instructional planning for the future. A mean score near 1 indicates poorly developed selection, use, and self-regulation of comprehension monitoring strategies. These students need explicit teacher explanation of: a) comprehension monitoring strategies, b) how, when, and why to use comprehension monitoring strategies, c) teacher modeling of comprehension monitoring strategy use, and d) guided practice applying selected comprehension monitoring strategies during the reading and discussion of stories in the classroom.

BACKGROUND KNOWLEDGE

Purpose

Children's background information and experiences are among the most important contributors or inhibitors of comprehension. Researchers have determined that students who possess a great deal of background information about a subject tend to recall greater amounts of information more accurately from reading than do students with little or no background knowledge (Carr & Thompson, 1996; Pearson, Hansen, & Gordon, 1979; Pressley, 2000). It also a well-known fact that well-developed background information can inhibit the comprehension of new information that conflicts with or refutes prior knowledge and assumptions about a specific topic. Thus, knowing how much knowledge a reader has about a concept or topic can help teachers better prepare students to read and comprehend successfully. One way that teachers can assess background knowledge and experience is to use a procedure developed by Langer (1982) for assessing the amount and content of students' background knowledge about selected topics, themes, concepts, and events.

Materials

Use the checklist and materials represented in Figure 10.9.

Procedure

Select a story for children to read. Construct a list of specific vocabulary terms or story concepts related to the topic, message, theme, or events to be experienced in reading the story. For example, students may read the story *Stone Fox* by John R. Gardiner (1980), about a boy named Willy who saves his grandfather's farm from the tax collector. Construct a list of 5 to 10 specific vocabulary terms or concepts related to the story. Use this list to probe background knowledge and experiences of the students about the story's message and plot. Such a list might include the following:

1. Broke
2. Taxes
3. Tax collector
4. Dogsled race
5. Samoyeds

Figure 10.9   Checklist of Levels of Prior Knowledge

Phrase 1	What comes to mind when. . . ?
Phrase 2	What made you think of. . . ?
Phrase 3	Have you any new ideas about. . . ?

Stimulus used to elicit student background knowledge _____

(Picture, word, or phrase, etc.)

	Much - (3)	Some - (2)	Little - (1)
	category labels	examples	personal associations
	definitions	attributes	morphemes
	analogies	defining characteristics	sound alikes
	relationships		personal experiences

Student name			
Maria	_____	X	_____
Jawan	X	_____	_____
_____	_____	_____	_____
_____	_____	_____	_____
_____	_____	_____	_____

Students are asked to respond to each of these terms in writing or through discussion. This is accomplished by using one of several stem statements, as shown in Figure 10.9, such as, "What comes to mind when you think of paying bills and you hear the term 'broke'?" Students then respond. Once students have responded to each of the specific terms, the teacher can score the responses using the information in Figure 10.9 to survey the class's or individual's knowledge and experience. Awarding the number of points that most closely represents the level of prior knowledge in the response is used to score each item. Divide the total score by the number of terms or concepts in the list (five in our example) to determine the average knowledge level of individual students. These average scores are compared against the *Checklist of Levels of Prior Knowledge* in Figure 10.9 for each student. By scanning the x's in the checklist, a teacher can get a sense of the entire class's overall level of prior knowledge. Information thus gathered can be used to inform both the content and nature of whole-group comprehension instruction.

STUDENT READING INTEREST SURVEY

Purpose

For many years researchers have found that reading comprehension is positively affected when children are interested in the reading materials (Asher, 1980; Corno & Randi, 1997).

Figure 10.10   Student Reading Interest Survey

In-School Interests

What is the title of your favorite book that you have read?

Do you have a favorite book title that someone has read to you?

What kinds of books do you like to read on your own?

Do you have favorite books, magazines, or comic books at home?

Do you ever read the newspaper at home? If so, what parts of the newspaper do you read?

What is your favorite school subject (other than recess and lunch)?

Have you ever done a special research project? What was the topic?

Out-of-School Interests

What do you do for fun on weekends or after school?

Do you have a hobby? If so, what?

What is your favorite TV show?

What is your favorite movie?

Do you play sports? If so, what?

Do you like animals or have a pet?

Do you have favorite video or computer games?

If you surf the Internet, what do you generally look for as you surf?

Have you ever collected something like coins, stamps, and so on? If you have, what?

This is so much the case that interest in reading materials has been shown also to compensate for children's lack of strategy, use, and ability in comprehension specifically, and reading generally (Sweet, 1997). Knowing how important student interests are in shaping and influencing students' reading comprehension, the *Student Reading Interest Survey* or *SRIS* (see Figure 10.10) provides teachers with an efficient and effective tool to gain insights into student interests.

Materials

You will need:

- One laminated copy of the questions found in the Student Reading Interest Survey
- One paper copy for recording individual student responses
- One paper copy for recording categories of class responses

Procedure

Once the necessary materials are in place, schedule a time during the day to meet with students individually. Using the laminated copy of the SRIS, seat the child comfortably next

Figure 10.11   Class SRIS Profile Recording Table

Student Names	Q1	Q2							

to you at a table in a quiet corner of the classroom. *(This survey may also be given by an aide or volunteer so long as he or she has been trained to completely record answers.)* Ask children each question and record the answers given. After each response, be sure to tell each child that if he or she remembers anything else to tell you, that child is welcome to share it at a later time.

After the entire class has been surveyed, compile the individual responses into a class survey response profile (see Figure 10.11). Record abbreviated answers to each question for each student in the class response profile. Look over the responses to each question by all of the children for categories of interests to be observed in your teaching and reading materials acquisition plan.

During the year, particularly if children's writing skills are well developed, distribute the SRIS to the entire group of children. Ask them to write their answers to the SRIS questions on their own copy and turn it in. Make any changes on the class profile sheet you discover throughout the year. This updated information about your students' reading interests will help you adjust your selection of topics and reading materials as the year progresses.

CONNECTING ASSESSMENT FINDINGS TO TEACHING STRATEGIES

Before discussing intervention strategies, we have constructed a guide connecting assessment to intervention and/or strategy choices. It is our intention to help you, the teacher, select the most appropriate instructional inventions and strategies to meet students' needs based on assessment data.

In the next part of this chapter, we offer strategies for intervention based on the foregoing assessments.

Intervention Strategy Guide for Story Comprehension

Intervention Strategy / Student Problem(s)	Interactive Read Alouds	Story Schema Lesson	Click or Clunk	Story Grammar Instruction	Summary Writing	Graphic Organizers	Comp Through Literature	Comp Strategy Framework	Reciprocal Teaching
Doesn't know story parts	+	+	-	+	+	+	*	*	*
Doesn't know or use story order	+	+	-	+	+	+	*	*	*
Doesn't remember important story elements	*	*	-	+	+	+	*	*	*
Makes poor strategy selections	*	*	+	-	-	*	+	+	+
Expresses feelings of inadequacy	*	*	*	*	*	*	+	+	+
Doesn't recognize when not understanding	*	*	+	*	*	*	+	+	*
Doesn't have or activate background knowledge	*	+	+	*	*	*	+	+	*
Seldom chooses to read voluntarily	+	*	-	*	*	*	+	*	*
Can't find a book to read of interest	+	*	-	*	*	*	*	*	*
Doesn't know what to do when he doesn't understand	*	*	+	*	*	*	+	+	+

Key: + excellent strategy
      * adaptable strategy
      – unsuitable strategy

INSTRUCTIONAL INTERVENTIONS AND STRATEGIES: HELPING EVERY STUDENT COMPREHEND STORIES

After a careful assessment of a student's story comprehension, one or more of the following strategies may be appropriately applied. Perhaps the most important thing to remember is that children with a poor sense of the structure of stories must be immersed in a multitude of reading-related activities and related strategy use. Authentic reading and writing experiences coupled with the informed guidance of a caring teacher or other literate individuals (e.g., parents, peers, and volunteers) can do much to help students learn about the structure of well-formed stories.

INTERACTIVE READ ALOUD

Purpose

Interactive Read Aloud is a strategy that helps young children internalize story structure knowledge through hearing and interacting with others about stories (Campbell, 2001; Martens, 1996; Martin & Reutzel, 1999; Schikendanz, 1990). Several of the chief benefits associated with interactively reading aloud are that children learn about literacy, develop new cognitive concepts and oral language, and are motivated to become readers themselves (Campbell, 2001). Although most read alouds in school take place with an entire class or group of children, Morrow (1988, 2001) reminded us not to overlook the benefits and importance of reading aloud to smaller groups and individuals. Children whose reading development is lagging behind their peers can be helped a great deal by teachers and parents who take time to read to them in small group or individual settings and talk through the text and about how the text is structured with children. During interactive read alouds (Campbell, 2001), it is expected that teachers and children will stop to ask questions, make comments, or respond to the story. Morrow (2001) suggested, when possible, individual or small group readings be recorded and analyzed to provide diagnostic information to inform instruction.

Materials

No special materials are needed, other than books correctly matched to students' interests and needs. It is best if you select stories that are well-formed narrative structures that have a clear beginning, middle, and end, or setting, problem, attempts, and resolution.

Procedure

Graham and Kelly (1997) and Campbell (2001) described how to get an Interactive Read Aloud started in the classroom. Campbell (2001) suggested that teachers need to 1) prepare for effective Interactive Read Alouds, 2) read the book aloud as a performance, and 3) ensure that children take part. Preparations for an Interactive Read Aloud can be divided into four sequential steps: 1) Select, 2) Plan, 3) Practice, and 4) Deliver (Graham & Kelly, 1997). Books selected should match the intellectual, social, and emotional levels of the children according to Trelease's *The New Read Aloud Handbook* (1995). In planning for the Interactive Read Aloud, decide on any resources or props that may be needed, decide how much of the book will be read aloud in one sitting, how to introduce the book, points to be raised for discussion, how to end the session if the book is not read in its entirety, and how to involve the children in the story reading. Campbell (2001) suggested the book be as a performance—this means that teachers should read the story aloud with enthusiasm and expression. Following the reading, demonstrate for children a quality retelling that contains all of the important story structure elements in the correct order. Explain that the best retellings include key story elements such as a description of characters, setting, and so forth. When you feel the students are ready to begin producing their own oral retellings of a story, let them know *before* you read aloud the story that you will want them to give retelling a try (Morrow, 2001). We have also found that it is best that students be encouraged to try out their retellings with peers prior to sharing it with the teacher or the group.

Schema Stories

Purpose

Watson and Crowley (1988), originators of this strategy lesson, described *schema stories* as a reading strategy lesson that helps readers "reconstruct the order of a text based on meaning and story grammar" (p. 263). This strategy helps students learn to anticipate such elements as setting, problem to be addressed by the characters, key events in the story, and resolution of the story (Simmons & Kameenui, 1998).

Materials

Start with stories that contain familiar beginning and ending phrases, such as *Once upon a time* and *They lived happily ever after.* After choosing an interesting story, prepare the schema story strategy lesson by making a photocopy of the text and physically cutting the photocopy into sections or parts that are long enough to contain at least one main idea. Usually, one or two paragraphs will be a sufficient length to accomplish this purpose.

Procedure

To begin the lesson, distribute a section or part of the story to each small group of students (four to eight students in each group is about right). Typically, one student is selected in each group to read the text aloud for her group. Once each group has read their story part, ask if any group believes they were given the section of the story that comes at the beginning of the story. Students who believe they have the beginning of the story are to raise their hands to respond. Those who raise their hands must state *why* they believe they have the beginning of the story. After the majority of the students agree as to which section or story part is first, the group proceeds to the next segment of the story. This process continues as described until all of the segments have been placed in a predicted order.

Schema story lessons make excellent small-group or individual activities that can be located at a classroom center or station devoted to developing a sense of story. All of the segments of a text can be placed into an envelope and filed in the center. Small groups of children or individuals can come to the center and select an envelope, working individually or collectively on reconstructing a story. A "key" for self-checking can be included in the envelope, as well, to reduce the amount of teacher supervision necessary in the center. As children work through a schema story strategy lesson, they talk about how language works, ways authors construct texts, and how meaning can be used to make sense out of the scrambled elements of a text or story.

Figure 10.12   Metacomprehension "Repair" Strategies

Broken Comprehension Repair Strategies

- **Read on.**
- **Reread** the sentence.
- **Go back** and reread the paragraph.
- **Seek** information from glossary or reference materials.
- **Ask** someone near you who may be able to help, such as one of your peers.

CLICK OR CLUNK AND FIX-UP STRATEGIES

Purpose

As described earlier in this chapter, the act of monitoring one's unfolding comprehension of stories and taking steps to "fix" comprehension when it is not occurring is referred to as metacognition or, sometimes, metacomprehension. The "Click or Clunk" strategy was designed to help students recognize when and where their comprehension of a story breaks down. Coupled with instruction on comprehension "fix-up" strategies, students can come to know what to do to detect and correct comprehension breakdowns. If readers fail to detect comprehension breakdowns, they will take no action to correct misinterpretations of the text. If students fail to correct misinterpretations of a story or text, their comprehension of stories or other texts will likely be both inaccurate and incomplete.

Materials

You will need:

- One book or story that children have read collectively or individually
- A poster display of the repair strategies shown in Figure 10.12 (adapted from Babbs, 1994)

Procedure

To help students develop the ability to monitor their own comprehension processes, Carr (1985) suggested a strategy called *Click or Clunk*. This strategy urges readers to reflect at the end of each sentence, paragraph, or section of reading by stopping and asking themselves if the meaning or message "clicks" for them or goes "clunk." If it clunks, what is wrong? What can be done to make sense of it?

Once a comprehension breakdown has been detected, it is important to know which strategies to select in repairing broken comprehension, as well as when to use these strategies. In fact, students may know that they need to take steps to repair comprehension, but they may not know which steps to take or when to take them. As a consequence, children should be introduced to several well-known repair options for repairing broken comprehension.

To demonstrate the use of a "fix-up" poster, model for students using a "think-aloud" process to help them develop a sense for when to select certain repair strategies for failing comprehension. Read part of a text aloud and, as you proceed, comment on your thinking. Reveal to students your thinking, the hypotheses you have formed for the text, and anything that strikes you as difficult or unclear. By doing so, you demonstrate for students the processes that successful readers use to comprehend a text. Next, remind them of the Click or Clunk strategy. Gradually release the responsibility for modeling metacognitive strategies to the children during follow-up lessons on metacognitive monitoring. Display the repair strategies in a prominent place in your classroom. Be sure to draw your students' attention to these strategies throughout the year.

GRAPHIC ORGANIZERS FOR STORIES

Purpose

Graphic organizers are visual representations of story elements and the interrelationships among these parts. Several researchers over the years have demonstrated the efficacy of using graphic organizers to teach children how stories are constructed to improve their comprehension of stories (Beck & McKeown, 1981; Reutzel, 1985; 1986). Graphic organizers like story maps or story webs have been used to effectively increase children's comprehension of stories (Boyle, 1996; Bromley, 1993; Reutzel, 1985, 1986).

Reutzel and Fawson (1989) designed a successful strategy lesson to be used with young readers' predictable storybooks for building children's understanding of story structure. A literature web is constructed from the major story elements in a predictable book by selecting sentences from a book that tell about each major element of the story (i.e., setting, problem, events, and resolution).

To cement or correct comprehension of text *after* reading, you may want to conduct a class discussion. Most class discussions tend to center around the teacher and a few vocal children, with the rest of the class passively listening, or worse, completely inattentive. A *discussion web* (Alvermann, 1991) is a practical technique for enhancing student participation and thought during class discussions after reading. Recent work by Merkley and Jeffries (2001) provided guidelines for implementing graphic organizers.

Materials

The following materials are needed for constructing a graphic organizer for stories:

- One well-formed story
- Sentence strips
- Hand-drawn or copied pictures from the selected story
- A chalkboard or other display area for posting the literature web
- A felt pen or marker for drawing lines of relationships

Procedure

Sentences from the story are copied onto strips. The title of the story is copied onto a sentence strip. The sentence strip with the title is placed in the center of the board or display area. The remaining sentence strips are placed in random order on the chalk tray or some other display area (see Figure 10.13 for an example). Prior to reading the story in a shared book experience, reading it aloud, or encouraging students to read it independently, the class or group reads the sentences aloud with the teacher. In the early part of the school year, the sentences selected for the web sentence strips are usually heavily augmented with hand-drawn or copied pictures from the book.

Organize children into small groups and give each group one of the picture/sentence cards from the board. The children are asked which group thinks it has the first part of the story. After discussion and group agreement is reached, the first sentence/picture card is placed at the one o'clock position on the literature web graphic organizer. The remainder

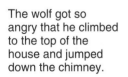 **Figure 10.13**   Random-Order Literature Web

One pig met a man carrying a bundle of sticks. "May I have those sticks to build myself a house?" asked the pig. "You may," answered the man.

And the three little pigs lived happily ever after in a brick house built for three.

One day the wolf came knocking at the door of the brick house. "Little pig, little pig, let me come in." "Not by the hair of my chinny chin chin," said the pig. "Then I'll huff and I'll puff and I'll blow your house in." But the house would not fall down.

The wolf fell, kersplot, into a kettle of hot water. He jumped out with a start and ran out the door and never came back again.

One day the wolf came knocking at the door of the straw house. "Little pig, little pig, let me come in." "Not by the hair of my chinny chin chin," said the pig. "Then I'll huff and I'll puff and I'll blow your house in." And he blew the house down.

Once upon a time, three little pigs set out to make their fortune.

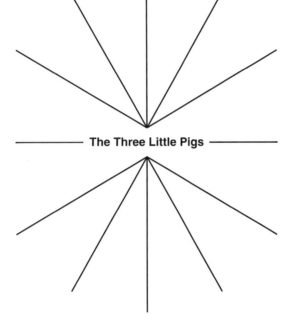

The Three Little Pigs

The wolf got so angry that he climbed to the top of the house and jumped down the chimney.

One pig met a man with a load of bricks. "May I have those bricks to build myself a house?" asked the pig. "You may," answered the man.

One pig met a man carrying a bundle of straw. "May I have that straw to build myself a house?" asked the pig. "You may," answered the man.

One day the wolf came knocking at the door of the stick house. "Little pig, little pig, let me come in." "Not by the hair of my chinny chin chin," said the pig. "Then I'll huff and I'll puff and I'll blow your house in." And he blew the house down.

of the groups are asked which sentence/picture combination comes next, and the sentence strips/pictures are placed around the graphic organizer in clockwise order. Figure 10.14 shows how one group of students rearranged a graphic organizer to confirm their predictions.

Figure 10.14   Literature Web Predictions

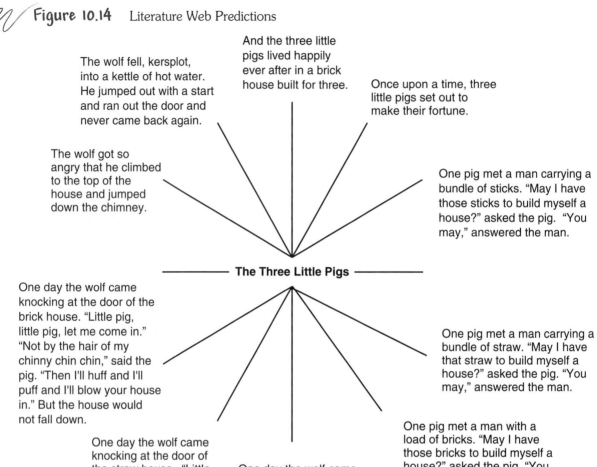

Next, the story is read aloud or silently from a traditional-sized trade book or from a big book in a shared reading. Children listen attentively to confirm or correct their graphic organizer predictions. After the reading, predictions are revised in the graphic organizer as necessary (see Figure 10.15). Children respond to the story, and these responses are recorded near the end of the graphic organizer. Other books similar to the one read may be discussed and comments recorded on the web. Finally, the children and teacher brainstorm together some ideas about how to extend the reading of the book into the other language arts while recording these ideas on the graphic organizer. Reutzel and Fawson (1991) also demonstrated that children having reading problems who participate in using a graphic organizer of a predictable book learn to read these books with fewer oral reading miscues, fewer miscues that distort comprehension, and greater recall. They attribute

Figure 10.15 Completed Literature Web

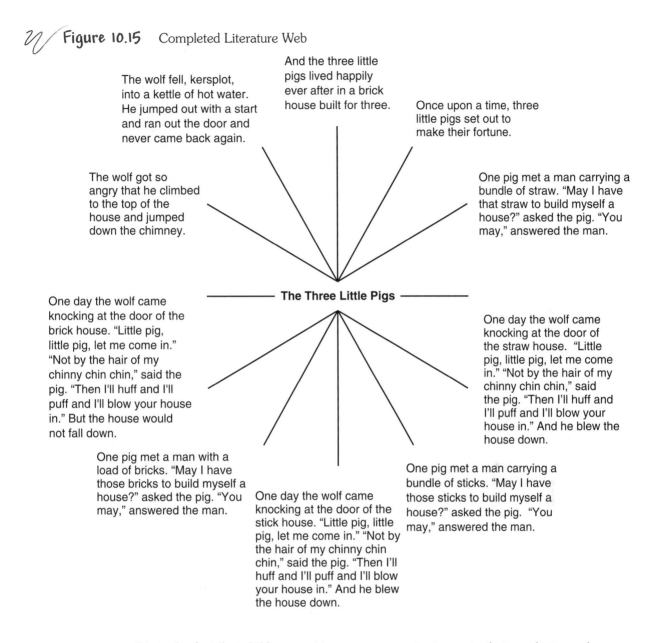

The wolf fell, kersplot, into a kettle of hot water. He jumped out with a start and ran out the door and never came back again.

And the three little pigs lived happily ever after in a brick house built for three.

Once upon a time, three little pigs set out to make their fortune.

The wolf got so angry that he climbed to the top of the house and jumped down the chimney.

One pig met a man carrying a bundle of straw. "May I have that straw to build myself a house?" asked the pig. "You may," answered the man.

The Three Little Pigs

One day the wolf came knocking at the door of the brick house. "Little pig, little pig, let me come in." "Not by the hair of my chinny chin chin," said the pig. "Then I'll huff and I'll puff and I'll blow your house in." But the house would not fall down.

One day the wolf came knocking at the door of the straw house. "Little pig, little pig, let me come in." "Not by the hair of my chinny chin chin," said the pig. "Then I'll huff and I'll puff and I'll blow your house in." And he blew the house down.

One pig met a man with a load of bricks. "May I have those bricks to build myself a house?" asked the pig. "You may," answered the man.

One day the wolf came knocking at the door of the stick house. "Little pig, little pig, let me come in." "Not by the hair of my chinny chin chin," said the pig. "Then I'll huff and I'll puff and I'll blow your house in." And he blew the house down.

One pig met a man carrying a bundle of sticks. "May I have those sticks to build myself a house?" asked the pig. "You may," answered the man.

this to the fact that children must impose an organization onto their predictions when using graphic organizers, rather than simply making random predictions from story titles and pictures.

To use a discussion web graphic organizer after reading a story, begin by preparing students to read a text selection or book as you normally would (see Figure 10.16.). Help them think of related background experiences and invite them to set a purpose for reading the story. You may want to ask an open-ended question about the story. For example, for *The Widow's Broom* by Chris Van Allsburg (1992), you might ask, "Do you think the widow Minna Shaw should have tricked her neighbors?" Group students in pairs and ask them to answer the question according to their own feelings and the facts they remember from the story. Help them focus on *why* a certain answer could be true. Ask students to think also

Figure 10.16   Discussion Web

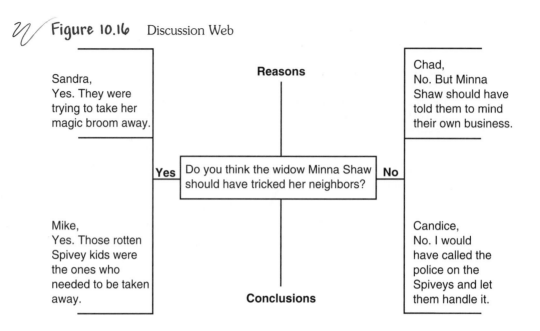

of some reasons the opposite answer could be true. For example, one student may say, "Yes, they were trying to take her magic broom away." A partner may add, "Yes, those rotten Spivey kids were the ones who needed to be taken away." In this example, these students have voiced two "yes" answers. Next, the teacher should ask the students to think of some "no" answers, as well.

After students have discussed their ideas in pairs, you may want to ask them to share their thinking with another pair of students. Ask each pair to choose their best answer to the question, as well as the strongest reason supporting their thinking. Then, bring the children together and ask one student from each pair to report their best answer and the reason supporting that answer. As each student speaks, include the reason in the diagram. After each pair reports, invite others to suggest additional ideas for the discussion web. You may want to reach a class conclusion, or you may want to stop just before a conclusion is reached to avoid a "right" or "wrong" feeling for the answers. (Note: Some teachers of very young students use the discussion web strategy in a whole-class setting, rather than grouping students in pairs. Vary the approach according to your teaching style and class needs.)

Merkley and Jeffries (2001) encouraged teachers to use the following guidelines in teaching with graphic organizers to help students improve their comprehension:

- Talk about the links or relationships among the concepts or events expressed in the visual.
- Provide opportunity for student input in shaping the content and order of the visual.
- Connect the new learning to past learning and to other stories to demonstrate relationships.
- Reference an upcoming story that will be read soon.
- Use the text in the visual of a graphic organizer to reinforce decoding and other word study skills.
- Although the graphic organizer may be distributed as a worksheet, the secret to success is to use graphic organizers to organize discussion, text talk, and thinking.

TEACHING COMPREHENSION STRATEGIES THROUGH LITERATURE

Purpose

The purpose of teaching comprehension strategies through literature is to integrate comprehension strategy instruction into literature reading and response activities. Teaching comprehension within the framework of reading literature is supported from the view that application of a skill or strategy is far more likely to transfer to another context when it has been taught in a meaningful context in the first place (Baumann, Hooten, & White, 1999; Headley & Dunston, 2000; Routman, 1991). A meaningful context is defined in four ways: 1) within the framework of quality literature, 2) within a setting of high utility for skill or strategy application, 3) within an instructional framework that is explicit and spontaneous, and 4) within reading materials that are of high interest to learners (Baumann et al., 1999; Wade, Buxton, & Kelley, 1999). "Teaching Comprehension Through Literature" was designed to provide students with what Pressley (2000) referred to as transactional comprehension strategy instruction because such comprehension instruction uses direct explanation of specific strategies embedded in a rich literary context.

According to Pressley and Wharton-McDonald (1997), singular comprehension strategies such as: predicting, activating prior knowledge, generating questions, seeking clarification, constructing mental images, relating text content to prior knowledge, and summarizing, when taught one at a time or together, were often used as vehicles for directing talk about texts. As such, individual comprehension strategies were explicitly taught and then applied in various forms of responses or "grand conversations" about text. This collection of effective, individual comprehension instructional strategies, when combined into a comprehension instructional framework, was to become known as *Transactional Strategies Instruction* because students transacted with texts and with others about texts in discussion and dialog.

During the decade of the 1990s, Pressley and his colleagues carefully studied the nature of comprehension instruction in schools and classrooms where there was evidence of *effective* comprehension instruction (El-Dinary, Pressley, & Schuder, 1992; Gaskins, Anderson, Pressley, Cunicelli, & Satlow, 1993; Pressley, Gaskins, Wile, Cunicelli & Sheridan, 1991). Studies of the effectiveness of *Transactional Strategies Instruction* across varying ages and abilities have demonstrated strikingly positive effects on students' comprehension (Anderson & Roit, 1993; Brown, Pressley, Van Meter, & Schuder, 1996; Collins, 1991).

Materials

You will need:

- One high-quality literature book containing a well-formed story
- One analysis of the challenges and opportunities the story offers for skill or strategy instruction
- One lesson plan for an "Elaborated" or "brief review" strategy lesson

Procedure

Locate a quality literature story for the lesson. As the teacher, read the book to determine which of several comprehension skills or strategy lessons the content and structure may best support. Determine which type of three comprehension lessons to prepare: 1) An Elaborated strategy lesson that is planned in advance and taught directly to students within the context of the book selected; 2) A Brief strategy lesson that is a planned review or extension lesson of a previously taught skill or strategy taught in the context of the book selected; or 3) An Impromptu strategy lesson that is an unplanned lesson taught "on the spot" in the context of reading or discussing the book selected. Comprehension strategies found to be most effectively taught within the framework of literature include: 1) predictions based on prior-knowledge activation, 2) question generation, 3) clarification seeking when confused, 4) constructing mental images, 5) relating prior knowledge to text content, and 6) summarization.

As you prepare the lesson, be sure to plan the lesson to include an explanation of the strategy. Next, model its use in the context of the story. Provide guided group and individual independent practice in the meaningful story context. See the model lesson for predicting and verifying in Figure 10.17.

Figure 10.17   Teaching Comprehension Strategies through Literature Lesson: Elaborated Strategy Lesson Plan

Strategy: **Predicting and Verifying**

Objective: Learn to connect text content and use prior knowledge to make and check predictions in stories.

Explanation: Making a prediction is to make a guess about what may be coming next in a story. Readers use the information they get from reading a story, their own experience, and their prior knowledge about stories to make predictions and to check or "verify" their predictions as they read.

Teacher Modeling: Using the story *The Biggest Bear* by Lynd Ward (1952), read aloud the text, "After he had gone quite a way into the woods, he came to a place where there was a big stump, and something seemed to be moving in the bushes behind it" (p. 14). Ask yourself the question aloud, "I wonder what is rustling behind the bushes?" "Could it be a squirrel, a raccoon, a deer, or maybe a bear?" Read on to check. "It was a bear alright" (p. 16).

Group Guided Practice: Continue reading aloud pages 18–22. On page 22, after reading, "Johnny's mother and father were a little surprised to see that Johnny had really brought a bear back with him. Johnny's grandfather said, 'Humph, I suppose you know what a bear likes to eat.'" Ask the children, "Why do you think Grandpa asked Johnny what bears like to eat?" Discuss ideas and predictions to the question. Then read on and list the things bears like to eat.

Individual Independent Practice: Tell students to stop at the end of specific pages and make predictions to answer the question you have placed on a large poster board. Also display the steps of predicting and verifying on a large poster board as shown:

> **Five-Step Process for Predicting and Verifying Predictions**
> 1. Read.
> 2. Make a prediction.
> 3. Check the prediction.
> 4. Change the prediction or make a new prediction.
> 5. Repeat these steps.

Assess Strategy Use: Ask children to write down one story prediction and write down the text they used to support and check their predictions.

QUESTION-ANSWER RELATIONSHIPS (QARs)

Purpose

Raphael (1982, 1986) identified four Question-Answer Relationships (QARs) to help children identify the connection between the type of questions asked of them by teachers and textbooks and the information sources necessary and available to them for answering questions: 1) *Right There,* 2) *Think and Search,* 3) *Author and You,* and 4) *On My Own.* Research by Raphael and Pearson (1982) provided evidence that training students to recognize question-answer relationships (QARs) results in improved comprehension and question-answering behavior. In addition, using the QARs question-answering training strategy is useful for another purpose: helping teachers examine their own questioning with respect to the types of questions and the information sources that students need to use to answer their questions. By using QARs to monitor their own questioning behaviors, some teachers may find that they are asking only *Right There* types of questions. This discovery very often leads teachers to ask other questions that require the use of additional or seldom-used information sources.

Materials

The materials needed include a variety of texts for asking and answering questions, a poster displaying the information in the classroom to heighten childrens' and teachers' awareness of the types of questions asked, and the information sources available for answering those questions. Figure 10.18 provides examples of each of the four types of Question-Answer Relationships (QARs).

Procedure

Instruction using QARs begins by explaining to students that when they answer questions about reading, there are basically two places they can look to get information: *In the Book* and *In My Head.* This concept should be practiced with the students by reading aloud a text, asking questions, and having the students explain or show where they found their answers. Once students understand the two-category approach, expand the *In the Book* category to include: *Right There* and *Putting It Together.* The distinction between these two categories should be practiced by reading and discussing several texts. For older students, Raphael (1986) suggested that students be shown specific strategies for locating the answers to *Right There* questions. These include looking in a single sentence or looking in two sentences connected by a pronoun. For *Putting It Together* questions, students can be asked to focus their attention on the structure of the text, such as cause-effect, problem-solution, listing-example, compare-contrast, and explanation.

Next, instruction should be directed toward two subcategories within the *In My Head* category: *Author and Me,* and *On My Own.* Here again, these categories can be practiced as a group by reading a text aloud, answering the questions, and discussing the sources of information. To expand this training, students can be asked to identify the types of questions asked in their basal readers, workbooks, content area texts, and tests; in addition, they can determine the sources of information needed to answer these questions. Students may be informed that certain types of questions are asked before and after reading a text. For example, questions asked before reading typically invite students to activate their own knowledge. Therefore, questions asked before reading will usually be *On My Own* questions. However, questions asked after reading will make use of information found in the text. Thus, questions asked after reading will typically focus on the *Right There, Putting It Together,* and *Author and Me* types of questions. As a culminating training activity for QARs, children are asked to write their own questions for each of the QAR categories.

 **Figure 10.18**   Illustrations to Explain Question-Answer Relationships (QARs) to Students

In the Book QARs

Right There
The answer is in the text, usually easy to find. The words used to make up the question and words used to answer the question are **Right There** in the same sentence.

> One day there was ~~~~
> ~~~~ ~~~~
> ~~~~
> So Jack rode a horse to school today!
>
> What did Jack ride to school today!

**Think and Search
(Putting It Together)**
The answer is in the story, but you need to put together different story parts to find it. Words for the question and words for the answer are not found in the same sentence. They come from different parts of the text.

> First you get some bread ~~~~
> ~~~~ ~~~~
> ~~~~
> Second you get a knife.
> Third you get the peanut butter
>
> How do you make a peanut butter sandwich?

In My Head QARs

Author and You
The answer is *not* in the story. You need to think about what you already know, what the author tells you in the text, and how it fits together.

On My Own
The answer is *not* in the story. You can even answer the question without reading the story. You need to use your own experience.

Source: From "Teaching Question Answer Relationships, Revisited" by Taffy E. Raphael, *The Reading Teacher,* February 1986. Reprinted with permission of Taffy E. Raphael and the International Reading Association.

STORY GRAMMAR INSTRUCTION

Purpose

Developing a sense of how stories are formed through story grammar instruction helps students having reading problems predict with greater facility, store information more efficiently, and recall story elements with increased accuracy and completeness.

Materials

Well-formed stories and a visual organizer (see Figures 10.2 and 10.13) to guide the introduction of story grammar concepts are the materials needed for this activity.

Procedure

A number of reading researchers have described instructional procedures for developing readers' story schema or *story grammar* awareness. Gordon and Braun (1983) recommended several guidelines for teaching story grammar. We have adapted these recommendations as follows:

1. Story grammar instruction should use well-formed stories such as "Jack and the Beanstalk." A visual organizer can be used to guide the introduction of the concept of story grammar. For the first story used in story grammar instruction, read the story aloud, stop at key points in the story, and discuss the information needed to fill in the diagram. For stories read after introducing the concept of story grammar, use the visual organizer to introduce the story and make predictions about the story prior to reading. During and after reading, a visual organizer can be used to guide a discussion.

2. Set the purposes for reading by asking questions related to the structure of the story. Questioning developed to follow the structure of the story will focus students' attention on major story elements.

3. After questioning and discussing story structure, specific questions about the story content can be asked.

4. For continued instruction, gradually introduce less well-formed stories so that students will learn that not all stories are "ideal" in organization.

Extend instruction by encouraging children to ask their own questions using story structure and to apply this understanding in writing their own stories.

SUMMARY WRITING

Purpose

The purpose of writing a summary is to extract main ideas from a reading selection. Good readers are constantly stopping themselves during reading to think about their comprehension and to take corrective action when necessary. Summaries are important because they help form memory structures that readers can use to select and store relevant details from their reading. Some readers do not spontaneously summarize their reading and, as a result, have poor understanding and recall of what they read (Brown, Day, & Jones, 1983).

Materials

A tradebook, basal, or textbook selection is needed, along with a chart displaying the rules for summary writing. An example based on the work of Hare and Borchordt (1984) is shown in Figure 10.19.

Figure 10.19 Five Rules for Writing a Summary

1. *Collapse lists.* If there is a list of things, supply a word or phrase for the whole list. For example, if you saw *swimming, sailing, fishing,* and *surfing,* you could substitute *water sports.*
2. *Use topic sentences.* Sometimes authors write a sentence that summarizes the whole paragraph. If so, use that sentence in your summary. If not, you'll have to make up your own topic sentences.
3. *Get rid of unnecessary detail.* Sometimes information is repeated or is stated in several different ways. Some information may be trivial and unnecessary. Get rid of repetitive or trivial information. Summaries should be short.
4. *Collapse paragraphs.* Often, paragraphs are related to each other. For example, some paragraphs simply explain or expand on other paragraphs in a selection. Some paragraphs are more important than others. Join the paragraphs that are related. Important paragraphs should stand alone.
5. *Polish the summary.* When you collapse a lot of information from many paragraphs into one or two paragraphs, the resulting summary sometimes sounds awkward and unnatural. There are several ways to remedy this: add connecting words such as *like* or *because,* or write introductory or closing statements. Another method is to paraphrase the material; this will improve your ability to remember what you read and enable you to avoid plagiarism—using the exact words of the author.

Source: From "Direct Instruction of Summarization Skills" by V. C. Hare and K. M. Borchordt, 1984, *Reading Research Quarterly 20* (1) pp. 62–78. Copyright 1984 by the International Reading Association.

Procedure

Begin by distributing copies of the tradebook or textbook selections to be read by the group. Have the students silently read the first few passages. Next, on an overhead transparency, model for the children how you would use the five summary rules in Figure 10.19 to write a summary. After modeling how you would write a summary, instruct the children to finish reading the entire chapter or passage. Next, organize students into cooperative-learning groups, or teams of five, to work on writing a summary together. Each student is assigned to take charge of one of the five summary writing rules. Move about the classroom to assist the groups as needed. You may want to have students use different colored transparency pens for each of the five summary rules to record their work. For example, green may be used for lists, red for eliminating unnecessary details, and so on. Share each group's summary writing processes and products with the entire class on the overhead projector. Be sure to provide additional practice on summary writing throughout the year with other books.

ADDITIONAL STRATEGIES FOR ENGLISH LANGUAGE LEARNERS

COMPREHENSION STRATEGY FRAMEWORK

Purpose

The purpose of the Comprehension Strategy Framework (Dowhower, 1999) is at least twofold. First, teachers chunk the text into smaller parts for teaching comprehension strategies. And second, the framework is intended to facilitate the teaching of a repertoire of skills and strategies to facilitate comprehension. It is clear that isolated comprehension strategy instruction is being replaced by an emphasis on learning a repertoire of strategies and coordinating and controlling the flexible use of those strategies (Collins-Block & Pressley, 2002; Duffy, 1993). The rationale for the structure of the CSF is found in five important principles of effective comprehension strategy instruction. First, the text is chunked into cycles of instruction including purpose setting, silent reading, and discussion. Second, a purpose is set for reading to guide and provide a purpose for students' reading. Third, students are encouraged to read silently inasmuch as silent reading has been shown to be better for facilitating comprehension processes over oral reading, which diverts attention away from comprehension to an accurate and lively performance of the text. Fourth, instruction is embedded in the discussion of literature. And finally, the discussion is focused around a theme because themes help students move beyond literal processes and toward constructing their own interpretations of texts.

Learning and orchestrating a repertoire of flexible comprehension strategies is critically important for ESL or LEP students. These students, similar to most students, but even more so because they have the additional challenge of learning English, need to experience comprehension strategy instruction within a consistent, reliable, and cohesive framework.

Materials

You will need:

- One well-formed story or storybook
- One copy of the *Comprehension Strategy Framework* (CSF) Overview shown in Figure 10.20.
- One copy of a lesson plan for using the CSF with the story selected

Procedure

Select a well-formed story for reading together as a class or small group. Chunk the text into sufficient segments to provide several cycles of practice using purpose setting, silent reading, and discussion. Remember to select a large enough text chunk for prereading to allow students to activate and relate the text to their prior knowledge as well as to provide an example of using a selected comprehension strategy for instruction such as *constructing visual images.* At the conclusion of the cycles of practice using text segments from the story, students are encouraged to engage in independent, follow-up activities. These might include a number of response activities such as those outlined in chapter 15. By using CSF for providing comprehension instruction of a varied repertoire of comprehension strategies, teachers can scaffold the comprehension instruction for LEP and ESL students in a more predictable and cohesive manner.

INCLUDING ALL STUDENTS

RECIPROCAL TEACHING

Purpose

Palincsar and Brown (1985) designed and evaluated an approach for improving the reading comprehension and comprehension monitoring of special-needs students who scored two years below grade level on standardized tests of reading comprehension. Their results suggested a teaching strategy called Reciprocal Teaching that is useful for helping students

Figure 10.20 Comprehension Strategy Framework Overview

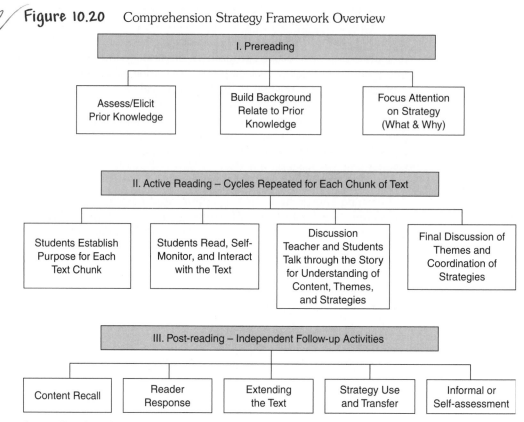

Source: Based on "Supporting a Strategic Stance in the Classroom: A Comprehension Framework for Helping Teachers Help Students to Be Strategic," by S. Dowhower, 1999, *The Reading Teacher, 52*(7), 672–683.

who have difficulties with comprehension and comprehension monitoring as well as those who are learning English (Casanave, 1988; Johnson-Glenberg, 2000; Rosenshine & Meister, 1994). Although Reciprocal Teaching was originally intended for use with expository text, we can see no reason why this intervention strategy cannot be used with narrative texts by focusing discussion and reading on the major elements of stories.

Materials

A tradebook, basal, or textbook selection is needed for this activity.

Procedure

Essentially, this strategy lesson requires that teachers and students exchange roles, which is intended to increase student involvement in the lesson. The Reciprocal Teaching lesson comprises four phases or steps. These are:

- *Prediction:* Students predict from the title and pictures the possible content of the text. The teacher records the predictions.
- *Question Generation:* Students generate purpose questions after reading a predetermined segment of the text, such as a paragraph, page, and so on.

- *Summarizing:* Students write a brief summary (see Figure 10.19) for the text by starting with "This paragraph was about. . . ." Summarizing helps students capture the gist of the text.
- *Clarifying:* Students and teacher discuss various reasons a text may be hard or confusing, such as difficult vocabulary, poor text organization, unfamiliar content, or lack of cohesion. Students are then instructed in a variety of comprehension fix-up or repair strategies.

Once teachers have modeled this process with several segments of text, the teacher assigns one of the students (preferably a good student) to assume the role of teacher for the next segment of text. The teacher may also, while acting in the student role, provide appropriate prompts and feedback when necessary. When the next segment of text is completed, the student assigned as teacher assigns another student to assume that role.

Teachers who use Reciprocal Teaching to help students with comprehension difficulties should follow four simple guidelines suggested by Palincsar and Brown (1985). First, assess student difficulties and provide reading materials appropriate to students' decoding abilities. Second, use Reciprocal Teaching for at least 30 minutes a day for 15 to 20 consecutive days. Third, model frequently and provide corrective feedback. Finally, monitor student progress regularly and individually to determine whether the instruction is having the intended effect. Palincsar and Brown (1985) reported positive results for this intervention procedure by demonstrating dramatic changes in students' ineffective reading behaviors. Other research has demonstrated the effectiveness of Reciprocal Teaching with a variety of students (Casanave, 1988; Johnson-Glenberg, 2000; Kelly, Moore, & Tuck, 1994; King & Parent-Johnson, 1999; Pressley & Wharton-McDonald, 1997; Rosenshine & Meister, 1994)

SELECTED REFERENCES

Alvermann, D. E. (1991). The discussion web: A graphic aide for learning across the curriculum. *The Reading Teacher, 45,* 92–99.

Anderson, V., & Roit, M. (1993). Planning and implementing collaborative strategy instruction for delayed readers in grades 6–10. *Elementary School Journal, 94,* 121–137.

Applebee, A. N. (1979). *The child's concept of story: Ages two to seventeen.* Chicago, IL: The University of Chicago Press.

Asher, S. R. (1980). Topic interest and children's reading comprehension. In R. J. Spiro, B. C. Bruce, & W. F. Brewer (Eds.), *Theoretical issues in reading comprehension* (pp. 525–534). Hillsdale, NJ: Erlbaum.

Babbs, P. (1994). Monitoring cards help improve comprehension. *The Reading Teacher, 38*(3), 200–204.

Bandura, A. (1986). *Social foundations of thought and action: A social cognitive theory.* Englewood Cliffs, NJ: Prentice Hall.

Baumann, J. F., Hooten, H., & White, P. (1999). Teaching comprehension through literature: A teacher-research project to develop fifth graders' reading strategies and motivation. *The Reading Teacher, 53*(1), 38–51.

Beck, I. L., & McKeown, M. G. (1981). Developing questions that promote comprehension: The story map. *Language Arts, 58,* 913–918.

Beck, I. L., Omanson, R. C., & McKeown, M. G. (1982). An instructional redesign of reading lessons: Effects on comprehension. *Reading Research Quarterly, 17,* 462–481.

Boyle, J. R. (1996). The effects of cognitive mapping strategy on the literal and inferential comprehension of students with mild disabilities. *Learning Disability Quarterly, 19*(3), 86–98.

Bromley, K. (1985). Precise writing and outlining enhance content learning. *The Reading Teacher, 38*(4), 406–411.

Bromley, K. (1993). *Webbing with literature: Creating story maps with children's books,* (2nd ed.). Boston: Allyn & Bacon.

Brown, A. L., Day, J. D., & Jones, R. S. (1983). The development of plans for summarzing texts. *Child Development, 54,* 968–979.

Brown, H., & Cambourne, B. (1987). *Read and retell.* Portsmouth, NH: Heinemann Educational Books.

Brown, R. Pressley, M., Van Meter, P., & Schuder, T. (1996). A quasi-experimental validation of transactional strategies instruction with low-achieving second grade readers. *Journal of Educational Psychology, 88,* 18–37.

Campbell, R. (2001). *Read-alouds with young children.* Newark, DE: International Reading Association.

Carr, E. (1985). The vocabulary overview guide: A metacognitive strategy to improve vocabulary comprehension and retention. *Journal of Reading, 28*(8), 684–689.

Carr, S., & Thompson, B. (1996). The effects of prior knowledge and schema activation strategies on the inferential reading comprehension of children with and without learning disabilites. *Learning Disabilities Quarterly, 19*(2), 48–61.

Casanave, C. P. (1988). Comprehension monitoring in ESL reading: A neglected essential. *TESOL Quarterly, 22*(2), 283–302.

Collins, A. M., & Quillian, M. R. (1969). Retrieval time from semantic memory. *Journal of Verbal Learning and Verbal Behavior, 8,* 240–247.

Collins, C. (1991). Reading instruction that increases thinking abilities. *Journal of Reading, 34,* 510–516.

Collins-Block, C., & Pressley, M. (2002). *Comprehension instruction: Research-based practices.* New York: Guilford Press.

Corno, L., & Randi, J. (1997). Motivation, volition, and collaborative innovation in classroom literacy. In J. T. Guthrie & A. Wigfield (Eds.), *Reading engagement: Motivating readers through integrated instruction* (pp. 51–67). Newark, DE: International Reading Association.

Dowhower, S. L. (1999). Supporting a strategic stance in the classroom: A comprehension framework for helping teachers help students to be strategic. *The Reading Teacher, 52*(7), 672–688.

Duffy, G. G. (1993). Rethinking strategy instruction: Four teachers' development and their low achievers' understanding. *The Elementary School Journal, 93,* 231–247.

El-Dinary, P. B., Pressley, M., & Schuder, T. (1992). Becoming a strategies teacher: An observational and inteview study of three teachers learning transactional strategies instruction. In C. Kinzer, & D. Leu (Eds.), *Cognitive strategy research: Educational applications* (pp. 133–156). New York: Springer-Verlag.

Gambrell, L. B., Pfeiffer, W., & Wilson, R. (1985). The effects of retelling upon reading comprehension and recall of text information. *Journal of Educational Research, 78,* 216–220.

Gardiner, J. R. (1980). *Stone fox.* New York: Scholastic.

Gaskins, I. W., Anderson, R. C., Pressley, M., Cunicelli, E. A., & Satlow, E. (1993). Six teachers' dialogue during cognitive process instruction. *Elementary School Journal, 93,* 277–304.

Gordon, C. J., & Braun, C. (1983). Using story schema as an aid to reading and writing. *The Reading Teacher, 37*(2), 116–121.

Graham, J., & Kelly, A. (1997). *Reading under control: Teaching reading in the primary school.* London: David Fulton.

Hare, V., & Borchordt, K. M. (1984). Direct instruction of summarization skills. *Reading Research Quarterly, 20*(1), 62–78.

Headley, K. N., & Dunston, P. J. (2000). Teacher's choices books and comprehension strategies as transaction tools. *The Reading Teacher, 54*(3), 260–268.

Henk, W. A., & Melnick, S. A. (1995). The reader self-perception scale (rsps): A new tool for measuring how children feel about themselves as readers. *The Reading Teacher, 48*(6), 470–482.

Johnson-Glenberg, M. C. (2000). Training reading comprehension in adequate decoders/poor comprehenders verbal versus visual strategies. *Journal of Educational Psychology, 92*(4), 772–782.

Keene, E. O., & Zimmerman, S. (1997). *Mosaic of thought: Teaching comprehension in a reader's workshop.* Portsmouth, NH: Heinemann Educational Books.

Kelly, M., Moore, D. W., & Tuck, B. F. (1994). Reciprocal teaching in a regular primary school classroom. *Journal of Educational Research, 88*(1), 53–61.

King, C. M., & Parent-Johnson, L. M. (1999). Constructing meaning via reciprocal teaching. *Reading Research and Instruction, 38*(3), 169–186.

Krauss, R. (1945). *The carrot seed.* New York: Scholastic, Inc.

Langer, J. A. (1982). Facilitating text processing: The elaboration of prior knowledge. In J. A. Langer & M. Smith-Burke (Eds.), *Reader meets author: Bridging the gap* (pp. 149–162). Newark, DE: International Reading Association.

Lindsay, P. H., & Norman, D. A. (1977). *Human information processing: An introduction to psychology.* New York: Academic Press.

Mandler, J. M., & Johnson, N. S. (1977). Remembrance of things parsed: Story structure and recall. *Cognitive Psychology, 9,* 111–151.

Martens, P. (1996). *I already know how to read: A child's view of literacy.* Portsmouth, NH: Heinemann.

Martin, L., & Reutzel, D. R. (1999). Sharing books: Examining how and why mothers deviate from the print. *Reading Research and Instruction, 39*(1), 39–70.

Merkley, D. M., & Jeffries, D. (2001). Guidelines for implementing a graphic organizer. *The Reading Teacher, 54*(4), 350–357.

Morrow, L. M. (1985). Retelling stories: A strategy for improving children's comprehension, concept of story structure and oral language complexity. *Elementary School Journal, 85,* 647–661.

Morrow, L. M. (1988). Young children's responses to one-to-one story reading in school settings. *The Reading Teacher, 23*(1) 89–107.

Morrow, L. M. (2001). *Literacy development in the early years: Helping children read and write* (4th ed.). New York: Allyn & Bacon.

Neuman, S. B. (2000). *The importance of the classroom library.* New York: Scholastic, Inc.

Noble, T. H. (1980). *The day Jimmie's boa ate the wash.* New York: Scholastic.

Palincsar, A., & Brown, A. (1985). Reciprocal teaching: A means to a meaningful end. In J. Osborn, P. T. Wilson, & R. C. Anderson (Eds.), *Reading education: Foundations for a literate America* (pp. 299–310). Lexington, MA: D. C. Heath and Company.

Paris, S. G., Wasik, B., & Turner, J. C. (1991). The development of strategic readers. In R. Barr, M. L. Kamil, P. Mosenthal, & P. D. Pearson (Eds.), *Handbook of Reading Research* (Vol. II, 641–668). New York: Longman.

Paris, S. G., & Winograd, P. (2001). *The role of self-regulated learning in contextual teaching: Principles and practices for teacher preparation.* Ann Arbor, MI: Center for the Improvement of Early Reading Achievement.

Pearson, P. D., Hansen, J., & Gordon, C. (1979). The effect of background knowledge on children's comprehension of implicit and explicit information. *Journal of Reading Behavior, 11*(3), 201–209.

Pereira-Laird, J. A., & Deane, F. P. (1997). Development and validation of a self-report measure of reading strategy use. *Reading Psychology, 18*(3), 185–235.

Pressley, M. (2000). What should comprehension instruction be the instruction of? In M. L. Kamil, P. B. Mosenthal, P. D. Pearson, & R. Barr (Eds.), *Handbook of Reading Research* (vol. 3, pp. 545–561). Mahwah, NJ: Erlbaum.

Pressley, M., Gaskins, I. W., Wile, D., Cunicelli, E. A., & Sheridan, J. (1991). Teaching literacy strategies across the curriculum: A case study at Benchmark School. In J. Zutell & S. McCormick (Eds.), *Learner factors/teacher factors: Issues in literacy research and instruction: Fortieth yearbook of the National Reading Conference* (pp. 219–228). Chicago: National Reading Conference.

Pressley, M., & Wharton-McDonald, R. (1997). Skilled comprehension and its development through instruction. *School Psychology Review, 26*(3), 448–466.

Raphael, T. E. (1982). Question-answering strategies for children. *The Reading Teacher, 36,* 186–191.

Raphael, T. E. (1986). Teaching question answer relationships, revisited. *The Reading Teacher, 39*(6), 516–523.

Raphael, T. E., & Pearson, P. D. (1982). *The effect of metacognitive training on children's question-answering behaviors.* ERIC Document Reproduction Service No. ED215315. Urbana, Ill: Center for the Study of Reading.

Reutzel, D. R. (1985). Story maps improve comprehension. *The Reading Teacher, 38*(4), 400–405.

Reutzel, D. R. (1986). Clozing in on comprehension: The cloze story map. *The Reading Teacher, 39*(6), 524–529.

Reutzel, D. R., & Fawson, P. C. (1989). Using a literature webbing strategy lesson with predictable books. *The Reading Teacher, 43*(3), 208–215.

Reutzel, D. R., & Fawson, P. C. (1991). Literature webbing predictable books: A prediction strategy that helps below-average, first-grade readers. *Reading Research and Instruction, 30*(4), 20–30.

Rosenshine, B., & Meister, C. (1994). Reciprocal teaching: A review of the research. *Review of Educational Research, 64*(4), 479–530.

Routman, R. (1991). *Invitations: Changing as teachers and learners K–12.* Portsmouth, NH: Heinemann.

Rumelhart, D. E. (1981). Schemata: The building blocks of cognition. In J. T. Guthrie (Ed.), *Comprehension and teaching: Research reviews* (pp. 3–26). Newark, DE: International Reading Association.

Sadow, M. W. (1982). The use of story grammar in the design of questions. *The Reading Teacher, 35,* 518–523.

Santa, C. M., & Hayes, B. L. (1981). *Children's prose comprehension: Research and practice.* Newark, DE: International Reading Association.

Schikendanz, J. A. (1990). *Adam's righting revolutions.* Portsmouth, NH: Heinemann.

Schunk, D. H. (1996). Goal and self-evaluative influences during children's cognitive skill learning. *American Educational Research Journal, 33,* 359–382.

Schunk, D. H., & Zimmerman, B. J. (1997). Developing self-efficacious readers and writers: The role of social and self-regulatory processes. In J. T. Guthrie, & A. Wigfield (Eds.), *Reading engagement: Motivating readers through integrated instruction* (pp. 34–50). Newark, DE: International Reading Association.

Simmons, D. C., & Kameenui, E. J. (1998). *What reading research tells us about children with diverse learning needs: Bases and basics.* Mahwah, NJ: Lawrence Erlbaum Associates.

Stein, N. L., & Glenn, C. G. (1979). An analysis of story comprehension in elementary school children. In R. O. Freedle (Ed.), *New directions in discourse processing* (pp. 53–120). Hillsdale, NJ: Lawrence Erlbaum Associates.

Sweet, A. P. (1997). Teacher perceptions of student motivation and their relation to literacy learning. In J. T. Guthrie & A. Wigfield (Eds.), *Reading engagement: Motivating readers through integrated instruction* (pp. 86–101). Newark, DE: International Reading Association.

Thorndyke, P. N. (1977). Cognitive structure in comprehension and memory of narrative discourse. *Cognitive Psychology, 9*(1), 77–110.

Trelease, J. (1995). *The new read aloud handbook* (4th ed.). New York: Penguin.

Van Allsburg, C. (1992). *The widow's broom*. Boston: Houghton Mifflin.

Wade, S. E., Buxton, W. M., & Kelley, M. (1999). Using think-alouds to examine reader-text interest. *Reading Research Quarterly, 34*(2), 194–216.

Ward, L. (1952). *The biggest bear*. Boston, MA: Houghton Mifflin.

Watson, D., & Crowley, P. (1988). How can we implement a whole-language approach? In C. Weaver, *Reading process and practice* (pp. 232–279). Portsmouth, NH: Heinemann Educational Books.

Watson, J. J. (1991). An integral setting tells more than when and where. *The Reading Teacher, 44*(9), 338–347.

Whaley, J. F. (1981). Readers' expectations for story structures. *Reading Research Quarterly, 17,* 90–114.

Chapter 11

Reading Comprehension: Information Texts

Millie is a fourth-grade student in Ms. Franklin's class. Millie is one of those kids that simply blasts their way through their first several years of school reading well above grade level in story and chapter books, poetry, and about everything else encountered in the basal reader. In short, through second grade Millie was a very good student in reading.

When Millie reached the last half of third grade and the reading selections and general curriculum took a decided swing toward informational texts, her performance began to falter. Especially in science, Millie seemed to now be having some serious difficulties with comprehension and vocabulary knowledge, and, worse yet, her motivation and excitement about school were beginning to fade. At a recent teacher-parent conference, Millie's father expressed some concerns about her not wanting to come to school on Monday mornings, what he called "Mondaynucleosis." Funny, but disturbing.

Ms. Franklin had seen this before and knew just what to do. She set aside time with Millie for a series of short assessments. From this information she was able to construct a profile of Millie's strengths and needs. Knowing just what Millie needed was critical, as she perused the "If-Then Chart," searching for just the right teaching interventions for Millie and the other children in her class having similar needs.

"A piece of cake!" mused Ms. Franklin as she planned her lessons that would help her young readers tackle the challenges of information-laden texts. "They're going to positively *love* this unit!" she whispered to herself.

Content classrooms (such as social studies, science, mathematics, and so on) are heavily populated with students for whom reading **informational texts** (also known as *expository* texts) is a challenge (Romine, McKenna, & Robinson, 1996). These students, who may be good readers otherwise, must sometimes think to themselves, "Why am I such a lousy reader in my classes when I am such a good reader otherwise?!"

The answer is relatively simple: expository texts use very different organizational structures and techniques to convey ideas than those used in narrative texts (i.e., stories). One of the most important tasks teachers have is to help students learn to strategically organize and construct new knowledge from content texts (Farnan, 1996; Simpson, 1996). Even though a number of effective strategies have been identified for use in content classrooms to help students succeed (see, for example, Alvermann & Moore, 1991; Guthrie,

Van Meter et al., 1996; Swafford & Bryan, 2000), startlingly few teachers actually use them (Irvin & Connors, 1989, Romine et al., 1996). In this chapter, we provide a short tutorial for teachers on expository text writing patterns, strategies for assessing reading problems with expository texts, and teaching methods to help students succeed when reading expository texts.

BACKGROUND BRIEFING FOR TEACHERS

In narrative texts the writer uses story grammar elements (i.e., setting, characters, problem, resolution, and so on) to tell the story. Expository writing, however, is intended to inform others about a subject rather than to tell a story (Cooter & Flynt, 1996, p. 226). Just as narrative authors use story grammars to communicate effectively, expository writers use what we call expository text patterns to effectively convey information. An important difference exists between story grammars and expository text patterns, however. In narrative texts, all story grammar elements are typically used; in expository texts, only a few of the patterns are generally used in any one content-area textbook or passage, depending on the nature of the information to be shared.

Researchers in the field of content-area reading (Armbruster & Anderson, 1981; Meyer & Freedle, 1984) describe five common patterns for presenting information: time order (sequence of events), cause-effect (showing how one event happened as a result of another), problem-solution (presenting a problem along with its possible solution[s]), comparison (also known as compare/contrast), and simple listing. Other researchers (Flood, Lapp, & Farnan, 1986; McGee & Richgels, 1985) have discovered that students can be taught about these patterns to better comprehend content texts and simultaneously improve their written communication skills.

Because of the varying and rather unique styles used by writers of expository text, students can have difficulty acquiring new or technical vocabulary, comprehending expository texts, retaining information over time, and monitoring their own learning. In this chapter, we offer a variety of classroom-proven strategies to help students succeed with expository materials.

A fundamental maxim of effective teaching is for teachers to assess what a student *knows* (and still needs to know) before offering instruction on a new skill. In the next section, we offer some suggestions for discerning which expository text patterns are known to students so that instruction can be planned strategically.

ASSESSING KNOWLEDGE OF EXPOSITORY TEXT PATTERNS

The key to effective expository text instruction lies in the accurate identification of the types of content or expository texts that students are able to read effectively, as well as the forms of expository writing that are difficult for them to comprehend. We have discovered that several rather common forms of reading assessment are easily adaptable to expository texts and can help teachers plan instruction. Offered in this section are some examples of each for your consideration.

EXPOSITORY TEXT FRAMES

Purpose

Expository text frames are useful in identifying types of expository text patterns that may be troublesome for students. Based on the "story frames" concept (Fowler, 1982; Nichols, 1980), expository text frames are completed by the student after reading an expository passage. Instruction can be focused much more precisely, based on student needs, as a result of this procedure.

Materials

You will need the textbook, a computer and word processing program, and a means by which to copy the expository text frames for students. Abbreviated examples of expository text frames for each of the primary expository text patterns are shown in Figures 11.1 through 11.5.

Procedure

Before reading the selection, list the major vocabulary and concepts. Discuss what students already know about the topic and display it on the chalkboard or on chart paper. Next, have students read an expository selection similar to the one you will ask them to read in class. Once the passage has been read, model the process for completing expository text frames using mock examples. Now have them read the actual selection for the unit of study. Finally, have students complete the expository text frame(s) you have prepared for this passage.

For students who have trouble with any of the frames, conduct a one-on-one reading conference to determine the thinking processes going on as the student completed the expository text frame.

Figure 11.1   Expository Text Frames: Description

Decimals are another way to write fractions when _____
_____
_____
_____

Figure 11.2   Expository Text Frames: Collection

Water Habitats

Freshwater habitats are found in _____, _____, _____, and rivers. Each freshwater habitat has special kinds of _____ and _____ that live there. Some plants and animals live in waters that are very _____. Others live in waters that are _____. Some plants and animals adapt to waters that flow _____.

Figure 11.3 Expository Text Frames: Causation

America Enters the War

On Sunday, December 7, 1941, World War II came to the United States. The entry of the United States into World War II was triggered by _____. Roosevelt said that it was a day that would "live in Infamy." *Infamy* (IN · fuh · mee) means remembered for being evil.

 Figure 11.4 Expository Text Frames: Problem/Solution

Agreement by Compromise
Events that led to the Civil War

For a while there were an equal number of Southern and Northern states. That meant that there were just as many senators in Congress from slave states as from free states. Neither had more votes in the Senate, so they usually reached agreement on new laws by compromise. One way that the balance of power was maintained in Congress was _____
_____.

Figure 11.5 Expository Text Frames: Comparison

Segregation

Many people said that the segregation laws were unfair. But in 1896, the Supreme Court ruled segregation legal if _____
_____. "Separate but equal" became the law in many parts of the country.

But separate was not equal. One of the most serious problems was education. Black parents felt _____
_____. Sometimes the segregated schools had teachers who were not _____ as teachers in the white schools. Textbooks were often _____,
if they had any books at all. But in many of the white schools the books were _____. Without a good education, the blacks argued, their children would not be able to get good jobs as adults.

Cloze Passages

Purpose

Cloze passages, from the word closure, are short passages (250 words) from expository books commonly used in the teacher's classroom that have certain words deleted (usually every fifth word) and replaced with a blank. Students are asked to read the cloze passages and fill in the missing words based on what they feel makes sense using context clues. If students are reading effectively and with adequate comprehension, usually they are able to accurately guess the missing words—or, at least, a word of the same part of speech. This helps the teacher know whether the student is able to use context clues when reading expository materials in the selected field of study, and whether he has a strong enough vocabulary to cope with the textbook being used. Following are the usual materials and procedures for constructing expository text cloze passages, followed by some examples from selected content texts.

Materials

Materials needed include the textbook, a computer and word processing program, and means by which to copy the cloze passage for students.

Procedure

Cloze tests cause students to use their background knowledge of a subject, their understanding of basic syntax (word-order relationships), and their word and sentence meaning (semantics) knowledge to guess what a missing or familiar word in print might be (Cooter & Flynt, 1996). We encourage teachers working with students having reading problems to first assess the student's performance using cloze passages created from narrative texts as a baseline indicator of general reading ability. This will help you to find out how well the student normally performs at reading narrative books, which are the main focus of reading instruction in the elementary years. This approach also helps students to practice the cloze procedure before being asked to take on the different—and perhaps more difficult—expository cloze passages.

Teachers may choose cloze excerpts that include each of the expository text patterns found in the textbook(s) currently used by students in their content classes. Results inform the teacher as to whether the text is likely to be at what is termed the independent level (easy to read), the instructional level (requiring some assistance from the teacher for student success), or the frustration level (far too difficult for the student). General instructions for the construction and scoring of cloze tests using content-area texts are as follows:

1. **Choose a passage of about 250 words from the class textbook.** It is usually best to choose a passage at the beginning of a chapter or unit so that needed introductory information is included.

2. **Prepare the cloze passage, preferably using a computer word processing program.** The first sentence should be typed exactly as it is written in the original text. Thereafter, beginning with the second sentence, delete one of the first five words and replace it with a blank, then repeat this procedure every 50th word. The process is complete when you have fifty (50) blanks in the cloze passage. After the 50th blank, finish typing the sentence in which the last blank occurred. Then, type at least one more sentence intact (no deletions).

3. **Have students read the passage all the way through once without attempting to fill in any of the blanks, then reread the passage and fill in the blanks to the best of their ability.**

4. **To score cloze passages, use the one-half/one-third formula.** Students who correctly complete one half (25 of 50) or more of the blanks are considered to be at the independent reading level, at least with the passage selected. Students who complete fewer than one third of the blanks correctly (17 out of 50 blanks) will probably find the text frustrating, or too difficult even with assistance. Those students falling somewhere between the one-third and one-half range will probably be able to succeed with the text if they receive some preparatory assistance from the teacher.

 **Figure 11.6**   Cloze Passage: Diamonds

Diamonds

A diamond is one of the most beautiful treasures that nature has ever created. And one of _____ rarest. It takes thousands _____ years for nature to _____ a chunk of carbon _____ a rough diamond. Only _____ important diamond fields have _____ found in the world, _____ India, South America, and Africa.

_____ first diamonds were found _____ the sand and grave _____ stream beds. These types _____ diamonds are called alluvial _____ . Later, diamonds were found _____ in the earth in _____ formations called *pipes*. These _____ resemble extinct volcanoes. The _____ in which diamonds are _____ is called *blue ground*. _____ even where diamonds are _____ it takes digging and _____ through tons of rock _____ gravel to find enough _____ for a one-carat _____ .

   Gem diamonds' quality is _____ on weight, purity, color, _____ cut. The weight of a diamond is measured by the carat. Its purity is determined by the presence or absence of impurities, such as foreign minerals and uncrystallized carbon.

Source: From *The Flynt/Cooter Reading Inventory for the Classroom*, 4th ed., by E. S. Flynt, & R. B. Cooter, 2001. Upper Saddle River, NJ: Merrill/Prentice Hall. Used with permission.

Figure 11.6 shows a partial cloze passage constructed using an excerpt from *The Flynt/Cooter Reading Inventory for the Classroom* (Flynt & Cooter, 2001).

MAZE PASSAGES

Purpose

Maze passages (Guthrie, Seifert, Burnham, & Caplan, 1974) are a modification of cloze strategies that may be easily adapted to content classroom needs. Maze passages tend to be less frustrating to students because the students have three possible answers to choose from; thus, students tend to get a larger percentage of the items correct. The purpose of maze passages is otherwise identical to cloze.

Materials

You will need the textbook, a computer and word processing program, and a means by which to copy the cloze passage for students.

Procedure

In our adaptation of maze, the criteria for the independent reading level is 85% or greater, the frustration level is 50 to 85%, and the instructional reading level is less than 50%. The procedure for constructing maze passages is identical to the construction of cloze passages, with the exception that, following each blank, three fill-in choices are included. One choice is a word that is the same part of speech as the missing word, but does not make sense; a second choice is usually one that does not make sense and is a different part of speech from the missing word; and the third choice is, of course, the correct choice. An example of a maze sentence follows (Berger, 1974, p. 183) using the content area of sociology and discussing the topic of conformity:

	conformist	
A straight _____	control	is the individual who has learned his
	ever	
place, has accepted it, and acts accordingly.		

SELF-RATING CHECKLISTS

Purpose

Cooter and Flynt (1996) suggested that quality assessment plans should include direct student input and self-perceptions via self-rating checklists. Students complete a checklist matched to specific reading skills especially useful in the content area studied. Students indicate whether they feel that they are Strong, Good, Getting by, or Not very strong in the areas specified. Figure 11.7 is a sample self-rating (Cooter & Flynt, 1996, p. 45) suggested for use in an Algebra I class.

Materials

You will need to develop a checklist keyed to the basic reading/study skills needed in your content area prepared on a computer using a word processing program, an enlarged version of the checklist (overhead transparency), and copies for all students.

Procedure

Use the overhead transparency to present your checklist to students. Model several examples, demonstrating the kinds of complete responses that you wish to solicit. Then distribute the checklist for students to complete. When the students have finished, collect and analyze their self-assessments.

CONTENT-AREA READING INVENTORY (CARI)

Purpose

The Content-Area Reading Inventory (CARI) (Farr, Tulley, & Pritchard, 1989; Readence, Bean, & Baldwin, 1992) is an informal reading inventory assessing whether students have learned sufficient reading/study strategies to succeed with content materials.

Materials

The CARI can be administered to groups of students and typically includes three major sections (Farr et al., 1989) that assess 1) student knowledge of and ability to use common textbook components (i.e., table of contents, glossary, index) and supplemental research aids (card catalog, reference books, periodicals); 2) student knowledge of important vocabulary and skills such as context clues; and 3) comprehension skills important to understanding expository texts. For the last two sections of the CARI assessment, students are asked to read a selection from the adopted text. Readence et al. (1992) suggested contents for a CARI, which are described (and slightly adapted) here:

PART 1: TEXTUAL READING/STUDY AIDS

    A. Internal aids
        1. Table of contents
        2. Index

Figure 11.7   Self-Rating Checklist

"Reading" Algebra

Name: _____   Class Period/Block: _____

Date: _____

Part I

Directions: Rate yourself according to your ability to do the following in past mathematics classes. Please be completely honest in your assessment, as this will help your teacher to plan the kind of instruction that meets your needs.

Your ability to. . .	Strong	Good	Getting by	Not very strong
Read the introduction of a new chapter and understand what the author is saying the first time.				
Translate familiar and new mathematical symbols into spoken language.				
Translate words in story problems into mathematical symbols.				
Write daily learning log entries that describe what you have learned and how to solve problems.				
Explain mathematical processes to another person orally.				
Perform complex addition problems.				
Perform complex subtraction problems.				
Perform complex multiplication problems.				
Perform complex division problems.				
Overall, how do rate yourself as a student of mathematics?				

Part II

In the space below, please explain what you hope to be able to do as a result of taking this class.

Source: Adapted from *Teaching Reading in the Content Areas: Developing Content Literacy for All Students,* by R. B. Cooter, Jr., and E. S. Flynt, 1996, Upper Saddle River, NJ: Merrill/Prentice Hall. Used with permission.

        3. Glossary
        4. Chapter introduction/summaries
        5. Information from pictures
        6. Other aids included in the text
    B. Supplemental research aids
        1. Card catalog
        2. Periodicals
        3. Encyclopedias
        4. Other relevant aids for the content area

PART II: VOCABULARY KNOWLEDGE
    A. Knowledge and recall of relevant vocabulary
    B. Use of context clues

PART III: COMPREHENSION SKILLS AND STRATEGIES
    A. Text-explicit (literal) information
    B. Text-implicit (inferred) information
    C. Knowledge of text structures and related strategies

Procedure

To develop a CARI, follow this process:

Step 1: Choose a passage of at least three to four pages from the textbook(s) to be used. The passage selected should represent the typical writing style of the author.

Step 2: Construct about 20 questions related to the text. Readence et al. (1992) recommended eight to ten questions for Part I, four to six questions for Part II, and seven to nine questions for Part III. We urge the use of questions based on writing patterns used in the sample selection; they should reflect the facts, concepts, and generalizations in the selection.

Step 3: Explain to students that the CARI is not used for grading purposes, but is useful for planning teaching activities that will help them succeed. Using a mini-lesson kind of format, walk students through the different sections of the CARI and model responses.

Step 4: Administer Part I first, then Parts II and III on separate day(s). It may take several sessions to work through the CARI. We recommend devoting only about 20 minutes per day to administering parts of the CARI, so that other class needs are not ignored during the assessment phase.

Readence et al. (1992) suggested the following criteria for assessing the CARI:

Percent Correct	Text Difficulty
86–100%	Easy reading
64–85%	Adequate for instruction
63% or below	Too difficult

From careful analysis of this assessment, teachers can plan special lessons to help students cope with difficult readings and internalize important information. Students can be grouped according to need for these lessons and practice strategies leading to success.

CONNECTING ASSESSMENT FINDINGS TO TEACHING STRATEGIES

Before discussing teaching strategies for expository texts, we want to share a guide we have constructed, connecting assessment to intervention strategy choices. It is our intention to help you, the teacher, select the most appropriate teaching strategies to meet your students' needs based on assessment data.

Indicators That a Reader Has Learning Needs

Poor comprehension

Fluency problems

Adjusting reading rate

Researching information

Notetaking

Perseverance

Motivation

Summarizing

Written products

In the next part of this chapter, we offer phonemic awareness/alphabetic principle strategies for intervention based on the foregoing assessments.

INSTRUCTIONAL INTERVENTIONS AND STRATEGIES: DEVELOPING READERS AND WRITERS OF EXPOSITORY TEXT

CONCEPT-ORIENTED READING INSTRUCTION (CORI)

Purpose

Guthrie et al. (1996) researched a teaching framework called the *Concept-Oriented Reading Instruction (CORI),* designed to improve students' learning in science. Easily applied to other content areas, CORI helps students become deeply engaged in new content, helps students crystallize and connect new knowledge to what is already known, and shows students how to demonstrate their learning in some interesting ways. The direct instruction components of CORI have also been shown to be effective with low-achieving students in elementary grades 3 and 5 (Guthrie et al., 1996; Swafford & Bryan, 2000). CORI provides a sound basic platform for teaching and learning in the content areas that can be modified to suit your instructional goals.

Materials

Frankly, it is a little difficult to generalize a specific list of materials for CORI, as that depends heavily on the subject area, content to be studied, and available texts for instruction. You will see what we mean as we move through our description, but typically the materials will include subject-linked textbooks, materials for the writing process, access to the Worldwide Web and Internet search engines, and other research tools usually available in the school library/media center.

Intervention Strategy Guide for Expository Text Reading

Intervention Strategy/ → Student Problem(s) ↓	CORI	Writing Process	I-Charts	Expos. Text Frames	Learning Logs	Reader Response Journals	Personal Word Lists	Big Books	Group Summa-rizing	Response Charts	Text Activ. Guides	Defin. Writing	Cartoons	Four-Step Summ. Writing
Compre-hension	+	+	+	+	+	+	+	+	+	+	+	+	+	+
Fluency	*	–	*	–	–	–	–	–	–	–	*	–	–	–
Adjusting Reading Rate	+	–	+	*	–	–	–	–	–	–	*	–	–	–
Researching Information	+	+	+	–	*	*	+	+	+	*	*	+	*	+
Notetaking	+	+	+	–	–	–	–	*	*	–	–	–	*	*
Perseverance	*	*	*	–	–	–	–	*	+	–	+	–	+	*
Motivation	+	*	+	*	*	*	–	+	+	*	*	–	+	*
Summarizing	+	+	+	–	*	*	+	+	+	*	*	+	+	+
Written Products	+	+	+	*	+	+	+	+	+	+	*	+	+	+

Key: + excellent strategy
* adaptable strategy
– unsuitable strategy

Procedure

CORI includes the following: real-world observations, conceptual themes, self-directed learning, direct instruction on strategies, peer collaboration, and self-expression of learning. The four parts of this instructional model are described next.

PART I: OBSERVE AND PERSONALIZE

Students are led through hands-on experiences designed to activate their prior knowledge that is relevant to the new topic and motivate them to want to know more. After the hands-on experience, the teacher leads students through a discussion about what they observed and helps them to form theories and generate questions for further study. The teacher-led discussion can help students move from concrete-only thinking into the more sophisticated forms of abstract thinking.

PART II: SEARCH AND RETRIEVE

In this stage, the teacher introduces search strategies for finding answers to students' questions. For each search strategy, the teacher provides a clear description, models using the strategy, and has practice sessions (guided practice) and collaborative group work. Strategies to be learned include *goal setting* (what they want to learn), *categorizing* (learning how information is organized and presented in books, and how to find information in the library or on the Internet), *extracting* (taking notes, summarizing, and paraphrasing information), and *abstracting* (forming generalizations).

PART III: COMPREHEND AND INTEGRATE

The goal here is to help students better understand the new information they have gathered in Part II. Teacher modeling and students' discussions about the following strategies usually occur: comprehension monitoring (metacognition), developing images or graphics, rereading to clarify, and modifying reading rate to match purpose and varying text types. Identification of central ideas and supporting details is also a priority in this stage of instruction. Guthrie et al. (1996) recommended the use of *idea circles* (student-led small-group discussions) and *group self-monitoring* as ways to transfer learning responsibility to students, leading to more productive discussions. This is especially useful when they discover information that is conflicting or when it contradicts their earlier hypotheses.

PART IV: COMMUNICATION

The "Communication" phase of CORI focuses on students sharing what they have learned. They often communicate their new understandings through debates, discussions, or written reports. Some students prefer more creative expressions such as Microsoft PowerPoint presentations, poetry, dramas, raps, songs, or graphic illustrations. As with the other phases of CORI, teacher support and modeling is critical in helping students develop effective communication skills to present their new knowledge and strengthen their social development (Swafford & Bryan, 2000).

The elements of Content-Oriented Reading Instruction (CORI) are summarized in Figure 11.8.

TEACHING EXPOSITORY READING SKILLS THROUGH WRITING

Purpose

Cooter and Flynt (1996) suggested that teachers utilize an expository text pattern writing process in helping students to become fluent readers and writers of expository text patterns and materials. The belief is that as students learn how to master the different expository text patterns as writers, they will automatically become better readers of the same

Figure 11.8   Content-Oriented Reading Instruction (CORI)

Part I: Observe and Personalize

1. Hands-on experiences
2. Relate hands-on experience to prior experiences
3. Teacher-led discussion
4. Form theories
5. Generate questions for further study

Part II: Search and Retrieve

Teacher introduces search strategies for finding answers to their questions . . .

1. *Goal setting* (what they want to learn)
2. *Categorizing* (learning how information is organized and presented in books and how to find information in the library or on the Internet)
3. *Extracting* (taking notes, summarizing, and paraphrasing information)
4. *Abstracting* (forming generalizations)

Part III: Comprehend and Integrate

Teacher modeling and students discussions about . . .

1. Comprehension monitoring (metacognition)
2. Developing images or graphics
3. Rereading to clarify
4. Modifying reading rate to match purpose and varying text types
5. Identification of central ideas and supporting details

Part IV: Communication

Communication of new knowledge through such media as . . .

Debates
Discussions
Written reports
Technology (e.g., Microsoft PowerPoint presentations)
Poetry
Dramas
Raps or songs
Graphic illustrations

types of text. As Lucy Calkins (1994) stated, it is when students become writers that they become "insiders" and, thus, become more perceptive readers. We feel that this applies not only to narrative texts, but to expository texts as well.

Materials

You will need examples of the expository text pattern(s) to be shared and learned, as well as the usual writing materials and word processing computer programs for this activity.

Procedure

The steps recommended by Cooter and Flynt (1996) are paraphrased and adapted as follows:

Step 1:   The teacher should learn and internalize knowledge about the various expository text patterns.

Step 2:   The teacher should teach students about expository text patterns commonly found in their textbooks.

Step 3:   The teacher should teach students to recognize and correctly identify expository text patterns in the reading materials they use in their content classes.

Step 4:   The teacher should teach students how to write summaries of their learning in content classes, using the various expository text patterns.

Most teachers would intuitively move students from Step 1 through Step 3, especially those students having difficulty with content materials. But it is Step 4—learning to write expository texts—that causes students to actually internalize their knowledge and to become better expository text readers.

I-CHARTS

Purpose

One of the most common assignments in content classes is the research report. Theoretically, students survey informational texts in a given area (research), read and synthesize the information, then construct a written report detailing their understanding of the subject under study. Many students have a great deal of difficulty going about these activities in a logical, orderly, and sequential manner, however, leading to much frustration and confusion. Information Charts, or I-Charts (Hoffman, 1992; Randall, 1996), provide a structure to help teachers guide students through these explorations.

The version we share here was adapted by Randall (1996, p. 537) for use in her eighth-grade language arts classes. It involves three components: preparing the charts, research and notetaking using the charts, and the completion of the final product using the charts.

Materials

You will need access to reference materials, ten copies of an I-Chart such as that shown in Figure 11.9, and multiple enlarged copies of the I-Chart on poster board.

Procedure

Planning for Your Research

1. **Topic identification and necessary skills.** Students first explore topics related to the new unit of study, brainstorming subjects of interest to them, and deciding what their individual topics might be. The teacher also offers minilessons on needed research-related skills such as skimming, scanning, paraphrasing, interviewing techniques, library skills, and how to write bibliographic entries.

2. **Writing topic proposals.** Students write their topic proposals for the teacher, including an explanation of their interest in their proposed topics. Also included is a tentative strategy for finding needed information. The teacher is then able to confer with students and/or make written suggestions to help guide them in shaping their topic proposals.

Figure 11.9   I-Chart

Student: _____   Topic/Subject: _____
Subtopic: _____
What I already know . . . _____
Bibliography #:

Other related information: _____
Important words: _____
New questions to learn about . . .

3. **Brainstorming questions.** Students generate specific questions to be answered. This is a great activity for cooperative learning groups. These questions should then be turned into subtopics to help students fine-tune their research efforts.

4. **Setting up I-Charts.** Provide students with about ten copies of the I-Chart. Students should write one subtopic/question at the top of each I-Chart, then complete the section titled, "What I already know . . ." for each subtopic. Sometimes students may know a good deal about a topic, while at other times they may simply write, "Nothing." Their I-Charts should be kept in a loose-leaf notebook for easy access during this process.

5. **Modeling.** As with all new learning experiences, it is important that students be able to *see* someone with expertise (the teacher, usually) modeling the task. Using the large poster board copies of the I-Chart, lead a class simulation pertaining to topics related to the unit of study. Complete each step on the I-Chart with the help of student volunteers.

Research and Notetaking

1. **Finding resources.** Randall (1996) advocated spending about a class period each day for a week in the school library. Make "house calls" (Reutzel & Cooter, 2000) on the students to make sure that each is using the I-Charts to guide his searches for information and to provide coaching as needed. Also, as homework, students should be encouraged to continue their quest for information at local public libraries, through governmental agencies that have relevant print information, and in interviews with experts.

2. **Answering research questions.** Students should have their I-Chart notebooks in front of them as they skim new information sources, pulling relevant I-Chart subtopics as they discover information that may be pertinent to their research (Randall, 1996, p. 539). The corresponding I-Chart should be pulled out of the notebook

as new information is discovered, then numbered and summarized on the I-Chart in the bibliography section. A line should be drawn between bibliographic entries and corresponding information to keep things straight.

3. **Making bibliographic entries.** For each bibliographic entry made on the various I-Chart forms, the student should make one complete bibliographic entry on a sheet labeled "References" at the end of the notebook. This will save him from having to make the same reference repeatedly on the different I-Chart forms when a reference is used more than once.

4. **Completing the I-Chart.** As students come across "Other related information" that is of interest but is not really pertinent to the subtopic or question, they can note it in the appropriate space. Sometimes this information can be included in a research report to make the report more interesting—like adding color to a black-and-white photograph. Likewise, "Important words" related to the subject—especially unusual words previously unknown to the student—should be noted in the space provided. Sometimes these words will require further research for clarity. Finally, "New questions to learn about . . ." that have arisen as a result of the research should be noted and answered before moving on to the final product stage.

5. **Critically evaluating research findings.** Sometimes students are not able to locate authoritative sources to complete their I-Charts. If they cannot locate print information or an expert to interview, then that particular I-Chart should be abandoned (Randall, 1996). Students should constantly evaluate whether they have accumulated enough information to consider a given I-Chart complete before moving on.

Completion of Final Products

1. Writing research papers. I-Charts create a natural bridge from research to outlining. They should be used (after considerable modeling by the teacher) to construct webs, traditional outlines, or structured overviews of the information. Timelines, maps, flowcharts, bar graphs, lists, and other graphic aids can also be constructed as prewriting tools to aid students in organizing facts, concepts, and generalizations. Each subtopic/I-Chart naturally becomes a category under the primary topic or generalization, with information noted in the "Bibliography" and "Important words" sections becoming concepts and facts in subordinate categories. Once an outline of the information is completed, students can begin their first drafts of their research papers.

EXPOSITORY TEXT FRAMES

Purpose

We know that students internalize reading processes on a much deeper level when they are able to apply their knowledge through writing. For example, students become much stronger readers and comprehenders of cause-and-effect-style texts when they have developed the ability to write cause-and-effect texts themselves. Thus, the goals of using expository text frames (Cudd & Roberts, 1989) are 1) to encourage the use of writing skills to enhance content-area learning, 2) to review and reinforce specific content in the subject area, and 3) to familiarize students with the different ways that authors organize material.

Materials

You will need the adopted content textbook or appropriate nonfiction trade books, expository text frames (such as those shown in the assessment section of this chapter), and writing materials.

Procedure

Step 1: Model the Process

1. Write a simple paragraph organized in the pattern of the content book (i.e., collection, cause-effect, and so on).
2. Copy the sentences on strips or transparency strips.
3. Review the topic and logical order embedded in the text.
4. Have students arrange sentences in the way in which they believe the paragraph should be organized.
5. Read the paragraph aloud, letting the students suggest any necessary changes.
6. Ask students to illustrate the details of the paragraph (optional).
7. After the students are more comfortable with the organization, practice the process with more paragraphs from the textbook or trade book.

Step 2: Add a Frame

1. Model the process of using the story frame with another paragraph from the text.
2. Discuss the transition and signal words used.
3. Let the students work through the rest of the process independently.
4. Ask students to illustrate the story frame (optional). Note: This can be an important visual connector for many children, especially those having reading problems.

Step 3: Optional Extensions of Story Frames

Extension A

1. Use a "reaction frame" as an extension of the story frame, letting the students respond to what they have learned.
2. When opinions are divided, the reaction frames lead nicely into group discussions for older students.
3. Reaction frames can be used either to bring in prior background with current knowledge or to see how new information can modify or revise old conceptual ideas.

Extension B

1. Students should use the comparison-and-contrast frames after they have worked with other types of paragraph frames because they are more complex.
2. Make the transition to this type of frame by discussing similarities and differences in a familiar paragraph.
3. Introduce comparison-and-contrast frames separately for younger children.
4. Illustrations are particularly useful for comparison and contrast.

LEARNING LOGS

Purpose

One of the problems students frequently have with expository texts is monitoring their own comprehension—they often do not know what they know or do not know. Students need to engage in a variety of writing activities to help them better understand such subjects as social studies and the sciences (Ediger, 2000). Journal writing has been effective with many students, probably because it causes students to be more directly engaged with the subject being studied (Emig, 1983; Strong, 1983). *Learning logs* (Commander & Smith, 1996) are a form of structured journal writing that not only aid a student's ability to gain new information from expository texts, but also can help him develop better awareness of his own comprehension (metacognition), and help a student connect with what he already knows from his experiences (Swafford & Bryan, 2000).

Materials

You will need to develop a learning log assignment sheet similar to the one shown in Figure 11.10 (adapted from Commander & Smith, 1996) that is keyed to the requirements of the unit of study. Also needed are about ten enlarged examples (overhead transparencies or on poster board) of learning log entries that conform to your expectations for students of this developmental level, for use in modeling activities.

Procedure

Pass out the learning log assignment sheet you created for this unit. After discussing the assignment sheet, walk students through several examples using the enlarged versions to model the thinking processes. Then distribute the first week's topic and discuss it. Follow the remaining procedure as described in the learning log assignment sheet example.

READER RESPONSE JOURNALS

Purpose

Many reading authorities have indicated in recent years that students need to respond to what they read in order to move them from passive to active learning. Reader response, as it is logically called, frequently involves writing about what has been read. However, many teachers have noted that, in the beginning, students often do not know what to write or how to respond without some sort of structure. Linda Berger (1996) developed a structure called the reader response journal for getting her junior high students started in more active learning.

Materials

Each student will require a notebook that can serve as his reader response journal (loose-leaf notebooks usually work best). A classroom chart, bulletin board, or handout similar to the one shown in Figure 11.11 to guide the students' early attempts at journal writing will also be needed.

Procedure

For a new chapter or unit of study, conduct usual prereading activities such as the following (see Cooter & Flynt, 1996, pp. 186–203): a structured overview, survey techniques, anticipation guides, prereading questions, semantic maps, or preview guides. Next, introduce the concept of reader response journals and share some teacher-made examples or

ν/ **Figure 11.10**   Learning Log Assignment Sheet

What is a learning log?

This learning log assignment will help you find out more about how you learn. We all learn in many different ways—listening, doing, thinking about what we already know, and learning from others. You will be able to use all of these ways of learning in your log.

Purpose of the assignment

Your daily entries will help you to know what it is you are learning and what you still need to learn. This will also help you to be able to share what you know with other students and the teacher. You will also learn important steps in knowing more about this subject, and how to be a better student in other subjects, as well.

Grade

Here are the important procedures for using your learning log as part of your grade this term:

- All learning logs will be collected each Tuesday at the beginning of the class period. They will not be accepted late, so be sure to have it ready to turn in.
- You can make log entries either daily or every other day. It is usually easier, though, to do it daily so that you do not fall behind.
- There will be ten separate topics assigned for you to respond to in your learning log each week. They will be awarded anywhere from 0 to 10 points based on the quality of your response. How much thought you put into your answers will be an important factor in determining your grade each time.

Format

Your response to the weekly question should be from one to two pages on notebook paper, or the same number double spaced, using a 12-point "Geneva" font on the computer. Again, *quality* of ideas, not *quantity* of pages, will determine your grade on this assignment.

Topics

Topics will be assigned each Tuesday, and your learning log entry must directly address the topic. Your response should include information from class discussions, cooperative learning activities, library assignments, presentations in the multimedia lab, and any other learning experience we have during that week.

Examples of learning logs

We will work through several learning log entries the first week to help you better understand what we are doing. Then, each Tuesday, the teacher will show you another example from the previous week's topic to better help you learn the process. The goal here is to get better at this as we go along. Please do not hesitate to ask a classmate or your teacher for help whenever you have a problem. Together we can learn a great deal this term!

examples from other classes the previous year. Distribute or display the information shown in Figure 11.10 and walk students through several more examples using each of the questions and accompanying examples. Each day, conduct a five-minute minilesson in which you highlight one of the questions and relate it to the unit by answering an aspect of that question. This kind of continuous modeling will help students learn and understand the process, and the unit!

Figure 11.11 Reader Response Journal: Guide Questions for Expository Tests

Reader Response Journal for Your Social Studies Textbook

DIRECTIONS: Skim your new chapter in social studies once using the methods we discussed in class. Then as you carefully reread the chapter, write a journal response each day using one or more of the questions below after each five (5) pages. Date each journal entry and be sure to mention the major headings, subheadings, and new vocabulary in bold print. I will collect your journal about every five to ten school days and write back to you. Your chapter and journal should be completed by _____ .

What do you notice that is new information for you?

Examples: Did you discover any cause/effect situations as you read? Could you identify a time sequence in what you read? (If so, you may want to sketch a timeline.) What key words or concepts did you come across? Can you compare and contrast with others not related to this unit that we have learned about?

What do you wonder about or question?

Examples: Do you wonder what a certain passage or paragraph might mean? (If so, which one?) Do you question if the author completely and accurately discussed one of the topics? Do you need to know more about something in the chapter to really understand it? Do you think the author may be biased? If so, why?

What do you feel?

Examples: Does any part of this section make you feel interested, confused, happy, annoyed, angry, or horrified? Which part, and why? Do you feel differently about a subject in this section than you did before? If so, why have your feelings changed? Do you want to read more about this subject? Why or why not?

What do you relate to?

Examples: Does anything in this section remind you of something from your own experience, a movie, a T.V. show, a song, or another book you have read? Talk about those ideas.

If your teacher could suggest a great book to read on this subject, such as a historical novel, would you be interested?

If so, write me a note and I'll see what I can find!

Source: Adapted from "Reader Response Journals: You Make the Meaning . . . and How" by L. R. Berger, 1996, *Journal of Adolescent & Adult Literacy, 39*(5).

PERSONAL WORD LISTS (VOCABULARY)

Purpose

Researchers have estimated that fluent readers have recognition vocabularies of anywhere from 10,000 to 100,000 words (Nagy & Herman, 1987). Students having reading difficulties, as well as those learning English as a second language (ESL), may have much smaller vocabularies—perhaps 5,000 words or fewer (Singer, 1981). This is not nearly enough for success with infrequently used or technical vocabulary. A personal word list (Johnson & Steele, 1996) is one strategy that a student can use to build his vocabulary, based on self-need.

Figure 11.12   Personal Word List

New Word	What I think it means . . .	Clues from the sentence	Dictionary definition (if needed)	My definition

Source: Adapted from "So Many Words, So Little Time: Helping College ESL Learners Acquire Vocabulary-Building Strategies" by D. Johnson and V. Steele, 1996, *Journal of Adolescent & Adult Literacy, 39*(5).

Materials

In addition to the reading materials to be used in the content area unit being studied, the student will require multiple copies of the chart shown in Figure 11.12. Each student should also have a notebook in which to keep his new vocabulary for review and as an aid to his writing assignments.

Procedure

Help students put together their vocabulary notebooks using multiple sheets such as the one shown in Figure 11.12. Model the use of the notebook with a practice passage that contains useful words that are not likely already known by the students. Demonstrate how these new "dictionaries" they are creating can be useful to them in compositions on the subject being studied, and quite likely in other assignments, as well. For the latter, however, students will need to pursue multiple meanings in the dictionary.

MAKING BIG BOOKS

Purpose

For many years, teachers have understood the value of student-made big books that summarize the content found in a unit of study. Constructing big books requires students to read, comprehend, and then "tell back" what they have learned. Big books can be especially motivating because they provide students with an opportunity to share with others what they have learned, such as when presenting their finished book to the rest of the class, or perhaps to a class of younger students. One school with which we worked in Nevada had an ongoing program wherein sixth-grade students each Friday would visit a first-grade class to share their big books and other literature response projects. This had

Dr. Robert Cooter (co-author) using a big book

a very positive effect on both older and younger students and stimulated much interest and reading. The following procedure is based on one offered by Snowball (1989) and is an easy-to-use version of this popular expository text response activity.

Materials

You will need appropriate content-area books, large paper (preferably heavy construction paper), markers, crayons, paints, colored pencils, and lined and unlined paper.

Procedure

1. Select a topic from the text that is likely to stimulate interest for students. As a prereading exercise, to call to mind background knowledge about the subject, write on the chalkboard or overhead projector topic-related words that children brainstorm.

2. Ask students to describe relationships between these words and the topic, and organize the words under headings or categories. A structured overview or semantic web format will work well with this part of the lesson.

3. The first time this process is used, the class should pick one topic to write about and the teacher should model the process. After they are familiar with the process, students may choose their own topic(s) and work in groups. In this stage of writing, the students should list what they know, what they would like to find out, and where they could find that information. This step is essentially a traditional K-W-L framework.

4. Relate new information to existing information and begin writing using visual displays of information. The teacher should demonstrate how to clarify and classify information using flowcharts, headings, subheadings, and so on.

5. Write a first draft of a big book that retells what the students have learned about the topic using the organization described as a guide. Early drafts should be written in pencil on 8 1/2- × 11-inch paper, complete with sketches of illustrations to be used. We have found that this makes drafting and revising relatively quick and painless for the students.

6. Write the final draft in big-book format for presentation to others.

GROUP SUMMARIZING

Purpose

Writing summaries of what has been learned helps make learning permanent (Swafford & Bryan, 2000). Oftentimes, however, students do not know where to begin in creating summaries. They benefit greatly from an initial structure for organizing ideas, as well as from having these structures modeled by the "classroom writing expert" (you, the teacher)! Following is a simple procedure for group summarizing adapted from one offered by Olson and Gee (1991).

Materials

The fundamental learning tools include well-written content books and writing materials (paper and pencil, and so on).

Procedure

Prior to reading about a subject, the class should read descriptions of the key topic(s) for the day. The teacher then divides the chalkboard into four sections relating to the topic. For example, if you are learning about an animal (say, alligators), your topics might be "Description," "Food," "Home," and "Interesting Facts." As the groups read, the students can write facts on the chalkboard under the different headings. After reading the text materials carefully, the students can discuss the facts they have listed, erase any duplicates, and write the facts in complete sentences. The class can then draft a summary using the above information as a guide.

RESPONSE CHARTS

Purpose

One of the characteristics of successful readers is that they frequently self-assess what they understand or do not understand, then make adjustments as needed (e.g., rereading sections of a book that they failed to grasp). Response charts (Richards & Gipe, 1992) provide initial "scaffolding" for students, helping them perform these metacognitive reflection and self-assessment activities. Not only do response charts help students interpret expository texts, they can also help the teacher understand which areas in the curriculum need more attention for planning instruction.

Materials

Aside from content books or other instructional texts, chart paper will be needed for making the response charts. For whole-class demonstrations and modeling, you will also need an overhead projector, blank transparencies, and watercolor markers.

Procedure

Using a minilesson format for instruction (remember, this series of activities will likely be spread over several sessions), begin by reading a short excerpt pertaining to the topic you wish to study. Next, explain that good readers regularly monitor their own comprehension. They ask themselves such questions as, "What do I already know about this subject?" "What did I not understand about what I just read?" "Did my mind wander as I read that last paragraph?" Explain that this kind of self-monitoring (metacognition) helps readers know when they need to take corrective actions, such as rereading that last section in which their mind wandered, so that any gaps in their learning can be filled.

Next, using a blank transparency and markers, draw a line down the middle of the transparency and write the headings YES and NO at the top (see Figure 11.13, illustrating a unit on comets). Then, using the passage you read at the beginning of the lesson for context, write under the YES column those things that the reader knows, appreciates, or understands about the topic. Explain as you go along what you know about the topic and how you chose the phrases to represent your knowledge. Repeat the parallel process under the NO column, describing points from the passage that you did not understand, any dislikes or disputes, and the strategies you might use to gain the needed information (i.e., ask a friend, reread the passage, ask a designated "classroom expert," check in the library for a clearer explanation, and so on).

As your minilesson series progresses, students will read a small section of the book or text. With your guidance, they should respond to what they do and do not like or understand by filling in an individual response chart labeled "My YES and why" and "My NO and why."

TEXTBOOK ACTIVITY GUIDES

Purpose

Textbook activity guides (Noyce & Christie, 1989) help students learn ways to read strategically and understand new information found in the text.

Materials

A teacher-constructed textbook activity guide pertaining to a new unit of study is needed. Also, a copy of the textbook activity guide on transparency for the overhead projector, blank transparencies, and watercolor markers will be needed for modeling activities.

 **Figure 11.13**   Response Chart

Yes	No
• mostly dirt and ice	• what makes them move?
• Halley's comet	• do they ever strike Earth?
• cause of superstitious tales	• what causes the tail?
• no life on them, most likely	• what's so special about Halley's
• have a "tail"	comet, anyway?

Procedure

After a thorough content analysis of the new unit of study (Reutzel & Cooter, 2000), develop questions for all major facts, concepts, and generalizations. For each question, decide whether students will best understand and retain the new knowledge through discussion with their partner (DP), predicting with their partner (PP), writing individual responses (WR), preparing semantic maps (MAP), or simply reading the passage quickly (SKIM). Write the appropriate abbreviation after each question as a guide to students' reading-study activities. Students should work in dyads or small groups, especially when just learning to use the guide, and should use the abbreviations to direct their efforts in discovering new information. As with all new learning strategies and processes, the first few times you use the textbook activity guide you will need to model the process.

DEFINITION WRITING

Purpose

In definition writing, students simply create definitions for specialized content vocabulary using their own language.

Materials

A list of words relating to the content unit being studied is needed.

Procedure

Make a list of new vocabulary words and concepts found in the new unit of study. You may want to ask students to make predictions about word meanings before reading the text in order to assess background knowledge and to focus their attention on the most important elements. After reading the text, make class dictionaries using the revised definitions.

CARTOONS

Purpose

Cartoons are used as a creative medium for students to demonstrate their understanding of the unit of study. (Note: This activity is especially functional in social studies, literature, and science courses.)

Materials

Textbook and other learning materials, markers, crayons, paints, art paper, and cartoon examples are needed.

Procedure

Prior to reading new text materials, explain to students that they will have an opportunity to complete a text response activity in lieu of taking a traditional test (this usually grabs their interest right off), and that the activity consists of working in small groups of two to construct a cartoon strip. The cartoon strip is to retell the important information found in the text in a creative way. If they wish, students can create a fictional situation as a context for presenting the information. Prepare and show partial examples of the kinds of products you hope to see (see Figure 11.14). Students should help you to construct an evaluation rubric prior to beginning the unit so that the expectations are clear. At the conclusion of the unit, teams will present their cartoon strips to the class. Many classes enjoy making

Figure 11.14 A Cartoon Created by a Student to Retell Key Points About a Passage

Author's note: Not to worry, the above story turned out to be about a child jumping to conclusions!

awards for such aspects as art quality, creativity, and accuracy and completeness of information presented.

FOUR-STEP SUMMARY WRITING

Purpose

Four-step summary writing serves to help students internalize a simple procedure for summarizing information.

Materials

A content textbook and writing materials are needed.

Procedure

We have found the following procedure by Noyce and Christie (1989) to be easy for most students from grade five on up. (Naturally, the teacher will need to model this process and then guide students as they work in groups discussing how to do it.) It is built on these four easy steps:

Step 1: Write a topic sentence, that is, one that summarizes in general terms what the content is about. Either select one that the author has written or write your own.

Step 2: Delete all unnecessary sentences, words, and other information from the entire passage.

Step 3: After sorting all terms into categories, think of a collective term(s) for those things that fall into the same category.

Step 4: Collapse paragraphs on the same subject down to one when they are largely redundant.

SELECTED REFERENCES

Alvermann, D. E., & Moore, D. W. (1991). Secondary school reading. In R. Barr, M. L. Kamil, P. B. Mosenthal, & P. D. Pearson (Eds.), *Handbook of reading research* (vol. 2, pp. 951–983). White Plains, NY: Longman.

Armbruster, B., & Anderson, T. (1981). *Content area textbooks* (Reading Education Report No. 23). Urbana–Champaign: University of Illinois, Center for the Study of Reading.

Berger, L. R. (1996). Reader response journals: You make the meaning. . . and how. *Journal of Adolescent & Adult Literacy, 39*(5), 380–385.

Berger, P. L. (1974). *Sociology: A biographical approach.* New York: Basic Books.

Calkins, L. (1994). *The art of teaching writing* (new ed.). Portsmouth, NH: Heinemann.

Commander, N. E., & Smith, B. D. (1996). Learning logs: A tool for cognitive monitoring. *Journal of Adolescent & Adult Literacy, 39*(6), 446–453.

Cooter, R. B., Jr., & Flynt, E. S. (1996). *Teaching reading in the content areas: Developing content literacy for all students.* Upper Saddle River, NJ: Merrill/Prentice Hall.

Cudd, E. T., & Roberts, L. (1989). Using writing to enhance content area learning in the primary grades. *The Reading Teacher, 42,* 392–403.

Ediger, M. (2000). Writing, the pupil, and the social studies. *College Student Journal, 34*(1), 59–68.

Emig, J. (1983). Writing as a mode of learning. In D. Goswami & M. Butler (Eds.), *The web of meaning: Essays on writing, teaching, learning and thinking* (pp. 122–131). Montclair, NJ: Boynton/Cook.

Farnan, N. (1996). Connecting adolescents and reading: Goals at the middle level. *Journal of Adolescent & Adult Literacy, 39*(6), 436–445.

Farr, R., Tulley, M. A., & Pritchard, R. (1989). Assessment instruments and techniques used by the content area teacher. In D. Lapp, J. Flood, & N. Farnan (Eds.), *Content area reading and learning* (pp. 346–356). Englewood Cliffs, NJ: Prentice Hall.

Flood, J., Lapp, D., & Farnan, N. (1986). A reading-writing procedure that teaches expository paragraph structure. *The Reading Teacher, 39,* 556–562.

Flynt, E. S., & Cooter, R. B., Jr. (2001). *The Flynt/Cooter reading inventory for the classroom* (4th ed.). Upper Saddle River, NJ: Merrill/Prentice Hall.

Fowler, G. L. (1982). Developing comprehension skills in primary students through the use of story frames. *The Reading Teacher, 36*(2), 176–179.

Guthrie, J. T., Seifert, M., Burnham, N. A., & Caplan, R. J. (1974). The maze technique to assess and monitor reading comprehension. *The Reading Teacher, 28*(2), 161–168.

Guthrie, J. T., Van Meter, P., McCann, A. D., Wigfield, A., Bennett, L., Poundstone et al. (1996). Growth of literacy engagement: Changes in motivations and strategies during concept-oriented reading instruction. *Reading Research Quarterly, 31*(3), 306–332

Hoffman, J. V. (1992). Critical reading/thinking across the curriculum: Using I-charts to support learning. *Language Arts, 69,* 121–127.

Irvin, J. L., & Connors, N. A. (1989). Reading instruction in middle level schools: Results of a U.S. survey. *Journal of Reading, 32,* 306–311.

Johnson, D., & Steele, V. (1996). So many words, so little time: Helping college ESL learners acquire vocabulary-building strategies. *Journal of Adolescent & Adult Literacy, 39*(5), 348–357.

McGee, L. M., & Richgels, D. J. (1985). Teaching expository text structure to elementary students. *The Reading Teacher, 38,* 739–748.

Meyer, B. J., & Freedle, R. O. (1984). Effects of discourse type on recall. *American Educational Research Journal, 21*(1), 121–143.

Nagy, W., & Herman, P. (1987). Breadth and depth of vocabulary knowledge: Implications for acquisition and instruction. In M. McKeown & M. Curtis (Eds.), *The nature of vocabulary acquisition* (pp. 19–35). Hillsdale, NJ: Erlbaum.

Nichols, J. (1980). Using paragraph frames to help remedial high school students with written assignments. *Journal of Reading, 24,* 228–231.

Noyce, R. M., & Christie, J. F. (1989). *Integrating reading and writing instruction.* Boston: Allyn & Bacon.

Olson, M. W., & Gee, T. C. (1991). Content reading instruction in the primary grades: Perceptions and strategies. *The Reading Teacher, 45,* 298–306.

Randall, S. N. (1996). Information charts: A strategy for organizing student research. *Journal of Adolescent & Adult Literacy, 39*(7), 536–542.

Readence, J. E., Bean, T. W., & Baldwin, R. S. (1992). *Content area reading: An integrated approach* (4th ed.). Dubuque, IA: Kendall/Hunt.

Reutzel, D. R., & Cooter, R. B. (2000). *Teaching children to read: Putting the pieces together* (4th ed.). Upper Saddle River, NJ: Merrill/Prentice Hall.

Richards, J. C., & Gipe, J. P. (1992) Activating background knowledge: Strategies for beginning and poor readers. *The Reading Teacher, 45,* 474–475.

Romine, B. G., McKenna, M. C., & Robinson, R. D. (1996). Reading coursework requirements for middle and high school content area teachers: A U.S. survey. *Journal of Adolescent & Adult Literacy, 40*(3), 194–198.

Simpson, M. (1996). Conducting reality checks to improve students' strategic learning. *Journal of Adolescent & Adult Literacy, 40*(2), 102–109.

Singer, H. (1981). Instruction in reading acquisition. In O. Tzeng & H. Singer (Eds.), *Perception of print* (pp. 291–311). Hillsdale, NJ: Erlbaum.

Snowball, D. (1989). Reading and writing in the content areas. *The Reading Teacher, 43,* 266–270.

Strong, W. (1983). Writing: A means to meaning or how I got from the Tastee Donut Shop to the Inn of the Seventh Mountain. *English Journal, 72,* 34–37.

Swafford, J., & Bryan, J. K. (2000). Instructional strategies for promoting conceptual change: Supporting middle school students. *Reading & Writing Quarterly, 16*(2), 139–161.

Chapter 12

Developing Research and Reference Skills

James McLeary is the great grandfather of Jon McLeary in my sixth-grade class, and came to share his experiences in the early twentieth century as an immigrant. He came to the United States an ocean of time ago from his homeland of Ireland at the age of 17. Mr. McLeary told us about seeing the Statue of Liberty for the first time, and his landing at Ellis Island with a clarity that made you feel you were there with him. Later, Mr. McLeary spoke of his trek to Chicago, his first jobs as a roofer and craftsman, and later as a policeman in a checkered cap. Tears appeared in his eyes when he spoke of first meeting his future wife of 53 years, Kathleen. The room was mesmerized.

The next day, I said to my class, "Mr. McLeary's story was a wonderful beginning to our study of world history this year. His testimony was what is called a 'primary source.' That is information that comes to us firsthand and we can witness it for ourselves. Over the next several weeks we will learn many interesting and important things about Ireland. We'll learn something about Ireland's history, its people today, and its conflicts. We will also take a close look at the influences Irish Americans have on the United States. Perhaps the most important thing we will learn about Ireland is how the story of Irish immigrants is so much like the stories of immigrants from other countries in South America, Africa, Asia, and Europe.

"Folks, we are also going to learn some very cool ways of gathering information about our world, what I call 'research tools.' These are tools that will save you a lot of time and make learning much easier. In fact, these are the tools you will need for the rest of your lives—in high school, college, and in your adult career. Best of all, these research tools are downright fun! Let's get started."

As students develop as fluent readers, they are challenged to apply their skills to learn more about the world in which they live. In chapter 11, we reviewed various ways students can apply their skills to read and comprehend expository texts. In this chapter, we describe ways students can be helped to acquire research and reference skills, the logical next step in conquering expository texts. These practical skills help students discover and draw upon various resources commonly found in library/media centers as they pursue knowledge in specific areas of interest.

BACKGROUND BRIEFING FOR TEACHERS

Readence, Bean, and Baldwin (2000) stated that the teaching of study strategies, which include research and reference skills, is crucial in helping students achieve independent learning. Research and reference skills include such diverse areas as notetaking, mapping known and unknown information areas, choosing sources for obtaining information (e.g., Internet search engines, reference materials, expert interviews, and so on), and searching card catalogs electronically and manually. Some of the key strategies offered in this chapter help students to choose areas to research, to organize new information, and to learn efficient ways to locate facts.

Much of what is contained in this chapter relates directly to *metacognition*—helping students to determine what they know or do not know about a topic. In addition, many of these activities help students understand *how* they know what they know and recognize which research and reference skills they have already partially internalized.

Another major component of this chapter is the presentation of tools that can help readers categorize known information, identify gaps in their knowledge, and self-select appropriate sources to fill those blank areas with pertinent facts.

We begin by suggesting ways that teachers can assess student knowledge of research and reference skills. In the latter part of the chapter, we suggest strategies for research/reference skill improvement that can easily be modeled for students to improve their skills.

ASSESSING STUDENT KNOWLEDGE OF RESEARCH AND REFERENCE SKILLS

Investigations conducted by researchers to help teachers determine what research and reference skills students possess are few. There are some informal strategies, however, that can help teachers determine what students know about a topic of study or survey the kinds of materials that students may be using in their research. We have included in this section the strategies that have been most helpful in our classrooms. When used as teaching activities, these strategies help students to recognize their own needs—an important motivational teaching practice.

RESEARCH LOGS

Purpose

An effective activity for determining the kinds of research methods and materials students are using is the research log. Research logs are a simple listing of materials used over time in the content classroom to complete research projects. By periodically reviewing research logs, teachers can survey patterns of reading/study behavior in their classrooms and plan instruction to help fill in gaps in students' knowledge about research resources.

Materials

Students will benefit from a structured research log form. A simple format for research logs is presented in Figure 12.1.

Figure 12.1   Research Log

| Name: _____ |
| Subject: _____ Period: _____ Homeroom: _____ |

Date	Assignment/ Topic	Materials Selected	Pages/ Programs Used	Notes

Procedure

First, develop a brief minilesson modeling how you would use a research log while completing a class assignment. Using a recent assignment as the context will save time in your minilesson and will lead students to contribute to the conversation. Once you have modeled how to record information on the log form, distribute copies of the research log to the students. If possible, introduce the research log just prior to beginning a new unit of study and provide a folder in which the logs may be kept. Check the logs at the midpoint of the unit of study to determine which research materials are being used, then offer research skills minilessons as needed. Review the logs again at the conclusion of the unit to determine student progress and for future lesson planning.

SELF-RATING SCALES

Purpose

It is often true that no one knows better how he is doing in reading than the reader himself. This is especially true when it comes to his ability to use research and reference materials in the library stacks. A teacher carrying out an assessment agenda should never overlook the obvious—ask the student what he is good at doing! Although this may be best achieved in a one-on-one discussion setting, large class sizes frequently make this impractical. A good alternative to one-on-one interviews for older elementary children is a student self-rating scale. In applying this strategy, students complete a questionnaire that is custom tailored to obtain specific information about the reader and his skills with research and reference tools—from the reader's point of view.

Materials

You will need to construct a self-rating scale that conforms to the research and reference skills you want each of your students to possess. Figure 12.2 shows an example of a self-rating scale.

Figure 12.2　Self-Rating Scale

Self-Rating Scale: Researching the "Evolution of Surgery"

Name: _____　Date: _____

Directions: Answer the following questions as they pertain to how you will find out more about the ways surgery has improved in the United States in the last 100 years.

The first three things I will do to find out more about how surgery has improved in the United States when I enter the library is:
1.
2.
3.

Three things I know about entries (cards) in the card catalog in the library are:
1.
2.
3.

Three sources of information I can use in this study of surgery are:
1.
2.
3.

I can organize the information and data I find by . . .

I feel I could use some help in understanding how to use library resources or research skills in these areas (check all that apply):
_____ using the card catalog
_____ taking notes
_____ finding periodicals from a particular time period or topic
_____ finding books that relate to our unit on surgery
_____ using the Internet to find information
_____ organizing information to write a report
_____ interviewing experts
_____ knowing where to begin my research
_____ locating information quickly in a book

Procedure

We prefer to use self-rating scales within the context of an actual unit of study about to commence or with a unit just completed. For example, let us assume that you are about to begin a new unit of study pertaining to "The Evolution of Surgery" in this country from 1900 to the present. After having a brief warm-up conversation with the students about the field of medicine and surgery, distribute the self-rating scale you have developed. Once the students have completed their self-rating scales, collect and analyze the scales to determine in a cursory way the skills the students feel that they possess. (Note: This is only a survey of student perceptions. You will also need to collect further observations as the students begin to actually use library resources to complete assignments.)

PREREADING PLAN (PREP)

Purpose

This three-stage strategy by Langer (1981) helps teachers assess and activate the prior knowledge of students about a topic of study. This assessment and instruction activity may be used with a whole class or small groups. The first step uses a question to determine any associations students might have with a topic, concept, or term to be studied. The second step asks students to review and interpret their first impressions. The final step has students work with the teacher to identify existing gaps in their knowledge to help guide their research into the topic.

Materials

There are no materials required to do the PreP activity beyond the usual paper, pencils, and chalkboards normally found in classrooms. However, large pictures or other artifacts that relate to the topic of study may help jog students' memories in the first activity.

Procedure

As noted, the first step is to ask students what they know about the topic to be studied. These initial associations provide insights into how much prior knowledge exists in the class and helps students to begin building concept-related associations about the topic (Cooter & Flynt, 1996). For example, in teaching a lesson about the Civil Rights movement of the 1960s, you might start off by asking your class, "What do you think of when you hear the words 'civil rights'?" Showing pictures from the 1950s and 1960s of lunch counter "sit-ins," the Little Rock, Arkansas, school desegregation incident, or of Rosa Parks and Dr. Martin Luther King, Jr. could be quite helpful in stimulating initial discussion. After recording students' first associations, the next step is to have students think about or reflect on their initial associations. During this reflection stage your goal is to have students discuss and explain why the associations they had about the topic came to mind—"What made you think of . . . ?" This interactive stage further taps prior knowledge, builds a common network of ideas about the topic, and facilitates a student-centered discussion.

The last stage of PreP is called reformulation of knowledge. Your goal is to have students recognize and define what they know about the topic before they begin research to learn more about it. We find that creating an outline or concept web about the topic helps many students see graphically what they already know, create categories for known information, and provoke questions about what must still be learned through the research process.

SEMANTIC MAPS

Purpose

Another useful strategy that can be used to activate students' prior knowledge of a topic and lead them to preview text material via student-centered discussion is the semantic map. Based on schema theory, semantic maps are essentially "road maps" of what is known by students with clusters of related information noted. Semantic maps can help students better understand metacognitively what is known and not known, as well as the research sources that can be employed to help find information. Because semantic maps depict known information in precisely the same way the brain stores information, they are inherently logical for students and can provide valuable insights for teachers.

Materials

You will need a large chart or tablet on an easel and colored markers to illustrate the semantic map. An alternative is to use an overhead projector, blank transparencies, and markers.

Procedure

The procedure starts with the teacher writing the topic on the chart or transparency. Similar to the PreP procedure discussed earlier, students are then asked to volunteer any information they associate with the identified topic. As the students offer them, the teacher lists their associations on the chart or transparency. Next, the teacher asks students to examine all headings, subheadings, and visuals in a textbook selection to be used as part of the introduction to gather more information. Students may do this work independently or with a partner. The new information is then added to the semantic map. At this time, students are asked to read the textbook selection carefully to provoke more discussion and to find more relevant information that can be added to the semantic map. A postreading discussion centers on the various questions that remain to be answered more completely and research sources that could be used in answering the questions. In Figure 12.3, we illustrate a typical semantic map that was created by students with teacher assistance regarding the Civil Rights movement topic mentioned earlier in the chapter. Note that a product that grew out of the semantic map's construction was a listing of research sources available for locating needed information.

CONNECTING ASSESSMENT FINDINGS TO TEACHING STRATEGIES

Before moving on to specific research strategies, we have constructed a guide connecting assessment findings to intervention and/or strategy choices. It is our intention to help you select the most appropriate instructional interventions and strategies to meet your students' needs based on assessment data. This is in keeping with the "If-Then" mode of thinking we discussed in chapter 2. Teaching strategies described in the next section are listed across the top of the grid on page 328. Potential problems are listed vertically in the left-hand column.

TEACHING STUDENTS RESEARCH AND REFERENCE SKILLS

Teaching students how to become effective researchers of knowledge is paramount if they are to become independent learners in later years. Thus, we must be good at setting up

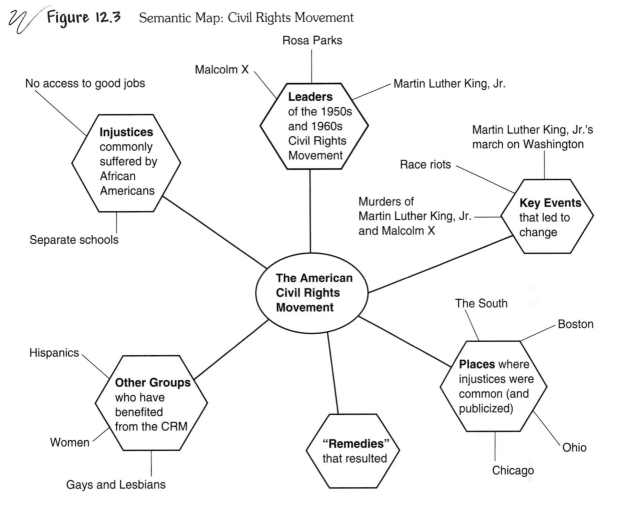

Figure 12.3 Semantic Map: Civil Rights Movement

Rosa Parks

Malcolm X

No access to good jobs

Martin Luther King, Jr.

Leaders of the 1950s and 1960s Civil Rights Movement

Martin Luther King, Jr.'s march on Washington

Race riots

Injustices commonly suffered by African Americans

Murders of Martin Luther King, Jr. and Malcolm X

Key Events that led to change

Separate schools

The American Civil Rights Movement

The South

Boston

Hispanics

Other Groups who have benefited from the CRM

Places where injustices were common (and publicized)

Women

Ohio

Gays and Lesbians

"Remedies" that resulted

Chicago

Questions to Answer

1. What are some of the greatest injustices suffered by African Americans that led to the Civil Rights Movement (CRM)?

2. Who were the Americans who seemed to have helped the CRM to be successful?

3. What were the key events that seemed to trigger the CRM?

4. Where were changes needed most in the United States?

5. What changes or remedies resulted?

Research Sources Available

History books, periodicals from that era, interviews with people who lived in the 1950s and 1960s, Internet searches, M.L. King Center in Atlanta, historians, card catalog entries, NAACP literature.

Intervention Strategy Guide for Developing Research and Reference Skills

Intervention Strategy/ → Student Problem(s) ↓	Graphic Organizers	Notetaking	SQ3R	Venn Hula Hoops	KWLS	KWWL
Organiz. Skills	+	–	+	+	+	+
Test Perform.	+	–	+	–	+	+
Problem Solving	*	*	*	+	*	*
Research Skills	*	+	*	–	+	+
Retaining Information	+	+	+	+	+	+

Key: + excellent strategy
* adaptable strategy
– unsuitable strategy

these kinds of learning experiences! Susan De la Paz (1999; Swanson & De la Paz, 1998) developed an effective process for teaching students the kinds of research and reference skills we discuss in the remainder of this chapter. We think you will see a familiar Vygotskian thread to this process she calls the **Self-Regulated Strategy Development Model (SRSD),** and highly recommend SRSD as the framework for introducing and practicing research strategies. Here is the gist of her recommendations:

1. **Describe the strategy.** Explicitly describe the strategy steps and discuss why and when they can be useful, and what they accomplish.

2. **Activate prior knowledge.** Review information the students may have already learned that may be useful in learning the new strategy.

3. **Review students' current level of functioning.** Provide information to students about their current performance levels and how this strategy can help them achieve a higher level of performance.

4. **Model the strategy.** Show the student how to use the strategy using multiple examples. Allow for student input and feedback.

5. **Provide collaborative practice.** Provide numerous opportunities for students to practice the new strategy in the whole group, small groups, pairs, and/or individually, depending on what you believe will be most effective. Teacher support will be faded out over time.

6. **Include independent practice.** Students should have ample opportunities to practice the strategy alone. They should have teacher or peer support available at first, but ultimately they should demonstrate proficiency in using the strategy alone.

7. **Generalize the strategy.** After learning has taken place, be sure to use the strategy routinely in future teaching and learning experiences. If the strategy is worth teaching, it is worth using and allowing it to become, as they say in the military, "SOP" (standard operating procedure).

GRAPHIC ORGANIZERS

Purpose

The purpose of research conducted by students is to gain and understand new knowledge about a topic. Many students struggle with this process and often seem to find disparate bits of information that they are unable to assimilate into what they already know. Without assimilation, no new learning is likely to result. *Graphic organizers* (GOs) can be used to help students comprehend new information, assimilate new information into what they already know, and recall that information later on when needed. Donna Merkley and Debra Jeffries (2001) developed guidelines for constructing and implementing GOs effectively in the classroom.

Materials

First, identify a fairly short (5–15 pages) expository text selection that is germane to the content curriculum. Next, follow the steps in the procedure section and analyze the selection identifying important key terms, descriptions, and concepts. Select a simple GO format and construct examples for classroom demonstrations/modeling with the GO in varying degrees of completion. We like to use overhead transparencies and an OHP (overhead projector) for this kind of modeling.

Procedure

Merkley and Jeffries (2001) summarized ways of 1) creating graphic organizers (GOs) and 2) implementing GOs in the classroom. We have adapted and combined these steps so that you can present them as a process tool to students. As always, extensive description and modeling on your part is essential. The goal is to have students internalize these processes so that they begin using GOs as tools in their research activities.

Step 1:   Show students ways of analyzing new information for important key words, descriptions, and global concepts. Verbalize relationships between concepts and key words. Provide opportunities for student questions and input.

Step 2:   Arrange key words into an illustration to show interrelationships and patterns of organization. As you construct a graphic organizer (GO), verbalize for students how their earlier work in Step 1 flows in a natural way into the selection of an appropriate GO design (see examples shown in Figures 12.8–12.13). Demonstrate how new knowledge can connect to their prior knowledge.

Step 3:   Review and evaluate the relationships in the GO for clarity, simplicity, and visual effectiveness. Demonstrate how the need for more information in some areas can help students formulate research questions leading to further reading and a search for missing links.

To summarize, the key elements to teaching students about GOs include (Merkley & Jeffries, 2001):

- *Verbalize relationships (links) among concepts by the GO.*
- *Provide opportunities for student input and questioning during your modeling and guided practice experiences.*
- *Connect new knowledge to prior experiences.*
- *Develop "need to know" questions that relate to upcoming readings and further research.*

NOTETAKING STRATEGIES

Purpose

There are many different systems for teaching students how to take notes as they listen (Cooter & Flynt, 1996). Among the notetaking systems that have been proposed are the Cornell System (Pauk, 2000) and the REST system (Morgan, Meeks, Schollaert, & Paul, 1986). Recommendations about how notes should initially be recorded, the need for subsequent reorganization and expansion of the notes, and a strong recommendation for frequent review exemplify the common threads of these systems.

Materials

Students will need a notebook that can be used exclusively for learning notetaking.

Procedure

Before discussing each of the components of effective notetaking, we would first like to suggest a couple of general guidelines derived from the work of Cooter and Flynt (1996). First, students should be asked to obtain a single notebook specifically for use in learning notetaking skills. Dedicating a notebook for this purpose will help them keep the notes organized and will make it easier for you to collect and examine the notes. Second, if note-taking is important to you, then some type of credit should be given to students who do a good job of recording and organizing their notes. Finally, adapt the amount and style of lecturing to your students' ability level. If you have an advanced class, more sophisticated lectures might be warranted. However, if your class has little experience with notetaking and effective listening techniques, you might want to begin slowly and use a lot of visuals, or perhaps a listening outline, to assist students in determining and writing important information.

Two traditional notetaking systems are the *Cornell System* (Pauk, 2000) and *A Notetaking System for Learning* (Palmatier, 1973). These systems share several features that we recommend for use in training students in how to listen and take notes on lecture information.

First, students should divide their notebook paper into two columns. The left column should be about 2 or 3 inches wide, or one third of the paper width. The remaining two thirds of the page is used for recording the notes.

Second, students should write information in a modified outline form on the right side of the page. Students should indent subtopics and minor ideas using letters and numbers. They should be encouraged to use abbreviations to minimize time spent in writing down information. Heavily emphasized points should be marked with asterisks or stars.

Third, students should organize and expand their notes as soon as possible. Early in the school year, considerate teachers provide in-class time for this task. At this time the students literally rewrite their notes on similarly lined paper. The purpose is for the students to write all abbreviations, expand phrases, and make sure that the information is sequentially organized. This is obviously a form of practice.

Fourth, students fill in the left margin for aid in study and review. As they reread their notes, students identify topics, key terms, and questions that might assist them in remembering the lecture information recorded on the right side of the paper.

Fifth, students use their notes for study and review. Students can now cover up the right-hand side of the paper and use the memory triggers they have recorded on the left-hand side for review. As they move down the left-hand side of the page, students use the headings, key terms, and questions as a means of assessing their ability to remember and paraphrase what they have recorded.

SQ3R

All effective reading/study strategies are metacognitive in nature because they cause readers to establish purposes for study, to determine whether they have been successful in satisfying their purposes, and to adjust their tactics if they have failed or fallen short in achieving their purpose for studying. Reading/study strategies require the students to actively attend to text information; respond to the text in some way (taking notes, underlining, answering questions); spend more time on task; and review the material for long-term retention. If one examines a reading/study "how to" book, one often finds a plethora of reading/study strategies that are touted as either effective or tailor-made for specific subject matter areas. They are usually presented by an acronym that reflects the various steps of the strategy. The most time-honored of all these reading/study strategies is SQ3R. Originally developed by Francis Robinson (1946) as a technique to help soldiers study manuals during World War II (Stahl & Henk, 1986), SQ3R has been used widely in schools as a way of providing students with a specific, albeit intense, method for independent study. SQ3R has spawned many other similar-looking reading/study strategies; however, because most of the other reading/study strategies reflect much of what SQ3R recommends, we will confine this discussion to SQ3R. First, we would like to present the steps of SQ3R and then discuss the strategy's relative usefulness in content reading and study.

Survey: Begin a new unit of study by quickly reading all chapter headings, subheadings, margin notes, words printed in bold, pictures and their captions, and charts or diagrams. This will draw one's attention to some of the major topics to be learned.

Question: Based on your "survey," write several questions that pertain to the headings, subheadings, words in bold, and margin notes you discovered. This will alert you to some of the key information while reading. (Note: We recommend that teachers model for students how to write questions on different levels of complexity, such as literal, inferential, and evaluative levels. Many students need a great deal of practice with higher order thinking skills.)

Read: Read the chapter. As you do so, try to pay careful attention to information that answers the questions you created in the previous step. After reading, go back and answer each question in writing, being sure to note specific details from the chapter.

Recite: After you have answered all questions in detail, give yourself a quiz over those same questions and try to write your responses from memory. Any questions that gave you difficulty should be practiced by rereading the questions and answers aloud. Continue this practice until all questions and answers can be rewritten from memory.

Review: Once information has been learned and can be recited from memory, it should be reviewed daily so that it becomes permanent. The amount of time spent for review each day will depend on the complexity of the unit of study, but about 20 minutes per day is generally a good rule of thumb.

As you can see, SQ3R may require a great deal of effort on the part of the student and the teacher. Estimates suggest that a minimum of 10 hours of teacher-led instruction is required for low-achieving students to utilize SQ3R effectively (Orlando, 1986). In addition, the overall benefit of SQ3R on student achievement is not clear (Caverly & Orlando, 1991). We feel that teachers should stress only those components of SQ3R that can best serve students with a particular assignment.

VENN DIAGRAM HULA HOOPS

Purpose

Venn diagrams have been used for many years to help students understand similarities, differences, and common features of information gleaned from reading assignments. Venn diagrams are simply overlapping circles used to graphically display three kinds of information. With Venn Diagram Hula Hoops (Cooter & Thomas, 1998), this concept is applied for students (elementary through high school) using the hula hoops first popularized in the 1950s.

Materials

You will need to purchase at least two hula hoops for each group of children (usually four students to a group) to be involved in this activity. For each group, sentence strips or tag board and watercolor markers are needed for use in writing information from the readings.

Figure 12.4   Venn Diagram Hula Hoops

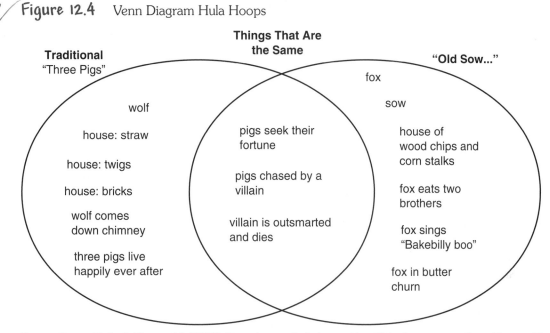

Source: Cooter, K. S., & Thomas M. (1998). *Venn diagram hula hoops.* Unpublished manuscript. Texas Christian University, Fort Worth, TX. Comparisons using the traditional telling of "The Three Little Pigs" and Richard Chase's (1948) "The Old Sow and the Three Shoats" from *Grandfather Tales* (Houghton Mifflin).

Procedure

With a simple passage, begin by modeling for the class how Venn diagrams are used. You can use a dry-erase board, chart, chalkboard, or overhead projector for your modeling. For younger children—and perhaps for older ones, too—an easy-to-use comparison is the traditional telling of "The Three Little Pigs" contrasted to *The True Story of the Three Little Pigs* by A. Wolf. Another version of the story we enjoy using is "The Old Sow and the Three Shoats" found in Richard Chase's classic *Grandfather Tales* (1948). In Figure 12.4, we display how similarities, differences, and commonalties could be portrayed in the teacher's modeling exercise using Chase's version and the traditional story.

Once students seem to grasp the Venn diagram concept, repeat the modeling exercise in a large open space using the hula hoops. Simply ask the children to gather around in a circle where they can see the hula hoops laid across each other to form the familiar Venn diagram configuration. Be sure to print on sentence strips the appropriate name/title for each circle and place the labels above the corresponding circle or center section (i.e., "Traditional Three Pigs Story," "Old Sow and the Three Shoats," "Both Stories"). Using the very same descriptors that you suggested in the modeling activity and wrote on sentence strips or tag board strips (in this case, using the "Three Pigs" story descriptors), lay the sentence strips where appropriate within the diagram. Ask a volunteer if she can explain what each descriptor means in each circle or in the overlapping section.

Once students have demonstrated an understanding of how to use Venn diagram hula hoops, broaden the experience using nonfiction expository reading selections. Be sure to model first, then ask the students to do the task in small groups.

K-W-L-S Strategy Chart

Purpose

The K-W-L strategy is effective in improving reading comprehension by causing students to activate, think about, and organize their prior knowledge as an aid to reading comprehension. Ogle (1986), originator of K-W-L, asserted that this strategy is best suited for use with expository text. Sinatra (1997) found success using K-W-L with informational texts when adding one additional step—asking students what they *still* want to know ("S") after the K-W-L routine has been completed. This addition to Ogle's original strategy helps create continuing interest in the topic under study, encourages a degree of metacognitive thinking (i.e., helping students realize what they know and do not yet know), and helps teachers assess student learning. We have adapted Sinatra's K-W-L-S Strategy Chart somewhat for use as a research tool.

Materials

Students will need a copy of the K-W-L-S Strategy Chart, such as the one shown in Figure 12.5.

Procedure

As with a standard K-W-L activity, this version is intended as a metacognitive exercise to help guide students' learning. Begin by displaying an enlarged version of the K-W-L-S Strategy Chart at the front of the group, using either large tablet paper or transparencies and an overhead projector. Define and explain what each letter in the K-W-L-S Strategy Chart means and how an awareness of what one knows or does not know can help guide one efficiently through a research experience. This latter timesaving point can be motivational for most of us who hope to keep library search time to a minimum.

Next, use the enlarged chart to "walk through" the K-W-L-S procedure once, using a combination of read aloud and group participation. For example, let's say you have chosen a passage from a health textbook pertaining to heart disease to illustrate how the K-W-L-S Strategy Chart can be used as an aid in health research.

Say to the students: "Before we try out the K-W-L-S Strategy Chart on our own, let's try it out once together. A topic we will be learning about next has to do with the human heart and ways to prevent heart disease. The first step in using a K-W-L-S Strategy Chart is to think about what we know about the topic. That is what the 'K' represents on the chart. Let's list some of the things we already know about the heart. Any volunteers?"

Begin to list things that are known in the first column. Note that we have included at the bottom of that column a question that pertains to reference tools that helped students know what they already know about a subject. This helps students immediately think about tools they have used in some manner in the past, or—in other columns—tools they could use as they progress in their research.

The next step is to complete the "W" column by answering the question, "What information about the human heart and its diseases would I want to know (or need to know)?" Once the "W" column has been completed, use student participation up to this point as a springboard to discuss in some detail the library/media center tools that can be helpful for locating information. Next, using one of the library/media center tools, instruct your students to listen as you read aloud a passage you have selected pertaining to your question (in this case, a passage on heart disease might be chosen). Once you have completed the reading, go back to the K-W-L-S Strategy Chart and complete the section "L", describing the additional information you learned from listening to the passage.

Figure 12.5   K-W-L-S Strategy Chart

Name: _____   Date: _____

Topic: _____

"K" What I "Know" . . .	"W" What I "Want" to Know . . .	"L" What I "Learned" . . .	"S" What I Am "Still" Needing to Know . . .
Reference tools that helped me know what I know:	**Reference tools** I will need to find out more:	**Reference tools** that helped me:	**Reference tools** I will need to find out more:

At this point in a standard K-W-L activity, the students would be finished. However, as Sinatra (1997) observed, there are usually many more facts yet to be learned and questions left unanswered; hence, the addition of the stage "S", which essentially asks, "What do I still need to know about this subject?" Unanswered questions from the "W" stage of the activity, as well as any new questions emerging from the read-aloud activity, should be listed in this column. This final category sends some very important messages to students: 1) there are always some unanswered questions in almost every research project, 2) as you learn more information, that information often spawns new questions, 3) there are sources of information in the library/media center to help me find answers to my questions, and 4) my teacher will help me to learn how to use these resources effectively.

K-W-W-L

Purpose

Another variation of the K-W-L (Ogle, 1986) strategy is K-W-W-L (Bryan, 1988). Much like Sinatra's (1997) K-W-L-S Strategy Chart, this activity helps students to identify starting points for their research.

Materials

Reproduce worksheets such as the one shown in Figure 12.6 for each student, as well as an enlarged version with which you can model the activity.

Procedure

Follow the same process as described for the K-W-L-S Strategy Chart; only use the K-W-W-L figure instead. We have included a partially completed K-W-W-L chart in Figure 12.7 for use in your modeling exercise.

SELECTED MAPS AND GRAPHIC ORGANIZERS FOR USE WITH INFORMATIONAL TEXT

Purpose

As noted earlier in the chapter, semantic maps and other graphic organizers (GOs) can help teachers assess what students know or do not know about a topic. They can also be used as a research and study tool to help students chart important knowledge they are acquiring, understand steps in a process or sequence, classify or categorize information, compare and contrast two or more features, determine causal patterns, and prepare and defend thesis statements concerning an area of study. In short, maps are a form of outlining that help students determine which areas they must research.

Materials

Figures 12.8 through 12.13 display each map as described in the next section.

Procedure

Sinatra, Gemake, Wielan, and Sinatra (1998) identified several map forms and their usefulness with informational text. We offer here an abbreviated summary of their research, targeting maps that we wish to emphasize.

Figure 12.6   K-W-W-L Chart

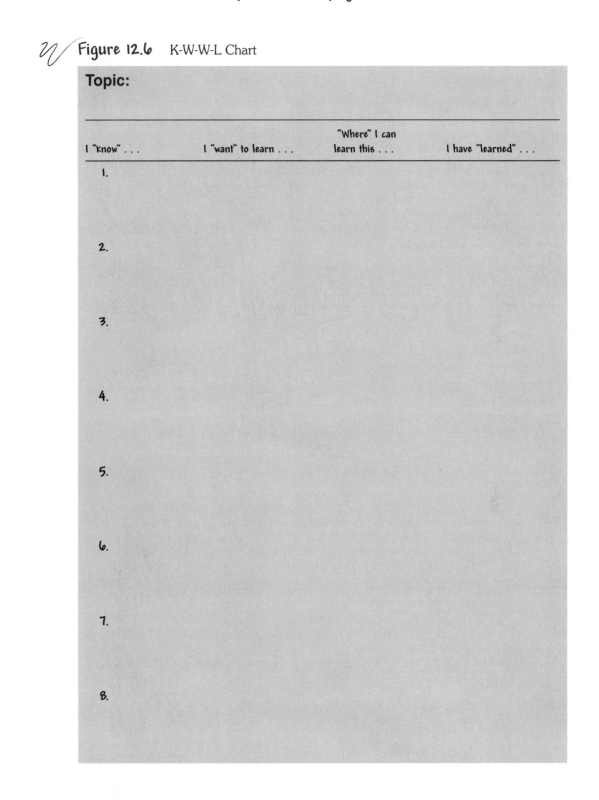

Topic:

I "know" . . .	I "want" to learn . . .	"Where" I can learn this . . .	I have "learned" . . .
1.			
2.			
3.			
4.			
5.			
6.			
7.			
8.			

Figure 12.7   K-W-W-L Chart Example

Topic: "Oceans"

I know . . .	I want to learn . . .	Where I can learn this . . .	I have learned . . .
1. Oceans have salt water.	What makes the ocean salty?	• encyclopedia • Internet search • ask a scientist	
2. Salt water burns your eyes.	Is salt water harmful to your eyes?	• ask a doctor • look for a book in the library on this subject	
3. There are many kinds of sharks.	Are all sharks "man eaters"?	• ask a marine biologist • check the Internet	
4. Oceans have waves and tides.	What causes the tides?	• look for a book in the library on oceans • ask a scientist at the university • call the TV station weather personnel	
5. Many kinds of fish live in the ocean.	What kinds of sea creatures live in the deep waters?	• look for a library book on fish • ask a scientist • check the encyclopedia • try an Internet search	
6. There are other forms of sea life found in the ocean.	What are some of the main kinds of sea life?	• same as #5	
7. Songs have been written about the sea.	How would I go about getting a list of songs about the sea?	• check with the music teacher • try a search on the Internet with <Amazon.com> for songs	
8.			

Notes:

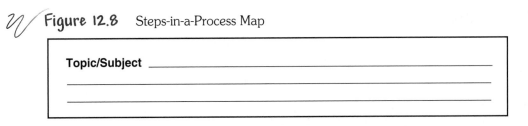

Figure 12.8 Steps-in-a-Process Map

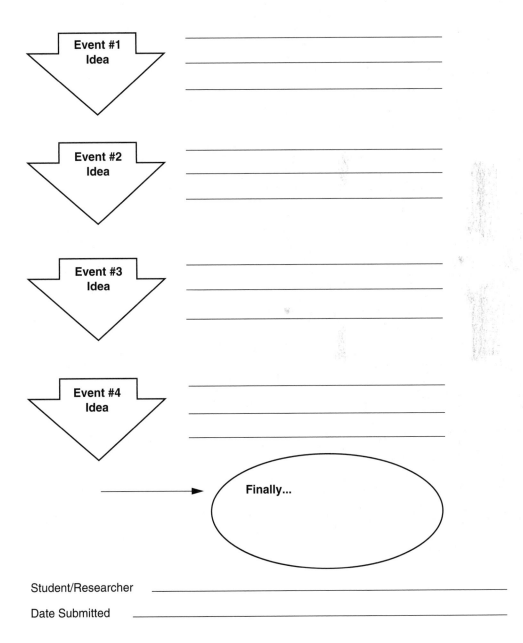

Topic/Subject _____

Event #1
Idea

Event #2
Idea

Event #3
Idea

Event #4
Idea

Finally...

Student/Researcher _____

Date Submitted _____

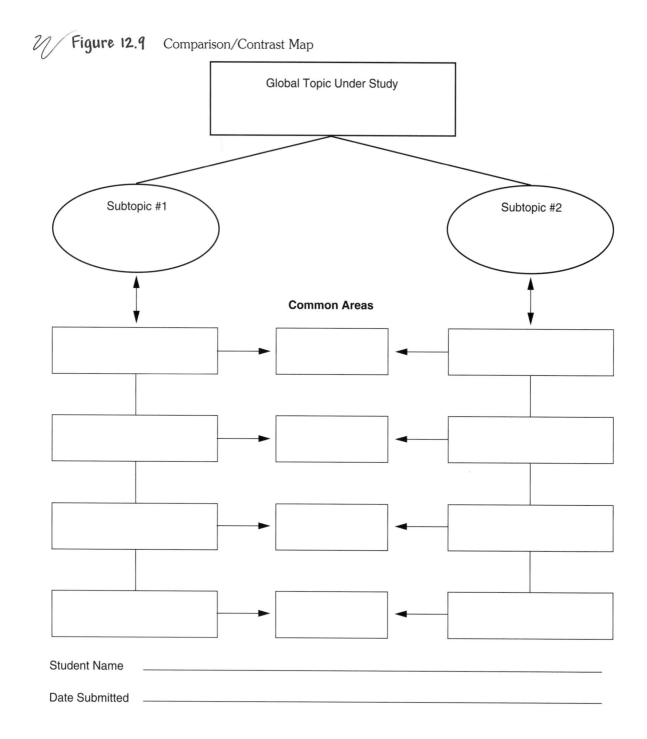

Figure 12.9   Comparison/Contrast Map

Global Topic Under Study

Subtopic #1

Subtopic #2

Common Areas

Student Name _____

Date Submitted _____

Figure 12.10 Same/Different Map

Topic or Main Idea _____

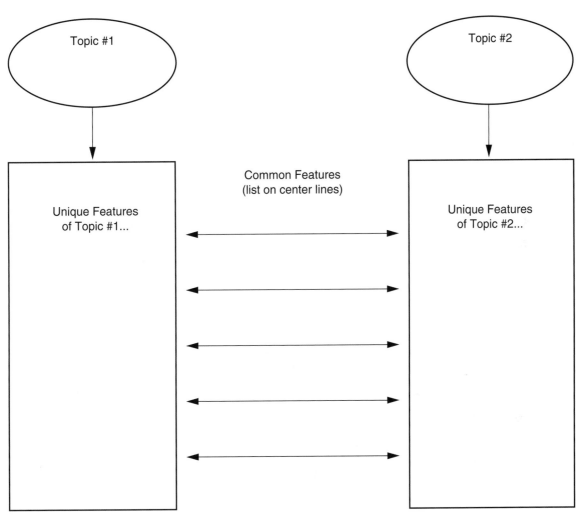

Student Name _____

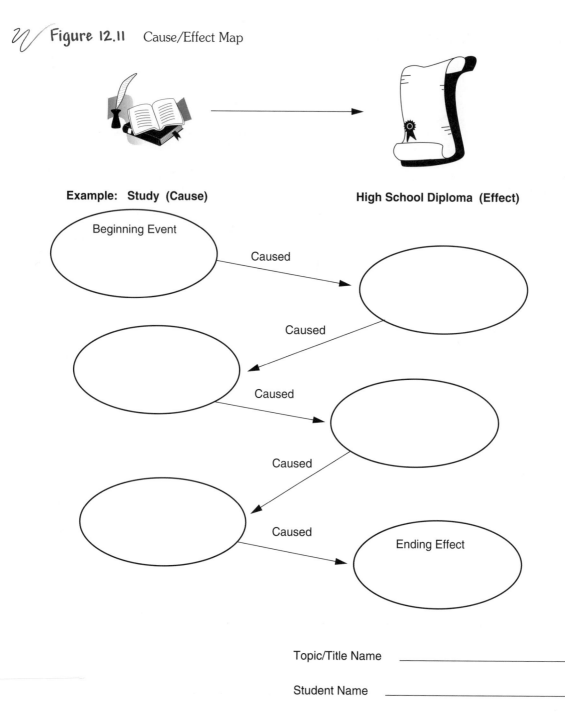

Figure 12.11 Cause/Effect Map

Example: Study (Cause)   **High School Diploma (Effect)**

Beginning Event

Caused

Caused

Caused

Caused

Caused

Ending Effect

Topic/Title Name _____

Student Name _____

𝒲 **Figure 12.12**   Persuasion by Point/Counterpoint Map

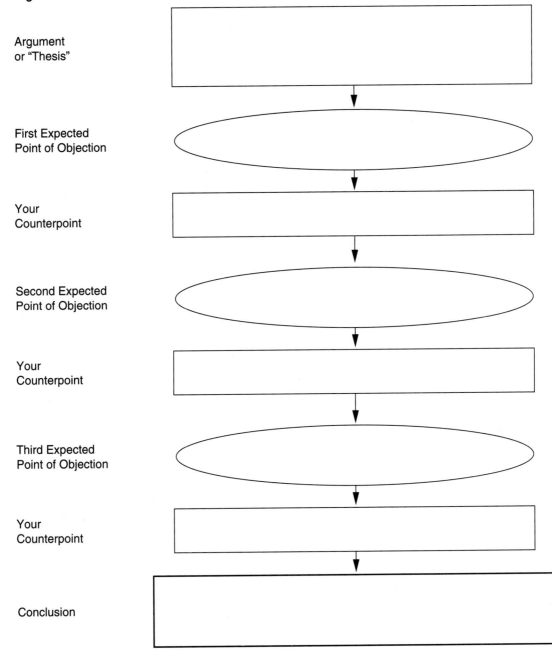

Argument
or "Thesis"

First Expected
Point of Objection

Your
Counterpoint

Second Expected
Point of Objection

Your
Counterpoint

Third Expected
Point of Objection

Your
Counterpoint

Conclusion

Figure 12.13 Turning Point Map

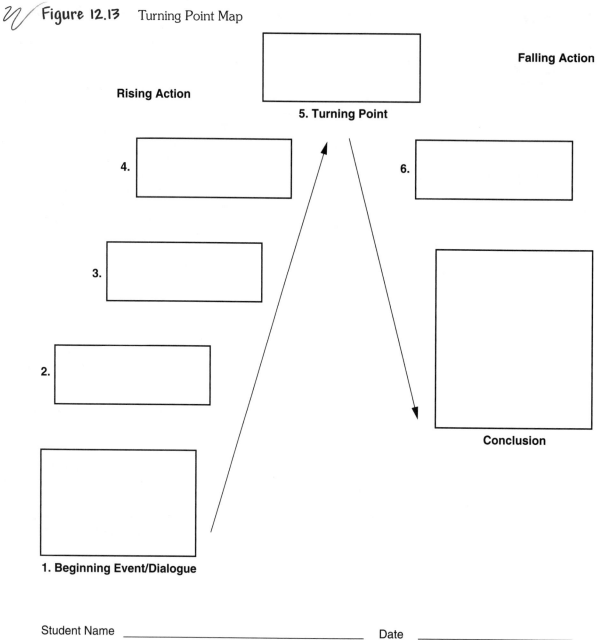

Rising Action

Falling Action

5. Turning Point

4.

6.

3.

2.

Conclusion

1. Beginning Event/Dialogue

Student Name _____ Date _____

Type of Map	Type of Text Structure	Type of Higher Order Thinking
Steps-in-a-Process	Time-related events with multiple episodes and/or a sequence of events, as with many science process steps or social studies events.	Students must be able to select and sequence events, describing processes in order. All are based on the student's ability to locate appropriate information sources.
Compare/Contrast *and* **Same/Different**	Comparison information structures found in many expository texts, particularly in the sciences, literature, social studies, health, and mathematics.	Often inferential or implied in texts, comparison requires students to identify qualities of sameness and differences. Thus, this activity provides a logical framework for identifying and using library/media resources.
Chain of Events	Causal patterns found in the text descriptions, most often the sciences, literature, and social studies.	Identification of causal events that trigger an (often predictable) outcome.
Persuasion by Point/Counterpoint	Derived typically from literature, social studies, and studies of the arts.	Identification of problems or issues, location of information to support a thesis/belief/judgment, charting opposing views, and formulating counterarguments in support of the thesis.
Turning Point Map	Useful primarily with literature and history texts.	Students are required to detect important events in sequence that contribute to a final outcome.

Note that students may be helped or "coached" by teachers to locate additional research materials or data bases to complete the map(s). In the end, it may be concluded that the construction of maps can indeed help students construct their own comprehension of the topic under study. Sinatra et al. (1998) urged teachers, as a next step, to challenge students to develop their own maps to represent new units of study, then present them to the class or group.

SELECTED REFERENCES

Bryan, J. (1998). K-W-W-L: Questioning the known. *The Reading Teacher, 51*(7), 618–620.

Caverly, D. C., & Orlando, V. P. (1991). Textbook strategies. In R. F. Filippo & D. C. Caverly (Eds.), *Teaching reading and study strategies at the college level* (pp. 86–165). Newark, DE: International Reading Association.

Chase, R. (1948). *Grandfather tales.* Boston: Houghton Mifflin.

Cooter, K. S., & Thomas, M. (1998). *Venn diagram hula hoops.* Unpublished manuscript. Texas Christian University, Fort Worth, TX.

Cooter, R. B., & Flynt, E. S. (1996). *Teaching reading in the content areas: Developing content literacy for all students.* New York: John Wiley & Sons.

De la Paz, S. (1999). Self-regulated strategy instruction in regular education settings: Improving outcomes for students with and without learning disabilities. *Learning Disabilities Research & Practice, 14*(2), 92–106.

Langer, J. (1981). From theory to practice: A prereading plan. *Journal of Reading, 25,* 152–156.

Merkley, D. M., & Jeffries, D. (2001). Guidelines for implementing graphic organizers. *The Reading Teacher, 54*(4), 350–357.

Morgan, R. F., Meeks, J., Schollaert, A., & Paul, J. (1986). *Critical reading/thinking skills for the college student.* Dubuque, IA: Kendall/Hunt.

Ogle, D. (1986). K-W-L: A teaching model that develops active reading of expository text. *The Reading Teacher, 39*(6), 564–570.

Orlando, V. P. (1986). Training students to use a modified version of SQ3R: An instructional strategy. *Reading World, 20,* 65–70.

Palmatier, R. A. (1973). A notetaking system for learning. *Journal of Reading, 17,* 36–39.

Pauk, W. (2000). *How to study in college.* Boston: Houghton Mifflin.

Readence, J. E., Bean, T. W., & Baldwin, R. S. (2000). *Content area reading: An integrated approach.* Dubuque, IA: Kendall/Hunt.

Robinson, F. P. (1946). *Effective study.* New York: Harper Brothers.

Sinatra, R. (1997). *Inner-city games CAMP-US: Literacy training manual.* St. John's University, New York.

Sinatra, R., Gemake, J., Wielan, O. P., & Sinatra, C. (1998). *Teaching learners to think, read, and write more effectively.* The 1998 ASCD Annual Conference (March 23, 1998). San Antonio, TX.

Stahl, N. A., & Henk, W. A. (1986). Tracing the roots of textbook study systems: An extended historical perspective. In J. A. Niles & R. V. Lalik (Eds.), *Solving problems in literacy: Learners, teachers, and researchers.* Thirty-fifth yearbook of the National Reading Conference (pp. 336–374). Rochester, NY: National Reading Conference.

Swanson, P. N., & De la Paz, S. (1998). Teaching effective comprehension strategies to students. *Intervention in School & Clinic, 33*(4), 209–218.

Chapter 13

Writing and Reading

Ms. Kathy, as her fourth graders know her, has begun teaching her students strategies for comparing and contrasting two stories. She has already done a considerable amount of modeling for the students, as well as several days of guided practice with the students working in pairs. Ms. Kathy is convinced that her students are ready to move into some individual practice sessions (with her "waiting in the wings" to help when necessary). She showed the students how to use a comparison grid to chart out similarities and differences, then use the grid to write a brief summary comparing and contrasting the two narratives. In other words, she has been gradually releasing responsibility to her young charges and is pleased with their progress.

"Girls and boys, we are now ready to practice our new compare-and-contrast skills on our own so that I can see how each of you is progressing individually. Here is what I want you to do. First, complete this blank comparison grid I am distributing for the two movies we have just seen together: *Shrek* and *The Grinch Who Stole Christmas*. We will, as we have done before, compare and contrast the two stories in terms of main character, setting, the character's main problem, ways he tries to solve the problem, and the resolution of each story. This should be fun!

"After you finish your grid, please come see me for a miniconference before you begin writing your summary, just in case I have any questions. Is everyone with me? Okay, let's rock 'n' roll."

Reading and writing are two sides of the same coin, or, put another way, they are *reflections* of the same language process (Squire, 1983). Reading is a *receptive* language process in that the reader *receives* the message of a writer for mental processing. Writing, however, is a *productive* language process in that the author is *producing* a message to be interpreted later by a reader. Reading and writing are even more closely linked than one might think initially, however. This point is further examined later in this chapter in a discussion on teacher knowledge base. In addition, the chapter focuses on specific ways of measuring writing development. Further, it includes suggestions for activities that help simultaneously foster the strengthening of reading and writing processes.

BACKGROUND BRIEFING FOR TEACHERS

Reading and writing are reciprocal processes (Shanahan, 1984): when teachers build students' skills in one process, the other tends to be strengthened, as well. For example, when students act in the role of writer, they also act as readers, because writers read and reread during writing. Similarly, when students read, they often notice and learn aspects of writing from the author, such as writing styles, interesting phrases, ways to write dialogue, new vocabulary, and methods of punctuation. Lucy Calkins (1994) stated that one of the great benefits of writing process instruction for students is that it helps them feel like "insiders" or peers with their favorite authors. Tompkins (1999), in summarizing research pertaining to reading-writing connections, concluded:

> Reading and writing are both meaning-making processes, and experience with one process provides a scaffold or framework to support the learning of the other. . . . Frank Smith (1983) reminds us that, in order for students to be writers, they must read like writers. (p. 2)

ASSESSING WRITING DEVELOPMENT

At least two writing assessment perspectives are commonly thought of when analyzing student compositions: qualitative (also known as descriptive) and quantitative (also known as numerical). Each will be briefly described, along with other ideas and an instrument useful in writing assessment.

QUALITATIVE ASSESSMENT

Qualitative assessments use written summaries rather than numbers in assessing student work samples. Descriptive assessment is anecdotal in nature, meaning that teachers make "field notes" on a student's work during classroom writing activities, which are later placed into the student's portfolio. Additionally, teachers summarize their impressions of student writing samples gathered during learning experiences. By accumulating informal classroom observations and analyses of writing samples over time, teachers develop a more complete picture of students' development in writing.

Purpose

Teachers compile written observations and interpretations of student accomplishments in writing that may be used in conjunction with other pieces of assessment evidence (i.e., quantitative measures) to form a more complete understanding of students' writing development.

Materials

Materials needed are a legal pad for notetaking by the teacher and student work samples.

Procedure

It is very difficult to describe in specific terms how best to carry out this form of assessment; nevertheless, we do have a few suggestions to offer based on our own experiences. Qualitative assessments are based on a thorough understanding of writing development coupled with classroom experience. Many teachers accustomed to performing qualitative writing assessments in their classrooms try to identify two students per day whom they will observe during writing activities (do not alert these students that they are the ones being studied). This permits most teachers to observe each student about once every two weeks or so. At the end of the day the teacher reviews the classroom observations, along with work samples collected by students in their writing folders, and attempts to draw some conclusions as to students' development.

Writing development may be said to encompass several broad abilities, including the capacity to transmit messages effectively and an understanding of the basic mechanics of writing. In the first aspect of writing development, students gain an understanding of the writing process: prewriting, drafting, revising, editing, and sharing or publishing. The mechanics of writing involve such aspects as spelling, punctuation, and appropriate use of reference materials. Of course, students' relative ability in each of these areas varies a great deal and is, by definition, developmental (one gets better at these skills with practice). The best advice we can offer is for teachers to read extensively about the writing process, then meet with colleagues to develop a kind of writing development checklist(s) to help in monitoring student progress. We find that Gail Tompkins' (1999) book, titled *Teaching Writing: Balancing Process and Product,* is an excellent resource for gaining basic information about the writing process and for developing writing observation checklists.

QUANTITATIVE ASSESSMENT: HOLISTIC SCORING

Quantitative assessments use numbers rather than words to describe student development and performance in writing. There are at least two forms of quantitative assessment: *holistic* and *analytic.* These two forms are closely related, with the chief difference being that holistic scoring seems to work best with a single criterion, whereas analytic scoring is intended for multiple criteria. In all instances, students should understand the assessment criteria for which they are being held accountable.

Purpose

The purpose of this assessment is to develop relatively objective measures of writing products using a numerical system.

Materials

An assessment form that includes a numerical scale for each criterion and student work samples, such as that shown in Figure 13.1, will be helpful.

Figure 13.1 Sample Holistic Scoring Form for Writing: Single Criterion

| Student name: _____ |
| Date: _____ |

Criterion:

	Not used				Used a great deal
Temporary (invented) spellings: Beginning and ending sounds	1	2	3	4	5

Comments/observations:

Procedure

Probably the most convenient way to conduct a quantitative assessment is for teachers to first construct an assessment instrument. This makes the process much more time efficient when trying to review more than one work sample. Because only one criterion is being assessed, all that is required is a place for the student's name, date, the criterion specified, and a numerical scale (usually 1 to 5) to rate student performance using the writing skill. In *group settings,* we recommend that teachers read all of the student compositions once without grading to get a feel for the range of development in the class before assigning numerical values to each paper.

Figure 13.1 shows an example of an assessment form for emergent writers in a first-grade classroom, focusing on students' use of temporary spellings (also called *invented spellings*) with at least beginning and ending sounds.

QUANTITATIVE ASSESSMENT: ANALYTIC SCORING

Analytic scoring methods are essentially holistic scoring systems for *multiple* criteria. Analytic scoring systems add a "weight" dimension for each criterion being measured, because the criteria tend to be of unequal value. For example, let's say a fifth-grade teacher has been teaching minilessons on using commas correctly, developing characters more fully in student-created stories, and completing a *prewriting outline* or *web* before writing a first draft. Let's also assume that, in this instance, the teacher feels that correct usage of commas is not quite as important (or as challenging) as is developing characters more fully. Further, if the teacher feels that developing characters more fully is more important than completing a prewriting outline or web (perhaps because her students have been creating webs and outlines since second grade, and the focus on characters is a newly introduced skill), then the weighting used in scoring a work sample will reflect that priority, as well. In any event, it is *easy* to see that the teacher feels that certain writing skills are somewhat more important or challenging than others.

When multiple criteria are being used in writing assessment, the teacher usually assigns a weighted value of 1 to the least important skill, 2 for the more important skill, and 3 for the next most important skill. As mentioned previously, the numerical scale frequently ranges from a low rate of 1 to a high rate of 5. Thus, for our example, the following assigned weights would apply:

Writing Skill/Criteria	Relative Weight or Value
Using commas correctly	1
Developing characters more fully	3
Prewriting outline or web	2

These teacher-determined weights are to be multiplied by the holistic scoring value (1–5) arrived at in the same way as described in the previous section on holistic scoring for a single criterion (i.e., a score of 1 to 5 is given based on the quality of the student's work on that criterion, say using commas correctly). Figure 13.2 presents an assessment form based on the above example. (Note that the figure for "Total possible points" (30) is arrived at by first multiplying the maximum possible score of 5 for each skill by the weighted value, then adding the total possible scores [5 + 10 + 15 = 30]).

Figure 13.2 Analytic Writing Assessment Form Using Three Criteria

Student name: _____
Date: _____

Criteria

	Not used				Used a great deal		Weighted value		Total points
Using commas correctly	1	2	3	4	5	×	1	=	_____
Developing characters more fully	1	2	3	4	5	×	3	=	_____
Prewriting outline or web	1	2	3	4	5	×	2	=	_____

A. Total points for assignment   _____

B. Total possible points   30

C. Percentage of points achieved (A divided by B)   _____

Comments/observations:

OTHER ACTIVITIES FOR ASSESSING READING-WRITING CONNECTIONS

In addition to the quantitative and qualitative strategies mentioned previously, the following activities have value as both assessment and writing activities. These activities remind us that good assessment is frequently synonymous with good teaching.

STORY PYRAMIDS

An activity popularized by teachers in the Rio Grande Valley area of south Texas is the *story pyramid*. It combines the use of story grammars as a means for assessing reading comprehension in narrative passages with writing (vocabulary knowledge) assessment. Story pyramids are interesting and simple to use, yet powerful in their assessment potential.

Purpose

The assessment purpose of story pyramids is twofold. First, they require students to recall key information from stories using a modified story grammar scheme (main character, setting, problem, attempts to solve the problem, and solution). Next, students are asked to survey their vocabulary knowledge to find just the right word or words to report the story grammar information in the pyramid.

Materials

The materials needed include paper and pen or pencil, one sheet of poster board, and a narrative book recently read by the student.

Procedure

Teachers usually create a poster or bulletin board depicting a pyramid. It should show the required information needed in a story pyramid and an example based on a book shared during a read-aloud experience. The following information and pattern for writing are used in the story pyramid:

Line 1:   One word for who the story is about (main character)
Line 2:   Two words describing the main character
Line 3:   Three words describing the setting
Line 4:   Four words stating the problem
Line 5:   Five words describing an event in the story
Line 6:   Six words describing an event in the story
Line 7:   Seven words describing an event in the story
Line 8:   Eight words describing the final solution

This activity not only assesses reading comprehension and vocabulary knowledge, but also encourages economy of language when students compose.

FLIP MOVIES

Using *flip movies* is an activity suggested for assessing students' understanding of a book by having them illustrate and bind a series of scenes together from a story. Flipping through the scenes quickly simulates the action (Pike, Compain, & Mumper, 1997). In our version of this activity, students create a series of pictures and captions that summarize a key story event. Flipping through the book quickly simulates scrolling text that retells part of the story.

Purpose

Flip movies assess students' ability to retell key events in a story using written captions matched to illustrations.

Materials

The student will need a book that she read recently. In addition, you will need to collect the following art materials in order for students to make flip movies:

- Index cards (5" × 8")
- Writing and illustrating materials
- Drawing paper cut to a rectangular pattern of about 3" × 8"
- Access to a photocopier machine
- Book-binding tape or a heavy-duty stapler

Procedure

Students begin by choosing a key event in a story that they read recently. Next, they create a single illustration of the setting and characters depicting this key event. The illustration should not be colored in at first, but created to look much like an uncolored coloring book page on a single sheet of 3" × 8" paper. On a separate sheet of paper (this can be a "messy copy") the student should write a caption that describes the key event. For example, a student who read *The Polar Express* (Van Allsburg, 1985) might draw an illustration depicting the child in the story receiving a bell from Santa's sleigh at the North Pole. Perhaps the caption reads "Santa handed the sleigh bell to me!" Next, take the single uncolored illustration and make the same number of photocopies of the illustration as there are words in the caption. (In our example, the teacher would make seven copies of the student's illustration, because there are seven words in the caption). The copies of the illustration are then given to the student so that the final phase can be completed.

Next, students carefully trim each photocopy of the illustration to match the size of the original (3" × 8") and color each one as desired, making sure to use the same color scheme on each photocopy to produce identical copies. Next, glue each illustration to the upper portion of 5" × 8" index cards so that the student now has multiple identical copies of the illustration mounted on index cards. On the first card, the student writes only the *first* word in the caption. She writes the first *two words* of the caption on the second card, the first *three words* of the caption on the third card, and so on. After this process is complete and the cards have been bound together using binding tape or heavy-duty staples, the pages in the flip book can be slowly thumbed through so that the text appears to scroll out across the bottom of the page word by word until the full sentence has appeared. Older students may want to alter this activity, slightly changing the illustrations so that the flipping action simulates movement in the illustration.

COAT-HANGER MOBILES

Coat-hanger mobiles are easy to construct and are an inventive way to combine reader response with writing. Students create illustrations and captions depicting important bits of information from a book they have read. Then, as a form of "publishing," these information bits are displayed on a common coat hanger that is hung from the ceiling as a mobile in the classroom. Coat-hanger mobiles work well with both narrative and expository texts.

Purpose

This activity is useful as a quick assessment of key ideas understood by the student after reading, and as an indirect assessment of descriptive vocabulary in writing (likewise, the acquisition of technical vocabulary in expository books).

Materials

A coat-hanger mobile can be constructed using a wire coat hanger (preferably one that has been coated in colored plastic), string or dark thread, a sheet of poster or tag board, assorted color markers for illustrating and writing captions, and a book that the child has recently read.

Procedure

Using the poster board, ask the student to create at least five illustrations and captions representing key ideas or events found in the book she has recently completed. Students often like to make the illustrations in the shapes of characters, settings, or objects that pertain to the book. Remind them that they will need to illustrate both sides of each shape so that, as the mobile turns, the illustration can be read from any direction. Have students attach each illustration/caption to their coat hanger using thread or string, as shown in Figure 13.3. Once it is completed, hang the mobile from the ceiling or from a light fixture.

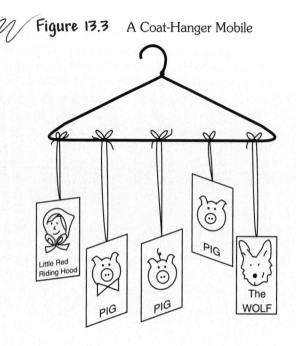

Figure 13.3   A Coat-Hanger Mobile

A Checklist for Middle School Writing Programs

Checklists help teachers maximize the efficiency of their contact time with students because of the checklist's built-in organization and structure. You should be aware, however, that, although checklists may be useful in many situations, they are certainly no panacea in writing assessment. In fact, they have somewhat limited use. But, Gail Tompkins (1999), in her book *Teaching Writing: Balancing Process and Product,* offers a number of checklists that we believe teachers will find useful. In this section, we offer an adaptation of a Tompkins checklist that can be of general use in the middle school.

Purpose

This activity is intended for the assessment of student compositions in order to review understanding of stages of the writing process.

Materials

A copy of the writing process checklist shown in Figure 13.4 is needed.

Procedure

As the teacher reviews samples kept in students' writing folders, she notes on the checklist evidence of the various writing process activities. Many teachers also note dates when different writing process activities were done. The result is that teachers can determine which writing process activities are being used by class members and which are not. Thus, the teacher can identify the writing skills that may be needed by some or all of the class members. Figure 13.4 offers a general form for this purpose.

Figure 13.4 Writing Process Checklist Form

Writing Process Checklist: Middle School

Name: _____

Date of writing folder review: _____

Title(s) of compositions: _____

Writing Process Stages and Activities

PREWRITING

1. Student develops a list of possible topics that are of high interest to him.

2. An organizational web or outline is constructed.

3. Student conducts research to gather necessary facts and information.

DRAFTING

4. Student produces one or more drafts before the final version.

5. Drafts are double- or triple-spaced to allow for editorial comments.

6. Evidence demonstrates that the student is more interested in ideas and content, rather than mechanics at this stage.

REVISING

7. Student shares the composition with others to obtain useful suggestions.

8. A new draft of the paper is generated incorporating suggestions offered by peers.

EDITING

9. Student again reviews composition, looking for ways to improve the mechanics of the piece (e.g., spelling, punctuation, etc.).

10. After improvements have been made mechanically, the student meets with the teacher for a writing conference.

SHARING

11. Student produces a final copy suitable for sharing.

12. An appropriate way of sharing the piece is chosen and carried out (e.g., author's chair, publication area in classroom or library, publishing in the school newspaper, others as appropriate).

Source: Adapted from *Teaching Writing: Balancing Process and Product* by G. E. Tompkins, 2000, Upper Saddle River, NJ: Merrill/Prentice Hall.

CONNECTING ASSESSMENT FINDINGS TO TEACHING STRATEGIES

Before moving on to specific research strategies, we have constructed a guide connecting assessment findings to teaching strategies. It is our intention to help you select the most appropriate instructional interventions and strategies to meet your students' needs based on assessment data. This is in keeping with the "If-Then" mode of thinking we discussed in chapter 2. Teaching strategies described in the next section are listed across the top of the guide. Potential problems are listed vertically in the left-hand column.

TEACHING STRATEGIES

We begin this part of the chapter with a presentation of ideas that could be called **interactive writing.** The idea is for the teacher to demonstrate new ideas about writing for learners in their zones of proximal development; ideas that bridge the reading and writing processes and help students grow in each language area. We begin with a very flexible method of writing instruction known as *Writing Aloud, Writing TO,* followed by activities that fit nicely into this paradigm. Later, we describe other activities that make writing connections with books and other texts for students followed by bookmaking ideas.

WRITING ALOUD, WRITING TO: A WAY OF STRUCTURING YOUR TEACHING

In *read-aloud* activities, teachers share books orally with students and use read-aloud sessions as opportunities to model such reading essentials as comprehension strategies and decoding skills. *Writing Aloud, Writing TO* (Cooter, 2002) is an adaptation of Routman's (1995) technique for getting students' attention and demonstrating various aspects of the writing process. *Writing Aloud, Writing TO* has been used with great success in The Dallas Reading Plan, a massive teacher education project in Texas, which has resulted in significant improvement in student writing and reading achievement levels. The "Writing TO" part of *Writing Aloud, Writing TO* comes from the notion of Writing TO, WITH, and BY; in a comprehensive writing program of instruction, teachers should engage daily in writing TO students (demonstrations and minilessons); writing WITH students (guided practice sessions where students implement new writing skills with the help of the teacher or a more skilled peer), and writing BY students (independent writing sessions where students practice their newly acquired skills).

The materials you will use depend greatly on the kinds of writing strategies you plan to model. In general, we like to use an overhead projector, transparencies, screen, and erasable markers for writing demonstrations with groups, or a large tablet on an easel. If it is a demonstration involving the computer, then it is usually best to do *Writing Aloud, Writing TO* sessions in small groups, unless you have access to a computer projection system.

As with materials, the strategies you will employ will be based on the writing/reading connections you will emphasize. Routman (1995) and Cooter (2002) did, however, provide us with some useful tips to remember for *Writing Aloud, Writing TO.*

- In *Writing Aloud, Writing To,* the teacher thinks aloud while writing in front of the students.

Intervention Strategy Guide for Writing and Reading

Student Problem(s) ↓ / Intervention Strategy →	Morning Message	Daily News	T-Shirts Etc.	Travels Class Mascot	Sell-A-Bration	Movie Rev.	Caps. Guide	Illus. Craft	Class. Characters	Fairy Tales	Feature Story	Resp.-Pict. Books	Pop-Ups	Accord. Books	Innov. Books
Emergent Writer	+	+	−	*	*	−	−	*	*	*	*	+	+	+	*
Written Correspondence	+	+	−	+	−	−	−	*	*	*	−	−	−	−	*
Spelling	+	+	*	+	*	+	*	−	+	*	+	*	+	+	+
Decoding	*	*	*	*	*	*	−	*	*	*	+	*	*	*	+
Comprehension-Narrative	−	−	−	−	−	*	+	−	+	+	−	+	+	+	+
Comprehension-Expository	−	*	−	*	*	−	+	*	−	−	+	+	+	+	+
Motivation	+	+	+	+	+	+	+	+	+	+	+	+	+	+	+

Key: + excellent strategy
 * adaptable strategy
 − unsuitable strategy

Figure 13.5   Writing Aloud, Writing TO

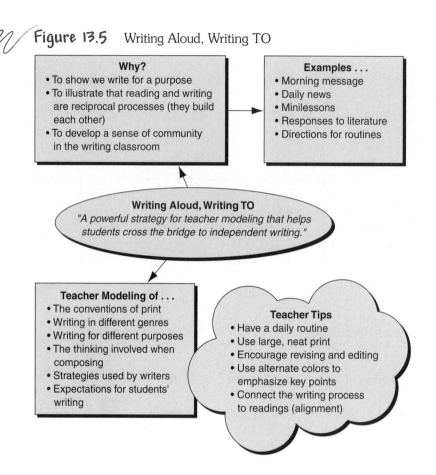

- Students watch the teacher as he writes, and sometimes read aloud with the teacher, as the teacher says explicitly what he is doing. This may include the writer's thinking processes, format that has been chosen and why, layout of the piece, spacing, handwriting, spelling, punctuation, and discussion of vocabulary.
- Teachers help students relate the spoken word to the written word at all times.
- The teacher often asks questions that relate to the conventions of writing or features of text.

A graphic was prepared for the Dallas Reading Academy (Cooter, 2002) that summarizes key elements of *Writing Aloud, Writing To* based on the work of Regie Routman (1995). It is shown in Figure 13.5.

Morning Message

Purpose

Another Writing TO activity that is basic to reading/writing instruction is the *Morning Message* (Cooter, 2002). The teacher writes about what will be happening that day in terms of schedule or activities, or about what will be happening in the teacher's or students' lives. Morning Message is inherently motivational and provides an excellent opportunity for students to learn new reading skills. The whole activity takes from five to seven minutes and

Figure 13.6   Morning Message

> Monday, January 15, 200_
>
> Dear Second Grade,
>
> Today will be an exciting day at Robert Spencer Elementary School. At 10 o'clock Easy Reader will come to our school and tell stories. He will come on his motorcycle and bring his favorite books!
>
> Yesterday, we learned that Toby Benson's mother is going to have a baby in August. He is very excited that he will soon have a baby brother or sister.
>
> Let's make this a great day.
>
> Your friend,

is a great way to reinforce skill lessons such as spelling conventions, punctuation tips, grammar rules, capitalization, and any parts of the writing process you may want to emphasize (Routman, 1995). An example is provided in Figure 13.6.

Materials

Morning Message is usually done at a reserved section of the chalkboard, or on large chart paper and easel. If using chart paper, we recommend picking up some highlighter tape and various colored markers.

Procedure

The teacher does the following during Morning Message:

1. Teachers should think aloud while writing the message. Students observe the writing procedures and may be invited to read along with the teacher aloud.

2. If you are working with emergent readers, compose the messages orally before writing. Demonstrate rereading to confirm that you have written what you intended (sometimes make deliberate errors to create "teachable moments"). This is also an opportune time to demonstrate strategies like "word rubber banding"—stretching out the sounds of a spoken word to hear phonemes and match appropriate letters. Students can also be helped to attend to conventions of print such as leaving spaces and rereading with finger pointing to illustrate a one-to-one match.

3. Teachers should be aware of group needs and model something noticed recently in the writing of students. For example, if students are struggling with the use of some homonyms (e.g., there-their), include these words in the Morning Message and mention in passing how you knew which word to use.

4. After the message is written and read together, take a few minutes to ask questions and familiarize students with the conventions of writing you have used. Ask students to explain the reasons for the conventions used, such as

   Why did I capitalize _____?   *What do you notice about _____?*
   Why did I use a comma here?   *Why did I begin a new paragraph here?*

Figure 13.7   Morning Message Innovation: A Skill Message

September 1, 200_

Dear Students,

Yesterday I had to shovel snow from my driveway for three hours. Then I conk<u>ed</u> out!

look<u>ed</u>   crash<u>ed</u>

help<u>ed</u>   walk<u>ed</u>

stack<u>ed</u>   play<u>ed</u>

---

5. After emergent readers "read" the Morning Message together, have students locate certain letters and words. Highlighter tape is great to use for this exercise when chart paper is used for Morning Message.

INNOVATIONS ON THE MORNING MESSAGE

Morning Message Innovation 1: Skill Messages

Create a "planned" *Skill Message* to highlight a particular word structure or phonic element. The bottom of the chart can be used as a kind of minilesson. Do Skill Messages on chart paper so that you can post them around the classroom as reminders. See the example in Figure 13.7.

Morning Message Innovation 2: Modified Cloze Messages

Modify the Morning Message using a kind of cloze technique that suits your instructional purpose. For example, you can modify a message to emphasize endings (-ed, -s, -ing), beginning sounds, ending sounds, and so forth. See Figure 13.8 for an example.

 Figure 13.8   Modified Cloze Morning Message (Endings)

<u>Directions: Look for words needing the following endings: -s, -es, -ed, -ing.</u>

October 3, 200_

Dear Girl_and Boy_,

I am excit__ about go____ to the zoo on Friday. It will be a little frighten____when we see the lion_, tiger_, and snake_!

We must all remember to bring our lunch__ so we can have a picnic at the zoo.

See you on Friday!

‍// **Figure 13.9**   The Mystery Message

> Ja__ kept climb___ th_ _ean st___ and t_king things fr__ __e gi__t. He g_t a sing___
>
> h__p, and a__n th__ l__s gold__ e_g_.

Morning Message Innovation 3: The Mystery Message

As a variation of Innovation 2 (see Figure 13.9), have students complete and submit in writing a summary of a story the children have just read or heard. See who is a good detective!

DAILY NEWS STORY

Purpose

The *Daily News Story* provides an opportunity for the class to discuss what is news to them and then record the information in a newspaper format. Some teachers like to glue a real newspaper front page header (i.e., *The Los Angeles Times, The Dallas Morning News, The Chicago Tribune,* and so on) to the chart paper used for writing the story.

Materials

Chart paper on an easel, newspaper front page headers from your local newspaper, and markers are all you will need.

Procedure

Introduce the activity by showing a newspaper and talking about how a newspaper tells us what is happening in our world. Give examples of what is news, such as someone's birthday, a visiting relative, guest speakers for the class, holiday activities, and so forth. Share some of your own special "news" as a model for the class.

The class may want to begin by talking about an event they have shared together, or by using the activity as a way to share personal news. After students have shared ideas for a while, the teacher should choose one or two topics that have been shared and begin writing sentences on the chart paper, saying each word as she writes. The teacher should "think aloud" as she writes to emphasize important new skills such as capitalizing the first letter of a person's name, matching letters to phonemes, and punctuation. Just don't overdo thinking aloud or the purpose of writing (constructing meaningful sentences in a fluid manner) will be lost.

We like to ask two students to illustrate the Daily News during center time. The requirements are that the illustration must match the message and fill up the space allotted. Display the story for students to read during the week as an ongoing vocabulary review. Also, you may want to type up the news stories at your computer and print copies of the text for students to take home each Friday for home review and practice. See Figure 13.10 for an example of the Daily News Story.

Figure 13.10 Daily News Story

The Nashville Tennessean		
Volume 1, No. 35	November 30, 200_	Free

Today is Thursday and we learned that Arnot's family got a new car. It is a station wagon, and it is blue. Arnot likes to ride in the very back and look out the rear window.

T-Shirts and Tapestries

Students love to make their own T-shirts and tapestries that display something of interest to the student (Pike et al., 1997). T-shirts and tapestries are easy to construct and can relate to such things as a student's soccer team, club memberships, favorite book characters, musical groups, or family members. Also, they are great for students who enjoy creating illustrations to accent their writing. Because the text that can appear on either a t-shirt or tapestry is limited by space, students must work with teachers to discover just the right words and thus to develop brevity in written communications.

Purpose

Making t-shirts or tapestries that include illustrations and captions helps students develop brevity in written communications. This activity may also be linked to the usage of such writing tools as the dictionary and thesaurus.

Materials

The materials needed include a plain white T-shirt in the student's size or a sheet of cloth suitable for a tapestry, as well as fabric crayons, paints, or liquid embroidery.

Procedure

It is best to begin by having students develop a diagram of their T-shirt or tapestry on paper. The usual steps in the writing process are quite helpful (prewriting, drafting, revising, editing). If this activity is used in a classroom setting, students should be encouraged to take part in peer conferences to share and refine their ideas.

Once the idea has been finalized and approved by the teacher, walk through the steps in creating T-shirt designs or tapestries. If a family member is available who has artistic expertise, by all means put him or her to work teaching the student(s) art skills! Finally, students use the liquid embroidery, fabric crayons, or paints to create their final products, as shown in Figure 13.11. "Publishing" is accomplished as students wear their T-shirts or display their tapestries in a place of honor.

Travels of Your Favorite Stuffed Animal (or Class Mascot)

A popular idea with early elementary students, this activity encourages students to write a story about the adventures (usually the student's own experiences that day) of their favorite stuffed animal through the school day, or of a class mascot on an imaginary adventure (Wiseman, 1992).

Figure 13.11   Student-Made T-Shirt

Purpose

The idea is to encourage students to write a creative composition about an imaginary journey or adventure taken by a stuffed animal.

Materials

In order to create an example for students to see, we recommend that you obtain a copy of the book *The Velveteen Rabbit* (Williams, 1922, 1958) and a stuffed animal—preferably one that is showing signs of wear—or a class mascot in the form of a stuffed animal.

Materials needed include the usual writing materials favored by students (markers and crayons), as well as magazine pictures, word cards, picture dictionary, index cards, lined and unlined paper, tape, stapler, paper clips, rubber bands, and scissors.

Procedure

Begin by reading and discussing *The Velveteen Rabbit* with student(s). Talk about how stuffed animals often seem real to us and how it is fun to fantasize about how our stuffed friends might have real adventures. Bring in a stuffed toy to serve as a class mascot (Wiseman, 1992), such as a teddy bear, and talk about how students could write stories about him—either real-life situations that may take place at school or fictitious adventures we might choose to create, like the author of *The Velveteen Rabbit* did. You might wish to choose a stuffed friend that is in some disrepair. For example, if an eye is missing, ask the children to create a story about how that could have happened.

Using a large tablet on an easel, begin an outline of the story the children are helping to generate, which will then be fashioned into a story following a kind of language experience format. Next, ask the children to bring in stuffed animals of their own on the following day to write about and share with the class. If a child does not have a stuffed animal, then let her use the class mascot. Completed stories, along with the associated stuffed animal friends, can be displayed in the classroom or school library as part of the publishing process.

2// Figure 13.12   Comparison Grid: Persuasive Writing/Propaganda Types and Examples

Prop.type/ Example	Cigarette ads	Sports car ads	Political ads	Student's choice
Image makers	Cowboys; athletic-looking people	Racing image; sexy, etc.	Fight-for-right image	
Bandwagon	"Liberated women do it!"	"Join the 'new generation'"	"Come along with us and elect _____."	
Testimonial	(No longer used)	Famous NASCAR racers	Person-on-the-street testimonials	
Plain folks	Farmers, cowboys, soldiers	Not appropriate to image desired	"I'm just a country lawyer...."	
Name comparisons	"If you *like* Marlboro, then you'll *love*...."	"Audi outperforms Porsche and BMW...."	"Like Lincoln, our candidate stands for...."	

SELL-A-BRATION

This activity helps students develop an understanding of persuasive writing (propaganda) strategies used by advertisers through reading and reviewing commercials in print and other media forms, then constructing their own ad campaigns using the writing process.

Purpose

The purpose is to teach students about persuasive writing while also inspiring interest in reading books, magazines, and other text forms they have not previously considered.

Materials

Materials needed include a variety of magazines and newspapers, video clips recorded on VHS/VCR tape from television commercials for popular products, radio commercials recorded on cassette tape, a videocassette recorder/player and television, and a cassette tape player/recorder.

Procedure

Prepare a minilesson about how persuasive writing strategies are used to sell necessities (such as soap, food products, clothing) and nonnecessities (such as computer games, sodas, and designer clothes). Conduct a classroom discussion about specific strategies used in advertising and the common features of each. A comparison grid such as the one shown in Figure 13.12 may be helpful for compare/contrast discussions.

Depending on the age group, you may need to talk about what would or would not be appropriate ways to sell things in your classroom. Some teachers appoint an advertising review committee made up of students who decide whether material is appropriate.

Have students review materials and make notes about the types of advertising strategies used. One strategy sometimes used in persuasive writing involves the use of humor (for instance, TV commercials for the fruit juice Tropicana Twisters, and many of the local commercials for automobile dealerships).

Finally, have students use the writing process to write their own commercials for real or created products. They might also write commercials for their favorite books read during Self-Selected Reading (SSR) periods. The commercials should be presented or performed for the class as a publishing/sharing experience.

Movie Reviews

One fun way for students to practice analytical reading skills and persuasive writing abilities is through *movie reviews*. In this activity, students read movie reviews and learn about writing styles used by critics, then construct reviews of movies they have recently seen.

Purpose

The movie review activity enables students to practice analytical reading skills, summarization abilities, and persuasive writing skills.

Materials

Collect several copies of past movie reviews, usual writing process materials, and blank comparison grids for compare/contrast.

Procedure

Conduct a minilesson series reviewing a current or popular movie that most students will be aware of and for which reviews can be found. In your minilesson, begin by first reviewing and summarizing the story line through discussions with the students. Next, produce several (3 or 4) authentic movie reviews of the selected film that can be read with the class, either using overhead transparencies or photocopies for students. Organize the differing points of view by completing a blank comparison grid on the chalkboard or on an overhead transparency, then discuss different perspectives and writing styles that each critic seems to use. Next, construct a prewriting outline from information contained on the grid. Finally, draft a new movie review of your own, mimicking the style of your favorite critic. At the conclusion of the minilessons, have each student write a review of a film that he or she has recently seen. The reviews can be displayed on a bulletin board dedicated to the cinema or compiled in a special edition class newspaper.

Capsulization Guides (Summarization)

In this activity, students create their own stories from brief, teacher-created summaries of short books called *capsulization guides* (Gauthier, 1989). Students then read the actual stories and compare.

Purpose

Using capsulization guides helps students learn and practice summarization and writing process skills.

Materials

Writing process materials, short books that the class has not heard before, and teacher- or student-generated capsulation guides are the essential materials for this activity.

Procedure

Step 1: *Choose a story or other form of text and write a summary or "capsuliza-tion guide."* Select a relatively short story or other text type (such as a non-fiction piece pertaining to science or social studies) and write a brief summary (also known as a capsulization guide) about the piece. For example, for the story *Gila Monsters Meet You at the Airport* (Sharmat, 1980), your cap-sulization guide might read: "A boy from New York City is moving to the West with his family. He talks about all the bad things he has imagined about the West and why he won't like living there." The capsulization guide may be writ-ten either by the teacher or, better yet, by another student from a different class or grade level. Once you have done this activity with students, you will begin to build a library of capsulization guides.

Step 2: *Share the capsulization guide with your students and ask them to write a composition.* After reading the capsulization guide with your students, ask them to write their own stories by expanding the information provided in the capsulization guide. Students should be expected to use writing process skills appropriate to their levels.

Step 3: *Have students share their compositions with peers.* Once compositions are completed, ask students to share their works with a group of students in an "author's chair" format or in pairs.

Step 4: *Share the original story or nonfiction text.* Now, read the full text of the original story or nonfiction text to the students. Compare and contrast the compositions that students constructed to the original version and discuss sim-ilarities and differences. For stories (narratives), it might be helpful to use a story grammar comparison grid such as the one shown in Figure 13.13.

Step 5: *Have students write their own capsulization guides.* As a final activity, have students select short books or passages of their own and write capsulization guides. Acting as the teacher, they are then paired with a peer and repeat the cycle above using their own capsulization guides.

WRITING CONNECTIONS WITH BOOKS: DRAWING STUDENTS CLOSER

We know that reading and writing are reciprocal processes and tend to strengthen each other the more the students engage texts, whether as a writer or reader. How can we do more to actually structure learning experiences that capitalize on this reciprocity? In this section, we share some strategies that do just that.

THE ILLUSTRATOR'S CRAFT

The *illustrator's craft* encourages students to read and learn all that they can about a fa-vorite illustrator, to create a composition reporting what they have learned, and then to share their report with the illustrator (optional).

Purpose

The illustrator's craft activity is intended to cause students to read, use the writing process as a summary tool for the investigation, and then share results with peers. Communica-tions with illustrators may also help students see the importance and purposes of letter-writing skills.

Figure 13.13   Story Grammar Comparison Table

	Original story	Your story
Setting		
Characters		
Problem(s)		
Attempts to solve problems		
Conclusion/Resolution		
Theme/Moral		

Materials

Materials needed include several books with the same illustrator, writing materials, addresses of the illustrators (optional), and materials such as markers, paints, and colored pencils for making a diary or journal.

Procedure

Spend time with your students discussing different illustrators and looking at some of their work. Tell an interesting fact about each illustrator you have chosen for these activities, in order to show something of the human side and motivations of the illustrators. For example, Rachel Isadora wrote and illustrated a Caldecott Honor book called *Opening Night* (1984), a story that grew out of her experience as a professional ballerina.

After students select an illustrator about whom they would like to learn more, have them design a portfolio of the illustrator's best work from favorite books. The portfolio might include discussions from the student's perspective as to why this is the illustrator's best work. Students could be creative in their presentation by adding captions to the illustrations or by writing a diary of the illustrator. Students should do some research into the illustrators, exploring how they create their illustrations, settings in which they like to work, and/or what was happening in the world at the time that might have influenced their work. After the portfolio is finished, have students make a copy and send it, along with a letter, to the illustrator.

An alternate version of this activity might be to have students review artwork by older high school students, to find one person's work they like, and then to interview that person. They could also construct a portfolio of the high school student's work and present it to the class.

CLASSROOM CHARACTERS

Classroom characters (Adams, 1991) is a great activity for making writing connections with books and other texts by having students corresponding with a book character whom they are getting to know during a daily read-aloud activity conducted by the teacher. Letters written to the character are mailed using a classroom mailbox, then the character's response comes back the next class meeting either in the form of a letter or through cartoon-like "bubble" responses appearing on a special bulletin board depicting the character.

Purpose

The classroom character activity is intended to interest students in writing and reading through interaction with a classroom character, providing a perceived audience for writing.

Materials

Many teachers use a character-for-the-month who appears in a book the student or class has read, letters and stories from the character to the students (provided secretly by older buddy students or the teacher), a bulletin board featuring an illustration of the character, speech "bubbles" with comments from the character to the students to be displayed each day on a bulletin board depicting the character, and writing materials for the students.

Procedure

Select a character—either from a book just read aloud to the class or a book used in a core book unit (Reutzel & Cooter, 2000)—who will interact with the student(s) each day. Sometimes you may decide to use a character associated with a seasonal or classroom theme, but we prefer to use characters from read-aloud or self-selected books (Keiser, 1991). The character should be displayed on a bulletin board or area on the classroom wall throughout the life of this activity. Students are encouraged to write to the character to find out more about him or her, to leave the character books to read, and to respond to letters or captions on the bulletin board each day "written by the character."

WRITING FAIRY TALES

After careful study of common story grammar patterns found in favorite fairy tales, students write their own fairy tales using these same common patterns. It is an interesting introduction to "formula story writing" that offers students yet another way of making writing connections with books and other texts.

Purpose

Writing a fairy tale helps students to develop an understanding of ways an author creates tales and to apply this knowledge in the construction of one's own tales.

Materials

Materials needed include fairy tales with traditional endings; pictures of a mixing bowl, wooden spoon or spatula, old boxes of baking soda, bags of flour or other ingredients used in baking; writing and illustrating materials; a baker's hat; and an artist's beret.

Procedure

Read aloud two or three fairy tales and discuss their common ingredients. For example, tales usually begin with "Once upon a time . . ." or "Long, long ago . . ." Fairy tales also generally have good and bad characters; many contain a commandment or rule, as well as a punishment for breaking the commandment. Sometimes a key incident occurs three times in fairy tales (three pigs have their homes threatened by the wolf three times). Also, there is often some kind of magic, and most end with a "happily ever after" situation.

Set up a writing center with a picture depicting a mixing bowl and spoons, along with ingredient boxes labeled Beginning, Good Character(s), Bad Character(s), 3 Times, Magic, and Ending. An office tray might be placed at the center with an organizational prewriting form using the same labels. Students visiting the center create their own fairy tales (and can wear a baker's hat, if desired). One could also have an illustrator's center, too, where the authors wear an artist's hat or beret and illustrate compositions on an easel.

WRITING A FEATURE STORY ABOUT A CENTRAL CHARACTER

This activity begins by reading several sensationalized "news" accounts of celebrities and other famous people as portrayed in tabloid publications (such as *The National Inquirer*). Students then choose from their free reading a book character and write newspaper articles (feature stories) about the character (based on Smith & Elliot, 1986). The stories are crafted onto a newspaper front page, complete with illustrations created by the student (or several students working in a group), for a fun and motivating writing experience.

Purpose

In writing a feature story, students construct a literature or expository text response in which a character or person from a self-selected book is described using a newspaper or feature story style (who, what, when, where, why, and how).

Materials

Materials needed include newspaper accounts of local or national personalities, a student self-selected book or other text(s) (may be fiction or nonfiction), writing and illustrating materials, and a sheet of poster board to serve as the "newspaper front page."

Procedure

Begin by showing and discussing actual newspaper articles about local or national figures. These may be legitimate press reports, but sometimes it is quite stimulating and fun for students when the teacher uses tabloid or "yellow" journalism. For example, one tabloid story we have used with students proclaims that a "Titanic Survivor Lived 20 Years On Iceberg" and, in the same issue (*Sun*, August 4, 1992), "Head of Goliath Found in Desert." Prepare a minilesson about the typical questions news reporters are interested in learning answers to: who, what, when, where, why, and how. In your minilesson, choose a character from a well-known book that both the student(s) and you have read, then write a feature story about the character. You may prefer to choose a real person or event to write about from a nonfiction selection.

As you work through your minilesson, ask students to choose a character from a book they have read and construct their own feature story. The student should write several stories about different events in the books, complete with a title that suggests the main idea of that event. It may be helpful to show the student the front cover of the book *The True Story of the Three Little Pigs! By A. Wolf* (Scieszka, 1989) as an example.

WRITTEN RESPONSE TO PICTURE BOOKS FOR OLDER STUDENTS

Upper-grade students write in response to picture books about sensitive subjects (Miletta, 1992). The forms of writing vary a great deal based on the subject being studied and the types of response that seem appropriate. Written responses may take the form of poems, songs, letters, essays, debates, one-act plays, video productions, and many more. The key to these writing activities is finding an emotional connection between the theme and the student.

Purpose

In writing in response to picture books about sensitive subjects, students write passionate compositions.

Materials

Materials needed include picture books relating to important and possibly controversial themes and writing supplies.

Procedure

Introduce picture books (those that rely heavily on illustrations to help get ideas across to readers) that portray emotionally powerful themes. Possible themes include war-and-peace issues, peer pressures, family relationships across generations (such as between grandparents and grandchildren), and health issues (abortion, AIDS, and so on). Try to select books that show different perspectives of the same issue in order to encourage debate. For example, for a theme related to "war and peace," one might choose *Hiroshima No Pika* by T. Maruki, *The Butter Battle Book* by Dr. Seuss (Geisel), *The Wall* by Edith Bunting, or *The Flame of Peace: A Tale of the Aztecs* by Deborah Nourse Lattimore. For a theme pertaining to "Relationships Between Generations" one might choose *Wilfred Gordon McDonald Partridge* by Mem Fox.

Written responses might take many forms. For controversial issues of the day, students may choose to debate positions and tactics or write letters to congressional leaders or platform positions for political parties. Issues that relate more to personal relationships could take the form of diary entries, letters, or discussions in a one-act play format.

It is important, however, to note that these books sometimes contain deep and emotional themes (child abuse and divorce, for instance). They are often controversial, and thus should always be previewed in order to make judgments about the appropriateness of the material.

BOOKMAKING AND PUBLISHING ACTIVITIES

This section presents several highly interesting ways that students can publish their compositions by turning them into books. In each of these activities, teachers stimulate reading and writing in students by showing them easy ways to publish their compositions. Other benefits to bookmaking include promoting creativity and problem-solving and decision-making abilities. Some of the following ideas have been adapted primarily from ideas by Routman (1995) and Yopp and Yopp (2000).

Pop-Up Books

Purpose

In this activity, children produce their own *pop-up books*—a fun and easy activity that stimulates students' interest in writing. An additional benefit is that pop-up books present parents with an impressive product documenting their child's literacy growth.

Materials

Materials needed include construction paper, glue, tape, scissors, and pictures to be used.

Procedure

Begin by sharing several pop-up books that have been commercially produced, as well as a sample the teacher or another student has produced. Next, have students illustrate the background for each page of their story and write in text. This step makes the finished product appear more professional and is less likely to frustrate young authors. It is possible to have one or more pop-up figures on a page by following these simple directions:

Step 1:   *Fold a sheet of construction paper in half and make two cuts an inch deep each and about an inch apart in the creased part of the paper.*

Step 2:   *Open the paper about halfway, push through the cut section carefully, and fold it inward.*

Step 3:   *Glue the picture to be used to the protruding cut section.*

Step 4:   *Fold each completed page in the closed position and stack the pages in order. The stack may be either glued or stitched together to complete the process. Don't forget to include an outside cover page.*

Accordion Books

Purpose

Accordion books are easy-to-construct books made of folded tag board that are displayed in special areas in the classroom. This activity has been suggested for group situations not only as a type of problem solving, but also as a means of putting together a composition in a sequence that makes sense.

Materials

Materials needed include multiple sheets of tag board, tape, and crayons or other colored markers for writing and illustrating.

Procedure

After the teacher shows an example of an accordion book, each group of students selects a composition that it wishes to retell in this format. Groups first decide which student will summarize each of the parts of the selection. Students then write a summary statement

Figure 13.14 Innovation Book *White Skeleton, White Skeleton*

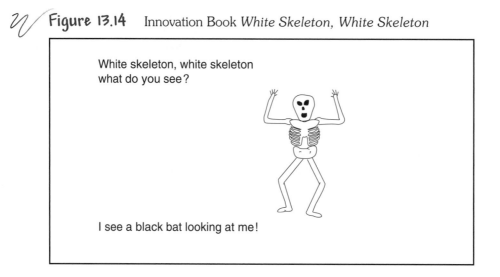

White skeleton, white skeleton
what do you see?

I see a black bat looking at me!

and draw an illustration on the tag board. Once group members have completed their assignments, the tag board or transparencies are taped together in sequence. The finished accordion book is then placed on a table in the classroom for other students to read.

INNOVATION BOOKS

Purpose

Many of the early reading books students encounter have memorable patterns, repeating verses, or other literary devices that make them highly predictable. Dr. Seuss (*Green Eggs and Ham*) and Bill Martin (*Brown Bear, Brown Bear, What Do You See?*) are two authors who have created many such books familiar to most English-speaking children. *Innovation books* are adaptations of popular predictable books using the same basic theme as the original book. They may be created by individual students as literature response projects using the writing process or generated in small-group settings with the assistance of the teacher.

Materials

Materials needed include regular 8-1/2″ × 11″ sheets of paper or construction paper, laminating materials, writing and illustrating materials, a hole punch, and metal clasps or rings.

Procedure

Choose a popular book that has a clear pattern. Two popular books that have been used for innovations in the primary grades are *Brown Bear, Brown Bear, What Do You See?* (Martin, 1983) and *If You Give a Mouse a Cookie* (Numeroff, 1985). For example, Miss Tims's first-grade class in Kansas took the *Brown Bear, Brown Bear, What Do You See?* pattern and used it to create a Halloween version using scary words, titled *White Skeleton, White Skeleton* (see Figure 13.14 for a sample page from the book). Innovation books also can be written by older students for younger ones, thus encouraging the older students to practice writing skills and to enjoy a new form of publishing.

The procedure can be followed in either small-group or whole-class formats. First, read aloud a book, song (such as "On Top of Old Smokey"), poem, rap, or chant that has the desired pattern. Next, challenge the student or group to brainstorm possible new verses. Record them on chart paper, the chalkboard, or on an overhead projector/transparency. Once the new text has been written, each student then writes and illustrates an assigned page that will be laminated upon completion. Assemble all the pages in the desired order, punch three holes along the binding edge of the aligned pages, then bind them with chrome rings or clasps. The innovation book is now ready to be shared.

SELECTED REFERENCES

Adams, T. (1991). Classroom characters. *The Reading Teacher, 45,* 73–74.

Brown, M. K. (1992). *Sally's room.* New York: Scholastic.

Bunting, E. (1992). *The wall.* Boston: Houghton Mifflin.

Calkins, L. M. (1994). *The art of teaching writing* (new ed.). Portsmouth, NH: Heinemann.

Cooter, R. B. (2002). *The reading academy instructor's guide.* Arlington, TX: Unpublished manuscript.

Fox, M. (1985). *Wilfred Gordon McDonald Partridge.* La Jolla, CA: Kane/Miller.

Gauthier, L. R. (1989). Using capsulization guides. *The Reading Teacher, 42,* 553–554.

Geisel, T. (Dr. Seuss) (1960). *Green eggs and ham.* New York: Random House.

Geisel, T. (Dr. Seuss) (1984). *The butter battle book.* New York: Random House.

Isadora, R. (1984). *Opening night.* New York: Greenwillow Books.

Keiser, B. (1991). Creating authentic conditions for writing. *The Reading Teacher, 45,* 249–250.

Lattimore, D. N. (1991). *The flame of peace: A tale of the Aztecs.* New York: Harper-Collins.

Martin, B. (1983). *Brown bear, brown bear, what do you see?* New York: Henry Holt.

Maruki, T. (1982). *Hiroshima no pika.* New York: William Morrow.

Miletta, M. M. (1992). Picture books for older children: Reading and writing connections. *The Reading Teacher, 45,* 555–556.

Numeroff, L. J. (1985). *If you give a mouse a cookie.* New York: Scholastic.

Pike, K., Compain, R., & Mumper, J. (1997). *New connections: An integrated approach to literacy.* New York: Addison-Wesley.

Reutzel, D. R., & Cooter, R. B. (2000). *Teaching children to read: Putting the pieces together* (3rd ed.). New York: Merrill/Prentice Hall.

Routman, R. (1995). *Invitations.* Portsmouth, NH: Heinemann.

Scieszka, J. (1989). *The true story of the three little pigs: By A. Wolf.* New York: Viking Kestrel.

Shanahan, T. (1984). Nature of the reading-writing relation: An exploratory multivariate analysis. *Journal of Educational Psychology, 76,* 466–477.

Sharmat, M. W. (1980). *Gila monsters meet you at the airport.* New York: Aladdin Books, Macmillan Publishing Company.

Smith, C. B., & Elliot, P. G. (1986). *Reading activities for middle and secondary schools.* New York: Teachers College Press.

Smith, F. (1983). *Essays into literacy.* Portsmouth, NH: Heinemann.

Squire, J. R. (1983). Composing and comprehending: Two sides of the same basic process. *Language Arts, 60*(5), 581–589.

Tompkins, G. E. (1992). Assessing the processes students use as writers. *Journal of Reading, 36*(3), 244–246.

Tompkins, G. E. (2000). *Teaching writing: Balancing process and product.* New York: Merrill/Prentice Hall.

Van Allsburg, C. (1985). *The polar express.* Boston: Houghton Mifflin.

Williams, M. (1922, 1958). *The velveteen rabbit: Or how toys become real.* New York: Doubleday.

Wiseman, D. L. (1992). *Learning to read with literature.* Needham Heights, MA: Allyn & Bacon.

Yopp, R. H., & Yopp, H. K. (2000). *Literature-based reading activities.* Boston: Allyn & Bacon.

Chapter 14

Reading Fluency

Mikhal, a third grader, walked reluctantly toward the chair placed next to his teacher, Mrs. Smith, carrying a tattered copy of his favorite book. He had practiced reading several pages in preparation for his regularly scheduled individual reading conference.

"Mikhal, I am glad to spend some time today listening to you read. Are you ready?" queried Mrs. Smith.

"Yah, I think so," answered Mikhal.

"So, what story are you going to read for me today?"

"I have a book called *The Boy Who Owned the School* for today."

"Great! I have your audiocassette tape here. I need to load it into the recorder, and then we can begin," remarked Mrs. Smith. "OK, I'm ready for you to read now, Mikhal. Where are you going to start reading?"

"I'm going to start on page 7, chapter 2. It's called *The Joys of Home Life.*"

"OK then, start when you are ready."

Mrs. Smith pushed the record button on the cassette tape recorder. Mikhal began reading.

"His father was a mechanical engineer who designed or invented a new drill bit for oil drilling, a self-cleaning, self-sharpening bit." When Mikhal finished his reading, Mrs. Smith praised how well he had done.

"Mikhal, you are reading very fluently. You sound just like you are speaking!" Mikhal beamed with pride.

"Thanks," he said quietly.

"Can you tell me what you remember from the pages you read?"

"I think so," responded Mikhal. Mrs. Smith turned the recorder back on. When Mikhal finished, Mrs. Smith praised him one more time.

"Would you like to hear what you said and add anything to it?" she questioned.

"Uh, huh." Mrs. Smith played the tape for Mikhal, and he added one more detail he had remembered as he listened to his oral retelling of his own reading.

That afternoon, Mrs. Smith looked at the running record she had made from Mikhal's earlier oral reading. He had read the text with 95% accuracy, so she knew that decoding this text wasn't a problem for Mikhal. Next, she timed his reading and figured out Mikhal's reading rate in words read per minute and compared this against a chart showing expected reading rate ranges by grade level. Mikhal was on the upper end of the range for his grade level. Next, Mrs. Smith listened to Mikhal's reading tape recording again, noting any problems with expression, pacing, smoothness, and phrasing. Again, Mikhal had performed well. Finally, Mrs. Smith listened to Mikhal's oral retelling of the pages he had read aloud. He had remembered the major ideas and a good number of the details, evidencing his comprehension of the text.

There was no doubt in Mrs. Smith's mind; Mikhal was progressing well toward the goal of becoming a fluent reader!

BACKGROUND BRIEFING FOR TEACHERS

For many years, *reading fluency,* the ability to read aloud smoothly at a reasonable rate and with expression, has been acknowledged as an important goal in becoming a proficient and strategic reader (Allington, 1983, 1984, 2001; Dowhower, 1991; Klenk & Kibby, 2000; National Reading Panel, 2000; Optiz & Rasinski, 1998; Rasinski, 2000; Rasinkski & Padak, 1996; Reutzel, 1996; Reutzel & Cooter, 2000; Reutzel, Hollingsworth, & Eldredge, 1994). However, with a shift in emphasis away from proficient oral reading in the early 1900s and toward silent reading for private and personal purposes, the goal of developing fluent oral readers all but disappeared from the reading curriculum. This was so much the case that it prompted Allington (1983, 1984) to declare reading fluency to be a neglected goal of reading instruction. Most reading methods textbooks and basal reader teacher's manuals today still provide little or no guidance for developing fluency as an important part of comprehensive reading instruction programs. Visits to many elementary school classrooms likewise reveal little attention to reading fluency in daily instruction.

How can teachers assess and assist all students in becoming fluent readers? First, they must understand *how* children develop fluency in reading. Second, they must be able to *assess* fluency to determine which parts of fluent reading require attention. And finally, teachers should know of successful and proven instructional alternatives available to use in assisting all children to develop fluent reading behaviors. This chapter is intended to develop teacher knowledge in the area of reading fluency, describe assessment strategies, provide a variety of successful instructional strategies, and connect assessment to best practices in developing reading fluency with all students.

WHAT IS FLUENCY?

What makes up the ability to read fluently? Although teachers and reading researchers have yet to agree on minor elements of reading fluency, some consensus has been achieved in recent years as to the major aspects (Allington, 2001; National Reading Panel, 2000; Richards, 2000). Typically, **fluency** is described as: 1) accuracy of decoding; 2) appropriate use of pitch, juncture, and stress (prosodic features) in one's voice; 3) appropriate text phrasing or "chunking;" and 4) an acceptable reading speed or rate. Thus, a fluent reader can decode the words in the text accurately and with relative ease, and also read with correct phrasing, appropriate intonation, and at a reasonably rapid rate so as to facilitate comprehension of the text. In *A Dictionary of Reading and Related Terms,* Harris and Hodges (1981) defined reading fluency as expressing oneself "smoothly, easily, and readily, with freedom from word identification problems, and possessing the ability to deal with words, and larger language units with quickness" (p. 120). In 1995, Harris and Hodges characterized reading fluency as reading smoothly, without hesitation, and with comprehension. Rasinski (1989) and Reutzel and Hollingsworth (1993) asserted that reading fluency contributes to better comprehension.

How readers achieve fluency in oral reading is a subject of contemporary concern (National Reading Panel, 2000; Snow et al. 1998). Several hypotheses offer potential insights into the question of how readers develop fluency. In 1983 and more recently in 2001, Allington discussed six hypotheses to explain how readers develop the ability to read fluently:

1. *(Modeling)* Being exposed to rich and varied models of fluent reading helps some children. In this case, parents or siblings spend significant amounts of time reading

aloud to these children. Through this process of modeling fluent reading children learn the behaviors of fluent readers. Other researchers have documented the significant impact of "modeling" upon the acquisition of fluent reading (Amarel, Bussis, & Chittenden, 1977; Durkin, 1966, 1974).

2. *(Quality of Instruction)* Good readers are more likely to get encouragement to read with expression than are students having reading problems (Gambrell, Wilson, & Gnatt, 1981). In comparison, students having reading problems are often directed to focus their attention on "sounding out" rather than on "making sense of the text" when reading orally (Allington, 1980b).

3. *(Volume of Reading)* Good readers are given more opportunities to read connected text and for longer periods of time than are students having reading problems. This dilemma led Allington (1977) to muse, "If they don't read much how they ever gonna get good?"

4. *(Access to Easy Reading Materials)* Proficient readers spend more time reading easier texts than students having reading problems (Gambrell et al., 1981). Reading easy books may help proficient readers make the transition from word-by-word reading to fluent reading, whereas poorer readers spend more time in reading materials that are relatively difficult. This practice denies students having reading problems access to reading materials that could help them develop fluent reading abilities.

5. *(Independent Reading)* The more time a student spends in silent reading, the greater her fluency is likely to be. Here again, proficient readers spend more time reading silently than do students having reading problems (Allington, 1980b; NAEP, 2000).

6. *(Self-Efficacy)* Fluent readers seem to view the reading process itself differently than do less fluent readers. Children who believe that reading is simply a process of decoding symbols to sounds, blending sounds together, and pronouncing words tend to be far less fluent in their reading than do students who believe reading should be meaningful, enjoyable, and above all, make sense.

An awareness of these six hypotheses can help teachers create optimal conditions for students to become fluent readers.

Rasinski (1989), Rasinski and Padak (1996), and Richards (2000) described six effective instructional principles to guide teachers in providing effective fluency instruction: 1) repetition, 2) modeling, 3) direct instruction and feedback, 4) support or assistance, 5) phrasing practice, and 6) easy materials. When students practice a single text repeatedly, the oral reading becomes fluent. Observing, listening to, and imitating fluent reading models help students learn how to become fluent readers themselves. Modeling fluent reading for students and pointing out specific behaviors as texts are read aloud, as well as and providing constructive feedback, can also help students become fluent. Supporting students using such strategies as choral reading, buddy or dyad reading, and computer-assisted reading can be most effective in a well-conceived reading fluency program. Finally, providing readers with easy reading materials for oral reading is essential for developing fluency.

Understanding the nature, quantity, and quality of teacher feedback during oral reading is a crucial part of helping students become fluent readers (Shake, 1986). The following self-assessment questions for teachers (see Figure 14.1) are provided to assist in this process.

Armed with an understanding of the problems, obstacles, and possibilities for helping students become fluent readers, we now turn our attention toward assessing students' reading fluency to inform and direct our selection of instructional strategies.

Figure 14.1   Teacher Verbal Feedback Think Questions

1. Am I more often telling the word than providing a clue?
2. What is the average self-correction rate of my students?
3. Do I assist poor readers with unknown words more often than good readers? If so, why?
4. Am I correcting miscues even when they do not alter the meaning of the text? If so, why?
5. Does one reader group tend to engage in more self-correction than other groups? If so, why?
6. Does one reading group have more miscues that go unaddressed than other groups?
7. What types of cues for oral reading errors do I provide and why?
8. What is *my* ultimate goal in reading instruction?
9. How do I handle interruptions from other students during oral reading? Do I practice what I preach?
10. How does my feedback influence the self-correction behavior of students?
11. Does my feedback differ across reader groups? If so, *how* and *why*?
12. Would students benefit more from a form of feedback different from that which I normally offer?
13. Am I allowing students time to self-correct (3–5 seconds)?
14. Am I further confusing students with my feedback?
15. Do I digress into "minilessons" midsentence when students make a mistake? If so, why?
16. Do I analyze miscues to gain information about the reading strategies students employ?
17. Does the feedback I offer aid students in becoming independent, self-monitoring readers? If so, how?
18. Do I encourage students to ask themselves, "Did that make sense?" when they are reading both orally and silently? If not, why not?
19. Do students need the kind of feedback I am offering them?

Source: Adapted from "Teacher Interruptions During Oral Reading Instruction: Self-monitoring as an Impetus for Change in Corrective Feedback," by M. Shake, 1986, *Remedial and Special Education, 7* (5), 18–24.

ASSESSING CHILDREN'S READING FLUENCY

Assessing fluency has for many years focused exclusively upon how quickly students could read a given text. This is known as "reading rate." Reading teachers have historically used a *words per minute* (wpm) figure to indicate reading rate, even though an optimum rate has never been determined or validated. Although this is one indicator of fluent oral/silent reading, it is only one. To adequately assess a student's ability to read fluently, one should consider at least four different areas: 1) automatic decoding of text, 2) reading rate or speed, 3) use of stress, pitch, and juncture (prosodic markers), and 4) mature phrasing or *chunking* of text.

Educators have in recent years begun to discuss how one might more *authentically* assess the ability to read fluently (Stayter & Allington, 1991). Most teachers feel that paper-and-pencil assessment tools appear to be inadequate or at least incomplete measures of fluency. One issue for many teachers today is accessing "ballpark" estimates of reading rates appropriate for children of differing ages and grades. In 1990, Harris and Sipay (see Figure 14.2) presented information about reading rates associated with several norm-referenced or standardized reading rate measures in the past.

Figure 14.2   Harris and Sipay (1990) Reading Rate Chart

Reading Rates by Grade Levels Expressed as Ranges of Words per Minute (WPM)

Grades	WPM
1	60–90
2	85–120
3	115–140
4	140–170
5	170–195
6	195–220
7	215–245
8	235–270
9	250–270
12	250–300

We offer a word of caution in strictly applying these ranges as the only assessment of fluency because other factors such as decoding accuracy, expression, and phrasing are also important. Furthermore, we do not believe that words per minute (wpm) is the best measure of reading rate as we shall explain later in this section on fluency assessment.

Several approaches to assessing readers' fluency in more authentic, naturalistic, and holistic ways are described in this section. None of these approaches are sufficient alone, but taken together offer a fairly complete picture of the fluency assessment. Before beginning the discussion of each of these assessment strategies, we refer the reader to chapter 2 where the processes for completing a **Running Record** are described.

AUDIO TAPING

Purpose

One of the simplest and most useful means of collecting fluency data for later analysis is through the use of audio recordings. The purpose of audio recording is to gather reading fluency samples of at-risk children over time in order to measure growth. In addition, these tapes function as miscue analysis documentation when conducting running records. Audio recordings may be kept and passed on from year to year through the student's elementary school experience. In one school where we have worked, the PTA provides 120-minute tapes for each child beginning with the first grade. Audio recordings are passed on through the grades until the children leave the elementary school. Parents are given these tapes when their child moves on to the middle school. Many parents consider these tapes as important as family photos and home videos. Audiotapes such as these are vivid demonstrations of a child's progress over time as well as the efforts of many dedicated teachers who have helped the child learn to read.

Materials

- One blank audiocassette tape per student (120-minute length strongly suggested)
- A portable audiocassette recorder with an internal microphone
- An audiocassette tape storage case

Procedure

The text to be read for the audio recording should be selected based on the nature and purpose of the information needed. For instance, information needed to document students' fluency progress over time will differ from information collected to compare one student's fluency to another. If a teacher wants to document a student's fluency progress over time, have the student select a favorite text to be practiced aloud or silently at least three times in preparation for audio recording. Record the oral reading of the practiced, self-selected text. Recording several readings of self-selected, favorite texts over a sufficiently long period of time provide both teachers and parents with useful longitudinal information regarding a student's fluency progress.

However, there may be a need mandated by school districts or governmental agencies to compare a student's fluency performance with that of others his own age or grade level. In this case, all students can be assigned the same text to be read, practiced at least three times, and recorded. Recording the same sample text for all students allows for collection of comparative fluency data. In either case, audio recording provides documentation of progress as well as data for more searching analyses of fluency to be made at a later date or time convenient to the teacher's schedule.

CURRICULUM-BASED ORAL READING FLUENCY NORMS FOR GRADES 2-5

One of the most common measures of oral reading fluency is that of reading rate or reading speed. In the past, reading rate was measured in terms of one of two existing scales—words per minute (WPM) and miscues or errors per minute (MPM). More recently, another measure has been developed to measure rate or fluency—*Words Correct Per Minute (WCPM)*. A WCPM measure has been carefully researched and related to a set of Oral Reading Fluency Curriculum-Based Norms for Grades 2–5 (Hasbrouck & Tindal, 1992). Data were collected to establish the oral reading fluency norms from 9,000 students over a nine-year period, 1981–1990, in grades 2 through 5 in five mid-western and western states. Students attended a wide range of schools including large urban and racially mixed to rural, isolated schools.

AGE/GRADE APPROPRIATE

Purpose

The purposes for assessing oral reading fluency are varied. Some reasons include the following:

- Screening students for special program eligibility
- Setting instructional goals and objectives
- Assigning students to specific groups for instruction
- Monitoring academic progress toward established goals
- Diagnosing special needs for assistance or instruction

Materials

- A teacher-selected passage of 200–300 words

Figure 14.3   Curriculum-Based Norms in Oral Reading Fluency for Grades 2–5 (Medians)

Grade	%ile	Fall WCPM*	Winter WCPM	Spring WCPM
	75	82	106	124
2	50	53	78	94
	25	23	46	65
	75	107	123	142
3	50	79	93	114
	25	65	70	87
	75	125	133	143
4	50	99	112	118
	25	72	89	92
	75	126	143	151
5	50	105	118	128
	25	77	93	100

* = Words Correct Per Minute

Source: Based on "Curriculum-Based Oral Reading Fluency Norms for Students in Grades 2 Through 5," by J. E. Hasbrouck and G. Tindal, 1992, *Teaching Exceptional Children,* (Spring, 1992), 41–44.

- Curriculum-based measurement procedures for assessing and scoring oral reading fluency
- Cassette tape player/recorder with blank tape
- Curriculum-Based Norms in Oral Reading Fluency for Grades 2–5 as shown in Figure 14.3.

Procedure
The procedures for collecting oral reading fluency information are shown in Figure 14.4.

MULTIDIMENSIONAL FLUENCY SCALE

Purpose
Zutell and Rasinski (1991) developed a good informal assessment of reading fluency known as the Multidimensional Fluency Scale (MFS). No audio recording is necessary to use this instrument, but it is recommended for accurate documentation. The purpose of the Zutell and Rasinski (1991) Multidimensional Fluency Scale is to provide a practical measurement of students' oral reading fluency that provides clear and valid information.

Materials
- A student self-selected passage of 200–300 words
- Multidimensional Fluency Scale
- Cassette tape player/recorder with blank tape

Figure 14.4 Curriculum-Based Measurement Procedures for Assessing and Scoring Oral Reading Fluency

Say to the student: *"When I say 'start,' begin reading aloud at the top of this page. Read across the page (demonstrate by pointing). Try to read each word. If you come to a word you don't know, I'll tell it to you. Be sure to do your best reading. Are there any questions?"*

Say: *"Start."*

Following along on your copy of the story, mark the words that are read incorrectly. If a student stops or struggles with a word for three seconds, tell the student the word and mark it as incorrect. Place a vertical line after the last word read within a one-minute time frame. Thank and praise the student.

The following guidelines determine which words are to be counted as correct:

1. Words read correctly. Words read correctly are those words that are pronounced correctly, given the reading context.
   a. The word "read" must be pronounced "reed" when presented in the context of "He will read the book," not as "red."
   b. Repetitions are not counted as incorrect.
   c. Self-corrections within three seconds are counted as correctly read words.
2. Words read incorrectly. The following types of errors are counted: (a) mispronunciations, (b) substitutions, and (c) omissions. Further, words not read within three seconds are counted as errors.
   a. Mispronunciations are words that are misread: dog for dig.
   b. Substitutions are words that are substituted for the stimulus word; this is often inferred by a one-to-one correspondence between word orders: dog for cat.
   c. Omissions are words skipped or not read; if a student skips an entire line, each word is counted as an error.
3. Use the three-second rule. If students struggle to pronounce a word or hesitate for three seconds, then the students are told the word; and it is counted as an error.

Source: Based on *Curriculum-based Measurement: Assessing Special Children* (pp. 239–240), by M. R. Shinn (Ed), 1989, New York: Guilford Press.

Procedure

We recommend that students rehearse a familiar self-selected word passage (200–300 words) at least three times prior to using the Multidimensional Fluency Scale shown in Figure 14.5. It may be informative for teachers to also observe the difference in a student's fluency with a practiced, self-selected, familiar text and the reading of an unpracticed, teacher-selected, unfamiliar text chosen at the child's approximate grade level. The Multidimensional Fluency Scale shown in Figure 14.5 can be used to assess each student's reading fluency.

Fluency ratings may be taken during individual reading conferences or during group dramatizations including plays, Reader's Theater, and radio plays (Reutzel & Cooter, 2000). For radio plays, students can prepare a text for reading and recording on a cassette tape player, complete with sound effects, if they wish! After taping, the teacher can analyze the performance of individual students and provide helpful modeling and feedback for future improvement.

𝒲 **Figure 14.5**   Zutell and Rasinski (1991) Multidimensional Fluency Scale MFS

Use the following scales to rate reader fluency on the three dimensions of phrasing, smoothness, and pace.

A. Phrasing

1. Monotonic with little sense of phrase boundaries, frequent word-by-word reading.
2. Frequent two- and three-word phrases giving the impression of choppy reading; improper stress and intonation that fails to mark ends of sentences and clauses.
3. Mixture of run-ons, midsentence pauses for breath, and possibly some choppiness; reasonable stress/intonation.
4. Generally well phrased, mostly in clause and sentence units, with adequate attention to expression.

B. Smoothness

1. Frequent extended pauses, hesitations, false starts, sound-outs, repetitions, and/or multiple attempts.
2. Several "rough spots" in text where extended pauses, hesitations, etc., are more frequent and disruptive.
3. Occasional breaks in smoothness caused by difficulties with specific words and/or structures.
4. Generally smooth reading with some breaks, but word and structure difficulties are resolved quickly, usually through self-correction.

C. Pace (during sections of minimal disruption)

1. Slow and laborious
2. Moderately slow
3. Uneven mixture of fast and slow reading
4. Consistently conversational

Source: "Training Teachers to Attend to their Students' Oral Reading Fluency," by J. Zutell and T. Rasinski, 1991, *Theory into Practice, 30*(3), 211–217. Reprinted by permission. Copyright 1991 by the College of Education, The Ohio State University. All rights reserved.

CONNECTING ASSESSMENT FINDINGS TO TEACHING STRATEGIES

Before discussing fluency intervention strategies, we have constructed a guide connecting assessment to intervention and/or strategy choices. It is our intention to help you, the teacher, select the most appropriate instructional interventions and strategies to meet your students' needs based on assessment data.

In the next part of this chapter, we offer strategies for intervention based on the foregoing assessments.

DEVELOPING READING FLUENCY FOR ALL CHILDREN

After a careful assessment of a student's reading fluency as outlined previously, one or more of the following fluency development strategies or lesson frameworks may be appropriately applied. Perhaps the most important thing to remember is that children with

Intervention Strategy Guide for Reading Fluency

Intervention Strategy / Student Problem(s)	Oral Recitation Lesson	Fluency Development Lesson	Repeated Readings	Assisted Reading	Choral Readings	Reader's Theater	Radio Reading	Imitative Reading	Caption TV	Neurological Impress
Accuracy of Decoding	+	+	+	+	*	–	*	*	–	*
Reading Rate	*	*	+	*	*	–	–	*	–	*
Expressive Reading	+	+	+	+	+	+	+	+	+	+
Smoothness of Reading	+	+	+	+	+	+	+	+	+	+
Phrasing the Text	+	+	+	+	+	*	+	+	+	+

Key: + excellent strategy
 * adaptable strategy
 – unsuitable strategy

poorly developed fluency must receive regular opportunities to read and reread for authentic and motivating reasons, such as to gather information, to present a dramatization, or simply to reread a favorite story. The strategies described in this section offer effective and varied means for teachers to help learners become more fluent readers in authentic, effective, and motivating ways!

ORAL RECITATION LESSON FRAMEWORK (ORL)

Purpose

Hoffman (1987) used a lesson format drawn from the one-room schoolhouse period of American education. During these early years of American education, teachers modeled reading aloud; students were assigned all or part of the text for practice; and later, students were asked to read aloud to the class using a practice called *"recitation."* The Oral Recitation Lesson shares many important theoretical and practical characteristics with the Shared Book Approach strategy described in chapter 3. According to Rasinski (1990a), the Shared Book Approach and the Oral Recitation Lesson are similar in respect to teacher modeling, repeated readings of text, independent reading, and the use of predictable and meaningful materials. Thus, the Shared Book Approach may be seen in many respects as a less formalized approach to developing fluency with children (Nelson & Morris, 1986). However, for some readers (and teachers) the Oral Recitation Lesson offers a degree of security through providing a predictable lesson structure for planning.

Materials

Student self-selected books appropriate for reading aloud are used.

Procedure

The Oral Recitation Lesson incorporates two basic components with each made up of several subroutines outlined here:

Components of the Oral Recitation Lesson

    I. DIRECT INSTRUCTION
        A. Three Subroutines
            1. Comprehension
            2. Practice
            3. Performance

    II. INDIRECT INSTRUCTION
        A. Two Subroutines
            1. Fluency Practice
            2. Demonstrate Expert Reading

Direct instruction consists of three subroutines: a comprehension phase, a practice phase, and a performance phase. When beginning an Oral Recitation Lesson, the teacher reads a story aloud and leads the students through an analysis of the story's content by constructing a Story Grammar Map and discussing the major elements of the story such as setting, characters, goals, plans, events, and resolution. Students are asked to tell what they remember about these parts of the story and the teacher records their responses on the Story Grammar Map. At the conclusion of this discussion, the Story Grammar Map is used as an outline for students to write a story summary.

During the second subroutine, Practice, the teacher works with students to improve their oral reading expression. The teacher models fluent reading aloud with parts of the text, then the students individually or chorally practice imitating the teacher's oral expressions. Choral readings of texts can be accomplished in a number of ways (see Wood 4-Way Oral Reading described in the section "Choral Reading"). Text segments modeled by the teacher during the practice phase may begin with only one or two sentences and gradually move toward modeling and practicing whole pages of text.

The third subroutine is the Performance phase. Students select and perform a part of the text for others in the group. Then, listeners are encouraged to comment positively on the performance. We suggest this activity by asking students to begin by stating what they liked about the oral reading by their peers. Next we ask questions about parts of the reading they liked less. Teacher modeling is very important with this latter activity. For instance, the teacher might model a question about a strange rendition of the Big Bad Wolf in the *Three Pigs* story by saying,

"I noticed that your voice had a nice and friendly tone when you read the Big Bad Wolf's part. I'm curious. Why did you choose to read his part that way when so many other readers choose to use a mean-sounding voice for that character?"

Many times the student has a perfectly logical reason for irregular intonation or other anomalies. Sometimes it is simply a matter of not enough practice time. If so, this regular format helps students be aware that there is some accountability to these lessons.

The second major component of the Oral Recitation Lesson is an indirect instruction phase. During this part of the lesson, students practice a single story until they become expert readers. Hoffman (1987) defined an expert reader as one who reads with 98% accuracy and 75 words-per-minute fluency. For ten minutes each day, students practice reading a story or text segment in a soft or mumble reading fashion. Teachers use this time to check students individually, what we term "house calls," for story mastery before moving on to another story. The direct instruction component creates a pool of stories from which the students can select a story for expert reading activities in the indirect instruction phase. In summary, ORL provides teachers with a workable strategy to break away from the traditional practice of round-robin oral reading.

FLUENCY DEVELOPMENT LESSON

Purpose

Based on the six principles of successful fluency instruction articulated by Rasinski (1989) and Rasinski and Padak (1996) earlier in this chapter, Rasinski, Padak, Linek, and Sturtevant (1994) and Rasinski and Padak (1996) described an instructional process known as the **Fluency Development Lesson (FDL).** The FDL is viewed by the authors as supplementary instruction aimed at helping special-needs readers develop fluency through reading of connected texts in addition to the regular instruction they receive in the classroom.

Materials

An assortment of highly predictable and easy-to-read stories, poems, jokes, and riddles are needed.

Procedure

Rasinski and Padak (1996) outlined steps for designing and effectively using a Fluency Development Lesson (FDL) as follows:

1. The chosen text is read by the teacher one or more times to the students and is followed by a brief discussion of the content and the teacher's reading.

2. Read the chosen text chorally one or more times with teachers and students together. Each student reads from his own copy of the text. Teachers vary the choral reading by including echo, antiphonal, and small-group choral reading in this part of the lesson.

3. Students work in pairs in different parts of the classroom and nearby hall, practicing the reading three times to the partner, who listens and provides feedback. After three readings by one partner, the roles are reversed.

4. Students return to the large group and are invited by the teacher to perform the text for each group. Individuals, pairs, trios, and quartets read for their own group or other audiences including other classes, the school principal and office staff, and other teachers.

5. Students engage in word bank practice and word play using words chosen from the day's text and previously read texts.

6. Students are encouraged to take the text home and read it to their parents and guardians who have been notified to expect and encourage their children to read to them and give positive feedback for their children's efforts.

Teachers may also choose to return to favorite texts from previous lessons for further reading and enjoyment. Rasinski et. al. (1994) found positive effects for the FDL over traditional fluency instruction on measures of fluency and reading achievement. The most pronounced positive effects were noted among special-needs readers.

Repeated Readings

Purpose

Repeated readings engage students in reading interesting passages orally over and over again. The basic purpose of repeated readings is to enhance students' reading fluency (Dowhower, 1989; Samuels, 1979). Although it might seem that reading a text again and again may lead to boredom, it can actually have just the opposite effect.

Materials

In the beginning, texts selected for repeated readings should be short, predictable, and easy. Examples of poetry we recommend for repeated readings with at-risk readers include those authored by Shel Silverstein and Jack Prelutsky. Stories by Bill Martin, such as *Brown Bear, Brown Bear,* or Eric Carle's *The Very Hungry Caterpillar* are also wonderful places to start this activity. When students attain adequate speed and accuracy with easy texts, the length and difficulty of the stories and poems can gradually be increased.

Procedure

In this exercise each reading is timed and recorded on a chart or graph. Students compete with themselves trying to better their own reading rate and cut down on errors with each successive attempt. Also, with each attempt, students' comprehension and prosody or vocal inflections improve (Dowhower, 1987; Reutzel & Hollingsworth, 1993). Students with reading problems find it reinforcing to see visible evidence of improvement. Figure 14.6 illustrates a graph of student progress in repeated readings.

Figure 14.6   Graph of Student's Fluency Progress

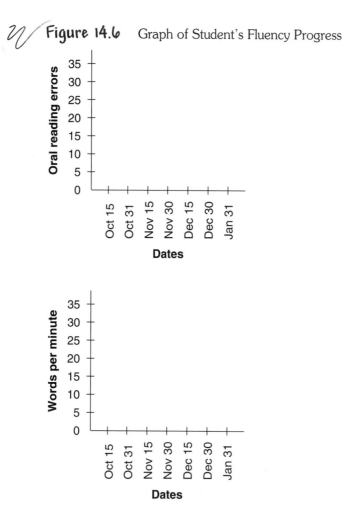

To increase reading rate, all students must learn to recognize words without having to sound them out. In Figure 14.6, both the amount of time it took to read the selection and the number of oral reading errors that occurred during each trial day has been graphed.

Repeated readings help students by expanding the total number of words they can recognize instantaneously and, as previously mentioned, help improve students' comprehension and oral elocution (performance) with each succeeding attempt. Improved performance quickly leads students to improved confidence regarding reading aloud and positive attitudes toward the act of reading. Additionally, because high-frequency words (the, and, but, was, and so on) occur in literally all reading situations, the increase in automatic sight word knowledge developed through repeated readings transfers far beyond the practiced texts.

One way of supporting readers during repeated readings is to use a tape-recorded version of the story or poem. Students can read along with an audiocassette tape to develop fluency similar to the model on the tape. Also, students can tape-record their oral reading performance as a source of immediate feedback. If two audiocassette tape player/recorders are available, ask students to listen and read along with the taped version of the text using headphones. At the same time, use the second recorder for recording the student's oral reading. The child can then either replay his version simultaneously with the teacher-recorded version to compare, or simply listen to his own rendition alone. Either way, the feedback can be both instant and effective.

You may use taped recordings of repeated readings for further analysis of each reader's improvement in fluency and comprehension. Also, using a tape recorder frees the teacher to work with other students, thereby conserving precious instructional time and leaving behind an audit trail of student readings for later assessment and documentation. On occasion teachers should listen to the tape with the reader present. During this time the teacher and student can discuss effective ways of reducing word recognition errors and increasing reading rate.

ASSISTED READING

Purpose

With *assisted* (also called *buddy, dyad, peer* or *paired*) *reading,* two students read the same text aloud in unison for mutual support (Eldredge & Quinn, 1988; Greene 1970; Topping, 1987; Topping & Ehly, 1998).

Materials

Initial dyad reading sessions should be structured so that the materials used are equally familiar and motivating for both students.

Procedure

Students can be paired according to their general reading level, but more importantly, they should be paired according to their ability to work well with one another. A spirit of teamwork and cooperation must be present so that when one reader stumbles, the other lends assistance. The dyad sessions can be tape-recorded and played back for the students and teachers to evaluate. Discussions or taped replays should center not just on word recognition accuracy, but also on reading rate, pausing, intonation, expressive oral interpretation, and comprehension of the text.

CHORAL READING

Purpose

In many classrooms, special-needs students are asked to read aloud in a solo, barbershop, or round-robin fashion. Round-robin oral reading carries with it significant instructional, emotional, and psychological risks for all children, but most especially for special-needs readers (Eldredge, Reutzel, & Hollingsworth, 1996; Opitz & Rasinski, 1998). Homan, Klesius, and Hite (1993) found that choral reading forms of fluency practice such as echoic and unison readings yielded excellent gains in fluency and comprehension for all children. Karen Wood (1983) suggested an approach for reading a story orally in a group called 4-way oral reading. Choral readings of this type alleviate some of the identified weaknesses of oral round-robin reading while adding variety to repeated readings.

Materials

One copy of a story, text, poem, song, or script is needed.

Procedure

In 4-way oral reading, Wood (1983) pointed out that the oral reading of a text should be varied by using four different types of oral reading: 1) unison choral reading, 2) echoic or *imitative* reading, 3) paired reading, and 4) mumble reading (Wood, 1983). All of these approaches to oral reading, except mumble reading, are described elsewhere in this chapter. Mumble reading, or reading quietly aloud, is typically heard among young readers as they are initially told to read silently. These young readers tend to "mumble" as they attempt to read silently. Teachers should model this approach to oral reading before asking students to mumble read.

To use 4-way oral reading, Wood (1983) suggested that the teacher introduce the story content and the varied methods to be used in reading it. The teacher should pause briefly during the oral reading of the story to help students reflect on the story and predict ahead of themselves to focus and improve comprehension. During 4-way oral reading students are called upon in random order to read, but none of them will be put on the spot because none of the 4-way oral reading strategies require that students read solo. Because of this, all students participate repeatedly throughout the oral reading of the story, thus helping them remain actively involved and keep their place in the story. Also students read together, often providing many minutes of reading aloud for pleasure and practice to support special-needs readers in becoming more fluent.

READER'S THEATER

Purpose

Reader's Theater is a strategy whereby students practice reading from a script, then share their oral reading with classmates and selected audiences (Allington, 2001; Opitz & Rasinski, 1998; Sloyer, 1982). Unlike a play, students do not memorize lines or use elaborate stage sets to make their presentation. Emphasis is placed on presenting an interpretation of literature read in a dramatic style for an audience who imagines setting and actions.

Materials

Literature selected for Reader's Theater should be drawn from tales originating from the oral tradition, poetry, or quality picture books designed to be read aloud by children. Selections should be packed with action, have an element of suspense, and comprise an entire, meaningful story or episode. Also, texts selected for use in Reader's Theater should contain sufficient dialogue to make reading and preparing the text a challenge as well as involving several children as characters. A few examples of such texts include Martin and Archambault's *Knots on a Counting Rope* (1987), Viorst's *Alexander and the Terrible, Horrible, No Good, Very Bad Day* (1972), and Barbara Robinson's *The Best Christmas Pagent Ever* (1972). Minimal props are often used in Reader's Theater, such as masks, hats, or simple costumes.

Procedure

If a story is selected for reading, students are assigned to read characters parts. If poems are selected for a Reader's Theater, students may read alternating lines or groups of lines. Reader's Theater In-the-Round, where readers stand around the perimeter of the room and the audience is in the center surrounded by the readers, is a fun and interesting variation for both the performers and audience.

Students often benefit from a discussion prior to reading a Reader's Theater script. The purpose of this discussion is to help students make connections between their own background experiences and the text to be read. Also, struggling students benefit from listening to a previously recorded performance of the text as a model prior to the initial reading of the script.

Hennings (1974) described a simplified procedure for preparing Reader's Theater scripts for classroom performance. First, the text to be performed is read silently by the individual students. Second, the text is read again orally, sometimes using choral reading in a group. After the second reading, children either choose their parts or the teacher assigns parts to the children. We suggest that students be allowed to select their three most desired parts, write these choices on a slip of paper to submit to the teacher, and that teachers do everything possible to assign one of these three choices to the requesting student. The third reading is also an oral reading with students reading their parts with scripts in hand. There may be several rehearsal readings as students prepare for the final reading or performance in front of the class or a selected audience.

Reader's Theater offers students a unique opportunity to participate in reading along with other, perhaps more skilled readers. Participating in the mainstream classroom with better readers helps students having reading problems feel a part of their peer group, provides them with ready models of good reading, and demonstrates how good readers, through practice, become even better readers. Working together with other readers fosters a sense of teamwork, support, and pride in personal and group accomplishment.

Radio Reading

Purpose

Radio reading (Searfoss, 1975) is a procedure for developing oral reading fluency in a group setting, a process that shields struggling students from the sometimes harsh emotional consequences from unkind peer feedback due to their limited reading abilities.

Materials

In radio reading, each student is given a "script" to read aloud. Selections can be drawn from any print media, such as newspapers, magazines, or any print source that can be converted into a news story.

Procedure

One student acts as a news broadcaster, and others act as listeners. Only the reader and the teacher have copies of the scripts. Because other students have no script to follow, minor word recognition errors will go unnoticed if the text is well presented. Students having reading problems have enjoyed radio reading from *Know Your World.* This publication is well suited for use in radio reading activities because the content and level of difficulty make it possible for older readers with fluency problems to read with ease and enjoyment.

Before reading aloud to the group, students should rehearse the story silently to themselves or aloud to the teacher until they gain confidence. Emphasis is first placed on the meaning of the story so that the students can paraphrase any difficult portions of the text. Students are encouraged to keep the ideas flowing in the same way as a broadcaster.

IMITATIVE READING

Purpose

The primary aims of *Imitative Reading* are to improve word recognition accuracy, fluency, sense of story, and intonation and phrasing (Allington, 2001).

Materials

Materials for this type of intervention can be selected from several sources. Perhaps the best sources for reading aloud are predictable trade books. The following segment was taken from *This is the Place for Me* (Cole, 1986).

> Morty walked and walked. He came to a good house. "I like this house," he said. "Oh, oh," Morty said. "This is not the place for me." He dried himself off. And went looking for a house again. He found one . . . but it was too small. He found another . . . but it was too thin. He found another . . . but it was too scary! Poor Morty! He was all alone in the world. He had no place to live.

Texts such as these provide students with predictable language and events as well as repetitive language they can feel successful with from the very start.

Procedure

In imitative reading, the teacher reads a segment of the text aloud while a student follows along silently (Huey, 1968). When finished, the student tries to echo or imitate what the teacher has read. In the early stages, very easy reading material should be used. More difficult reading material can be introduced gradually, as the length of the teacher-modeled oral reading segments increases.

To begin, the teacher should read only small segments of text. Most students can begin with a sentence, but sometimes it will be necessary to limit the segments read to phrases. When text is broken up in this way, the student should be required to echo whole sentences before the teacher continues reading.

ADDITIONAL STRATEGIES FOR ENGLISH LANGUAGE LEARNERS

CLOSED-CAPTION TV

Purpose

Several researchers (Koskinen, Wilson, & Jensema, 1985; Neuman & Koskinen, 1992) have found that closed-caption television is a particularly effective tool for motivating students who are learning English as a second language to improve fluency and comprehension. Closed-caption television, which uses written subtitles, provides students with meaningful and motivating reading material.

Materials

Teachers should carefully select high-interest television programs, record and preview programs before making final selections, then introduce the program(s) to students with attention to vocabulary and prior knowledge factors (Koskinen et al., 1985).

Procedure

Three elements should be considered in a successful closed-caption lesson. First, watch a part of the captioned TV program together as a group (5–10 minutes). Stop the recorded tape and ask students to predict what will happen next in the program. Then, continue showing the program so that students can check their predictions. Second, watch a segment of the program that has examples of certain kinds of phonic patterns, word uses, or punctuation. For example, students can be alerted to the use of quotation marks and the fact that these marks signal dialogue. Students can then watch the remainder of the tape to identify the dialogue using their knowledge of quotation marks. Third, after watching a closed-caption TV program, students can practice reading aloud along with the captions. If necessary, both the auditory portion and the closed captioning can be played simultaneously to provide students with fluency problems support through their initial attempts to read. At some later point, students can be allowed to practice reading the captioning without the auditory portion of the program. Koskinen et al. (1985) added that they "do not recommend that the sound be turned off if this, in effect, turns off the children. The major advantage of captioned television is the multisensory stimulation of viewing the drama, hearing the sound, and seeing the captions." (p. 6)

INCLUDING ALL STUDENTS

NEUROLOGICAL IMPRESS

Purpose

The neurological impress method (NIM) involves the student and the teacher in reading the same text aloud simultaneously (Heckleman, 1966, 1969; Hollingsworth, 1970, 1978). The use of multiple sensory systems associated with using NIM is thought to "impress" upon the student the fluid reading patterns of the teacher through direct modeling. It is assumed that exposing students to numerous examples of texts (read in a more sophisticated way than the at-risk students could achieve on their own) will enable them to learn the patterns of letter-sound correspondence in the language more naturally. This assumption stands to reason when viewed in light of more recent advances in learning theory, especially those espoused by Vygotsky (1978).

Materials

Each NIM session is aimed at reading as much material as is possible in 10 minutes. As mentioned previously, the reading material selected for the first few sessions should be easy, predictable, and make sense for the reader. However, other more challenging materials can be used rather quickly.

Procedure

To use the NIM, the student sits slightly in front and to one side of the teacher as they hold the text. The teacher moves her finger beneath the words as they are spoken in near-unison fashion. Both try to maintain a comfortably brisk, continuous rate of oral reading. The teacher's role is to keep the pace when the student starts to slow down. Pausing for analyzing unknown words is not permitted. The teacher's voice is directed at the student's ear so that the words are seen, heard, and said simultaneously.

In the first few NIM sessions, students should become acquainted with the process by practicing on short, familiar texts. Because most students with reading problems have not read at an accelerated pace before, their first efforts often have a mumble-like quality. Most students with reading problems typically take some time to adjust to the NIM; however, within a few sessions they start to feel at ease. Many students with reading problems say they enjoy the NIM because it allows them to read more challenging and interesting material like "good readers."

At first, the teacher's voice will dominate the oral reading, but in later sessions it should be reduced gradually. This will eventually allow the student to assume the vocal lead naturally. Usually three sessions per week are sufficient to obtain noticeable results. This routine should be followed for a minimum of 10 consecutive weeks (Henk, 1983).

The NIM can also be adapted for group use (Hollingsworth, 1970; 1978). The teacher tape-records 10 minutes of her own oral reading in advance. Individual students can read along with the tape while following the text independently, or the tape can be used in a listening center to permit the teacher to spend individual time with each student as others participate in reading with the tape. Despite the advantages of the prerecorded tape format, teachers' one-to-one interactions with individual students result in a better instructional experience.

SELECTED REFERENCES

Allington, R. L. (1977). If they don't read much, how they ever gonna get good? *Journal of Reading, 21*, 57–61.

Allington, R. L. (1980a). Poor readers don't get to read much in reading groups. *Language Arts, 57*, 872–876.

Allington, R. L. (1980b). Teacher interruption behaviors during primary grade oral reading. *Journal of Educational Psychology, 72*, 371–377.

Allington, R. L. (1983). Fluency: The neglected reading goal. *The Reading Teacher, 36*(6), 556–561.

Allington, R. L. (1984). Oral reading. In R. Barr, M. Kamil, & P. Mosenthal (Eds.), *Handbook of reading research*. New York: Longman.

Allington, R. L. (2001). *What really matters for struggling readers: Designing research-based programs*. New York: Addison-Wesley/Longman.

Amarel, M, Bussis, A., & Chittenden, E. A. (1977). *An approach to the study of beginning reading: Longitudinal case studies*. Paper presented at the National Reading Conference, New Orleans, LA.

Cole, J. (1986). *This is the place for me*. New York: Scholastic, Inc.

Dowhower, S. (1987). Effects of repeated readings on second-grade transitional readers' fluency and comprehension. *Reading Research Quarterly, 22*, 389–406.

Dowhower, S. (1991). Speaking of prosody: Fluency's unattended bedfellow. *Theory into Practice, 30*(3), 158–164.

Dowhower, S. L. (1989). Repeated reading: Research into practice. *The Reading Teacher, 42*(7), 502–507.

Durkin, D. (1966). *Children who read early: Two longitudinal studies*. New York: Teachers College Press.

Durkin, D. (1974). A six year study of children who learned to read in school at the age of four. *Reading Research Quarterly, 10*, 9–61.

Eldredge, J. L., & Quinn, D. W. (1988). Increasing reading performance of low-achieving second graders with dyad reading groups. *Journal of Educational Research, 82*, 40–46.

Eldredge, J. L., Reutzel, D. R., & Hollingsworth, P. M. (1996). Comparing the effectiveness of two oral reading practices: Round-robin reading and the shared book experience. *Journal of Literacy Research, 28*(2), 201–225.

Gambrell, L. B., Wilson, R. M., & Gnatt, W. N. (1981). Classroom observations of task-attending behaviors of good and poor readers. *Journal of Educational Research, 74*, 400–404.

Greene, F. P. (1970). *Paired reading*. Unpublished manuscript, Syracuse University, New York.

Harris, T. L., & Hodges, R. E. (Eds.). (1981). *A dictionary of reading and related terms*. Newark, DE: International Reading Association.

Harris, T. L., & Hodges, R. E. (Eds.). (1995). *The literacy dictionary: The vocabulary of reading and writing*. Newark, DE: International Reading Association.

Harris, T. L., & Sipay, E. R. (1990). *How to increase reading ability* (9th ed.). New York: Longman.

Hasbrouck, J. E., & Tindal, G. (1992). Curriculum-based oral reading fluency norms for students in grades 2 through 5. *Teaching Exceptional Children*, (Spring), 41–44.

Heckleman, R. G. (1966). Using the neurological impress remedial reading technique. *Academic Therapy, 1*, 235–239, 250.

Heckleman, R. G. (1969). A neurological impress method of remedial reading instruction. *Academic Therapy, 4*, 277, 282.

Henk, W. A. (1983). Adapting the NIM to improve comprehension. *Academic Therapy, 19*, 97–101.

Hennings, K. (1974). Drama reading, an on-going classroom activity at the elementary school level. *Elementary English, 51*, 48–51.

Hoffman, J. V. (1987). Rethinking the role of oral reading in basal instruction. *The Elementary School Journal, 87*(3), 367–374.

Hollingsworth, P. M. (1970). An experiment with the impress method of teaching reading. *The Reading Teacher, 24,* 112–114.

Hollingsworth, P. M. (1978). An experimental approach to the impress method of teaching reading. *The Reading Teacher, 31,* 624–626.

Homan, S. P., Klesius, J. P., & Hite, C. (1993). Effects of repeated readings and nonrepetitive strategies on students' fluency and comprehension. *The Journal of Educational Research, 87*(2), 94–99.

Huey, E. B. (1968). *The pyschology and pedagogy of reading.* Cambridge, MA: MIT Press.

Klenk, L., & Kibby, M. W. (2000). Re-mediating reading difficulties: Appraising the past, reconciling the present, constructing the future. In M. L. Kamil, P. B. Mosenthal, P. D. Pearson, & R. Barr (Eds.), *Handbook of Reading Research,* vol. 3. Mahwah, NJ: Lawrence Erlbaum Associates.

Koskinen, P., Wilson, R., & Jensema, C. (1985). Closed-captioned television: A new tool for reading instruction. *Reading World, 24,* 1–7.

Martin, B., & Archambault, J. (1987). *Knots on a counting rope.* New York: Henry Holt.

National Assessment of Educational Progress. (2000). *The nation's report card: Reading 2000.* Washington, DC: Department of Education.

National Reading Panel (NRP). (2000). *Report of the National Reading Panel: Teaching children to read.* Washington, DC: National Institute of Child Health and Human Development.

Nelson, L., & Morris, D. (1986). *Supported oral reading: A year-long intervention study in two inner-city primary grade classrooms.* Paper presented at the annual meeting of the National Reading Conference, Austin, TX.

Neuman, S. B., & Koskinen, P. (1992). Captioned television as comprehensible input: Effects of incidental word learning from context for language minority students. *Reading Research Quarterly, 27*(1), 94–106.

Opitz, M. F., & Rasinski, T. V. (1998). *Good-bye round robin: 25 effective oral reading strategies.* Portsmouth, NH: Heinemann.

Paulsen, G. (1987). *Hatchet.* New York: Scholastic, Inc.

Rasinski, T. (1989). Fluency for everyone: Incorporating fluency instruction in the classroom. *The Reading Teacher, 42*(9), 690–693.

Rasinski, T. (1990a). Effects of repeated reading and listening-while-reading on reading fluency. *The Journal of Educational Research, 83*(3), 147–150.

Rasinski, T. (1990b). Investigating measure of reading fluency. *Educational Research Quarterly, 14*(3), 37–44.

Rasinski, T. (2000). Speed does matter. *The Reading Teacher, 54*(2), 146–51.

Rasinski, T. V., & Padak, N. (1996). Five lessons to increase reading fluency. In L. R. Putnam (Ed.), *How to become a better reading teacher: Strategies for assessment and intervention.* Columbus, OH: Merrill/Prentice Hall.

Rasinski, T. V., Padak, N., Linek, W., & Sturtevant, E. (1994). Effects of fluency development on urban second-grade readers. *The Journal of Educational Research, 87*(3), 158–165.

Reutzel, D. R. (1996). Developing special needs readers' oral reading fluency. In L. R. Putnam (Ed.), *How to become a better reading teacher: Strategies for assessment and intervention.* Columbus, OH: Merrill/Prentice Hall.

Reutzel, D. R., & Cooter, R. B. (2000). *Teaching children to read: Putting the pieces together* (3rd ed.). Upper Saddle River, NJ: Merrill/Prentice Hall.

Reutzel, D. R., & Hollingsworth, P. M. (1993). Effects of fluency training on second grade students' reading comprehension. *The Journal of Educational Research, 86*(6), 325–331.

Reutzel, D. R., Hollingsworth, P. M., & Eldredge, J. L. (1994). Oral reading instruction: The impact on student reading development. *Reading Research Quarterly, 29*(1), 40–62.

Richards, M. (2000). Be a good detective: Solve the case of oral reading fluency. *The Reading Teacher, 53*(7), 534–539.

Robinson, B. (1972). *The best Christmas pageant ever.* New York: Harper & Row.

Samuels, J. (1979). The method of repeated reading. *The Reading Teacher, 32,* 403–408.

Searfoss, L. W. (1975). Radio reading. *The Reading Teacher, 29,* 295–296.

Shake, M. (1986). Teacher interruptions during oral reading instruction: Self-monitoring as an impetus for change in corrective feedback. *Remedial and Special Education, 7*(5), 18–24.

Sloyer, S. (1982). *Reader's theater: Story dramatization in the classroom.* Urbana, IL: National Council of Teachers of English.

Snow, C. E., Burns, M. N., & Griffin, P. (1998). *Preventing reading difficulties in young children.* Washington: National Academy Press.

Stayter, F., & Allington, R. (1991). Fluency and the understanding of texts. *Theory into Practice, 30*(3), 143–148.

Topping, K. (1987). Peer tutored paired reading: Outcome data from ten projects. *Educational Psychology, 7,* 604–614.

Topping, K., & Ehly, S. (1998). *Peer-assisted learning.* Mahwah, NJ: Lawrence Erlbaum Associates.

Viorst, J. (1972). *Alexander and the terrible, horrible, no good, very bad day.* New York: Atheneum.

Vygotsky, L. S. (1978). *Mind in society.* Cambridge, MA: Harvard University Press.

Wood, K. D. (1983). A variation on an old theme: 4-way oral reading. *The Reading Teacher, 37*(1), 38–41.

Zutell, J., & Rasinski, T. (1991). Training teachers to attend to their students' oral reading fluency. *Theory into Practice, 30*(3), 211–217.

Chapter 15

Literature Response

"Boys and girls, I'd like to share several books with you today. Listen carefully as I tell you about each so that you can vote on which literature circle group you would like to join."

Mr. Jackson shared three book titles, *Tuck Everlasting, Fog Magic,* and *The Great Gilly Hopkins,* with his third-grade class by giving a brief "book talk" about each. Children were handed a ballot containing the titles of the three books to rank in order from their first choice to their last choice. After voting, Mr. Jackson collected the ballots. He tallied the votes to form three literature circle groups with between eight and ten students each. Students, wherever possible, were given their first choice literature circle selection. Next, Mr. Jackson met with each of the three groups for about five minutes to decide how many pages in the books each group will read before the next literature circle meeting and how students will respond to their reading. After the meeting of the second group, Mr. Jackson overhears a conversation between two children.

"Wow, this is going to be fun. We get to read books we choose. We get to talk about the books and do projects of all kinds. I think I'm going to like this."

"Me too," intones the other student.

The teacher in this class realizes the multiple benefits of "marinating" children in books and talk about text.

BACKGROUND BRIEFING FOR TEACHERS

Basal readers have dominated reading instruction in the United States for many years. More and more teachers in America's classrooms are using children's literature as a primary vehicle for teaching literacy skills (Morrow & Gambrell, 2000). Several researchers have documented a 20% increase in the use of literature as the primary means for providing reading instruction over a period of the past two decades (Gambrell, 1992; Strickland, Walmsley, Bronk, & Weiss, 1994). This trend is also evident in current basal reading series that contain many reprinted excerpts of award-winning literature (Hoffman et al., 1994; Reutzel & Larsen, 1995). One of the leading basal publishers, in fact, paid well over $50 million in royalties to children's book authors to cover the cost of reprinting their stories!

One of the most exciting changes in today's literacy instruction is a movement away from the traditional assumption that each text holds only one correct meaning or interpretation. For both the child and the teacher, this change transforms the act of reading and reading instruction from a pursuit to discover an author's (or, very often, the teacher's) single correct message to discovering meaning based, at least in part, on one's own life experiences.

An alternative approach, called **reader response,** provides for a much more active role for students (Bleich, 1978; Rosenblatt, 1978, 1989). Reader response advocates suggest that there are many possible meanings in a text, depending upon the reader's background and reaction to the text. Instruction guided by reader response seeks balance by considering the reader's background experiences, beliefs, and purposes for reading, as well as the author's style and intended meaning. The role of the teacher is to assist each child to develop a creative product—usually a written response in some form—that explains her understanding of the author's message.

Literature-based instruction is characterized by four major elements: 1) a knowledgeable teacher who guides children enthusiastically through the literature, 2) a classroom environment and teaching practices that encourage talk about the literature, 3) a teacher who encourages students to make choices about books, and 4) time and access to materials to read and respond (Galda, Cullinan, & Strickland, 1993). Literature-based reading instruction, coupled with reader response activities, seems to hold great promise for readers having learning problems as well as for mainstream learners (Morrow, 1992; Morrow, Pressley, Smith, & Smith, 1997; Reutzel & Cooter, 1990; Reutzel et al., 1989). Increasing numbers of teachers who work with struggling readers are catching the spirit and excitement of using children's literature and response activities to spark reading among reluctant readers. Excellent results are reported from around the nation where students having reading problems are discovering anew the joy of reading and writing with real books rather than struggling to learn to read with the often sterile, controlled readers used in the past (Goatley, 1996; Goatley, Brock, & Raphael, 1995; Goatley & Raphael, 1992; Tunnell & Jacobs, 1989).

This chapter provides teachers with the information necessary to understand the shift in focus from text-centered instruction to a more balanced reading approach that brings quality texts and an active reader together. We begin with assessment tools that can help teachers determine where students are in their reading development and comprehension. This chapter also offers appropriate strategies for helping students to respond to written text in ways that greatly enhance their reading comprehension and to develop insights into different forms of writing and authoring.

READER RESPONSE THEORY

Many teachers were reared with the tenets of *Critical Formalism* or *New Criticism* in their elementary, secondary, and postsecondary experiences with literature study. As undergraduate and graduate students, we were taught to love and admire the close and critical reading of poetry and prose. As we read, the text was considered an isolated object that we should objectively and dispassionately prepare to discuss and analyze. This process of literature study was almost like examining a glass prism and considering it from all possible points of view by carefully turning it about in space. If we merely turned it and handled it, we would not alter the work's integrity. Hence, literature was to be processed as an object separate from its social, political, or historical context. This was literature study without the influence of the reader or the writer. It was a rather sterile analysis of the text with attention directed toward genre and structure, as well as to such stylistic devices as mood, imagery, and metaphor. Christenbury (1992) captured the feeling of this approach when he wrote, "What for us was a celebration of the intricate art of literature for our students became a repugnant dissection of an already difficult text, robbing it of joy, making it a task, not a connection to life" (p. 34).

Out of an increasing sense of dissatisfaction with the *New Criticism* approach to literature study, Norman Holland (1975) and David Bleich (1978) proposed a more subjective position, called *Subjective Criticism,* that stated that the reader was most important. This position, however, became as untenable as the former position that emphasized the singular importance of the text.

Rosenblatt's (1978) *transactional theory* declared reading and literature study to be a carefully orchestrated relationship between reader and text. Reader response evolved, in part, out of the work of Rosenblatt (Kelly, 1990). A *transaction* suggests a special type of relationship between the reader and the text—an act that causes the reader to be motivated to construct a personal meaning for a particular text. Situational conditions, such as time, mood, pressures, reason, intents, and purposes for reading, influence a reader's stance, or attitude, toward a piece of literature. Rosenblatt described two stances—efferent and aesthetic—in discussing how readers may choose to focus their attention during reading.

Efferent Stance

When readers focus their attention on information to be remembered from reading a text, they are taking an **efferent stance.** For example, reading the driver's license manual in preparation for an upcoming driving examination exemplifies an efferent stance toward a text. Reading a novel for the purpose of writing a book report that summarizes the plot is another example of taking an efferent stance toward text. However, when readers assume an efferent stance toward a novel, the focus of their attention is upon memorizing or gleaning from the text to pass a test rather than upon enjoying and learning from the experience. Obviously, there is a need for another type of reader stance or motivation for reading a text—an aesthetic stance.

Aesthetic Stance

When adopting an **aesthetic stance,** the reader draws on past experiences, connects these experiences to the text, often savors the beauty of the literary art form, and becomes an integral participant in the unfolding events of the text. When reading John Scieszka's *The True Story of the Three Little Pigs* to students—even college students—they never remark how the text follows accepted narrative form or contains three major repetitive plot episodes! Instead, they connect the zany perspective of the wolf's account and their own past experiences with the original tale of "The Three Little Pigs." Arising from the bizarre twist of perspectives represented between the two stories, the humor of these perspectives often produces gales of laughter among students as they see the story through the eyes of the character "A. Wolf." Assuming an aesthetic stance toward a text leads to making personal connections and reporting feelings and images, as well as ideas about how the story may occur in our own lives.

The quality or validity of readers' responses is often a concern for teachers who have been schooled in the "single correct" interpretation of *New Criticism.* "How can we determine if a response to a text is valid?" is an oft-asked question. Karolides (1992) explained that the validity of a response depends on the degree to which an individual response

- includes the various features of the text and the nuances of language,
- includes aspects that do not reflect the text, and
- leads the reader to create a coherent reaction.

Discussion of texts as a whole class or sharing responses in small groups, called *Literature Circles,* lead students into *Grand Conversations* about literature (Daniels, 1994; Peterson & Eeds, 1990; Tompkins 2001). During these *Grand Conversations,* students are exposed to a range of responses to a text. Such discussions can motivate students to extend, clarify, and understand their own reactions to the text read. Further, comparing their responses to those of peers can help students to recognize that there can be more than one valid interpretation of a text.

In the next part of this chapter, a listing of various informal tasks for assessing reader response is presented. These may be used to determine the quality of thought, preparation, diligence, and attitudes toward literature study and reader response.

ASSESSING READERS' RESPONSES TO LITERATURE

Assessing children's responses to literature focuses on several different dimensions. First, responding to literature is intended to assure that children deepen and broaden their comprehension of the materials they read. Second, individual and group preparation for and participation in literature response groups or literature circles are another dimension of assessment. Third, literature response participation is expected to positively influence children's attitudes toward reading. So, assessing students' attitudes is an important part of examining the impact of literature response participation on students. We provide some tools for observing students' interactions with books during literature discussion and during independent reading time. And finally, we provide a tool for assessing student cooperation and teamwork during literature response group meetings. By using these assessment tools, teachers can gain a comprehensive understanding of their students' engagement with literature and literature discussions.

LITERATURE RESPONSE READING COMPREHENSION ASSESSMENT

Purpose

Teachers building balanced reading programs using trade books quickly find that they must construct minilessons and assessment strategies to account for reading skills to be taught. Angeletti (1991) developed a way to engage children in a blend of reading, writing, and talking about books that yielded the necessary skill-based accountability demanded by many schools, districts, states, and basal readers. Although conceived of as teaching strategy, Angeletti's approach to questioning is quite effective as an assessment procedure.

Materials

For this activity, you will need standard-sized white letter paper, 11" × 14" colored construction paper, and a marker. If available, a computer with a word processing program and printer with large font or type size should be used for best results. Question cards should be produced similar to those shown in Figure 15.1.

Procedure

Begin by printing the question cards on white paper and mounting each question card on a colored construction-paper backing. Next, pick a type of questioning you wish to emphasize. During shared reading or literature circle study, ask children questions of this chosen type for several days. After this, show the children the question card you have

𝒲 **Figure 15.1**   Question Cards

Comparison and contrast card 1
Choose two characters from one story. Do the characters look alike? How are they alike? How are they different? What problems do the two characters have that are the same? How are the feelings of the characters different?

Comparison and contrast card 2
Choose two stories. How were the places where the stories took place alike or different? How were the stories the same? How were they different? How were the story endings different? Which story did you like better? Why? Which character did you like better? Why?

Opinions
What did you like about the main character? What did the character do that made you like him or her? What did you think about the ending? Was anything surprising to you in the story? What was it? Why were you surprised?

Inference
Look at the pictures and at the title. What do you know about the story before you begin to read it? Read the story. Think about the ending. If the story had continued, what might have happened? Why?

Drawing conclusions
Draw a picture of your favorite character. Tell as much as you can about what kind of person your character is. Tell things he or she did in the story. Is this a nice person? Why or why not? Would you like to have this person for a friend? Why or why not?

Characters
As you read a story, you learn about the characters by what they say and do. Choose a character from your story. What kind of person is your character? Do you like him or her? Why? How would he or she act if you were with him or her?

Author's style
Every writer has his or her own way of writing, called *style.* When we learn the author's style, we know what to expect from that writer. We often know whether books written by a particular author will be easy picture books or chapter books. We know what kind of characters are typical of the writer—animals that talk, or people like us. We might know whether there will be a happy ending. We know whether we would enjoy reading another book by the same author. Choose an author whose style you know and tell what you know about the author's style of writing. Give examples from books you have read by that author.

Author's purpose
Sometimes authors write a story to teach you something. Sometimes they tell a story about something that happened to them. Sometimes they just want to entertain you. Or, they may have another reason for writing. Tell in one sentence why you think the author wrote the story you read. Then tell how you knew the author's reason for writing the story.

Type of literature
Tell what kind of book you are reading. Look for clues that let you know. If it is *fantasy,* or *fiction,* for example, there may be animals that talk, or magic things may happen. If it is *realistic fiction,* there may be real people in the story and the story could have happened, but the author made it up, perhaps using ideas from his or her own life. If you find rhyming words, short lines, and writing that makes every word count, you are reading *poetry.* Or, you may be reading facts from a book like an encyclopedia. If so, the book is *factual.* Think about what section of the library you would go to in order to find the book. Then put your book into one group and tell what clues let you know which type of book it is.

Source: Adapted from "Encouraging Students to Think About What They Read" by S. R. Angeletti, 1991, *The Reading Teacher, 45*(4), 288–296. Copyright 1991 by the International Reading Association.

selected for emphasis. Model with a book how the question could be answered. Follow-up with whole-class practice with a shared book. Finally, practice in small groups and individually. Encourage students to select a question card to guide the construction of their responses in a literature log. Each of these responses to question cards can be judged against the type of "comprehension skill" represented by the question for documenting skill acquisition and instruction.

INDIVIDUAL LITERATURE RESPONSES ASSESSMENT

Purpose

Although many teachers recognize the value of literature study groups (also called literature study circles), they often feel a need to satisfy the political realities of documenting student progress and growth as a result of their teaching. One means for doing this is to develop a checklist outlining the expectations for those who participate in literature study groups. Such a checklist can be used to assess student readiness or preparation prior to participation in the literature study group as well as to yield qualitative information about each student's participation during the literature study group (Peterson & Eeds, 1990).

Materials

The *Literature Study Preparation and Participation Evaluation Record* shown in Figure 15.2 is the main item needed for this activity.

Procedure

One form should be duplicated for each student in the literature study group. We recommend that the "Preparation" section be completed prior to participation and reevaluated at the conclusion of the literature study session. The "Participation" section should then be completed at the end of the literature study to evaluate each participant. Other items may be added to Figure 15.2 to tailor its use to individual classroom needs.

GROUP LITERATURE DISCUSSION ASSESSMENT

Purpose

Although many teachers are coming to recognize the value of literature-based reading instruction, they also feel a need to satisfy the political realities of documenting student progress as a result of using literature to teach children to read (Hoyt, 1999). One means for doing this is to use a group checklist that outlines the qualities of young children's participation in quality literature discussions before, during, or after interactive read aloud or shared reading sessions. Such a checklist is used to assess overall student participation in the literature discussion as well as to yield qualitative information about each student's participation (Peterson & Eeds, 1990; Vogt, 1996).

Materials

The *Group Literature Discussion Checklist* shown in Figure 15.3 is the main item needed for this activity.

Procedure

One form should be duplicated for each student in the literature study group. We recommend that each participant complete the form at the conclusion of the literature study

Figure 15.2   Literature Study Preparation and Participation Evaluation Record

Record of Preparation for and Participation in Literature Study*			
Name: _____	Date: _____		
Author: _____	Title: _____		
Preparation for Literature Study			
Brought book to group	Yes _____		No _____
Contributed to developing a group reading plan	Yes _____		No _____
Worked according to group reading plan	Yes _____		No _____
Read the book	Yes _____		No _____
Took note of places to share (ones of interest, ones that were puzzling, etc.)	Yes _____		No _____
Did nightly assignments as they arose from the day's discussion	Yes _____		No _____
Participation in Literature Study			
Overall participation in the dialogue	Weak _____	Good _____	Excellent _____
Overall quality of responses	Weak _____	Good _____	Excellent _____
Referred to text to support ideas and to clarify	Weak _____	Good _____	Excellent _____
Listened to others and modified responses where appropriate	Weak _____	Good _____	Excellent _____
_____ **	Weak _____	Good _____	Excellent _____
_____ **	Weak _____	Good _____	Excellent _____
_____ **	Weak _____	Good _____	Excellent _____

*We suggest using this form at the end of each literature study to evaluate each participant.

**The rest of the items are intended to tailor this evaluation to your individual students. Choose appropriate items to complete the form from those listed in the Response to Literature Checklist in Figure 15.4 or add those you think are most appropriate.

Source: From *Grand Conversations: Literature Groups in Action,* by R. Peterson and M. Eeds, 1990, New York: Scholastic.

session. After reviewing the completed forms, the teacher should lead a discussion of the group's evaluation of the session and point out areas where improvement can be made in the future.

Student Literature Response Assessment

Purpose

Teachers want to know if children are making personal connections between their own lives and experiences and those recorded in the books they are reading. Some teachers may want to assess whether students are interpreting and making meaning, or are gaining insights in a story as they read. Peterson and Eeds (1990) developed a *Response to Literature Checklist* that we have found particularly helpful in providing documentation of the way in which children respond to particular stories or books within that programmatic framework.

Figure 15.3   Group Literature Discussion Checklist

Title of Book Discussed _____   Author _____

Date _____

Put an "X" on the face that tells what you feel.

Everyone was prepared to discuss the book.   😊   😐   ☹️

Everyone contributed to the discussion.   😊   😐   ☹️

We kept our talk focused on the book.   😊   😐   ☹️

We asked good questions that helped us all think.   😊   😐   ☹️

We used the book to support our opinions and ideas.   😊   😐   ☹️

We were respectful of others having a turn to talk.   😊   😐   ☹️

We invited our peers to talk and express their ideas.   😊   😐   ☹️

We talked about how the author had structured
the writing.   😊   😐   ☹️

We talked about how the author used words
and language.   😊   😐   ☹️

Materials

Copies of the Response to Literature Checklist in Figure 15.4 are needed for each student for this activity.

Procedure

A copy of the checklist should be made for each student. We recommend that the teacher not try to evaluate all students in every area of the checklist daily. Instead, select one or two students each day to observe (preferably without their knowledge). For example, you might decide to observe two students as they select and read books during Silent Sustained Reading (SSR) time while they are at their seats or in a reading nook. Then, for each of these students, you could complete Section I of the checklist: Enjoyment/Involvement. Another example of applying the checklist might include reading a student's reading log entry. You could determine whether the student was making sense of the reading or making personal connections. In this case, Sections II and III—Making Personal Connections and Interpretations/Making Meaning—would be used to assess the student's response to literature. Thus, the checklist should be used flexibly; teachers should not feel obligated to complete the checklist for every child during every observation. Instead, observations should be focused and selective.

STUDENT READING ATTITUDE SURVEY

Purpose

Developing positive attitudes toward reading and writing is the primary instructional goal for teachers of children. This is particularly true for teachers who work with readers having learning problems. Assessing the impact of using *real* books on their student's reading and writing attitudes, however, can be challenging.

Over the years, several informal attitude measures have been developed and validated for classroom use. Heathington and Alexander (1978) developed a primary and intermediate scale of reading attitude assessment. More recently, McKenna and Kear (1990) developed and validated a new instrument that is simple and effective for measuring reading attitudes. They incorporated into this instrument the Garfield cartoon character, but other characters, or figures ranging from smiling faces to frowning faces, may be substituted.

Materials

For each student, materials needed include one copy of the Reading Attitude Survey shown in Figure 15.5 and one copy of the Attitude Survey Scoring Sheet shown in Figure 15.6.

Figure 15.4 Response to Literature Checklist

I. Enjoyment/Involvement

_____ Is aware of a variety of reading materials and can select those he enjoys reading
_____ Enjoys looking at pictures in picture story books
_____ Responds with emotion to text: laughs, cries, smiles
_____ Can get "lost" in a book
_____ Chooses to read during free time
_____ Wants to go on reading when time is up
_____ Shares reading experiences with classmates
_____ Has books on hand to read
_____ Chooses books in different genres

II. Making Personal Connections

_____ Seeks meaning in both pictures and the text in picture story books
_____ Can identify the works of authors that he enjoys
_____ Sees literature as a way of knowing about the world
_____ Draws on personal experiences in constructing meaning
_____ Draws on earlier reading experiences in making meaning from a text

III. Interpretation/Making Meaning

_____ Gets beyond "I like" in talking about story
_____ Makes comparisons between the works of individual authors and among the works of different authors
_____ Appreciates the value of pictures in picture story books and uses them to interpret story meaning
_____ Asks questions and seeks the help of others to clarify meaning
_____ Makes reasonable predictions about what will happen in a story
_____ Can disagree without disrupting the dialogue
_____ Can follow information important to getting to the meaning of the story
_____ Attends to multiple levels of meaning
_____ Is willing to think about and search out alternative points of view
_____ Values other perspectives as a means for increasing interpretative possibilities
_____ Turns to text to verify and clarify ideas
_____ Can modify interpretations in light of "new evidence"
_____ Can make implied relationships not stated in the text
_____ Can make statements about an author's intent drawn from the total work
_____ Is secure enough to put forward half-baked ideas to benefit from others' response

IV. Insight Into Story Elements

_____ Is growing in awareness of how elements function in story
_____ Can talk meaningfully about
        characters
        setting
        mood
        incident
        structure
        symbol
        time
        tensions
_____ Draws on elements when interpreting text/constructing meaning with others
_____ Uses elements of literature in working to improve upon personal writing
_____ Is intrigued by how authors work
_____ Makes use of elements in making comparisons

Source: From _Grand Conversations: Literature Groups in Action,_ by R. Peterson and M. Eeds, 1990, New York: Scholastic.

Figure 15.5   Elementary Reading Attitude Survey

School: _____   Grade: _____   Name: _____

1. How do you feel when you read a book on a rainy Saturday?

2. How do you feel when you read a book in school during free time?

3. How do you feel about reading for fun at home?

Note: GARFIELD © PAWS

continued

Figure 15.5   Continued

4. How do you feel about getting a book for a present?

5. How do you feel about spending free time reading?

6. How do you feel about starting a new book?

Note: GARFIELD © PAWS

continued

Figure 15.5   Continued

7. How do you feel about reading during summer vacation?

8. How do you feel about reading instead of playing?

9. How do you feel about going to a bookstore?

Note: GARFIELD © PAWS

continued

Figure 15.5   Continued

10. How do you feel about reading different kinds of books?

11. How do you feel when the teacher asks you questions about what you read?

12. How do you feel about doing reading workbook pages and worksheets?

Note: GARFIELD © PAWS

continued

W **Figure 15.5   Continued**

13. How do you feel about reading in school?

14. How do you feel about reading your schoolbooks?

15. How do you feel about learning from a book?

Note: GARFIELD © PAWS

continued

Figure 15.5   Continued

16. How do you feel when it's time for reading class?

17. How do you feel about the stories you read in reading class?

18. How do you feel when you read aloud in class?

Note: GARFIELD © PAWS

continued

Ⱳ **Figure 15.5**   Continued

19. How do you feel about using a dictionary?

20. How do you feel about taking a reading class?

Source: Elementary Reading Attitude Survey, by Michael C. McKenna, and Dennis J. Kear, 1990, May. Measuring attitude toward reading: A new tool for teachers. *The Reading Teacher 43*(9), 626–639. Copyright © 1990 by Michael C. McKenna and the International Reading Association. All rights reserved.

Procedure

Instructions for the instrument in Figure 15.7 are those described by McKenna and Kear (1990). We suggest that you follow these instructions carefully so that the interpretive information found in Figure 15.8 can then be used.

DAILY READING RECORD

Purpose

Simple and easy-to-keep records of daily reading can give teachers an idea about how well students are progressing in developing positive reading habits. By using a version of the *Daily Reading Record* shown in Figure 15.9, students also develop a greater sense of their own reading habits. Thus, these records provide documentation of how well students use their time for reading as well as inducing in students a sense of pride in what they are accomplishing.

Figure 15.6   Elementary Reading Attitude Survey Scoring Sheet

Student name: _____

Teacher: _____

Grade: _____   Administration date: _____

Scoring guide

4 points	Happiest Garfield
3 points	Slightly smiling Garfield
2 points	Mildly upset Garfield
1 point	Very upset Garfield

Recreational reading

1. _____
2. _____
3. _____
4. _____
5. _____
6. _____
7. _____
8. _____
9. _____
10. _____

Raw score: _____

Academic reading

11. _____
12. _____
13. _____
14. _____
15. _____
16. _____
17. _____
18. _____
19. _____
20. _____

Raw score: _____

Full scale raw score (Recreational + Academic): _____

Percentile ranks   Recreational

Academic

Full scale

Source: From Elementary Reading Attitude Survey, by Michael C. McKenna, and Dennis J. Kear, 1990, May. Measuring attitude toward reading: A new tool for teachers. *The Reading Teacher,* 43(9), 626–639. Copyright © 1990 by Michael C. McKenna and the International Reading Association. All rights reserved.

W/ **Figure 15.7** Attitude Survey Directions

Directions for Use of Elementary Reading Attitude Survey
The *Elementary Reading Attitude Survey* provides a quick indication of student attitudes toward reading. It consists of 20 items and can be administered to an entire classroom in about 10 minutes. Each item presents a brief, simply worded statement about reading, followed by four pictures of Garfield. Each pose is designed to depict a different emotional state, ranging from very positive to very negative.

Administration
Begin by telling students that you wish to find out how they feel about reading. Emphasize that this is not a test and that there are no "right" answers. Encourage sincerity.

Distribute the survey forms and, if you wish to monitor the attitudes of specific students, ask them to write their names in the space at the top. Hold up a copy of the survey so that the students can see the first page. Point to the picture of Garfield at the far left of the first item. Ask the students to look at this same picture on their own survey forms. Discuss with them the mood Garfield seems to be in (very happy). Then move to the next picture and again discuss Garfield's mood (this time, a little happy). In the same way, move to the third and fourth pictures and talk about Garfield's moods—a little upset and very upset. It is helpful to point out the position of Garfield's mouth, especially in the middle two figures.

Explain that together you will read some statements about reading and that the students should think about how they feel about each statement. They should then circle the picture of Garfield that is closest to their own feelings. (Emphasize that the students should respond according to their own feelings, not as Garfield might respond!) Read each item aloud slowly and distinctly; then read it a second time while students are thinking. Be sure to read the item number and to remind students of page numbers when new pages are reached.

Scoring
To score the survey, count four points for each leftmost (happiest) Garfield circled, three for each slightly smiling Garfield, two for each mildly upset Garfield, and one point for each very upset (right-most) Garfield. Three scores for each student can be obtained: the total for the first 10 items, the total for the second 10, and a composite total. The first half of the survey relates to attitude toward recreational reading; the second half relates to attitude toward academic aspects of reading.

Interpretation
You can interpret scores in two ways. One is to note informally where the score falls in regard to the four nodes of the scale. A total score of 50, for example, would fall about midway on the scale, between the slightly happy and slightly upset figures, therefore indicating a relatively indifferent overall attitude toward reading. The other approach is more formal. It involves converting the raw scores into percentile ranks by means of Figure 15.8. Be sure to use the norms for the right grade level and to note the column headings (*Rec* = recreational reading, *Aca* = academic reading, *Tot* = total raw score). If you wish to determine the average percentile rank for your class, average the raw scores first; then use the figure to locate the percentile rank corresponding to the raw score mean. Percentile ranks cannot be averaged directly.

Source: From Elementary Reading Attitude Survey, by Michael C. McKenna, and Dennis J. Kear, 1990, May. Measuring attitude toward reading: A new tool for teachers. *The Reading Teacher, 43*(9), 626–639. Copyright © 1990 by Michael C. McKenna and the International Reading Association. All rights reserved.

Figure 15.8   Interpretive Information for Survey

Midyear Percentile Ranks by Grade and Scale

Raw Scr	Grade 1 Rec Aca Tot	Grade 2 Rec Aca Tot	Grade 3 Rec Aca Tot	Grade 4 Rec Aca Tot	Grade 5 Rec Aca Tot	Grade 6 Rec Aca Tot
80	99	99	99	99	99	99
79	95	96	98	99	99	99
78	93	95	97	98	99	99
77	92	94	97	98	99	99
76	90	93	96	97	98	99
75	88	92	95	96	98	99
74	86	90	94	95	97	99
73	84	88	92	94	97	98
72	82	86	91	93	96	98
71	80	84	89	91	95	97
70	78	81	86	89	94	96
69	75	79	84	88	92	95
68	72	77	81	86	91	93
67	69	74	79	83	89	92
66	66	71	76	80	87	90
65	62	69	73	78	84	88
64	59	66	70	75	82	86
63	55	63	67	72	79	84
62	52	60	64	69	76	82
61	49	57	61	66	73	79
60	46	54	58	62	70	76
59	43	51	55	59	67	73
58	40	47	51	56	64	69
57	37	45	48	53	61	66
56	34	41	44	48	57	62
55	31	38	41	45	53	58
54	28	35	38	41	50	55
53	25	32	34	38	46	52
52	22	29	31	35	42	48
51	20	26	28	32	39	44
50	18	23	25	28	36	40
49	15	20	23	26	33	37
48	13	18	20	23	29	33
47	12	15	17	20	26	30
46	10	13	15	18	23	27

continued

W Figure 15.8 Continued

Midyear Percentile Ranks by Grade and Scale

Raw Scr	Grade 1			Grade 2			Grade 3			Grade 4			Grade 5			Grade 6		
	Rec	Aca	Tot	Rec	Aca	Tot	Rec	Aca	Tot	Rec	Aca	Tot	Rec	Aca	Tot	Rec	Aca	Tot
45			8			11			13			16			20			25
44			7			9			11			13			17			22
43			6			8			9			12			15			20
42			5			7			8			10			13			17
41			5			6			7			9			12			15
40	99	99	4	99	99	5	99	99	6	99	99	7	99	99	10	99	99	13
39	92	91	3	94	94	4	96	97	5	97	98	6	98	99	9	99	99	12
38	89	88	3	92	92	3	94	95	4	95	97	5	96	98	8	97	99	10
37	86	85	2	88	89	2	90	93	3	92	95	4	94	98	7	96	99	8
36	81	79	2	84	85	2	87	91	2	88	93	3	91	96	6	92	98	7
35	77	75	1	79	81	1	81	88	2	84	90	3	87	95	4	88	97	6
34	72	69	1	75	78	1	75	83	2	78	87	2	82	93	4	83	95	5
33	65	63	1	68	73	1	69	79	1	72	83	2	77	90	3	79	93	4
32	58	58	1	62	67	1	63	74	1	66	79	1	71	86	3	74	91	3
31	82	53	1	56	62	1	57	69	0	60	75	1	65	82	2	69	87	2
30	44	49	1	50	57	0	51	63	0	54	70	1	59	77	1	63	82	2
29	38	44	0	44	51	0	45	58	0	47	64	1	53	71	1	58	78	1
28	32	39	0	37	46	0	38	52	0	41	58	1	48	66	1	51	73	1
27	26	34	0	31	41	0	33	47	0	35	52	1	42	60	1	46	67	1
26	21	30	0	25	37	0	26	41	0	29	46	0	36	54	0	39	60	1
25	17	25	0	20	32	0	21	36	0	23	40	0	30	49	0	34	54	0
24	12	21	0	15	27	0	17	31	0	19	35	0	25	42	0	29	49	0
23	9	18	0	11	23	0	13	26	0	14	29	0	20	37	0	24	42	0
22	7	14	0	8	18	0	9	22	0	11	25	0	16	31	0	19	36	0
21	5	11	0	6	15	0	6	18	0	99	20	0	13	26	0	15	30	0
20	4	9	0	4	11	0	5	14	0	6	16	0	10	21	0	12	24	0
19	2	7		2	8		3	11		5	13		7	17		10	20	
18	2	5		2	6		2	8		3	9		6	13		8	15	
17	1	4		1	5		1	5		2	7		4	9		6	11	
16	1	3		1	3		1	4		2	5		3	6		4	8	
15	0	2		0	2		0	3		1	3		2	4		3	6	
14	0	2		0	1		0	1		1	2		1	2		1	3	
13	0	1		0	1		0	1		0	1		1	2		1	2	
12	0	1		0	0		0	0		0	1		0	1		0	1	
11	0	0		0	0		0	0		0	0		0	0		0	0	
10	0	0		0	0		0	0		0	0		0	0		0	0	

Figure 15.9 Daily Reading Record

Student Reading Record Sheet

My Reading Record

Name: _____

Date	Pages read	Title	Author	Time Spent Reading

A daily reading record should have a place to list the author(s) and title of the book as well as the date, time, and pages read. In addition, a brief written response may be encouraged, but is not usually required on the Daily Reading Record.

Materials

For each child, one copy of the *Daily Reading Record* form, found in Figure 15.9, is needed.

Procedure

A time at the end of each day's literature study period should be allocated for student record keeping. During this brief period of 2–4 minutes, students should log into their Daily Reading Records the information required and be encouraged to write a brief response if they desire. The teacher should review students' Daily Reading Record forms at least weekly. We encourage teachers to avoid giving undue emphasis to the numbers of books read, recognizing instead the quality of the reading experience. Remember that "savoring" a good book takes time, just as fine food should be relished with appreciation.

OBSERVING STUDENT INTERACTION WITH BOOKS ASSESSMENT

Purpose

Teachers often observe the frequency and types of books students choose to read, but many do not keep records about when children choose to read, how frequently they read, and what types of books they select. To monitor and assist children in their book selections, we provide the *Observing Student Interactions With Books* assessment checklist. This checklist can be used to determine if children are selecting books that present them with an appropriate level of challenge as well as linking to their interests (See chapter 10 for a student interest survey). And teachers can, by using this assessment tool, observe how children use books as models for writing and as support for discussion in literature circles (Daniels, 1994; Hoyt, 1999; Spiegel, 1998).

Materials

One copy of the *Observing Student Interactions With Books* assessment checklist for each child in the classroom, shown in Figure 15.10, is needed.

Procedures

Observe children at least twice each reporting period (nine weeks) using the *Observing Student Interactions With Books*. Make note of the areas where children are progressing and where students need assistance, instruction, or encouragement. This checklist is also useful as a part of individual reading conferences held as a part of the reading workshop.

GROUP FEEDBACK ON LITERATURE DISCUSSIONS

Purpose

Sometimes it is important for students to see their own learning and participation through the eyes of their peers. For some students, such a process is not only a reality check, but also an opportunity to interact in positive ways to support and extend individuals within the

Figure 15.10 Observing Student Interactions With Books Checklist

Student's Name _____ Date of Observation _____

1. Child chooses to read when finished with assignments.

    Often   Sometimes   Seldom

2. Child selects books that are appropriate and interesting.

    Often   Sometimes   Seldom

3. Child talks about the books selected with others.

    Often   Sometimes   Seldom

4. Child explains why he likes or dislikes a book.

    Often   Sometimes   Seldom

5. Child listens to other children talk about books.

    Often   Sometimes   Seldom

6. Child responds to reading books in a variety of ways.

    Often   Sometimes   Seldom

7. Child talks about the author's writing.

    Often   Sometimes   Seldom

8. Child explains how the book is organized.

    Often   Sometimes   Seldom

9. Child can retell the major points of the book.

    Often   Sometimes   Seldom

10. Child connects to his own experience when discussing a book.

    Often   Sometimes   Seldom

group. By engaging in peer feedback and accountability, literature discussion groups and the individuals within these groups create and maintain a spirit of healthy interdependence (Johnson & Johnson, 1995; Slavin, 1999).

Materials

An example of a teammate individual feedback form is shown in Figure 15.11. This or a modified version can be duplicated and distributed to teams to be completed at the conclusion of daily cooperative group activities.

Procedure

The *Group Feedback on Literature Discussions* form shown in Figure 15.11 is given on a periodic (usually weekly) basis to students within a group or partnership to be filled out on another individual. Next, partners or teammates share their comments and rating with the individual they evaluated. Encouragement in weak areas should be given and praise should be offered for the many and varied contributions the partner or teammate makes to the successful completion of group goals and tasks. Teachers should first model the types of responses and verbal feedback to be offered during discussions.

Figure 15.11   Group Feedback on Literature Discussions

Student Peer Name _____

Evaluator Name _____

1. My friend offers facts, opinions, or ideas to help the group discussion.

   Usually   Frequently   Seldom   Never

2. My friend expresses a willingness to cooperate with other group members.

   Usually   Frequently   Seldom   Never

3. My friend supports group members who are struggling to participate in the group.

   Usually   Frequently   Seldom   Never

4. My friend listens carefully and respectfully to others in the group when they express themselves.

   Usually   Frequently   Seldom   Never

5. My friend evaluates the contributions of other group members in terms of usefulness and correctness.

   Usually   Frequently   Seldom   Never

6. My friend takes risks to express new ideas and feelings during a group discussion.

   Usually   Frequently   Seldom   Never

7. My friend expresses awareness of and appreciation for the gifts, talents, abilities, and skills of other group members.

   Usually   Frequently   Seldom   Never

8. My friend offers support and help to other team members.

   Usually   Frequently   Seldom   Never

9. My friend shares materials, books, resources, or information with others to help in the completion of tasks or solving problems.

   Usually   Frequently   Seldom   Never

10. My friend is open and willing to share and participate in the group.

    Usually   Frequently   Seldom   Never

CONNECTING ASSESSMENT FINDINGS TO TEACHING STRATEGIES

Before discussing reading response strategies, we have constructed a guide connecting assessment to intervention and/or strategy choices. It is our intention to help you, the teacher, select the most appropriate instructional interventions and strategies to meet your students' needs based on assessment data.

In the next part of this chapter, we offer strategies for intervention based on the foregoing assessments.

RESPONDING TO READING FOR ALL CHILDREN

After a careful assessment of each student's or each group's reading responses, comprehension, work habits, and attitudes as outlined previously, one or more of the following

Intervention Strategy Guide for Literature Response

Intervention Strategy / Student Problem(s)	Imagery	Lit. Circles	Response Journals	Art as Response	Intertextuality	Cooperative Group Rotation	Collaborative Reasoning	Book Club	Author Studies	Story Telling	Drama
Poor Comprehension	+	*	*	*	+	-	+	*	*	*	*
Poor Preparation	-	+	+	+	-	+	-	+	*	*	*
Poor Participation	*	+	*	+	-	+	-	+	*	+	+
Poor Attitudes	*	*	*	*	*	*	*	*	*	*	*
Lack of Accountability	-	*	+	+	*	+	*	*	*	*	*
Lack of Collaboration	-	*	-	-	-	+	*	*	*	*	*
Lack of Engagement With Books	*	+	*	*	+	-	*	+	+	*	*

Key: + excellent strategy
* adaptable strategy
- unsuitable strategy

Figure 15.12 Imagery Hints

Hints on Imaging

1. Inform students that making pictures in their minds can help them understand what a story or passage is about. Specific directions, depending upon whether the text is narrative or expository, may be helpful. For example, "Make pictures in your mind of the interesting characters in this story." "Make pictures in your mind about the things that happened in this story." "Make a picture in your mind of our solar system." Using visual imagery in this manner encourages students to integrate information across the text as they engage in constructive processing.

2. Inform students that, when something is difficult to understand, it sometimes helps to try to make a picture in their minds. Using visual imagery can help students clarify meaning, and it encourages them to think about whether they are comprehending.

3. Encourage students to make visual images about stories or information they want to remember. Tell them that making pictures in their minds can help them remember. As a follow-up to story time or the silent reading of basal stories, have students think about the visual images they made and encourage them to use their images to help them retell the story to a partner (or, as homework, to retell the story to a parent or sibling). This activity will help students realize the value of using visual imagery to enhance memory.

reading response strategies or lesson frameworks may be appropriately applied. Perhaps the most important thing to remember is that children who do not respond or who respond poorly must receive regular opportunities to talk about books, stories, and texts for authentic and motivating reasons, such as to gather information, to present a dramatization, or simply discuss a favorite story. The strategies described in this section offer effective and varied means for teachers to help children respond to reading in authentic, effective, and motivating ways!

IMAGERY: MAKING MENTAL MOVIES OF TEXT

Purpose

When students make visual images about what they read, the mental "movies" provide an effective framework for organizing, remembering, and constructing meaning from text (Sadoski & Quast, 1990; Wilson & Gambrell, 1988). Unfortunately, some readers with learning problems do not spontaneously create mental movies as they read and thus miss out on the comprehension-monitoring boost that mental movies can give them (Gambrell & Bales, 1986). Wilson and Gambrell (1988) indicated that specific instruction in how and when to apply *imagery* as a comprehension tool can be extremely helpful for students.

Materials

Activities and materials proposed by Wilson and Gambrell (1988) are summarized in Figure 15.12.

Procedure

Because research on visual imagery tells us that some students do not spontaneously use visual imagery, but can when directed to do so, teachers need to provide guidance and practice in the use of imagery. Wilson and Gambrell (1988) recommended the following considerations when selecting materials to be used to encourage visual imagery:

1. For modeling and teacher-guided practice activities, select brief passages of about paragraph length.
2. Choose passages that have strong potential for creating "mental movies" (i.e., those that typically contain rich descriptions of events and objects).
3. Point out that not all text material is easy to visualize—especially when the material is about unfamiliar and abstract concepts. Tell students that in those instances they should select another strategy that would be easier to use and more helpful (be prepared with suggestions that better fit some of the text types they are likely to encounter). With minimal guidance and practice, students can learn and enjoy using visual imagery to enhance their reading experiences.

LITERATURE RESPONSE GROUPS (LITERATURE CIRCLES)

Purpose

The purpose of *literature response groups* (also known as *literature study circles*) is to emphasize the importance of reading and discussing children's literature or trade books (Daniels, 1994; Eeds & Wells, 1989; Peterson & Eeds, 1990; Reutzel & Cooter, 2000; Samway et al., 1991; Short, Harste, & Burke, 1988). Samway and others (1991) reported that many students who participate in literature response groups often go through dramatic changes in just one year:

> We noticed that in literature study circles the students naturally and spontaneously compared books and authors; initiated and sustained discussion topics as they arose; built their literary repertoires; and made associations between events and characters in books and their own lives. (p. 205).

Additionally, our own experiences with literature response groups/study circles have caused us to become great believers in this teaching and learning option.

Materials

You will need six to eight copies of four or five books that will interest students and duplicated choice ballots as shown in Figure 15.13. You will also need to prepare a book talk on each of the four or five books selected.

Figure 15.13   Choice Ballots

Literature Response Groups Choice Ballot

Name: _____

1st choice: _____

2nd choice: _____

3rd choice: _____

Procedure

To initiate literature response groups, begin by selecting four or five books that will engender interest and discussion among students. Next, give a book talk on each of the four or five titles selected, enthusiastically presenting and describing each book to the students. Then, ask students to individually select their top three book choices they want to read. After the student ballots have been collected, make an assignment sheet for each book title. Give each student her first choice. If too many students want the same title, go to each student's second choice as you compile the assignments list. This system works well, because students always know that they get to read a book of their own choosing. After books are distributed the next day, give the students a large block of uninterrupted reading time in class to read. At the beginning of the year, students can read about 20 minutes without undue restlessness. However, later in the year children can often sustain free reading for up to one full hour.

As students complete several hours of independent reading, each literature response group (comprising those students reading the same title, and thus interest based) meets on a rotating basis for about 20 minutes with the teacher. Group members discuss and share their initial reactions to the book. We have found that meeting with one literature response group per day—with a maximum of three days independent reading between meetings—works quite well.

Based on the group discussion, an assignment is given to the group to extend the discussion of the book into other interpretive media (i.e., writing, art, drama, and so on). Each member of the Literature Response Group works on this assignment before returning to the group for a second meeting. This sequence of reading and working on an extension response assignment repeats until the entire book is completed. We recommend that the first extension assignment focus on personal responses and connections with the book. Subsequent assignments can focus on understanding literary elements (i.e., characterization, point of view, story elements, role of the narrator, and so on). At the conclusion of the book, the literature study circle meets to determine a culminating project (Reutzel & Cooter, 2000; Zarillo, 1989). This project captures the group's interpretation and feelings about the entire book as demonstrated in a mural, story map, diorama, character wanted posters, and so on.

RESPONSE JOURNALS AND LOGS

Purpose

Children grow as readers as they learn to use their knowledge, experiences, and feelings to construct a personal response text. *Response journals and logs* offer students "an active and concrete means of participating in the text" (Tashlik, 1987, p. 177). When personal responses are encouraged, students feel an innate need to share their ideas, feelings, and questions (Parsons, 1990; Stillman, 1987). Journal writing results in more complete and elaborate responses to literature than questions provoke and, most importantly, facilitates students' growth, confidence, and motivation to read (Wollman-Bonilla, 1991a).

Materials

Collect reading materials 1) of high interest to students, 2) of high-quality literary merit, 3) within the reading abilities of the students, and 4) with text that helps integrate language arts within discipline-based content learning areas. Each student will also need a response journal. This can consist of almost any type of bound, lined, or unlined paper (e.g., loose-leaf paper, spiral notebook, composition notebook, stenographer's notebook, and so on).

Procedure

Using an overhead projector, begin by showing students several sample journal or log entries that reflect a range of possible responses. Text selections already familiar to students work best. Be sure to include honest feelings, questions, and reflections. Consider the following suggestions to guide responses based on Wollman-Bonilla (1991b, p. 22):

1. What you like or disliked and why
2. What you wish had happened
3. What you wish the author had included
4. Your opinion of the characters
5. Your opinion of the illustrations, tables, and figures
6. What the text reminds you of
7. What you felt as you read
8. What you noticed about how you read
9. Questions you have after reading

Once students begin using journals or logs, teachers need to find time to respond to students' responses. This sends a clear message that journal responses are not simply a required exercise, but that someone cares about how the students feel about reading.

Perhaps the most important reason for replying to students' journal entries is to teach and support students. Finding time to do so is relatively easy. Do not feel that you must respond to each student every day, but simply respond on a rotating basis. As you do so, consider the following ideas:

- Share your own ideas and feelings about the book.
- Provide additional information where needed.
- Develop students' awareness of reading strategies and literary techniques.
- Model elaborated responses.
- Challenge students' thinking.
- Offer alternative perspectives on the student's observations from a book.

Journals and logs provide students with important evidence of their own growth in reading as well as substantial assessment data for teachers. Students can be brought to higher levels of thinking, greater strategic use of reading strategies, deeper understanding of literature, and improved skill in communicating their ideas through journal and log responses to literature. But the most important frequent outcome of journaling is an increase in the desire to read!

ART AND LITERATURE

Purpose

Drawing helps students understand that there are ways to respond to their reading, such as through music, art, drama, writing, and movement. Siegel (1983) claimed that by translating and expressing what we know and feel from one communication system (written language, for example) into another (say, music, dance, or art), new knowledge and understanding are created. This process of "recasting" knowledge or feeling into another form of expression is called *transmediation*.

Figure 15.14   Art Literature Response Ideas

Responding to Books Through Art
- Construct a mobile of your favorite characters from a book.
- Build a 3-D model of the setting from your favorite story.
- Draw a wanted poster for your favorite story character.
- Design a new book jacket for your favorite book.
- Construct an author mobile showing the titles and illustrations of your favorite author.
- Make flannel characters to support a retelling of your favorite story.
- Make a frieze to illustrate a book.
- Make an illustrated timeline mural of events occurring in the book.
- Make a stained-glass window replica using tissue paper and cellophane.
- Make illustrated bookmarks.
- Make a TV Cranky of the book's plot with a box and rollers.
- Carve soap sculptures for a book's characters.
- Illustrate placemats from a favorite book.
- Make a mask for a character in a book.
- Construct a paper-bag puppet for a character in a book.
- Illustrate a mural-sized story map showing the setting and events of a book.

Materials

Artistic media of all varieties (e.g., paints, markers, brushes, easels, paper, pencils, chalk, crayons, cloth, and so on) are the materials needed for this activity.

Procedure

Figure 15.14 lists suggestions for art activities. An almost infinite number of possibilities exist for using art to respond to literature.

EXPLORING MULTIPLE TEXTS AND MAKING CONNECTIONS

Purpose

For students to become lifelong readers, they need to regularly enjoy rich and satisfying experiences with great books. It is sometimes difficult, however, to help students find books that offer positive experiences for every class member. Consequently, it is important to offer as many choices for students as possible (Poe, 1992), especially for comprehension instruction.

Reading comprehension instruction has often been viewed traditionally in terms of having individual students recount the story line or the main idea of the passage (Hartman, 1992; Hartman & Allison, 1996). This is actually contrary to what better readers do, namely, comprehending text along a somewhat zigzag path. When reading is understood as a complex, layered process that cuts across the boundaries of single passages, stories, or texts, then using multiple texts to intensify readers' transactions takes on increasing importance. Hence, using multiple texts on a single topic or theme not only helps readers to develop and appreciate individual responses to books but also helps to develop their capacity to make intertextual links between different books.

Materials

Once a theme is chosen, you will need a selection of related texts to support that topic or theme. You will also need to develop a procedural minilesson on using multiple texts for literature study, as discussed in the procedures section.

Procedure

To begin, invite students to write in their journals about the selected theme (e.g., grandparents). Students should express in their journals their feelings, thoughts, and associations concerning this concept. These prewriting entries can be used at the end of a literature study to compare their pre- and postreading thoughts and knowledge levels. Next, select three or four novels on the theme of grandparents, such as *Grandparents: A Special Kind of Love; Childtimes: A Three-Generation Memoir; Grandmother Came From Dworitz;* and *Grandpa, Me and the Wishing Star.* Introduce the three or four novels about grandparents by giving a brief book talk on each. Tell the children they will be reading these books to explore their own response.

During the weeks in which students are reading the novels, they should discuss them periodically in small literature discussion groups. Each group should comprise a mix of students who are reading the given book based on choice. In other words, their grouping should not be based on assumed ability levels. Students should decide, as a group, which days will be reading days and which will be discussion days. In these groups, students should share and expand upon their responses, developing understanding about why they and others in their group reacted as they did. Teachers should sit in on these discussions regularly to evaluate students' participation in this important aspect of the unit. As students finish their books, they should write their response to the work as a whole. Whole-book responses give students an opportunity to synthesize their thoughts and feelings about the book, reflect on their experiences with it, and self-evaluate what they gained from reading it.

After writing whole-book responses, groups gather for a class discussion and presentation. Students in each group lead a panel discussion of each person's responses to their group's book. When all groups have finished their presentations, students are invited to make comments that connect the commonalities among the three or four books read by members of the class. A comparison grid is often helpful for making these comparisons (Reutzel & Cooter, 2000). One example of a comparison grid is shown in Figure 15.15.

Finally, individual students usually engage in personal response projects intended to make stronger their connections to the text read. They often create a project that appropriately expresses their responses to an aspect of the book they read. Students share their projects with the class by explaining the relationship between their project, the book, and their feelings or thoughts about the book.

COOPERATIVE GROUP ROTATION

Purpose

By using *cooperative group rotation* (Mermelstein, 1994), students have access to a variety of quality literature books and to nonfiction trade books in small-group settings. Children participate actively in gathering and using information to create projects that demonstrate their growing knowledge of subject matter.

Figure 15.15   Comparison Grid for the Grandparents Theme

	Grandparents: A Special Kind of Love	Childtimes: A Three-Generation Memoir	Grandmother Came from Dworitz	Grandpa, Me and the Wishing Star
Grandparent				
Significant other				
Problem				
Resolution				
Theme/Moral				

Materials

You may want to design a poster that describes the expectations and processes of the *Cooperative Group Rotation,* such as the one shown in Figure 15.16. Also needed are topic, subject, or theme-related trade books sufficient in number for each group.

Procedure

Begin the process by dividing the students into groups of four or five. Next, the group assigns the major roles at the beginning of each day's sessions: *reader, note taker,* and

Figure 15.16   Cooperative Group Rotation

Cooperative Group Rotation
1. Get together with your assigned group or team.
2. Decide who will fill the roles of reader, note taker, and leader for today. *(Remember this should change each day.)*
3. The "reader" should get the book for the day and read it aloud to the rest of the group.
4. The "leader" reminds the reader to stop at the end of each page and ask the group members to answer the question, "What do you think was important on the page?"
5. The "note taker" writes down the group's answers to the question, "What do you think was important on the page?"
6. Select a project from the following list for today's book:
   - Composing different kinds of poetry
   - Drawing a picture showing the topic or subject
   - Writing a paragraph about the subject
   - Creating an adjective word web
   - Writing a creative story about the subject
   - Making a puppet
   - Creating a diorama
7. Choose your favorite project to display when the group has finished reading the book.

leader. Next, select at least enough books on a selected subject, topic, or theme for each group to have one book per group. The student selected for the role of the reader reads the book aloud to the rest of the group, stopping at the end of each page. The student selected as the leader reminds the reader to stop at the end of each page and asks the group members to answer the question, "What do you think was important on the page?" After this, the student selected to fill the role of the note taker writes down the group's answers to the question. When the group has finished reading the book, each student selects a project about the topic using the book and the note taker's list as resources. For the next day's sessions, the remaining books are rotated around the groups, so that all of the groups will have an opportunity to read the books. After the group reads all the books, the students complete their individual projects for each book. Finally, each student selects his favorite project to be displayed in a class portfolio, display area, or bulletin board.

COLLABORATIVE REASONING DISCUSSIONS

Purpose

"Collaborative reasoning (CR) is an approach to literature discussion intended to stimulate critical reading and thinking and to be personally engaging" (Chinn, Anderson, & Waggonner, 2001, p. 383). During CR discussions, children take a position on a central question raised by a story. Then they present reasons and evidence for and against their positions. Using a collaborative reasoning (CR) discussion has been shown to increase student engagement in reading and in discussion. It has also been shown to induce students to use higher-level cognitive processes than other forms of discussion (Chinn et al., 2001).

Materials

A list of possible central questions about the story or text, around which different positions may be taken, is needed.

Procedure

A CR discussion begins with the students reading a story or text silently at their seats. After reading, students and teacher gather as a group. The teacher begins the discussion with a single, central story question about a significant issue related to the story or text. It is possible to write more than one question about a significant issue related to the text or story. For example, *The Paper Bag Princess* (Munsch & Munsch, 1988) is a story about a princess who has fallen in love with a prince who is kidnapped by a fire-breathing dragon. Elizabeth, the princess, takes off on a long quest to find her prince charming in a paper bag because her clothes were burned up when the dragon carried off her prince. At the end, the princess looks a mess but rescues her prince from the clutches of the dragon. When the prince sees her, he tells her to come back when she looks more like a princess. The question for this story might be, "Should Elizabeth marry the prince anyway?" After the question is asked, children raise their hands to share their positions. They may adopt a "yes" or "no" position or they may say, "the prince needs to apologize and then the princess should forgive him." Some children might suggest that the princess date someone else for a while to make the prince jealous. Other students may support these positions or take their own. When disagreements come up, they challenge one another with counterarguments and present text-based evidence. During the CR discussion, the teacher says little or nothing during long stretches of time. When teachers do enter the discussion, they should ask students to clarify their ideas, prompt students to present evidence, and model clear arguments and counterarguments. During this time, students speak without raising

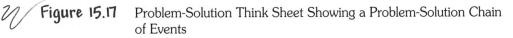

Figure 15.17 Problem-Solution Think Sheet Showing a Problem-Solution Chain of Events

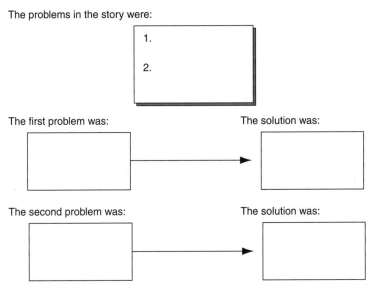

their hands in an open participatory structure. In the end, the interpretative authority for the story rests with the students. Books on how people work in collaborative settings may be a good prerequisite for using CR discussions (See Wood, Roser, & Martinez, 2001).

Book Clubs

Purpose

Book Clubs provide teachers a structure for providing groups of students engaging experiences with books, opportunities to talk about books as a community of learners, time to teach specific strategies and skills, and a way to foster an enjoyment of and appreciation for reading. During Book Club (BC) meetings, students read, write, respond, and participate in instruction. Book Clubs not only enable children to develop their literacy abilities, they also encourage a desire to read and an appreciation of texts because children have extended opportunities to read, write, and discuss their stories and texts (McMahon & Raphael, 1997).

Materials

Select a quality book recommended by others, with a reputable author, and on a topic of interest to the students and the teacher. Use a focused, short writing assignment (See Figure 15.17).

Procedure

A Book Club meeting begins with the selection of a quality text or book for discussion. To be effective, Book Club books must be quality literature, reflect character diversity (ethnicity, gender, class, and race), and meet curricular needs. To meet curricular needs, Book Club books must meet the needs of students and address the skills and strategies included in the district curriculum guide. Once a quality book is chosen, the Book Club begins with reading the book. During the Book Club time, teachers and students read books aloud to model fluent reading. The teacher may begin reading a part of the book to set the example and the tone for reading. Frequently following the teacher, students read silently. In some cases, students read in pairs, taking turns. Students are also encouraged to keep their Book Club books handy for reading when they have free time, at recess, and lunch. Students must complete the same amount of reading to participate in discussions. So, if Book Club time is insufficient to complete the amount of reading needed to participate in the discussion, then students must plan their reading to include additional time out of school or during the day.

During Book Club reading, students are given the choice of where they read. They can read their books anywhere in the room or in the adjacent hallway, as long as they read. They can sit on the floor, lie under a table, or stand in a corner, so long as they are comfortable and are reading. Students who struggled with reading are provided additional support during the Book Club reading time. Some are given additional time to read. Some are given individual or small group instruction with the teacher focusing on particular needs.

Once the reading assignment is completed, students engage in a reading-writing connection. Writing within the Book Club takes two primary forms: 1) short, focused writing and 2) extended writing projects. Short, focused writing could be done in the student's "Reading Log" or using a "Think Sheet" focusing on a particular writing procedure using prompts. Extended writing projects typically take the form of theme essays, stories within the genre of the Book Club book, and informational writing (i.e., articles or reports).

Having read and written about the reading assignment, all students are ready to discuss the assigned portion of the Book Club book. During discussions, the teacher focuses students' conversations around literary elements such as characters, sequence of the story, or text elements, making intertextual links between the book being read and others read previously. Daily writing assignments may be focused on helping students consolidate their understanding of story/text characters, story elements, and connections with other books after the discussion concludes and a new book or portion of a book is to be read by the next meeting date. In many ways, the Book Club structure parallels the *Reading Workshop* described in chapter 4.

AUTHOR STUDIES

Purpose

Author studies involve learning about the author as a person and a writer, and becoming acquainted with his published works (Kotch & Zackman, 1995). Studying an author and sharing books written by an author can bond every member of the class into a community of learners. Sharing an author's techniques and strategies helps students gain insights into the author's craft as a writer. Choosing authors whose works spans various genres facilitates curriculum integration across subject fields.

Materials

Select three or four books published by a single author.

Procedure

When selecting an author, students' interests, reading and writing needs, and attitudes need to be considered. Once the author has been identified, information about that author can

Figure 15.18   Example of a Language Chart for a Literacy Unit

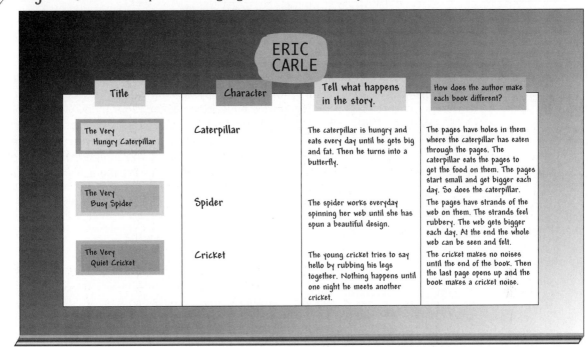

be obtained from publishers, Internet sites, books, and tapes. Some of these resources are listed here:

- *Meet the Authors and Illustrators, Vols. I & II.* Deborah & James Preller. (1991, 1993) Scholastic.
- *Meet the Authors, Vol. 1–5.* Rozanne Williams. (1993). Creative Teaching Press.
- *Scholastic Authors on Tape,* Scholastic

Roser, Hoffman, and Farest (1990) offered the use of a Language to Literacy Chart to compare authors' works along the lines of genre, themes, illustrations, special effects, characters, settings, episodes, and resolutions. Language to Literacy charts are constructed from large pieces of butcher paper ruled into a lattice or matrix with headings that help to focus children on relations among various books read in a unit or in various response groups. In Figure 15.18, the chart includes headings on title, characters, the goals or purposes of the characters, and how the author makes each of his books special or different. Children are invited to respond to each of Eric Carle's books separately under the first three headings. Under the final heading, children respond to the books by comparing the techniques the author used to make each book distinctive. One way to minimize the risk of language charts limiting the range of responses is to begin by simply recording students' initial, unorganized responses to literature in a *collection* language chart. Then, another more *focused* language chart with specific categories drawn from the collection language chart could be used to organize a chart as shown in Figure 15.18.

ADDITIONAL STRATEGIES FOR ENGLISH LANGUAGE LEARNERS

DRAMA AS LITERATURE RESPONSE

Purpose

McCaslin (1990) asserted that *creative drama* is an art, a socializing activity, and a way of learning. Drama as an art form to satisfy human needs and to foster the development and learning of children has been recognized by leading educators for many years (Rhodes & Dudley-Marling, 1988; Siks, 1983). As an oral and interpretive response to literature, Lynch-Brown and Tomlinson (1993) strongly recommended creative drama for use with children of all ages and abilities. McCaslin (1990) specifically recommended creative drama activities for students with learning problems. Creative drama is the act of informal play-making comprised of several distinct techniques:

- Plays
- Movement and rhythms
- Pantomime
- Improvisation
- Puppetry and mask making
- Reader's and chamber theater

Creative drama offers teachers and children a wide array of possibilities for responding to literature through dramatic interpretation. McCaslin (1990) recommended that teachers bear in mind the following as they use creative drama for interpretive responses to literature:

1. Creative drama activities should be based on literature.
2. Authors create the dialogue and scripts are not prepared or memorized.
3. Improvisation is a critical feature of creative drama.
4. Acting is primarily through improvisation and movement; there is minimal use of props.
5. Creative drama is for the benefit of the performers, not for the approval of an audience.
6. No one dramatic interpretation of a story is correct. Several interpretations are to be encouraged.

Materials

Materials needed for dramatic interpretations include a good story, chapter, or literature book, and perhaps an assortment of props such as hats, glasses, puppets, clothes, etc. (optional).

Procedure

Creative drama is an enjoyable literature response alternative that makes use of children's imagination and oral language. Some educators have said, "Drama comes in the door of the school with every child" (Siks, 1983, p. 3). Literature-based drama may reenact a single scene from a chapter, a short picture book, or a brief story. It is best to begin with simple, short stories with two to six characters and a great deal of action. Folktales and fairy tales tend to fit this description well. When using creative drama to interpret literature responses, the following steps should be kept in mind:

1. Students listen to or read the story selected.
2. Students determine if this is a story they would like to act out. If so, they then read or listen to the story again, paying particular attention to the characters, action, and sequence of the story episode.
3. Students list the events on the board or on chart paper to review their sequence.
4. Students cast the play.
5. Actors use the list of sequenced events to plan actions, dialogue, and props suitable for the dramatization.
6. The cast of actors takes a few minutes to decide how the play will be presented and then rehearses it.
7. After the first performance, other students or groups can be invited to evaluate the success of the first performance. Actors in the performance can also self-evaluate their performance.

Based on McCaslin (1990), we suggest the following questions to guide the evaluation of dramatic interpretations of books and stories:

- Did the performance tell the story?
- What did you like about the opening scene?
- Did the characters show they were excited and interesting?
- When we play it again, can you think of anything that would improve the performance?
- Was anything important left out?

Including All Students

Storytelling as Literature Response

Purpose

Storytelling is first and foremost an art form (Sawyer, 1970). Cooter (1991) explained that storytelling—an ancient art form—is enjoying renewed attention nationally in language arts classrooms. Goodlad (1984), in his book, *A Place Called School,* punctuated the need for breaking the emotional neutrality of most American classrooms. Storytelling appears to offer a solution to this problem.

Although teachers may enjoy storytelling as an exciting teaching strategy, children can also find increased joy in responding to their reading through storytelling. We say this for at least two major reasons. First, children can learn more about the richness of our language through storytelling. And second, they can reach out to their environment and other persons through storytelling (Ross, 1980). Teaching students how to select and tell stories well is an important means of dramatically responding to literature and exploring new modes of self-expression.

Materials

Construct a poster showing the four steps to becoming a storyteller, as described in Figure 15.19.

Figure 15.19   Storytelling Poster

Steps to Becoming a Storyteller
- Find a story that is just right for *you*.
- Prepare the story for telling.
- Use books, props, and voices.
- Get the audience involved.

Procedure

Tell children that a storytelling response to a story begins by selecting a story that suits their personality and preferences. The storyteller and the story must become emotionally linked to be believable. Therefore, children should not select storytelling as a reader response unless the story truly interests them. Next, encourage each child to prepare to tell the story by "picturing" the events, characters, setting, and episodes in the story in her mind's eye. She should read the story repeatedly until the story line is fully committed to memory . . . like a "mental movie." If a story has a specific sequence or linguistic dialect, children should learn the language of the story verbatim. Tell each child that practicing the storytelling alone in her bedroom or in front of a mirror allows for seeing herself as she is seen.

After rehearsing, some storytellers enjoy selecting props such as eyeglasses, hats, makeup, or puppets. Children storytellers can be invited to consider various simple props for telling their story. In addition, using different voices to tell a story is very effective. Varying the pitch of one's voice, adjusting the speed of speech, or using dialects or foreign accents establishes story characters as real and believable. However, subtlety is an important key, because extreme variations of one's voice can also detract from the story.

Finally, arrange a legitimate audience for children storytellers. Groups of classroom peers or younger children are the most readily available audiences for child storytellers. For some children, a performance at home with their families may be a sufficient audience. Encourage young storytellers to get their audiences involved in parts of the story. This can be accomplished by copying a repeated phrase in the text onto a large cue card for the audience members to read at various points in the storytelling. For example, in "The Gingerbread Man," the cue card might read: Run, run as fast as you can. You can't catch me, I'm the Gingerbread Man.

To bring a storytelling event to closure, teachers may wish to ask a child storyteller to construct a storytelling map modeled after a story grammar map (see chapter 10) in order to review the parts and plot of the story in a visual graphic form for display in the classroom.

SELECTED REFERENCES

Angeletti, S. R. (1991). Encouraging students to think about what they read. *The Reading Teacher, 45*(4), 288–296.

Bleich, D. (1978). *Subjective criticism.* Baltimore, MD: Johns Hopkins University Press.

Chinn, C. A., Anderson, R. C., & Waggonner, M. A. (2001). Patterns of discourse in two kinds of literature discussion. *Reading Research Quarterly, 36*(4), 378–411.

Christenbury, L. (1992). The guy who wrote this poem seems to have the same feelings as you have: Reader response methodology. In N. J. Karolides (Ed.), *Reader response in the classroom: Evoking and interpreting meaning in literature.* New York: Longman.

Cooter, R. B. (1991). Storytelling in the language arts classroom. *Reading Research and Instruction, 30*(2), 71–76.

Daniels, H. (1994). Literature circles: Voice and choice in the student-centered classroom. York, ME: Stenhouse.

Eeds, M., & Wells, D. (1989). Grand conversations: An exploration of meaning construction in literature study groups. *Research in the Teaching of English, 23,* 4–29.

Galda, L., Cullinan, B. E., & Strickland, D. S. (1993). *Language, literacy and the child.* New York: Harcourt Brace.

Gambrell, L., & Bales, R. J. (1986). Mental imagery and the comprehension-monitoring performance of fourth- and fifth-grade poor readers. *Reading Research Quarterly, 21*(4), 454–464.

Gambrell, L. B. (1992). Elementary school literacy instruction: Changes and challenges. In M. J. Dreher & W. H. Slater (Eds.), *Elementary school literacy: Critical issues* (pp. 227–239). Norwood, MA: Christopher-Gordon.

Goatley, V. J. (1996). The participation of a student identified as learning disabled in a regular education book club: The case of Stark. *Reading & Writing Quarterly: Overcoming Learning Difficulties, 12*(2), 195–214.

Goatley, V. J., Brock, C. H., & Raphael, T. E. (1995). Diverse learners participating in regular education "book clubs." *Reading Research Quarterly, 30*(3), 352–380.

Goatley, V. J., & Raphael, T. E. (1992). *Non-traditional learners' written and dialogic response to literature: Fortieth yearbook of the National Reading Conference* (pp. 313–322). Chicago: National Reading Conference.

Goodlad, J. I. (1984). *A place called school: Prospects for the future.* New York: McGraw-Hill.

Hartman, D. K. (1992). Eight readers reading: The intertextual links of able readers using multiple passages. *Reading Research Quarterly, 27*(2), 122–123.

Hartman, D. K., & Allison, J. (1996). Promoting inquiry-oriented discussions using multiple texts. In L. B. Gambrell & J. F. Almasi (Eds.), *Lively discussions: Fostering engaged reading* (pp 106–133). Newark, DE: International Reading Association.

Heathington, B. S., & Alexander, J. E. (1978). A child-based observation checklist to assess attitudes toward reading. *Reading Teacher, 31*(7), 769–771.

Hoffman, J. V., McCarthey, S. J., Abbott, J., Christian, C., Corman, L., Curry, C., et al. (1994). So what's new in the new basals? A focus on first grade. *Journal of Reading Behavior, 26*(1), 47–73.

Holland, N. N. (1975). *5 readers reading.* New Haven, CT: Yale University Press.

Hoyt, L. (1999). *Revisit, reflect, retell: Strategies for improving reading comprehension.* Portsmouth, NH: Heinemann.

Johnson, D. W., & Johnson, R. T. (1995). *Learning together and alone: Cooperative, competitive, and individualistic learning* (5th ed.). Boston: Allyn & Bacon.

Karolides, N. J. (1992). *Reader response in the classroom: Evoking and interpreting meaning in literature.* New York: Longman.

Kelly, P. R. (1990). Guiding young students' response to literature. *The Reading Teacher, 43*(7), 464–471.

Kotch, L., & Zackman, L. (1995). *The author studies handbook: Helping students build powerful connections to literature.* New York: Scholastic.

Lynch-Brown, C., & Tomlinson, C. M. (1993). *Essentials of children's literature.* Boston: Allyn & Bacon.

McCaslin, N. (1990). *Creative drama in the classroom.* New York: Longman.

McKenna, M. C., & Kear, D. J. (1990). Measuring attitude toward reading: A new tool for teachers. *The Reading Teacher, 43*(9), 626–639.

McMahon, S. I., & Raphael, T. E. (1997). *The book club connection: Literacy learning and classroom talk.* New York: Teachers College Press.

Mermelstein, B. (1994). Cooperative group rotation. *The Reading Teacher, 48*(3), 281–282.

Morrow, L. M. (1992). The impact of a literature-based program on literacy achievement, use of literature, and attitudes of children from minority backgrounds. *Reading Research Quarterly, 27*(3), 251–275.

Morrow, L. M., & Gambrell, L. B. (2000). Literature-based reading instruction. In M. L. Kamil, P. B. Mosenthal, P. D. Pearson, & R. Barr (Eds.), *Handbook of Reading Research (Vol. 3,* pp. 563–586). Mahwah, NJ: Lawrence Erlbaum.

Morrow, L. M., Pressley, M., Smith, J. K., & Smith, J. (1997). The effect of a literature-based program integrated into literacy and science instruction with children from diverse backgrounds. *Reading Research Quarterly, 32*(1), 54–76.

Munsch, R. N., & Munsch, M. (1988). *The paper bag princess.* Toronto: Annick Press.

Parsons, L. (1990). *Response journals.* Portsmouth, NH: Heineman.

Peterson, R., & Eeds, M. (1990). *Grand conversations: Literature groups in action.* New York: Scholastic.

Poe, E. A. (1992). Intensifying transactions through multiple text exploration. In N. J. Karolides (Ed.), *Reader response in the classroom: Evoking and interpreting meaning in literature.* New York: Longman.

Reutzel, D. R., & Cooter, R. B. (1990). Whole language: Comparative effects on first-grade reading achievement. *Journal of Educational Research, 83*(5), 252–257.

Reutzel, D. R., & Cooter, R. B. (2000). *Teaching children to read: Putting the pieces together* (3rd ed.). Upper Saddle River, NJ: Merrill/Prentice Hall.

Reutzel, D. R., & Larsen, N. S. (1995). Look what they've done to real children's books in the new basal readers! *Language Arts, 72*(7), 495–507.

Reutzel, D. R., Oda, L. K., & Moore, B. H. (1989). Developing print awareness: The effect of three instructional approaches on kindergartners; print awareness, reading readiness, and word reading. *Journal of Reading Behavior, 21*(3), 197–217.

Rhodes, L. K., & Dudley-Marling, C. (1988). *Readers and writers with a difference*. Portsmouth, NH: Heinemann.

Rosenblatt, L. M. (1978). *The reader, the text, and the poem*. Carbondale, IL: Southern Illinois University Press.

Rosenblatt, L. M. (1989). Writing and reading: The transactional theory. In J. M. Mason (Ed.), *Reading and writing connections*. Boston: Allyn & Bacon.

Roser, N. L., Hoffman, J. V., & Farest, C. (1990). Language, literature, and at-risk children. *The Reading Teacher, 43*(8), 554–561.

Ross, R. (1980). *Storyteller*. Columbus, OH: Charles E. Merrill Publishing Company.

Sadoski, M., & Quast, Z. (1990). Reader response and long-term recall for journalistic text: The roles of imagery, affect, and importance. *Reading Research Quarterly, 24*(4), 256–272.

Samway, K. D., Whang, G., Cade, C., Gamil, M., Lubandina, M. A., & Phommanchanh, K. (1991). Reading the skeleton, the heart, and the brains of a book: Students' perspectives on literature study circles. *The Reading Teacher, 45*(3), 196–205.

Saywer, R. (1970). *The way of the storyteller*. New York: Penguin Books.

Short, K., Harste, J., & Burke, C. (1988). *Creating classrooms for authors*. Portsmouth, NH: Heineman.

Siegel, M. (1983). *Reading as signification*. Unpublished doctoral dissertation, Indiana University.

Siks, G. B. (1983). *Drama with children*. New York: Harper & Row.

Slavin, R. E. (1999). *Cooperative learning: Theory, research, and practice* (2nd ed.). Boston: Allyn & Bacon.

Spiegel, D. L. (1998). Reader response approaches and the growth of readers. *Language Arts, 76*(1), 41–48.

Stillman, P. (1987). Of myself, for myself. In T. Fulwiler (Ed.), *The journal book* (pp. 77–86). Portsmouth, NH: Heineman.

Strickland, D. S., Walmsley, S., Bronk, G., & Weiss, K. (1994). *School book clubs and literacy development: A descriptive study*. (Rep. No. 2.22). Albany, NY: State University of New York, National Research Center on Literature Teaching and Learning.

Tashlik, P. (1987). I hear voices: The text, the journal and me. In T. Fulwiler (Ed.), *The journal book* (pp. 171–178). Portsmouth, NH: Heineman.

Tompkins, G. E. (2001). *Literacy for the 21st century: A balanced approach*. Upper Saddle River, NJ: Merrill/Prentice Hall.

Tunnell, M. O., & Jacobs, J. S. (1989). Using "real" books: Research findings on literature based reading instruction. *The Reading Teacher, 42*, 470–477.

Vogt, M. E. (1996). Creating a response-centered curriculum with literature discussion groups. In L. B. Gambrell & J. F. Almasi (Eds.), *Lively discussions: Fostering engaged reading* (pp. 181–193). Newark, DE: International Reading Association.

Wilson, R. M., & Gambrell, L. B. (1988). *Reading comprehension in the elementary school*. Boston: Allyn & Bacon.

Wollman-Bonilla, J. E. (1991a). Reading journals: Invitations to participate in literature. *The Reading Teacher, 43*(2), 112–113.

Wollman-Bonilla, J. E. (1991b). *Response journals*. New York: Scholastic Inc.

Wood, K. D., Roser, N. L, & Martinez, M. (2001). Collaborative literacy: Lessons learned from literature. *The Reading Teacher, 55*(2), 102–111.

Zarillo, J. (1989). Teachers' interpretations of literature-based reading. *The Reading Teacher, 43*(1), 22–29.

Chapter 16

Getting Families Involved: A Primer

"M. J." is Ruth Adams' mother and she has come in for a parent-teacher conference.

"I want to help Ruth become a better reader, but there's one big problem," said M. J. rather sheepishly, "I don't read so well myself. Y'know, I never finished high school."

"Oh, M. J., that's quite alright. There are lots of things you can do to help Ruth become a better reader and writer," I began. "For one thing, children *love* to read out loud to their mom. All you have to do is be a good listener and ask a few questions. And that's just the beginning. Let's talk about some of the other things you can do for Ruth that will really make a difference!"

M. J.'s face lit up as we talked about three powerful ways she could help Ruth at home.

Later, I said, "M. J., we're trying to organize a community reading program and I need some help. Would you be interested?"

I could tell by her expression that I had a new "recruit"!

Families, in sending their children to our schools each day, send to us the best and most precious gift they have. When we are able to offer them quality suggestions of ways they can help their children succeed, they deeply appreciate the assistance; they are the bedrock of support for their children.

A "failure analysis," a process first invented in the 1960s by NASA for the space shuttle program, conducted by the Dallas (TX) school district concluded that parent and community involvement are essential for student success in reading (May & Rizzardi, 2002). Between birth and the age of 19, children spend just 9% of their lives in school, and 91% elsewhere. Paul Barton (1992, 1994) of the Educational Testing Service estimated that 90% of the difference among students and their schools across the United States could be explained by five factors: numbers of days absent from school, number of hours spent watching television, number of pages read for homework, quantity and quality of reading materials in the home, and the presence of two parents in the home. That fifth factor is supremely important because it is apt to decisively influence the other four (Will, 2002). Barton (1992) concluded that school success is heavily dependent on the platform of readiness and support of learning created in the home.

If we are to maximize the learning potential of every child, we must enlist the aid of family members. We cannot afford to overlook the needs, strengths, contributions, and perspectives that family members can bring to school programs (Handel, 1999, p. 127). Recognition of adult family members as a valuable resource is evident nowadays in such federal legislation as the 1998 Reading Excellence Act, the Workforce Investment Act, and President Bush's No Child Left Behind Act.

In this chapter, we share several ideas that have been shown to be effective in getting families involved in their children's literacy development. Because this chapter is quite *unlike* our others (there is no real diagnosis of reading problems to be done), we simply summarize key research briefly, then share some great ideas used in effective classrooms. We do, however, include a chart that explains which ideas are appropriate for each age group.

BACKGROUND BRIEFING FOR TEACHERS

Sara Williams (2001), in an extensive review of the research concerning family involvement in children's education, offered some valuable insights. First, it is important that we understand that many families are rather passive in their children's education; not necessarily because of a lack of interest in their child's future, but often due to a lack of knowing just *what* to do. Sadly, one study (Garshelis & McConnell, 1993) concluded that families having the greatest needs (i.e., poverty issues, children with severe handicaps, and so on) are less likely to feel they have input in their child's education. Williams' (2001) second research finding was that "professionals [teachers] should serve a more facilitative and empowering role for families" (p. 10). Given that so many family members lack either the knowledge or financial resources to provide books and reading opportunities in the home, it is incumbent on the teacher to help bring resources and information to the primary caregiver. Although many might argue that this is not necessarily the role teachers should play, it is clear that inaction will lead to more of the same and jeopardize student success. Finally, Williams (2001) concluded that there is a need for further training and education for teachers in this area. Few teachers are prepared to take charge of family involvement programs, but the need is clear. Therefore, teachers should receive extensive professional development, support, and necessary materials to encourage family involvement.

In this section, we take a look at other important research findings that relate to family involvement.

MORE ACCESS LEADS TO MORE READING

In his book *The Literacy Crisis: False Claims, Real Solutions,* Jeff McQuillan (1998) made a powerful case for increasing student access to books in the home. In summarizing a number of rigorous research studies on the topic of access, McQuillan came to the following conclusions:

- More access to reading materials leads to more reading, and subsequently higher reading achievement.

- In a study of parental attitudes among a group of African American families where such variables as speaking to children about certain topics, telling children how to pronounce words correctly, teaching names of countries and states, and so forth were discussed, the *only* behavior that correlated significantly with reading scores was the number of books in the home. Thus, providing reading materials to low-income African American families, concludes this study, may be one of the most important things schools can do.

- In a study of middle school reluctant readers, the primary reason for students' infrequent reading was not a dislike of reading necessarily, but because they did not have access at home to the kinds of reading materials that interest them (e.g., comics, magazines, books on relevant topics). In another study, reading performance was improved at elementary and junior high schools when students were given two free subscriptions to magazines of their choice.

THE NEED FOR COMMUNITY INVOLVEMENT

Families can be approached either directly or indirectly. For example, an indirect way of getting the attention of adult family members is through community-wide efforts. Cooter, Mills-House, Marrin, Mathews, and Campbell (1999) reported success in gaining community involvement in reading through a number of strategies, which we highlight later in this chapter. Here is a brief summary of the types of activities they found helpful.

- *Summer Food and Reading Programs*—Efforts involving community religious organizations provide food to children of poverty and also nourish their minds with books. Volunteers work with children in motivational read alouds, DEAR time (Drop Everything And Read), and discussion groups.
- *Public Access Television*—School districts in metropolitan areas are allotted free public access airtime on television, time that often goes unused. A "Reading Channel" that brings reading ideas into the living rooms of families can be put together inexpensively.
- *Web Pages*—The Internet is rapidly becoming a commonplace tool in many homes and businesses. Sponsorship of a community web page by such groups as the Rotary, Chambers of Commerce, and local corporations can be quite effective.
- *Citywide DEAR Time*—Imagine a day each month when the entire city stops at an appointed time just to pull out a book and read as a sign of solidarity and recognition of the necessity of reading. Citywide Drop Everything and Read (DEAR) accomplishes just that.

FAMILY INVOLVEMENT AND ENGLISH LANGUAGE LEARNERS

A rapidly growing segment of the school population is the English Language Learner (ELL): students who are learning English as their second language. Indeed, in many southwestern school districts in the United States, ELL learners are the majority. The question then arises, *How can we assist the family members of ELL children in reading development?* This can be quite a challenge for teachers who are not bilingual themselves.

One avenue that shows a great deal of promise relates to adult education as part of family involvement with children. It is a well-known and accepted research finding that the mother's level of education correlates positively with the school achievement of her children (McQuillan, 1998). Many mothers of ELL children in urban areas, however, have low levels of education and often cannot speak English themselves. Therefore, there is a double challenge: helping mothers increase their own literacy levels while also teaching them ways to assist their children in reading. Yarosz and Barnett (2001) concluded from their research that parent education programs targeting those with the least education might be especially valuable in trying to improve the literacy levels of children.

A successful research project known as the *Harvest America's Family Reading Program* (Lanteigne & Schwarzer, 1997) provides us with a splendid prototype that can work in many communities. Adult English classes are held in a local library having an extensive collection of adult education and ESL materials. Each week, six children's books are selected that would interest both adults and children. The books are read aloud and discussed as part of the adult class. The focus is on ways of reading aloud to *children* and strategies for discussing the content, new vocabulary, and reactions to the stories. Test results confirmed that the reading proficiency levels of both children *and* adults in the program (many men participate as well as moms) improved dramatically.

BE PROACTIVE

Williams (2001) concluded that teachers must be proactive in seeking family involvement using an *enablement model.* Teachers, she said, should:

1. *Offer supportive assistance* to adult family members, rather than wait for a problem in students' reading to emerge.

2. *Help families set reading goals* such as turning off the television at a designated time each night for family reading.

3. *Suggest materials and activities that will not be an uncomfortable burden* for the family in terms of time or financial resources. You do not want costs to outweigh benefits.

4. *Offer aid that can be reciprocated,* if desired. Some families, particularly those from poverty, are more likely to respond if they can "give something back" to the school for what they have received. Even illiterate adults as parent volunteers can be good listeners for children reading aloud, for example.

5. *Try not to interfere with the family's natural supports.* School efforts should not supplant or interfere with a family's own ability to provide reading resources for themselves.

ACTIVITIES MATCHED TO GRADE LEVELS

Following is a listing of the Family Outreach Activities found in the remainder of the chapter matched to appropriate grade levels for your convenience. Note that many can be adapted for different levels.

FAMILY AND COMMUNITY INVOLVEMENT ACTIVITIES
PART I: PROVIDING MATERIALS AND STRATEGIES FOR THE HOME

START OUT RIGHT: CONTACT THE FAMILY

Harry Wong has a superb book that we highly recommend to teachers, titled *The First Days of School* (Wong & Wong, 1998), in which he explains how to get your school year off on the right foot. One of his ideas is to send home a letter that tells parents the following*:

- That you are looking forward to having their child in your class

- Asks them to put the dates of the school's open house on their calendar, and explains that it is important for them to attend as you will be explaining homework, grading, discipline, classroom procedures, and *what they can do at home to help their child succeed*

- Include a list of materials the child will need at school, *and at home.*

*Note: the parts in italics we have added

Intervention Strategy Guide for Getting Families Involved

Intervention Strategy → Student Problem(s) ↓	Refrig-erator Reading	Family Projects	Voice Mail	Reading Backpacks	Class-books	Writing Briefcase	Buddy Journals	Wishbone Video	DEAR City	Ed Major Pen Pals	Summer Food/ Read	Reading Channel	Internet Home Page
K–2	+	+	*	+	+	+	+	+	+	+	+	+	+
3–4	+	+	+	+	+	+	+	+	+	+	+	+	+
5–8	*	*	+	*	*	*	+	–	+	+	+	*	+

Key: + excellent strategy
     * adaptable strategy
     – unsuitable strategy

At the first open house, use that time to "train" your parents on strategies they can use at home that will help their child grow in reading and writing abilities. In this section are strategies and tools you might consider for parent involvement.

REFRIGERATOR READING

Purpose

Whether engaging in a major reading initiative in a large urban center or in a single classroom, communication with families is critical. Many times adults will say to teachers, "I would love to help my child become a better reader . . . I just don't know what to do. Can you help me?" Cooter et al. (1999) found that monthly newsletters for families are a great vehicle for communicating easy-to-do activities to primary caregivers. Theirs is called *Refrigerator Reading,* a reference to the age-old practice of putting important school papers on the refrigerator for everyone to see.

Materials

Refrigerator Reading newsletters are typically put together on a computer, then photocopied for each child to take home. Thus, you will need access to a computer, printer, and photocopier.

Procedure

The idea is to send home tips for parents on ways they can help their child develop in reading and writing in both Spanish or English, if necessary. You may choose to include such areas as helping your child self-select high-interest books using the "rule of thumb" method, how to do read alouds, how to encourage recreational writing, being a good listener when your child reads, conducting retellings, questioning after reading, study tips, ways to become involved in your child's classroom as a volunteer, and humorous tales about school life (like one principal's "No whining" rule).

Reports from Cooter and his colleagues (1999) were that some parents collect *Refrigerator Reading* newsletters and mail copies to grandmas and new moms, confirming the usefulness of this easy-to-do medium.

FAMILY PROJECTS

Purpose

Andrea Burkhart (2000), a teacher at a school on the south side of Chicago, asked parents to help her come up with ideas for family-school projects. They responded with many great ideas that she incorporated into her curriculum as *family projects* that get adults at home actively involved.

Materials

Plan on constructing a monthly newsletter with a full description of the family project assignment and "deliverables" (products you would like for the students to bring in to school when the project is done). Sometimes parents are willing to come in with their child to present their product!

Figure 16.1   Family Projects Curriculum

September: Family Tree
Parents and students work together to trace their family roots. They should create a visual display and present an object that reflects their family history, such as an antique picture, clothing, food, music, or literature.

October: Weather
Parents and students predict weather patterns for the next month. They will watch weather reports to compare their predictions and keep track of their work in a journal.

November: Family Reading Month
Parents and students read to or with each other daily. The books read and the amount of time spent reading will be recorded in a daily log and turned in at the end of November.

December: Biographies
Students learn about biographies and how they are constructed in class. They then create interview questions and interview a parent or primary caregiver. Students write a biography of that person and share it with their family.

January: Measurement
Parents and students predict the measurement (length, width, area, etc.) of an object or distance two or three times each week. After actually measuring each object, a journal entry is completed, showing the predicted measurement and the actual measurement.

February: Poetry Month
A book of family poetry is created. Students are responsible for educating their families about poetry, collecting the poems, and compiling them into a book.

March: Plants
Each student will take home two plants in milk cartons. The student will care for one, and an adult family member the other. One plant will be given light and the other plant will not. The progress of each plant will be tracked by the child and adult together and their progress recorded in a journal entry regularly.

April: Decisions
Two or three times per week students will take home a proposed (hypothetical) question that requires a decision. Topics might include issues related to drugs, gangs, honesty, or others proposed by parents. The parent and child will discuss options together and create a written response.

May: Simple Machines
After learning about simple machines in class, students will construct a simple machine with the guidance of a parent.

Source: From "Breaking the Parental Barrier" by A. L. Burkhart, in T. V. Rasinksi and N. D. Padak, et al. (Eds.), 2000, *Motivating Recreational Reading and Promoting Home-School Connections* (pp. 110–113), Newark: DE: International Reading Association.

Procedure

In Figure 16.1 is an outline of the topics Burkhart (2000) developed for her class. You will want to adapt and expand the descriptions to suit your needs and fit grade-level expectations.

VOICE MAIL

Purpose

Many teachers have access to their school district's voice mail system and usually have their own account/number. Willman (2000), a remedial reading teacher, used voice mail during the summer break to keep in contact with her students. They report back to her verbally about books they have chosen to read, and parents are often involved. We feel this strategy could be used throughout the school, as well as during summers for developing readers.

Materials

The primary tools needed for this activity are books for self-selection by students, a touch-tone phone, a voice mail account, and writing materials. For summer use, the students will need three books apiece; two fiction, one nonfiction (Willman, 2000).

Procedure

Begin by creating a letter to the parents explaining how the assignment will work, how to access the voice mail system, and what your expectations include. If you will be using this activity during the school year (as opposed to summer only), plan on conducting this briefing in person at the first open house.

In Willman's (2000) model, she asked students to call in to the voice mail and read aloud for three minutes or summarize a chapter from the book they are reading. It is also recommended that you have specific questions for each book for student response. They can answer these questions when they call in to read.

Another adaptation is for students to call in to the school's homework hotline to hear the teacher read aloud portions of the book. This provides a fluent reading model for students. However, a better idea is for parents to read aloud a portion of the book regularly for their child.

Willman (2000) reported that the summer voice mail program succeeded in its inaugural year in preventing all remedial readers from losing ground, and one student actually increased his reading level by a half year!

READING BACKPACKS

One of the challenges is getting high-quality books into the hands of children at home. Many families are economically disadvantaged and simply do not have books for their children to read. The *Reading Backpacks* strategy (Cooter et al., 1999) gets books of appropriate interest and reading levels into each child's home at least once per week.

Materials

Five backpacks per classroom (with the school logo or mascot, if possible), leveled books that can be sent home, writing materials, card stock, and markers are the required materials.

Procedure

Based on the Traveling Tales Backpacks concept (Reutzel & Cooter, 2000; Reutzel & Fawson, 1990) for promoting writing, Reading Backpacks contain a supply of trade books on varying topics and readability levels (often in both English and Spanish), easy activities for parents to do with their children on printed card stock adapted from Mooney's (1990) *Reading To, With, and By* strategies, a copy of the *Wishbone*™ video (discussed later in this chapter), and materials for written responses (markers, colored paper, scissors, and so on). Also included is a simple Family Report Form for adults to note which books were read by the child and to whom, as well as any reader response activities they are able to do at home. In this way, teachers are able to track student interests and, to a degree, outside reading habits.

Reading Backpacks are regarded as a wonderful success in many schools and are treasured by young readers.

CLASSBOOKS

Purpose

Laura Lee Scott (2000), a second-grade teacher, recommended the construction of *classbooks* by students to send home with children for reading and sharing with parents. Contributions for the classbook are made by each student using the writing process, or by the class as a whole using the language experience approach.

Materials

You will need writing materials for individual students to use in the writing process; or an easel, markers, and chart paper for use during a language experience with the class. Photocopies of the final classbook for each child will also be needed.

Procedure

Each student composes a contribution (i.e., story, poem, expository passage about a topic of interest, song, and so on) for the classbook independently; or the class writes together using a language experience approach. After working through the revising and editing process, copies of the classbook are taken home by students to share with adult family members. The book can be read *by* students to adults, or *to* students by the adult.

Some classbooks have emphasized academic subjects like science and social studies, as well as other topics of personal interest. Titles of student contributions included "If I Could

Be a Dinosaur," "My Mom," and "When I Grow Up." Classbooks constructed by the whole class in a language experience format have included "Halloween Stories" and "Christmas Memories."

Scott (2000) reported a great success using classbooks, including an increase of parent volunteers during her writing workshop period!

THE WRITING BRIEFCASE

Purpose

The *writing briefcase* (Miller-Rodriguez, 1992) is a brilliant idea that helps parents become more involved with their child's literacy learning. In our interpretation of this activity, students periodically take home a briefcase containing materials helpful in the creation of new compositions. We see the writing briefcase as especially useful for emergent writers and readers in the early grades and as a tool for involving parents in their child's literacy learning at home.

Materials

You will need an old briefcase (a backpack works just as well), stickers and other decorations for the outside of the briefcase, a laminated letter to the family member, markers, crayons, magazine pictures, word cards, picture dictionary, index cards, lined and unlined paper, tape, stapler, paper clips, rubber bands, scissors, and any other writing and illustrating materials of your choice, as well as easy-to-read books of various kinds that might inspire different text types (e.g., poetry, songs, stories, and so on).

Procedure

A different child takes home the briefcase each night and writes (or completes, in some cases) a story and illustrates it. She also reads her story, as well as the other books enclosed, to family members. A letter included in the briefcase is directed to family members, explaining the activity and the importance of their involvement. This letter ideally serves as a follow-up refresher course on the writing and other literacy-learning processes previously described by the teacher at the beginning of the school year in a parent meeting expressly held for that purpose. Figure 16.2 is a sample letter to family members.

Finally, students may wish to have their own writing briefcase or backpack that they can use throughout the year in which to take their compositions and writing materials home. Some students like to emulate adults by "taking work home from the office."

BUDDY JOURNALS

Purpose

Buddy journals (Klobukowski, 2000) are a version of reading logs that have students and parents read the same book together, silently or orally (whatever works best), then respond to each other in a journal. Parents often make superb models of fluent reading and respond well to this activity.

Materials

Two copies of the book that will be sent home with the child are needed, as well as two spiral notebooks to serve as buddy journals.

Figure 16.2   Sample Letter for the Writing Briefcase

Sarah Cannon School
711 Opry Place
Nashville, TN 37211

Dear Family Member:

Children in our class are becoming more and more interested and excited about their abilities as writers and readers. I am interested in helping them realize that writing and reading are not just school activities, but are also skills they can use and enjoy at home and in other places.

This writing briefcase allows your child to experience writing at home using the different tools enclosed. I'd like for you to encourage your child to create a story, poem, song, recipe, rap, or any other composition. You might want to encourage your child to take the briefcase and write outside, perhaps in a favorite hiding place.

Please allow your child to try out the enclosed materials. It would be especially helpful if you would take time to listen to your child's finished products. The product may not look like a story or other composition, but you will find that your child can read and understand it. Please have your child return the written composition, along with the writing briefcase, tomorrow.

Sincerely,

Procedure

The procedure is simple. The adult family member and child each read the book, or portions of the book, then respond in their journals. Then, the adult and child swap journals, read the entry, and respond to the entry. Here are some further suggestions from Klobukowski (2000):

- Encourage parents to reread portions of the text orally, if they are not already reading the book aloud, so that the child can have a reading role model.
- When parents are making entries in their buddy journal, ask them to relate what happened to book characters to themselves and their family, and help their child understand these connections.
- Encourage both parents and students to identify the feelings of the characters and share in their journals what they think the characters should do.
- Ask parents to help their child find information in the text and clarify for them any misunderstandings they detect in the buddy journal entries.
- Urge parents to give their child lots of positive reinforcement and praise for what they can do, and avoid negative criticism.
- Parents should try to include humor in their responses.
- Let parents know that this activity will work best if there is an appointed time to complete the task at home. This avoids last minute rushes to complete a "homework" assignment.

Reading With Wishbone™: Video Tapes for Parent Outreach

Purpose

This is a fantastic 18-minute video available to teachers at very low cost featuring the popular PBS television character, *Wishbone,*™ giving parents ideas about ways they can help their children become better readers.

Materials

There is a VHS video tape that can be ordered for your classroom or school use. It is available in both English and Spanish. Ordering information follows at the end of the chapter.

Procedure

The creation of Lyrick Studios, *Wishbone*™ is a popular character who is a promoter of great books on Public Broadcasting (PBS) stations in the United States. *Wishbone*™ is a lovable Jack Russell terrier who each week reenacts a famous classic novel for viewers. Fully costumed in period clothing appropriate to the book being highlighted, *Wishbone*™ draws youngsters and adult viewers alike into the wonderful world of books.

Two great products have arisen from *Wishbone's*™ collaboration with the Dallas schools (Cooter et al., 1999) that benefit not only Texas children, but also interested teachers across America. The primary product is a high-quality video tape (VCR) titled "DEAR Families: Paws to Read . . . with *Wishbone*™" which features *Wishbone*™ in captivating vignettes extolling the virtues of recreational reading. In essence, it features *Wishbone*™ acting out a series of book talks and offering advice to children and adults for choosing books for family DEAR time. This humorous tale (or is it *tail?!*) is appropriate for children, PTA and civic groups, and especially for families. The other product is an audio tape that features the voice of *Wishbone*™ giving students useful reading tips. Both products are highly motivational.

Teachers everywhere who are interested in motivating parents to read with their children can take advantage of this *Wishbone*™ video, too. Arrangements have been made so that teachers can order the *Wishbone™* video at a very minimal cost for their classroom or school. Ordering information follows at the end of the chapter. It is a great way to "unleash" the power of reading!

PART II: COMMUNITY INVOLVEMENT

D.E.A.R. "CITY"!

Purpose

Research indicates that young children average reading only about seven to eight minutes during the school day (Anderson et al., 1985, p. 76). Yet we know that the development of fluent reading requires massive amounts of practice in order to satisfy student interest, build fluency, increase vocabulary, and improve comprehension. Clearly, some sort of sustained silent reading on a daily basis is needed. *D.E.A.R. your city's name here* (Cooter et al., 1999) sets up a designated day and time, usually by a mayoral proclamation, where every business, school, and corporation stops for five minutes to pull out a book and read as a sign of their unified commitment to the importance of reading.

Materials

This project requires political support, newspaper coverage (an "Op-Ed" piece), media coverage, and a lot of volunteer workers to spread the word.

Procedure

The goal of *D.E.A.R. "City"!* (modeled after the *Drop Everything And Read* classroom strategy) is to get everyone in the city to join local schools in making a dramatic statement in support of reading. The original vision in Dallas Public Schools (Cooter et al., 1999) was that citizens would stop whatever they were doing for just 10 minutes at an assigned time (10:00 to 10:10 A.M. on March 6) and read a book, newspaper, or magazine just for fun. Publicity was arranged in cooperation with local newspapers, television, and radio stations, and with the city buses that would travel about the city brandishing large advertising banners (see Figure 16.3) to help spread the word.

Who joined the original *D.E.A.R. Dallas* citywide effort? Nearly everyone. The mayor proclaimed March 6 as "D.E.A.R. Dallas Day" and joined in by reading with all teachers and children of Dallas in grades K–12. The police chief, also a strong supporter of children and education in Dallas, joined in along with downtown businesses and corporate offices as an act of solidarity. Then Governor George W. Bush, seeing *D.E.A.R. Dallas!* as consonant with his statewide reading initiative, issued a statement praising the effort and reiterating how we must all encourage our children to read everyday for fun and to strengthen their literacy skills for improved life choices.

Getting D.E.A.R. time started at the classroom or school level is really quite simple. It begins with an understanding that time set aside for pleasure reading is not a frill, but a necessity in a comprehensive reading program. Teachers should set aside about 20 minutes per day for students to self-select and read books.

We teach students to self-select books using the "Rule-of-Thumb" method (Reutzel & Cooter, 2000): after choosing a book of interest, open the book to any page with a lot of words and count the number of words you do not know. If you use all five fingers to count unknown words on one page, the book is too difficult; put it back and choose another you

Figure 16.3   DEAR Dallas Poster

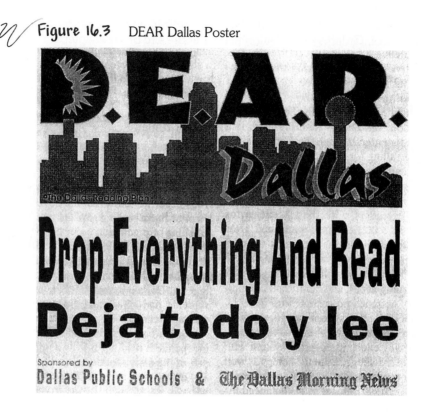

like just as well. Schoolwide D.E.A.R. time can be achieved with the principal's support. Simply set aside a time daily where everyone drops everything to read. It is a truly powerful tool that can have magnificent results so long as everyone participates.

Education Major Pen Pals

Purpose

Education major pen pals (Flickenger, 1991) is a slight variation on the pen pals theme that has met with great success in many areas. Its only substantive difference is that, instead of pairing students with other students or peers, education major pen pals matches students (usually elementary level) with young adults majoring in education at a local college or university. A final book project based on the elementary student is completed jointly between the youngster and the university student.

In addition to providing an audience and reason for writing, this form of pen pals gives students other motivational reasons for reading: the anticipation and receiving of letters, personalized books, or other compositions from the student teachers. Education students are likewise given opportunities as new professionals to connect with students in a way that offers valuable insights.

Materials

Begin by obtaining a list of education majors interested in working with your students. This may be obtained from a local college or university professor (usually specializing in reading, literacy, and/or language arts education) interested in such a project. Materials needed include writing center materials for final drafts of letters, such as writing paper, envelopes, pens, and stamps; bookmaking materials, such as laminating materials, stiff cardboard for book covers, and art materials for illustrations; first draft (messy copy) writing materials (paper and pencils) for the elementary students; transparency-making equipment and materials for the construction of overhead projector examples of each of the writing process stages as they pertain to the composition of letters; and, if possible, a word processor/computer on which students can type letters and other compositions.

Procedure

This activity is essentially the same as with the standard pen pals activity, except that students correspond with student teachers attending education classes at the local college or university. Students in early elementary grades are encouraged to use invented (we prefer the term "temporary") spellings. Elementary students are encouraged to talk and/or draw about families, interests, friends, and special events taking place in their lives at school and at home.

One expectation, which takes the form of a book project, is that university students write books (text only) for their pen pals using what they have learned about their pen pals' interests. The university students bind the nearly finished books, but leave room on each page for illustrations. Then, the elementary students illustrate their personalized books and send them back to the university students. After making one or more copies of the finished books, the university students return the original books to their pen pals.

An additional teacher education benefit is that university students are able to use the letters and other compositions written by their pen pals for analysis of writing development and discovery of children's learning.

SUMMER FOOD AND READING PROGRAM

Purpose

One of the great concerns of urban communities is the welfare of children during the summer months. When schools are out, for example, many children regress in their literacy development. Another worry is that some of the children may not have access to the kind of nutritious meals available to them during the school year. To respond to both of these needs, one community developed a *Summer Food and Reading Program* (Cooter et al., 1999). They discovered that a city with numerous bored 5–12-year-olds, comfortable space available at local churches, a pool of enthusiastic volunteers, and thousands of "gently used" donated books can provide all the ingredients needed for a successful summer "reading and feeding" program.

Materials and Resources

This project requires at least five books per child to be served, volunteer workers, and coordination by a local community group.

Procedure

Many have selected the *Reading To, With, and By* model (Mooney, 1990) to train volunteers and involve the more reluctant readers. Several teachers usually design and deliver interactive training for the volunteers in effective balanced reading instruction. Making reading *fun* is one of the basic tenets of the training model for the volunteer tutors. Volunteers are taught ways to read aloud favorite poems and stories, encourage buddy reading using big books, make big books, and support strategies for encouraging children's oral reading. Volunteers are also taught how to establish a print-rich environment using primarily children's work.

To start your own summer reading and nutrition program, we suggest contacting local church leaders, social support agencies, and youth organizations (boys and girls clubs, the local Y, and so on). Urban centers have a number of such agencies looking to leverage their resources through partnering. Business-oriented clubs, such as Rotary International and Kiwanis, can also be helpful in recruiting volunteers and securing funding.

THE READING CHANNEL

Purpose

The purpose is to use a public access television channel available to a school district as an outreach tool for reading development in the home.

Materials and Resources

This primarily requires official contacts and negotiations between the local PBS network provider and the local school district leadership. At least one full-time equivalent teacher will be needed to organize the Reading Channel and serve as liaison with the television station personnel.

Procedure

One of the tools many large urban school districts have at their disposal is one or more "public access" cable television channels from the local providers. The *Reading Channel* (Cooter et al., 1999) can be organized as a support for families in raising literate children. One way this is accomplished is to air each evening during prime time (6–9 P.M.) alternative television offerings oriented toward positive literacy habits. As part of the Public Broadcasting System (PBS) and cable television charters, school districts having a public access channel can rerun at no charge any PBS program from the prior year. Thus, such programs as *Reading Rainbow, Mr. Rogers' Neighborhood, Sesame Street,* and *Wishbone* can be aired on a new *Reading Channel.* A regular slate of offerings can be planned so that the *Reading Channel* can become a welcomed friend to families in the region.

School districts interested in taking advantage of public access channels should do several key things. First, check with the central office administrator in your school district responsible for communications and distance learning initiatives. This person is a valuable resource who will know the details for public access initiatives in your district and the procedures to get things started. If your district is new to this kind of enterprise, then contact the cable television provider in your area directly and inquire as to the public access provisions in their charter. Finally, if you are interested in rebroadcasting PBS television programs like the ones mentioned, get in touch with your area Public Broadcasting affiliate to learn about how you can partner with them to make your plan a reality.

READING INTERNET HOME PAGE

Purpose

As computers in the home, public libraries, workplace, and schools have become increasingly commonplace, many organizations are establishing an Internet home page.

The purpose of the *Reading Internet Home Page* is to create another tool for your students that is tailor made to your curriculum.

Materials

If your school district has a technology department, ask for assistance in setting up an Internet web page of your own. If not, most large business equipment retailers carry software packages for creating web pages.

Procedure

We prefer to persuade a talented "web master" (a techie already on the school district payroll) to help us design a new home page as a distance learning tool for parents, teachers, college researchers, foundations, business leaders, and others frequently asking for more information on reading. The web page enables people from literally around the world to access at any time information on upcoming learning events, how to contact teachers and resource professionals, support materials for assisting children in becoming literate in the home, links to other related Internet web sites, and many other options.

The home page is a living document that is constantly under construction and revision (pardon our dust!) and is a terrific tool for serving all stakeholders in the balanced literacy reform effort.

SELECTED REFERENCES

Anderson, R. C., Hiebert, E. F., Scott, J. A., & Wilkinson, I. A. G. (1985). *Becoming a nation of readers: The report of the commission on reading.* Washington, DC: The National Institute of Education.

Barton, P. (1992). *America's smallest school: The family.* Princeton, NJ: Educational Testing Service.

Barton, P. (1994). *Becoming literate about literacy.* Princeton, NJ: Educational Testing Service.

Burkhart, A. L. (2000). Breaking the parental barrier. In T. V. Rasinski, N. D. Padak, et al. (Eds.), *Motivating recreational reading and promoting home-school connections* (pp. 110–113). Newark, DE: International Reading Association.

Cooter, R. B., Mills-House, E., Marrin, P., Mathews, B., & Campbell, S. (May, 1999). Family and community involvement: The bedrock of reading success. *The Reading Teacher, 52*(8), 891–896.

Flickenger, G. (1991). Pen pals and collaborative books. *The Reading Teacher, 45,* 72–73.

Garshelis, J., & McConnell, S. (1993). Comparison of family needs assessed by mothers, individual professionals, and interdisciplinary teams. *Journal of Early Intervention, 17,* 36–49.

Handel, R. D. (1999). The multiple meanings of family literacy. *Education & Urban Society, 32*(1), 127–144.

Klobukowski, P. (2000). Parents, buddy journals, and teacher response. In T. V. Rasinski, N. D. Padak, et al. (Eds.), *Motivating recreational reading and promoting home-school connections* (pp. 74–78). Newark, DE: International Reading Association.

Lanteigne, B., & Schwarzer, D. (1997). The progress of Rafael in English and family reading: A case study. *Journal of Adolescent & Adult Literacy, 41*(1), 36–45.

May, F. B., & Rizzardi, L. (2002). *Reading as communication.* Upper Saddle River, NJ: Merrill/Prentice Hall.

McQuillan, J. (1998). *The literacy crisis: False claims, real solutions.* Portsmouth, NH: Heinemann.

Miller-Rodriguez, K. (1992). Home writing activities: The writing briefcase and the traveling suitcase. *The Reading Teacher, 45,* 160–161.

Mooney, M. E. (1990). *Reading to, with, and by children.* Katonah, NY: Richard C. Owens.

Reutzel, D. R., & Cooter, R. B. (2000). *Teaching children to read: Putting the pieces together.* Upper Saddle River, NJ: Merrill/Prentice Hall.

Reutzel, D. R., & Fawson, P. C. (1990). Traveling tales: Connecting parents and children in writing. *The Reading Teacher, 44,* 222–227.

Scott, L. L. (2000). Classbooks: Linking the classroom to the home. In T. V. Rasinski, N. D. Padak, et al. (Eds.), *Motivating recreational reading and promoting home-school connections* (pp. 93–94). Newark, DE: International Reading Association.

Will, G. (2002, January 6). Mom and dad mean more than Miss Wormwood. Fort Worth *Star-Telegram,* 4E.

Williams, S. G. (2001). *Participation of families in interventions.* Unpublished manuscript, George Peabody College of Vanderbilt University, Nashville, TN.

Willman, A. T. (2000). "Hello, Mrs. Willman, it's me!": Keep kids reading over the summer by using voice mail. In T. V. Rasinski, N. D. Padak, et al. (Eds.), *Motivating recreational reading and promoting home-school connections* (pp. 51–52). Newark, DE: International Reading Association.

Wong, H. K., & Wong, R. T. (1998). *The first days of school.* Mountain View, CA: Harry Wong.

Yarosz, D. J., & Barnett, W. S. (2001). Who reads to young children?: Identifying predictors of family reading activities. *Reading Psychology, 22*(1), 67–81.

WISHBONE™ VIDEO AND AUDIO TAPES

DEAR Families: Paws to Read . . . with Wishbone™!—video tape/English (order # 4517)

DEAR Families: Paws to Read . . . with Wishbone™!—video tape/Spanish (order # 4518)

DEAR Schools: Paws to Read . . . with Wishbone™!—audio tape (for announcing DEAR time over the school intercom in Wishbone's own voice!!!)/ English (order # 4519)

Big Feats! Entertainment
P.O. Box 9523
Allen, TX 75013–9523 (USA)
Phone: 1–800–888-WISH
Fax: 972–390–6039

Name Index

Subject Index